Our Catholic Roots

Old Churches East of the Mississippi

Walter H. Maloney

Drawings by Thomas P. Maloney

Our Sunday Visitor Publishing Division
Our Sunday Visitor, Inc.
Huntington, Indiana 46750

Acknowledgments

All photographs and line drawings in this work were provided by the author and Thomas P. Maloney with the exception of the rendering of St. Mary's, Chicago, Illinois, which was made available through the courtesy of Rael D. Slutsky & Associates of Chicago.

If any copyrighted materials have been inadvertently used in this book without proper credit being given, please notify Our Sunday Visitor in writing so that future printings of this work may be corrected accordingly.

Copyright © 1992 by Our Sunday Visitor Publishing Division
Our Sunday Visitor, Inc.

ALL RIGHTS RESERVED

With the exception of short excerpts for critical reviews, no part of this book may be reproduced in any manner whatsoever without permission in writing from the publisher.
Write:
Our Sunday Visitor Publishing Division
Our Sunday Visitor, Inc.
200 Noll Plaza
Huntington, Indiana 46750

International Standard Book Number: 0-87973-463-9 (softcover)
International Standard Book Number: 0-87973-541-4 (hardcover)
Library of Congress Catalog Card Number: 92-80496

Cover design by Rebecca J. Heaston

PRINTED IN THE UNITED STATES OF AMERICA

TO
Walter and Madeline Maloney,
who provided me with my roots
and with a lively affection
for churches, old and new

1 ● Holy Cross, Christiansted, St. Croix, U.S. Virgin Islands [1755]
2 ● St. John Baptist Cathedral, San Juan, Puerto Rico [1522]
3 ● Holy Cross Cathedral, Boston, Massachusetts [1788]
4 ● St. Augustine, Boston, Massachusetts [1868]
5 ● Immaculate Conception, Salem, Massachusetts [1821]
6 ● St. John the Baptist, New Bedford, Massachusetts [1871]
7 ● Immaculate Conception Cathedral, Portland, Maine [1856]
8 ● St. Patrick, Newcastle, Maine [1808]
9 ● St. Bruno, Van Buren, Maine [1838]
10 ● St. Mary, Claremont, New Hampshire [1823]
11 ● St. Mary, Newport, Rhode Island [1828]
12 ● St. Mary, New Haven, Connecticut [1834]
13 ● St. Peter, New York, New York [1785]
14 ● St. Patrick's Cathedral, New York, New York [1809]
15 ● St. James Cathedral, Brooklyn, New York [1822]
16 ● Most Holy Trinity Chapel, West Point, New York [1899]
17 ● St. John the Baptist Cathedral, Paterson, New Jersey [1820]
18 ● St. Joseph, Philadelphia, Pennsylvania [1732]
19 ● St. Mary, Philadelphia, Pennsylvania [1763]
20 ● Sts. Peter and Paul Cathedral, Philadelphia, Pennsylvania [1846]
21 ● St. Mary Magdalen de Pazzi, Philadelphia, Pennsylvania [1852]
22 ● Most Blessed Sacrament, Bally, Pennsylvania [1743]
23 ● St. George, Shenandoah, Pennsylvania [1891]
24 ● St. Michael (Byzantine Rite), Shenandoah, Pennsylvania [1884]
25 ● St. Mary, Lancaster, Pennsylvania [1742]
26 ● Sacred Heart Basilica, Conewago Township, Pennsylvania [1741]
27 ● St. Michael, Loretto, Pennsylvania [1799]
28 ● St. Ignatius, Chapel Point, Maryland [1641]
29 ● Sacred Heart, Bowie, Maryland [1741]
30 ● St. John the Evangelist, Silver Spring, Maryland [1774]
31 ● Basilica of the Assumption, Baltimore, Maryland [1806]
32 ● St. Peter the Apostle, Baltimore, Maryland [1844]
33 ● St. Francis Xavier, Baltimore, Maryland [1864]
34 ● St. Mary, Annapolis, Maryland [1822]
35 ● U.S. Naval Academy Chapel, Annapolis, Maryland [1854]
36 ● Holy Trinity, Washington, D.C. [1794]
37 ● St. Matthew's Cathedral, Washington, D.C. [1840]
38 ● St. Mary, Alexandria, Virginia [1796]
39 ● St. Peter, Harpers Ferry, West Virginia [1833]
40 ● St. Mary, Charleston, South Carolina [1789]
41 ● St. John the Baptist Cathedral, Savannah, Georgia [1799]
42 ● Shrine of the Immaculate Conception, Atlanta, Georgia [1849]
43 ● St. Augustine Cathedral, St. Augustine, Florida [1565]
44 ● St. Mary, Star of the Sea, Key West, Florida [1852]
45 ● Immaculate Conception Cathedral, Mobile, Alabama [1702]
46 ● St. Patrick, Cleveland, Ohio [1848]
47 ● St. Joseph, Somerset, Ohio [1818]
48 ● St. Peter in Chains Cathedral, Cincinnati, Ohio [1826]
49 ● St. Joseph, Bardstown, Kentucky [1816]
50 ● Abbey of Our Lady of Gethsemani, Trappist, Kentucky [1848]
51 ● Ste. Anne, Detroit, Michigan [1701]
52 ● Sts. Peter and Paul, Detroit, Michigan [1844]
53 ● Holy Name of Mary, Sault Ste. Marie, Michigan [1834]
54 ● Basilica of St. Francis Xavier, Vincennes, Indiana [1749]
55 ● Sacred Heart, Notre Dame, Indiana [1848]
56 ● St. Mary, Chicago, Illinois [1833]
57 ● Holy Name Cathedral, Chicago, Illinois [1849]
58 ● St. Stanislaus Kostka, Chicago, Illinois [1867]
59 ● St. John Cathedral, Milwaukee, Wisconsin [1847]

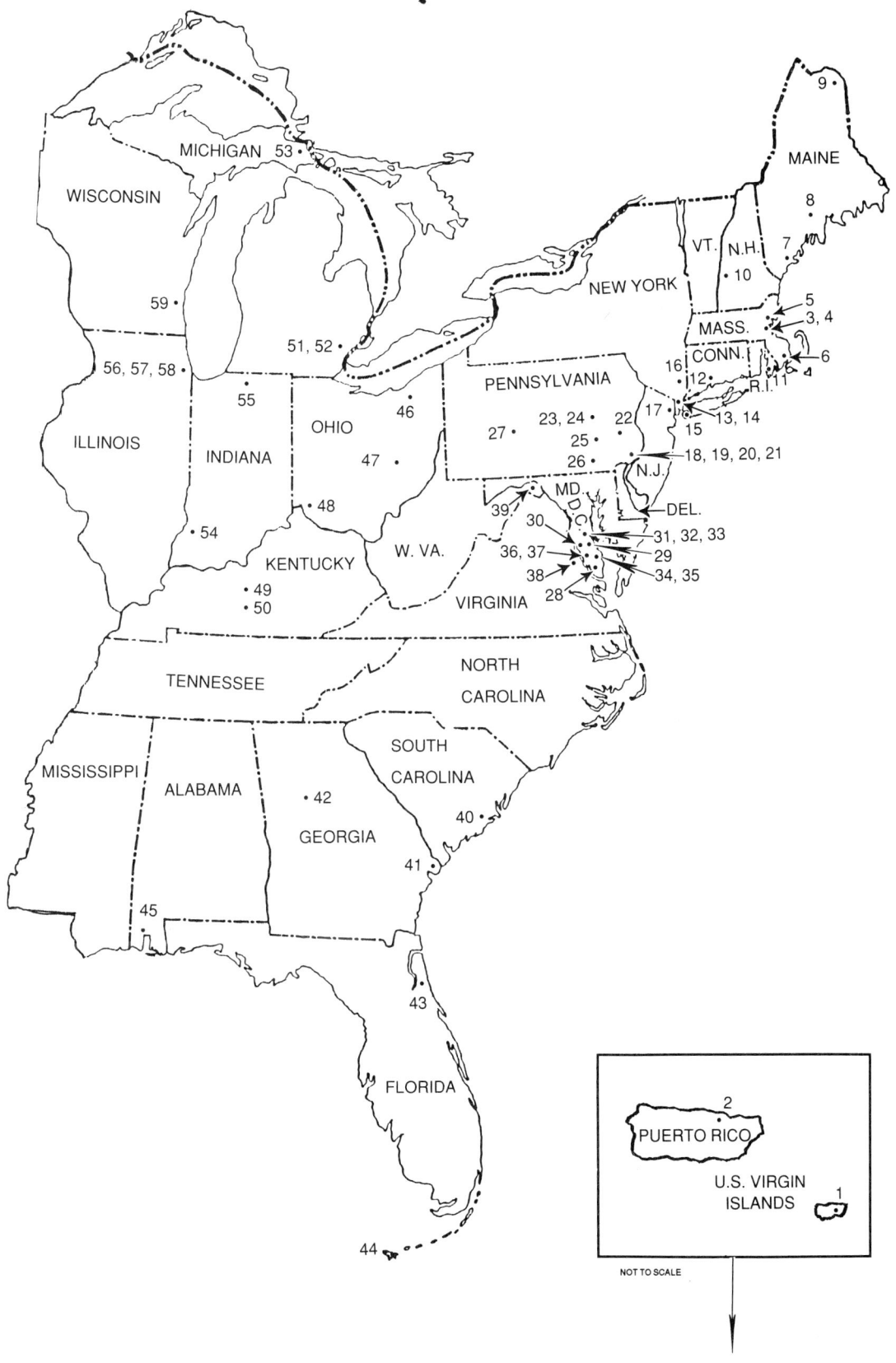

CONTENTS

Foreword / 9

Taking Root / 14

1 / Holy Cross, Christiansted, St. Croix, U.S. Virgin Islands / 33

2 / St. John Baptist Cathedral, San Juan, Puerto Rico / 45

3 / Holy Cross Cathedral, Boston, Massachusetts / 55

4 / St. Augustine, Boston, Massachusetts / 63

5 / Immaculate Conception, Salem, Massachusetts / 69

6 / St. John the Baptist, New Bedford, Massachusetts / 75

7 / Immaculate Conception Cathedral, Portland, Maine / 83

8 / St. Patrick, Newcastle, Maine / 89

9 / St. Bruno, Van Buren, Maine / 97

10 / St. Mary, Claremont, New Hampshire / 103

11 / St. Mary, Newport, Rhode Island / 109

12 / St. Mary, New Haven, Connecticut / 117

13 / St. Peter, New York, New York / 125

14 / St. Patrick's Cathedral, New York, New York / 143

15 / St. James Cathedral, Brooklyn, New York / 165

16 / Most Holy Trinity Chapel, West Point, New York / 179

17 / St. John the Baptist Cathedral, Paterson, New Jersey / 187

18 / St. Joseph, Philadelphia, Pennsylvania / 195

19 / St. Mary, Philadelphia, Pennsylvania / 203

20 / Sts. Peter and Paul Cathedral, Philadelphia, Pennsylvania / 215

21 / St. Mary Magdalen de Pazzi, Philadelphia, Pennsylvania / 221

22 / Most Blessed Sacrament, Bally, Pennsylvania / 227

23 / St. George, Shenandoah, Pennsylvania / 233

24 / St. Michael (Byzantine Rite), Shenandoah, Pennsylvania / 247

25 / St. Mary, Lancaster, Pennsylvania / 253

26 / Sacred Heart Basilica, Conewago Township, Pennsylvania / 259

27 / St. Michael, Loretto, Pennsylvania / 265

28 / St. Ignatius, Chapel Point, Maryland / 273

29 / Sacred Heart, Bowie, Maryland / 277

30 / St. John the Evangelist, Silver Spring, Maryland / 283

31 / Basilica of the Assumption, Baltimore, Maryland / 287

32 / St. Peter the Apostle, Baltimore, Maryland / 299

33 / St. Francis Xavier, Baltimore, Maryland / 303

34 / St. Mary, Annapolis, Maryland / 309

35 / U.S. Naval Academy Chapel, Annapolis, Maryland / 313

36 / Holy Trinity, Washington, D.C. / 321

37 / St. Matthew's Cathedral, Washington, D.C. / 329

38 / St. Mary, Alexandria, Virginia / 337

39 / St. Peter, Harpers Ferry, West Virginia / 343

40 / St. Mary, Charleston, South Carolina / 349

41 / St. John the Baptist Cathedral, Savannah, Georgia / 365

42 / Shrine of the Immaculate Conception, Atlanta, Georgia / 379

43 / St. Augustine Cathedral, St. Augustine, Florida / 385

44 / St. Mary, Star of the Sea, Key West, Florida / 403

45 / Immaculate Conception Cathedral, Mobile, Alabama / 415

46 / St. Patrick, Cleveland, Ohio / 429

47 / St. Joseph, Somerset, Ohio / 433

48 / St. Peter in Chains Cathedral, Cincinnati, Ohio / 441

49 / St. Joseph, Bardstown, Kentucky / 449

50 / Abbey of Our Lady of Gethsemani, Trappist, Kentucky / 463

51 / Ste. Anne, Detroit, Michigan / 475

52 / Sts. Peter and Paul, Detroit, Michigan / 479

53 / Holy Name of Mary, Sault Ste. Marie, Michigan / 485

54 / Basilica of St. Francis Xavier, Vincennes, Indiana / 497

55 / Sacred Heart, Notre Dame, Indiana / 509

56 / St. Mary, Chicago, Illinois / 519

57 / Holy Name Cathedral, Chicago, Illinois / 529

58 / St. Stanislaus Kostka, Chicago, Illinois / 541

59 / St. John Cathedral, Milwaukee, Wisconsin / 555

Bibliography / 566

Index / 572

Foreword

Anyone who goes searching for his roots is taking a chance. The hope of course is to find an array of princes and poets whose presence on the family tree will enhance the family name and serve to explain its many inestimable qualities. The risk is that one will also find an occasional sheep stealer whose presence will also serve to explain a thing or two. The risk is even greater when a search for roots is undertaken on a group rather than an individual basis. One may very well uncover a thing or two that might not make for pleasant reminiscences, but the rewards greatly outweigh that peril.

In recent years, Americans have been making great efforts to find their roots, and that is all to the good. Regrettably, some may start out thinking they are on a sentimental journey into a romanticized past and come away quite upset to uncover stories of hardship, privation, and distress. Indeed, if our forebears could be heard on this subject, they might very well question why all this effort in the first place. With all the material comforts and blessings a modern American can enjoy, why go poking around into the days when life was unrelentingly hard and the future promised only more of the same? The answer is that in the midst of material blessings we now have problems and perplexities that did not confront our predecessors, and Catholics are no exception. Our ancestors had fixed points of reference to guide them and to give their lives meaning and perspective. A search into a collective past can assist in inserting some of those guideposts into our own lives.

Catholics can derive a secondary benefit from such an effort. Despite the fact that Catholics first set foot on what is now American soil in 1493, over the centuries they have been treated as if they were really strangers in their own land. In reality, Catholic roots in many communities in this country reach back to the very inception of those communities and, in some instances, provide some of the few tangible reminders of their beginnings. In almost all parts of the country, Catholics helped to shape the growth and development of what exists today, and their role may have been more prominent than what we have been led to believe. Looking into a Catholic past can readily uncover a historical truth that has been greatly overlooked, namely that Catholics have been an integral and important part of the American experience from its very beginning, and even before.

This book is intended to assist over fifty-eight million Roman Catholics in the United States in finding their roots. If others find it of interest or benefit, then so much the better. Set forth are the stories of fifty-nine old Catholic churches located east of the Mississippi River whose stories disclose many of those roots. Hopefully, we can continue this journey into the Catholic past of the land west of the Mississippi at another time. This is not a book about architecture or religious artifacts. It is a book focused upon present communities in all parts of the country that are the living results of the efforts of Catholics who have long since passed to their rewards. Such a search is intended to provide modern Catholics with a perspective that I fear many may have acquired only in the sketchiest form. I trust that these findings will establish some additional benchmarks that will aid them in understanding both themselves and the world they now confront.

Old churches were selected for this purpose because they provide ready and tangible vehicles for a journey into the past. If there is one thing with which a modern Catholic can still identify, it is a parish church, even if he does not attend one with the frequency he knows he should. Anyone who says he is a Catholic but cannot name the parish he lives in is bluffing about his religion. If there is a problem in using old parish churches for this purpose (and a couple of churches in this volume technically do not qualify as parish churches), it is that there are so many of them. At last count, this nation had about 19,971 Catholic parishes located in 199 dioceses and eparchies. Each has a story worth telling; however, the effort would result not in a single volume but several file drawers full of computer printouts. A hard job of selecting out had to be done, and I cannot insist that it was done with total objectivity or comprehension. There are other parishes that should have been represented in this volume but were omitted simply because there was not enough room.

In selecting the "old" churches to be discussed, I established a flexible cutoff date to determine exactly what should be meant by "old." With three or four exceptions, made for what are obvious reasons, the end of the Civil War was used as the end of antiquity. The Civil War is widely regarded as the great watershed of American history. Without more, it would have served handily as a dividing line. For Catholics the Civil War era serves particularly well as the turning point from the old to the new. In 1790, when Bishop John Carroll assumed office as the first Catholic bishop in the United States, he was confronted with the task of administering a diocese that extended from Canada to Florida and from the Atlantic to the Mississippi River. At that time, there were between twenty-five thousand and fifty thousand Catholics in the United States and its western territories. They constituted about one percent of the total population. To accomplish this task Bishop Carroll had fewer than twenty-five priests to assist him. By 1850, Roman Catholicism had become the largest religious denomination in the United States. It has never relinquished this position. By the end of the Civil War — within the lifetime of one person — the Catholic Church in America had grown to forty dioceses and some three and a half million members, who constituted about thirteen percent of the total population. This was the era when most Catholic roots were sunk deeply into the soil of this nation (or, having been sunk in colonial times, were extended), so the end of this historic conflict makes a most convenient and logical breaking-off point for the selection.

It is not possible to say much about Catholic history in the United States and to say it accurately without mentioning controversy, both among Catholics and between Catholics and others. Some people get upset by controversies, especially internal ones. They shouldn't. During the debates in the 1960s at the Second Vatican Council, someone asked Pope John XXIII if he was upset by the intensity with which some of the disputes were being aired by the bishops who had assembled in Rome. He replied that the debates did not upset him at all, adding that the bishops taking part in the council were not exactly choirboys. The same description should be applied to Catholics who hacked their way into the wilderness and built primitive church buildings or who supervised the building of churches for the masses of immigrants who settled our major cities. These were not jobs for choirboys, and it is not surprising that those who had what it took to do such jobs occasionally became involved in controversy. Some comfort can be taken in the fact that most of these disputes did not linger on. When looked at from a late twentieth-century perspective, we can barely appreciate what some of them were all about. More to the point, when compared with the fierceness with which some of the issues of our Catholic past were fought, the controversies of our own day involving the Catholic Church seem tame indeed, even if the stakes are often a good deal higher.

Any view of American Catholic history should not conclude, however, that controversy was the main problem or preoccupation of Catholics of yesteryear. The major enemies of American Catholics in the formative years of the Church in this country were neither other Catholics nor other Christians, and it would be revisionist history to suggest otherwise. Then, as now, the major enemies of American Catholics were the world, the flesh, and the devil.

One disconcerting realization developed as the parish profiles in this volume were being put together. As one might expect, many older churches dating back a century or more are to be found in the central parts of major cities. In comparing the parish lives of these parishes today with what they formerly were, there is no doubt that a great many are not what they once were. The question might then arise in the minds of some: What has become of the Catholic Church in America?

The answer in most cases is quite simple. Large numbers of Catholics have moved to the suburbs where they currently support large churches, large schools, and large mortgages. A more cogent question would be: What has happened to the central portions of our major cities? Many have become largely uninhabitable, so the old Catholic churches that remain stand as reminders of the fact that people once inhabited these areas on a full-time, not just a part-time, basis. There exists in most cities something called urban renewal, but it has not provided the kind of revitalization necessary for attractive urban living. Public urban renewal has often torn down existing housing to build freeways and government buildings, while private urban renewal, always demanding "more bang for the buck," concentrates on office buildings, shopping malls, and an occasional high-rise condominium. Neither has provided the kind of family-oriented community life upon which a lively parish must depend. In these situations, Catholic churches have developed different ministries to cope with what they find, but any large-scale Catholic renewal in such areas must await more meaningful and comprehensive urban renewal, which includes affordable residences for families of ordinary means.

In searching out their roots, American Catholics would be remiss if they ignored

American saints, whose conspicuous success stories are only now beginning to be told. They are the taproots of the American Catholic Church. Their gravesites dot the map of this country in churches and chapels from New York City to California. Many have recently been canonized while some are merely beatified, but this canonical distinction is a small matter from the standpoint of telling the American Catholic story. Father Isaac Jogues, Kateri Tekakwitha (the "Lily of the Mohawks"), Mother Elizabeth Seton, Mother Frances Cabrini, Bishop John Neumann, Mother Rose Philippine Duchesne, Father Junípero Serra, and Father Damien de Veuster are not plaster figures representing a remote European past. They were here among us. Their tombs are, for the most part, readily accessible to any pilgrim, and their biographies are recent reminders of what the Church is all about. I have tried to acknowledge these facts while telling the stories of old churches.

It is customary to recognize the assistance of those who have helped bring a writing effort to fruition. Anyone who has even dabbled in the area of American Catholic history owes a large debt of gratitude to Dr. John Gilmary Shea, the dean and forerunner of all American Catholic historians. Although Dr. Shea has been dead for nearly a century, his remarkable four-volume history of the Catholic Church in the United States is a wellspring of information and insight into the activities of Catholics in the first three centuries of settlement on this continent. Without his diligence, dedication, and talent, much information we have today about our Catholic roots would doubtless be lost or veiled in obscurity. I cannot repay this debt, but I can at least acknowledge it. I would also like to thank a large number of priests and parish personnel who took time out of their busy schedules to tell a stranger who dropped in at their rectories the story of what's happening now in their old churches and who took the time and trouble to review individual parish profiles and to offer helpful comments. In particular, I would like to thank Father Michael J. Roach, pastor of St. Peter's in Baltimore and visiting professor of American Church History at Mount St. Mary's Seminary in Emmitsburg, Maryland.

I cannot fully express my gratitude to the publishers and copyright holders of those sources mentioned in the bibliography from which material has been excerpted or has served (either quoted verbatim or paraphrased) as the basis for portions of this work.

I would like to thank my wife, Cecelia, and my six adult children, Tim, Eileen, Kathy, P. J., John, and Ann Marie, for their assistance, interest, and encouragement. I can only begin to acknowledge my debt to my brother, Thomas P. Maloney. Pat's drawings of several of these old churches are pieces of artistry that add a unique luster to this volume. Long ago, Father Peyton told us that the family that prays together stays together. The same can be said for a family that takes a lively interest in a common project.

In profiling old churches, I have decided to follow the sun from east to west, starting on the island of St. Croix in the U.S. Virgin Islands and traveling westward. The reader will pardon me if the sequence he finds does not always track the rays of the sun precisely as they traverse this land each day. History does not unfold with such mechanical regularity, so an approximation will simply have to do.

But enough of explanations. The sun is already high in the sky, and it is time we got on with our journey.

Walter H. Maloney
BELTSVILLE, MARYLAND

Taking Root

The individual stories of the fifty-nine churches that are profiled in this volume can best be appreciated in the context of the general development of the Catholic Church in America, which took place in three distinct cultures — Spanish, French, and English — and in a later context that is uniquely American. These stories can also be better understood after reflecting generally upon how the Catholic Church goes about planting its roots and growing in a land where it did not previously exist.

Organizing a Worldwide Mission Effort

From 1493, when Columbus first set foot on what is now American soil, until 1908, the Catholic Church in America was officially regarded as a mission church. Not until 1908 was the Church in the United States and southern Canada as well as in several Protestant nations of Europe reclassified by the Holy See and placed in the same administrative category as the Church in other nations. Being a mission church for over four hundred years meant many things. Mission status meant that the primary focus of its activity was evangelization, the attempt to Christianize people who were not Catholic. It meant that the Church was in an expansionist mode, sending priests and nuns into areas where priests and nuns had never gone before and erecting churches in areas that had never before seen a Catholic church. Mission status also meant that the American clergy and laity operated under the direct control of a department of the Catholic Church in Rome known for centuries as the *Propaganda Fide* — the Sacred Congregation of the Propagation of the Faith, now called the Congregation for the Evangelization of Peoples.

The Propagation of the Faith, as a separate department or congregation of the total church administration, grew out of a suggestion made in 1568 to Pope Pius V by St. Francis Borgia, the second superior general of the Jesuit order. He saw the need for centralized and specialized oversight of the Church's missionary efforts, which by then were beginning to take shape not only in the Western Hemisphere but also in the Near and Far East. Several temporary commissions were established over a period of time; but, in 1622, Pope Gregory XV established a permanent congregation to take charge of the Church's entire missionary activity and to operate it on a supranational basis. The establishment of the Propagation of the Faith (which we will refer to simply as "the Propagation") was designed to promote some degree of uniformity in the methodology of evangelizing widely disparate groups of people. In North America, the object of its efforts were Indians; in the Near East, Arabs; and in the Far East, Japanese, Chinese, Indians, and Polynesians. The Propagation tried to eliminate or modify "turf disputes" between and among national clergy and various religious orders and to see to it that the missionary effort of the Church remained a spiritual undertaking, not an offspring of Spanish, Portuguese, or French colonial ambitions. It faced serious problems in its worldwide program of evangelization — an insufficient number of priests, a lack of knowledge of native languages and native cultures, and even a lack of instructional texts and prayer books translated into native languages. No one knew how to say the Lord's Prayer or the Hail Mary in Apache or Iroquois, for example.

Priests sent to the New World by Catholic monarchs sometimes tended to be indifferent to native values and customs. They often felt that they were being dispatched to remote regions of the globe to promote the particular culture and the political aspirations of their own country. It was a fixed policy of the Propagation to respect and to accommodate local practices and customs insofar as they did not conflict with Catholic doctrine and moral precepts. The Propagation also had a policy of sending priests of various nationalities into a single area, regardless of which nation was trying to colonize it, both to fill an immediate need and to demonstrate the universal character of the Church. To carry out its functions, in 1627 the Propagation established a seminary in Rome, called the Urban College (now known as the Pontifical Urban University), to train missionary priests. It began to operate a printing press and to establish examinations for priests who wished to be sent to mission lands. The Propagation also required annual reports from all missionaries, regardless of nationality or religious order, set up an inspection program for the national seminaries in Rome that trained missionary priests, and went about the difficult job of recruiting both men and money to support a global activity involving the subjects of many nations and kingdoms.

In order to assist the Propagation in its worldwide ministry, the Holy See conferred upon it ecclesiastical powers that, at least in theory, superseded powers normally exercised by bishops and heads of religious orders. For instance, the Propagation had the power to make rules and regulations for the operation of the Church in mission lands and to supplement existing regulations found in the canon law. The Propagation had great flexibility in creating, changing, or abolishing local church jurisdictions anywhere in the mission world and to pass upon the appointments of local bishops and mission pastors. With exceptions discussed later, nominations for bishop in mission dioceses were normally made to the pope through the Propagation.

One of its most important powers was the right to grant or withhold faculties, that is, permission to act as a priest, in all mission areas. The Catholic Church does not function with a free-lance priesthood. Upon ordination, a priest is normally subject to the bishop in whose diocese he is incardinated or enrolled, or to the head of a religious order to whom he must give a vow of obedience. A priest may not, simply by virtue of ordination, exercise a ministry in any particular nation or locality. He must first obtain faculties from the local bishop or other official to say Mass, preach, or hear confessions in any particular area. Restrictions in this regard were much tighter during the early days of the American Church than they are today. The Propagation exercised some control over its far-flung activities by its global power to grant faculties both to bishops and to priests.

This was the theory for operating a supranational mission church on the North American continent (or anywhere else) in the seventeenth and eighteenth centuries. The powers and the activities of the Propagation in Rome often ran afoul of special national arrangements with the pope. These special arrangements were often required by Catholic monarchs who were insistent that the spiritual activities of priests operating in their colonies also advance their colonization efforts. In French, Spanish, and Portuguese areas, missionary activity was undertaken with direct and substantial assistance from public authorities. In English colonies, it took place despite opposition and harassment by public authorities. Both situations presented special and vexing problems. These problems were compounded by other problems, particularly the hostility of Indians themselves, who did not take kindly to European explorers and their religious auxiliaries. For more than a century and a half missionary activity anywhere in North America was perilous work. The martyrology of the Church was greatly enlarged with the names of priests from various nations and religious orders whose preaching of the Gospel was met with torture, brutalization, and death at the hands of native tribes. St. Isaac Jogues was put to death in Upper New York State in 1646. He and seven other French missionaries — six Jesuit priests and two lay assistants — were killed by Indians. They were canonized in 1930. However, these French Jesuit martyrs were merely representatives of a great many others who met similar fates in the effort to evangelize the Western Hemisphere. Some twenty-two French Jesuits and sixty-nine Spanish Franciscans were killed by Indians while on the mission trail. To that figure one should add several secular priests and members of other orders as well as a number of laymen.

Organizing a Mission Effort in New Spain

Throughout the mission period, both Spanish and Portuguese monarchs enjoyed special privileges from the Holy See concerning the control of mission activities in the New World. These privileges often conflicted with the policy and desire of the Church to centralize the control of mission activities under the auspices of the Propagation. Known in Spanish as *patronato real*, or royal patronage, their Most Catholic Majesties were given what they regarded as a concession to evangelize the natives of all islands and lands they might occupy. In 1508, Pope Julius II gave Spanish kings, not Spanish bishops, the right to appoint missionaries to the Indies, as the Spanish were accustomed to describing their holdings in Central and South America. *Patronato real* extended to Florida, Texas, the Southwest, and to California when Spanish missionary activity expanded into those areas. *Patronato real* was later claimed by the Mexican government after Mexico broke away from Spain and was even involved in litigation over control of the New Orleans cathedral long after Louisiana had become an American state.

The extent and meaning of *patronato real* was enlarged upon from time to time by unilateral interpretations by Spanish kings who insisted, among other things, that they had received from Pope Julius a personal grant of power that could not be revoked by subsequent popes. Under this power, Spanish kings had the right to present to the pope candidates for bishop and heads of monasteries in New Spain and to veto appointments made by the Holy See to which they objected. They had the right to construct churches and missions and assumed the obligation to support these activities from public funds. All communications from Rome to Spanish missions had to be "visaed," that is, passed, through government officials in Madrid and Mexico City. These officials might not choose to forward these messages to local clergy if they did not like the contents of the communication. Missionary bishops and priests were forbidden to communicate directly with Rome and had to submit reports and requests through Spanish government channels. For more than a century all clergy sent to New Spain were Spanish subjects and in a sense were regarded as an ecclesiastical branch of the royal civil service. For many years Spanish officials refused to permit the recruitment of priests and nuns among mestizos, the local populace that was part Indian and part Spanish. This policy directly conflicted with a basic aim of the Propagation to develop native clergy. Whenever a new mission or church was to be constructed, official permission had to be obtained from the viceroy or the royal governor.

Toward the end of the seventeenth century, Spain relaxed its insistence upon using only Spanish priests for Spanish missions simply because the government could not obtain enough priests who were Spanish nationals. Eventually, German names came to be found among Spanish missionaries in California, Arizona, and elsewhere. In the latter part of the eighteenth century, King Carlos III recruited Irish priests to minister to English-speaking Catholics who lived in Louisiana and Florida. The Propaganda established and directly controlled so-called apostolic colleges in various parts of Mexico. These colleges supplied missionaries sent to Texas and California. Both Jesuits and Franciscans tried to develop sources of revenue apart from the royal treasury in order to lessen their dependence on the Spanish government and its control over their activities. However, the Spanish crown kept close control over the Church in its possessions in the New World until it lost the last of those possessions following the Spanish-American War of 1898.

Organizing a Mission Effort in New France

The relationship between the Catholic Church in France and their Most Christian Majesties was also close but not so rigidly structured as the *patronato real*. Using a theory called Gallicanism, French kings tried to limit papal authority both in France and its colonies.

The first permanent French settlement in North America was established in 1608 in Quebec. Franciscan Recollects, a branch of the Franciscan order, were chaplains to Samuel de Champlain in that undertaking. They established a small church in the old town of Quebec near the St. Lawrence River, just beneath the bluffs where France eventually met its fate at the hands of General James Wolfe in 1759. Cardinal Jean du Plessis Richelieu, the French secretary of state, offered them the opportunity to supervise Catholic missionary effort throughout New France. However, the Recollects declined the offer because they did not have the manpower to fulfill the mission. Since the Recollects were unable to accept, the Jesuits became the principal French missionaries for the next one hundred fifty years. New France was headquartered at Quebec, but it extended into New York State, the Ohio Valley, Michigan, Illinois, and down the Mississippi River to its mouth. Like their Spanish counterparts, French missionaries frequently accompanied soldiers and explorers on expeditions; but, in the case of the French, the cross often preceded the flag with the fleur-de-lis. New France was originally made a part of the archdiocese of Rouen, but distance and poor communications made this arrangement impractical. In 1658, Quebec was created as a diocese and Monsignor François Laval, a prominent figure in Canadian history, was appointed the first bishop. His diocese ultimately reached Mobile and New Orleans.

The French government was expected to support French missionaries in the field, but disputes often arose between officials such as Frontenac, La Salle, and Cadillac, and various missionaries, especially the Jesuits. On some occasions, when disputes became serious, civil officials asserted their authority by cutting off financial support from priests. The official government opinion of the Jesuits was not shared by the bishop of Quebec. In 1663, Monsignor Laval designated Father Claude Allouez, S.J., to be his vicar general in the West. This meant that Father Allouez was second in command of the Quebec diocese and in charge of all Catholic activities in the Ohio and Mississippi Valleys. In his letter of appointment, Monsignor Laval wrote: "We cannot sufficiently praise God on beholding the zeal and charity with which all the Fathers of your Society continue to employ their lives in this new Church to advance the glory of God and the Kingdom of Jesus Christ, and to secure the salvation of souls whom He has confided to our care."

In 1718, France gave to a semipublic corporation, known as the Company of the West, an exclusive franchise to develop the Mississippi Valley. The Duc d'Orleans, the French viceroy, insisted that its charter impose a responsibility on the part of the company to construct churches and support missionaries. The company complied with this obligation for a while, but it often reneged, leaving missionaries stranded and destitute in the wilderness.

France lost the Seven Years War (called the French and Indian War in North America) and ceded the Louisiana Territory to Spain before a general peace conference could be called to dispose of the rest of its holdings. With the departure of the French government, French priests were replaced in the Mississippi Valley by Spanish priests, but this exchange did not always take place immediately. After 1763, all that was left of French Catholic influence in America were a few small settlements such as Detroit, Vincennes, Cahokia, Kaskaskia, and New Orleans. The area east of the Mississippi River was British territory and was off limits to Catholic missionaries and to colonial American settlers as well.

Facing Persecution in British Colonies

The British sphere of influence, stretching from Maine to Georgia, initially extended westward only as far as the Appalachian Mountains. Catholics in British colonies faced vastly different problems. With two short-lived exceptions, all reigning monarchs of Great Britain since 1534 have been not only members of the Church of England but the head of that Church as well. Because civil and religious authority was intertwined in the same civil ruler, dissent from the established church was for many years deemed to be either treason or some lesser but serious crime. Not until the Catholic Emancipation Act of 1829 were all of these civil disabilities removed from British law.

Throughout the time when the British settlement of North America was taking place, Englishmen were subject to what were collectively called penal laws. Beginning in 1534, those who refused to take an oath recognizing the king as head of the Church of England were subject to punishment, including death. Later, the scope of penal laws was enlarged. The Anglican Book of Common Prayer was established by statute as the basis for any lawful public worship; any criticism of that book was prohibited. Accordingly, saying or hearing Mass or receiving the sacraments meant that a Catholic had to recuse himself (that is, decline) from participating in official worship. Thus he became a "popish recusant."

Queen Elizabeth made it treason to reconcile a Protestant to the Catholic Church and a lesser crime to import into England any article that had been blessed by the pope. Catholics were forbidden from leaving England without permission, forbidden to live abroad without official permission, and forbidden to send their children abroad to receive an education. Neglecting to attend Anglican services brought with it a fine, as did keeping a schoolmaster who did not attend Anglican services. In what was styled an "act against Jesuits, Seminary Priests, and other such like disobedient persons," it became a crime for a priest to enter or to remain in England. Later, penal laws forbade anyone who had recused himself from taking the Oath of Allegiance on religious grounds (a "popish recusant") from holding public office, obtaining a commission in any of the armed services, acting as a guardian, or filing a civil lawsuit. Anyone married outside the Anglican Church was deprived of any interest in his or her spouse's property. In 1673, the Test Oath was enlarged from a declaration recognizing the religious supremacy of the king to a renunciation of certain fundamental Catholic theological doctrines, such as belief in the transubstantiation. Later, penal laws prohibited recusants from inheriting land or acquiring title to land in any other manner. In light of the loose use of the word "treason" that existed in English law in those times, it is easy to see why the Founding Fathers were so particular in placing a precise definition of "treason" in the American Constitution and preventing that designation from applying to any conduct other than what was contained in the constitutional definition.

There was some doubt as to whether penal laws enacted by the English Parliament had any legal effect outside England, so the Scottish and Irish parliaments, sitting at Edinburgh and Dublin, enacted similar laws for their own jurisdictions. So did colonial assemblies in North America, using the accumulation of English penal laws as prototypes. In Massachusetts Bay, Jesuits were forbidden from entering the colony and were banished if they did. In New York, an act of the legislature was passed in 1700 according to which a Catholic priest was "deemed and accounted an incendiary and disturber of public peace and safety, and an enemy of the true Christian religion, and shall be adjudged to suffer perpetual imprisonment." Anyone who harbored a priest was subject to a fine of £250 and three days in the pillory (that is, the public stocks). In 1704, the Maryland General Assembly passed an act "to prevent the growth of popery within this province." It forbade priests from baptizing children "other than such who have popish parents," outlawed the saying of Mass, and prohibited the attempts to convert Protestants. It precluded Catholics from inheriting or purchasing land and outlawed the practice, often resorted to by Maryland Catholics, of sending their children abroad to be educated. The assembly also made it a crime to import an Irish Catholic into Maryland. At this point, Queen Anne, whose father was the last Catholic king of England, intervened to decree that priests in Maryland could continue to exercise their ministry so long as they did it "in a private family of the Roman Communion, but in no other Case whatsoever."

Later acts of the Maryland General Assembly in the eighteenth century made Catholics ineligible to vote or hold public office. The assembly also divided up each county into parishes and levied a tax of forty pounds of tobacco each year on every landowner, regardless of religion, to be paid to the wardens of the local Anglican church for its support. Attendance at Anglican churches was mandatory; only the Book of Common Prayer could be used at any lawful public worship. When the English Parliament passed an Act of Toleration for members of certain religious groups, the Maryland General Assembly applied it only to Protestant dissenters, such as Methodists and Quakers. Various bills aimed at Catholics were introduced in the lower house of the general assembly but did not pass. One such bill was designed to inquire into the affairs of Jesuits and particularly into the manner by which they held title to land. A bill that did pass was a fundraising measure aimed at supporting the British Army in the French and Indian War. Enacted in 1756, it imposed an annual real-estate levy on Catholics at twice the regular rate. The double tax remained in effect until the American Revolution twenty years later.

In Virginia, Catholics were forbidden from holding office and from owning a horse valued at more than £5; anyone failing to attend the Anglican church could be fined £20. Priests were forbidden from entering Virginia and, if found, were required to leave upon five days' notice. In order to vote in colonial Virginia, a man had to receive Communion three times a year in an Anglican church. There were few penal laws in Pennsylvania where Catholics were given the widest freedom to practice their religion. One restriction that did exist was a prohibition on holding land for the purpose of erecting a hospital or other charitable institution. Another law prevented the naturalization of foreign Catholics, but there is evidence that this law was often ignored by magistrates who administered oaths of allegiance to German Catholic immigrants. In Georgia, there were no penal laws because there were no Catholics. The royal charter in effect until 1752 in that province simply forbade Catholics from living in Georgia, and there is no evidence that any did.

The government of the Catholic Church in the American colonies was entrusted to a church official known as the vicar apostolic for the London district. England had been divided by the Holy See into four districts, each of which was under the supervision of a vicar apostolic. Each vicar apostolic was a bishop, but during penal times his jurisdiction did not have the dignity of a full-fledged diocese. During this era, England was regarded as a mission country just as its colonies were, so its Catholic churches also came under the jurisdiction of the Propagation of the Faith. The American colonies were simply given to the London vicar as an adjunct to his regular duties.

The extent of the control exercised by the vicar apostolic over Catholics in America was necessarily slight. The distance between him and the twenty-five thousand Catholics in his vicariate in America was enormous. Communications were slow and uncertain, so colonial Catholics were pretty much on their own. Moreover, the vicar himself often had to contend with many immediate difficulties that left little time or energy for people who were three thousand miles away. One example of these difficulties could be found in the career of Bishop Bonaventure Giffard. He was the London vicar apostolic in the late seventeenth and early eighteenth centuries, just after the removal of Catholic King James II from the throne of England. During the short reign of James II, Bishop Giffard was chaplain to the king as well as president of Magdalen College at Oxford. When William and Mary became ruling monarchs, Bishop Giffard was imprisoned in Newgate jail and later in Hertford jail. Sometime after he had been released from confinement, a bounty was placed on his head, so priest hunters eagerly sought him out. During one year, he had to relocate his London address fourteen times to evade recapture.

The Catholic Church in the American colonies was actually a Jesuit mission band of about twenty priests who were headquartered at St. Thomas Manor in southern Maryland. The head of this mission band was the deputy or vicar general for the vicar apostolic. He was in charge of the entire Catholic Church from New England to Georgia.

Although penal laws both in England and in America were Draconian measures, they were frequently left unenforced. However, they remained as legal disabilities under which Catholics were required to live and which could be invoked from time to time, depending upon the internal and external political pressures of the moment and often depending upon nothing more substantial than the disposition or whim of a royal governor. In 1715 and again in 1745, anti-Catholic sentiment broke out because the Catholic branch of the deposed Stuart family tried to recapture the throne by uprisings incited among residents of the Scottish Highlands. Since the Stuart pretenders were Catholic, Protestant supporters of incumbent kings were afraid that Catholics throughout England and its colonies would automatically join in these rebellions and depose the king, as they themselves had done in 1688. These potential acts of rebellion did not materialize, but the possibility was enough to trigger an increase in anti-Catholic sentiment and piecemeal enforcement of penal laws.

A year after "Bonnie Prince Charlie," the last of the Stuart pretenders, was defeated at the Battle of Culloden Moor, Governor Thomas Bladen of Maryland issued the following proclamation at Annapolis: "Whereas I have received certain information that several Jesuits and other Popish priests and their emissaries have presumed of late, especially since the unnatural rebellion broke out in Scotland, to seduce and pervert several of His Majesty's Protestant subjects from their religion and to alienate their affections from His Majesty's royal person and government, although such practises are high treason, not only in priests or their emissaries but also in those who shall be seduced or perverted, I have therefore thought it fit, with the advice of His Lordship's Council of State, to issue this, my Proclamation, to charge all Jesuits and other Popish priests and their emissaries to forbear such traitorous practises and to assure such of them as shall dare hereafter to offend, that they shall be prosecuted according to law. And all magistrates within this province are hereby strictly required and charged, when and as often as they shall be informed, or have reason to suspect, of any Jesuit or other Popish priests, or any of their emissaries offending in the premises, to issue a warrant or warrants against such offender or offenders to take his or their examinations, and the examinations or depositions of the witnesses against them; and if need be, commit such offender or offenders to prison, until he or they shall be delivered by due course of law."

Sporadic enforcement of anti-Catholic penal laws came about for other reasons and sometimes involved people who were not Catholics or who had not even been offered an opportunity to take the Test Oath. In 1740, Governor James Oglethorpe of Georgia published letters in New York and elsewhere warning residents of Northern cities that the Spanish, whom he was fighting in Florida, had spies in the North, led by a priest, who were attempting to start an insurrection against the British crown. During the hysteria created by these charges, an Anglican clergyman and several black Spanish slaves who had been brought to New York were put on trial in New York for treason and sedition. No priests could be found in New York to fit Oglethorpe's warning, so New York authorities did the next best thing — they indicted a nonjuring clergyman, John Ury, as the leader of this conspiracy. The term "nonjuring clergyman" was applied at that time to certain Protestant ministers who, like Catholics, recused themselves from taking the Oath of Allegiance in the prescribed form but for reasons that were slightly different from those entertained by Catholics. This type of dissent was enough to bring down the wrath of public officialdom upon Ury and to influence a jury to return a guilty verdict within fifteen minutes after being instructed by a hostile judge. On August 15, 1741, Ury and the alleged Spanish insurrectionists were hanged. Fifteen years later, an asserted refusal of French Catholics to take the Oath of Allegiance, most of whom had never been given the opportunity either to take or refuse it, resulted in the forced evacuation of seven thousand people from Acadia and the forfeiture of their lands.

Pressure against Maryland Catholics prompted Charles Carroll of Annapolis, father of the signer of the Declaration of Independence and uncle of the future archbishop of Baltimore, to go to Paris in 1752 to ask King Louis XV for land along the Arkansas River, then within the French colonial domain, so that Maryland Catholics could escape from British rule and migrate en masse to a new home west of the Mississippi. He may have asked for too large a grant. In any event, Louis XV denied the request.

Anti-Catholic hysteria welled up a few years later during the French and Indian

War. The French were Catholics, some English colonists reasoned, and they and their Indian allies were just over the Allegheny Mountains at Fort Duquesne. If the French were able to advance east of the mountains, Catholics in English colonies might join with their co-religionists against the British crown. The Berks County commissioners, meeting near Reading, Pennsylvania, sent a petition to the governor of Pennsylvania warning him of just such a possibility and urging him to take measures against Catholics in their area. Actually, most Catholics in the Susquehanna River valley were German immigrants who had no more liking for the French than did their Protestant neighbors. However, the perception of Catholics as an alien and untrustworthy element in the community arose once more during a time of public distress and turmoil. Here again these fears proved to be groundless.

Finding Men and Money for the Missions

Expressed in the simplest terms, the goal of the mission church was to establish territorial dioceses, supervised by bishops (known as ordinaries), who could assign diocesan or secular priests to serve as pastors of territorial parishes within each diocese. This checkerboard design is quite familiar to Catholics today. It did not exist in colonial times. Even after accommodations were made with various governmental authorities that would permit the colonial Church to pursue its mission, the Church was still confronted by its initial problem: how to begin parishes and dioceses that did not exist, with diocesan priests who could not be found except in a few missionary seminaries in Rome, Paris, and Quebec. This predicament meant calling upon religious orders who had their own seminaries, their own recruitment programs that were organized on a supranational basis, and their own financial resources. They also had the flexibility to respond rapidly when the call came. It was to these task-oriented fraternities of priests that the Church turned during this period in its existence.

The principal responses to the Church's call for missionaries came from Jesuits and Franciscans, although Recollects, Capuchins, Dominicans, and Discalced Carmelites were also among the earliest priests to arrive in America. Most of them had members among the nationals of all three major powers who were claiming a share of the North American continent. After the United States was founded, these orders were followed by members of other orders that in many instances were not even in existence when the mission effort began. In the latter part of the eighteenth and nineteenth centuries, Sulpicians, Vincentians, Redemptorists, Resurrectionists, Holy Cross Fathers, and Benedictines all joined in this effort, as did some native American religious orders such as the Paulists and the Josephites. After the penal laws were relaxed in Ireland, St. Patrick's Seminary at Maynooth and All Hallows' Seminary in Dublin provided hundreds of secular priests to staff the increasing number of dioceses in the United States.

The other necessary element of any mission undertaking was money. One principle normally followed during the mission era was that the Church did not look for financial support from the people it was evangelizing or from Catholics who lived at mission stops and mission parishes. Funds had to be obtained from other sources. Stipends provided by the Spanish and French governments were never enough to support missionaries in the field. Some orders began to operate plantations to obtain funds. English Jesuits in Maryland raised tobacco while French Jesuits in Louisiana grew sugar cane and oranges. The vicar apostolic in London was the recipient of a bequest from a wealthy Catholic Englishman, Sir John James. This bequest was applied in part for the relief of the poor in London and in part to the support of missionaries in Maryland and Pennsylvania. In Mexico, the Jesuits established what they called the Pious Fund, donations that they invested so that the interest could be used to support their missions in the American Southwest and in northern Mexico.

In 1819, a French laywoman, Pauline Jaricot, organized in Lyons the Society for the Propagation of the Faith. Its function was to collect money in France to support missions all over the world. Between 1822 and 1861, the society supplied more than seven million dollars to American missions. In pre-Civil War America, a large percentage of the priests on the mission as well as a significant number of American bishops were French. The society made a determined effort to recruit missionary clergy as well as to collect money. One prospectus, sent out in 1825, read: "We offer you: no salary, no recompense; no holidays; no pension. But: much hard work; a poor dwelling; few consolations; many disappointments; frequent sickness; a violent or lonely death; an unknown grave." Despite the forbidding nature of the want ad, it drew applicants.

Since that time, the society has expanded into many parts of the world, including the United States, and now collects funds in this country and other developed nations to support mission activities in Africa, the Near East, the islands of the Pacific, and South America. In 1828, Father Frederic Résé, an Austrian missionary, returned to Vienna from Cincinnati to organize the Leopoldine Society whose function was to provide financial support for German parishes in the United States. When it ceased to function in 1921, the Leopoldine Society had provided more than $700,000 to assist German Catholic immigrants in the United States. When the first synod, or convention, of American priests was called in Baltimore in 1791 by Bishop Carroll, one of the resolutions it adopted was that collections should be taken up at all the Masses in every Catholic parish each Sunday. This all seems pretty routine today; in 1791, it was a startling and innovative proposal.

If there is another fixed policy that has always governed the missionary activity of the Church, it is that a mission is not forever. Jesuits in southern Maryland and Franciscans in California always knew that someday they would be replaced, although the California Franciscans might not have anticipated that their missions would be brought to an end so rudely and abruptly. For the most part these missionaries have been replaced, as secular priests from established dioceses have moved in to take charge of the churches that others established long ago. Meanwhile, members of missionary orders have gone on to other mission fields. Occasionally, someone expresses regret that the Jesuits are no longer a large presence in southern Maryland or that the Franciscans have left most of their Spanish missions, but this is pure nostalgia. If one wants to find Jesuit missionaries today, he should look in northern Alaska, not in southern Maryland. Jesuits are now establishing and manning parishes at the Arctic Circle just as they did three hundred fifty years ago at the point where Port Tobacco Creek flows into the Potomac. Franciscans can be found in many places, including large, busy churches in the heart of major cities such as Boston, New York, and Chicago. Far from being the cause of regret, these changes simply demonstrate that colonial missionaries accomplished the tasks that were set before them, so the American Church has been able to move on to a permanent mode of existence in formally established parishes.

As old dioceses grow, additional ones are created in areas formerly served by the mother diocese, and the original one usually becomes an archdiocese presided over by an archbishop or metropolitan. The group of dioceses over which an archbishop presides is called an ecclesiastical province. It is within this framework that over a period of 200 years, one diocese in Baltimore and another created during Spanish rule in New Orleans have grown into 199 dioceses and archdioceses and 33 Roman Rite ecclesiastical provinces.

Suppressing the Jesuits

A series of events of considerable consequence to the Catholic Church took place just before the outbreak of the American Revolution which had a direct and serious impact throughout the colonies of all of the major powers who had holdings in the Western Hemisphere. As a result of the vicissitudes of European politics, between 1759 and 1773, Jesuits were expelled from several European countries. Whenever they were expelled from the mother country, they were also expelled at the same time from its colonies in the New World. The causes of these attacks on the Society of Jesus were many and varied. Jesuits championed the rights of the pope against various monarchies. This brought upon them the wrath of Catholic royal families, especially the Bourbons. The spirit of the Enlightenment, a heresy known as Jansenism, and the jealousy of other clerics were other factors that contributed to a forty-year suspension of the Jesuits. This effort began with the expulsion of the Society of Jesus from Portugal, Spain, and France, with the Kingdom of the Two Sicilies following suit. In France, Jesuits were allowed to remain if they ceased to function as an order and were content to become secular or diocesan priests. The campaign to eliminate the society was climaxed by a papal bull, a directive issued in 1773 by Pope Clement XIV, which dissolved the order in every country whose monarch allowed it to be promulgated. Catherine the Great, empress of Russia and an Orthodox Catholic, was the only important European ruler who forbade the promulgation of the papal order. As a result, many Jesuits took refuge in Russia and remained under her protection for several decades.

During the two centuries of exploration and missionary activity that took place prior to the order of suppression, some 3,500 Jesuits had served the Church in the Western Hemisphere; of this number, 329 were French, 144 were English, and the rest were either Spanish or Portuguese. The first expulsion took place in 1759 in Portugal. This event affected Jesuits in Brazil. In 1763, they were suppressed in France. At that time, about a dozen Jesuits in the Mississippi Valley were rounded up by French soldiers, placed on a ship in New Orleans, and sent back to France. Their property was confiscated and, in some instances, their churches were razed. Some twenty-nine Jesuits were serving in northern Mexico and in the American Southwest in 1767 when King Carlos III ordered them expelled. They were arrested at their mission stations by Spanish soldiers, put aboard prison ships, and sent back to Spain to await an uncertain fate.

Ironically, the place where this campaign had the least impact was the English colonies where Jesuits were already an outlawed order in an outlawed Church. The *coup de grace* for English Jesuits landed when Pope Clement dissolved the order in 1773. In that decree, Jesuits everywhere were required to submit to the order of dissolution in writing. They were instructed to make themselves available to local bishops as diocesan priests and to turn over all community property to those bishops. Pope Clement never explained the reason for his action, stating only that it "was suggested to Us by the principles of prudence which We retain concealed in Our breast." In the English colonies in North America, Father John Lewis, the Jesuit superior, and about twenty-five others complied with the decree and signed the documents of submissions presented to them by the vicar apostolic Bishop Richard Challoner. They continued to act as parish or missionary priests under his remote supervision. Technically, they owned no property in the name of the community because of the penal laws, so they claimed that they had no property to turn over to the bishop. This contention gave rise to a sharp dispute forty years later.

The impact of the decree of suppression on English Jesuits can be appreciated by the reaction of John Carroll, who had joined the order in 1753. He had been teaching in the English College at St. Omer's in French Flanders, a school operated under the patronage of the king of France by English Jesuits for the sons of English Catholics. After the French expulsion of Jesuits in 1763, the English College moved a few miles across the border into Austrian Flanders where it continued to function in Bruges under the patronage of the empress of Austria. (There was no Belgium in those days.) When the order of suppression from the Holy See was published in Austria, the English College at Bruges was closed and Carroll and his fellow priests were placed under house arrest. Their property and personal papers were seized and they were interrogated by Austrian officials concerning the location of other property. Carroll was released only when an English lord interceded with the Austrian government on his behalf. In referring to the news of the papal suppression, Carroll wrote: "I am not, and perhaps never shall be, recovered from the shock of this dreadful intelligence. The greatest blessing which, in my estimation, I could receive from God would be immediate death, but if He deny me this, may His holy and adorable designs on me be wholly fulfilled. Is it possible that Divine Providence should permit to such an end a body wholly devoted, and I will still aver, with most disinterested charity, in procuring every comfort and advantage to their neighbors, whether by preaching, teaching, catechizing, missions, visiting hospitals, prisons, and every other function of spiritual and corporal mercy?"

Carroll lived to see the Jesuit order revived in the year before his death. In 1814, when Pope Pius VII had returned to Rome after serving five years as a prisoner of Napoleon Bonaparte, he decided that he needed the support of an order like the Jesuits, so he issued a papal bull restoring the Society of Jesus to its previous status in the Church.

Involvement in the American Revolution

As the clouds of revolutionary war gathered, British leaders were confronted with an acute political problem. They wished to prevent 60,000 French settlers, living in lands acquired from France in 1763, from making common cause with 4,000,000 Englishmen in 13 English colonies who were thinking about leaving the Empire. As a means of securing the allegiance of their French subjects, the British tried religious toleration and it worked. On June 13, 1774, the House of Commons, by a vote of 56 to 20, enacted what was called the Quebec Act. It stated in part: "And, for the more perfect security and ease of the minds of the inhabitants of the said province, it is hereby declared, that His Majesty's subjects, professing the religion of the Church of Rome of and in the said province of Quebec, may have, hold, and enjoy the free exercise of the religion of the Church of Rome, subject to the King's supremacy, declared and established by an Act made in the first year of the reign of Queen Elizabeth...."

The Quebec Act not only granted religious toleration to Catholics but also gave formal recognition to certain rights that the institutional Church might enjoy. Catholic clergy would be entitled to tithes from Catholics. The Oath of Allegiance to the crown was revised so that Catholics might take it in good conscience, title to Catholic Church properties was recognized, and penal laws were repealed.

What is sometimes overlooked is that the Quebec Act applied not only to what we now call Quebec but extended as well to all British territory west of the Appalachian Mountains, including the Ohio Valley, the Northwest Territory, and the Mississippi Valley as far south as Natchez and Mobile. This was land to which several colonies had laid territorial claims, however insubstantial, and to which many English settlers in the original colonies had aspired to migrate. In terms of keeping the French loyal to the British crown, this measure succeeded. In 1776, when Benjamin Franklin, Charles Carroll of Carrollton, and Father John Carroll journeyed to Canada to enlist the support of French inhabitants in the American cause, they were rebuffed. However, in English colonies, the Quebec Act ignited a firestorm of protest. Like the Stamp Act and the Tea Act, it was included among the "usurpations" of the British government to which colonists took strong exception.

Cartoons appeared in New England publications depicting dancing bishops celebrating the enactment of the Quebec Act. "No Popery" flags were flown in New York. A prominent journal, the *Pennsylvania Packet*, denounced the Quebec Act as "in an extreme degree dangerous." In another article, it warned: "We may live to see our churches converted into masshouses and our lands plundered of tythes for the support of a Popish clergy. The Inquisition may erect her standard in Pennsylvania, and the city of Philadelphia may yet experience the carnage of St. Bartholomew's day." The First Continental Congress, meeting in Philadelphia, also reacted strongly to the Quebec Act, prompted in no small part by John Jay, a delegate from New York and a prominent politician of the time. In later years, he would come to be the first chief justice of the United States and then governor of New York. He gained historical prominence as one of the three authors of the *Federalist Papers*. He also authored a resolution, adopted by the Continental Congress on October 14, 1774, which stated: "We think the Legislature of Great Britain is not authorized by the Constitution to establish a religion, fraught with sanguinary and impious tenets, or to erect an arbitrary form of government in any quarter of the globe. . . . By another act the dominion of Canada is to be so extended, modelled, and governed, as, that being disunited from us, detached from our interests by civil as well as religious prejudices, that, by their numbers daily swelling with Catholic immigrants from Europe, and by their devotion to administration so friendly to their religion they might become formidable to us, and on occasion to be fit instruments in the hand of power to reduce the ancient free Protestant colonies to the same state of slavery with themselves."

At the time of the American Revolution, Catholics constituted only one percent of the population of the colonies. Their impact on these events was a minor one. However, no group in the colonies gained more from the success of the Revolution than did Catholics. Of considerable importance was the foreign assistance obtained by the Continental Congress in support of the colonial cause. It came mostly from two Catholic countries, France and Spain. Foreign military leaders who lent their expertise to the Revolution — Kosciuszko, Pulaski, Rochambeau, and Lafayette — were all Catholics. Shortly after the Battle of Saratoga, both France and Spain accorded formal diplomatic recognition to the Continental Congress, and Catholic envoys soon arrived in Philadelphia to make up a fledgling diplomatic corps accredited to the colonial government. These ministers represented European powers whose interests had previously been regarded as hostile to English colonists. They brought with them to Philadelphia Catholic chaplains who were, in effect, part of their diplomatic delegations.

In 1781, Spain took advantage of the weakness of its historic rival to recapture from the British Spain's former possessions in Florida. Although the assistance of France and Spain was dictated by obvious motives of national advantage, the fact that the interests of two Catholic nations could coincide with those of English colonists was itself a revolutionary development. Some three thousand miles from the battle front, Father Junípero Serra, *Padre Presidente* of the Spanish missions in California, instructed priests along the Camino Real to chant a "Te Deum" — a formal public prayer of thanksgiving — to celebrate the defeat of the enemies of the king of Spain at Yorktown. The same Latin prayer was also being offered at Old St. Mary's in Philadelphia by its pastor,

Father Robert Molyneaux, and Father Séraphin Bandol, chaplain to the French minister to the Continental Congress.

Organizing the Church in a New Nation

After the American colonies ceased to be a part of the British Empire, the vicar apostolic in London resigned his responsibilities for the Catholic Church in America. This left a temporary leadership vacuum that was filled when the Propagation of the Faith in Rome appointed Carroll as prefect apostolic. This appointment placed Carroll at the head of the American Church. While serving as American envoy to the king of France during the 1780s, Benjamin Franklin spoke to the papal nuncio in Paris to urge the appointment of his old friend John Carroll as bishop. At first, American clergy, many of them ex-Jesuits, were opposed to the installation of a bishop in the United States, feeling that the presence of a bishop might pose a challenge to the titles to properties then held in trust by individual priests for the benefit of the defunct society. Then, in 1788, the Propagation convened all of the American clergy at Sacred Heart Church in White Marsh (now Bowie), Maryland, to select a candidate for bishop. They recommended Carroll by a vote of 24 to 2. On November 6, 1789, Pope Pius VI issued a bull entitled *Ad Futuram Rei Memoriam* in which he created an American diocese that included all American territory as far west as the Mississippi River. He designated Baltimore as its headquarters and appointed John Carroll to be its bishop. Carroll went to England to be consecrated and returned to Baltimore on December 7, 1790, where, as old record books would phrase it, he "took possession of his See." At this point in time, the Catholic Church in America took on its own unique existence and began a development and expansion which, by any standards, has been truly remarkable.

The Arrival of New Catholics

It is at this point that the story of the Catholic Church in the United States can be coherently told by reviewing the histories of certain old parishes in various parts of the country that prominently recount the history of that Church. In 1790, some 17 churches profiled in this volume were already in existence; another 36 began in the ensuing 75 years. One development of paramount importance to the growth of the American Church during the following century deserves a few words of general attention, namely the arrival on these shores of large numbers of immigrants from various Catholic countries. Between 1830 and 1860, some 4,910,000 people immigrated to the United States. About forty percent came from Ireland; another thirty percent came from states and principalities now known as Germany. Almost all of the Irish and about a third of the German immigrants were Catholics. During these three decades, the Catholic population of the United States increased tenfold, from about 300,000 to more than three million.

The first of these immigrants were twenty-nine priests who came to the United States between 1791 and 1800 as refugees from the anticlerical laws of the French

Revolution. Their arrival had the effect of doubling the size of the American Catholic clergy. Many stayed and others followed. French names like Cheverus, Flaget, Dubourg, Lefevere, Verot, Marèchal, Dubois, Portier, Loras, Miège, and Bruté can be found among the members of the early American Catholic hierarchy. Some were post-Revolution émigrés; most were founding bishops of their dioceses. The presence of such a large French hierarchy in this country brought talent and experience to the new American Church, but it also resulted in occasional friction with new Irish immigrants, who were fast becoming the main body of Catholics in the United States.

One of many instances of this early ethnic friction can be found in the mixed emotions of Ambrose Marèchal, a French Sulpician and the third archbishop of Baltimore, who had trouble not only with the Irish but with the Jesuits and the Propagation itself. In a formal report to Rome in 1818, he wrote: "Indeed it gives me great joy that many of this race [the Irish] are in my diocese; I would gladly receive many more of them with open arms. But alas, so many priests who have come hither from Ireland are addicted to the vice of drunkenness, and I cannot place them in charge of souls until after a mature and thorough examination. For when they have once obtained faculties from us, it is hard to say what harm they would bring down upon the Church of God, if they should fall back into the vice of drunkenness. Nor would there be much of a remedy left to us by which we could put an end to their scandals. For if we should take away their faculties or attempt to do so, they would shake off the yoke completely and trouble the American Church with unbelievable seditions. They can do nothing among the faithful who are Americans, English, or belong to the any of the European nationalities. These indeed flee from them. But it is truly surprising how much authority these drunkard [sic] priests exercise among the lowest classes of their own race. For since these consider drunkenness only a slight imperfection, they strenuously defend their profligate pastors, associate with them, and enter into and remain with them in schism." Thus he described the forerunners of a conservative and rigorous Irish clergy of several following generations of American Catholics who, in their turn, had to contend with newly arrived Catholics from cultures with which they had difficulty in coping. The pages ahead contain several such examples.

The importance of the Catholic Church in facilitating the settlement and the integration into American society of these millions of newcomers can hardly be overstated. This work is still going on. These newcomers eventually came to make up the bulk of the Catholic Church in America, and the bishops recognized this fact early on. Recognition of this development can be found in this volume in the profiles of certain ethnic parishes — often the first parish to be established in the United States by a particular nationality. In these old ethnic parishes, millions of Americans find their roots today.

In 1852, 1866, and 1884, the Catholic Church in the United States convened plenary councils in Baltimore at which bishops from all over America gathered to discuss and to formulate policies and regulations for the Catholic Church in this country. In 1852, the First Plenary Council adopted a regulation requiring all parishes and missions to have stated geographical boundaries. Thus it established the checkerboard pattern of territorial parishes in territorial dioceses that was previously mentioned. However, an important exception to that pattern was made to accommodate immigrant Catholics. They authorized national churches — churches without fixed boundaries administered by priests who spoke the language of a particular immigrant group. They were assigned to these churches to minister to the needs of Catholics who could not be reached by English-speaking priests in territorial parishes.

The first national parish had already been established in Philadelphia in 1789 at the request of German-speaking Catholics. This practice was greatly expanded in the latter half of the nineteenth century and continues today. As a result, one can see today in various towns and cities in the Northeast and the Middle West clusters of Catholic churches built within short distances of each other and designed to serve a particular language and ethnic constituency. As this country becomes more suburbanized and more homogenized, hard choices may have to be made concerning the future of some of these parishes. Some can be viewed as victims of their own success, having served as a vehicle for integrating millions of immigrants to these shores into the mainstream of American life. The children and grandchildren of the founders of these parishes have, by now, made their way into ethnically mixed neighborhoods where they are part of the parish life of churches that have no distinct national identity other than American. As for now, they continue to find support from Catholics for whom ethnic identification has ceased to be a matter of invidious distinction and has come to be a source of family roots and personal identity in a society they may well find to be increasingly rootless and impersonal.

1
Holy Cross

Christiansted

ST. CROIX, U.S. VIRGIN ISLANDS

Each morning, the sun's rays first strike the United States as well as its territories and possessions (excluding Guam) at Udall Point, the eastern tip of the island of St. Croix in the U.S. Virgin Islands. A few miles west of this point, Christopher Columbus, the first Catholic to set foot on future American soil, landed on the north shore of the island on November 13, 1493, during his second trip to the New World. He was in search of fresh water for his expedition. The name of his landing place, Salt River, suggests that he may have experienced some difficulty in his quest.

St. Croix, the largest of the U.S. Virgin Islands, is located about forty miles south of the island of St. Thomas where the capital of this territory is now located. St. Croix contains some eighty square miles and made its living from sugar-cane plantations until the twentieth century when it began to develop the tourist trade that now supports its economy. Before leaving St. Croix, Columbus named it in honor of the Holy Cross — Santa Cruz in Spanish — and one hundred fifty years later the French carried on this name. It has survived in the French form to this day. Later, the Spanish named the entire collection of Caribbean islands, of which St. Croix is a part, in honor of St. Ursula, a fifth-century Saxon martyr, and her eleven thousand virgins, some of whom met their deaths with St. Ursula near Cologne at the hands of Hun invaders.

Like many Caribbean islands, control of the Virgin Islands changed hands often during the four hundred years that elapsed following the discovery by Columbus. Some changes came about through naval conquest and others by purchase. Dutch and English settlers came first to St. Croix, followed by the French. By 1651, the French controlled the island through a trading company, the French West Indian Company. There is evidence that two Catholic churches were built on the island by Dominican missionaries during the French period. Other evidence suggests that religious ministrations to French Catholics were conducted only on an occasional basis by French missionaries from Martinique. One relic of the French period still standing in the central square at Christiansted is an old building originally built as a Catholic church. In 1753, when the Danish crown took over this island, the Catholic church was transformed into a Lutheran church. It is now a museum.

The French government took direct control of St. Croix in 1674 but abandoned the island about twenty years later. Until well into the eighteenth century, St. Croix stood uninhabited. Meanwhile, in 1666, King Frederik III of Denmark decided to occupy the island of St. Thomas and turned control of that island over to the Danish exploration and trading arm, the West Indian and Guinea Trading Company. In 1672, the first Danes arrived on St. Thomas. Denmark officially recognized and supported the Lutheran Church. There is doubt that any Catholics resided on St. Thomas during the first fifty years of Danish occupation, although Spanish priests from nearby Puerto Rico occasionally visited the island to look after slaves owned by Danish settlers. The Danish trading company adopted a regulation designed to promote the settlement of the island. It provided that "a gentleman who will establish himself there and take an estate . . . is to be granted freedom of conscience . . . and is not to be hindered in whatever nation and religion it may be." In 1685, Denmark granted private toleration to Catholics and Jews, meaning that they were free to worship in their own homes but not to erect public churches and synagogues. This limited grant of religious toleration had little immediate impact on the Danish West Indies, as the Virgin Islands were then called, since they had no Catholic or Jewish inhabitants until well into the eighteenth century.

In 1733, the French relinquished title to St. Croix to the Danish West Indian and Guinea Trading Company. Immediately, Moravian missionaries began colonizing the island, as did British planters. When the Danish crown bought the island from the trading company in 1755, it was inhabited by ten thousand people who were engaged in raising sugar, cotton, tobacco, and indigo on three hundred seventy-five plantations.

In the late 1740s, Nicholas Tuite, an Irish Catholic plantation owner residing on the British island of Montserrat, wanted to start a sugar plantation on St. Croix. Before bringing his household, including his slaves, to St. Croix, he wanted to be assured of the existence of a Catholic church on the island both for them and for a large number of Irish and English Catholics whom he intended to place in charge of the plantation. Like many Caribbean planters, Tuite spent only a small amount of time in the West Indies, preferring to live several months each year in London. He sought permission from the king of Denmark to bring priests to St. Croix and limited permission was granted. On September 20, 1754, the royal Danish government published an order that read: "The King grants that 'papists' on St. Croix, St. Thomas, and St. John practice freely their religion, build as many churches, and have as many priests (but no Jesuits) as may be necessary."

The decree went on to state that any Jesuits already on the islands would have to leave as soon as replacements could be found. This exception proved an embarrassment to Tuite, since he had already arranged with the English province of the Society of Jesus to send priests to St. Croix. One of them, Father Bernard Cross, had already arrived before the decree was published and a second Jesuit, Father Richard Ellis, was on his way. When he arrived, he was forced to leave by the Danish governor but returned the following year. He was on the island only three weeks when, like so many other missionaries to the Caribbean during this era, he died of a fever. Father Cross left a few years later. After the departure of the Jesuits, Tuite was able to obtain the services of Irish Dominicans. Two of them, Father Hyacinth Kennedy and Father Dominic Allen, arrived in 1758. They died within three years of unspecified fevers, as did another Dominican, Father James Flynn.

Christiansted was selected by the Danes as the capital of their West Indian islands and was platted and laid out as a town. It remained the capital of the Danish West Indies until the islands were ceded to the United States in 1917. In 1755, Tuite built a small church at Christiansted on Prindsens Gade (street), between Dronigens Gade and Company Gade. It was a few blocks from the center of the town. A plat map of Christiansted, dated 1779, shows a Catholic church and rectory at the site now occupied by Holy Cross Church. Tuite's church is the oldest functioning Catholic church in the Virgin Islands. Father Allen lived next door to the church while Father Kennedy resided a few miles away on the Tuite estate where he ministered to both white and black inhabitants of the plantation.

In 1760, Father Kennedy described the Christiansted Catholic church, as it was then referred to, and the condition of its two hundred fifty parishioners as follows: "The chapel in town is a large, spacious one but is no way finished inside as yet. No altar, nothing but a table. Their cares and temporal calls prevent their attention to it. Mr. [Father] Allen has a house by the chapel where he resides. . . . There is no stairs at either of the three doors, one of which is at the end of the church; the others are at each side of the church. In a word, it is roofed and floored and that is all. There is enclosed about a quarter of an acre of ground from the church to the house for the priest to live in, without offices requisite such as are necessary in this part of the world. The dwelling house is adjacent to the church. It contains a large hall below and a back room, and two small rooms above facing one of the few streets we have here."

Father Allen, who lived next door, painted a less flattering picture of the premises: "Our church is only the bare shell without an ornament. It is exceeding modelled [torn] and was ill finished; would make a genteel figure tho' indeed it cost sufficient to complete had it been duly taken care of. I can't expect it will be perfected too soon as this is an infant settlement and those three years past vastly severe, which, of course, must retard the gentlemen's subscriptions."

Shortly after Father Allen died from fever, Father Kennedy wrote to a Dominican colleague in Ireland: "All I have to say is, if I depart, that you acquaint Corpo Santo [in Portugal] and the house on Bridge Street [another Dominican establishment] that they may pray for my soul. I dread sudden death, though the God of Mercy may be gracious and pleased to allow me some years yet to live. All is in His hands, but I fear my days are short. I wish I may make good use of my time, since Mr. Tuite was pleased to give to our Order the care of this mission. . . . If I depart, let others more fit than me come, and let the attempt of a mission be undertaken. As for my part, I was very unworthy and unfit for it. I [have] done but little. However, the God of Mercy, I hope, will pardon me. All I could do was among poor black slaves who groped in the dark of ignorance. I [have] done what I could. They were my flock and, at this moment, I would lay down my life for them if it would conduce to the salvation of their souls." He died of a fever just a little more than a year after writing this letter during an epidemic that claimed forty members of the Christiansted parish.

Father Kennedy's letter did result in the sending of three more Dominicans to St. Croix. They arrived in 1761 after managing to avoid capture en route by French pirates. The leader of this mission, Father Thomas Devenish, was an energetic and imaginative priest who conceived of the idea of purchasing a small sugar plantation to be operated by the Dominicans for the support of their activities, both in St. Croix and elsewhere in the Caribbean. Several Catholic plantation owners pledged to support his project, but when the land for the Dominican plantation was purchased, they did not redeem their pledges so the plan fell through. Disgusted with the leading Catholics on St. Croix, Father Devenish left the island and started another mission at Grenada, leaving the care of Catholics at St. Croix to the other priests who had accompanied him from Ireland.

The Dominicans left St. Croix in 1771. For the next one hundred twenty years the Christiansted parish was placed in the hands of secular priests, except for a brief two-year period when it was staffed by Redemptorists. The first secular priest to head the mission was Father Christopher McEvoy, who was appointed to this position by the Propagation of the Faith in Rome. During his tenure, he became involved in a dispute with Danish authorities because he had baptized four blacks who had formerly been members of the Moravian, or Brethren, Church. The royal governor published a decree instructing Catholic priests to refrain from making converts among either white or black Protestants. It also informed the superiors of the Roman Catholic congregation that the newly baptized Moravians had to "be returned to the congregation, . . . of which they first became members by baptism," within fourteen days. The government ban on religious conversions extended to any children born of Protestant parents. It forbade either free blacks or slaves from joining the Catholic Church, whether voluntarily or otherwise. Catholic priests were instructed to keep proper church records for government inspection and were directed to file with government authorities their letters of appointment, which had to include information concerning which religious order they belonged to and the name of the church to which they were being assigned.

During this period of time, the nearby island of St. Thomas was also growing in population and was attracting a varied group of settlers. This number included both French Catholics and Sephardic Jews. The latter had come to the Danish West Indies after first escaping from Spain and Portugal and then being forced to leave the Portuguese city of Pernambuco in Brazil.

The initial establishment of a Catholic church at St. Thomas was prompted, in no small part, by an effort on the part of the Danes to recapture runaway slaves. Slavery was harsh in Danish, Dutch, and English colonies as well as in the pre-Civil War United States. Although still an undesirable status, the position of slaves in Spanish territories was considerably better, largely due to the influence of the Catholic Church. In Spanish colonies, slaves could marry freemen as well as other slaves, even against the will of their masters, so long as they remained slaves. Such marriages were regarded as sacramental in character and hence inviolable. The Church attempted to ensure that masters placed married couples together. If this was not possible, the Church would buy one of the slaves so that he or she would be able to remain with the individual who remained in bondage. Masters were forbidden to injure or kill slaves, and slaves had redress in civil courts for the misconduct of their masters. If misconduct was proven, the judge was required to sell the slave and turn the purchase price over to the former master. Any slaves held by Muslims or Jews could gain their freedom by being baptized. The Church assisted in the enforcement of these rules and, in extreme cases, would excommunicate a slaveholder who was guilty of violating them. The same ecclesiastical punishment was imposed on slaveholders who failed to provide for the religious education of their subjects. None of these protections existed in the Danish West Indies.

From time to time, slaves escaped from St. Thomas to nearby Puerto Rico, a Spanish territory. Spain was reluctant to return any slaves who were baptized into the Catholic Church because there were no churches on St. Thomas where Catholics could practice their religion. Danish slaveholders became profoundly disturbed that runaway slaves were gaining their freedom by going to Puerto Rico. They requested diplomatic intervention to arrange for the return of such individuals. Spain finally agreed to cooperate in the return of runaway slaves from St. Thomas if a Catholic church were built on the island so that Catholic slaves could receive the sacraments and attend Mass. Denmark agreed and permitted the establishment of a Catholic church on St. Thomas as well as on St. Croix. Beginning in 1773, a Catholic church, later named in honor of St. Peter and St. Paul, was erected at St. Thomas. With the exception of brief periods when it was closed because of fire, hurricanes, or schism, that parish has existed continuously to this day. In 1960, when the U.S. Virgin Islands became a prelature and received its own bishop, Sts. Peter and Paul Church was designated a cathedral.

In 1793, Father Mathieu Herard was appointed pastor of the Christiansted Church.

Father Herard had escaped from France during the anticlerical excesses of the Revolution and made his way first to Cayenne in French Guiana where he again encountered the same hostility. Father Herard then went to New York and later to Guadaloupe where the Revolutionary government imprisoned him. He escaped and made his way to the British island of St. Kitts and then to St. Croix where he remained until 1819.

In 1804, the Holy See placed the Danish West Indies under the supervision of Bishop John Carroll in Baltimore. Bishop Carroll already had a diocese that extended to the Mississippi River and had also been given the responsibility of administering the New Orleans diocese when the Louisiana Territory was ceded to the United States. This responsibility extended all the way to Montana, so there was little that he could do to promote the interest of the Church in the Danish West Indies. He appointed Father Henry Kendall, pastor of the newly established church at Frederiksted, St. Croix, as prefect of the Church in the Danish West Indies and gave Father Kendall permission to administer the sacrament of confirmation, a function normally reserved to bishops. Father Herard at Christiansted was appointed vice-prefect.

In 1819, the Holy See created a new Caribbean diocese at Port of Spain, the capital of the British island of Trinidad. All British, Danish, and Dutch islands were placed in this diocese, so Catholics on St. Croix no longer had to look to Baltimore for leadership. However, it was many years before the new bishop came to St. Croix. In 1838, Bishop Richard Smith, the second bishop of Port of Spain, visited the Christiansted church and administered confirmation. He reported to the Holy See that there were about eight thousand Catholics on the entire island, almost all of whom were slaves, and noted that "both churches there are in a bad state, both built in stone, 70 ft. by 35 ft. The Catholic landowners agreed to support a second priest so they should request an assistant to Fr. J. F. O'Kennelly, who is a very good priest."

A census of the Danish West Indies taken during the mid-1830s disclosed that there were forty-three thousand inhabitants on three major islands of what are now the U.S. Virgin Islands. Of this number some twenty-seven thousand were slaves. St. Croix was far and away the most heavily populated island, having twenty-seven thousand residents. Catholics were the largest denomination on St. Croix, constituting about thirty percent of the population. The others were Moravians, Episcopalians, and Lutherans. Whites predominated in St. Thomas, a large number of whom were French-speaking. In 1848, an event of momentous importance took place in St. Croix. On July 3 of that year, Royal Governor Peter Von Scholten, in defiance of instructions from Copenhagen, issued an order freeing all of the slaves in the Danish West Indies. He took this action to head off a slave revolt that was brewing in St. Croix. Although slavery was abolished, poverty was not, and it continued to plague the island for generations. At times, lack of work has brought about precipitous declines in population as Cruzians have left their homes to find employment elsewhere. By 1880, the 1835 population figure had dwindled to eighteen thousand.

In 1848, Father Thomas E. Butler, the pastor of the Christiansted church, completed the first renovation of that structure which had been attempted since it was originally built. A new wing was constructed over the cemetery adjacent to the north wall of the original building. A cornerstone was placed in the enlarged church that read: "The Holy Catholic Apostolic Church of the Holy Cross, erected 1849." This was the first reference to the title "Holy Cross" for the Christiansted church. In 1850, a new diocese was created at Roseau on the British island of Dominica and the diocese of Trinidad became an archdiocese. The Danish West Indies were assigned to the Roseau diocese and became part of the responsibility of its new bishop, Michael Monahan. In 1851, Bishop Monahan came to Christiansted and dedicated its enlarged church to the honor of the Holy Cross and the Virgin Mary.

Events in the mid-1850s brought to St. Thomas and St. Croix the Redemptorist Fathers, a missionary congregation whose work has been an integral part of the growth of the Church in the Virgin Islands since that time. In 1856, the pastor at Holy Cross dropped dead at the altar while saying Mass on Passion Sunday, leaving only one priest on the island of St. Croix. Sts. Peter and Paul Church at St. Thomas experienced an upheaval that was even more dramatic. Sts. Peter and Paul had grown to nearly five thousand parishioners and was one of the largest parishes in the entire Caribbean area. Father S. P. Giorgetti, a young Corsican priest, had been assigned to assist its ailing pastor, a Father Pratt. Father Giorgetti succeeded in alienating many of the parishioners from supporting their pastor, so the latter resigned. Father Giorgetti was then reassigned to Trinidad, much to the displeasure of many parishioners. In December of 1855, Monsignor George Talbot, a papal legate, was visiting the island en route to Trinidad. Many parishioners staged a torchlight parade to the place where Monsignor Talbot was staying to voice their displeasure over the transfer of Father Giorgetti. Monsignor Talbot promised to inform the archbishop of Trinidad of their feelings.

Notwithstanding this protest, the archbishop assigned a Father Orsini, Father Giorgetti's uncle, to be the new pastor of Sts. Peter and Paul's parish. When Father Orsini arrived, the trustees locked and barred the church building and seized the parish records, so he was forced to say Mass in a private home. When Monsignor Talbot returned to Rome, he recommended to Pope Pius IX that the Redemptorists be sent to the Virgin Islands. This suggestion had originally been made by the new bishop of Roseau, Michel Vesque, an admirer of the Redemptorist congregation. The Holy Father agreed. The Redemptorist superior general, Father Nicholas Mauron, was reluctant to send his men into such a controversial situation but was afraid that, if he declined the Holy Father's request, the Redemptorists might be given an even less desirable assignment, so he consented and turned the responsibility for the mission over to the American Redemptorists who had just established their provincial headquarters at Baltimore.

In 1857, Bishop Vesque visited St. Thomas and was not allowed by the wardens to enter the Catholic church. He simply stood before it and prayed. After French Catholics on the island had prompted diplomatic intervention by the French government to bring about the reopening of the church, the Danish governor, flanked by the French, Spanish, and Venezuelan consuls to the Danish West Indies, marched to the church with Father Orsini and a contingent of troops and reopened it. The whole procession was met with hoots and stone throwing on the part of the schismatics who supported the wardens. At the church, Father Orsini received the keys to the building for the first time in the eighteen months he had been at St. Thomas and services were resumed. However, armed guards were placed in front of the church for some time and Father Orsini did not walk about the city without being accompanied by two policemen.

Father Joseph Prost, a former superior of the Redemptorists in the United States, was sent to the Danish West Indies in 1858 as the superior of the mission. He was then living in Austria. He told his superiors that he would have volunteered for the assignment if he were younger, but he felt he was too old for the assignment and lacked any fluency in French, a helpful asset for any priest assigned to St. Thomas. They sent him despite his objections. He was instructed, upon arriving in St. Thomas, to go directly to Roseau to consult with the bishop and to travel "incognito" while in transit in the Virgin Islands. After arriving in Roseau, he was assigned to St. Croix and went immediately to take up that mission.

A regrettable difference of opinion grew up between the bishop and the Redemptorists concerning the extent of the Redemptorist mission. It arose simply out of their different points of view and different responsibilities. Bishop Vesque had several vacant parishes to fill, both in the Danish West Indies and elsewhere. He needed priests both at St. Croix and St. Thomas and asked the Redemptorists to staff both parishes. The Redemptorists insisted that they were missionaries, not curates. They would operate a parish only because it provided them with a foundation from which they could send missionaries throughout the Caribbean to conduct what amounted to revivals aimed at restoring lax Catholics to the active observance of their religious duties. They insisted that they simply did not have the manpower to staff two parishes. They would be glad to staff one parish at whatever place the bishop might designate, but one parish was the limit of their capabilities.

For many years Catholic priests serving in the Danish West Indies were obligated by Danish law to take a written oath that they would conform themselves to the laws and ordinances of Denmark and the orders of the Danish authorities and to comport themselves "in such a manner as is becoming an honorable clergyman." Bishop Vesque advised Father Prost to take the oath upon arriving in St. Croix and he did so without hesitation. However, other priests assigned to the colony refused to do so and they were supported by the Holy See, which somehow saw in this oath an implied promise that Catholic priests would not make converts from members of Protestant denominations. Such was the opinion of a Redemptorist missionary who was sent to St. Croix to assist Father Prost. Moreover, Danish authorities came into possession of an ancient decree published by the Austrian emperor that referred to the Redemptorists as a branch of the Jesuit order. The information was wholly erroneous, but it was enough to cause the Danish governor to attempt to apply the old ban on Jesuits to the newly arrived

Redemptorists. Although Danish officials had no objection to the existence of Catholic churches and the maintenance of those churches as conventional parishes, they did not like the idea of a parish church serving as the headquarters for priests traveling throughout the Caribbean on missionary errands. This raised the specter of a Catholic effort aimed at proselytizing Protestants, a definite prohibition in a nation that officially recognized the Lutheran Church.

Father Prost wrote a thirty-page letter to the governor, trying to allay his fears and suspicions on all of these matters. It also praised the manner in which Great Britain, also a Protestant nation, dealt with the Catholic Church. Father Prost assured the governor that Catholics did in fact read the Bible and did not worship images. He also insisted in this letter that sacramental confession was instituted by Christ himself. With respect to the missionary efforts of the Redemptorists, he informed the governor that Redemptorists were less likely to make converts of Protestants than were other priests, since the institute of the Redemptorist congregation principally directed its members to seek out neglected and abandoned Catholics, not members of other denominations.

A party of four Redemptorists — two priests and two Brothers — was sent to the Danish West Indies late in 1858 to assist Father Prost. While en route, one of the members of the party, Brother Vincent Soleau, contracted smallpox and died. He was buried at sea and the vessel on which they were traveling was briefly quarantined by public officials when it arrived in St. Thomas. The remaining Redemptorists were dressed in civilian clothes as they went to their hotel, but when their identities were discovered, several supporters of the dissident faction supporting the church wardens denounced them as "Jesuits," a handy pejorative term they applied to anyone who was supporting the efforts of the bishop to reopen Sts. Peter and Paul Church. Eventually, the church was opened and the Redemptorists accepted the responsibility for staffing it. (They remained at the parish until 1989 when the diocese of St. Thomas was able to staff its cathedral with diocesan priests.) In St. Croix, Father Prost was recalled to Austria and the Redemptorists turned the parish back to the bishop of Roseau. They resumed their service to Holy Cross parish in 1897 when Belgian Redemptorists came to St. Croix, later to be replaced by American Redemptorists during World War I. They are still at Holy Cross parish today and at St. Patrick's parish in Frederiksted.

For over fifty years the United States government had been negotiating with the Danes to purchase the Virgin Islands. Just after the Civil War, Secretary of State William Seward, who had engineered the purchase of Alaska from the Russians, entered into a treaty to buy the islands of St. Thomas and St. John from the Danes, but the U.S. Senate refused to ratify the treaty. In 1902, the matter was brought up again and this time it was the Danish parliament that refused to go along. After the opening of the Panama Canal, the Virgin Islands came to have greater strategic importance to the American position in the Caribbean. A purchase price of twenty-five million dollars was agreed upon by both parties for all three major islands and on March 31, 1917, the Danish flag was lowered for the last time at St. Croix and elsewhere in the Danish West Indies.

Even before this occurred, American Redemptorists were starting to replace the Belgian members of their congregation at St. Croix and elsewhere in the Virgin Islands. Their coming was viewed by many Danes on the islands with hostility, since the American priests were seen as a harbinger of a complete American takeover. Although there was no connection between the two events, it is a fact that American Redemptorists started to come back to the islands about five years before the American flag was raised. In 1918, the replacement of Belgian Redemptorists by Americans was completed.

By 1918, the population of St. Croix had declined to about eleven thousand people. Its chief industries then were corn and cotton. For those who could find work, men were paid about 20 cents a day and women received about 12 to 15 cents. Superstition, such as the use of wooden hex dolls, abounded; there was widespread concubinage and many children were illegitimate. Holy Cross parish had about twenty-two hundred parishioners, of whom twelve hundred lived in Christiansted while the remainder lived in the surrounding countryside. In 1915, Belgian nuns, the Canonesses of St. Augustine, opened St. Mary's parochial school at Christiansted. Before the Danes left, the Danish government contributed two dollars per pupil per year to the operation of this school. Later, the same order opened a second school in the center of the island at St. Ann's, a church that was built in 1825 as an estate chapel and grew into a regular parish. After a hurricane destroyed St. Ann's School in 1928, the two schools were consolidated with the assistance of the Virgin Islands government, which bussed children from St. Ann's to St. Mary's. Notwithstanding the many problems confronted by the Church on St. Croix, the parochial school was well attended and the number of Communions received by Holy Cross parishioners increased dramatically.

On December 2, 1956, a fire of undetermined origin gutted the interior of Holy Cross Church. It did about $60,000 worth of damage that took nearly two years to repair. When the new church [**pictured above**] was rededicated, the ceremony was attended by the apostolic delegate to the United States and the bishop of the newly created diocese of St. Thomas. Additional improvements to the church building were made in 1975. The most recent calamity to befall the parish occurred throughout the night of September 17-18, 1989, when Hurricane Hugo, having winds of up to two hundred miles an hour, swept the Virgin Islands, leaving homes and buildings demolished and trees uprooted. Holy Cross Church suffered less than many of the homeowners on St. Croix. Damage inflicted on St. Mary's School next door, including the destruction of the roof, caused classes to be suspended for three weeks. St. Joseph's High School was demolished.

Some five hundred years after Columbus arrived at St. Croix, the island has slightly more than fifty thousand inhabitants, of whom a third are Catholics. There are four parishes, two of which are operated by Redemptorists. Attendance at the five weekend Masses at Holy Cross includes about five hundred year-round parishioners and a large number of tourists during the winter months. The Spanish Mass said each weekend is well attended. About ninety percent of the regular parishioners at Holy Cross are black, including a significant number of immigrants who have recently come to St. Croix from other Caribbean islands in search of work.

The parish buildings house the Catholic Social Center, an organization formed in 1959 to provide a number of social-welfare programs. It serves free lunches three times a week to some twenty to thirty people who visit its soup kitchen. Help is given to a large number of poor and elderly to assist them in applying for public assistance benefits, such as food stamps. The 4'Cs (Christian Community Conscious Center, Inc.) is looking forward to establishing a home for the significant number of homeless teenagers who live on St. Croix. One of its principal activities is a federally funded pregnancy-aid program for teenage girls. In St. Croix, there is a high illegitimacy rate. However, both adoption and abortion are culturally unacceptable. The extended family of a newborn child is expected to care for the child. Since the principal responsibility falls on the youthful mother, this organization also provides prenatal care as well as instruction in nutrition and child care. Recently, the bishop of St. Thomas has opened two homes for the homeless, one on St. Croix and the other at St. Thomas.

2
St. John Baptist Cathedral

San Juan

PUERTO RICO

Far and away the oldest church on American soil is the cathedral located in old San Juan, two blocks from the ancient port that was constructed by the Spanish at San Juan Bay. The building of the original church began at this site in 1522. This was eight years after Puerto Rico was established as a diocese, five years after Martin Luther pinned his famous ninety-five theses on the cathedral door at Wittenberg, and twelve years before King Henry VIII secured passage by the British Parliament of the Act of Supremacy severing the Church of England from the Church of Rome. Both the San Juan and Santo Domingo dioceses were established by the Holy See at about the same time. Both continue to this day and both served the Catholic Church during Spanish rule until Spain lost most of its holdings in the Western Hemisphere nearly four hundred years later during the Spanish-American War. Since December 19, 1898, the American flag has flown over Puerto Rico. At that time, the last in a line of more than fifty Spanish bishops withdrew and were replaced by a series of American bishops, most of whom had distinctly English or Irish names. In 1965, a native Puerto Rican, Luis Aponte Martínez, was appointed archbishop of San Juan. He became Puerto Rico's first cardinal in 1973.

Columbus discovered Puerto Rico on November

19, 1493, during his second voyage to the New World. At that time, the island was inhabited by fierce Carib Indians who harassed European settlements throughout the Caribbean area. Columbus named the entire island in honor of St. John Baptist — San Juan Bautista. The name has survived for its capital and for the island's first cathedral, which, according to *The Official Catholic Directory*, is Catedral de San Juan Bautista. Among the members of the second Columbus expedition was Juan Ponce de León, who returned to Puerto Rico in 1508 as royal governor. In that position, he founded a settlement near the present city.

By a papal bull issued on July 28, 1508, Pope Julius II conferred upon the Spanish monarchy all ecclesiastical benefices in Spanish possessions in the New World and, in effect, the right to control the Church in those colonies. Three years later, the Holy See created three dioceses in the Caribbean — at Santo Domingo, Haiti, and Puerto Rico, all under the Spanish archdiocese of Seville. The archdiocese of Puerto Rico can trace its origins to this date, although the original diocese existed largely on paper for the next few years.

The capital of the Spanish colony was moved to San Juan in 1521. In the following year, Bishop Alonso Manso, the first bishop of San Juan, erected a wooden church on the hill where the present cathedral now stands. Four years later, the original church was destroyed by a hurricane, one of many storms that have devastated the cathedral over the centuries. By 1529, a new church, built of stone and adobe, was completed. In the same year, the first ordination of a bishop to take place in North America was held in the new cathedral.

The cathedral has experienced almost constant rebuilding and renovation throughout its long life. Its greatest enemy has been the elements. One of its most abiding problems has been poor construction due to lack of sufficient funds. During centuries of Spanish control, it had two principal sources of financial support. One source was the kings of Spain, who financed church construction and maintenance either from the royal treasury or from grants of taxing authority, the proceeds of which were earmarked for church support. The other source was donations by various bishops of San Juan who, from time to time, made generous grants from their own personal assets. In 1533, some 4,000 pesos in Bishop Manso's estate were applied to improvements made on the cathedral during the next few years. For this construction, stone was quarried at Toa Baja, located at the mouth of the Toa River, and used for the wall on the eastern side of the building and for the church tower. Church officials hoped that by substituting stone for wood they would be spared the problem of making constant repairs. Bishop Manso's successor, Bishop Bastidas, asked King Carlos V for a royal donation to carry on the construction. Apparently, the donation was insufficient because work on the building came to a halt for several years. However, over a period of twenty-five years, Bishop Bastidas was able to finish most of the great chapel and to erect stone walls as high as the cornices. About 1580, one of his successors, Bishop Diego de Salamanca, built the steps in front of the church out of his own funds. The steps lead to La Caleta, a narrow, cobble-stoned street which goes down to the old port. For centuries sailors arriving in San Juan climbed La Caleta to the cathedral to offer their thanksgiving for a safe voyage.

Bishop de Salamanca wrote King Philip II to report that the poverty of his church was so great that he felt sure that the monarch would be moved to make a contribution. He informed the king that he had not received from public officials certain funds that had been allotted for that purpose by the king from the proceeds of unclaimed estates. In making this charge, the bishop touched upon another recurring problem that the Church faced in Puerto Rico, namely the fact that royal officials often impeded works of religion by diverting funds belonging to the Church to other purposes. Bishop de Salamanca told Philip II that he had repeatedly asked royal judges for the money that had been officially set aside for the cathedral but was told on each occasion that there was no money to be had. He asked the king to order local officials to pay over the amount that was due so that repairs could be made.

In this letter, the bishop also said that the Church in Puerto Rico was so poor that tne cathedral clergy possessed neither an alb nor a chasuble, nor did they have any altar linens that were not in eight pieces. He also reported that his cathedral had no organ, no choir books, and nothing in the way of donations or benefices for the clergy. He complained that cathedral income was insufficient to buy wine, flour, or candle wax with which to say Mass, and that the church did not even have any oil for the vigil lamp. According to the bishop, the cause of this financial distress was the fact that any money received had to be applied to the support of slaves whom the king had given to the cathedral to assist in the building project. He complained that most of these slaves were so old that they were useless.

By the beginning of the seventeenth century, the present outlines of the cathedral had taken shape. By this time, the western side of the building had been completed in stone, as well as the central nave from the main altar to the front entrance. The eastern façade had yet to be finished in stone.

The diocese administered from this cathedral was enormous. It included not only the island of Puerto Rico but several Caribbean islands off the coast of South America, such as Margarita and Trinidad. It also included Guyana and all of Venezuela as far south as the Orinoco River. In fact, this diocese, one of the largest in the whole Catholic Church, had no fixed southern boundary and stretched as far as Spanish settlements extended into the northern part of the South American continent. The diocese was extremely difficult to administer, not only because of the slowness and uncertainty of communications and travel but also because of dangers posed by hostile Indians and by pirates who hovered off the coast of South America and throughout the Caribbean to plunder the Spanish Main. It was not until 1791 that the boundaries of the San Juan diocese became restricted to the island itself.

Early in the development of the city, another church was built just two blocks up the Cristo Street hill from the cathedral. It has been the neighbor of the cathedral for over four hundred fifty years. Ponce de León gave Bishop Manso land for this church, now called San José, and the bishop drew up plans for its construction about the same time that he was planning the cathedral. The walls of San José were completed in 1532 and its sanctuary in 1539. The wall behind the main altar is nearly three feet thick while the wall on one side of its sanctuary is nearly seven feet thick. High on the wall the coat of arms of Ponce de León has been inscribed. For about three hundred years this church served as the chapel of a Dominican monastery. The Dominicans called it St. Thomas Aquinas and built their monastery around it. For centuries they conducted a school on this site. After the Dominicans left in 1838, the Jesuits took over the church and operated it for many years. It is now the home for the Institute of Puerto Rican Culture.

For three centuries the remains of Ponce de León rested at San José. The founder of Puerto Rico was wounded in 1521 by Indians during an expedition to western Florida. He died and was buried in Cuba. In 1559, his grandson brought his remains back to the Dominican church where they were reinterred under the steps of its main altar. In 1908, Bishop William Jones removed them to the cathedral and they were placed in the crypt where they now lie.

The cathedral is also a short distance from Morro Castle, the famed fortress that the Spanish placed at the point of the peninsula on which the old city was constructed. By reason of its location, the cathedral has been a part of several sieges and invasions that have occurred over the centuries. In 1597, British privateers, led by Sir Francis Drake, occupied the city but were forced to withdraw, not so much by force of arms as by a serious attack of dysentery that afflicted the invading crews. In 1625, the Dutch attacked the city, sacked the cathedral, and burned its library. In 1797, during the Napoleonic wars, the Spanish crown was allied with the French against the British. A British expedition landed at Torrecilla, about twelve miles from San Juan, and proceeded to lay siege to the city. They ultimately withdrew. A modern statue commemorating the withdrawal of the British has recently been placed near the rampart. It honors Puerto Rican women who, with the encouragement of the bishop, gathered there to offer prayers through the intercession of St. Ursula and her eleven thousand virgins for the lifting of the siege. The last time that shots were fired in anger at San Juan was during the Spanish-American War in 1898. American naval artillery did not harm the cathedral but blew several holes in the façade of San José Church.

Throughout the history of the cathedral a group that exercised a considerable influence over its activities was the cathedral chapter, a body composed of clergymen known as canons. They performed various pastoral functions both for the parish and for other Catholic institutions, such as the hospital. The position of canon was a prestigious one and carried with it certain benefices. Often, during the absence of the bishop or during interim periods when the see of Puerto Rico was vacant, the cathedral chapter ran the cathedral parish. Sometimes these interim periods between the death or resignation of one bishop and the appointment of another were extended ones because it was often difficult for the Spanish king and the Holy See to find a suitable replacement who was willing to take the post. Under the system of *patronato real* (royal patronage), in effect during the Spanish era, the Council of the Indies (the agency of the Spanish government that administered the affairs of the Spanish West Indies) proposed the names of several candidates for bishop to the king, who would then select one name and forward it to the Holy See under a treaty arrangement known as the right of presentation. Normally, the pope would then issue a papal bull nominating the king's choice. On some occasions nominees declined these appointments because of the remoteness of the diocese and the precarious financial support that was available to it.

In the early seventeenth century, the cathedral received several large donations that permitted construction to be completed. In 1609, Bishop Martín Vásquez de Arce left 20,000 ducats to the church in his will, but after his estate was administered, the church itself received only a portion of the bequest because the bulk of the money was divided up between the canons of the cathedral chapter. In 1615, King Philip III donated 4,000 ducats to repair the roof, which had been blown away by a hurricane. The cathedral canons were able to siphon off some of this money, but most of it went to repair the transept and to build an arch and two pillars in the central nave. In 1627, Bishop Bernardo de Balboa left a bequest to the cathedral in his will containing a stipulation that the money was to be used to build a chapel in the sacristy honoring his patron, St. Bernard. By the 1640s, all of the main body of the building, from the transept to the front door, had been completed with solid material. For the next several decades additional construction focused on interior improvements. About 1665, Bishop Biento Rivas built a chapel dedicated to the holy martyrs and later, around 1710, another chapel, honoring Our Lady of Sorrows, was completed. The king recognized the importance of the San Juan Cathedral to the Catholic Church in New Spain by conferring upon it a coat of arms that depicted a lamb, adorned with diadems, whose body was pierced by a cross. Surrounding this design was a circle bearing the motto "John Is His Name."

As late as 1700, complaints were still being made to the king as to the condition of the cathedral. Nicolás F. Correa, the principal master of the cathedral, asked for help from the king because no other funds were available from any other source for needed improvements. It appeared that the royal governor of the province had kept part of the government funds designated for cathedral maintenance and had diverted them for maintenance of the military presidio. In 1706, Bishop Pedro de la Concepción was transferred from Mexico to San Juan. In that portion of the Spanish domain, the mining of gold and silver had resulted in the lavish decoration of churches, and Bishop de la Concepción was not accustomed to the poverty with which the Church in Puerto Rico had to contend. He wrote the king that improvements were necessary in order to celebrate the liturgy with proper decorum and was able to obtain sufficient financing to rebuild a portion of the cathedral from the transept to the front door. However, the interior was still whitewashed and contained only a choir, a baptistry, and a few ornaments.

In 1774, the cathedral chapter informed the governor that the roof was threatened by termites. The existence of the problem was confirmed by a detailed examination, and work of an emergency nature was performed on the heads of beams that posed the gravest danger to the structure. The royal governor sent to Spain a reconstruction plan drawn up by Thomas O'Daly, the commander of the army engineers in Puerto Rico. However, the threat of war made building plans difficult to carry out. The plan drawn up by O'Daly followed a Gothic design. However, the rear of the church was not sufficiently strong to support anything but a wooden roof, so interior pillars had to be erected to provide support for a more durable roof. In 1785, additional repairs costing about 75,000 pesos were proposed by Governor Juan Dabán. Again the church looked to the generosity of the king for this sum. Unfortunately, the generosity of the king toward works of charity and religion was spread thin and had to include a hospital, a home for wayward women, and other charitable institutions. More to the point, such capital expenditures had to compete with the ongoing work of fortifying the city not only with a large fortress located at its most prominent point but also by a lengthy wall surrounding the old town along which were located other smaller fortifications. In August 1789, the king sent back word to spend only what was necessary on the church. By 1793, the threatened destruction of the roof was so advanced that Bishop de la Cuerda wrote to the king to tell him that the cathedral was in such bad shape that the king would have to see it to believe it. Tiles were missing and bats were starting to nest in the roof.

Since efforts to charge the royal household for additional construction expenses bore little results, church officials realized, during the first part of the nineteenth century, that they would have to look to local sources. Governor Torio de Montes decided to impose a sales tax, amounting to one maravedí (one sixth of a cent) on each loaf of bread baked and sold in Puerto Rico to meet the renovation cost of the cathedral. Unfortunately, his successor, Governor Meléndez, diverted the proceeds of this tax to the construction of a royal jail, which he built in the rear of the cathedral chapter house. In 1811, when the Spanish Cortes (parliament) in Madrid heard about this diversion, it levied a tax of two cuartos (about eight maravedís) on each loaf and directed that it be paid to the cathedral for construction. A committee composed of both church and government officials decided to auction off a plot of ground adjacent to the cathedral that had been used for an old cemetery and to apply the proceeds to the renovation and enlargement of the cathedral. The sale provided nearly 19,000 pesos for this purpose. With this kind of support, further improvements could be made on the aging cathedral, which, by then, was more than two hundred years old.

A Tuscan-style church [**pictured above**] emerged from the nineteenth-century renovation. The design was made by the royal engineer commander, Manuel Soriano. The actual construction was placed in the hands of Manuel de Zayas, the architect who supervised much of the ongoing work on the fortification of the town. At one time, there were as many as twelve altars within the cathedral, in two groups of three on either side of the main altar. One altar was eventually removed to provide for a baptistry and another was eliminated to permit a vestibule to be built. De Zayas built a new main altar of rough masonry and constructed an elliptical arch of bricks. New choir stalls for the cathedral canons were built in a semicircle at the rear and a large bishop's chair was installed near the great altar. Eight elaborate Doric columns were built on the sides of the transept. In 1867, the tower, which had been seriously damaged by an earthquake, was rebuilt.

It is doubtful that the Catholic Church could have survived in New Spain during this era without the active support and assistance of the government. However, for this support and assistance it had to pay a price in terms of irritation and interference with church affairs. On the other hand, local bishops, who regarded themselves as the king's servants as well as the pope's, did not hesitate to make recommendations to the government on purely secular matters and to report to Madrid the shortcomings and misconduct of local governors. In some instances, conflicts between church and civil officials were of some consequence; in other instances, they were indescribably petty.

The operating expenses of the Church in Puerto Rico were derived from two sources, *diezmos* (tithes) and *premicias* (harvest taxes). In 1774, Governor Muesas complained to the king that because he had not turned over to the dean and the cathedral chapter certain surplus tithes the king had been subjected to a calculated insult at the Good Friday services. In previous years, when the Blessed Sacrament was removed and the tabernacle left open, the key to the tabernacle was then ceremonially handed over to the governor for safekeeping. On this occasion, the cathedral canons told the governor, in advance of the ceremony, that they were not going to give him the key during the Good Friday liturgy, so the governor boycotted the ceremony. In his mind, the action on the part of the cathedral canons was an insult to the king because it was an insult to his local representative. The governor felt it was being taken in reprisal for his refusal to remit the surplus tithes. The canons of the chapter replied that they were merely following a change in the Holy Week ritual derived from a book of ceremonies that had been adopted two years earlier in Madrid, according to which the tabernacle key was given to the celebrant of the Holy Thursday Mass, not to the governor. They also complained to the king that the governor had behaved in a haughty manner in church by refusing to kneel at benediction as other governors had done in previous years. Bishop Jiménez, who was not at the cathedral on this occasion, assured the governor, when he heard about this dispute, that the cathedral chapter was not acting out of spite but promised that it would not happen again and that the governor would be presented with the tabernacle key at future Good Friday ceremonies.

The same governor issued an order forbidding any clergyman from leaving the city without an official pass. When a Dominican priest from St. Thomas Aquinas tried to go to Toa Baja on an approved errand, a guard at the city gate refused to let him pass. Bishop Jiménez complained to the governor that, according to the royal cedula of August 25, 1768, any priest authorized by the bishop to be absent from the city for a period of time up to three months could leave without permission of public authorities. Apparently, the governor relented. On another occasion, the governor complained to the bishop that at solemn high Mass he was given the kiss of peace by a subdeacon, whereas the kiss of peace should have been imparted by a priest wearing a surplice and stole, as befitted his stature as a royal official. Bishop Jiménez dismissed the complaint, citing Law XX, Title XV, Book III, of the Recodification of the Laws of the Indies as his authority, and adding that if it was not possible for a priest dressed in surplice and stole to perform this rite, then the sacristan could do it just as well.

A more serious confrontation arose when, in August 1775, several soldiers who had been condemned to death at the San Juan presidio escaped and took refuge in the cathedral. The governor demanded that they be turned over to the army immediately, but the bishop refused, insisting that the soldiers had a right of sanctuary. A meeting of theologians and canon lawyers was held at the episcopal palace, with the military judge in attendance. The clerics decided that they would extend the right of asylum to the fleeing soldiers. Thereafter, the bishop directed that the cathedral and all parish churches in Puerto Rico would be regarded as places of asylum. The governor denounced this action as merely an expression of the "theology of Puerto Rico." Later, papal decrees were issued granting the right of sanctuary in certain churches but not in all parishes.

There was cooperation as well as conflict between Church and State officials, especially in a time of public need. When the British threatened San Juan in 1797, the governor asked Bishop Juan Bautista Cengotiti for a loan of the money set aside for construction of the cathedral because there was a deficit in the royal bank account and funds were immediately needed for the defense of the city. The bishop not only gave the governor 3,000 pesos from rents payable to the church but also gave him an additional 5,000 pesos from his own capital account. He later gave the governor a second loan of church funds. He granted a dispensation from hearing Mass on holy days because the city was in imminent danger of attack. When he learned that the British had landed at Torrecilla, the bishop went in search of the governor and offered the assistance of all the priests of the dioceses. He offered to allow the bishop's house to be used as a garrison and for the storage of munitions. He ordered all priests to pray for the success of Spanish forces and directed priests to bury the dead at night without any ceremonies and without ringing church bells. He also directed the distribution of Holy Viaticum when bombs and artillery shells began to fall.

The bishop visited dangerous locations along the city fortification wall to encourage the troops and issued a pastoral letter urging all Catholics to act in the public defense and to guard against pillaging and robbing. When, on May 1, the defenders of the city learned that the British were reboarding their ships to leave the island, he offered a solemn "Te Deum" and Mass at the cathedral attended by both civil and military authorities. Later, he visited outlying areas and offered whatever material assistance his means would allow to people who had suffered destruction because of the conflict. For his assistance in the defense of San Juan, Bishop Cengotiti was later awarded the Cross of the Royal Order of Charles III by the king of Spain.

With the replacement of Spanish rule by American rule, the Church in Puerto Rico gained freedom from government interference in its activities and lost financial support from public revenues. The same freedom brought to Puerto Rico Spanish Protestant

Evangelicals and Pentecostals, groups who were unknown on the island before 1900 but are now quite active. Today, approximately eighty percent of Puerto Rico's 3.2 million inhabitants are Catholic. The San Juan cathedral is the principal church in the archdiocese of San Juan, which now has about one hundred forty parishes. In addition, there are four other dioceses in Puerto Rico covering those portions of the island that lie outside the San Juan metropolitan area.

In 1978, the cathedral was designated a minor basilica. The shops, restaurants, and historical sites of the old city attract large numbers of tourists, but the area has relatively few permanent residents, so the parish has little in the way of community life. Three Masses are offered each weekend at the cathedral itself. Many of those in attendance are either tourists or reside in other parts of the city. (Many Catholic tourists from the American mainland are surprised to find that Holy Communion may not be taken in the hand at the cathedral or anywhere else in Puerto Rico and are also surprised to learn that Catholics on the island observe only four holy days of obligation — Christmas, New Year's, Epiphany, and Corpus Christi.) Priests who assist the rector also say Mass each weekend at two chapels in the locality, San José and Santa Ana. About six hundred people, mostly residents of the area, attend Mass at these locations each week. All liturgies are conducted in Spanish. A large number of weddings are held each year at the cathedral, involving, in most instances, couples residing in other parishes who ask to be married there. Cathedral parish records extend back to the sixteenth century. Those compiled during the past two hundred years are retained at the rectory; the earlier ones have been turned over to the archdiocesan archives in Santurce, a suburb of San Juan.

There are small independent Catholic elementary schools in old San Juan but none that are supported by the parish itself. The cathedral parish is developing plans to provide catechism instruction, a youth organization, and a program of continuing religious education. The same problems that faced the cathedral chapter three hundred years ago still plague the present parish administration, namely how to provide for the maintenance of an old building on a very limited budget. Although the king and his royal governors no longer dictate construction plans, any current changes in the architecture of the building must be approved by the Institute of Puerto Rican Culture. In September 1989, Hurricane Hugo did about $150,000 worth of damage to the structure, destroying the doors and some of the stained-glass windows as well as causing widespread water damage because of holes made in the roof. Repairs are being undertaken so that a fully restored church may be an integral part of the 1992 celebration marking the 500th anniversary of the arrival of Christopher Columbus in the New World. Of all of the churches and other buildings now standing in the Western Hemisphere, none has a date of origin that more closely approximates the arrival of Columbus than the Cathedral of St. John Baptist at San Juan.

3
Holy Cross Cathedral

Boston

MASSACHUSETTS

Catholic churches simply could not be found in Boston during the first one hundred sixty years of its existence. Dr. John Gilmary Shea noted that, in 1631, Sir Christopher Carder was seized and exiled from the city on suspicion of being a Catholic. In 1647, the Pilgrim Fathers in the Massachusetts legislature enacted a law forbidding Jesuits from entering the colony, banishing them if they did, and subjecting them to capital punishment if they returned. The first Catholics who came to Boston in any numbers were French-speaking Acadian refugees. They had been forcibly removed from their homes in Nova Scotia in 1755 by the British Army and scattered about the Atlantic and Gulf Coast areas by the British Navy. Bostonians, who were already growing restive under the Crown, regarded the Acadians as objects of pity so they were allowed to stay and work in certain areas. However, in general, Catholics in the American colonies were largely confined to Maryland and Pennsylvania, so no Catholic churches exist today in Massachusetts that rival in antiquity those established farther south.

The first public Mass to be offered in Boston or anywhere in post-colonial New England was said by a French Navy chaplain, one Abbé de la Poterie, who jumped ship in 1788, stayed in Boston, and for a short while had permission from Father John Carroll, the prefect apostolic, to remain and establish a church. This Mass was said on November 2, 1788, before a group of French and Irish inhabitants who gathered in an abandoned Huguenot church on School Street for the occasion. Father de la Poterie did not last long as a pastor, but he did leave with the congregation a relic of the true cross. It remains with the parish to this day and is the basis for naming it in honor of the Holy Cross. The original congregation was small and impoverished but initially was able to obtain the use of the School Street premises for free. They appealed to the archbishop of Paris for vestments and sacred vessels with which to say Mass, and they received a donation from him for that purpose.

The second pastor, Father Louis de Rousselet, did not last long either. After becoming embroiled in an internal dispute involving an assistant pastor and a conflict between Irish and French members of the congregation, he left and went to the French island of Guadaloupe where he was ultimately put to death at the guillotine in 1794 by French revolutionaries who had seized the island.

The small parish on School Street, the first of five locations for Holy Cross Church, began to achieve stability in 1792 with the appointment of Father Francis A. Matignon who served as its pastor for twenty-six years. Father Matignon was a refugee from the French Revolution. Before coming to the United States, he had been a professor at the Sorbonne in Paris. During his tenure as pastor, Holy Cross parish grew from a church with about one hundred twenty parishioners to a cathedral and the largest Catholic church in New England. Father Matignon administered the parish with the assistance of his friend Father John de Cheverus, who was often absent on missionary visits to Indians in Maine. Later, in 1808, Father Cheverus was named the first bishop of Boston when it became a diocese embracing all of New England. Father Cheverus was the most prominent figure in the early days of the Catholic Church in New England. After serving as a missionary and then as a bishop for fifteen years, he was recalled to France where he became archbishop of Bordeaux and ultimately a member of the College of Cardinals.

By 1799, the Holy Cross congregation had increased from 120 to between 600 and 700 people and had outgrown the building on School Street. Moreover, their lease was about to expire. In the face of a tight real-estate market, the parish was able to purchase a 70-by-100-foot plot of land for $2,500 at the end of Franklin Square, which the parish committee felt was "remote from noise, especially on Sunday." Charles Bulfinch, architect of the Massachusetts State House, designed the Franklin Street church, but work on the building, which began in 1800, was halted because Father Matignon ran out of money and was reluctant to build on credit. He went up and down the East Coast soliciting funds and sent appeals as far away as Martinique and Kentucky. About one hundred forty Protestants contributed to the drive to build the first Catholic church in New England. This number included former President John Adams, who donated $100, a handsome sum in those days. In 1803, Bishop John Carroll, in whose diocese the Holy Cross Church was located, came from Baltimore to dedicate it. A few years later, when Bishop Carroll began to build his own cathedral in Baltimore, Boston Catholics reciprocated the generosity of Marylanders by donating $1,200 in cash and lotto tickets toward the construction of that building.

Father Cheverus had acquired a reputation as a preacher, and this reputation drew large crowds to Mass at Holy Cross, including substantial numbers of Protestants. In 1804, a small school was started next to the church that for a short period of time provided elementary education to a large number of poor Catholic girls in the city.

In 1808, when Boston became one of four cities in the United States to acquire a bishop, Holy Cross became its cathedral and has remained such until this day. The prospects of the Catholic Church in New England were not well regarded at that time. Nativist hostility, especially among evangelical Protestants, was intense. Bishop John England, who became the first Catholic bishop in South Carolina, once wrote that he felt the prospects of the Church were far greater in the South than in New England because of Puritan opposition. In 1824, when Bishop Cheverus returned to France, there were only nine Catholic churches in all of New England, five of which did not have resident pastors. The total Catholic population of the region was around forty-five hundred, about three thousand of whom lived in Boston and were members of the cathedral parish.

Then, as now, the biggest problem was a shortage of priests. Today, the archdiocese of Boston, which includes only the city and four surrounding counties, has 1,848,000 Catholics and 820 priests serving 408 parishes. This phenomenal growth cannot be attributed to conversion but to immigration, which then was only beginning to occur. Other cities to the south, especially New York and Philadelphia, had experienced a wave of Irish immigration long before Boston did, but immigrant population growth eventually arrived there as well. First came the Irish, but a large number of other groups followed. An archdiocesan history published in 1944 stated that, at that time, the Boston area had 29 French-Canadian, 15 Italian, 14 Polish, six Lithuanian, and three Portuguese parishes. The most recent immigrant group to arrive are Hispanics and Southeast Asians.

In 1860, the same development that took place in 1803 repeated itself. The Franklin Street cathedral became too small for the parish population, so new and larger premises were sought. Before the Civil War the diocese had purchased, over a period of a few years, four Protestant churches for the purpose of establishing new parishes. In order to accomplish these purchases, it was forced to employ straw parties to represent it and to insert penalty clauses in real-estate contracts so that sellers could not easily renege on their agreements once they found out that the Catholic diocese was the real purchaser. This it did when it bought a Unitarian Church at Washington and Castle Streets (where the Massachusetts Turnpike is now located) and installed a procathedral that functioned there from 1862 to 1875. Between Franklin Street and this location, Holy Cross also conducted services for two years at the Melodeon Theater at Lafayette and Washington. In the years following the Civil War, the diocese was dedicating eight to ten new churches each year.

Bishop John Fitzpatrick determined that the new cathedral should be located in Boston's South End, an area never to be confused with South Boston. In the 1860s, the

Neck, as it was called, became filled in, and a large and well-to-do residential area was being built upon land recently reclaimed from the sea. In 1867, construction began on the present cathedral building under the supervision of Patrick C. Keely, a church architect from Brooklyn who, as noted elsewhere in this volume, built nearly six hundred churches throughout the United States. Over twenty-five thousand people attended the ceremony at which the cornerstone was laid. Over the next nine years, the present English Gothic cathedral **[pictured above]**, made of Roxbury pudding stone and trimmed with granite and sandstone, was erected on Washington Street at a cost of $1.5 million. It is today one of the largest churches in the United States, having about forty-six thousand square feet. It seats twenty-five hundred people and another thousand can be squeezed in. The high altar from the original Franklin Street cathedral was relocated to this spot and placed in the lower level of the Blessed Sacrament Chapel, which was opened in 1870.

The new cathedral was dedicated in 1875, but Bishop Fitzpatrick never lived to see the event. By this time, Boston had become an archdiocese. The first archbishop to occupy Holy Cross Cathedral was John J. Williams. Years later, a parochial school was opened and, in 1927, Cathedral High School across the street held its first classes.

As Back Bay became filled in, the center of real-estate development in Boston shifted to that area nearer the Charles River, and the South End began to suffer. By the early 1900s, old mansions began to be subdivided into tenements and the Holy Cross parish changed in its constituency. The construction of the Orange Line of the elevated railway, which opened just a few years after the cathedral was dedicated, ran right past its front door and had a detrimental effect both on the beauty of the surroundings and the tranquillity of public worship. The railway company paid the archdiocese a small amount of money for consequential damages caused by the construction and operation of this railway line, but the payment was merely token recognition of the harm it did.

Just north on the parish boundaries is Boston's famed "Combat Zone" where city zoning authorities have concentrated an array of porno shops, sleazy burlesque theaters, and cheap bars. If you now travel south along Washington Street from the Combat Zone in the direction of the cathedral you will encounter a hodgepodge of warehouses, boarded-up stores, crumbling apartment buildings, and small factories. The residential component of this area includes some public-housing units, homes for the elderly, and two large shelters for the homeless that were placed in this area by the city. In a form submitted by the parish to the Archdiocesan Office of Religious Education in 1987, the parish was asked, "What are the diverse cultural minorities in your parish?" The reply was, "Hispanic, blacks, Orientals, Italian, Irish, Syrian, and gays." The parish has many minorities but no majority to lend it character or cohesiveness.

There are also pockets of considerable wealth, such as Union Park, a couple of blocks west of the cathedral, where older houses once selling for $20,000 to $30,000 are now selling for $400,000. For the most part, though, the South End is an area of extreme poverty and great wealth and nothing in between. The Holy Cross parish population is now estimated to be six hundred twenty registered households. The grammar school has about two hundred students, who are equally divided among blacks, Hispanics, Orientals, and "Anglos." A majority of its enrollment is not Catholic. Cathedral High School has about three hundred students, of whom some fifty-eight percent are not Catholic. At one time, Cardinal Cushing allowed Hispanics in the area to operate what was, in effect, their own "parish within a parish." This experiment has come to an end, and Hispanics are once again integrated into the rest of the parish.

On occasion, the cathedral has been the site of some large civic, national, or archdiocesan meeting. For instance, the Boston Symphony commemorated the death of President John F. Kennedy at the cathedral by playing Mozart's "Requiem." In 1979, Pope John Paul II addressed the clergy of the archdiocese from the bishop's chair. These events are the exception, not the rule. There are only three Masses each Sunday, one in Spanish and the other two in English. The English Masses are normally said in the Blessed Sacrament Chapel on the side of the cathedral while the Spanish Mass is said in the lower church. Mass is also said at different developments for the elderly. A parish self-study indicated that, on a Sunday in 1986 selected as typical, only thirty-nine parishioners used the weekly envelopes to make their contribution. From time to time, especially on major feast days, the full cathedral is used for services. However, it is ironic that in one of the largest Catholic cities in the United States the red hats of Cardinals O'Connell and Cushing hang suspended from the ceiling in a great cathedral that is normally locked and empty.

The simple fact is that when the neighborhood it serves is hurting, the parish hurts. Something called urban renewal has been on the books since 1965, but it has a long way to go in the South End. At least the obnoxious elevated railway tracks have been removed and have been replaced by a bus line. The good news is that real-estate values have started to increase dramatically, signaling the fact that the area has been "rediscovered" and over the years will be undergoing private redevelopment on a piecemeal basis. The proximity of the South End to downtown Boston almost guarantees that this trend will continue apace. The bad news is that as prices go up, living accommodations for the poor disappear and they must scramble for affordable housing elsewhere.

In the midst of this distressing situation, both the parish and the archdiocese continue to make a response. The parish did not decide to flee to the suburbs or to become a museum or another stop on a walking tour of historic Boston. About eighty percent of the Holy Cross annual budget of $600,000 is an archdiocesan subsidy, an amount that was increased significantly in the past few years. Parish activities have been adapted to the situation that exists. For instance, the Legion of Mary has, for fifteen years, operated a shelter providing temporary refuge for women who are trying to escape from the Combat Zone and its sordid establishments. The parish also sponsors a whole host of cultural and educational programs, including lectures and tours as well as essentially religious exercises.

It is a long road back for the South End to regain social and economic viability, but a parish that has just completed its 200th anniversary has seen a great many ups and downs and will obviously be around for the long haul. At this point in its long life, Holy Cross has come full circle and is once again the gathering place for a relative handful of largely impoverished persons, as it was back on School Street at the end of the eighteenth century. Holy Cross's current needs as servant of the poor are far more extensive than a few vestments and plate with which to say Sunday Mass, but its resources are also greater. It has demonstrated the will to remain and to devote those resources to alleviate the needs, both spiritual and material, that it continues to witness each day.

4
St. Augustine

Boston
MASSACHUSETTS

"Southie" is the spiritual home of the Boston Irish, and St. Augustine's, on Dorchester Avenue, is one of several parishes in South Boston, all with fiercely loyal congregations who claim to personify the spirit of that locality. Parishes like Gate of Heaven, St. Brigid's, St. Monica, and Sts. Peter and Paul are also just as Irish and just as much a part of the South Boston tradition as St. Augustine.

In 1818, Bishop John de Cheverus purchased a tract of land about two blocks from the present St. Augustine Church as a cemetery. He wished to find a suitable resting place for his great friend, Father Francis A. Matignon, the long-time pastor of Holy Cross Cathedral, who had died of consumption. Father Matignon was one of four Catholic priests in all of New England at the time of his death. Shortly after the burial, Bishop Cheverus built a small French Gothic chapel, some thirty-five feet by twenty feet, near Father Matignon's grave. A few years later, the chapel was extended to a length of eighty-six feet so that it would incorporate the grave within its walls.

The cemetery was named in honor of an Irish Augustinian, Father Philip Larissey, who reputedly could preach fire-and-brimstone sermons in his native Gaelic that were every bit the match of those ascribed to Cotton Mather and other Puritan divines. The cemetery chapel was the only Catholic establishment in South Boston for a number of years, so it was used by priests from the cathedral to say Mass for Catholics in the area. In 1831, the sacristy of the chapel was dedicated and a resident priest was assigned, although St. Augustine's, as a parish, was not formally established until 1868.

South Boston was a farming community during the American Revolution. It was a peninsula known as the Dorchester Neck. In 1803, a number of Yankee real-estate speculators, realizing the value of land in the area near the growing port of Boston, bought up large acreage in South Boston and petitioned the city to annex it. The annexation vote won, although historians note that the election was tainted by fraud. However, Boston has always been able to make the best of such situations, and its extension of municipal services in the newly annexed area helped the city to grow southward. More of South Boston was annexed in 1855.

At that time, the port was busily engaged in what was known as the "triangular trade." Yankee clippers left Boston for Africa for the purpose of buying slaves, who were taken to the Caribbean and exchanged for sugar or molasses. Molasses was then brought to Boston where it was made into rum and sold to obtain money to buy more slaves. South Boston's role in this activity was to make the rum. The money was collected across the Fort Point Channel by Yankees on Beacon Hill. A foundry, a glassworks, and other small industries also came to be established during the same period of time.

The same port that brought in molasses also served as a place of embarkation for thousands of Irish trying to escape the hunger and oppression of their homeland. By 1850, some fifty thousand Irish had migrated to Boston. At first, they took refuge in the tenements of the central city, but they eventually found their way to "Southie" as well. South Boston was not popular at first with the Irish. In fact, it was a Yankee stronghold until the Civil War. A workhouse known as the House of Industry was located there, and those who could not find employment were confined in this grim establishment. There was also an almshouse at City Point. An Asiatic cholera epidemic struck Boston in the early 1830s, as it did other major American cities, and its impact upon the poor was particularly devastating.

Services at St. Augustine's cemetery chapel were discontinued in 1844 when Sts. Peter and Paul was formally established. However, when Sts. Peter and Paul burned almost to the ground in 1848, services at the chapel were resumed. Anti-Catholic feeling had a way of breaking out from time to time in unexplained ways in various parts of Boston. In 1849, Bishop John Fitzpatrick was summoned before a grand jury to answer a complaint that he was maintaining a nuisance in South Boston. The nuisance in question was St. Augustine's cemetery. Ultimately, the complaint was dropped.

Two events brought mass migration into South Boston. One was the Civil War, during which a great deal of industry associated with the war effort settled in the area. The other was the great fire of 1874, during which a large number of tenements in the central city burned to the ground, forcing the inhabitants of these burned-out buildings to seek other shelter. Many came to South Boston. By 1900, the Irish acquired majority status in the area, although large numbers of Poles, Germans, Lithuanians, Italians, and Albanians began to move in and reduced the Irish majority to something less than half.

In the 1860s, the diocese purchased a plot of ground about two blocks from the cemetery chapel next to a public cemetery owned by the city of Boston. There it erected the red brick Gothic church **[pictured above]** that was started in 1868 and completed in 1874. The church cost $200,000 and was paid for within ten years. In 1893, St. Augustine's opened a parochial school that is still operating today. At one time, the school had two classes for each grade, one for the boys and one for the girls. Today, there is only one class per grade.

By 1900, St. Augustine was the largest parish in South Boston. In addition to the normal activities of a parish ministry, it established a lyceum — which provided opportunities for debates, lectures, and various entertainments — and sponsored an annual field day for athletic events. During its formative years, the parish was under the guiding hand of Father Denis O'Callaghan, who served as pastor for fifty years until his death in 1913. Years after his death, stories of Father O'Callaghan's legendary charity linger on.

South Boston's most prominent contribution to the Church was Cardinal Richard Cushing, who served as archbishop of Boston for twenty-six years. He represented and personified the spirit of the parishioners of St. Augustine's and all of its neighbors. He was the product of working-class immigrant parents and was not bashful about saying so. His father worked a seventy-five-hour week over a forge as a blacksmith for the Boston Elevated Railway Company. In extolling the values of a college education, Cardinal Cushing told a graduating class in 1947 that not one member of the American hierarchy at that time, including himself, had parents who were college graduates.

Cardinal Cushing had a reputation for being a prodigious fund-raiser. During his years as archbishop, he built over eighty new parishes and twenty Catholic high schools. He also brought sixty religious orders of men and women to Boston to staff the many new institutions that were established. However, his efforts did not stop there. Throughout his priesthood he supplied large sums to support missionaries in South America and once raised one million dollars to ransom captives of Fidel Castro following the attempted Bay of Pigs invasion that had been improvidently authorized by his friend John F. Kennedy. Cardinal Cushing once stated that he had spent over two hundred million dollars to support the expansion of the archdiocese and, in doing so, had been called upon to raise about $35,000 a day (in 1960 dollars).

However, it was not as a builder that Cardinal Cushing caught the popular imagination. Boston Catholics had seen builders before. He succeeded in office the aristocratic and austere Cardinal William O'Connell, referred to in hushed tones by Boston Catholics simply as "Number One." Cardinal Cushing was cut from different cloth. He would march energetically through South Boston in parades singing "Southie Is My Home Town." He once referred publicly to his cardinal's vestments as a Santa Claus suit and shocked the Roman Curia when a photo was printed in a Roman English-language newspaper showing him dancing an Irish jig with an old lady at a Thanksgiving Day party. He publicly threatened to come home from the worldwide meeting of bishops at Vatican Council II because he could not understand the deliberations in Latin. He then changed his mind and decided to stay and to provide his colleagues with simultaneous running translations of the discussions similar to the ones enjoyed by delegates to the U.N. He once offered to Pope John XXIII his resignation as archbishop, saying that he would like to spend his remaining years as a priest in the South American missions. The Holy Father declined. A combination of personal humility, administrative astuteness, and popular appeal made him as much a folk hero as a prelate, and nowhere more than in his native South Boston.

The Red Line in the Boston transit system runs through St. Augustine's parish as it does through all of South Boston. Its ultimate terminus is Harvard Square. Generations of South Bostonians have taken that trip or similar ones to Boston College and other colleges and universities to find their way up the ladder, a path that often takes them out of South Boston for keeps. For many others Southie is the ultimate terminus, and that attachment to turf serves to explain the intensity of feeling that occurs when South Bostonians perceive that their turf is being threatened.

St. Patrick's Day is homecoming in "Southie." Years ago, some savant discovered that on March 17, 1776, General William Howe, commander of British forces in Boston during the American Revolution, evacuated the city and sailed away. That footnote in colonial history has long served as the basis for a public holiday. The fact that Evacuation Day is a mere pretext for honoring St. Patrick is all to the good, and the fact that it also commemorates the British departure is so much the better. On St. Patrick's Day, Mass is celebrated in the old cemetery chapel, as is the case with all major feast days, on an altar built over the tombs of the deceased pastors of the parish. Later, the parade starts along Broadway and eventually wends its way down Dorchester Street right past St. Augustine's. Afterward, there are hundreds of open houses thrown by South Bostonians to greet relatives and friends who have returned for the annual celebration. If a good time is not had by all, it's not for lack of trying on the part of everyone willing to come forward and acknowledge his roots in Southie's hard-working past.

5
Immaculate Conception

Salem

MASSACHUSETTS

The city of Salem, located on the Massachusetts North Shore about twenty miles from Boston, can date its history back to 1626. During the first one hundred sixty-four years of its existence, the city did not take kindly to Catholics. In 1634, John Endicott, the leader of the original village, publicly cut the cross from the middle of the British flag, denouncing this part of the design of the Union Jack as a symbol of popery. One of the nineteen victims of the famous Salem witchcraft trials of 1692 was Mary Dyer, an Irish Catholic. She was found guilty of witchcraft and sent to the gallows on Witches Hill on the basis of evidence, adduced at her trial, that she could not recite the Lord's Prayer in English and could only say it in her native Gaelic or haltingly in Latin. When French Acadians were removed from Nova Scotia in 1755 by British troops, a significant number were brought to Salem as well as to other ports along the Atlantic seaboard. They were allowed to remain in the city but were forbidden to make any public display of Catholicism. Many simply chose to leave.

The first Mass said in Salem was celebrated on May 6, 1790. At that time, the city had about seventy-nine hundred inhabitants compared to Boston's eighteen thousand. Father John Thayer, who was then stationed at Holy Cross Church in Boston, was able to obtain a license from the board of selectmen which permitted a public Mass to be said. The city fathers, at that time headed by a Quaker, extended such liberality not only to Catholics but to Methodists, Presbyterians, and Episcopalians as well. To arrange for this event, Father Thayer contacted Reverend William Bentley of Salem, a Unitarian minister who, during the next thirty years, went out of his way to befriend Catholics. In reply to Father Thayer's request for assistance, Dr. Bentley wrote back that it was his "desire that every man enjoy his religion, not by toleration but as the inalienable right of his nature." Dr. Bentley resided in an old frame house known as the Crowninshield Mansion and arranged for Father Thayer to lodge there during his visit. In all probability, the first Mass in the city was offered at this location. In attendance was an assembly of individuals of various nationalities who either resided in Salem or happened to be in port at the time. Before returning to Boston, Father Thayer left a large number of Catholic books with Reverend Bentley and asked that he give them to a local bookstore where they could be offered for sale.

When Father Thayer returned from Boston a few weeks later, he obtained permission to deliver a public address at the courthouse. During his speech, he spoke at length on various aspects of Catholic doctrine. However, he had the poor judgment of concentrating his attention on subjects that would prove most controversial to Protestant listeners. His remarks were carried in the press and had the predictable effect of generating a dispute. In 1791, when Father Thayer again visited the city, he administered baptism there for the first time. For many years to come, Salem's Catholics were served by similar missionary visits that occurred only at irregular intervals. Among those making such visits was Father (later Bishop) John de Cheverus, who reported in his journal that three persons received their Easter Communion in 1798. Between 1797 and 1810, only twenty-nine Salem residents were baptized, although it is possible that some received this sacrament by journeying to Boston. Dr. Bentley wrote that Bishop Carroll came to the city in 1803 during the course of an episcopal visit to Boston.

During the early 1800s, Bishop Cheverus and Father Matignon from Boston began to visit Catholics in Salem about two or three times a year, and thereafter such visits increased in number and regularity. It was reported that Bishop Cheverus usually took the stagecoach from Boston but occasionally crossed the Charles River by ferry and walked the remaining distance, satchel in hand, so that he could save the price of a stagecoach ticket and devote the savings to the relief of the poor. When priests came to Salem in those days, Mass was offered at the home of a Mr. Connolly, who resided on Herbert Street, or a Mr. Campbell, whose home was on Daniels Street.

In 1813, Bishop Cheverus bought a tract of land at Washington and Federal Streets for the purpose of building a church, but this land was sold four years later without any construction taking place. From 1818 to 1823, Father Paul McQuade regularly visited Salem from Boston on a monthly basis. In 1820, Bishop Cheverus purchased another piece of land for a church, and actual construction started to take place shortly thereafter. At that time, there were about one hundred twenty Catholics in Salem and they constituted only a minuscule portion of the population. Many of these individuals personally helped with the construction, coming by after work each day to donate an hour or two of their time. By the fall of 1821, they had completed the building of the first church, which they called St. Mary's. It seated about three hundred fifty people. The first Mass was said in the new church on October 14, 1821, an event that was reported in the Salem *Gazette* as follows: "Bishop Cheverus performed the services of the Romish Church and preached a sermon at the Catholic Church in this town on Saturday last, when one hundred and seventy-seven dollars were contributed for the completion of the house, an instance of a liberal and tolerant spirit, which our forefathers, who sought the true faith through a different medium, would hardly have anticipated."

The church was still not plastered on the inside or painted on the outside. It was not completed until 1826, at which time it was formally dedicated. It was the fourth Catholic church to be completed in all of New England. Bishop Benedict Fenwick described the building at that time as "a neat and handsome frame church . . . not quite finished. The congregation consists of about 150 or 200 souls. They have no pastor; the Bishop or the Rev. Mr. Byrne, to afford them an opportunity of frequenting the sacraments, pays them a monthly visit. The Catholics of this town are generally very poor, scarcely able to support a clergyman."

In 1826, St. Mary's received its first resident pastor but his responsibilities extended far beyond Salem. The parish included such towns as Marblehead, Lynn, Newburyport, Lowell, and Dover, New Hampshire. One writer recounts that in 1829, when Bishop Fenwick again visited Salem to administer confirmation, "many Protestants were present . . . and when they had departed upon request of the Bishop at the close of the ceremony, he addressed the population on the strict duty of supporting their pastor, which they seemed not fully to understand."

With the opening of the Erie Canal, the importance of the port sharply declined, although nearby Marblehead continued to be a home for whaling vessels. Yankee clippers no longer plied the China Sea in order to bring their Oriental cargoes home to Salem, so the town had to find an alternative means of supporting itself. It turned to manufacturing and, over the next fifty years, developed into a busy New England mill town. The principal industry was the Naumkeog Cotton Mills. This change in economy meant opportunity for Irish and other immigrants who arrived in great numbers to fill railroad and factory jobs. In 1836, St. Mary's had its first parish rectory. In 1837, the first Sunday school was started. By 1838, the parish had grown to 1,000 members in a city of 15,000 inhabitants and reported 59 baptisms; between 1845 and 1850, when the potato famine was in full swing, the parish grew by 3,500 people.

During this era, St. Mary's had several pastors who engendered varying degrees of popularity. Father James Strain lasted only one year because of dissension during his pastorate. His successor, Father Thomas O'Flaherty, was described as a "controversialist" because of several religious disputations that he had with Protestant clergymen. Apparently, he ruled his own congregation with an iron hand. On one occasion, a parishioner who was guilty of "gross neglect of his family and unchristian conduct" was required to appear personally before the entire congregation, holding an unlighted candle, beg forgiveness of God, the Church, and the congregation, and promise that he would be faithful to his wife and children in the future. Father O'Flaherty was followed by Father James Conway, who displayed a totally different temperament. During Father Conway's eleven years as pastor, he erected a second church in Salem, St. James, brought the Sisters of Notre Dame to the city to open a girls' school, enlarged the existing St. Mary's Church, and erected a sacristy along with a transept and a choir loft. In 1856, the flooring timbers in the old building began to give way, so he immediately undertook to build a new church. Ground was broken for this purpose in 1857, but Father Conway did not live to see the completion of his project. On May 26, 1857, all the mills and businesses in Salem were closed to observe his funeral, and more than six thousand people lined the streets to pay their final respects as his funeral cortege passed by.

The present church [**pictured above**] was dedicated in 1858 and named in honor of the Immaculate Conception, a doctrine of the Catholic Church that had just been proclaimed in 1854. The altar from the old church was removed and placed in the basement of the new building. On the same day, St. James Church on Federal Street was also formally dedicated. For a short period of time St. James functioned under the pastor at Immaculate Conception, but this arrangement soon proved to be impractical and was discontinued. The old St. Mary's Church was used a short while as a boys' school, but the building was eventually torn down and the land on which it stood was sold.

In 1863 and 1864, improvements were made to the interior of Immaculate Conception Church. A new altar was installed that was supported by eight marble columns between which were placed panels depicting various scenes in the life of Christ. Other portraits and statuary were also installed. In 1864, the new altar was consecrated.

In 1866, the parish opened an orphan asylum staffed by the Grey Nuns from Montreal. The Sunday school had nearly two hundred in regular attendance. Many of these children were provided with shoes and clothing by the parish so that they could be suitably dressed when attending Mass.

One visitor of note who came to Salem before the Civil War was the celebrated temperance crusader, Father Theobald Mathew. Father Mathew traveled extensively in Ireland and America, devoting his energies to preaching against what the Irish usually referred to as "the problem." As their old lament put it, God made whiskey to keep the Irish poor. Father Mathew drew large crowds when he spoke, possibly because so many families had one or more members who were afflicted by "the problem." In the British Isles, he spoke before more than 200,000 people in the course of his temperance crusade and led them in "taking the pledge." During his American tour, he visited twenty-five states and led more than 600,000 listeners in publicly swearing off the use of alcohol. On September 19, 1849, Father Mathew came to Salem at the invitation of the Henfield Division of the Sons of Temperance. The members of this organization gathered at St. Mary's, donned green badges, and then marched as a body to the Danvers township line to meet their guest. Father Mathew was escorted to the Salem town hall where he was formally received by the mayor and made a guest of the city. He preached both at the town hall and at St. Mary's before throngs whom he led in "taking the pledge."

Father Mathew directed his fire principally at the consumer. He paid little attention to interdicting the importation of liquor or prohibiting its manufacture and sale. His views set the tone for Catholic responses in later years to efforts aimed at curbing alcoholism by prohibiting its sale. Drawing a sharp distinction between temperance and prohibition, Catholics generally supported the former and voted against the latter. In 1887, long after Father Mathew died, a large statue was erected in his honor at the Central Square in front of Immaculate Conception Church where it has remained for over a hundred years.

As members of various Catholic national groups began to move into Salem, additional churches were established within the territorial boundaries of Immaculate Conception so that priests could minister to those individuals in their own languages. In 1872, a French congregation began to meet in the basement of Immaculate Conception Church and did so until it could establish its own parish, which was named in honor of St. Joseph. St. Joseph's still functions a few blocks from Immaculate Conception, as do Italian and Polish churches. By 1890, Immaculate Conception had 6,000 members and reported 180 baptisms; at that time, some 30 parishes, having about 130,000 Catholics, had been erected in the territory that old St. Mary's had served 65 years before.

Today, Immaculate Conception is the second oldest of the four hundred three churches in the Boston archdiocese. The parish finds itself in an older area of Salem, near the port, which consists of restored homes, such as the Nathaniel Hawthorne house across the street and similar houses with varying numbers of gables. This fact means that prices in the neighborhood have skyrocketed and severely limited the economic groups who can move into the area. The parish now numbers about one thousand people, still mostly Irish with a fair number of French and Italian members. It consists largely of older families or young professional people who can commute to work in Boston. The parochial school was closed in 1972, so parochial school students must attend a nearby school still operated by St. Joseph's parish. Because of the integration of its nationality group into the total community, this originally French church no longer offers services in French but does have a Spanish Mass each weekend to accommodate the Spanish population that has recently come to Salem.

Among the many parish programs instituted by Immaculate Conception is an ecumenical healing ministry by which the parish, in cooperation with an Episcopal church and a Jewish synagogue, has retained the services of a nurse to assist in medical aspects of health care such as health counseling, giving blood pressure examinations, and visiting the sick. The scope of the ministry extends to drug, nicotine, alcohol addiction, and other health problems. Clergymen work with the nurse to provide their respective congregations with spiritual assistance in the healing process. Immaculate Conception is also undertaking an effort to evangelize both lapsed Catholics within its parish boundaries and other residents who have no particular religious affiliation.

6
St. John the Baptist

New Bedford

MASSACHUSETTS

St. John the Baptist in New Bedford, Massachusetts, is the oldest Portuguese Catholic church in America. It was founded in 1871 to accommodate the religious needs of a growing number of Portuguese immigrants who had come to America, principally from the island of Pico in the Azores and who had settled in this New England seaport city. Long before the Civil War, New Bedford had become a center of the New England whaling industry. By 1857, some 327 whaling ships used New Bedford as their home port; at that time, the industry employed about 10,000 seamen, of whom an estimated 1,000 were Portuguese. It was at the Seamen's Bethel in New Bedford, a Protestant church on Johnnycake Road, that Herman Melville worshiped and meditated, saw the memorials to those who had lost their lives working at this hazardous calling, and received the inspiration to write his celebrated novel, *Moby Dick*.

Whaling ships, usually captained by Yankee owners, made regular stops in the Azores and at Madeira, islands located off the west coast of Portugal. They stopped for both supplies and seamen who were recruited from landless agricultural workers struggling for existence on St. Michael, Pico, Fayal, and other islands that make up the Azorean archipelago. There is a suggestion by some writers that not all Portuguese seamen were recruited voluntarily. Many ultimately found their way to New

Bedford and other Massachusetts cities while others sailed for Monterey and Carmel in California and manned ships leaving for Alaskan waters from those ports. Some went as far as Hawaii where they initially engaged in the same occupation. Portuguese immigrants also came to America by more conventional means, not only from the Azores but from the Spanish Canary Islands and Cape Verde, the latter being a group of Portuguese islands off the west coast of Africa. It was not until the twentieth century that continentals — Portuguese from mainland Portugal — began coming to the United States in significant numbers.

Until St. John the Baptist parish was founded in 1871, there was only one Catholic church in New Bedford. Originally called St. Mary's, it was established as a mission in 1821 by an Irish Augustinian, Father Philip Larissey, and was dedicated in that year by Bishop John de Cheverus of Boston. Before that date, Catholics in New Bedford saw only an occasional visiting priest who went from house to house, hearing confessions and distributing Communion. They often took their children to Boston to be baptized at Holy Cross Cathedral.

The original St. Mary's Church was a wooden frame building containing twenty-four pews. It was surrounded by a high wooden fence and cost $800 to build. Until 1844, it had no resident pastor and was served by priests coming from Newport, Rhode Island. In 1843, the Hartford diocese was created. It included Newport but not New Bedford. Hence, other arrangements had to be made to minister to the sixty or seventy members of St. Mary's parish and to other Catholics living in such southeastern Massachusetts towns as Sandwich and Wareham. To fill this need the bishop of Boston sent Father Patrick Byrne to St. Mary's as its first resident pastor.

The building that housed the original St. Mary's Church was abandoned in 1849 when the parish bought the former Universalist church located at Pleasant and School Streets. It remained the only Catholic church in New Bedford for the next fifteen years. It was to this location that Portuguese Catholics came to worship as an incidental part of an Irish congregation presided over by English-speaking pastors. Following the Civil War, Father Lawrence McMahon, a former Union Army chaplain and future bishop of Hartford, was sent to New Bedford where he built a new church to replace St. Mary's, naming it after his patron, St. Lawrence Martyr. St. Lawrence Church, dedicated in 1866, stands today as the mother church of all Catholic parishes in and about New Bedford. At the time of its dedication, it had about eight hundred Portuguese members, most of whom were recent immigrants. Most could not speak English and many were illiterate. The presence of a large Portuguese community in an English-speaking parish was wholly unsatisfactory from many standpoints. One predictable effect was that many Portuguese Catholics simply did not come to church and were developing attitudes of indifference and neglect toward their religious duties. This was in marked contrast to the attitudes and practices of Portuguese Catholics living on the islands they had recently left, where Catholic religious observances and practices had been an integral part of daily life since Prince Henry the Navigator settled those islands long before the time of Columbus.

In 1869, Father João Ignácio Azevedo Encarnação arrived in New Bedford from the Azores and founded the first Portuguese parish in the United States. It was and remains a national parish, meaning that it does not have territorial boundaries. It was formally established on September 10, 1871, and named in honor of São João Baptista — St. John the Baptist — a saint especially revered in Portuguese tradition. Father Encarnação bought a tract of land at Wing and Pleasant Streets for $3,098 and undertook to build the first church to be occupied by the new parish. The cornerstone was laid on September 27, 1874, and it was completed and opened for services the following June. By that time, Father Encarnação had left New Bedford and had gone to seek out Portuguese Catholics living in such cities as Fall River, Providence, Provincetown (at the tip of Cape Cod), the island of Martha's Vineyard, and Boston. His successor, Father Antonio Freitas, took over in 1873 and remained until 1885 when, like several of his successors, he returned to the Azores and retired because of ill health.

As St. John's was being founded in New Bedford, other Portuguese parishes were beginning to be formed in other cities on both coasts. Father Freitas founded a mission for Portuguese Catholics in nearby Fall River called Senhor Santo Cristo dos Milagres — Lord Holy Christ of the Miracles. It became a parish in its own right in 1892. On the West Coast a number of Portuguese had come to California to participate in the gold rush. Instead of coming across the United States in covered wagons, they signed on as seamen aboard whaling vessels leaving New Bedford, sailed around Cape Horn and up the Pacific coasts of South and North America, and then jumped ship in California. After trying their luck in the gold country, they settled around Oakland, San Jose, and Hayward. Father Manuel Francisco Fernandes, an ex-shepherd from Pico Island, came to Santa Barbara, California, to be ordained. After becoming a priest, he tried to revive religious activities among Portuguese Catholics in California, Hawaii, and even in Macao, a Portuguese colony off the China coast. He founded St. Joseph's Portuguese Catholic Church in Oakland in 1892. By sheer persistence, he prevailed upon the bishop of Honolulu to recruit the services of Portuguese priests in California to tend to the needs of Portuguese Catholics in Hawaii. These missionary priests included Father Stephen Alencastre, a native of Madeira, who many years later was consecrated bishop of Honolulu, the first Portuguese cleric to become a member of the American hierarchy.

During the final decades of the nineteenth century, Portuguese immigrants entered the United States at the rate of about twenty thousand a year. About a third came to Massachusetts and most of these settled in and about New Bedford, Fall River, and Taunton, and on Cape Cod. A Portuguese newspaper called the *Luso-Americano* was published in Boston and New Bedford from 1881 to 1889. In the 1890s, a Portuguese Methodist church and a Portuguese Baptist church were organized in New Bedford. Their presence in this overwhelmingly Catholic Portuguese community served as a spur, here as elsewhere, to Catholic bishops to look to the needs of Portuguese Catholics because new immigrants were often reluctant to attend a church having an English-speaking pastor.

The economic base of New Bedford changed radically after 1870. With the discovery of oil in Pennsylvania in 1859, petroleum came to replace whale oil as a source of fuel and light, so whaling rapidly disappeared. Beginning in 1875 and continuing until about 1930, the cotton textile industry came to be the principal source of jobs. At its height, this industry employed about twenty thousand people. As the latest arrivals among immigrant groups, the Portuguese took the worst-paid jobs and occupied the lowest rung on the economic ladder. Above them were English-speaking immigrants of various nationalities and French-speaking Canadians, who for many years were the principal foreign-language group in New Bedford. French Canadians founded their own church, St. Joseph's, as did the Germans at St. Boniface and the Poles at Our Lady of Perpetual Help. By 1900, there were twenty-three Catholic churches in New Bedford and some fifty-one percent of its total population was Catholic.

Portuguese immigrants retained a close attachment to others who came from the same towns and islands in the old country. Each group spoke Portuguese with a distinct accent and had special local customs that they brought with them to New Bedford. Those from Fayal settled in the south end of the city. Portuguese from St. Michael settled in the north end near the textile mills along the Acushnet River. Madeirans settled in Immaculate Conception parish. Each group had its own clubs and associations, even within a particular parish. Most distinctive were the Cape Verdeans, who came from former Portuguese islands near the African mainland. Cape Verdeans are partly black, have a separate culture, and speak their own dialect, Crioulo, which is not understandable by someone who knows only Portuguese. In 1905, they formed their own parish, Our Lady of the Assumption, and that parish continues to date as a Cape Verdean national parish, one of two in the United States. However, by now most of its two thousand members are completely Americanized and Masses are said in English, except for one Mass each Sunday at which some Crioulo and some Portuguese is used.

The growth of the Portuguese community in New Bedford reached the point in 1902 where a second Portuguese national church, Mount Carmel, was established. Later, Immaculate Conception was founded. Today, the city has three Portuguese national churches and one Cape Verdean church. For several generations it was necessary for American bishops in the new Fall River diocese and elsewhere to obtain Portuguese-speaking priests from Europe. One of them, Father Humberto Medeiros, a native of St. Michael in the Azores, became archbishop of Boston and a member of the College of Cardinals.

In 1908, the original St. John's Church at Pleasant and Wing Streets was almost totally consumed by fire, so the parish was forced to meet temporarily in the basement of St. James Church. The pastor, Father Antonio G. Neves, bought land a few blocks away at County and Wing Streets and started to build the church [pictured above]. It was completed and dedicated in 1911 and consecrated on May 30, 1913. Father Neves also bought land about a mile away for St. John's cemetery.

The new St. John's Church was constructed from locally quarried granite. It has a Byzantine style, influenced by Romanesque design found in many Portuguese churches. Among the artifacts are statues that can be found in all Portuguese churches, a statue of St. Anthony of Padua (who was actually a native of Lisbon) and one depicting Our Lady of the Immaculate Conception, the patroness of Portugal. Later, St. John's and other Portuguese parishes began to display statues of Our Lady of Fátima to commemorate the apparition of the Blessed Virgin in 1917 to three shepherd children who lived in Cova da Iria, a mountain village in central Portugal.

In 1927, Father Manuel G. Salvador, who was pastor for twenty-seven years, bought the Grinnell estate on County Street and opened St. John's Academy. It was placed in the hands of the Sisters of Mercy. In 1951, the parish received its first native-born pastor, Monsignor John A. Silvia. By that time, many Portuguese-speaking residents of southeastern Massachusetts were second- or third-generation Americans and were beginning to provide the diocese of Fall River with bilingual clergy, born in the United States but able to serve at a Portuguese church. Father Silvia enlarged the old St. John's cemetery. Having about five hundred burials a year, it has now become the final resting place not only for members of the parish but for Portuguese Catholics from the New Bedford area. In 1957, Father Silvia built a new school building, still in use today, and initiated a fund-raising drive that provided $150,000 for the renovation of the church.

Any profile of a Portuguese parish would be incomplete without mentioning *festas*, annual celebrations that take place with parish sponsorship and are religious, cultural, and social in character. They began to be held at St. John's about the turn of the twentieth century as new immigrants sought to re-create, in small part, the religious and cultural life they left behind in the Azores. The largest of these *festas* in New Bedford is not at St. John's but at Immaculate Conception. Its *Festa do Santissimo Sacramento* (Feast of the Most Holy Sacrament) — Corpus Christi — has grown from a parish function to a community event that attracts patronage from all over southern New England and from as far away as Canada and California. It began in 1915 when Madeiran members of the parish organized a three-day weekend devotion featuring a procession in which the Blessed Sacrament was carried through the streets of the parish. It grew to include a carnival, fireworks, a concert, and a banquet. Eventually, the secular component of the celebration became so prominent that the bishop of Fall River stepped in and forbade the carrying of the Blessed Sacrament in the parade. However, as a fund-raiser for the parish and principally for charitable activities, it has continued as *festeiros* (festival committee members) each year make every effort to outdo the *festa* that was staged by their predecessors the year before. As many as 200,000 have attended this *festa*, which has not entirely lost its religious aspect. The weekend is still an occasion for many to visit the church to leave *esmolas* (alms) and to redeem a *promessa*, to make an act of thanksgiving, for the granting of a favor received during the preceding year.

Not to be outdone, the *Micaelense* — members of the parish from the island of St. Michael in the Azores — organized their own *Festa do Senhor da Pedra*, a feast akin to Senhor Santo Cristo dos Milagres. This Azorean observance dates back to the sixteenth century and features a figure of Christ, known as the *Ecce Homo* (Latin for "Behold the Man"), that portrays his suffering prior to the Crucifixion. According to legend, a crate was washed ashore at Ponta Delgada, the capital of St. Michael, in which was found a stone bearing the *Ecce Homo* image. The stone was preserved in a chapel on the island and *Senhor da Pedra* (Lord of the Rock) became a venerated religious object. In 1924, the *Micaelense* started this *festa* at Immaculate Conception, which includes many of the same activities as the Madeiran *festa* earlier in the month but not on so large a scale. The *Senhor da Pedra* events attract about twenty-five thousand spectators and, as with the other celebration, provide additional revenues for the parish.

At St. John's, other *festas* are held but on a much simpler scale. The most important is the *Festa do Espirito Santo* — the Holy Spirit festival. This *festa* is one of the most popular and widely observed celebrations in American Portuguese parishes. It traces its origin to St. Elizabeth of Portugal, who died in 1336. She was a pious and charitable woman who was often berated and criticized for her generosity by her husband, sometimes portrayed as the cruel king, Don Diniz. According to legend, she was in the habit of smuggling bread out of the royal castle to feed the poor. On one occasion, as she was leaving the castle on a charitable errand, her husband stopped her and asked what she was carrying in her basket. She replied, "Roses." When he opened the basket to inspect its contents, he found only flowers because the small loaves of bread *(rosquilhas)* had been transformed into flowers. At the same moment, a dove, representing the Holy Spirit, lighted on the queen's hand, signifying divine approval of her action. (Interestingly enough, this same story is told about her great aunt, St. Elizabeth of Hungary, who lived two generations before her Portuguese namesake.)

The Holy Spirit festival is not a weekend event but stretches over the seven weeks between Easter and Pentecost. A crown and scepter are taken each week to a different home in the parish where, at stated times, members gather for recitation of the rosary and for a social event that follows. The *festa* ends on Pentecost with the crowning of the *mordomo* — the festival chairman — and a procession from the school to the church for Mass. Thereafter, a celebration takes place that includes the serving of specially prepared *sopas* (soups) and an auction for the benefit of charity. *Pensões* — gifts of wine, bread, and meat — are prepared and delivered to the poor. Then a drawing is held for the selection of the *mordomo* for the following year's *festa* as well as the parishioners who will serve as hosts for the Holy Spirit symbols the following year. Whoever hosts the Holy Spirit symbols on the first Sunday after Easter keeps the crown at his home throughout the year until the following Easter, when the activity commences anew. In addition to the Holy Spirit *festa*, a celebration in honor of the parish patron, St. John the Baptist, occurs each year on the third Sunday of June. This event includes Mass, a short procession through nearby streets, and entertainment, which includes ethnic foods and music.

Three waves of immigration have brought Portuguese to the United States. The first, starting about the time St. John's was founded in 1871, ended around 1920 when new immigration laws were enacted having nationality quotas that sharply curtailed Portuguese immigration. Notwithstanding the quotas, during the 1930s there was another upsurge in Portuguese immigration that brought to this country a number of continentals from the mainland. A third began in 1960. Three years earlier, a serious earthquake took place on the island of Fayal that nearly destroyed it. Another destructive quake hit the island of São Jorge in the Azores in 1964 and destroyed twenty-five thousand homes. In 1958, Congress passed a special relief act permitting fifteen hundred Fayalenses to enter the United States. It was amended in 1960 to permit an additional immigration from these islands. In 1965, the Immigration and Nationality Act raised the Portuguese quota to twenty thousand a year and permitted the pooling of national quotas. Thereafter, about twelve thousand new arrivals began to enter the United States annually. The 1970 census reported that there were 318,000 first- and second-generation Portuguese living in this country, of whom 108,000 resided in Massachusetts. As in the case of their predecessors, many of the newcomers to Massachusetts settled in the southeastern part of the state. A new development is the fairly recent arrival on Cape Cod of about three thousand Brazilians for whom religious services in Portuguese must be provided.

Today, a majority of the populations of Fall River, Taunton, and New Bedford are of Portuguese ancestry, although many are members of families who have been in the area for several generations. Both St. John's and the other Portuguese parishes have a substantial number of recent immigrants. However, Mount Carmel, with its four thousand families, has more new arrivals than St. John's. Most newcomers earn their livelihoods working in small factories, although there has been a revival of the fishing fleet in New Bedford harbor. For the last several years, it has been the most prosperous fishing port in the country. The fleet has about two hundred forty vessels, almost all manned by Portuguese seamen. These successors to the Moby Dick tradition set sail in search of scallops, not whales.

Today, there are about thirty Portuguese Catholic churches in New England — twelve in the Fall River diocese (including the four in New Bedford) and others in Providence, Hartford, and Boston. There are also Portuguese Catholic churches in New York City, Newark, and in various parts of California. St. John's, the mother church of all of them, has about fourteen hundred families. Half of the parishioners speak English and the other half speak Portuguese. There are five Masses each weekend, three in English and two in Portuguese. Two parish bulletins are published each week; the one with the red cover is in English and the one with the blue cover is in Portuguese. Some parishioners take both bulletins, the red one for younger members of the family and the blue one for older ones.

In addition to normal parish activities, St. John's provides the residence for a chaplain at St. Luke's hospital. The parochial school, which it shares with St. James parish, has two hundred twenty-five students, about a third of whom are of Portuguese ancestry. Ethnic identity is not as important in Catholic churches in New Bedford as it used to be. St. John's has a few Irish and French families while many former Portuguese parishioners have moved to the suburbs to take their places in the multiethnic territorial parishes that have been erected there in recent decades. However, their roots go back to St. John's, even though they now extend far beyond the church where they were planted well over a century ago.

7
Immaculate Conception Cathedral

Portland

MAINE

Shortly after Maine became a state in 1820, Portland, a seaport and its largest city, became the capital and remained as such for a dozen years. At that time, there were only about forty Catholics in the city. They were served by occasional missionary visits by priests from Boston. On those occasions, Mass was said at the home of Nicholas Shea on Fore Street. A collection was taken up in Boston for the parishes in Maine that netted about $2,900, and a portion of this sum was spent for the construction of St. Dominic's Church, the first Catholic church in Portland. It was opened in 1830 and dedicated in 1833 when the Catholic population of the city had grown to about two hundred people. In 1853, Maine and New Hampshire were removed from the Boston diocese and placed in the newly created diocese of Portland. At that time, there were only six priests and eight Catholic churches in both states.

The first bishop of Portland, David W. Bacon, was installed at St. Dominic's Church on May 31, 1855. Immediately thereafter he set about to build a new cathedral for his diocese. The project was ill-starred from the very outset and might not have been accomplished for many years without his energy and determination. When Bishop Bacon came to Maine, there was a great deal of hostility, both overt and otherwise, toward Catholics throughout the area. In the year that Bishop Bacon was installed at Portland, two Catholic churches, one in Bath and another in Manchester, were burned by mobs. When he traveled to Bath to lay the cornerstone for a new church, he was prevented from doing so by another mob that had assembled for the occasion. In the following year, a third Catholic church at Ellsworth was vandalized and later burned under circumstances strongly suggesting arson.

In 1856, Bishop Bacon purchased the Senter estate on Cumberland Street in Portland, along with an adjacent strip of land. There he erected a chapel with a seating capacity of six hundred people. It was at this location that he decided to erect the Portland cathedral. The dedication of the chapel took place in the middle of a severe storm that prevented many invited guests from attending the ceremony. For a number of years Bishop Bacon used this chapel as his cathedral while residing nearby in a house on Brackett Street.

Weather was not the only problem he encountered. Bishop Bacon was originally from New York and was able to raise about $30,000 from friends in Brooklyn for his project. However, most of that money went to pay for the construction of the chapel and a parochial school that he was also building. He was not able to break ground for the cathedral itself until 1860. Shortly thereafter, the Civil War broke out. During the war, money, materials, and qualified workmen were either scarce or nonexistent, so construction was interrupted. In the meantime, he was able to complete the parochial school for the cathedral parish and opened it in 1864 under the supervision of Notre Dame Sisters from Montreal. Relations at that time between the Irish and the French in Maine were not always cordial, so the bishop introduced French-speaking nuns into Portland for the purpose of attempting to bridge this gap. They opened an academy for tuition-paying girls and also began to teach at St. Aloysius, as the parish school was called. By 1867, the academy had sixty girls while the parish school had four hundred students of both sexes.

In May 1866, the cornerstone of the new cathedral was laid. By July, the walls of the building were in place. On July 4, 1866, a fire broke out that destroyed most of Portland; someone had thrown a firecracker into a boat builder's shop on Commercial Street, near the wharf, and it spread throughout the entire city, destroying fifteen hundred buildings and leaving ten thousand residents homeless. The cathedral complex was leveled — the chapel, the church under construction, the bishop's residence, the Notre Dame convent, and the parochial school. For some time thereafter, Mass was said each Sunday on Grand Trunk wharf and later in a temporary building near the cathedral site.

Bishop Bacon immediately began the work anew. He spent two months traveling in Canada and along the Eastern seaboard to raise funds. One source was friends in Brooklyn who had contributed to his building fund ten years earlier. Another source was Protestants in Portland, some of whom made donations to this project. Six months after the fire, the cathedral chapel and the school had been restored. On September 8, 1869, the cathedral [**pictured above**] was dedicated. On the night of the dedication, a storm arose, blowing the steeple from the top of the church and onto a nearby house. Happily, no one was injured, and the steeple was promptly replaced.

The bishop's house was completed at the same time. A three-story Victorian mansion, it was constructed on such a scale as to offer priests of the diocese a place to stay in Portland when they came to the cathedral for their annual retreat. The old house has a lookout tower on the roof that provides a view of the entire harbor. The house has been redecorated on several occasions and part of it now serves as a rectory for the cathedral parish. There are plans afoot to use it as a home for retired priests.

The cathedral has one tower, which is two hundred three feet high. Until the construction of large office buildings in downtown Portland, the tower was one of the main features of the Portland skyline. The cathedral has a large rose window and twenty-one small clerestory windows containing biblical scenes relating to the gospel writers. In the early 1900s, Bishop William O'Connell installed an eighteen-section Munich stained-glass window that depicts various episodes in the life of the Blessed Virgin.

Bishop Bacon died in 1874 after nineteen years of service to the Portland diocese. At the time of his death, the diocese had grown to 63 churches and had 52 priests, 23 parochial schools, and a Catholic population of about 80,000, a far cry from the frontier church that he had encountered when he first came to New England. His successor, James A. Healy, was an unusual figure in American Church history. Bishop Healy was born on a plantation in Macon, Georgia, owned by his father, an Irish immigrant. His mother was a mulatto slave. Under the laws of Georgia in effect at the time, James Healy and his seven brothers and sisters were deemed to be slaves. His father sent him north at an early age to be educated and most of his brothers and sisters eventually followed. He attended a seminary in Montreal and was ordained in Paris. After serving as a priest in Boston for twenty years, he was appointed bishop of Portland in 1875 and served in that post for twenty-five years. Two of his brothers became priests. One of them, Patrick Healy, joined the Jesuits and was appointed president of Georgetown University not long after Bishop Healy came to Portland.

The principal ongoing problem that confronted him during his administration was coping with the growth of the diocese, brought on both by immigration from abroad and by the migration of French-speaking Catholics from Canada who came south to Maine after the Civil War to work in lumber camps and cotton mills. At the end of his tenure, the diocese had 96,000 Catholics, 54 churches with resident pastors, and 32 mission churches.

Bishop William O'Connell served only six years in Portland before going on to Boston to become archbishop and later a cardinal. Shortly after the conclusion of the Spanish-American War, the Holy See was interested in appointing American bishops to dioceses in the Philippine Islands and offered Bishop O'Connell the post of archbishop of Manila. After consulting with public officials in Washington, he turned the offer down on the basis that he had opposed the Spanish-American War and was not interested in going to a territory that had been acquired by conquest as a result of that war.

Immaculate Conception Cathedral is still the principal Catholic church in Maine. Each summer, busloads of Catholics from all over the state come to visit the church in recognition of its stature and importance. Every year on Holy Thursday, priests from all over the diocese are present to receive holy oils consecrated by the bishop for use during the following year in all of the churches in the state. The parish itself is smaller in population than it used to be, having experienced the phenomenon commonplace to downtown churches of seeing some its congregation move to the suburbs. In this case, it is South Portland that has many former parishioners. A few years ago, nearly one hundred fifty houses near the cathedral were removed to permit the construction of a feeder road to an arterial highway, and among those forced to move were a large number of cathedral parishioners. The congregation has an ethnic mix of Irish, French, Polish, and Italian. Its four Masses each weekend serve about eight hundred people. The school, still staffed by the Sisters of Mercy after many years, has less than one hundred students, a situation dictated in no small part by the fact that tuition fees have placed parochial school education out of the reach of many families with limited incomes. Each year on Pentecost, the cathedral participates with nearby Episcopal and Methodist churches in a Christian Unity service, an event that symbolizes a vastly different attitude from the one that greeted Bishop Bacon when he undertook the construction of the building now standing on Cumberland Street as a monument to his dedication.

8
St. Patrick

Newcastle

MAINE

St. Patrick's Church, on the Academy Hill Road near Newcastle, Maine, was constructed in 1808 and is the oldest Catholic church building now standing in all of New England. Located near another old settlement called Damariscotta Mills, St. Patrick's was constructed in a remote section of the Maine district of Massachusetts by two Irish-born merchants, James Kavanagh and his partner, Matthew Cottrill. It was built to serve a Catholic community that had begun to settle on the banks of the Damariscotta River, about twenty miles from where that river meets the Atlantic Ocean at Pemaquid Point, the oldest settlement in Maine. St. Patrick's parish has maintained a continuous existence from 1808 until the present time.

Efforts of Catholics to settle in Maine began as early as 1583 and were uniformly unsuccessful for about two hundred years. In 1583, Sir George Peckham and Sir Thomas Girard, two English noblemen of the Elizabethan era, sent four ships to the New World for the purpose of establishing a refuge for English Catholics. Their vessels reached Newfoundland and later came to the Norumbega River, but the expedition turned back to England when one of the four vessels was lost at sea. In 1605, a Captain Weymouth sailed from Southampton aboard the *Archangel*, a ship financed by another Catholic nobleman, Lord Thomas Arundell. This ship arrived first at Cape Cod and journeyed on to Booth Bay, which its members named Pentecost Harbor. It ventured up the Penobscot River, but the party became torn by dissension and was unable to establish a permanent settlement.

The French also tried settling the Maine coast at about the same time. Pierre du Guast sailed from Le Havre in 1605 under the banner of the king of France with a party that included Samuel de Champlain. After reaching Nova Scotia in the summer of 1604, this party sailed on to an island in the Scoodic River that they named St. Croix. At this point, they established a small settlement, which included both a fort and a chapel. However, it lasted for only a year because some thirty-five of the seventy-nine members of this expedition died as the result of privation suffered during the rigors of a New England winter they were ill-prepared to meet. One of the members of the expedition, Father Nicholas Aubry, said what is believed to be the first Mass ever offered in New England. Regrettably, he was one of the members of the party who perished during the harshness of the winter of 1604-05. In 1613, the French tried another expedition to Maine, but it also proved to be unsuccessful. The members of this party reached Penobscot Bay and landed at Mount Desert Island, which they called St. Sauveur, but they did not stay long.

Before settling in Maryland, Sir George Calvert, better known as Lord Baltimore, obtained a charter from the king of England for a colony on Newfoundland that he hoped to establish for the benefit of English Catholics. In 1627, he arrived there and began to establish a settlement. However, he soon realized that the possibility of constant warfare with the French and the rigors of northern winters might prove too much for his followers, so he sailed south and sought permission from the governor of Virginia to found a Catholic settlement in Virginia south of the James River. Permission was refused, so Calvert ultimately obtained a charter for his settlement farther south in Maryland. Actually, he never came to Maryland, having died before the original expedition was formed in 1634, but his son carried on the project that he had envisioned. The only English settlers who were able to carve a religious refuge out of the New England wilderness was a group of dissenters who sailed from Holland in 1619 aboard the *Mayflower* and landed at Plymouth. Their colony at Massachusetts Bay took root and flourished.

For nearly one hundred fifty years Maine was a battleground in ongoing border warfare with the French. Recurring hostilities took place until the French lost all of their possessions on the North American continent in 1763. Caught in the middle of this warfare were French Jesuit and Capuchin missionaries who regularly traveled south from Quebec along the Penobscot and Kennebec Rivers to establish missionary outposts among the Abnaki, Passamaquoddy, and Penobscot Indians. What is believed to be the first Catholic church built in New England was constructed at an Indian village along the Penobscot River, called Old Town. It was named in honor of Ste. Anne, as were so many French churches of that era, but it did not last. The Massachusetts Bay colony claimed the area for England and enacted a statute in 1692 making it a crime for French

Catholics to settle in any coastal town in Maine. They also brought pressure to bear on the Indians to renounce the French missionaries, but the Indians regularly refused.

From time to time, Massachusetts militiamen backed up the English claim by repeated expeditions aimed at driving out the French. These minutemen played for keeps. In the fall of 1724, a Colonel Westbrook of the militia led a military force up the Kennebec River to Indian Old Point, sometimes called Norridgewock, and destroyed an Indian mission that had been functioning there for twenty-five years under the supervision of Father Sebastian Rasle, a French Jesuit. In the course of their efforts, they killed Father Rasle, scalped him, and brought his scalp back to Boston along with twenty-six similar trophies.

After Independence and the establishment of a Catholic church in Boston in 1788, priests traveled from Boston to the Indian missions, especially to Old Town on the Penobscot. One missionary who frequented the area was Father John de Cheverus, who usually stopped at Damariscotta Mills to visit Catholics at this location on his way to the Indian villages. During some of these stopovers, he said Mass in a barn owned by Matthew Cottrill. A small wooden church overlooking the mill was erected about 1790. There is evidence that Bishop John Carroll visited this chapel during a trip from Baltimore to New England in 1800.

Father Cheverus was actually given a small yearly stipend from the Massachusetts General Court, or legislature, for ministering to the Indians in Maine. However, when he administered the sacraments to white Catholics in Newcastle, he got into trouble. A Massachusetts statute forbade anyone from performing a marriage ceremony outside Boston unless he was either a justice of the peace or a clergyman residing in the county where the wedding took place. Since there were no Catholic priests residing in Lincoln County where Newcastle and Damariscotta were located, the impact of this statute was that Catholics in that locality could not be married in accordance with the requirements of the Church. On January 1, 1800, Father Cheverus officiated at a wedding of two Catholics at Newcastle and, for this offense, was criminally prosecuted. He escaped punishment when a majority of the court before which he was tried suspended sentence on the basis that he was a clergyman from Boston, though not from the locality; however, he was told by one member of the court that if he ever did it again, he would be fined £80 and sentenced to stand in the pillory.

During the early days of the Republic, Massachusetts levied what it called a ministerial rate, a local tax designed to support Congregational clergymen in each locality except Boston. Father Francis Matignon, the associate of Father Cheverus at Holy Cross parish in Boston, frequently came to Damariscotta and, on one occasion, brought a lawsuit in Lincoln County on behalf of local Catholics, asking that they be exempt from the tax, since they supported their own clergyman. In the alternative, he asked that the word "minister" in the state constitution be construed to include the support of Catholic priests as well as Congregational ministers. The case went all the way to the Massachusetts Supreme Judicial Court, which disagreed with Father Matignon and required the tax to be paid. In a decision issued on March 5, 1801, the court stated that "the constitution obliges everyone to contribute to the support of Protestant ministers alone. . . . Papists are only tolerated. And as long as their ministers behave well, we shall not disturb them, but let them expect no more than that. . . ."

In 1804, a French priest, Father James Romagne, was assigned full time to the Indian missions in Maine and came to Damariscotta occasionally. In 1808, Kavanagh and Cottrill donated three acres of land and $1,000 apiece toward the construction of St. Patrick's Church. The total cost of the building was about $3,000. In a letter to Bishop Carroll, Father Cheverus reported that there was also enough land available for a rectory, a garden, and an orchard for a resident priest. He also noted that a resident priest could always stay with the Kavanaghs, who had a large house nearby and had always demonstrated great hospitality to the clergy. Father Cheverus dedicated the church [**pictured above**] on July 17, 1808. He told Bishop Carroll that it "is called St. Patrick's; the name seemed to gratify our friends here; I liked it myself, because it proclaims that our church here is the work of Irish piety." However, he also noted that many of its parishioners were converts and suggested that any priest assigned to the parish be able to speak English.

St. Patrick's Church — which has withstood more than 180 New England winters — boasts brick walls that are two feet thick enclosing an area some 50 feet by 25 feet, has a ceiling that is about 30 feet high, and seats some 125 people on the main floor and in the small gallery above the rear door. For many years the only seats were wooden benches without backs. During Mass, men sat on the left and women on the right, much in the manner of a Quaker meeting. Pews were not introduced until 1896. The stations of the cross still seen in the church today are fourteen gold-leaved crosses placed in each of fourteen arches above the windows. They date back to the time the church was constructed.

Originally, the church had only clear glass windows, but they were replaced in 1896 by stained glass. Directly above the altar is a painting of the Descent from the Cross, which was probably donated by Father Cheverus's mother. A notable feature is a bell in the tower, donated by Cottrill in 1818, which was cast in Boston by the noted silversmith and bell maker, Paul Revere, made famous in the poem "Paul Revere's Ride" by Henry Wadsworth Longfellow. It is two feet high and has a circumference of three and a half feet at the top and seven feet at the bottom. In the vestibule beneath is an inscription that reads: "The living to the Church I call. And to the grave, I summon all."

Despite Father Cheverus's urgings, St. Patrick's did not have a full-time resident pastor until 1818 when Cheverus, now bishop of Boston, assigned Father Dennis Ryan to the parish. Father Ryan founded another parish some seventeen miles away at Whitfield and divided his time between these two churches, as did his successors for many years. The area prospered and so did the Kavanaghs and the Cottrills. These settlers first came to Newcastle as merchants but became shipbuilders as well, constructing about twenty-seven ships in their yard on the Damariscotta River. The mill was used for various purposes, including lumbering, and the lumber produced was used in part to build ships.

James Kavanagh's son, Edward, became a prominent public figure in Maine and remained so for several decades. In 1820, when Maine came into the Union as the silent partner in the Missouri Compromise, a convention was held to draft a new state constitution. As a delegate to that convention, Kavanagh was able to prevail upon the delegates to omit from the state constitution some of the civil disabilities against Catholics that were still found in the Massachusetts constitution. Kavanagh was a Jacksonian Democrat and was later appointed to serve in a diplomatic post in Portugal. After returning to Maine, he became acting governor in 1843 when the incumbent resigned to accept a seat in the United States Senate. The Kavanagh home in Newcastle is older than St. Patrick's Church; it is located only a few hundred feet down the road and still remains in private hands after two centuries.

Antagonism toward Catholics endured beyond the Civil War. Shortly after the Civil War, a populist protest group known as the Barnburners was formed in various parts of the country. To some degree it was the Northern equivalent of the Klan. Despite the name, this group did not always content itself with burning barns. On one occasion, its members in the Newcastle area decided that they would burn down St. Patrick's Church. Some measure of the general tolerance that had grown up in the area is reflected in the fact that, when this plan was formed, a member of the group reported it to Catholic neighbors who immediately informed public authorities. When an effort was made to attack St. Patrick's Church, the sheriff of Lincoln County was ready with a posse made up of both Catholics and Protestants who were able to thwart the action.

There is little in and about St. Patrick's Church today that would suggest the tumultuous beginnings of the Catholic Church in Maine. The church still stands along the old Pond Road in the midst of a woodland and is surrounded by its own cemetery and by stands of pine trees. The Newcastle-Damariscotta-Pemaquid Point area is now an upscale part of the Maine coastline and is home to many retired persons as well as to a large colony of "summer people" who stay for the season. About the only old occupation that still remains is some lobstering that takes place off the coast. Perhaps the greatest threat to the tranquillity of the churchyard is the increase in residential development in the general area.

The parish now has about two hundred fifty families who live in the area year-round. This number more than doubles in the summer. The parish is growing at the rate of about ten families a year, and many of these families have small children, as evidenced by the existence of an active Confraternity of Christian Doctrine (CCD) program. The old church was restored in recent years by a professional architectural and remodeling firm that specializes in the reconstruction and restoration of old buildings. A new parish center has been constructed on the far side of the cemetery and is used both for social and educational activities. Three Masses are offered each weekend. However, because the church only seats about one hundred twenty-five people, the ten o'clock Mass in the summer is said outside under the trees. From the old steeple Paul Revere's bell still sounds its call through the pine forest summoning people to Mass as it did when the Kavanaghs and Cottrills first erected the building nearly two hundred years ago.

9
St. Bruno

Van Buren

MAINE

St. Bruno's Church, located at the northeasternmost tip of Maine less than half a mile from the Canadian border, was founded in 1838 and is the oldest Catholic church in northern Maine. The Catholic community in this area antedates the Catholic settlement along the Maine coast at Damariscotta that formed St. Patrick's parish. In 1755, when the British deported French Acadians from a portion of Nova Scotia, a few escaped to more remote regions of that province and established another settlement. After the American Revolution, British loyalists moved from the newly freed colonies to this area and, in 1784, formed a separate province of New Brunswick. They wanted the Catholic Acadians out, so the British government accommodated them, deporting these Acadians for the second time in thirty years. This time they offered twenty French Catholic families land grants closer to Quebec near where the Madawaska River flows southward into the St. John's. French-speaking Catholics relocated to this area and settled on both sides of what was later to become the American-Canadian border.

Despite the provisions of the Treaty of 1783, which ended the American Revolution and purported to settle the boundaries of this country, the boundary question remained in dispute for another sixty years in northern Maine. The Acadian Catholics who had just moved into the area had little use for either government but, when push came to shove, they sided with the Americans. However, they regarded themselves as Madawaskans, the inhabitants of a portion of the 12,000-square-mile area on both sides of the present frontier. As time went on, more French Canadians moved into the area, as did Irish, Scotch, and New England Yankees. As the Madawaska district became more densely populated, the location of the border, and with it the enforcement of criminal laws and recognition of land titles, became more important. The bishop of Quebec provided religious services to Catholics, who were still the predominant group in the area. He did so because the nearest American bishop was in Baltimore, and Bishop Carroll was quite happy to have the bishop of Quebec send mission priests to Madawaska. In 1792, acting on a petition submitted by Catholics living at St. Basile on the north side of the St. John's River, the bishop of Quebec established St. Basil's Church, which, in the course of time, became the mother church of all Catholic churches in the area. For years St. Basil's did not have a resident pastor and was served by Father Francis Ciquart, a missionary whose parish extended westward from St. Basile for some fifty miles to St. Francis, Maine, on the south side of the river, and southward for more than one hundred miles to Woodstock, New Brunswick. St. Basil's Church did not have a resident pastor until 1808.

The same pattern of growth took place in Madawaska that was followed by the Catholic Church elsewhere. Mission chapels served by St. Basil's Church were established to take care of the farthest reaches of the parish, and those chapels ultimately became independent parishes. In 1828, the bishop of Quebec established a small chapel on the south side of the St. John's River about twenty miles from St. Basile at a location later called Van Buren. It is from this chapel that St. Bruno's parish grew. However, for several years formal parish records for St. Bruno's were kept at St. Basil's. It was not until 1838 that St. Bruno's parish was formally established. Five years later, the bishop established another church, St. Luce, in the western part of St. Basil's parish at Frenchville, Maine. That church is still in existence today. Father Antoine Gosselin became the first resident pastor at St. Bruno, serving for fourteen years. During his pastorate in this large and predominantly Catholic area extending to both sides of the American-Canadian border, the "Aroostook War" took place and the boundary question was finally resolved.

The "Aroostook War" was a locally generated dispute between Maine and New Brunswick that ultimately came to involve their two principals, the governments of the United States and Great Britain. In the background of this dispute were antagonisms between the descendants of those who fought for the American Revolution and those who opposed it. In the spring of 1839, General Winfield Scott arrived at Fort Kent with troops prepared to do battle, but no battle ever took place. Instead, American Secretary of State Daniel Webster and British Foreign Minister Lord Ashburton resolved the question by a treaty that bears their names. According to the Webster-Ashburton Treaty, concluded in 1842, the Madawaska district was divided approximately in half, with the St. John's River serving as the boundary between the

United States and Canada. One result of the Webster-Ashburton Treaty was that St. Bruno's parish extended into two nations.

Although the political boundaries of the area were finally established, the ecclesiastical boundaries were not adjusted until 1870. The entire area on the American side remained briefly in the Fredericton diocese and then came into the diocese of St. John, New Brunswick, but these matters were of modest consequence. Neither the American bishop in Boston nor the Canadian bishop in St. John's was in a position to provide much for this remote area, so the bishop of Quebec continued to send priests to minister to Catholics in all of Madawaska. During the 1850s, St. Bruno's was temporarily without a resident pastor, so it was served again from St. Basil's on the Canadian side of the St. John's River. In the 1860s, when St. Bruno's again received a resident pastor, he not only administered his own parish but established two chapels on the Canadian side of the border at Grand Falls and at Tobique in New Brunswick.

Most of St. Bruno's early pastors were Canadians and all were French-speaking. During the Civil War, some one hundred fifty residents of the area joined the Union Army. During this period, an American consciousness began to develop in the Maine portion of Madawaska, as a result of which Catholics in the area petitioned to have the American part of the Canadian diocese made into a separate vicariate under the control of an American vicar general. The Holy See never directly acted upon this request; but, in 1870, the year of the First Vatican Council, it redrew diocesan boundaries and placed the entire American portion of Madawaska and of St. Bruno's parish in the diocese of Portland where it remains today. During the First Vatican Council, which proclaimed the doctrine of papal infallibility, Bishop David Bacon of Portland, the first American bishop of the Madawaska area, was one of nineteen American bishops who petitioned the pope not to make papal infallibility an article of faith. The doctrine was proclaimed but fortunately it did not extend to the Holy See's knowledge of North American geography in dealing with American and Canadian diocesan boundaries.

One of the most serious ongoing problems encountered by residents of the Madawaska district in the late 1800s was the lack of schools, either public or parochial. Madawaskans earned their living from either farming or working in lumber mills and pulp mills. Later, potato plantations began to prosper. Many of the French-speaking inhabitants were unfamiliar with American laws and customs, most could not speak English, and many were illiterate. All were strongly family-oriented, and many families were quite large. The area was largely isolated from the outside world, so tourism and vacationing did not begin to develop as staples of the economy until many decades later.

When the Madawaska area was assigned to the diocese of Portland, Bishop Bacon became immediately involved in the affairs of St. Bruno's parish. Two or three years earlier, the bishop of St. John's, New Brunswick, had assigned the Holy Cross Fathers to St. Bruno's parish, with the thought in mind that they would eventually establish a college at or near Van Buren. Apparently, Bishop Bacon did not want members of religious orders to staff parishes in his diocese. A few Jesuits who had been in Maine in previous years had since departed. He reassigned the parish to Father Stanislas Vallee, a priest of the Portland diocese, and supported a decision to relocate the parish church to another site on the outskirts of Van Buren. The old church near the St. John's River had become much too small for the congregation, and another building was badly needed. However, a controversy had arisen as to its location. Bishop Bacon determined that it should be constructed at its present location, and a new church was opened there in 1873. The old rectory was lifted from its foundation, mounted on props, and transported to a new foundation next to the new church building. The successor to Father Vallee, a Father Richer, made several improvements in the new church, placing a bell in the tower and constructing a chapel that could seat a hundred people in the sacristy. Heating was always a problem in Maine, and the new chapel obviated the necessity of heating the entire church when large congregations were not present. Father Richer also built mission churches at Caribou, some twenty miles to the south, and at Hamlin, some nine miles southeast along the St. John's River. Both of these missions ultimately became independent parishes.

Bishop James Healy, who came to Portland in 1875, had a completely different attitude toward religious orders in his diocese from that of Bishop Bacon. He welcomed the assistance of congregations of men and women. He arranged with the Marist Fathers to take over St. Bruno's parish, with the understanding that they would also establish a college at Van Buren. The plan was similar to the one that had been contemplated at an earlier date with the Holy Cross Fathers. In 1886, the Marists took control of St. Bruno's parish, and they have been there ever since.

In the following year, the Marists opened St. Mary's College at Van Buren to thirty-five students. The college had a regular curriculum and offered A.B. degrees. It was one of Bishop Healy's hopes that the presence of St. Mary's College at this location would serve to heal an estrangement that had grown up between the two largest groups in his diocese, the French and the Irish. The Marist Fathers who ran the college were, for the most part, French, but Bishop Healy saw to it that several Irish priests also served on its faculty. The college attracted students both from Maine and from New Brunswick. However, the growth of Holy Cross and Boston College in Massachusetts ultimately proved to be too much competition for a limited potential clientele; so, in 1926, St. Mary's College closed its doors for economic reasons.

In 1891, the Good Shepherd Sisters came to St. Bruno's and opened a convent. Later, they also opened the Sacred Heart School in Van Buren and began to teach at this school as well as at several girls' grammar schools and high schools in northern Maine. When St. Mary's College closed in 1926, the Marists stayed on at Van Buren and continued to operate the facility as a public high school. It was closed in 1932 and reopened in the 1940s, remaining open until about 1970. In the 1920s, St. Joseph's mission at Hamlin received a resident pastor and became an independent parish, as did St. Remi in nearby Keegan, another mission of St. Bruno's parish.

Shortly after World War II, structural defects began to appear in the church building that had served the parish since 1873, so a new church **[pictured above]** was built next to it. The foundation and basement for the new church were completed in time to celebrate midnight Mass at Christmas in 1946, but it was not until 1952 that the entire structure was finished. The interior includes a large stained-glass window, a marble floor, and fixtures made from imported Italian marble. These improvements were made after the new church was dedicated and functioning.

St. Bruno's parish and the entire Madawaska area have not been immune from the winds of secularization that began to blow in Quebec and in the United States in the 1960s. It has affected parish life among French Americans as well as French Canadians. One concrete manifestation of this phenomenon is the fact that St. Joseph's in Hamlin, once a mission and then a separate parish, is again a mission of St. Bruno's, and the pastor of St. Remi's lives at the St. Bruno rectory because his own parish cannot support a separate rectory.

In 1988, St. Bruno's celebrated its sesquicentennial as a parish and staged a series of events to mark this milestone. Today, it has slightly more than 1,000 families and provides services to 190 families at St. Remi's and 110 families at St. Joseph's. The parish is still predominantly French in background, but Masses are said only in English. One Mass each weekend is offered in French at St. Remi's, and Masses in French are occasionally said at a large home for the aged located in Van Buren. Most parishioners under the age of forty do not even understand the language of their ancestors. An effort to recall the French roots of the area has been made by introducing old French hymns at various liturgies. The anniversary celebration focused on the French heritage of the area in such matters as cooking and costumes. However, a real contrast exists in regard to cultural assimilation between Van Buren and its twin city just across the St. John's River. In St. Leonard, New Brunswick, as a result of a determined public policy throughout Canada, French is offered in the schools and French signs appear on the roadways. French is commonly spoken, so French Masses are offered at St. Leonard Parent Church, located just a few hundred yards across the river from St. Bruno's. There is no similar public policy in Maine. Traditionally, French Canadians have sought to preserve their identity through *la langue et la foi* — language and faith. Now that language is ceasing to be an identifying characteristic for French Catholics in the United States, the faith is what must be relied upon in order to preserve their roots.

10
St. Mary

Claremont

NEW HAMPSHIRE

The oldest Catholic church in New Hampshire is St. Mary's in Claremont, a Connecticut River valley industrial town located in the western part of the state. In colonial times and in the early days of the United States, Jesuit missionaries occasionally passed through New Hampshire and Vermont to reach Indian tribes located in the region but no permanent religious establishments grew out of those efforts. In 1795, Reverend Daniel Barber, a Revolutionary War veteran, came to Claremont and was installed as the fourth minister of the Union Episcopal Church. He served as pastor for twenty-four years. Here began one of the most extraordinary family sagas in the history of the Catholic Church in the United States. In 1812, Daniel Barber attended a convention of Episcopal ministers in Boston and, while there, met the Roman Catholic bishop of that city, John de Cheverus. Bishop Cheverus and Daniel Barber had a lengthy discussion on the history of the Catholic Church and the question of apostolic succession. Bishop Cheverus lent Barber some books on the subject, which he took back to West Claremont with him. After studying these materials, Daniel Barber decided that he would take further instructions and join the Catholic Church. On November 15, 1818, he preached his last sermon to the Episcopal congregation over which he had been pastor for twenty-four years and parted company amicably. Some years later, his wife became a convert to the Church, having made this decision when her son, a seminarian, paid a visit to her in Claremont along with Father Charles D. Ffrench (sic), a Dominican priest.

The conversion of the Barber family did not end at this point. In addition to providing Bishop Cheverus's books to his wife, Daniel Barber gave them to his son, Virgil, who was then living in Fairfield, a town in Upstate New York near Utica. Reverend Virgil Barber was then the pastor of an Episcopal church and was also headmaster of an academy that he operated in conjunction with the church. After reading the literature supplied by his father, Virgil Barber also decided to become a Catholic, as did his wife, Jerusha. He contacted Father (future Bishop) Benedict Fenwick, S.J., who was then serving temporarily as administrator of the New York diocese, and related to Father Fenwick his interest in becoming a Catholic. In 1817, Father Fenwick suggested to the Reverend Mr. Barber that he resign his pastorate, close his school, and come to New York City, promising him "scholars" if he wished to open a school in the city. Virgil Barber did so, relocating his wife, his small son, and four daughters to New York where he opened a school with the assistance of Father Fenwick.

After becoming a Catholic along with the other members of his immediate family, Virgil Barber then decided that he wanted to become a priest. Today, certain limited exemptions from the rule of celibacy exist that permit Episcopal clergymen to enter the Catholic Church and to become ordained without leaving their families. In 1817, no such latitude existed. When Virgil Barber made his wishes known to Father Fenwick, the latter consulted with Father John Grassi, the Jesuit provincial and with Bishop Leonard Neale, who was then living in Georgetown. They devised a plan whereby Virgil Barber and his wife declared that they would no longer live together as man and wife. Barber then entered the Jesuits and his wife entered the Visitation Convent in Georgetown to live as a cloistered nun. The girls entered various convents and eventually became nuns. Their son Samuel went to Georgetown College where he eventually joined the Jesuit order. The youngest daughter was placed with Father Fenwick's mother, who raised her until she was old enough to join a convent. As a Jesuit scholastic, Virgil Barber went to Rome for a year to study and returned to Boston in 1822 to be ordained by Bishop John de Cheverus.

With the consent of the Jesuits, Bishop Cheverus sent Father Virgil Barber back to Claremont to establish a Catholic church to be called St. Mary's. Father Barber did so in 1823, right across the road from the Episcopal church where his father had ministered for nearly a quarter of a century. He also opened a school at St. Mary's and asked his parents to return from southern Maryland to help him run it. Father Barber traveled to Canada and elsewhere to raise funds for the new church and obtained sufficient financing to erect the plain brick edifice **[pictured above]**. In 1825, Father Barber's mother died in Claremont and became the first person to be buried in the large cemetery that surrounds the old church. In 1827, the Jesuits recalled Father Barber to Georgetown. Since the bishop of Boston had no replacement, Father Barber had no choice but to close the church and deliver the keys to the bishop. His father returned to southern Maryland and lived the remainder of his life as a resident of the Jesuit house at St. Inigoes in St. Mary's County.

In the next few years, priests visited St. Mary's only on rare occasions. The small Catholic congregation was financially unable to support a full-time resident priest. In 1833, Father John Daly was assigned to St. Mary's but did not spend all of his time at that location. The church became the base for his missionary activity, which extended throughout the state of New Hampshire. The saga of Father Virgil Barber ended in 1847 when he died at Georgetown College of paralysis (probably a stroke). During the twenty-four years of his priesthood, he frequently served as a missionary to various Indian tribes in Maine and was also assigned to the Jesuit parish at Conewago, Pennsylvania. He kept in touch with his family. His daughters were located at convents that were great distances apart. Two were at Ursuline convents in Quebec City and Three Rivers, Canada, and another was assigned to a convent operated by the Sisters of Charity at Kaskaskia, Illinois. He occasionally came into contact with his son, who was a member of the same Jesuit province as his father. His correspondence points out that his path happened to cross that of his youngest daughter, Mary Josephine, when both were in Frederick, Maryland, at the same time. In an unusual father-daughter reunion, Father Barber heard her confession on that occasion.

For a number of years St. Mary's was a mission parish of another church in Keene, New Hampshire. In 1870, it obtained a resident pastor and has continued without interruption since that time as a functioning parish. Father Patrick Finnegan, its pastor for the better part of thirty years, relocated the site of the church to the central portion of the town of Claremont, about five miles from the location of Father Barber's old church. He was able to construct a brick church with granite trim on Central Street that was dedicated in 1874. He also purchased two large houses across the street from the new church that had been the residences of two of Claremont's wealthier families. These buildings eventually became a convent and a school and one now serves as the parish rectory. Between 1881 and 1884, Father Finnegan refurbished the church, adding a spire and bells. A parochial school was opened in 1890 by the Sisters of Jesus and Mary. When they returned to Canada in 1896, the Sisters of Mercy replaced them and continued to operate the school, expanding it into a high school in 1921.

Claremont has always been a mill town and is well off the beaten path of New England tourism. In recent years, it has been economically depressed. During the past century, large numbers of French Canadians have come to Claremont in search of work in the mills. They form the largest single ethnic group within the parish. There is also a Polish parish in the city. Today, St. Mary's has about 1,675 families. Its school is staffed by Sisters of Charity, Sisters of Mercy, and a number of lay teachers. It has about one hundred sixty children. Despite the fact that tuition has gone up by more than $200 a year and now approximates $1,100 a year per pupil, its enrollment in this economically depressed community has increased dramatically by virtue of an aggressive job of salesmanship undertaken by the Sisters who teach there. Their principal sales point when talking with prospective parents is the strict discipline that they impose in the classrooms. This has convinced many who are far from affluent that the best allocation of limited family funds is a parochial school education for their children.

Acting in conjunction with other churches in the community, St. Mary's helps to sponsor a soup kitchen that operates five days a week in Claremont. About five percent of the gross income of the parish, some $20,000 a year, goes directly to charitable activities such as the St. Vincent de Paul Society and providing supplements to utility payments made by individuals. Often local social-welfare agencies refer clients to St. Mary's for emergency care while the wheels of the bureaucracy are turning to provide long-term assistance.

Although the parish is still predominantly French, Masses have not been said in French for more than a decade. The parish is composed, in significant part, of older persons. Priests from St. Mary's regularly make the rounds of five large public and private nursing homes in Claremont. The old church building on the outskirts of town is still in use. During summer months, Mass is said there every Saturday morning. Father Barber's church seats only fifty people on the main floor and an additional fifteen in the gallery. It is often used on special occasions such as baptisms, small weddings, and funerals, and is frequently visited by tourists who make a special trip to Claremont to see it. Despite limited resources and the enormous demands that are placed on them, St. Mary's is undertaking a $120,000 renovation program to ensure that the religious and educational mission that Father Barber began early in the nineteenth century will continue effectively into the twenty-first.

11
St. Mary

Newport

RHODE ISLAND

About two thirds of Rhode Island's 950,000 inhabitants are Roman Catholics, but in the first two centuries of the state's existence, that proportion remained at much less than one percent. In 1680, Colonial Governor Paley Sanford told the board of trade that "as for Papists, we know of none among us." Unlike other New England colonies, Rhode Island and Providence Plantation began its existence dedicated to the practice of religious liberty. Roger Williams, Anne Hutchison, and William Caddington left Massachusetts Bay because of the close entanglement of civil and religious authorities in that colony. They established a settlement in 1636 in what is now Rhode Island in order to avoid the impact of such entanglements. A royal charter obtained from King Charles II in 1663 provided expressly for "full liberty of religious concernments," stating that no person "shall be any wise molested, punished, disquieted, or called in question for any difference in opinion in matters of religion." Like William Penn two generations later in Pennsylvania, Williams did not insist upon religious liberty because he had any particular affection for Roman Catholics. He did not; but, like Penn, he was willing to accord to Catholics the same freedom from government interference with religious beliefs that he claimed for himself. Years later, when the Digest of Laws was published in Rhode Island in

1719, the government apparently backtracked on this charter guarantee. The digest stated that "all men professing Christianity and of competent estates, and of civil conversation who acknowledge and are obedient to the civil magistrate, though of different judgments in religious affairs (Roman Catholics only excepted), shall be admitted freemen and shall have liberty to choose and be chosen officers in the colony, both military and civil." This provision was reaffirmed in three later enactments made in the ensuing forty years, but it was removed from the laws of Rhode Island in 1783 at the conclusion of the American Revolution. However, the effect of such legislation was minimal because there were practically no Roman Catholics in Rhode Island to whom it could apply.

The first Catholic to visit Rhode Island was Giovanni da Verrazano, an Italian navigator and privateer who sailed for the king of France. In 1524, he sailed up Narragansett Bay from the Atlantic Ocean, spent two weeks at what is now Newport, and left. No significant numbers of Catholics could be found in the colony until July 11, 1780, when French Count de Rochambeau, an ally of George Washington, came ashore at Newport with six thousand French troops. They stayed nearly a year before sailing off to Virginia where they participated in the defeat of Cornwallis at Yorktown. During their stay in Newport, the French occupied the Old Colony House and fitted it out as a hospital to accommodate a large number of troops who were suffering from scurvy.

The French were popular in Newport. Not only were they allies, but, more to the point, they paid cash for room and board in contrast to the British troops who had preceded them and who insisted on being quartered for nothing. A number of Catholic chaplains accompanied the French troops. They established a chapel in the makeshift hospital. The Blessed Sacrament was reserved in this chapel and what is believed to be the first Masses said in Rhode Island were offered there by French Army chaplains. The first public display of the Catholic religion in Rhode Island occurred when the admiral commanding the French fleet offshore died and was buried with a Catholic ceremony at the local Episcopal cemetery. French chaplains also said a field Mass for Indian converts who came to Newport to confer with their allies of years past.

When the French Army finally evacuated Newport, a few deserters remained and began to live with some Acadian refugees who had been there a number of years. In 1793, about fifty additional French refugees arrived from Santo Domingo where a slave uprising was in progress. Along with a few Irish immigrants, they constituted the Catholic population of Rhode Island, and specifically of Newport, at the beginning of the nineteenth century.

Catholic religious services did not take place in Rhode Island regularly until almost 1830. Bishop John de Cheverus, Father Francis Matignon, or another priest from Boston would come through Providence from time to time to say Mass for Catholics living in that city. It is reported that Bishop John Carroll once visited Newport in 1803, quite by accident. On a sea voyage back to Baltimore from Boston he was forced to come ashore during a storm. While in Newport, he baptized several children. From about 1813 to

1816, a church was maintained in Providence in an old schoolhouse on Sheldon Street, which local Catholics living in the Fox Point section rented for that purpose, but the building was destroyed in a windstorm in 1816 and was not replaced.

In 1824, the U.S. government began to construct Fort Adams on Aquidneck Island to guard the entrance to Narragansett Bay. A large number of Irish immigrants arrived to work on the project, and others came to nearby Portsmouth to work in a coal mine. In 1827, Father Patrick Byrne was sent by Bishop Benedict Fenwick of Boston to make a survey of the religious needs of Catholics in Rhode Island. He reported that one hundred fifty people had received Holy Communion at Easter in Newport and another thirty did so in Portsmouth.

Following the survey, Bishop Fenwick sent a newly ordained priest, Father Robert D. Woodley, to Rhode Island in 1828 to investigate the feasibility of establishing Catholic churches in that state. Father Woodley purchased a building for $1,100 on Barney Street in Newport that had formerly been used as a schoolhouse. It held about four hundred to five hundred people. He renovated the building and began to say Mass there once a month. Bishop Fenwick dedicated the building in November of 1828, and it became the first Catholic parish to be established in Rhode Island. The parish extended into nearby sections of Massachusetts and into the entire state of Connecticut.

At this time, Father Woodley's parish included Taunton, Massachusetts, all of Rhode Island, and part of Connecticut. He lived in Taunton and conducted missionary visits from that point. He also set about establishing a church at Pawtucket, in the opposite corner of Rhode Island from Newport. Instead of purchasing a building for church use, the two hundred fifty Catholics living in Pawtucket were able to obtain a donation of land from David Wilkinson, an iron manufacturer, who wanted to see a Catholic church built in that area for the benefit of employees who had come to the area to work in his mill. A small white wooden church with a green door was constructed on this lot. Father Woodley said the first Mass in this church on Christmas Day, 1829, and it became the first Catholic church constructed for that purpose in Rhode Island. St. Mary's in Pawtucket and St. Mary's in Newport dispute which is the oldest Catholic church in Rhode Island but the matter is essentially one of defining terms. Both churches had the same founding pastor but their development over the ensuing one hundred sixty years has been quite different because of the areas that they serve.

Bishop Fenwick was not happy with the building that Father Woodley had purchased on Barney Street in Newport, so he arranged to buy an adjacent lot to permit expansion. Father Woodley, a native Virginian, had some difficulty in relating to the impoverished Irish who began to pour into Rhode Island. He eventually returned to Georgetown where he had been educated and entered the Jesuit order. Bishop Fenwick replaced him with Father John Corry, an Irish immigrant. Father Corry took over the expansive parish, choosing to administer it from Providence rather than from Taunton. In Newport, Father Corry built a new church on the land adjacent to the original building. It was large enough to accommodate eight hundred people. The effort took four years. At that time, there were an estimated seven hundred Catholics in Newport, about five times the number that Father Byrne had mentioned a decade earlier.

The fact that Newport had a new church did not mean that it had either a resident pastor or Mass every Sunday. It was not until 1844 that the parish acquired its first resident pastor and it was not until 1848 that Mass was said at St. Joseph's every Sunday. During this period, Newport was experiencing a mixed impact on its economy. Construction work on Fort Adams had been discontinued because the U.S. War Department ran out of money, so many Irish laborers had to go elsewhere. The growth of railroads had reduced the importance of the city as a seaport. However, Newport began to attract wealthy visitors during the warmer weather and its existence as a summer colony was starting to take shape. Southerners and Spaniards from Cuba began to come to the city "during the season" to avoid the oppressive heat in their own localities. One regular summer visitor was Mrs. Catherine Harper, daughter of Charles Carroll of Carrollton, who at his death was reputed to be the wealthiest man in America. She and her daughter taught Sunday school at the parish during the summer months. She donated $4,000 to buy land for another church, raised $3,000 more for its construction, and later donated to the parish the land where the convent now stands.

In 1848, construction began on the brownstone Gothic church [**pictured above**]. It was designed and built by Patrick C. Keely. Lieutenant William Rosecrans, later a Union Army general, was stationed at Fort Adams at the time and donated his services as engineer overseeing the actual construction of the building. The cost of the project was reduced by members of the parish who donated their services digging the original foundation. On July 25, 1852, the new church was dedicated and renamed the Church of the Holy Name of Mary, Our Lady of the Isle — St. Mary's for short.

St. Mary's first resident pastor was Father James Fitton, who began his duties in 1844. Father Fitton's name looms large in the history of the Catholic Church in New England. Before coming to Newport, he had founded parishes in Norwich and New London, Connecticut, and in Cranston, Rhode Island. He had also established a college at Worcester, Massachusetts, originally called Mount St. James but later known as Holy Cross. After taking up residence in Newport, he was able to prevail upon the Sisters of Mercy to take over the operation of a parochial school that had been started by laymen in 1846. The Sisters began teaching in 1853 and had about fifty or sixty girls in the parish school. In 1867, they opened an academy nearby that provided secondary education for girls.

The Sisters of Mercy had only recently been founded in Ireland in 1831. They expanded their efforts into the United States just a few years later. By the early 1850s, they had started four convents in Rhode Island, one of them at Newport. At that time, Protestant ministers controlled the public school boards in each of the state's four districts. Although public schools were nominally neutral in matters of religion, one of the leaders of the Rhode Island public school system wrote in 1856 that the public schools were "an arm of our common republican Christianity" and stated that their aim was to make the entire population "homogeneous." Catholics perceived this policy as simply an effort to employ public funds to proselytize Catholic children so they came to regard the establishment of Catholic schools as essential in preventing the "homogenization" of their children. The Sisters of Mercy were an integral part of this early effort. In one publication, they were denounced as "female Jesuits." In 1855, considerable agitation arose in Providence concerning the alleged kidnapping by the Sisters of a postulant named Rebecca Newell. The Mercy nuns were accused of holding her captive in their convent in Providence. Egged on by the Providence *Journal*, a mob of about two thousand gathered in front of the convent in an effort to "rescue" this recruit. Bishop Bernard O'Reilly, often called "Paddy, the Priest," appeared in front of the convent, confronted the mob, denounced it to its face, and was able to prevail upon its members to disperse without causing any damage. The upshot of this incident was that the Rhode Island legislature, then under the control of the Nativist and Know-Nothing Parties, enacted a convent inspection bill requiring all private institutions to submit to periodic inspections by "sniffing committees" whose job it was to see that no one was being confined in such places against her will. Refusal to submit to inspection meant loss of tax exemption.

As early as 1835, the Rhode Island legislature had enacted a law extending tax exemptions only to those religious and charitable institutions that held property and operated in a corporate form. The original deeds to St. Mary's transferred title personally to Father Woodley and to the bishop of Boston. St. Mary's and all other Catholic churches in Rhode Island eventually had to organize in corporate form under the state's general incorporation laws, which required that property be held by trustees or directors in the same manner as a commercial organization. As a result, St. Mary's and all Catholic churches in Rhode Island are each owned by a separate corporation governed by five-member boards of trustees. To avoid the problems that lay trusteeship had caused elsewhere in the country, these boards are composed of the bishop of Providence, his vicar general, and the pastor, each of whom are *ex officio* members, and two lay trustees who are periodically elected by the incumbent board members, with the approval of the bishop.

At the beginning of the Civil War, St. Mary's had fifteen hundred parishioners. This number temporarily increased when the Naval Academy was relocated from Annapolis to Newport during the hostilities. Support for the war received mixed enthusiasm from the Irish in Rhode Island. Over five thousand foreign-born soldiers made up eight Union regiments who were recruited from the state, including such units as the Aquidneck Rifles, who came from the Newport area. However, when marshals came to serve draft notices in Newport's Ward 5, a neighborhood made up of poor Irish immigrants, they were pelted with coal and mud thrown by women who did not want to see their husbands conscripted. Fortunately, no disturbances occurred in Rhode Island similar to the draft riots in New York City where public authorities threatened to use troops to serve conscription notices. Immigrant Irish instinctively disliked New England abolitionists. Not only were their austere mannerisms offensive, but the Irish soon came to realize that many of the political groups and public figures who were supporting the abolition cause were the same people who had been leading Nativist and Know-Nothing campaigns aimed at restricting Irish immigration and depriving recent immigrants of political rights and job opportunities.

In the 1890s, the Vanderbilts, the Morgans, and other wealthy industrialists and financiers began to erect massive summer homes at Newport. It became the summer playground of high society. Few if any of these families attended St. Mary's but their Irish servants did. As time went on, most of these mansions were either sold or donated to charitable and philanthropic organizations, as later generations sought cheaper and less ostentatious forms of summer relaxation. Many of these mansions are now stops on the tourist rounds of Newport. One brush with high society occurred in 1953 when St. Mary's saw the wedding of Senator John F. Kennedy and Jacqueline Bouvier. After the ceremony, they proceeded from the church to a reception at Hammersmith Farm, the former Newport home of the Auchincloss family.

Today, St. Mary's is one of four Catholic churches in Newport. It has about 1,450 families during the winter and accommodates more Catholics who visit Newport during the summer months. Its parishioners are a mix of ethnic and age-groups and include a substantial number of retired persons. The parochial school has closed but the religious education program serves about two hundred thirty-five students from preschool through grade 10. It has an active music program and a weekend liturgical program that involves over one hundred twenty laymen as ministers of hospitality, eucharistic ministers, lectors, choir members, and altar servers. It also sponsors a hot-lunch program for the needy and has a regular visitation program for shut-ins and residents of nursing homes.

12
St. Mary

New Haven
CONNECTICUT

Catholics constitute the largest religious denomination in Connecticut today but there is nothing in the early history of the state to suggest that such a development would take place. The first Catholics who came to Connecticut did not do so willingly. After Oliver Cromwell invaded Ireland in 1649, he deported 6,400 Irish to New England over a period of 36 months and later deported about 100,000 Irish to the West Indies. Many of these exiles were children. The purpose of the deportations was to remove possible opposition to English rule in Ireland and to provide farmers and plantation owners a source of free labor. The lot of these indentured servants was no better than that of black slaves who were being imported to the New World from Africa.

Connecticut received its share of these deportees. The practice of importing "parcels of Irish servants . . . to be sold cheap," as an ad in the Connecticut *Gazette* put it, continued until well into the 1700s. Later emigrations from Ireland in the eighteenth century were technically voluntary but with such voluntariness was prompted by complete destitution at home. The attitude of Connecticut residents toward these new immigrants and their religion was expressed in a petition forwarded by Connecticut colonists to King William of Orange shortly after he ascended the British throne in 1689 by defeating the Catholics at the Battle of the Boyne in Ireland: "Great was the day when the Lord who sitteth upon the floods did divide His and your adversaries like the waters of Jordan, and did begin to magnify you like Joshua, by the deliverance of the English dominions from Popery and slavery." Years later, British soldiers supervised another deportation, this one involving several thousand French Catholics from Acadia. Some four hundred twenty-seven Acadians were transported to Connecticut where the general assembly passed a resolution further distributing them among the various towns of the colony. New Haven received nineteen. These exiles were treated as paupers and were forbidden from leaving the town to which they had been assigned without permission of civil authorities.

Despite the presence of Catholics in Connecticut from its earliest days, they had no organized religious life. Until 1830, some fifty years after Independence, priests visited the state only sporadically. As early as 1651, Reverend Gabriel Druillettes, S.J., an emissary from Canada, came to New Haven briefly on a formal diplomatic mission. In January 1798, a French priest visited the city and resided for a short period of time in a boarding house on Chapel Street. In 1823, Bishop John de Cheverus from Boston was present one Sunday before leaving the United States to return to his native France. On that occasion, he said Mass at the home of a French professor at Yale who resided on York Street. In 1827, Father John Power from New York was in New Haven on a return trip from the Enfield Canal at Windsor Locks where he was making a pastoral call on Irish laborers who were employed on that project. While in New Haven, he said Mass in a barroom with the shades drawn because the Catholics who had invited him could not obtain the use of a seaman's chapel at the wharf. In responding to their request for use of the chapel, the owners of the building simply stated: "We have no popery and we don't want any." The next priestly visit recorded did not take place until 1829 when Father Robert D. Woodley, then assigned to Rhode Island, said Mass in New Haven in a barn at the corner of Chapel and Chestnut Streets. The barn was so dilapidated that the wind whistled through crevices in the wall.

The first permanent Catholic church in Connecticut was Holy Trinity, which was erected in 1829 in Hartford, some thirty-five miles from New Haven. It later served as Connecticut's first cathedral when Hartford became a diocese. Beginning in 1830, a priest from Holy Trinity came to New Haven occasionally to minister to a handful of Catholics who were living there. An early visitor was the famous Father James Fitton, the second pastor at Holy Trinity. One of his visits took place on Christmas Eve, 1831, when he drove to New Haven by sleigh from Hartford to say midnight Mass at the residence of a Mr. Finnegan. The snow gave out a few miles north of town, so he had to leave horse and sleigh and walk the rest of the distance along a frozen road carrying a valise over his shoulder. When he arrived at New Haven, he said Mass but was chilled by the elements and barely able to preach. However, he made the return trip to Hartford that night without breaking the eucharistic fast so that he could be in Hartford to say a second Mass on Christmas morning.

Christ Church in New Haven, the forerunner of St. Mary's, was established in

1834. Two years earlier, Father James McDermot, a newly ordained priest, was assigned to assist Father Fitton in Hartford and was then reassigned to New Haven. At that time, New Haven had about two hundred Catholics. He was the city's first resident priest. Father McDermot was also given the responsibility of attending mission stations at Bridgeport, Waterbury, Danbury, Meriden, Norwalk, and several other towns and cities. One of his major tasks was to build a church in New Haven.

In 1833, Father McDermot bought a lot at York and Davenport Streets where St. John's Church is now located. The lot cost $100. He also purchased a second lot next door, which ultimately became New Haven's first Catholic cemetery. A frame church, some 65 feet by 35 feet and 22 feet high, was built at this location; it contained one gallery. At the dedication ceremony, which took place on Ascension Thursday, 1834, the gallery collapsed, killing two people and injuring others. The collapse was attributed to the fact that although the building plan called for two columns to be erected to support the gallery, the carpenter who undertook the work decided that trussing would be sufficient and did not install the columns. His judgment proved disastrous.

A second calamity befell the new church that year. In October, it was robbed and vandalized. A crucifix and a silver chalice were stolen. A number of Protestants living in the area expressed their dismay at this occurrence by presenting Father McDermot with another silver chalice to replace the one that had been stolen. St. Mary's retains this chalice today among its prized religious artifacts.

In 1843, the Catholic population of New Haven had increased to the point where Christ Church had to be enlarged. This work was undertaken, extending its length to eighty-five feet and its width to seventy-five feet. Five years later, the enlarged church was destroyed by fire. Arson was suspected but the culprit was never apprehended. Although the building was insured, the policy limit fell far short of what was necessary to construct a replacement. For several months church services were held in a tent until the parish was able to buy a Congregational church and redecorate it appropriately for Catholic worship. This church was dedicated on December 18, 1841, under the title of St. Mary's, and that title has remained to this day, although the church itself was relocated following the Civil War.

Efforts to establish a Catholic school in New Haven began in 1834 at the time of the dedication of the first Christ Church but met with limited success. In 1848, a school was opened on the ground floor of the new church. A Mr. Looby was assigned to instruct the boys and Miss Elizabeth Meagher took charge of the girls. The following year, Patrick Morrissey, recently arrived from Ireland, took over the duties of instructing boys and continued in that job for eleven years. In 1852, the Sisters of Mercy, also just arrived from Ireland, took charge of the girls and, in 1860, assumed responsibility for both sections. During this decade, the Catholic population of New Haven had increased to the point where two additional churches, St. Patrick (1851) and St. John's (1858), were formed from the territory formerly comprising St. Mary's parish.

Notwithstanding these spinoffs, St. Mary's continued to grow to the point where the parish was in need of a third and larger building. Moreover, the area surrounding its location had become commercialized and increasingly unsuited for a religious institution. With the assistance of City Clerk William Downes, the only Catholic lawyer then in New Haven, Father Edward O'Brien, the pastor in the early 1870s, bought a vacant lot next door to a house owned by a Dr. Hillhouse, on a street that still bears his name. Construction of the church **[pictured above]** began in 1870 and was completed in 1874 at a cost of $120,000. Upon its completion, New Haven, which forty years earlier had no Catholic churches, then had five.

The construction of St. Mary's Church on Hillhouse Street did not meet with universal acceptance. An article appearing in the *New York Times* in 1879 told of the relocation of the parish under a headline subtitle that read: "How an Aristocratic Avenue was Blemished by a Roman Church Edifice — The Parish Badly in Debt — Efforts to Dispose of the Valuable Property."

The article went on to describe Hillhouse Avenue as the most aristocratic street in New Haven where the president and several deans of Yale University maintained stately residences. They were, in the estimation of the *Times* reporter, "representative of this City's best society." However, "several years ago an inventor who suddenly acquired wealth bought the only vacant lot on the avenue and intended to build a house for himself there. But his money did not hold out and he had to sell. He offered the lot to the residents of the avenue, but they would not give him his price. Intimations that he might sell to undesirable persons did not cause them to raise their figure. He then offered the lot to the Roman Catholics, and it was bought by St. Mary's Parish, then worshipping in a cheap building on Church Street. . . . When the residents of this aristocratic avenue discovered that they were in danger of seeing a Roman Catholic Church spring up among them, with all that the establishment of such a church implied, they bestirred themselves to oppose the project." However, by that time, it was too late and the present church building was constructed.

The large debt that was undertaken to build the church and the interest that it required proved to be a great burden to the parish. It weighed heavily on the next two pastors, both of whom died with broken health at comparatively youthful ages. Bishop Lawrence McMahon asked the Dominican Fathers if they would take charge of St. Mary's. Over the centuries, the Dominicans have made it a practice to maintain houses of studies at or near prominent universities so the proximity of St. Mary's to the Yale University campus made it especially attractive. Bishop McMahon turned the parish over to the Dominicans, saying that he "expected great things" from them. One of the things he hoped for was that they could pay off the debt on the church.

On May 16, 1886, the first Dominican Fathers arrived at St. Mary's. They have been there ever since, celebrating their 100th anniversary in the parish in 1986. When they arrived, they found a parish of about five thousand members, predominantly Irish but with a large mix of other nationalities, which had a debt of about $150,000. Within two years they had reduced this figure by one third, and in ten years had reduced it to practically nothing. In 1890, they enhanced the church by installing stained-glass windows, made in Munich, which portrayed the mysteries of the rosary and the lives of several Dominican saints.

Shortly before the arrival of the Dominicans, an event of lasting importance, both to the parish and to the American Church, occurred at St. Mary's. In the fall of 1881, Father Michael J. McGivney, the assistant pastor, called together a few parishioners to organize a fraternal benefit society designed to protect widows and orphans of workingmen whose deaths would otherwise leave them destitute. This aspect of industrial life was commonplace in an era when there were no workmen's compensation laws and no social security death and disability benefits. It was Father McGivney's hope that, by providing families with such benefits through insurance, many members of his parish could be spared the financial devastation that normally accompanied the loss of a breadwinner. On February 8, 1882, an organization designed to carry out this program was formally established. It was incorporated under the laws of Connecticut a week later. Thus, St. Mary's Council No. 1 of the Knights of Columbus came into existence. As a laymen's organization, it continued to function at St. Mary's long after Father McGivney was transferred to another parish. It soon spread throughout Connecticut and eventually to the rest of the nation. The Knights of Columbus was organized along the lines of a fraternal organization, with a special ritual and bylaws, so that in addition to providing its members with insurance, it could also serve as a Catholic response to various secret societies that were popular at the time, some of which had a definite anti-Catholic bias.

Today, the Knights of Columbus, or K. of C., has a membership of 1,456,000 who reside in 63 different jurisdictions throughout the United States, Canada, Mexico, and the Philippine Islands; St. Mary's Council No. 1 was the first of the organization's 11,669 local councils. The international headquarters, known as the Supreme Council, remains in New Haven and occupies a twenty-two-story office building that was recently constructed. The K. of C. has over one thousand insurance agents throughout the country and in various foreign nations to sell and service fraternal insurance polices. Today, there are 1,021,650 such policies in effect that have put in force more than thirteen billion dollars' worth of insurance. The K. of C. now has assets in excess of 2.2 billion dollars, thus ranking it among the top four percent of all insurance companies in the United States. Over the years, it has paid out more than 445 million dollars in death benefits to the widows and orphans of its members and more than twice that figure in dividends, interest, and annuities.

The K. of C. does not think of itself as an insurance company. It regards itself principally as a religious and fraternal organization of Catholic men who are devoted to promoting Catholic values and activities. From New Haven it sends out a monthly magazine, *Columbia*, which has far and away the largest circulation of any Catholic magazine in America. The activities of the Supreme Council and its 11,669 affiliated-member councils defy classification. They might extend to cleaning the façade of St.

Peter's Basilica in Rome, providing the Vatican with state-of-the-art broadcasting facilities, cooperating with Yale University to publish the complete works of St. Thomas More, sponsoring pro-life activities (including the support of local pregnancy-aid centers), or offering college scholarships. Local councils have their own special projects, in addition to providing social and recreational activities for members and their families.

There has always been a special bond between St. Mary's Church and the Knights of Columbus. The 7:30 Mass each morning at St. Mary's is offered for deceased Knights from councils located all over the world. Until recently, Council No. 1 held its regular meetings in the church basement, much as it did in Father McGivney's day. The Supreme Council recently helped to renovate the church. In this effort, they engaged the services of Kevin Roche, an internationally known architect who, in 1984, won the Metzger Award as architect of the year. State and provincial councils have donated replicas of their seals to mark the pews. There is a new rosewood floor imported from Thailand. Parts of the roof were replaced and the interior woodwork was restripped and refinished. The Knights were responsible for constructing a steeple that parishioners could never afford to build. In the belfry hang three 1,000-pound bells bearing the K. of C. seal, which ring out the "Angelus" each day in downtown New Haven. Hanging over the altar is a six-foot, 400-pound Carolingian crucifix similar to one that the K. of C. installed in a chapel beneath the main floor of the Basilica of St. Peter's in Rome. A pipe organ containing 2,994 pipes, originally at St. Alphonsus Church in lower Manhattan, was dismantled and brought to St. Mary's in 1869 where it was rebuilt by a consortium of organ builders. All of these improvements were undertaken in preparation for the reentombment of Father McGivney, whose remains were removed from St. Joseph's cemetery in Waterbury. On March 29, 1982, at the 100th anniversary celebration of the K. of C., his remains were taken to St. Mary's and were placed in a polished granite sarcophagus located at the rear of the church. This occasion marked the consecration of the church by Archbishop John Whealon of Hartford. In August of the same year, eight cardinals and fifty-five bishops and archbishops gathered at St. Mary's to commemorate the anniversary.

Each year, top officials of the K. of C. in each state and province, known as state deputies, meet in New Haven and incorporate into their agenda a ceremony at the tomb of their founder. Other ceremonies conducted by the Supreme Council, various Connecticut councils, and other affiliated organizations within the body of the K. of C. occur at St. Mary's. One of the long-range programs of the Knights is to promote the cause of Father McGivney for canonization.

The residential component of St. Mary's parish has been dramatically reduced because Yale University, the abiding presence in downtown New Haven, has purchased most of the real estate within the parish boundaries and has converted it to university purposes. Only one street of residential properties remains. About fourteen hundred attend Mass each weekend at St. Mary's. Approximately one third of this number are members of the student body, staff, and faculty at Yale (including professors at Yale

Divinity School). Many are older Catholics who grew up in the parish and regularly come back to St. Mary's on weekends from suburban locations, and the remainder are tourists. The St. Thomas More Newman Club at Yale attends to the spiritual needs of Catholic students, but those who prefer a more traditional church setting come to St. Mary's.

At present, there are seven Dominicans living at the priory next to the church. Some are assigned to parish work and others may be graduate students at Yale or teachers at Albertus Magnus College, a Dominican college founded in New Haven in 1925. At one time, members of a Dominican mission band made their headquarters at the priory. Members of the priory elect their prior for three-year terms. The prior may or may not be the same individual whom the bishop has appointed as pastor. In keeping with their monastic tradition, the Dominicans gather each day, either in the church or the priory chapel, to chant matins at 7:00 A.M. and vespers at 4:45 P.M. The noon Mass each Sunday is a sung Mass using Gregorian chant.

The parish closed its grammar school which was staffed from 1896 to 1987 by the Dominican Sisters. However, priests from the parish serve as chaplains for a nearby girls' high school of three hundred students taught by Dominican nuns. One of the ongoing responsibilities of the parish is assistance in the operation of Columbus House, which provides free meals for homeless people in downtown New Haven. After one hundred fifty years, the nature of its ministry has changed dramatically; but, in changing, the ministry of St. Mary's has become extended, directly and indirectly, far beyond its territorial borders.

13
St. Peter

New York

NEW YORK

St. Peter's Church, now nestled close to the twin towers of the giant World Trade Center in lower Manhattan, dates back to 1785 and is the oldest Catholic church in New York State. It was founded just before the adoption of the U.S. Constitution and was taking shape as a parish at the time that New York City was serving as the first capital of the United States. George Washington maintained his first residence as president a few blocks away on lower Broadway. Indeed, Mass was offered at St. Peter's on April 30, 1789, to mark the inauguration of President George Washington, which took place a few hours later just a few blocks away. The emergence of St. Peter's parish at that time followed nearly one hundred fifty years of periodic suppression of Catholics in New York, first by the Dutch and then by the English.

When New Netherlands was a Dutch colony, the Dutch Reformed Church was the official state church. The New Charter of Patroonship granted by the Dutch republic to the Dutch West India Company stated that "no other religion (was to) be publicly tolerated or allowed in New Netherlands, save that then taught and exercised by authority in the Reform Church in the United Provinces." In 1662, Peter Stuyvesant and his council passed an ordinance that levied a fine of 50 guilders against any individual who attended a religious meeting other than one conducted by the Dutch Reformed Church. Notwithstanding these laws, Presbyterians and Congregationalists were actually tolerated but Quakers and Catholics were not. The official policy of excluding Catholics did not prevent Dutch authorities from rescuing Father Isaac Jogues and other French Jesuits who had been tortured by the Iroquois. They ransomed these priests from the Indians and provided them with assistance until they recovered from their wounds and were able to leave Fort Orange in what is now New York City.

From 1683 to 1688 — most of which is included in the reign of the last British Catholic monarch, James II — Catholics in New York enjoyed full religious freedom. The royal governor, Thomas Dongan, was a Catholic and prevailed upon the general assembly to pass a law stating that "no person or persons which profess faith in God by Jesus Christ shall at anytime be anyways molested, punished, disquieted, or called in question for any difference of opinion or matter of religious concernment, who do not actually disturb the civil peace of the province." His action is commemorated in a plaque on the front of St. Peter's Church.

During this brief period, Father Thomas Harvey, S.J., came to New York and, with other English Jesuits, established a Latin school. He said the first Mass ever offered in New York City in a room in the governor's house, then located at Fort James at the southern tip of Manhattan Island in an area now known as the Battery. When Governor Dongan was removed from office by King William, the Jesuits were forced to close their school and leave the city.

In 1691, the New York Assembly passed another charter of religious liberty, but it had a proviso "that nothing herein mentioned or contained shall extend to give liberty to any persons of the Romish religion to exercise their manner of worship, contrary to the laws and statutes of their Majesty's Kingdom of England."

The English Test Oath of 1673 was then applied to New York, as a result of which Catholics were precluded from holding office, since any officeholder was called upon, by virtue of the oath, to renounce certain fundamental doctrines of the Catholic Church. In 1700, the assembly passed a penal law through the efforts of the governor, the First Earl of Bellamont. It stated:

> Whereas divers Jesuits ... and popish missionaries have of late come and for sometime have had their residence in the remote parts of this province and other of his majesty's adjacent colonies, who by their wicked and subtle insinuations industriously labor to debauch, seduce, and withdraw the Indians from their due obedience unto his most sacred majesty and to excite and stir them up to sedition, rebellion, and open hostility against his majesty's government,
>
> * * *
>
> (every priest should be) deemed and accounted an incendiary and disturber of the publick peace and safety and an enemy to the true Christian religion and shall be adjudged to suffer perpetual imprisonment, and if any person being so sentenced and

actually imprisoned shall break prison and make his escape and be afterwards retaken, he shall suffer such paines of death, penalties, and forfeitures as in cases of felony.

There were few Catholics in New York until the time of the American Revolution. Writing in 1757, Bishop Richard Challoner, the vicar general of the London district and the Catholic prelate in charge of the Church in the North American colonies, stated that Catholics existed here and there in New York and New England but ventured the opinion that priests would not be permitted to come into those regions because many of the inhabitants were strict Presbyterians and were as much opposed to Catholics as were British authorities.

One priest who did venture into New York during colonial times was an Austrian Jesuit missionary, Father Ferdinand Steinmeyer, who had changed his name to Farmer. Father Farmer visited New York City from Pennsylvania and, on occasion, said Mass at the home of Joseph Idley on Wall Street. The shutters were always drawn on these occasions so that the event could not be detected. Aside from these visits, any Catholic in New York City who wished to attend Mass or go to confession had to take a two-day trip to Philadelphia. Occasionally, some did in order to fulfill their Easter duty.

When Father John Carroll was named prefect apostolic of the Catholic Church in America in 1783, there were about twenty-four thousand inhabitants in New York City and about 200,000 in the entire state. In a letter to the Propagation of the Faith, he estimated that there were about fifteen hundred Catholics in the entire state. The combination of a disastrous fire and the departure of British loyalists caused a serious decline in the city's population. Although official sanctions against the practice of the Catholic faith disappeared with the evacuation of British troops, there was still no permanent place to say Mass in New York City. Father Farmer said Mass in a loft over a carpenter's shop on Barclay Street, not far from where the present St. Peter's Church is located. He also said Mass in a house on Water Street and at Vauxhall Gardens. There were about 200 Catholics in New York City during the 1780s but only about 20 or 25 were active. The impetus for the foundation of St. Peter's parish came, in large part, from Spanish and French diplomatic personnel who then made their consular offices in the city. The French legation had a small chapel and a Catholic chaplain. When the French consul departed, the chaplain stayed on in the service of the Spanish consul, saying Mass in the consul's front parlor.

Don Diego de Gardoqui, the Spanish ambassador to the American government, also resided in New York City. He prevailed upon King Carlos III to grant $1,000 toward the construction of the first St. Peter's Church. Assistance in this effort was also provided by the new French consul, Hector St. John de Crèvecoeur. On behalf of the city's Catholics, he drew up a petition to New York's common council asking for the grant or lease of land on which to build a church. His participation in this effort was remarkable because Crèvecoeur was not a New Yorker, not an American citizen, and, according to some, not even a Catholic. The common council referred his petition to Trinity Church, the ancient

Episcopal church still standing at the foot of Wall Street. The trustees of Trinity Church replied that they owned some lots on Barclay Street that they would be willing to lease for the purpose of erecting a Catholic church. They did so for an annual ground rent of 150 Spanish milled dollars. The property in question was located a block from St. Paul's Episcopal Chapel, operated by Trinity Church. St. Paul's was constructed in 1766 and is the oldest building in continuous use in New York City. It has remained the neighbor of St. Peter's since the laying of the cornerstone at St. Peter's, an event that occurred on October 5, 1785.

Finding a building site was easier than organizing a parish and obtaining the services of a priest who could get along with his parishioners. The first pastor, Father Charles Whelan, was an Irish Capuchin with an unusual background. He had served as a French Navy chaplain and, while in the service of the French government, was taken prisoner of war by the British and held captive in Jamaica. After his release, he came to New York in October 1784. He described the state of Catholicism in the city upon his arrival as follows: ". . . heretofore a priest who celebrated Mass and administered any sacrament would have incurred the death penalty; hence, there are many here married, without having received baptism, or any instruction when joining our religion. The Catholics here are very poor but very zealous, being for the most part Irish. They are not able to build a chapel, nor even to buy a place for saying Mass, only a Portuguese gentlemen has allowed us part of his house for that purpose. I hope that Providence will provide another place for us before next May, as this gentleman [José Roiz Silva] cannot after that oblige us."

In writing to the Propagation of the Faith in Rome to obtain faculties to act as a priest, Father Whelan told the cardinal prefect that "it is necessary for a priest in this place to know at least Irish, English, French, and Dutch, since our congregation is composed of people of these nationalities, as also of Portuguese and Spaniards." Father Whelan was granted faculties and became the first pastor of St. Peter's parish.

The fact that Father Whelan became pastor at St. Peter's did not mean that he assumed control of the parish any more than it did in the case of several of his successors. In 1784, the New York Assembly passed an incorporation law that permitted lay boards of trustees to be formed for the purpose of operating religious institutions in a corporate name. This format suited most Protestant congregations, but it was totally at odds with the basic structure of the Catholic Church. At St. Peter's, as in many other parishes, the trustee system gave rise to repeated conflicts, both among parishioners and between the trustees and the priests. The New York law conferred upon trustees, not upon the bishop or the pastor, the power to own church land and to sell and encumber the land. It also gave the trustees the sole power to collect money, pay bills, regulate the renting of pews, fix the salaries of ministers, and "alter or change the religious constitutions or governments . . . so far as respects or in any wise concerns the doctrine, discipline, or worship thereof." A group called "The Trustees of the Roman Catholic Church in the City of New York" was formed under the provisions of this law for the purpose of establishing

St. Peter's parish. It was this lay corporation that began the construction of the church and the employment of its pastor.

Shortly after the establishment of St. Peter's Church, Father Andrew Nugent, another Irish Capuchin, arrived in New York. He was permitted to serve as Father Whelan's assistant. Within a month after this arrangement was in place, factionalism broke out. The two priests did not get along. Father Nugent was a more eloquent preacher than Father Whelan. In an age when the effectiveness of a priest was gauged almost exclusively by his ability to deliver a sermon, many of the parishioners sided with Father Nugent. The prefect apostolic in Baltimore, Father John Carroll, sided with the pastor whom he had appointed and withdrew Father Nugent's faculties. However, Father Carroll was not yet a bishop and he lacked both the power and the prestige of a bishop in dealing with refractory priests.

The Nugent faction at St. Peter's continued to take up the collection at Sunday Mass and to keep the money. Father Whelan announced from the altar that Father Nugent had no power to hear confessions but the Nugent faction ignored this warning. They even threatened to go to court to remove the pastor. Father Carroll wrote several letters to the principals in this dispute, warning the trustees that, if they went to court to oust the pastor, the church would have no priests at all. As an overture toward peace, he offered to make both priests joint chaplains, but Father Whelan left the city to avoid a further dispute, so Father Carroll had no immediate alternative but to restore Father Nugent's faculties and permit him to stay on at St. Peter's.

Not long after these events occurred, Father Nugent got into a dispute with the trustees over his salary. They offered him $300 a year and he insisted on $400. This ongoing controversy forced Father Carroll to come to New York and make a personal investigation. He again withdrew Father Nugent's faculties and was able to obtain the services of an Irish Dominican, Father William O'Brien. He appointed Father O'Brien as pastor. Father Nugent refused the order to leave and told Father Carroll that he would not permit his replacement to say Mass at St. Peter's. The following Sunday, when Father Carroll began to say Mass at the church, he was interrupted by Father Nugent who insisted that he would not leave unless Father Carroll agreed not to mention his name during the sermon. Father Carroll refused his demand and, as one writer put it, "a violent tumult ensued." Father Carroll suspended Father Nugent as priest on the spot, warned the congregation not to attend any Mass that Father Nugent might say, and proceeded from the church to the chapel of the Spanish ambassador where he finished the Mass he had begun.

Father Nugent ignored the order and continued to say Mass that morning at St. Peter's for the members of the minority faction who supported him. During the following week, the majority of the trustees placed a lock on the church door to prevent Father Nugent from entering. However, the next Sunday, Father Nugent and his supporters took possession of the church and once again Father Carroll was forced to say Mass in the chapel at the Spanish embassy. The trustees then took legal action to remove Father

Nugent and prevailed in court, but Father Nugent rented a house and continued to say Mass in defiance both of the majority of the trustees and the prefect apostolic. Eventually, he left New York City and went to France, where he died in 1795 at the age of fifty-five.

While this dispute pitted church authorities and trustees against a dissident priest, later trustee disputes found church authorities and lay trustees in opposite camps. The dispute at St. Peter's gave great impetus to American Catholics to apply to the Propagation of the Faith for their own bishop, and their request was granted in 1788. By 1790, Bishop John Carroll was installed as the first bishop of Baltimore, with authority over both New York and the rest of the United States. At St. Peter's, Father O'Brien continued to serve as pastor for nearly twenty years. He was described as an intimate of Bishop Carroll and was able to bring a measure of tranquillity and ordered growth to the parish during its difficult formative years.

In 1789, Father O'Brien went to Cuba and Mexico to raise money for the construction of an altar, a pulpit, pews, and galleries, and to reduce the parish debt. He returned with more than $4,000. Despite his success, the trustees fell behind in the rent and, in 1792, had to ask the trustees of Trinity Church for a rent abatement. The Trinity trustees forgave £150 in back rent provided St. Peter's stayed current in its ongoing obligation. St. Peter's had trouble in meeting this stipulation and, in 1796, went back to the Trinity trustees with a request for another abatement. The parties finally agreed that, for £1,000, Trinity Church would convey title to the premises to St. Peter's. This is what took place as to the land on which the church had been built. However, title to adjacent properties was not relinquished until ninety years later. Annual receipts at St. Peter's were about $1,500, coming mostly from pew rentals, and annual expenses were slightly less, but the church owed about $6,500, mostly to its trustees. While the trustee system provided several controversies at St. Peter's, it is doubtful that the original church could have been built except for the generosity of these men. One of the trustees, Thomas Stoughton, kept the deed from Trinity Church as security for the repayment to the trustees of the parish debt so the deed was not recorded until 1820.

In addition to returning from Mexico with money, Father O'Brien also brought back a picture of the Crucifixion, painted by José María Vallejo, which still hangs behind the altar of the present church. It was this painting that St. Elizabeth Seton focused upon in her meditations when she joined the Catholic Church in 1805. In addition to his regular parish duties, Father O'Brien was called upon to bring spiritual comfort to yellow-fever victims during plagues that struck the city in 1795, 1798, and again in 1805. In the first plague, some five hundred people died, and two thousand perished during the second epidemic.

In a letter to Bishop Carroll written in 1800, Father O'Brien described the operation of St. Peter's parish, then in its fifteenth year, as follows: "We have, thanks to God, given an impulse to the mind of the congregation and an organ, organist, and choir are on foot and a singing master attends to and directs the children, many of whom would surprise you by their performance. All is conducted on the plan of Philadelphia and Baltimore and our church is crowded. We have catechism twice a week previous to the singing and in train for preparing for first communion. The organ is more than paid of (550 dollars) and answers very well; and we have a crimson damask curtain for the altar to correspond with that which fronts the choir and organ. In a word, I believe all promises as you would wish. The next object is a charity school."

In 1801, he wrote the bishop that "(the congregation) vastly increased and even now would fill two churches. We will finish our steeple in the ensuing spring. I purchased a bell. Our church yard is nearly paid for. We will put a new iron railing to the steps of the church and open another door. Could we erect a chapel of ease in the extremity of the city where most of the poor Catholics are thronged? It would make us most happy."

In 1800, St. Peter's opened the first free Catholic school in New York State. It was the forerunner of St. Peter's parochial school, which remained in existence until 1940 when it was closed because the residential component of the parish had almost completely disappeared. It must be remembered that New York City did not have a public school system until 1842, although public schools existed elsewhere in the state long before that date. In 1800, school-age children in New York City received their education either from tutors, religious congregations, or not at all. The state established what was called the Common School Fund, financed from the sale of public lands and the interest on money derived from such sales. Grants from the Common School Fund were made to private schools. Educational activities were also supported by local taxation and by tuition payments. Initially, St. Peter's rented rooms for its Free School. In 1803, it moved students into a building that had been constructed for school purposes. By 1805, St. Peter's had one hundred students and was the largest school in the city, so the parish trustees approached the managers of the Common School Fund to ask for financial assistance. Before this date, such assistance had been given only to Protestant schools.

In 1805, the Common School Fund paid St. Peter's $1,560 toward the support of its school. This support was discontinued until 1814 when it was renewed at a comparable sum. By 1817, another Catholic school, operated at St. Patrick's parish, was opened and both received public support until 1823. In that year, public support was permanently discontinued in the wake of a controversy that served as the prototype of all of the public versus parochial funding disputes that have arisen in this country in the past one hundred fifty years.

Until the establishment of the original St. Patrick's Cathedral in 1809, St. Peter's was one of two Catholic churches in New York State. St. Peter's became the center of anti-Catholic sentiment in New York that manifested itself in different forms. Following the outbreak of the American Revolution, New York adopted the state constitution of 1777. One of its principal draftsmen was John Jay, later a delegate to the federal constitutional convention in Philadelphia, a minor author of *The Federalist* (a series of essays supporting the Constitution), and first chief justice of the United States. Jay tried to insert in the 1777 state constitution a provision requiring every officeholder to take an oath that he did not believe that any person had the power to absolve sins through sacramental confession. The proposal, obviously aimed at keeping Catholics from holding office, failed. However, he was able to insert a provision requiring any naturalized citizen to renounce his allegiance to any foreign power "in all matters ecclesiastical and civil." This provision was aimed at keeping Catholic immigrants from obtaining voting rights. In 1801, this requirement was extended to all persons taking the oath prescribed for either state or local office in New York.

Two members of St. Peter's board of trustees were elected to public office. Andrew Morris became assistant alderman for the first ward in New York City and Francis Cooper was elected to the state assembly, the first Catholic to win election to the legislature. He refused to take an oath renouncing his allegiance in ecclesiastical matters to any foreign power, meaning of course Pope Pius VII. The parishioners of St. Peter's Church drew up a petition, dated January 6, 1806, and containing thirteen hundred signatures, and sent it to the state assembly. In the petition, they asked that the restrictive oath requirement be removed from the law. The assembly enacted a bill removing this provision but not without a bitter debate, during which many members, especially Federalist delegates, insisted that the restriction be retained.

On Christmas Eve of the same year, a mob of about fifty men, calling themselves the Highbinders, gathered in front of St. Peter's expecting that midnight Mass would take place. None was scheduled. Disappointed that they could not provoke a confrontation, they returned the next evening when they were met by a large number of Irish parishioners who had gathered in front of the church. The Highbinders threatened to tear down the houses of Irish inhabitants and, in the course of a fight, a constable was killed. Mayor (and later Governor) DeWitt Clinton arrived on the scene with reinforcements and was able to quell the disturbance before additional injuries took place.

In the midst of a myriad of problems brought on by growth, rapid immigration, poverty, disease, and anti-Catholic hostility, St. Peter's parish was uniquely touched by the presence of two people of conspicuous holiness, one of whom has been canonized and another whose cause for canonization is well advanced. There is no hard evidence that Elizabeth Bayley Seton and Pierre Toussaint ever knew each other, since they came from vastly different walks of life. However, it is altogether possible that they did, since both were active members of St. Peter's parish at the same time.

Elizabeth Seton was the granddaughter of an Anglican minister and the daughter of a prominent physician. In 1794, she married William Magee Seton, a New York merchant and importer, and bore him five children. The Setons went abroad to Italy because of William's poor health. He died in Italy in 1803, and Elizabeth stayed on a few months with her friends, the Filicchis. It was during this period of time that she was introduced to the Catholic Church.

After returning to New York, she began to read tracts that both supported and opposed the claims of the Catholic religion. She consulted Dr. Henry Hobart, the chaplain at St. Paul's, who understandably advised her not to convert. In addition to presenting arguments drawn from history and Scripture, he also warned her that the Catholics in New York were "the offscourings of the people" and a "public nuisance." Mrs. Seton was also in correspondence with Bishop Carroll and with Father John de Cheverus in Boston. She wrote her friend Antonio Filicchi that, during this period of indecision, she sometimes visited St. Paul's Chapel to pray and "got into a side pew which turned my face toward the Catholic church in the next street, and twenty times found myself speaking to the Blessed Sacrament there, instead of looking at the naked altar before me, or minding the routine of my prayers."

Mrs. Seton lived in the Seton home at the tip of lower Manhattan overlooking New York Harbor. (It is now the rectory of Our Lady of the Rosary Church.) On February 27, 1805 — Ash Wednesday — she made her way up Broadway past St. Paul's, where she was married and had often worshiped, and turned the corner at Barclay Street toward St. Peter's and toward sainthood. Upon entering St. Peter's for the first time, she told Father Matthew O'Brien, the assistant pastor, that she wanted to join the Catholic Church. Two weeks later, she took an oath formally renouncing Protestantism and agreeing to adhere to the tenets of the Catholic faith. A week later, she made a general confession and, on March 25, 1805, the Feast of the Annunciation, she made her first Communion.

Mrs. Seton might just as well have taken an oath to renounce her entire past life when she entered the Church at St. Peter's. Most of her family and her husband's family were bitterly opposed to her action and treated her as a pariah. However, her sister-in-law and her children followed her into the Church. Three years later, she left New York and opened a school in Baltimore. Shortly thereafter, she founded a religious order that later adopted the rule of St. Vincent de Paul and relocated to Emmitsburg, Maryland, where the first foundation of the Daughters of Charity was established. After many difficult personal and financial struggles, punctuated by periods of poor health, Mother Seton died in 1821, having set in motion the parochial school system in the United States. She was canonized in 1975, the first native American to be so honored.

Pierre Toussaint, in contrast, was born a slave on the plantation of the Berard family in Saint Domingue, now known as Haiti. To avoid an oncoming slave revolt, his master brought the Berard family and Toussaint to New York in 1787 and established a home on Reade Street in lower Manhattan. New York was then a slave state and did not abolish slavery until forty years later. The Berards encouraged Toussaint to apprentice himself to a hairdresser in order to learn a trade. He did so and became quite adept at this calling. Over the years, he developed a thriving business, serving as the hairdresser to the wives and daughters of some of the wealthiest and most prominent families in New York. As the fortunes of the Berards waned, Toussaint became the financial support of the family and filled that role cheerfully. In 1807, his mistress granted him his freedom on her deathbed. However, he continued to support the household, which by then consisted of her second husband and others who came to live at the Reade Street address.

Toussaint purchased the freedom of his sister and his future wife and brought them to live at the Berard home. After the death of his sister, he raised her daughter because the girl's father had abandoned the family. The girl died of tuberculosis at the age of fourteen, an event that proved to be one of the major sorrows of Toussaint's entire life. The Toussaints had no children, but he regularly allowed black boys in the area to live in the basement of the home, assisting them in learning trades that they could use to support themselves.

Toussaint attended daily Mass at St. Peter's for more than sixty years. His papers indicate that he rented pew number 24 for more than twenty years. Because of his contacts with the wealthy of New York and because of the fact that he had a steady income, Toussaint was frequently called upon as a fund-raiser for various charities that St. Peter's was sponsoring. In fact, priests from other cities came to know of Toussaint's generosity and often asked him for help when they visited New York. Toussaint gave money to assist in the founding of St. Vincent de Paul Church, established in New York for the large number of French-speaking Catholics who resided in Manhattan. In 1817, St. Patrick's Catholic Orphan Asylum was founded in a small wooden building on Prince Street. Toussaint raised much of the money that went toward the construction of a new and larger building built nearby for the orphanage. Before her death, Mother Seton, now in Emmitsburg, sent three members of the Daughters of Charity back to her old hometown to staff the orphanage, which soon grew to have one hundred sixty residents.

When he died in 1853 at the age of eighty-seven, Toussaint was honored by a well-attended funeral at St. Peter's and laid to rest in the cemetery next to old St. Patrick's Cathedral on Mulberry Street. In 1990, after careful research and excavation, Toussaint's grave was located and his remains were exhumed as part of the canonization process. He was reburied beneath the altar at the new St. Patrick's Cathedral on Fifth Avenue next to the tombs of the former archbishops of New York.

In 1808, New York City had grown to sixty thousand inhabitants, of whom fourteen thousand were Catholics. This number far exceeded the capacity of the church. Priests from St. Peter's were beginning to make missionary visits to Paterson in northern New Jersey, to Enfield near Windsor Locks in Connecticut, and to Brooklyn and elsewhere on Long Island. At that time, there was only one other established Catholic church in New York State, St. Mary's in Albany, which had been founded in 1797. However, St. John's in Utica would soon be built, and Catholics living along the Hudson River were in need of priests. Most of them looked to St. Peter's for help. In this year, New York became one of four cities in the United States to be named the central city of a new diocese. The diocese of New York that was created included the entire state and all of eastern New Jersey. Archbishop Carroll declined to recommend to the Propagation of the Faith any candidate for bishop, saying that he did not feel that there were any priests in the diocese who were qualified for the position. He suggested that the new diocese remain vacant and be placed under the supervision of Bishop Cheverus, who had been appointed bishop of Boston. The Propagation thought otherwise; but, as events would have it, no bishop actually took office in New York for another seven years.

Father Richard L. Concanen, an Irish Dominican, was named the first bishop of New York. He lived in Rome, serving as the representative of the Irish bishops to the Holy See, and was consecrated bishop in that city. However, the forces of Napoleon Bonaparte were occupying the Italian peninsula and they refused to allow ships to leave that were bound for American ports. Bishop Concanen waited two years for passage to New York and died in 1810 before being able to depart for his new assignment. Eventually, the Holy See appointed another Irish Dominican, Father John Connolly, to be bishop of New York. He too was consecrated in Rome. The ceremony took place in the fall of 1814, but Bishop Connolly did not arrive in New York until the end of the following year because he wanted to wait for the signing of the peace treaty ending the Napoleonic wars before leaving Europe.

In the meantime, the diocese of New York was being administered by the pastor of St. Peter's Church, Father Anthony Kohlmann, S.J., who had been appointed vicar general. Father Kohlmann was an Alsatian who had first joined the Capuchins and then became a member of the Fathers of the Sacred Heart. In 1801, he joined the Russian province of the Society of Jesus, although he never went to Russia. The Jesuits were not fully restored as a religious order throughout the world until Pope Pius VII returned to Rome in 1814 after having been held captive by Napoleon for five years. However, the Jesuits were never suppressed in Russia, so priests from various countries, including the United States, who wished to become Jesuits were granted membership in the Russian province, although they performed ministries in other countries.

Father Kohlmann spoke three languages. He brought several Jesuits to New York with him and, in addition to taking charge of St. Peter's parish, started a school called the New York Literary Institution. It lasted only about five years. However, he was able to bring about improvements in the religious life of Catholics in lower Manhattan. He revived the tone of spiritual activity in St. Peter's parish. He also undertook the construction of the second church in New York City, old St. Patrick's Cathedral. It was built on cemetery property owned by the trustees of St. Peter's Church at Prince and Mott Streets, about a mile from St. Peter's. This church became the cathedral of the New York diocese when Bishop Connolly arrived in the city late in 1815 to become its first resident bishop.

Concerning St. Peter's parish, Father Kohlmann wrote to his Jesuit superior, Father John Grassi: "The congregation chiefly consists of Irish, some hundreds of French & as many Germans, in all according to common estimation, some 14,000 souls. Rev. Mr. Fenwick [later bishop of Boston], a young father of our Society, distinguished for his learning and piety, has been sent along with me. I was no sooner arrived in this city, &, behold the Trustees, though before our arrival they had not spent a cent for the reparation & furniture of their clergyman's house, laid for the sole purpose above $800. All seems to revive at the very name of the Society though yet little known in this part of the country. The scandals given in this congregation as almost everywhere else by the clergymen, have brought it very near its ruin. Our immediate predecessors, although respectable in every regard, could not prevent its speedy decay. Almighty God seems to have permitted this to furnish the Society with an opportunity of diffusing the good odour of it & of disposing the minds to favour its establishment. May we be so happy as to produce these desirable effects upon the public mind!"

Later, he wrote: "The communion rail daily filled, though deserted before; general confessions every day (for the majority of this immense parish are natives of Ireland many of whom have never seen the face of a priest since their arrival in this country); three sermons, in English, French, and German, every Sunday, instead of the single one in English; three Catechism classes every Sunday, instead of one; Protestants every day instructed and received into the Church; sick persons attended with cheerfulness at the first call, and ordinarily such as stand in great need of instruction and general confessions; applications made at all houses to raise a subscription for the relief of the poor, by which means of three thousand dollars have been collected, to be paid constantly every year."

However, peace was not to reign at St. Peter's forever. The Jesuits relinquished the parish in 1818 and responsibility was given to Father Charles D. Ffrench, an Irish Dominican, to serve as pastor. (As mentioned in a previous chapter, "Ffrench" is the correct spelling.) Father Ffrench was the son of the Anglican bishop of Galway and a convert to the Church. He was assigned as an assistant to Father Peter Anthony Malou, S.J., who also had an unusual background. Father Malou was the son of a Belgian merchant. Long before entering the priesthood he had married the daughter of a prominent banker and had become a wealthy merchant. The Malous had two children. In 1790, he became a leader in the Belgian war of independence against the Austrian House of Hapsburg and was exiled to the United States. He briefly engaged in the banking business in this country before returning to Europe. His wife had remained behind in Belgium and died while Malou was still in America. He was devastated by his wife's death and, a few years later, entered a Sulpician seminary. He did not remain but joined the Jesuits in White Russia as a lay Brother. He was later ordained. At the age of fifty-eight, he was sent to New York as a prefect in the school that Father Kohlmann had established. After a brief stay at the school and then at Georgetown, he came back to New York as an assistant at St. Peter's.

A dispute broke out at St. Peter's between the trustees and Bishop Connolly. Father Ffrench and another assistant, a Father Carby, supported the bishop while Father Malou and yet another assistant, a Father Taylor, sided with the trustees. The background of this dispute was ethnic friction between Irish parishioners who supported the bishop and better-educated French and other parishioners, who basically looked down on the Irish. The trustees, citing powers conferred upon them by the 1784 New York incorporation act, claimed the right to control the operations and the finances of St. Peter's parish, while the bishop insisted on his powers as the ordinary of the diocese.

The matter came to a head when financial difficulties beset both St. Peter's and St. Patrick's. Until 1817, the St. Peter's trustees controlled both parishes because St.

Patrick's did not acquire a separate corporate existence until nearly a decade after it was founded. To save money the trustees threatened to withhold the salaries of the priests at both churches and even to withhold the salary of Bishop Connolly. The annual elections of trustees became heated political disputes between the two ethnic factions in the course of which the priests took sides.

In 1818, the Malou-anti-Connolly trustee faction won. During the campaign, Father Malou circulated sample ballots for his slate of trustees. The bishop countered by taking to the altar to read a letter disclaiming any responsibility for such electioneering. At this election, four policemen stood guard to keep the peace.

The following year, during the 1819 campaign, Father Ffrench appeared at the election meeting and asked to be heard. He wanted to present his own slate of candidates. He was denied the floor by the incumbent Malou faction that controlled the meeting and the meeting broke up in angry confusion. The incumbent trustees then cut off Father Ffrench's salary and sent a demand to the bishop that Father Ffrench be removed as pastor. The bishop refused and began to pay Father Ffrench out of funds drawn from St. Patrick's parish. Father Ffrench continued to campaign for his slate, accusing the incumbent Malou trustees of withholding from the parish a financial statement that would have demonstrated the precarious condition of parish accounts. He also accused Father Malou of circulating false charges of impropriety against him regarding the circumstances under which he had left the Quebec diocese a few years earlier.

The Malou trustees sent Father Taylor to Rome to press their point of view to the Propagation of the Faith. They also submitted a petition, signed largely by French parishioners, blaming the problems of the parish on Irish parishioners and charging that Bishop Connolly, an Irishman, was a weak leader who had allowed himself to be ruled by others. French-speaking Bishop Joseph Plessis of Quebec was sent to New York by the Propagation of the Faith to investigate the trustee dispute. He rendered a report to Rome in which he described the supporters of the bishop and Father Ffrench as *canaille irlandaise* — Irish riffraff. While awaiting a response from Rome, their position was weakened by the fact that at the next trustee election the Connolly-Ffrench faction won a majority of seats on the board of trustees.

When Father Taylor returned to New York, he was deprived of his faculties by Bishop Connolly, so he decided to apply to the bishop of Boston for a position. He was accepted and left New York. In 1821, the Propagation resolved the question by directing that both Father Ffrench and Father Malou be required to leave New York under pain of suspension in the event of refusal. Father Ffrench resigned as pastor of St. Peter's and eventually became a priest of the Boston diocese. Father Malou refused to leave the city and was suspended, both by Bishop Connolly and by the Jesuits. Years later, after Bishop Connolly's death, Father Malou's suspension was removed and he returned to the service of the Church as a secular priest.

For most of the next twenty-seven years Father John Power served as pastor at St. Peter's. Like Father William O'Brien in the 1790s, he was able to restore a sense of order and civility to the life of the parish. In 1826, a third Catholic church, St. Mary's, was established in New York City to relieve some of the pressure of the ever-increasing number of parishioners at St. Peter's. Regrettably, St. Mary's was burned down five years later by an anti-Catholic mob, but it was rebuilt and continued to function thereafter in lower Manhattan. Like some of his predecessors, Father Power was called upon from time to time to administer the entire diocese as vicar general during the absence of the bishop. When he came to New York in 1831, Alexis de Tocqueville visited Father Power and made the following notation in his diary:

> There are 95,000 Catholics in New York. There weren't as many as 30 fifty years ago. Mr. Powers (sic), grand vicar, says that their number increases daily through conversions. They already form the most numerous communion.
> What struck me most in Mr. Powers' conversation is:
> 1. That he appears to have no prejudice against republican institutions.
> 2. That he regards education as favorable to morality and religion.

By 1836, St. Peter's was so crowded that half the congregation had to stand in the vestibule at Mass. Its problems increased when part of the ceiling of the old church fell in.

Father Power decided that the time had come to build a new church, so he started to take up a collection for that purpose. The old church was surrounded by a small cemetery containing the remains of some of the earliest Catholics in New York City. The graves were removed and the bodies were reburied in the cemetery that surrounded old St. Patrick's because the land was needed to build the new church. Years later, when the basement of the new church was being renovated, additional graves were found. (Those individuals were then reinterred in the basement under a common grave marker.) The new church **[pictured above]** was designed in Greek Revival style and has six large Ionic columns across its portico. It took three years to build and was completed in 1840. The first Mass was said in its basement in 1837. By the time the new St. Peter's was completed, New York City alone had nine Catholic churches and sixty thousand Catholics.

The fact that the new church had been completed did not mean that it was paid for. A debt of $116,000 was incurred, and the inability of the trustees to curtail it meant that the accumulation of unpaid interest increased the obligation to $135,000. In 1844, the trustees went bankrupt and executed an assignment for the benefit of creditors. The church was placed on the auction block and was sold for $46,000, just a third of the amount owed. Archbishop John Hughes bought in at the auction to keep the building from falling into commercial hands. Immediately, he was beset by creditors who challenged the sale. They went to the chancery court with a request that court trustees be appointed to collect pew rents and other income and account to the court and the creditors for the management of these funds.

The embarrassment of the entire Catholic Church in New York for the events at St. Peter's became widespread and was heightened by newspaper articles that were severely critical of the management of the parish. Ultimately, St. Peter's sold thirty-five vacant lots that it owned in the suburbs at Fifth Avenue and 50th Street, near the present St. Patrick's Cathedral, and used the money to discharge its obligations. In 1852, after the debt was cleared, Father William Quinn, the pastor, held a special Sunday service and sang a "Te Deum" in thanksgiving. Of equal if not greater importance than the retirement of the debt was the fact that title to the property was in the hands of church authorities and sixty-five years of trustee control was at an end. Technically, title to St. Peter's parish is still in the hands of five trustees, but the trustees consist of the archbishop, the vicar general of the archdiocese of New York, the pastor, and two laymen appointed by the archbishop; although the legal form remains, the substance that gave rise to endless controversies does not.

The Daughters of Charity began to operate the girls' section of St. Peter's Free School in 1831 while laymen taught the boys. In 1874, the Christian Brothers took over the boys' department and operated it until the mid-1930s. In 1873, a building costing $200,000 was opened for the operation of the school, which then had eight hundred fifty pupils. This building is now the parish rectory. Since New York City did not begin to provide public high schools until 1897, St. Peter's parochial school had the equivalent of ten grades of schooling.

Over a period of years, the increased commercialization of lower Manhattan resulted in the decline of the residential base of the parish. Monsignor James J. McGean was the pastor at St. Peter's for forty-five years, starting in 1881. When the church was scheduled to be consecrated in 1885 at its 100th anniversary, a number of parishioners approached the archbishop, Cardinal John McCloskey, with the thought that it might make good business sense to sell St. Peter's and invest the money in a Catholic parish somewhere else. Skyscrapers, sometimes five or ten stories high, were beginning to be built in the area, and it was obvious that the land would bring a good price. Cardinal McCloskey had been baptized in the old St. Peter's in 1810. He told the delegation: "St. Peter's Church will never be alienated. Go on, therefore, with your contemplated work of preparing for the consecration."

The process of changing St. Peter's into a business or transient parish was well under way at the turn of the twentieth century. One type of business that sprang up in the locality was that of supplying Catholic books, religious vestments, and a variety of church goods and religious artifacts. For many years the name "Barclay Street" was synonymous with Catholics throughout the country as the biggest and best source of such items. These stores are now gone from Barclay Street, replaced by high-rise office buildings housing such enterprises as Dun and Bradstreet and Woolworth's.

In a public statement made by Monsignor McGean in 1905, he observed: "St. Peter's church is visited daily by many hundreds of devout Catholics, who are employed in the vicinity and who take the opportunity, when passing, of spending a few moments in the house of God. At any time of the day, but especially in the noon hour, may be seen men and women, young, aged, and in the prime of life, kneeling in the pews, praying, with bowed heads to their maker, or passing from station to station, making the Way of the Cross. The church is always open during the day and evening and is visited regularly by many times more people than reside in the parish. On last Holy Thursday the number of people who visited the Repository in St. Peter's numbered fully 20,000."

It is easy to forget that, until comparatively recent years, the existence of the strict eucharistic fast required both the celebrant of a Mass and anyone wishing to receive Communion to abstain from both food and water from the previous midnight onward. This rule made it impossible to hold noon or evening Masses. Accordingly, other midday services had to be held. These included a Holy Hour and similar exercises. Special permission for the exposition of the Blessed Sacrament was given to St. Peter's parish early in the nineteenth century. This devotion continues on a regular basis every afternoon following the midday Masses.

In 1921, near the end of his tenure as pastor, Monsignor McGean was quoted as saying that "when I came to St. Peter's, I had a flock of some 25,000 souls, most of them Irish. It has dwindled to 7,000 souls of twenty nationalities, most of them Polish and Ruthenian." Several national parishes, including Eastern Rite parishes, have had their origins at St. Peter's, using its facilities before being able to build their own churches. This number includes a Melchite parish for Syrians and a Maronite parish for Lebanese.

Today, St. Peter's retains its predominantly commuter-oriented character. However, contemplated changes in lower Manhattan suggest clearly that the parish will have a growing residential component. It is still a territorial parish, running from Canal Street on the north to Battery Park City and Pier A on the west and south and from Broadway to Rector Street. As already noted, within this area are the two 107-story skyscrapers built by the New York Port Authority called the World Trade Center where fifty thousand people go to work each business day. The PATH (for Port Authority Trans-Hudson Corporation) trains coming from northern New Jersey bring 150,000 commuters to a station within a few blocks from the church. A substantial number of these commuters are Catholics who find their way to St. Peter's, either for Mass, confession, or meditation. The church at Barclay and Church Streets has only four Masses each weekend, drawing about three hundred people. However, it has six Masses every weekday and thirty-five Masses on holy days of obligation. Such Masses begin every fifteen minutes and are celebrated both in the main church and in a downstairs chapel. Confessions are heard for six hours each business day. About one thousand attend Mass on an average weekday and about eighty-five hundred on a holy day. On Ash Wednesday, about ten thousand hear Mass and receive their ashes. A regular feature of each weekday Mass is the two-minute homily, a restriction rigidly imposed on the five priests assigned to the parish so that persons going to and from work will not be unduly detained. Many of the lectors and eucharistic ministers live in New Jersey or elsewhere in New York and make St. Peter's their religious home away from home. With the permission of their residential pastor, St. Peter's will marry them or baptize their children. The parish now has twelve to fifteen baptisms per year, whereas there were none a few years ago. It has almost no funerals.

Battery Park City is a complex of high-rise apartments built along the North River not far from St. Peter's. It occupies ninety-two acres of land reclaimed from the river by material excavated from the foundation of the World Trade Center. Many more apartments are expected to be built in the future. Moreover, several loft buildings in lower Manhattan have been converted into dwellings. These developments provide both an existing and an expanding residential Catholic community. However, it is difficult for St. Peter's to determine exactly how many Catholics reside in these buildings. The parish census has to be taken by mail because security-conscious New Yorkers in barricaded apartments will not permit any outsider to get past the doorman to conduct a survey, even if it is the parish priest making his rounds. Since 1983, St. Peter's has maintained a chapel in space rented at Battery Park City. Known as St. Joseph's Chapel, it takes its name from a nearby Maronite church that was closed. It is supported, in part, by interest on the money derived from the sale of the former St. Joseph's Church. About two hundred fifty people attend Mass each weekend at St. Joseph's Chapel and about four hundred fifty attend one of four Masses said every business day. Most of the congregation at the chapel are either single individuals or are young married couples. As the residential component of the parish grows, St. Peter's will be increasing the number and kind of activities normally found in a residential Catholic parish.

St. Peter's was once the only Catholic church in an area that now includes five dioceses in New Jersey and eight dioceses in New York. It is the mother church of all of the four hundred twelve churches in the archdiocese of New York. Although the character of its present ministry differs somewhat from what is offered in a conventional residential parish, its efforts continue to touch the lives of many thousands of Catholics in the nation's largest business and financial center who try to make of their religion something other than a Sunday-only activity.

14
St. Patrick's Cathedral

New York

NEW YORK

St. Patrick's Cathedral, now dwarfed by the skyscrapers of midtown Manhattan, is undoubtedly the best-known Catholic church in the United States. It is the largest Catholic cathedral in the United States. The story of St. Patrick's is actually the story of two churches with the same name, located about five miles apart in the nation's largest city and constructed some fifty to sixty years apart. Together they have served, one following the other, as the principal churches of the diocese and later the archdiocese of New York since 1815.

In 1801, the trustees of St. Peter's Church, then the only Catholic church in New York City and one of two in New York State, purchased nine lots at the corner of Prince and Mott Streets for a cemetery. Until that time, Catholic burials had taken place either in St. Peter's churchyard or in the cemetery surrounding Trinity Episcopal Church at the foot of Wall Street. In 1803, the St. Peter's trustees bought ten adjacent lots for the same purpose. They were located in the far northeast end of the inhabited part of Manhattan Island, about a mile from St. Peter's and actually beyond the city limits. Those limits were then at Canal Street, a boundary that was little more than a drainage ditch leading from a water-collection pond. Some of the gravestones still remaining at Old St. Patrick's date back to 1801.

In 1808, Archbishop Carroll sent Father

Anthony Kohlmann, a Jesuit from Alsace, to St. Peter's as its pastor. The newly formed diocese of New York was without a bishop and would remain without one until 1815, so Father Kohlmann was designated the vicar general. He ran the diocese as well as St. Peter's parish, which had nearly sixteen thousand members. Because of this overcrowding, he was able to convince the trustees to build a new church in the suburbs to serve as the cathedral for the new diocese. The newly acquired burial ground was deemed an appropriate location as soon as sufficient graves could be relocated to make room for a building site. On June 8, 1809, Father Kohlmann, along with the other Catholic clergy, the St. Peter's trustees, and the choir, walked in procession through the woods and fields from St. Peter's to the cemetery and laid the cornerstone for what is now known as Old St. Patrick's Church. The ceremony was witnessed by about three thousand spectators.

The new church took about six years to build. It was named in honor of St. Patrick at the suggestion of Archbishop Carroll. He wanted to recognize the large number of Irish who were beginning to come to New York, even at this early date and well in advance of the construction of the Erie Canal, and long before the potato famine in Ireland. These were the two developments that, in the next forty years, would bring mass immigration from Ireland to New York, both city and state.

Times were especially tough in New York during the first decade of the nineteenth century, so the construction of a new church ran into serious financial difficulties. Every economy was invoked to permit construction to go forward. Joseph Mangin, a prominent architect, was retained to draw the plans. The church was designed to be 120 feet by 80 feet and about 70 feet in height. However, the trustees decided to omit a steeple in order to save money. They engaged Peter Morte, a mason and master builder, as superintendent and agreed to pay him two dollars a day. He was authorized to hire an assistant at fourteen shillings a day.

To pay for the new church, Father Kohlmann organized the Patrician Society, whose object was to solicit small contributions ranging from twenty-five cents to one dollar a month. The promise given to members of the Patrician Society was that their names would be "carefully preserved on the church books, and . . . prayed for to time immemorial in said church." He even asked the trustees of Trinity Episcopal Church for a donation but received a polite letter of refusal stating that Trinity was having financial difficulties of its own and simply could not afford to help St. Patrick's. Construction was suspended during the War of 1812 but was resumed in time to permit the dedication to take place on May 4, 1815. By that time, the enterprise had cost $90,000.

The second bishop of New York, an Irish Dominican named John Connolly, had delayed coming to the city until the treaty was concluded ending the Napoleonic wars. Being Irish, he was a British subject and was afraid that he might be regarded as an enemy alien if he arrived in America while hostilities were still possible. Accordingly, Bishop John de Cheverus of Boston dedicated the new cathedral. The ceremony took place in the presence of about four thousand people, including Mayor DeWitt Clinton. At the time of its dedication, Old St. Patrick's was the largest church building in New York City.

As the new cathedral was under construction, Father Kohlmann made another purchase that had long-term implications for St. Patrick's. He first rented a house on Mulberry Street across from the cathedral grounds as a site for a classical school and organized what he called the New York Literary Institution. The school was soon moved around the corner on Broadway and grew to an enrollment of thirty-five students. At that point, Father Kohlmann decided to relocate it to the suburbs and bought land along Fifth Avenue at 50th Street across from the Elgin Botanical Gardens. That site, owned by Columbia College, is where Rockefeller Center now stands. The land, running from 50th to 51st Street and from Fourth Avenue (now Park Avenue) to Fifth, was obtained for $11,000, with title being placed in the hands of two trustees. A loan was obtained to construct school buildings, and a mortgage was placed on the property to secure the loan.

There the school grew to about seventy-five boarding students, including children of prominent Protestant families. Among its teachers were several Jesuits who had accompanied Father Kohlmann to New York. However, in 1813, the Jesuit superior in Maryland, Father John Grassi, closed the school because he felt that it was operating in competition with Georgetown and he had only enough men to staff one institution. After the New York Literary Institution was closed, the Trappists, who had come from the Midwest, occupied it briefly and maintained an orphanage for thirty children. However, the orphanage was soon closed because the Trappists were ordered to return to France. Thereafter, the property remained unoccupied for several years. A few years later, the Jesuits sold their fee interest in the mortgaged property, two city blocks at 51st Street and Fifth Avenue, for $1,900. It was surely one of the most ill-advised business transactions in the entire history of the society.

In the fall of 1815, Bishop Connolly, who had been consecrated in Rome, arrived in New York and took possession of his cathedral. His entire diocese, including all of New York State and half of New Jersey, had only three churches and four priests. This number included three Jesuits and one Dominican. Two of his priests were French and could not preach in English. His cathedral on Mulberry Street was described by visiting Bishop Joseph Plessis of Quebec as follows: "... it has not yet a steeple, a sacristy, an enclosure nor out-houses. It has not even any plaster outside; the joints are not drawn, although the very common stone of which it is built requires one or the other. In return, the interior is magnificent. Six clustered columns on either side divide the body of the edifice into three naves crowned by Gothic arches, forming a *coup d'oeil*, all the more imposing that a painter has figured on the plain wall ending the church behind the altar a continuation of these arches and columns which seem to vanish in the distance and create such an illusion on strangers ignorant of the fact, as to persuade them at first sight that the altar is placed at only half the length of the church, although it is really at the very end. The wonderful effect produced makes this church pass for the finest in the United States."

John McQuaid grew up in Old St. Patrick's parish. He was destined to be consecrated bishop of Rochester at its altar some fifty years after Bishop Plessis wrote the above description. Bishop McQuaid had a slightly different recollection of the premises:

"The elders of the congregation, whose memories go back to that which this church edifice was before its extension under Bishop Hughes, remember, no doubt, the high, straightbacked pews, constructed apparently with a view to uncomfortableness, the freezing temperature of a winter's morning in a building without fire, and the dim light at a Lenten evening's service, that came from the candles in tin sconces hung on the columns, and just enough to show the darkness. The methods and arrangements of those times, and of our fathers, were more remarkable for simplicity and economy than for comfort and brilliancy."

Whatever its architectural and ornamental virtues, Old St. Patrick's still had to be paid for. Upon completion, there was a debt of $53,000 accumulating interest at seven percent. This was reduced by some $37,500 derived from the sale of one thousand pews. Those located nearest the altar brought $1,000 each, while pews farther away sold for less. The trustees organized door-to-door collection efforts and, on occasion, stood on the front steps of the cathedral asking for money from parishioners as they left after Mass.

Bishop Connolly immediately took on the role of a parish priest as well as bishop of the diocese. He made parish visits, heard confessions, and taught catechism. He once wrote that he was so busy he scarcely had time to say his Office. A major concern was the trustees. In 1813, an act of the general assembly was passed creating a joint board to operate both St. Patrick's and St. Peter's. When Bishop Connolly refused to appoint a priest to their liking, the trustees threatened to cut off his salary; so, in 1817, he obtained another act of the assembly separately incorporating the trustees of St. Patrick's parish. This move brought only temporary peace at St. Patrick's.

Cornelius Heeney, an old Irish bachelor who had made a fortune in the fur business with John Jacob Astor, provided much of the financial support to Old St. Patrick's during its formative years. He contributed $18,000 toward the opening of an orphanage across the street from the church, made generous donations toward the church itself, and, upon his death, left an estate to the diocese of New York that was generating an income of $25,000 a year well into the next century. Trustees such as Heeney made the trustee system workable if not desirable during this era. It was large donations such as Heeney's, coming from an emerging number of well-to-do Catholics, that permitted the Church in New York to move beyond a hand-to-mouth existence during the early decades of the nineteenth century. Although Heeney himself was buried in Brooklyn, in the catacombs beneath Old St. Patrick's can be found burial vaults containing the remains of many of these old Catholic families whose contributions can be seen in what the writers of that era referred to as the "temporalities" of the Church.

In 1817, St. Patrick's opened a school in the basement of the church. For years it was taught by laymen. Until 1823, it received a pittance from the Common School Fund, ranging from $600 to $1,200 a year. This sum was not enough to support the school, whose annual expenditures were once calculated to be $3.02 per pupil. However, even this nominal contribution to the education of several hundred students stirred determined opposition from secular school advocates who felt that they should have all of the education money available from public authorities. In 1837, the school was moved to a two-story building nearby and eventually took over the orphanage building. Both the school and the orphanage were staffed by the Daughters of Charity from Emmitsburg, Maryland. Until the Christian Brothers came in 1849, the boys' "department" was taught by laymen, who received a salary of about $400 a year, while the girls' "department" was taught by nuns. At a later point in time, Bishop John Hughes asked the Daughters of Charity to teach both boys and girls. However, such activity violated the rules of their order, so permission was refused by the motherhouse in Maryland, whereupon Bishop Hughes organized a New York offshoot of the order whose rules were not so restrictive.

During the first years of St. Patrick's Cathedral, there was a shortage of priests so that Masses were said only on alternate Sundays with St. Peter's. After Bishop Connolly's death, Father John Power became rector and was temporarily designated as vicar general of the diocese. Father Power established the first Catholic paper in New York, the *Truth Teller*. The paper continued publication until 1855 when it merged with another paper, the *Irish-American*. The *Truth Teller* came into existence just as various Protestant papers were being established in New York for the express purpose of attacking the doctrines and practices of the Catholic Church. As early as 1824, Protestant Irishmen staged an Orangemen's Day parade in Greenwich Village, using anti-Catholic slogans and molesting bystanders whom they suspected were Catholics. More attacks in the pulpit, the press, and in the streets were to follow.

The Holy See named Father John Dubois, a French Sulpician and president of Mount St. Mary's College in Emmitsburg, Maryland, as the third bishop of New York. His appointment was a particular disappointment to the Irish of New York, who felt that their bishop should be one of their own. It was also a disappointment to Father Power. However, in the next fifteen years Bishop Dubois was able to pacify national pride and clerical ambition in administering the diocese. In 1829, he made a trip to Europe and was able to obtain funds for the diocese and particularly for the establishment of a seminary that he hoped to erect at Nyack on the Hudson. He tried to elevate the quality of devotional life by organizing the Confraternity of the Blessed Sacrament and by calling the priests of the cathedral together each day to say their Office with him, similar to the practice of cathedral chapters in Europe and monastic orders.

The first ordination took place at Old St. Patrick's in 1820. They continued thereafter, initially at the rate of about one a year. In 1836, Bishop Dubois ordained an unassuming immigrant priest from Bohemia named John N. Neumann and sent him off to western New York State as a missionary to German Catholics living near Niagara Falls. Father Neumann later became bishop of Philadelphia and, in 1977, was canonized as a saint of the universal Church.

In 1829, the trustees of both St. Peter's and St. Patrick's felt that more land was necessary for a Catholic cemetery. (By 1833, the cemetery surrounding Old St. Patrick's had over thirty-two thousand graves and was closed thereafter for interments except for

1850, new dioceses had been created in Albany, Buffalo, and Hartford. These areas, in addition to Boston, were formed into the ecclesiastical province of New York, and Old St. Patrick's became the seat of an archdiocese. John Hughes became its first archbishop. Three years later, Newark and Brooklyn became dioceses, at which time the archdiocese of New York was reduced to the territory it presently occupies.

The trustee system that had so troubled the early days of the Church in New York and elsewhere began to unravel in New York in the 1840s, not so much because of on-going hostilities as from incompetence on the part of parish trustees. In many instances, the trustees were simply not able to pay the bills so the parishes they controlled became the subjects of foreclosure actions by creditors. Five of the eight Catholic churches in New York City went on the auction block and were sold to pay parish debts. At that time, there were about sixty thousand Catholics in the city and most of their places of worship were in serious jeopardy. To prevent the loss of these churches, Bishop Hughes bought in at the foreclosure sales with money he was able to borrow and took title to these properties in his own name. At one time, he owned fifty-eight tracts of church land and became the object of public criticism, especially among those who were already antagonistic to the Church or to the man they called the "pope of New York." His action in taking title to church property in his own name was reminiscent of the practice of Jesuit missionaries in colonial times who, being unable to put title to church properties in the name of the Society of Jesus, took title in their own names and then executed wills leaving the property to the provincial or to their successor at a particular mission so that collateral heirs would be precluded from laying any claims. Newly installed bishops in Albany and Buffalo were forced to resort to the same practice.

Archbishop Hughes asked the New York Assembly for general legislation to permit the creation of a legal form known as a corporation sole, an ancient common-law practice used widely today in the Catholic Church throughout the United States. A corporation sole is simply a legal device whereby an individual can incorporate himself and hold title to property as a corporation, not as an individual. Thus corporate property is immune from judgments arising out of a bishop's personal debts and also from claims by his heirs, since title passes at death or resignation to his corporate successor.

Not only did the legislature in Albany refuse his request, it passed a law in 1855 forbidding any individual from taking title to property in his own name for the benefit of any church group. The law provided further that if an individual tried to do so, upon his death the property would revert to a trustee group elected by the pewholders of the church organization. Voting membership for trustees did not depend upon subscribing to any set of doctrinal or moral tenets nor was voting membership limited by this law to people who attended church services or received the sacraments. If such a trustee group was not formed, then upon the death of the individual property holder title to church property would pass to the state of New York, as in the case of any individual who died without heirs.

The new law was directly aimed at the Catholic bishops of the three New York dioceses. It sprang from anti-Catholic nativism, but it also had the support of at least one Catholic board of trustees, at St. Louis Church in Buffalo, which was locked in a bitter dispute with the first bishop of that city. They had recently been excommunicated by Bishop John Timon for their obstinacy and were getting even by supporting legislation that would curb his temporal powers. State Senator Erastus Brooks said on the floor of the New York State Senate in support of the measure: "In the remarks I propose to make, I shall aim to show that the political state is Protestant in character, if not in its constitution — that its republican success has been mainly founded upon its Protestant religion, that other systems of faith are not in harmony with true civil and religious liberty, that the bill before us is a legitimate subject of legislation, and that we are called upon to uphold and encourage all who are seeking to secure civil and religious independence from the control of a despot power...."

No new Catholic boards of trustees were formed in the next eight years under the provisions of the law; so, in 1863, after Know-Nothing agitation had died down, the state assembly passed another bill permitting church property to be owned by clerically controlled boards of trustees. Today, under that procedure, Catholic churches in New York are owned by boards of trustees, usually five in number, among whom are the bishop, the vicar general, and the pastor. The other two are usually laymen appointed by the bishop. Thus, the trustee question was finally put to rest but not until after a great deal of strife had taken place both inside and outside the membership of the Church. In this dispute Archbishop Hughes was the leading protagonist.

The archbishop became involved in another prominent public controversy during his early years at Old St. Patrick's. New York City did not institute a conventional public school system until 1842, long after other communities in the state had done so. As noted elsewhere, before that time education was publicly but indirectly supported from what was called the Common School Fund, that is, money controlled by the city council and derived from taxation and other sources. Beginning in 1813, the legislature directed that payments from this fund in New York City be made to the trustees of a nonsectarian group calling itself the Free School Society and to the Orphans Asylum Society, the Society of the Economical School, the African Free School, and any incorporated societies that operated so-called charity or free schools. Initially, St. Peter's and St. Patrick's received money from the Common School Fund for their parochial schools, as did the Bethel Baptist Church and other Protestant church schools.

Irregularities in the management of funds by the Bethel Baptist Church prompted the Free School Society, which had always opposed any sharing of funds with religiously connected schools, to ask the legislature to eliminate religious societies from any share of the Common School Fund in New York City. The legislature passed the question to the New York Common Council (City Council) which, in 1825, enacted an ordinance excluding religious schools from public support. The Free School Society then changed its name to the Public School Society, although it operated schools that charged tuition from pupils to supplement public funding.

Schools operated by the Public School Society used the King James Version of the Bible as a reading text and conducted simple devotional exercises at the opening of each school day. They campaigned against the use of liquor and employed as a text a book written by two Protestant clergymen called the Universal Non-Sectarian Catechism. Many Catholics in New York City thought the Public School Society textbooks, especially its history texts, were biased against Catholics and that the atmosphere in these schools was offensively anti-Catholic. For that reason, by 1840 they had built and were operating a total of eight Catholic parochial schools having an aggregate enrollment of five thousand children.

In 1840, Bishop Hughes went before New York's board of aldermen to ask for a share of the Common School Fund for the city's parochial schools. Hearings lasted two days and generated a firestorm of opposition, especially from the Methodist Church and from the Public School Society. Like other bishops of his time, Bishop Hughes was accused of trying to drive the Bible out of the public schools. A pastor of the Dutch Reformed Church opposed Hughes' request, testifying that "public schools were Protestant institutions and Protestants could not yield to the Catholic claim." A Presbyterian minister told the board of aldermen: "[Bishop Hughes] has sought to prove that the present system leads to infidelity. Now, sir, let no man think it strange that I should prefer infidelity to Catholicism. Even a mind as acute as Voltaire's came to the conclusion that, if there was no alternative between infidelity and the dogmas of the Catholic Church, he should choose infidelity. I would choose, sir, in similar circumstances, to be an infidel tomorrow."

Bishop Hughes then responded for three and a half hours. He summed up his case as follows: "There is, then, but one simple question — will you compel us to pay a tax from which we can receive no benefit, and to frequent schools which injure and destroy our religious rights in the minds of our children and of which, in our consciences, we cannot approve? That is the simple question."

The board of aldermen was unrelenting, so Bishop Hughes went back to Albany asking Governor (future U.S. Secretary of State) William Seward and the state assembly for relief. Seward was always regarded as a friend of Catholics. He was a friend of the archbishop for many years. He recommended to the assembly that it establish separate schools for Catholics, a recommendation that, as noted earlier, generated political and other reactions finding their way into the streets of New York and the grounds of Old St. Patrick's Cathedral. Both political parties were asked for pledges to oppose the use of public funds for parochial schools, a move that prompted Bishop Hughes to organize his own political ticket.

The assembly refused to follow Governor Seward's request but it voted to extend the statewide public school system into New York City, thus terminating the influence and the operations of the Public School Society. Bishop Hughes expressed his disappointment at the exclusion of Catholic schools from public support but said he was gratified at the establishment of a board of education and a general public school system.

He agreed to wait and see how the new system would accommodate the needs of Catholic children and the consciences of their parents. Meanwhile, he continued the effort to expand the parochial school system. Between 1840 and 1864, a total of thirty-eight parochial schools were established in New York City, and the bishop was forced to go to Europe to recruit members of religious orders to come to New York to staff them.

In 1853, an event occurred in New York that demonstrated how a routine act of church administration could develop into a *cause célèbre* owing to latent anti-Catholic feeling looking for any excuse to erupt. Pope Pius IX sent Archbishop Gaetano Bedini, the papal nuncio to Brazil, to the United States to see if he could resolve trustee disputes in Philadelphia and Buffalo. During his seven months in the United States, Archbishop Bedini traveled widely to secure information on the development of the American Church that the Holy See was interested in obtaining. He visited Old St. Patrick's and presided over the consecration of three bishops. His presence in the United States infuriated anti-Catholic newspapers and provided them with an excuse to whip up public fears of papal encroachment on American life and institutions. Hostility to the papal nuncio also stemmed from the activities of Italian and German supporters of political causes that had provoked revolutions in various European countries in 1848. They wanted to vent Old World antagonisms in a New World setting. Riots broke out frequently when Archbishop Bedini appeared. An assassination plot was uncovered and thwarted, but he traveled in fear of his life.

Upon taking leave of the United States, Archbishop Bedini was scheduled to depart for Rome by a steamship sailing from the port of New York. Shortly before embarking, he was warned by the mayor of New York to try to leave town quietly so that a riot might not take place. Heeding this warning, the archbishop went secretly to Staten Island and boarded the outgoing vessel at that point rather than at the regular passenger dock in the city.

Shortly after New York was designated an archdiocese, Archbishop Hughes announced his intention of building a new cathedral. He had recently purchased a seven-acre tract of land on Fifth Avenue between 51st and 52nd Streets, a block north of the cemetery property that had been acquired by the St. Patrick's and St. Peter's trustees in 1829. The new tract was slated to be used for the construction of two orphanages. (It was eventually sold in 1891.) Archbishop Hughes decided that this general area would be an appropriate place for a new cathedral and selected the old cemetery land between 49th and 50th Streets for this purpose. At that time, 34th Street was the city limit, so many called the proposed project at such a remote suburban location "Hughes' Folly." In 1858, when the project was beginning to take shape, New York City had 25 Catholic churches, 60 priests, and 200,000 Catholics. The archbishop felt that the size of the city, its future prospects, and the prestige of Catholics in that city required an elaborate expression in the form of a cathedral.

He had already acquired an architect but he needed "seed money" with which to begin. Legend has it that St. Patrick's on Fifth Avenue was built with the nickels and dimes of Irish working girls. It required a little more. On July 14, 1858, the archbishop sent a circular letter to about one hundred forty wealthy Catholics, telling them that he needed $100,000 to begin the project. He asked each of them for $1,000 as their initial and immediate contribution, stating in his letter that he had already set Sunday afternoon, August 15, at 4:00 P.M. as the date and time for laying the cornerstone. He told these prospective contributors that, if he had the required upfront money in hand by that date, he would proceed with construction and borrow the rest. On the other hand, if he did not have the money he would still proceed to lay the cornerstone and then erect an iron fence around it and wait for better days. The archbishop followed up his circular letter with personal calls on each of the addressees.

By the date set for laying the cornerstone, he had collected some $73,000 of his goal of $100,000, so, at the appointed hour, some 100,000 people gathered to witness the scheduled event. New York City was then experiencing a serious depression. Just a year before, the city government had undertaken a massive public works project, just nine blocks north of the cathedral site, which it had placed under the general supervision of Frederick Law Olmstead. One of the purposes for laying out Central Park at that time was to provide work for many in dire economic straits. This condition was mentioned by Archbishop Hughes in the course of his address: "You have given one hundred and three thousand dollars toward the building of a temple which can add nothing to the Glory of God; for His is the earth and the fullness thereof. On the other hand, this money might have been given to the poor. All this might be thrown at you by those who are of this world and have no comprehension of what is real faith, and what is real charity, and it is significant that you would seem to belong in this to the school of Christ, when He bore with the extravagance of Mary Magdalen pouring ointment on His sacred feet; and your accusers, if it were not almost uncharitable to say so, would seem to belong to the school of him who carried the purse and looked upon the penitent Mary's offering as if it were defrauding the poor. It comes up at a time when they are unusually depressed. Your charity will give honorable employment to a considerable extent; as the world is now constituted, compensation for honest labor is much better than alms for the relief of poverty under unavoidable pressure, which imposes idleness by necessity on the working classes. Now when you are reproached with your extravagance, ask your accusers whether it is in fact a crime to provide employment and compensation for the mechanic and laborer, who really belong to the substantial portion of society in all countries."

Archbishop Hughes never lived to see the completion of St. Patrick's Cathedral but his architect did. In those days, architects who specialized in designing Protestant churches in New York refused to accept commissions to design Catholic churches. In other cities, notably Boston and Baltimore, such was not the case. Archbishop Hughes selected James Renwick, Jr., the wealthy son of a Columbia College professor, to design and supervise the building of St. Patrick's. Renwick was a lifelong Episcopalian. He had never received any formal training as an architect but had completed the building of Grace Episcopal Church in Manhattan a few years before undertaking the assignment given to him by Archbishop Hughes. At that time, Renwick was working as the assistant engineer in the construction of the Croton Reservoir at 42nd Street and Fifth Avenue, a few blocks south of the cathedral site.

In the years to come, Renwick was to distinguish himself by designing the Smithsonian Institution building in Washington, D.C., several Protestant churches in New York, and the homes of many wealthy clients both in Manhattan and in Newport. During his lifetime, he amassed a large art collection which he placed in the gallery in Washington that bears his name. Notwithstanding all of these accomplishments, Renwick regarded the construction and furnishing of St. Patrick's Cathedral to be his most important and notable achievement and spent much of the next thirty-five years in this undertaking.

Renwick produced a Gothic Revival design for St. Patrick's, something that was rare if not unheard of in the construction of American churches of that era. The exterior resembled the cathedral at Cologne and the interior resembled the cathedrals at Rheims, Amiens, and several cities in England. He convinced Archbishop Hughes and the trustees to use white marble because of its durability, beauty, and long-term economy, despite the fact that white marble would cost about $50,000 more than three alternative materials. He also convinced the trustees to purchase, in their own names, the quarry sites in Eastchester and in Massachusetts to be used as sources for this stone so that production difficulties would not take place and interrupt the building of the cathedral. A railroad spur was built directly to the jobsite so that the marble could be delivered rapidly and cheaply.

The church that Renwick designed was 332 feet long, 132 feet wide, and had an interior height of 112 feet; its transept was 174 feet in length, though it is somewhat longer today. The twin steeples were not completed until nearly ten years after the cathedral was dedicated. They are each three hundred thirty feet high. The contractor and Renwick estimated the total cost of construction at $850,000. The archbishop told prospective donors that it might cost as much as a million dollars. Some thirty-five years later, Renwick estimated the cost at that time was running between two million and two and a half million dollars. By the time the east end chapels and the Lady Chapel were complete, the total had reached about four million dollars. Construction was halted when the Civil War began in 1861. At that time, the exterior walls had been constructed to a height of about fourteen feet.

During the Civil War, Archbishop Hughes directed that the American flag be flown over Old St. Patrick's. The Lincoln Administration, doubtless because of Hughes' old friend Secretary of State Seward, sent the archbishop on a vaguely defined mission to Europe for the purpose of counteracting the efforts of Confederate agents abroad who were pressuring the British and French governments to grant diplomatic recognition to the Confederate States of America. He was gone from New York for ten months. Upon his return, Lincoln thanked him for his efforts, said that they had been successful, and told the archbishop that he was going to ask Pope Pius IX to make him a cardinal.

Whether Lincoln actually recommended him for a red hat is unknown; in any case Hughes did not receive one.

On August 17, 1862, shortly before the Battle of Antietam, Archbishop Hughes delivered a sermon in Old St. Patrick's supporting the Union cause and urging the conscription of soldiers into the Union Army. In July of the following year, draft riots broke out in New York City when the lottery was held to put the draft into effect. Many were Irish immigrants who resented the fact that wealthy young men could purchase a substitute for $300 and thereby exempt themselves from military service. Many had arrived in this country only a few years earlier and felt that the war was simply not their fight. During the riots, Archbishop Hughes appeared on the balcony of his residence at 36th Street and Madison Avenue and spoke to a crowd of four thousand. It was his last public appearance. He urged them to remain peaceable, to support government authorities, and to return quietly to their homes. Those who heard him complied with the request. Many others took another course. The riots were finally quelled by military authorities but not before much violence and destruction had taken place. Other Irish immigrants in New York supported the Union cause. In the spring of 1864, a ceremony was held at Old St. Patrick's to honor the soldiers of the Irish Brigade which had suffered heavy casualties in the Battle of Fredricksburg when they tried unsuccessfully to storm Marye's Heights.

Between the end of the Civil War and the dedication of the new cathedral in 1879, a number of events of importance continued to occur at Old St. Patrick's before it was decommissioned as a cathedral. Three provincial councils, made up of bishops from the entire northeastern part of the United States, met and deliberated within its walls. Five diocesan synods, composed of priests and bishops of the archdiocese of New York, also took place there.

On October 6, 1866, Old St. Patrick's was substantially destroyed by fire. Sparks from a building fire on Broadway were carried by a high wind and landed on the church roof. The fire spread so fast that nothing could save the building. The Blessed Sacrament was removed, as were vestments and sacred vessels, but when the fire subsided, all that was left standing were the walls. Happily, the burial vaults in the basement were spared. The building was insured, but its destruction meant that the archdiocese was being called upon to build two St. Patrick's cathedrals at the same time. Services resumed at Old St. Patrick's the following Easter and the church was rededicated on St. Patrick's Day, 1868.

In 1864, New York Catholics received their first native-born archbishop, John McCloskey. He was born in Brooklyn, served much of his priestly life in New York City, was appointed the first bishop of Albany, and was Archbishop Hughes' coadjutor bishop during Hughes' latter years. Archbishop McCloskey had a markedly different temperament from his predecessor. He was quiet, easygoing, and not given to public controversies. In 1875, he was named the first American cardinal. The last major ceremony to take place in Old St. Patrick's occurred on April 27, 1875, when papal emissaries, some twenty-seven archbishops and bishops, several hundred priests, and several thousand laymen gathered to witness the conferring of the *biretta rosa* — the red hat — on Cardinal McCloskey.

On May 25, 1879, the present St. Patrick's Cathedral at 50th Street and Fifth Avenue was dedicated at a ceremony every bit as elaborate if not quite so large as the one that took place when the cornerstone was laid twenty-one years earlier. Since that date, the cathedral has not closed its doors a single day. Old St. Patrick's then became a territorial parish in a part of lower Manhattan that developed into an Italian tenement district. In recent years, New York's expanding Chinatown has extended into the parish, so its parochial school now has a large number of Chinese students.

Madison Avenue was cut through the property owned by the new cathedral. The eastern portion of the tract was developed into upscale housing. On the west side, at both corners flanking the cathedral, the parish rectory and the archbishop's residence were constructed. In 1882, St. Patrick's opened a parish school on what is now Park Avenue. It remained in operation until 1940, although not always at the same address. Changes in midtown Manhattan caused the enrollment to decline to the point where there was no longer any practical way to maintain it. While it was in operation, the Christian Brothers taught the boys and the Sisters of Charity taught the girls.

Originally, the parish boundaries extended from the East River westward to Seventh Avenue. By 1900, the parish had twelve thousand parishioners in an area that was dramatically diverse. Fifth Avenue and Madison Avenue both became rows of mansions for the very wealthy. After the New York Central Railroad tracks were covered over, Park Avenue followed suit. Other sections were not so well fixed. These included "Dutch Hill," a German section along the East River, and a number of Irish shantytowns on the west end nearer the Hudson River. Eventually, the mansions gave way to fashionable apartments, and the area became highly commercialized. Middle-class flight from midtown Manhattan began in the 1920s. The future of the area around St. Patrick's as a center of large and prominent office buildings became fixed in the 1930s when Rockefeller Center was erected across Fifth Avenue from the cathedral on land still owned by Columbia University.

One economy that Archbishop Hughes had ordered was the omission of a chapel in the apse of the cathedral behind the main altar. In 1900, as the result of a bequest by Mrs. Eugene Kelly, the cathedral was lengthened about fifty-six feet, and the Lady Chapel was erected in the new extension. The first Mass was said in the Lady Chapel on Christmas, 1906. It is now frequently used for weddings.

During the first decade of the twentieth century, New York's fourth archbishop, Cardinal John Farley, wished to remove the remaining debt from the church so that it could be consecrated on or about the 100th anniversary of the founding of the New York diocese. He was able to accomplish this goal by prevailing upon the trustees, all very wealthy business and professional men, to assume the remaining cathedral debt as their own personal obligations so that the cathedral itself would become debt-free. The amount in question was $400,000.

Because of its unique status and resources, St. Patrick's was able to undertake activities that lie far beyond the means of most parishes. William R. Grace, founder of Grace Lines and a cathedral trustee, donated a large sum of money in 1897 to establish Grace Institute, a vocational school for women which the Sisters of Charity began to operate on West 60th Street. By 1960, some seventy thousand women had taken courses at this school, either to prepare themselves for employment or to train in domestic arts. In an era when public library facilities were scarce, the cathedral opened a large lending library that ultimately was absorbed into the public library system as the Cathedral Branch of the New York Public Library. Monsignor Michael Lavelle, who was rector of the cathedral for fifty-two years, assisted in the establishing of the Catholic School for the Blind. Both he and Cardinal Farley were members of the board of trustees of the Catholic University of America. In conjunction with the university, St. Patrick's started a summer school in New York offering college courses.

During World War I, New York's fifth archbishop, Cardinal Patrick Hayes, was given the additional duty of military ordinary of a worldwide church jurisdiction composed of members of the armed forces of the United States. This duty was also assumed by his successors in office. The chancery of the military ordinariate was established near St. Patrick's and remained there until a separate military archdiocese was established in 1985 and its headquarters relocated to a suburb of Washington, D.C. During World War II, St. Patrick's Cathedral operated a canteen for military personnel passing through New York City.

Other activities include a glossy monthly magazine, started originally in 1922, and still published monthly under the title of *Alive and Well*. It contains articles about parish life, messages from the cardinal, and general religious topics. In 1905, the cathedral opened a high school that received its charter from the New York State Board of Regents in 1910. For twenty years it remained a parish school; however, in 1927, it was turned over to the archdiocese. Originally, it occupied the same building that housed the parish elementary school, but it has been relocated on at least two occasions. As noted previously, it now occupies a part of the same office building on First Avenue that contains the offices of the archdiocese.

Both because of its stature and its location, St. Patrick's has been the focal point for many events of general interest in New York during the past one hundred years. Military parades, suffragette marches, and other events on Fifth Avenue have passed right by its doors. Protest actions, such as a bomb scare at the outset of World War I and a sit-in by gay rights activists in 1989, have occurred on its premises. New York has witnessed two hundred forty St. Patrick's Day parades. For many years its line of march has proceeded down Fifth Avenue, passing in review before the smiling eyes of a succession of archbishops bearing distinctly Irish names, who have regularly witnessed the annual event from the front steps of the cathedral. The annual Columbus Day parade by Italians receives equal billing. Although it is hardly a Catholic event or even a matter of religious significance, the New York's storied Easter Parade ambles past St. Patrick's as well.

It would be impossible to catalog the names of all of the famous visitors to New York who have come to St. Patrick's. Most prominent have been three popes: in 1936, Cardinal Eugenio Pacelli, then Vatican secretary of state and later Pius XII; in 1965, Pope Paul VI during his visit to the United Nations; and in 1979, Pope John Paul II during the first of his two whirlwind visits to the United States. Foreign dignitaries such as Churchill, Adenauer, Gronchi, Kohl, and Andreotti have visited St. Patrick's, as have Kremlin representatives Nicolai Novikof and Andrei Vishinski. Ambassadors to the United Nations are frequent visitors to the cathedral. Special Masses are said at St. Patrick's on the patronal feasts of many South and Central American nations. Presidents Lyndon B. Johnson and Richard M. Nixon have visited the cathedral, and President Ronald W. Reagan paid a visit to Cardinal Terence Cooke at the archbishop's residence next door when the cardinal lay dying of leukemia.

St. Patrick's has hosted several ecumenical gatherings. One included the Anglican archbishop of Canterbury and another was held when the Dalai Lama came to New York. A number of prominent Catholics have been buried from St. Patrick's. In 1944, former Governor Alfred E. Smith, the first Catholic to run for president of the United States, lay in state in the cathedral. Funerals have also been conducted for former Postmaster General and legendary Democratic political leader James A. Farley, a member of the parish, and for Mayor Robert F. Wagner, Senator Robert Kennedy, and theatrical and sports personalities such as former Yankees Roger Maris and Billy Martin. Weddings of socially prominent New Yorkers regularly occur at the cathedral, but parish officials decline to disclose the names of these individuals in order to preserve their privacy.

The cathedral has been host to a variety of musical events and performances over the years. These have included concerts by Pavarotti, Domingo, and Carreras as well as groups such as the Vienna Boys' Choir, the Vienna State Opera Chorus, an African folk group from Upper Volta, and the Metropolitan Opera Orchestra conducted by Leopold Stokowski. Every Sunday afternoon there is an organ recital or some other musical performance. The cathedral now has a mixed choir of more than one hundred voices to assist at the numerous liturgies that are presented. Special Masses and celebrations are regularly held for Catholics in many walks of life: the New York Police and Fire Departments, radio and television network employees, State Department employees residing in New York, the Knights of Malta, the Catholic Daughters, and many others.

The doors of the cathedral are unlocked each morning about 6:30 and are normally locked each evening at 9:00, although they are often open much later for nocturnal adoration or an evening service, such as midnight Mass on Christmas Eve. Each week about sixty thousand people pass through those doors. Some come to pray while others come just to look. For those who come to pray, the church has pews that seat about twenty-five hundred people. There are eight Masses each weekday, having an average attendance of about 1,500 people, and nine Masses each weekend with an attendance that ranges from 6,000 to 8,000. The 10:15 Mass each Sunday morning is the cardinal's

Mass and for it there is usually standing room only. Confessions are heard daily. The first televised Mass from St. Patrick's took place in 1948. Since that time, midnight Mass on Christmas Eve has always been televised nationally.

Parish boundaries now extend from 44th to 59th Street and from Third to Seventh Avenue. There are only about three hundred resident parishioners, but this number fails to tell the story of a large number of New Yorkers (and New Jersey residents as well) who regard St. Patrick's as their spiritual home. Its volunteer program is well organized. As in the past, there are wide disparities in what remains of the residential community in midtown Manhattan. The parish boundaries include penthouses in the Waldorf Astoria Hotel and one hundred or more welfare hotels and rent-controlled apartments, especially near Times Square. Seventy or more volunteers regularly participate in a program called "Our Neighbors." They visit about two hundred elderly residents in these low-income residences, take them shopping or to medical appointments, and to an occasional recreational outing. The cathedral has always had an active young adults' club to reach out to the large number of career-minded single people who come to New York. For them the club presents both spiritual and social programs.

The trustees of the cathedral still have an active function in managing the "temporalities" of the cathedral. The ex-officio chairman of the board is the cardinal. Its membership is made up of prominent Catholic business and professional men who do not necessarily reside within the parish. One of their main functions is to supervise the operation of the cemeteries of the archdiocese to which legal title still reposes in the board. This is the New York version, on a grand scale, of managing the country churchyard that in quieter times typically surrounded a parish church. The cathedral has nearly thirty employees and, for this reason, has an operating budget that has always been difficult to meet.

For those who come to St. Patrick's only to look, the cathedral presents one of the premier tourist attractions in New York City. Each presiding archbishop since 1879 has added one or more new features or has improved upon an earlier one. One of the earliest improvements, completed about 1904, was the introduction of electric lighting. Some twenty-five hundred electric lights were installed to replace the eighteen hundred gas jets that had provided illumination since the time the cathedral opened.

When the cathedral was dedicated, it had five altars. It now has seventeen, each having a unique feature or history of its own. The high altar was installed in 1942 by Cardinal Francis Spellman. The previous altar was removed and given to Fordham University. The high altar is covered by a bronze canopy, or baldachin, whose arcs are thirty-eight feet above the pavement of the altar. The canopy is fifty-seven feet above the floor and is supported by four bronze pillars on which are bronze statues having the Redemption as their theme.

To the right of the Lady Chapel in the apse of the church is the altar of St. Elizabeth. The only altar constructed abroad, it was designed and built by the firm of Paoli Medici in Rome. After the Medici family lost the power that during the Middle

Ages brought members of the family to the papacy, it went into the church-restoration business in Italy. One of the products of that business can now be found at St. Patrick's. To the right of the Lady Chapel is the altar of St. Michael and St. Louis, the only known altar to be designed and built by Tiffany and Company, whose reputation was won by its expertise in stained-glass artistry rather than architecture. Underneath the high altar is the crypt which contains the remains of all of the archbishops of New York, two of the rectors of the cathedral, and Archbishop Fulton J. Sheen, the noted television personality and bishop of Rochester who frequently preached from the pulpit at St. Patrick's. As noted elsewhere in this volume, the remains of Pierre Toussaint were recently translated to this crypt.

Renwick actually designed the pulpit to the south of the high altar, the original baptistry, and the altars in the chapel of St. Veronica, St. John the Evangelist, and St. Anthony. He also designed the stained-glass window in the south transept which, in one scene, depicts St. Patrick, Archbishop Hughes, and Renwick himself.

In 1897, Archbishop Michael Corrigan blessed the nineteen bronze bells that constitute the cathedral carillon before they were installed in the north tower. The bells weigh from 173 pounds to 6,063 pounds and are named for various saints. Originally operated by compressed air, they were attached to an electric keyboard in 1952. Archbishop Corrigan also installed the stations of the cross, made in Holland, which contain figures that are two-thirds life-size. Three of these stations won first prize for religious art in the 1893 Chicago World's Fair.

In the 1920s and 1930s, Cardinal Hayes undertook the first of several renovations of the cathedral. It was a risky effort, since the Great Depression made it difficult to raise funds for such a purpose. During that era, there were occasions when the rector and the priests of the parish personally took up the collection on Sundays just to emphasize to the congregation the critical need for donations even to meet the operating expenses of the parish. Among the improvements that Cardinal Hayes was able to make was the installation of three organs. The great organ, installed in 1930, has 7,380 pipes, the longest of which is 32 feet; the chancel organ in the front of the church, installed in 1928, has 2,500 pipes.

In 1949, five bronze doors were placed in the entrances in the front and in the two towers. They are sixteen feet high and operate on specially designed pivots set on ball bearings and roller bearings sealed in oil. Each leaf of the central doors weighs ten thousand pounds. The various doors contain carved representations of American saints, of St. Joseph and St. Patrick, and symbols of the Christian faith.

In 1972, Cardinal Cooke began a multimillion-dollar renovation of both the inside and the outside of the cathedral. It took seven years to complete. One of the principal accomplishments of this renovation was to restore the original white marble exterior that had been covered over by a century of grime.

The cathedral originally had thirty-seven stained-glass windows; it now has seventy-one. At the time it was opened, those windows for which stained glass was not available were filled with what was known as cathedral glass composed of colored geometrical figures. The cathedral glass has been replaced incrementally over the years. The original stained-glass windows were designed and constructed either in Nantes or in Chartres. Most of the newer windows were made in the United States, principally in Boston. Most notable of these windows is the titular window, depicting twenty-five events in the life of St. Patrick; the window of the Blessed Virgin, depicting eighteen events in the life of the Blessed Virgin; and the Rose window, installed in 1947. The Rose window was designed by Charles Connick, one of the most noted stained-glass artists of the twentieth century. It has a motif that centers on heavenly beings, portraying angels, archangels, seraphim, and cherubim. The fifteen stained-glass windows in the Lady Chapel portray the fifteen mysteries of the rosary.

One problem in viewing the windows at St. Patrick's was never anticipated or addressed by the builders of medieval cathedrals in Europe. A full appreciation of this particular artistry depends upon the presence of rays of sunlight pouring through the glass at various times of day. This necessary backdrop has been severely inhibited by the construction of skyscrapers that now completely surround St. Patrick's and either block out or greatly diminish the amount of sunshine that can strike the cathedral.

In 1850, when he first proposed plans for the construction of St. Patrick's, Archbishop Hughes also announced the purpose of the new cathedral: "For the glory of Almighty God, for the honor of the Blessed and Immaculate Virgin, for the exaltation of Holy Mother Church, for the dignity of our ancient and glorious Catholic name, I propose to erect a cathedral in the city of New York which may be worthy of our increasing numbers, intelligence, and wealth as a religious community, and as a public architectural monument of the present and prospective greatness of this metropolis of the American continent." While he never lived to see the completion of this monument, hundreds of millions have. They have also seen it continue to fulfill the purposes the archbishop set out for it.

15
St. James Cathedral

Brooklyn

NEW YORK

Between 1636, when the first Dutch settlements were planned for Long Island, and 1801, when the village of Brooklyn was established at the western end of the island, the extent of organized Catholic activity on Long Island can be summed up very succinctly. There was none. The existence of a few individual Catholics on the island at that time can be inferred from the existence of a few Irish and French names on tax rolls and in old newspaper articles. There was an incident reported in 1657 when a local resident refused to pay the required tax to support the Dutch Reformed Church and was fined 12 guilders. His excuse — that he would not pay because he was a Catholic — was dismissed by a Dutch judge as being "frivolous." When Acadians were dispersed from Nova Scotia in 1755, some were put ashore on Long Island and were absorbed into the general populace, most of whom were either Presbyterian or Dutch Reformed. During the French and Indian War, French Army prisoners were temporarily confined on Long Island. Presumably, most of them were Catholics. However, this was the extent of a Catholic presence in an area where nearly three million Catholics now live.

In the first decade of the nineteenth century, after St. Peter's began functioning in lower Manhattan, a few priests from that parish occasionally crossed the East River to visit Catholics in Long Island. These included Father Louis Sibourd, Father John Byrne, and Father William O'Brien, the priest who brought Elizabeth Bayley Seton into the Church. However, any Catholic living in Brooklyn or elsewhere on Long Island who wished to attend Sunday Mass had to take the horse ferry or use a rowboat to cross the East River and then walk to St. Peter's on the western side of Manhattan. In winter months, ice floes made the river crossing a hazardous journey. After 1815, the land trip on Manhattan Island was somewhat shortened with the opening of Old St. Patrick's on Mulberry Street. One Brooklyn family who made this trip on a regular basis was that of Patrick McCloskey, an overseer at the Pierrepont Distillery in Brooklyn. His son, John, born in Brooklyn and baptized at St. Peter's, became America's first cardinal.

Brooklyn began to grow when the Navy Yard was established in 1801 and when additional ferry lines from Manhattan were added to supplement the original Main Street ferry that began in 1795. Some business and professional men began to find Brooklyn a pleasant residential area and erected large and imposing homes in Columbia Heights, now Brooklyn Heights, overlooking New York Harbor. Much of the new local population consisted of Navy Yard employees, artisans, and shopkeepers, many of whom were Irish. Reputedly, the first Mass said in Brooklyn was offered in the home of William Purcell just two blocks from the Navy Yard. Purcell was a Navy Yard employee who also kept a tavern. Mass was also said from time to time at Dempsey's Hotel on Fulton Avenue where an organization known as the Roman Catholic Society was formed. In 1816, Brooklyn village was enlarged. Its new boundaries far exceeded the limits of the old village.

Credit for establishing St. James Church is usually given to Peter Turner, an Irish immigrant who superintended a gun carriage shop at the Navy Yard and also operated a grocery store. Years later, Turner's son was to become rector of St. James Cathedral and vicar general of the Brooklyn diocese. A statue commemorating his efforts can be found in the small graveyard to the right of the entrance of the church.

On New Year's Day, 1822, Turner sent a circular letter to Brooklyn Catholics, asking them to attend a meeting the following week for the purpose of establishing a Catholic church in the city. The meeting took place in the long room at Dempsey's Hotel. It was estimated that at the time there were only about seventy Catholic householders in Brooklyn who would be financially able to contribute to the erection of a church. Other meetings took place shortly thereafter, and events moved swiftly toward the construction of a church. Bishop John Connolly of New York gave his support and approval to this enterprise, although he was not in a position to contribute any money.

In March of 1822, eight lots at the corner of Chapel and Jay Streets were purchased for $700. The trustees put $400 down and gave back a mortgage to secure a $300 note. The land was conveyed to seven named individuals as trustees for an organization known as the "Church in the Village of Brooklyn." The plot was blessed by Father Richard Bulger, a priest who was also instrumental in establishing the first Catholic church in northern New Jersey. A great deal of "sweat equity" went into the building of the original St. James Church. The building was designed to be sixty-three feet by forty-two feet, made of brick, and had four Gothic windows, one front door, and no tower. Mechanics and craftsmen would often go to the site in the evening after dinner and contribute a few hours' work before the sun set. When it was completed the following year, the inside of the church was still unplastered. The total amount of money spent during construction was about $7,000. Upon completion, a debt of $3,000 was still owed.

On August 23, 1823, Bishop Connolly came to Brooklyn to dedicate the church. It was the sixth church to be built in New York State and the third in what is now New York City. However, at the time, there were only eight priests in the entire New York diocese. Bishop Connolly could not afford to send one to St. James as a resident pastor, and initially the parishioners could not afford to support one. For instance, the collection on one Sunday in April 1825 was reported to be only $1.93. For the first two years of its existence St. James was served by priests from Manhattan who came to Brooklyn whenever they could be spared.

The parish did retain the services of Jeremiah Mehaney for the sum of $60 a year. Mehaney had the combined functions of sexton, cemetery caretaker, and schoolmaster of a school that was opened in the basement of the church just a few days after the dedication in 1823. Mehaney's place was taken three or four years later by John Murray, who remained at St. James for more than twenty years, fulfilling all of the assignments given to his predecessor. His principal function was to conduct the boys' section of the parish school after the Sisters of Charity arrived in Brooklyn to teach the girls' section.

In 1825, St. James received its first pastor, Father John Farnan. At that time, the total population of the city was about eight thousand. Father Farnan was an Irish immigrant who had been assigned to St. John's in Utica, the first Catholic church in western New York State. He was an energetic individual and promoted various Irish organizations, such as the Erin Fraternal Association and the Friends of Ireland. The latter had as its purpose Irish independence from Great Britain. In addition to his duties at St. James, he said Mass at Flushing, in Queens, at Fort Hamilton along the southwest shore of Brooklyn, and at Sag Harbor, a village at the far eastern end of Long Island about a hundred miles from St. James. In September 1829, Father Farnan was suspended by Bishop John Dubois because he reportedly showed up drunk at vespers. He appealed his suspension to the provincial council that was then meeting in Baltimore but to no avail.

While Father Farnan was forced to leave St. James, he did not leave Brooklyn. He attempted to organize his own church, which he called the "Independent Catholic Church," and began to collect money to erect a building a few blocks from St. James. His efforts ceased when funds ran out. Years later, the bishop of New York purchased these premises and organized the Church of the Assumption at that location. In 1847, Father Farnan was reinstated and allowed to join the new diocese of Detroit where he was assigned to serve an Irish parish. He died at the bishop's residence in Detroit in 1849.

The second pastor of St. James, Father John A. Walsh, was also an Irish immigrant.

He was sent to the parish in 1829 from Old St. Patrick's after Father Farnan left. By that time, the parish had grown to five thousand members. Father Walsh continued Father Farnan's practice of saying Mass in other localities when the opportunity presented itself and extended his missionary efforts to Astoria, Jamaica, and Williamsburg, which was then outside the Brooklyn city limits. Father Walsh encouraged cultural as well as religious activities at St. James. He held concerts of sacred music at the church, started a library, and organized the Young Men's Library Association. During his pastorate of twelve years, he was instrumental in sending a number of young men from St. James to the seminary at Mount St. Mary's in Emmitsburg, Maryland.

Visitors were beginning to come to St. James parish from elsewhere to make appeals for money to support churches, orphanages, and other Catholic institutions in other cities. They usually went away with generous donations. It was about this time that the city of Brooklyn received the title of City of Churches. The name could not have been prompted by the presence of many Catholic churches because there was only one. However, the title was a reflection of the fact that Brooklyn was a growing and attractive residential community that had been spared some but not all of the problems of its neighbor across the East River. One such problem was a cholera epidemic that broke out in 1832. It claimed the lives of two hundred seventy-four people, more than fifty of whom were buried in St. James cemetery.

In 1829, the Orphan Asylum Society was organized by Peter Turner, the man who had provided the impetus for organizing the parish itself, and it began to collect money for the establishment of an orphanage in Brooklyn. In 1831, the Sisters of Charity arrived at St. James to teach the girls in the parish school. Father Walsh bought additional land next to the church and erected a convent. For a number of years the Sisters lived at the convent and took in orphan girls as well. By 1838, the orphanage, called St. Mary's Asylum, had some eighteen girls living with the nuns. To support the parish and its school and orphanage, Father Walsh occasionally delivered lectures. Other fund-raisers were also conducted, such as a charity ball at Washington Hall, an art exhibit at the Brooklyn Lyceum, and a fair that was held in the meeting room at the Apprentices' Library where the Brooklyn Common Council held its meetings before the city hall was constructed.

One problem that Father Walsh had to confront repeatedly during his twelve years at St. James involved outbreaks of anti-Catholic agitation. One source of this antagonism was the Long Island *Star*, a newspaper that occasionally praised the work of Brooklyn Catholics when it was interested in soliciting Irish votes for its endorsed candidates. However, on other occasions it denounced Catholicism in venomous terms. Another source of anti-Catholicism revolved around certain Protestant ministers. In 1829, some seventy-three ministers organized the New York Protestant Association and founded a weekly paper called *The Protestant*. The purpose of the organization and its paper was to "expose the vile acts of Popery" and "the incompatibility of the Roman Catholic Religion with republican principles." Their paper circulated Maria Monk stories recounting alleged misconduct in a Montreal convent. These stories were also reprinted in the *Star* in serialized form. Later, an investigation of the charges was made, and they were exposed as a hoax; so, to its credit, the *Star* printed the results of the investigation as well.

The New York Protestant Association met regularly in several Brooklyn churches as well as in public school rooms. On two occasions, Father Walsh debated members of the association before large paying audiences. One question he debated was "Are the Clergy of the Roman Catholic Church justified in either withholding or forbidding their members to read the Holy Scriptures except through the medium of their Church?" At other public meetings, there was no debate but merely unanswered harangues on such topics as "Is the Roman Purgatory a Fiction?" or "Is the Roman Mass an Idolatry?" Some believe that the public disaffection of Father Farnan, a well-known fact in Brooklyn in the 1830s, added fuel to the fire of anti-Catholic sentiment. At this time, actual violence broke out in Manhattan, but there was none in Brooklyn until twenty years later. However, the anti-Catholic agitation had a political effect in Brooklyn. It drove Irish Catholics from the Whig and Nativist Parties and into the arms of the Democratic Party where they remained for many generations.

In 1805, Cornelius Heeney, who had aided many Catholic efforts in lower Manhattan, bought seventeen acres of land in Brooklyn on which he built his summer home. The property ran from the East River to Court Street. When St. James parish was being organized, he offered a part of this tract to the board of trustees of St. James Church, but they declined the offer because the land was too far from the center of population. In 1836, the trustees were ready to establish a second church at the far southwest corner of the city because St. James was becoming too crowded. They accepted an offer of land from Heeney for this purpose and undertook to organize St. Paul's parish at Court and Congress Streets, the second Catholic church in Brooklyn. The old brownstone building with its tall steeple, now the combined parish of St. Peter, St. Paul, and Our Lady of Pilar, stands today where the St. James trustees built it one hundred fifty years ago. Next to it, the Orphans Asylum Society built an orphanage on land also donated by Heeney. The orphanage was staffed for many years by the Sisters of Charity and, at one time, housed more than five hundred girls. The Sisters later opened a parochial school at St. Paul's.

Originally, the St. James trustees engaged Father Richard Waters to be pastor of the new church, but they soon fell into a disagreement with him so he was removed, at their request, by Bishop Dubois. The parish was then turned over to the Augustinian Fathers who remained about seven years. The new Augustinian pastor described the new parish rectory as follows:

> It is a fine airy place, and as a summer residence delightful. Our house is situated in about the centre of Brooklyn — I mean, as it stands on paper; but though we have fine houses scattered "far between" along the streets that stretch out on either side, we

are half a mile from the city proper and, were it not for the lamps and paved highways, I should fancy myself in the country altogether.

* * *

Our district embraces a circuit from seven to seventeen miles in diameter. The [Flatbush] Almshouse is five miles distant from us and we have frequent calls to that receptacle of human misery in every form. Besides, we are required to attend baptisms in the home of the parents and the fact is we cannot do without a horse and gig . . . [but] we go afoot and have no horse.

Heeney, the benefactor of the new church, died in 1846 and was laid to rest in St. Paul's churchyard.

At St. James, Father Walsh acquired more land. When the Sisters of Charity moved out of what was St. Mary's Asylum to the new orphanage at St. Paul's, he began to use the building as a rectory. Years later, when Brooklyn became a diocese, the building also served as the bishop's residence and remained as such for many years. Father Walsh left St. James in 1841, telling his congregation that he was going to enter a Trappist monastery in Ireland. It is understandable that the tranquillity of such a setting might have appealed to him after twelve hectic years in Brooklyn. However, after two years of peace and quiet, he returned to New York and was appointed pastor of a church in Harlem where he remained until his death in 1853.

In 1844, St. James Church was greatly enlarged to accommodate a rapidly growing parish. The building **[pictured above]** is eighty feet by one hundred fifteen feet. During the remodeling, it acquired a tower, a transept, and a new vestibule. A new wooden altar was also installed. The extension of the church was built over many graves and was elevated on pillars so that the grave markers would not be totally obscured. Three years later, the cemetery, which then held more than five thousand graves, was permanently closed, and a new Catholic cemetery, Holy Cross, was opened in Flatbush.

A boys' school was still being operated in the basement of the church until a new building, some thirty-five feet by sixty feet, was completed and the school placed in the hands of the Christian Brothers. In addition to an elementary school, the parish also conducted the Male Evening School to provide the rudiments of an education to a vast number of illiterate immigrants who were then pouring into Brooklyn. The Sisters of Charity, who had already moved out of the convent, ceased operating the girls' school in 1846. For a while it was turned over to a laywoman who had been conducting what was called a seminary for young ladies. In 1854, the Sisters of St. Joseph were retained to operate the girls' school, and they remained at the parish for many years until population changes in downtown Brooklyn made it impractical to continue to operate a parochial school.

In 1846, another of St. James's mission stops began to develop into a parish of its own. For years Catholics in Williamsburg, about three miles north, came to Mass at St. James across the Wallabout Causeway or they took an East River ferry to go to church at St. Mary's in Manhattan. Many were German and felt the need for a pastor who could speak their language. Bishop John Hughes sent Father John S. Raffeiner to Williamsburg to establish a German national parish, Most Holy Trinity. Father Raffeiner, an Austrian immigrant, had been educated as a physician and had fought in the Austrian Army against Napoleon before entering the priesthood. He had established a German parish in Manhattan before coming to Williamsburg and was given the title of vicar general for the Germans, a title that he retained in Brooklyn. During his ministry, Father Raffeiner visited German Catholics throughout the East Coast and is credited with founding over thirty German parishes during his lifetime.

In 1853, Brooklyn became a diocese that included all of Long Island. St. James became its cathedral. At that time, the Brooklyn diocese had about sixty thousand Catholics, twenty-four priests, and eight churches. Its first bishop was John Loughlin, who was born in Northern Ireland, grew up in Albany, and was ordained at Old St. Patrick's in 1840. He helped to found the St. Vincent de Paul Society at Old St. Patrick's and was vicar general of New York when he was appointed bishop of Brooklyn. Upon taking office as bishop, he moved into St. James rectory and lived there for the next thirty-seven years.

Bishop Loughlin participated in the life of the parish as well as administering his diocese from its rectory. Each Sunday for some thirty-five years he said the 7:00 A.M. Mass at St. James. He was an unprepossessing individual. He avoided controversy, kept what today would be called a low profile, and worked prodigiously. In his *History of the Diocese of Brooklyn*, Monsignor John K. Sharp described Bishop Loughlin as follows:

> Opposite the ancient church stood the old double red-brick house at 250 Jay Street, the first part of which was built in 1832. It had served as a convent, orphanage, rectory, and episcopal mansion. It was three stories and basement, and the upper floors had five windows on Jay Street. It had no modern conveniences.
>
> Here, from 1853 to 1888, Bishop John Loughlin maintained his residence. Anyone could call on him. One simply walked up the steps and struck the knocker above the door plate that read: "Rev. John Loughlin." As likely as not, he himself would open the door for the visitor and point out a place on the benches which lined the two sides of a somewhat shabby hall that served as a reception room. On the right was a library of 3,000 to 4,000 books, with an open coal-grate for the winter. When one's turn came, the caller entered the office on the left of the hall. It was stacked with old newspaper files and its desk was littered with papers. The bishop would transact business quickly and would accompany his visitor to the door as he addressed the assorted array of waiting people with the words, "Who's next?"
>
> The statement that John Loughlin worked harder than any of his priests is thoroughly credible. In fact, he was parish priest as well as bishop. He heard confessions on Saturday nights, preached at his early Sunday Mass, and often gave a catechetical instruction at afternoon vespers. He would confirm as often as three times a day. Many entries of baptisms and marriages at St. James' are in his fine handwriting.

Daily he crossed the street to say the early Mass and about nine o'clock walked to the post office for his mail. When he was not busy with callers, he traveled about the city visiting the institutions or conducting the financial and legal business of the diocese. He often carried a black telescope bag and, if he used the horse-drawn trolley, he preferred to stand and chat with the conductor at the rear platform. Later, he used a one-horse coupe. He did not care for civic functions and made almost no social engagements. . . .

Although Bishop Loughlin was one of the most prominent men in the old City of Brooklyn, his modest, unostentatious life made him one of the least known personally. Under an apparently rough exterior there beat a warm, fatherly heart; in the great qualities of charity and prudence, he was preeminent. Yet he was austere in his personal tastes and habits.

Bishop Loughlin arrived in Brooklyn just as anti-Catholic turmoil was about to break out again. This time, nativist sentiment became crystallized here, as in so many other places, in the emergence of the Know-Nothing Party, which had as its targets immigrants in general and Catholics in particular. The principal fomenters of trouble in Brooklyn were street preachers and pulpit preachers, who were aided by the press. Alessandro Gavazzi, an ex-priest and follower of Garibaldi, gave public talks both in Williamsburg and in Brooklyn during which he denounced the Catholic Church for opposing the placing of Protestant Bibles in public schools. The presence of Papal Nuncio Archbishop Gaetano Bedini in New York, as mentioned earlier in this volume, was another occasion for anti-Catholic hostility. The Long Island *Star* denounced the archbishop as a "notorious butcher" and "man skinner." In May of 1854, a number of street preachers were able to gather crowds on successive Sunday evenings on Atlantic Avenue, about a mile from St. James's and near St. Paul's, and to treat their listeners to strong denunciations of Catholics and Catholic teachings and practices. On one occasion, some three hundred Know-Nothings, who had taken the ferry to Brooklyn from Manhattan for the occasion, followed up the preaching by marching through the streets of Brooklyn beating up any Irish residents they came across. When the Irish were able to gather their forces, they chased the Know-Nothings to the Catherine Street ferry slip and forced them to take the boat back to Manhattan.

During the following week, rumors abounded that fifteen hundred men were coming to Brooklyn from Philadelphia to attack St. James's and St. Paul's Churches. For several days armed parishioners stood guard around each church building, but the rioters from Philadelphia did not appear. On Sunday, June 4, after listening to a street preacher lecture about the vices and errors of Romanism, a crowd of visiting Know-Nothings from New York, accompanied by two thousand Brooklyn supporters, began another march through the streets of Brooklyn. A crowd of twenty thousand soon gathered. To quell the mob, police fired into the crowd and the crowd retaliated with clubs and stones. The militia was then summoned and eventually restored order but not until after one person was killed and sixty were wounded. Bishop Loughlin instructed his pastors to warn parishioners to stay away from possible riot corridors, but this warning did not succeed in keeping peace.

On Sunday, June 11, during another anti-Catholic tirade by a street preacher named "Angel Gabriel" Orr, several in attendance who disagreed with him began to pelt him with paving stones. A pitched battle ensued and, in the course of the melee, several were injured; luckily, on this occasion, no one was killed.

The following November in Williamsburg, election-day disturbances occurred. Know-Nothings, assisted by deputy sheriffs, attacked Catholics as they went to the polls. During these riots, two were killed. Two nights later, mobs swirled through the streets of Williamsburg and threatened to destroy Catholic churches. The mayor summoned the militia, and a combination of four hundred soldiers and a rainstorm finally brought the disturbance to an end.

During this era, the most prominent church in the City of Churches was the Plymouth Congregational Church, located just a few blocks from St. James. Its presiding minister was the noted abolitionist, Henry Ward Beecher, whose father, Lyman Beecher, had stirred up mobs in Boston in 1834 that attacked the Charlestown convent of the Ursuline nuns. Beecher did not engage in street preaching, but he frequently made public statements from his pulpit or in the press attacking and disparaging Catholics, thereby lending a note of respectability to what was happening elsewhere. He was particularly vocal when Catholics did not support his candidate, John C. Fremont, who was running for president of the United States on an abolitionist platform. It was leaders like Beecher that made abolitionism highly suspect among Catholics of that day. They felt that it was hypocritical to seek to free slaves while at the same time trying to oppress others. Abraham Lincoln apparently shared that view. On August 24, 1855, he stated: "I am not a Know Nothing; how could I be? How can anyone who abhors the oppression of negroes be in favor of degrading certain classes of white people?"

During the Civil War, Bishop Loughlin and most Brooklyn Catholics supported the Union cause. The bishop directed that the American flag be flown over Catholic churches in his diocese. Draft riots, which caused many deaths and enormous destruction just across the East River in Manhattan, did not take place in Brooklyn where the Navy Yard was busily engaged in constructing and fitting out ships for the Union Navy. The St. Vincent de Paul Society from St. James Church engaged in welfare work to assist sailors stationed at the Navy Yard. Several Irish regiments, including the Fighting 69th, were organized in Brooklyn and saw service in many prominent battles. It has been estimated that one third of the Union troops recruited in Brooklyn were Catholics.

Bishop Loughlin was known as an astute purchaser of diocesan real estate. One purchase that he made seriously threatened the standing of St. James as the cathedral church of the Brooklyn diocese. In 1860, he bought the Sprader farm, about a mile east of St. James, at Lafayette and Clermont Avenues, to use as a site for a new cathedral. The land was purchased for $72,500 through a straw party. From the farm one could then see Coney Island and, after 1883, the Brooklyn Bridge. When it became known that the Catholic Church had actually bought the property, there was considerable public commotion and the Spraders tried to get their property back. They were unable to do so.

At the time, the archdiocese of New York was getting ready to move its own cathedral from lower Manhattan to the suburbs along Fifth Avenue, so Bishop Loughlin decided that Brooklyn would also build a new cathedral. He commissioned the design of a French Gothic cathedral, 350 by 160 feet, with a 180-foot transept, which would rise 350 feet into the air. The estimated cost was over a million dollars. It would be named in honor of the Immaculate Conception.

On Sunday, June 21, 1868, a procession began to gather in the heart of old Brooklyn and marched more than a mile to the laying of the cornerstone. There, some twenty thousand people, including prominent Catholic clergymen from all over the United States, gathered to hear Bishop Loughlin extol "a newer beauty, and another glory, and another honor, and another source of pride to what is already renowned as the city of churches." The Cathedral of the Immaculate Conception was never built. Unlike its counterpart in Manhattan, the diocese of Brooklyn simply ran out of money and had too many other demands on its limited resources to permit the construction of a church that would be only slightly smaller than St. Patrick's. All that was ever built were walls up to a height of fourteen feet, and St. John's Chapel, which served as the parish church for the locality until it was replaced by another church forty years later.

Bishop Loughlin's successor, Bishop Charles E. McDonnell, hired another architect in the early 1900s to complete the job. He also redesignated St. James as a procathedral, meaning that it was to be regarded only as a temporary cathedral until another, permanent one could be erected. Nothing happened, and the walls of Immaculate Conception Cathedral stood only partly finished for nearly fifty years, looking much like a medieval ruin in the midst of a growing residential neighborhood. The death knell for this project rang with finality when Brooklyn's first auxiliary bishop, George Mundelein, later archbishop of Chicago and "Cardinal of the West," was assigned to be pastor of Queen of All Saints Church and built another church right across the street from the projected cathedral. The new parish church was opened in 1913. In 1921, Bishop Thomas E. Molloy decided to use the walls and foundations of the "cathedral that never was" in order to build a high school. He finished the construction of the projected cathedral as a school building and named it after the bishop who had laid the cornerstone in 1868. Yet St. James still continued to be designated only as a procathedral.

One of the most prominent Catholics ever to have lived in St. James parish was Patrick C. Keely, whose name appears repeatedly in this volume. Keely was born in Ireland in 1816, learned the carpenter's trade from his father, and emigrated to Brooklyn in the 1830s. Without any formal training he set up shop as an architect specializing in the design and construction of Catholic churches. It was a fortunate choice of occupations, since large-scale construction of Catholic churches was getting under way and, in some areas, architects who designed Protestant churches would not accept a commission on a Catholic church. It is estimated that during his lifetime Keely designed and built 16 cathedrals and an additional 600 to 700 other churches; in his home diocese of Brooklyn alone, he designed about 50 churches and other Catholic buildings.

His first commission was in his own parish, St. James. He designed the entire reconstruction of the church that occurred between 1844 and 1846 as well as the wooden altar that was placed inside the new building. Of all the many churches he designed, the Immaculate Conception Cathedral in Brooklyn was to be his masterpiece. His initial rendering looked very much like St. Patrick's in New York. Keely lived the latter years of his life on Clermont Street, just across the street from the partially built edifice. He attended Mass at St. John's Chapel, the only part of the building to be completed. It must have seemed ironic that, in the final years of an extraordinary career, he had a reminder just outside his front door of his most important project but one that would never be finished. Keely was buried from St. John's Chapel in 1896.

In the years following the Civil War, St. James Church underwent a number of structural changes. In 1872, it received new floors, pews, windows, frescoes, and a side gallery. In 1883, a fire broke out and destroyed, among other interior furnishings, the old altar that Keely had painstakingly designed and installed, as well as the sanctuary and the window frames. Six years later, a bizarre calamity befell the church when two bolts of lightning struck within a ten-minute interval, cutting a hole in the roof and setting fire to the interior of the building. Mass was offered in the basement until the interior could be restored.

Several wealthy benefactors believed that St. James rectory was an inadequate residence for the bishop of Brooklyn, so they constructed a forty-room mansion near the "cathedral that was never built." Bishop Loughlin did not want to leave St. James and he waited for eighteen months after the new mansion was completed to do so. However, he eventually moved in and lived by himself in the new bishop's residence for the last years of his life. In October of 1890, to commemorate his fiftieth anniversary as a priest, the diocese of Brooklyn staged a mammoth celebration. As a part of it, the neighborhood around St. James was hung with bunting and a triumphal floral arch was constructed from the rectory across Jay Street to the church. The jubilee Mass was attended by prominent clergy from all over the United States. In the evening, a parade — including 50,000 laymen, 700 sailors from the Navy Yard, and 100 bands — marched through the streets of the city and passed in review to pay their respects to the city's first bishop. A year later, Bishop Loughlin died and was laid to rest in a crypt in the basement of the procathedral.

In 1898, Brooklyn ceased to be a separate city and became absorbed into the city of New York as one of its five boroughs. During this era, the area around St. James Church was beginning to change dramatically from residential to commercial and industrial. Many of its residential areas had already been demolished to provide access roads to the Brooklyn and Manhattan Bridges. To use Monsignor Sharp's description, the area was taking on the appearance of "shabby gentility." However, the parish still had eight thousand members. The boys' school had an enrollment of five hundred and the girls' school had an equal number of students. These changes in the character of the area did not prevent the parish from undertaking a substantial building program. A large and commodious rectory was built behind the church. The old rectory was torn down and replaced by a four-story building for the school, and the old boys' school that was built in the 1850s was removed and replaced with a park. The interior of the church was also renovated. One notable addition was an elaborate altar, made of various shades of marble, which was donated in the memory of Hugh McLoughlin, a Brooklyn political leader for many decades, who was buried in the cathedral churchyard.

In 1972, to celebrate the 150th anniversary of the church, St. James was again refurbished. At that time, Bishop Francis J. Mugavero announced that it would no longer be designated as a procathedral but would regain its original title as the principal church of the Brooklyn diocese. By that time, the Brooklyn diocese was composed only of Kings and Queens Counties, since the rest of Long Island was placed under the jurisdiction of the bishop of Rockville Centre. In referring to St. James, Bishop Mugavero remarked that "it is small and simple compared to many of our grand and beautiful churches, but it is rich in history and especially dear to the hundreds of priests who have been ordained at its altar."

During his tour of New York City in 1979, Pope John Paul II paid a visit to St. James. Three years later, he conferred upon it the status of a minor basilica in recognition of "its own religious and liturgical influence" and because "from it, legions of newly ordained priests have gone into the world and many other parishes have arisen."

The changes in the area that began at the turn of the century continued unabated. The area now includes both federal and state courts, government offices, a college, a large clothing factory, and other institutional establishments. The major residential component of the parish is Concord Village, an eleven-hundred-unit cooperative for senior citizens located just across the street from the church. The parish has only about one hundred fifty regular members and is supported, in part, by a diocesan subsidy. It hosts most functions that normally take place at a cathedral, such as the Holy Thursday chrism Mass and ordinations. Over the years, it has been the site of concerts, celebrations by various groups, and national conferences, such as one that took place in 1979 when representatives of sixty-five dioceses met to discuss the question of "cathedral revival."

The area once served by St. James alone now has a total of three hundred fifty churches and nearly twelve hundred priests working in two dioceses. The roots that began here in 1822 have grown into a tree that has extended far beyond Brooklyn.

16
Most Holy Trinity Chapel

West Point

NEW YORK

The United States Military Academy is located on a promontory in the Hudson Highlands where the river cuts through the Appalachian Mountains to make its way to the ocean. Located on the west side of the Hudson, West Point had military significance long before Congress decided that it would make a fitting site to train the officer corps of the United States Army. General George Washington sent Colonel Thaddeus Kosciuszko to West Point to construct a system of forts designed to secure the area from the British Army. Three years later, West Point formed the centerpiece of Benedict Arnold's unsuccessful plan to deliver the Hudson Valley and the New England colonies to the crown to which he had transferred his loyalties. Colonel Kosciuszko and a detachment of French-Canadian soldiers who assisted him in constructing and manning these Revolutionary War forts were the first Catholics to make their way into this region. When the Revolutionary War was over, they left.

The academy was established by an act of Congress in 1802; however, it was not until more than fifteen years later that it achieved any permanence as a military institution or recognition as a school of higher learning. Credit for this achievement is given to Sylvanus Thayer, who, as superintendent from 1817 to 1833, organized its curriculum and discipline, established standards for entrance and graduation, and improved its standing to the point that he is referred to as the "Father of the Military Academy." Colonel Thayer's brother, Father John Thayer (who is mentioned earlier in this volume), was a convert to Catholicism and an ordained priest. Colonel Thayer remained a Protestant, and the chaplain service that began shortly before he came to West Point remained a Protestant service. The first chaplain at West Point, the Reverend Adam Empie, was a minister who was appointed to his post in 1813. A civilian, Reverend Empie was required to teach history, geography, and ethics in addition to engaging in a religious ministry. It was not until 1896 that the academy was authorized a full-time chaplain. A chapel made of locally quarried granite, built in Classic Revival style, was erected on the military post in 1837 and was used throughout the nineteenth century. When the present Cadet Chapel was completed in 1910, the old Cadet Chapel was relocated to the edge of the post cemetery where it is still used from time to time for weddings, funerals, and other religious services.

The first Catholic graduate from the academy was Pascal Vincent Bouis, one of several French Catholics whom Thomas Jefferson appointed to West Point from the Louisiana Territory. Since his appointment in 1806, there have been Catholic cadets and Catholic officers, instructors, and enlisted men at the academy continuously, although their numbers were comparatively small until recent years. In the early 1800s, there were no Catholic churches or chapels either on or in the vicinity of this five-thousand-acre post. Records indicate that as early as 1830 Catholics at West Point crossed the Hudson to attend Mass at Our Lady of Loretto Church in Cold Springs or at another mission church over the hills in Arden, New York. Superintendents also permitted priests who came to the area to enter the post to attend to the religious needs of cadets and others assigned to West Point. In 1870, the archdiocese of New York established Sacred Heart parish in Highland Falls, a small town just outside the main gate. Contributions for building this church were obtained in part from Catholic personnel at the academy. In 1884, the Sacred Heart pastor, Father Thomas J. Early, wrote to the archbishop of New York informing him that four Masses were being said every Sunday, two in town and two on the post.

In 1890, Father Cornelius G. O'Keeffe was appointed pastor of Sacred Heart. Educated in Rome, Father O'Keeffe was a fluent linguist and, for a time, served as secretary to Pope Leo XIII. In 1896, when the U.S. War Department assigned a full-time Protestant chaplain to the academy, Father O'Keeffe wrote the academy superintendent requesting permission to erect a Catholic chapel on post. At that time, there were between twenty-five and thirty Catholics in the cadet corps, six Catholic professors, and a substantial number of Catholics among the enlisted personnel assigned to West Point. In the congressional debate that ultimately ensued from his request, the facilities then accorded to Catholics were described as a little chapel in a hollow that was "nothing more than an old ramshackle barn," located "down under the hill in a place needed for the storing of coal and other things." In this building, a temporary altar was erected and then removed after Mass was celebrated. For a while Catholic cadets were allowed to leave the post to attend Mass at Sacred Heart, just outside the gate, but this practice was contrary to normal academy discipline, which required cadets to stay on post unless given special permission to leave.

Father O'Keeffe proposed to the superintendent that the archdiocese of New York be given permission to erect and maintain a chapel at its own expense and to staff it with priests from the archdiocese. The request was approved by the superintendent and West Point's board of visitors, but it ran into a snag with the army judge advocate general, who felt that there was no statutory authority that would permit the secretary of war to issue a revocable license permitting the erection of a private church or chapel on a military reservation. Notwithstanding the judge advocate general's opinion, the outgoing secretary of war, on the final day of the Cleveland Administration, issued such a license, which contained several conditions, including the following. Any chapel erected at West Point would have to be constructed and maintained at private expense. Its location could not interfere with any military activities and its design would have to blend in with the prevailing architecture at the academy. The license further provided that it could be revoked at any time by the secretary of war, at which time the license holder would be obligated to dismantle and remove the chapel at his own expense. When the McKinley Administration took over, the license was renewed.

These actions did not anticipate the opposition of the American Protective Association (APA), whose function at the turn of the century was to protect the United States from Catholics. The APA regularly circulated tracts in which it misrepresented Catholic religious doctrines and practices and portrayed the Church as a public menace. It also acted as a pressure group to oppose Catholic activities and any type of public assistance that might benefit Catholics. The APA launched a campaign throughout the country to prevent the establishment of a Catholic chapel at West Point. It brought enough pressure upon the McKinley Administration that the license was revoked. The excuse for doing so was an opinion issued in May 1897 by Attorney General Joseph McKenna, himself a Catholic, that there was no legal authority in the United States Code for the issuance of such a license. The effect of this action was to toss a political hot potato into the lap of Congress.

Congressman Benjamin Odell, who represented the West Point area of New York in the House of Representatives, introduced a bill authorizing the secretary of war to grant a license to Catholics to erect a chapel at its own expense on the West Point military reservation. When the bill was reported to the floor of the House on June 29, 1898, it had been expanded to apply to any religious denomination. Representative William Sulzer of New York, the chairman of the committee on military affairs, expressed the hope that his colleagues would pass the bill without opposition. He was disappointed in this request. Representative Sulzer stated that "in my opinion, no fair-minded man can object to it or will object to it." He went on to say that the bill was absolutely necessary to permit a great many people at the United States Military Academy to enjoy the right to worship God according to the dictates of their own consciences. "I make bold to say that I do not believe there is a man in this House who is so illiberal, so bigoted, and so narrow minded that he is not willing to give his fellow man the same religious rights he enjoys. . . . I have only pity for the bigots in these closing years of the Nineteenth Century who would deny them that right."

He found such a man in Representative Stephen Northway of Ohio. Stating that he was not a member of any church, Representative Northway argued, "If you authorize the Secretary of War to allow a great Catholic Cathedral to be built there — and we are told that is what is to be done — you array all the Protestant churches of America quietly against that school. It is an entering wedge that will not, I tell you, cease to be felt in its effects for the next generation. This Government ought not to interfere with the building of churches." When Representative Northway was reminded that the government had already built a Protestant church at West Point, his reply was: "No sir; it is a Government church." Perhaps the most cogent comment uttered during the debate came from Representative David Henderson of Iowa, who called the whole controversy a "tempest in a teapot." The argument that carried the day was that all cadets were required by academy rules to attend religious services each Sunday, so it was only fair that they should be allowed to attend a service of their own choosing. The bill passed by a vote of 134 to 25, but the interesting feature of the roll call is that sixteen members answered "present" while one hundred eighty did not vote at all. Plainly, many congressmen were ducking a hot issue, just as the Administration had done. The debate in the Senate was milder and shorter. The House bill unanimously passed the Senate a week later and was signed into law by President William McKinley on July 8, 1898. On April 2, 1899, a new license, containing all of the restrictions found in the previous licenses, was issued by the secretary of war. It is still in effect.

The superintendent of the academy designated a tract of land located on a hillside overlooking the Hudson as the site for the new chapel. At that time, it was at the outskirts of the post, a ten-minute walk from the barracks and the classrooms. It is now well within the developed portion of the reservation. The chapel, named in honor of the Most Holy Trinity, was built of granite and modeled after St. Ethelred's Carthusian Abbey Parish Church in Essex, England, the first church to be restored to Catholic worship after the Reformation in that country. The original chapel seated about two hundred seventy-five people. There are Tiffany stained-glass windows on the right side of the chapel and other stained-glass windows on the left side of the chapel depicting military saints, such as St. Louis IX, St. Barbara, St. Martin of Tours, St. Joan of Arc, and St. Michael the Archangel as well as various military orders of the Catholic Church. On June 10, 1900, it was formally dedicated. Speaking at the dedication was Father George De Shon, who graduated from West Point in 1843 and was a classmate of Ulysses S. Grant. Father De Shon was formerly an instructor at the academy who had resigned his commission in the army to enter the priesthood. At that time, he was superior general of the Paulist Fathers.

The chapel was operated as a mission of Sacred Heart Church in Highland Falls until 1926 when it was canonically erected as a territorial parish of the archdiocese of New York. Its boundaries were and remain the West Point military reservation. This means that the pastor is not a military chaplain but a parish priest responsible for the spiritual welfare of all Catholics living within his parish. As such, Most Holy Trinity is quite different from chapels found on the grounds of other service academies and on military, naval, and air bases throughout the world. These chapels are built and maintained by the government, are interdenominational in character, and are staffed by clergymen who serve as military officers assigned to the various corps of chaplains.

In 1926, Father John A. Langton was appointed the first pastor of Most Holy Trinity parish. He found that he had no rectory, so he rented a room at the Hotel Thayer, a government hotel located at the entrance of the post, and established a rectory in his hotel room. In 1932, his successor asked and received permission to erect a residence adjacent to the chapel. As in the case of the chapel itself, the rectory was constructed at private expense.

In 1958, the number of Catholics in the cadet corps had increased to about seven hundred fifty. In addition, there were about two hundred fifty Catholic single officers and enlisted men on post as well as one hundred seventy-five Catholic families. The chapel was proving to be inadequate to service this expanding parish, so permission was obtained to enlarge its seating capacity to five hundred fifty. Another license was required for this purpose but it was issued by the district engineer of the Army Corps of Engineers without the controversy that followed the issuance of the original license. A campaign among West Point alumni, led by Lieutenant General J. Lawton Collins, class of 1917, raised enough money to pay for the enlargement.

The Chapel of the Most Holy Trinity **[pictured above]** is one of five chapels located at West Point. In 1910, the new Cadet Chapel, an enormous granite Gothic church, was built at public expense in a prominent location overlooking the central portion of the grounds. Among its many noteworthy features is an organ with eighteen thousand pipes, which was donated by West Point alumni. It is the largest pipe organ in North America. The Cadet Chapel is maintained and staffed at public expense and is used exclusively for Protestant services, as is the Post Chapel that was constructed during World War II to accommodate Protestant soldiers and staff and their families. Near the Catholic chapel is a Jewish synagogue that was completed in 1984. It was built by private subscription but was turned over to the army and is now maintained and staffed at public expense.

Until 1972, cadets were required to attend religious services. The academy regulations then in effect provided: "Attendance at Chapel is part of a cadet's training; no cadet is exempt. Each cadet must either attend the Cadet Chapel, Catholic Chapel, or Jewish Chapel services each Sunday, according to announced schedules." The U.S. Air Force and Navy academies had similar regulations. These regulations provided for excuses from attendance in cases of bona fide personal convictions of students opposed to church attendance. However, facts adduced at a lawsuit brought to challenge these regulations indicated that no cadet at West Point had ever been excused from chapel attendance and that only three midshipmen at Annapolis had been granted such excuses over a period of forty years. A class action affecting the U.S. Army, Navy, and Air Force academies was filed in federal court claiming that their regulations were an unconstitutional establishment of religion. The government responded by insisting that these traditional practices, going back in some instances for more than a century, were an integral part of the formation of an officer. In a 2 to 1 decision in *Anderson* v. *Laird*, the U.S. Court of Appeals for the District of Columbia sided with the plaintiffs and held that chapel attendance requirements at all of the academies were unconstitutional. The Supreme Court refused to review the case. Accordingly, since 1972, the Long Gray Line has not marched to Mass or to any other religious observance.

Today, the academy has eighteen hundred Catholic cadets. They constitute about thirty-eight percent of the entire cadet corps. This figure is somewhat lower than the forty-six percent that existed in 1980. Catholics also constitute a large proportion of the cadet and midshipmen corps at the other service academies. In 1988, those figures were: U.S. Naval Academy at Annapolis, Maryland, 47 percent; U.S. Coast Guard Academy at New London, Connecticut, 50 percent; U.S. Air Force Academy near Colorado Springs, Colorado, 42 percent; and U.S. Merchant Marine Academy at Kings Point, New York, 47 percent. Most Holy Trinity also serves an additional nine hundred single officers and enlisted men as well as about three hundred fifty families who live on or near the post. The ninety-year-old chapel is in need of substantial repairs to its leaky roof, cracked limestone, loose tiles, and decaying copper, so it has undertaken a $350,000 private fund-raising effort among parishioners and West Point alumni to meet this need.

No figures exist that show the exact number of Catholic Cadets who have attended Holy Trinity Chapel since it was dedicated in 1900. Over two thousand West Point alumni are among contributors to its fund-raising campaigns, but this figure is only a fraction of the number of Catholics who have graduated from West Point. At least twenty-one academy graduates have been ordained to the priesthood. The first was Father James Clark (1829 graduate and a classmate of Robert E. Lee), who resigned his commission, entered the Jesuits, and went on to become president of Holy Cross College and thereafter vice-president and treasurer of Georgetown University. The parish believes there are other priests among West Point graduates but their identities are presently unknown. Although cadets are no longer required to attend religious services, a very high percentage of the Catholic student body does so voluntarily. Most Holy Trinity maintains the full range of activities both for them and for its other parishioners that are normally found at civilian parishes, including a CCD program that has enrolled more than two hundred children. Since 1977, the Department of the Army has provided a military chaplain to augment the Catholic program and to assist the pastor and his associates. The latter are still supplied by the archdiocese of New York.

West Point has always believed that higher education consists of something more than offering students a smorgasbord of facts and ideas. It also includes character formation. The West Point anthem expresses the hope that "then, may that Line of Gray increase from day to day." As the Line of Gray has increased in recent decades, its Catholic proportion has also dramatically increased. As this has occurred, Most Holy Trinity Chapel has continued to grow in order to assist the academy in providing Catholic cadets with the vital element of character formation they are expected to receive on their way to becoming officers and gentlemen.

17
St. John the Baptist Cathedral

Paterson
NEW JERSEY

In colonial times, New Jersey was not a hospitable place for Catholics. There is a record indicating that Catholic baptisms were performed at Woodbridge and that priests from New York visited the colony during the reign of James II (1685-88). However, this practice ceased when Britain's last Catholic monarch was removed from the throne. There are no Catholic establishments in New Jersey dating back to that era. In 1680, William Douglas was elected to the New Jersey General Assembly from Bergen. When it found that he was a Catholic, the general assembly expelled him and declared his seat vacant.

In 1738, New Jersey became a crown colony separate and apart from New York. Instructions issued from London to the new governor, Lewis Morris, stated, "You are to permit a Liberty of Conscience to all Persons (except Papists)." This was in sharp contrast to the treatment being accorded to Catholics west of the Delaware River by William Penn and his descendants. In 1756, Bishop Richard Challoner, the vicar general of the London district (and hence the principal Catholic official for all of Britain's American colonies), wrote: "There are about 12 missionaries in Maryland, and, as they say, about 16,000 Catholics, including children, and in Pennsylvania about six or seven thousand under five missioners. Some of these also make excursions in one direction into the neighboring province of Jersey, and on the other into that of Virginia, and secretly administer the sacraments to Catholics residing there."

This reference to occasional visits included visits by Father Theodore Schneider, a German Jesuit residing at Goshenhoppen, Pennsylvania. In 1743, he said Mass at the home of Maurice Lorentz. Later, he went to the Glass House, near Salem, New Jersey, and to the home of Matthew and Adam Geiger in Salem County. The Geiger home became one of his regular mission stops. Father Schneider also established another mission stop at Bound Brook, New Jersey. Before coming to the American colonies, Father Schneider had received some medical training, so he often passed himself off as a medical doctor while making missionary rounds.

Beginning in 1757 and continuing until his death in 1786, another Jesuit missionary, Father Ferdinand Farmer, also visited New Jersey on a regular basis, using Old St. Joseph's Church in Philadelphia as his base of operations. (As mentioned earlier in this volume, Father Farmer, whose name pops up occasionally, changed his name from Steinmeyer.) He traveled south from Philadelphia to Salem and north to Ringwood, a mining area inhabited by German Catholics along the New Jersey-New York border. Catholics from the Black Forest region in Germany arrived in this area as early as 1764. These visits took place twice a year and ultimately involved such mission stops as Charlottesburg, Pilesgrove, Cohansey, Long Pond (now Greenwood Lake), Mount Hope, Gloucester, and Pompton. St. Joseph's parish in West Milford has sacramental records dating back to these mission stops, although it did not have a parish church until 1829.

Hostility toward Catholics in New Jersey continued well into the Revolutionary War era. A state constitutional convention was meeting at Burlington, about fifty miles north of Philadelphia, at the same time the Continental Congress was meeting at the Pennsylvania State House to draft the Declaration of Independence. On July 2, 1776, two days before the signing of the Declaration of Independence, a provision was adopted into the proposed New Jersey state constitution by the Burlington convention that read: "Art. XVII . . . that no protestant inhabitant of this colony shall be denied the enjoyment of any civil right merely on account of his religious principles; but that all persons professing belief in the faith of any protestant sect who shall demean themselves peaceably under the government, as hereby established, shall be capable of being elected to any office of profit or trust, or being a member of either branch of the legislature." Similar restrictions against Catholics in public office could be found in the New Jersey state constitution until the 1840s.

The first Catholic church established in New Jersey was founded in 1814 in Trenton, which by then had become the capital of the state. Catholic services had been held in Trenton as early as 1799. The parish was originally called St. John's but is now known as Sacred Heart. Until 1830, it was served by Augustinian missionaries coming from St. Augustine's Church in Philadelphia. After that time, it acquired a permanent resident pastor.

In a certain sense, St. John the Baptist Cathedral in Paterson might be considered the oldest parish in New Jersey inasmuch as it had, as its first pastor, the first resident priest to be assigned to any Catholic parish in New Jersey. The cathedral [**pictured above**] is the third church to be built at St. John's in its one hundred seventy years and occupies the third site to be used for a parish church. Catholics who first came to northern New Jersey in the early 1700s from the Black Forest in Germany worked in an iron mine in the Ramapo Mountains of Passaic County. As already noted, Father Ferdinand Farmer, a German-speaking Jesuit missionary from Philadelphia, occasionally visited Catholics in nearby Macopin and elsewhere in the region in the era that immediately preceded the American Revolution. While he was prefect apostolic, Father John Carroll came to Macopin in 1785 to administer confirmation.

Water power from the Passaic River provided the first incentive for manufacturing in the area. In 1791, when he was U.S. secretary of the treasury, Alexander Hamilton obtained from the New Jersey legislature a charter providing for an organization known as the Society for Establishing Useful Manufactures (SUM). This organization bought land and tried to develop the Paterson area. The city's first industry was a grist mill, but it was followed by cotton, linen, paper, and machinery manufacturing. Later in the 1800s, silk-manufacturing firms settled in the city and became its principal industry until they fell victim to synthetic substitutes, labor problems, and the lure of the South for runaway shops that desired to leave the area to take advantage of low wage scales elsewhere. However, Paterson still claims the title of the Silk City.

The first Mass said in Paterson was offered in 1817 by Father Philip Larissey, an Irish Augustinian, who conducted services in the Gillespie home on Market Street. Soon thereafter, Mass was said from time to time at the McNamee home on Broadway by Father Arthur Langdill from New York City, who followed a mission route that took him at regular intervals to Paterson, Macopin, and Newark. At that time, there were more Catholics in Paterson than in any other part of northern New Jersey.

Paterson's first resident priest was Father Richard Bulger, a young Irish immigrant and a graduate of Kilkenny College. He obtained land from SUM, which was then headed by Roswell C. Colt, and built a single-story building, twenty-five feet by thirty feet, at Market and Mill Streets in 1820. In order to stimulate development, SUM made land grants to various religious denominations but attached to each deed a requirement that the land be used for religious purposes or revert to the corporation. The first St. John's Church had a plain altar, wooden benches without backs, and seated about fifty people. The congregation was composed of about thirteen families. In addition to saying Mass in Paterson each Sunday, Father Bulger administered a parish that included several counties. This same area now comprises the diocese of Paterson, which, some 170 years later, has 367,000 Catholics served by 450 priests in 111 parishes.

Father Bulger died in 1824, just nine years after he was ordained, and was replaced by Father John Shanahan, who also died at an unusually early age. As work began on the Morris and Essex Canal, more Irish moved into the area to work on the project so that the population of St. John's parish increased dramatically. A gallery was constructed in the frame church building when it was not large enough to accommodate the growing congregation. Bishop John Dubois of New York prevailed upon Colt and SUM to allow the parish to sell the Mill Street property, notwithstanding the reverter clause in the deed, so it could buy other land for a larger church. The request was approved, and Colt indirectly made a $2,000 gift to the parish to help buy land on Oliver Street on which the second church was built. A brief factional dispute occurred among the trustees as to whether the old church should be enlarged or whether a new one should be built. The latter view prevailed, after which a new building, some fifty-five feet by one hundred feet, was erected. It was later enlarged, and galleries were added in order to increase its seating capacity to thirteen hundred.

At the time of the Civil War, Paterson had grown to twenty thousand inhabitants. The Oliver Street church proved to be too small for the rapidly growing Catholic population, so plans were drawn for a third structure, to be located at Grand and Main Streets. Sixteen lots were purchased from SUM for this purpose at the unheard-of price of $10,000, but the members of the congregation, flush with wartime prosperity, were able to raise the amount in two months. The development of St. John's for the next two generations was placed in the hands of one of the many old Irish monsignors whose vision, determination, and single-minded dedication guided the destinies of many Catholic parishes in the United States during this period of immigration and rapid expansion. Born in Ballyshannon, Ireland, Father William McNulty spent fifty-nine of his ninety-four years as pastor of St. John's parish in Paterson. He became dean of the Catholic clergy in Paterson and was usually addressed by that title. In 1865, Dean McNulty assisted in laying the cornerstone of the present church. It was constructed of brownstone hauled by canal from Little Falls and had a roof made of slate imported from England. The church seated 1,750 people and took five years to build. It cost $232,000 at the time of its completion in 1890, a sum that Dean McNulty was able to raise over a period of twenty years. He relocated the altar from the Oliver Street church, imported stained-glass windows from Austria, and installed a pipe organ with nineteen rows of pipes. The organ was enlarged half a century later to include about two thousand pipes. Although a diocese had been created in nearby Newark in 1853, Dean McNulty believed that Paterson would someday have its own bishop and St. John's would be his cathedral. He was right, but he never lived to see that day.

The parish had opened a small orphanage in 1850, some years before Dean McNulty came to Paterson, but the Civil War created many more orphans in Paterson so he enlarged it in 1867 to accommodate children of deceased soldiers. He did so by purchasing a large farmhouse near a cemetery that he was establishing at the same time on the outskirts of the city. He converted the farmhouse into an orphanage and prevailed upon the Sisters of Charity from Convent Station, New Jersey, to operate it. The old orphanage was made into a twelve-bed hospital, called St. Joseph's. It was relocated the following year and, at its new site, eventually grew into the largest Catholic hospital in the state of New Jersey.

St. John's opened the first parochial school in New Jersey in 1835. It is still in operation. For twenty years it was taught by laymen, then by a diocesan order of nuns, the Sisters of Charity from Convent Station. They remained until 1974, at which time there were replaced by the Salesian Sisters. The Christian Brothers were employed to teach the boys at the elementary school. They remained in the parish until 1923. In the 1880s, Dean McNulty built a three-story brick building on Oliver Street to permit the school to be enlarged. In 1895, the parish opened a high school that it operated for more than eighty years until it was consolidated with Paterson's Regional Catholic High School. Today, St. John's elementary school is over 150 years old and has more than 875 students; added to this number are about 250 preschoolers in the day-care center the parish now operates for working mothers.

Over the years, Paterson began to acquire heavy industry. The Colt Manufacturing Company began to make firearms that were used in the Mexican War. By 1880, the city was producing locomotives. Many years later, the Wright Aeronautical Company made airplane engines used in World War II. The industrialization of the area brought prosperity to some and poorly paid jobs to others. About the turn of the century, Dean McNulty was able to start St. Francis Residence for working girls who were employed in the various factories in the city and were badly in need of a home away from home. He also brought the Little Sisters of the Poor to Paterson where they opened a home for the elderly poor. In addition to these charities, the parish sponsored athletic teams and a large number of cultural events, such as dramatic performances and debating. It had a large laymen's club called the Entre Nous, which promoted these programs and also conducted religious education classes for Catholic children attending public schools.

At least eight parishes were established in Paterson as outgrowths of St. John's and Dean McNulty had a hand in helping each of them get started. In addition to these territorial parishes, national parishes for Italians, Poles, Lithuanians, and Syrians can trace their origins to St. John's Lady Chapel, which was made available to them, each in turn, until these groups could afford to build their own parishes. When Dean McNulty died in 1922, all the factories and businesses in the city closed their doors for a day. It was said that when the front part of his funeral cortege reached Holy Sepulchre cemetery, which he had established fifty years earlier at the edge of the city, the end of the procession was still leaving the church. In 1924, Dean McNulty was reinterred in front of the cathedral at the same time a statue honoring his memory was unveiled. Instead of using a triumphal ecclesiastical pose, the sculptor, a Paterson resident named Gaetano Frederici, captured the old man sitting in a chair chatting with a young boy standing next to him. (Years later, this same sculptor contributed a statue on the opposite side of the church honoring Paterson's first bishop, Thomas H. McLaughlin.)

In 1937, Paterson became a diocese and St. John's was designated to be its cathedral. The church was renovated and landscaped in anticipation of this event. Major diocesan functions take place at the cathedral on principal holidays, and ordinations occur here as well. While vocations have declined recently here as elsewhere, a parish history written in 1970 pointed out that at that time St. John's parish and its high school had, over the years, produced more than sixty priests and nearly one hundred nuns.

It is estimated that the population of Paterson, now about 150,000, will soon be more than ninety percent black and Hispanic. This demographic fact has had considerable impact on a parish that is located in the heart of the city. St. John's now has about nine hundred registered families and serves many more who are not formally affiliated with it. As early as 1965, the parish began to have a Mass said in Spanish. Today, two Masses each weekend are in English and two are in Spanish; all are filled to capacity. Older Irish parishioners, many of whom now live beyond the parish, come back each Sunday for the English Masses. Most of the parish is composed of members of sixteen different Hispanic nationalities, principally Peruvians, Puerto Ricans, and Cubans. These national groups each have their own individual celebrations throughout the year. Peruvians, who are among the most active, have five celebrations each year involving parades in which they carry statues of saints in procession throughout the streets of downtown Paterson.

The parish conducts CCD classes both in English and in Spanish and has weekend classes for adults who wish to learn English as a second language. These classes are popular and have enrolled more than sixty people. During the registration period provided in recently enacted changes to the immigration laws, the parish was active in encouraging eligible undocumented aliens to apply for amnesty. Hispanic residents constitute both the younger and less affluent portions of the parish population. Teams of these parishioners regularly go from door to door in Hispanic neighborhoods in downtown Paterson in an effort to evangelize other Hispanics who are cultural Catholics but have been lax in meeting their religious obligations.

In 1987, the cathedral was closed for a period of time so that it could be totally renovated and redesigned to meet the requirements of the revised liturgy of Vatican II. One immediate problem that St. John's is trying to remedy is one facing many downtown parishes, namely lack of parking space that discourages older residents and those living some distance from the church from attending Mass. St. John's uses its community building not only as a center for evangelization but for holding cursillos, retreats, and charismatic services. Its myriad current activities, directed toward the needs of a totally different population from the one that built the parish, carry on a parish tradition of activism the old dean set in motion more than a century ago. In so doing, St. John's is assisting another group of Catholic immigrants to establish its roots in America.

18
St. Joseph

Philadelphia
PENNSYLVANIA

There is a suggestion in some histories that public Masses were said in Philadelphia as early as 1707 and that complaints concerning such activities were registered with British officials. It is certain that in 1729 Father Joseph Greaton, a Jesuit missionary, purchased property at 206 Chestnut Street and said Mass privately in his dwelling. In 1731, Father Greaton purchased additional property on the south side of Walnut Street, between Third and Fourth Streets, and erected a house on this site. He then built a small chapel, about eighteen feet by twenty-eight feet, adjacent to the house, near a small passageway running from Third to Fourth Street known as Willing's Alley. Like several "Mass houses" that were built in colonial America, the original St. Joseph's Church was constructed to resemble a private residence. Under the English penal laws it was permissible to say Mass in a private dwelling but not in a public oratory. Under this pretext, he began to say Mass in St. Joseph's Chapel in 1732 in what was actually the kitchen of his residence. Eleven people attended the first Mass.

Deputy Governor Patrick Gordon complained to the provincial council of Pennsylvania about the "scandal" that public Masses were in fact being said in Father Greaton's chapel. Father Greaton's response was to go public: "We have an open and public chapel back of Walnut Street where Mass is publicly celebrated and all the practices of religion publicly performed by right of Charter of William Penn. Our land is in Pennsylvania, not in Maryland, and we are and of right ought to be free and independent of all civil authority retarding, restricting, or debarring our religion. It is not toleration we claim. It is freedom we demand and will maintain."

The provincial council, which was made up in large part of Quakers, noted in the minutes of its meeting of July 25, 1734, that "the Governor then informed the Board that he was under no small concern to hear that a house lately built in Walnut Street, in this City, has been set apart for the exercise of the Roman Catholic religion, and is commonly called the Romish Chappel where several persons, he understands, resort on Sundays to hear Mass openly celebrated by a Popish priest; that he conceives the tolerating of the publick exercise of that religion to be contrary to the laws of England." The council, relying on William Penn's Law of Liberty of Conscience of 1701, agreed with Father Greaton and decided to take no action against the maintenance of the chapel. As a result, it became the only church in England's North American colonies where the Catholic religion could be practiced both publicly and lawfully.

In 1757, the next pastor, Father Robert Harding, S.J., built a larger chapel, some forty feet by sixty feet, to replace the one that Father Greaton had erected. At that time, Father George Hunter, the Jesuit provincial, wrote that "we count about 10,000 customers" in Maryland and Pennsylvania, employing the code word for communicants that the missionaries used at the time to describe the Catholics under their care. There were about four hundred "customers" in Philadelphia. As noted in the following chapter, Father Harding bought additional land for a cemetery and also built a larger chapel at the cemetery site, sometimes referred to as "Mission No. l" or St. Mary's. The new chapel came to be used on Sundays and for large celebrations while St. Joseph's Chapel was relegated for use during the week.

One event that took place during the Revolutionary War at St. Joseph's Chapel was a memorial service conducted in honor of Don Juan Mirales, the Spanish envoy to the Continental Congress, who died at George Washington's camp across the Delaware River at Morristown, New Jersey. As a public event honoring the representative of a foreign nation, the service was well attended by members of Congress and other high officials, including General Benedict Arnold. A few months later, when Arnold decided to switch to the British cause, he wrote a letter to the officers and soldiers of the Continental Army, dated October 2, 1780, in which he attempted to induce them to abandon the Revolutionary cause. As one of his arguments, he stated: "Do you know that the eye which guides this pen lately saw your mean and profligate Congress at Mass for the soul of a Roman Catholic in purgatory, and participating in the rites of a Church against whose anti-Christian corruptions your pious ancestors would have witnessed with their blood?"

During the colonial era, priests from St. Joseph's visited mission stations throughout Pennsylvania, New Jersey, and in parts of New York. As noted previously, Father Ferdinand Farmer, a German Jesuit, was stationed at St. Joseph's and also visited New York City. Because of the suppression of the Jesuit order by the Holy See in 1773, St. Joseph's ceased to have either Jesuit or ex-Jesuit pastors by about 1800, when Father Leonard Neale, soon to be ordained as John Carroll's auxiliary bishop, departed for Georgetown. Moreover, with the formation of an active parish at St. Mary's and its designation by Bishop Michael Egan, Philadelphia's first bishop, as his cathedral, St. Mary's became the center for Catholic activity in Philadelphia for twenty years. Old St. Joseph's function was limited to providing a rectory for priests of St. Mary's parish.

The effect of the schism that occurred when Bishop Henry Conwell placed St. Mary's Cathedral under interdict in 1822 was to revive St. Joseph's as a parish for the first time since colonial days by providing Bishop Conwell and his followers with a place of worship. Immediately upon placing St. Mary's under interdict, Bishop Conwell enlarged St. Joseph's Chapel in 1821 so that it could accommodate the large numbers who remained loyal to him. Among the priests stationed at St. Joseph's during the stormy days of the 1820s was Father John Hughes, who later became archbishop of New York. The parish was able to rent out all of its one hundred fifteen pews, one of which was taken by Joseph Bonaparte, brother of Napoleon and former king of Spain, who lived in the parish. His son was baptized by Bishop Conwell at St. Joseph's. Records indicate that in 1827 Bishop Conwell confirmed 700 at the Church and that in 1829 the parish was the site of 119 marriages, 347 baptisms, and 200 funerals. It had a very busy parish life.

By 1833, Bishop Francis P. Kenrick had solidified his position as bishop of the Philadelphia diocese. For a while he lived at St. Joseph's, as did the aging Bishop Conwell, who persisted in referring to his successor as "that boy." Bishop Kenrick found other quarters and began to look for help in running his diocese, which now had 100,000 Catholics in Pennsylvania and southern New Jersey. To assist him in this task he had only thirty-eight priests, twenty-nine of whom were diocesan, and he welcomed the Jesuits in taking back their old parish on South Fourth Street so he could place the secular clergy then at the parish in other assignments. In April of 1833, the Jesuits again took charge of St. Joseph's and have been there since that time. Since that date, St. Joseph's and St. Mary's have existed as separate parishes. Both are territorial parishes, divided by Fourth Street, with St. Joseph's boundaries running eastward to the Delaware River and St. Mary's territory running westward to Ninth Street.

The church building that the Jesuits regained was described by a contemporary writer as a "lowly edifice, tottering to decay." A meeting was held in 1838 to raise funds for a new church; funds were solicited from all of the other parishes in the city. The old chapel was demolished and the cornerstone of a new church was laid on June 4, 1838. The present church [**pictured above**] was consecrated in February 1839, an event indicating that the entire building had been paid for by that time. Father Felix Barbelin, S.J., became an assistant pastor in 1838 and was appointed pastor in 1844. He served in that position until his death in 1869. During his stewardship, the parish was fully revived, notwithstanding the fact that the area surrounding St. Joseph's was becoming more and more commercialized and was gradually losing many of its parishioners as a result of the elimination of residential areas. For a number of years the parish had operated a girls' school on Locust Street that had nearly one hundred students. The first parish sodality to be established in the United States was founded by Father Barbelin at St. Joseph's in 1840. The parish began to operate a home for working girls and a St. Vincent de Paul Conference supervising and coordinating charitable activities. In 1851, the rectory was enlarged to provide schoolrooms for sixty-five students who were enrolled in a night school established for adults. The night school grew into St. Joseph's University, now located on City Line Avenue, which currently has an enrollment of nearly six thousand students. Some years later, a popular devotional magazine, *Messenger of the Sacred Heart*, began to be published at the parish.

Several parishes in Philadelphia had their beginnings at St. Joseph's. A meeting to form the first Italian parish, St. Mary Magdalen de Pazzi, took place at St. Joseph's in 1852. Some years later, Father Barbelin purchased a tract of land at 17th and Stiles and helped to found the Gesu parish at that location. The first black Catholic congregation in Philadelphia met at St. Joseph's and established a school for black children. In 1852, the Sisters of St. Joseph came to the parish to operate a parochial school, which they continued to do until 1959, when the school was closed and its students sent to a consolidated interparochial school established to serve downtown Philadelphia.

The revival of St. Joseph's parish in the 1840s took place against a background of anti-Catholic hostility that swept Philadelphia in a most destructive form. The excuse for the rioting that took place in 1844 was an allegation that Catholics were trying to prevent the use of the Bible in public schools. The charge was untrue, but at the time it was pointless to try to deny it to nativist agitators bent on destruction. In 1842, Bishop Kenrick wrote a letter to the board of controllers of the public schools in the city and county of Philadelphia (which in those days was not the same thing), asking that Catholic children in the public schools be excused from the use of Protestant Bibles. He requested that they be allowed to use Catholic Bibles, having appropriate annotations always found in an authentic Catholic Bible, in any public school classes or exercises. The controllers acceded to this request, at least in theory, and directed public schoolteachers to permit the use of Catholic Bibles by Catholic children in their classrooms. In the agitation that followed, the request that Catholic children use Catholic Bibles became translated in the minds of nativist groups, already hostile to the Irish, into a request to ban the use of Bibles entirely in the public schools. Mob violence erupted, as it so often did in Philadelphia during that era.

Anti-Catholic riots had occurred before in the United States but not of the size and fury of those that erupted in Philadelphia. In Boston in 1834, a nativist mob became fired up at the Bunker Hill Tavern and set about burning down the Ursuline Convent and School in Charlestown. Serious as it was, that episode involved a single event that was limited to one evening. It resulted in property damage and the dislocation of eighty Charlestown schoolchildren and their teachers but no loss of lives occurred.

In May of 1844, mobs with similar animosity swirled through the streets of Philadelphia for a week, seeking and finding targets of opportunity. Interestingly, these mobs bypassed German Catholic churches without incident and concentrated on churches used by Irish Catholics. On May 6, a nativist rally in the Kensington section resulted in a conflict with Catholics that first involved merely stone throwing and then deteriorated into an exchange of gunfire. One person was killed and several houses were torched. Two days later, the mob returned to this area and, though it was under military patrol, burned down St. Michael's Church, its rectory and convent, and several nearby houses to the accompaniment of a fife and drum corps playing Northern Irish Orangemen battle songs. Later that evening, the mob descended upon St. Augustine's Church, a few blocks north of St. Joseph's, burned down the church and rectory, and then started a bonfire in which books from St. Augustine's extensive library were destroyed. Here again a military guard surrounding the area proved inadequate to the task of protecting a church.

The following day the mayor called a large rally at the state house for the purpose of generating public opinion against this activity. Governor David Porter declared martial law and sought the assistance from the militia and from naval personnel aboard a ship then docked at Philadelphia Harbor. This enlarged force was stationed near every Catholic church in the city and was able to prevent the destruction of St. Joseph's and St. Mary's Churches on South Fourth Street. Bishop Kenrick suspended all Catholic church services in the city and directed that the Blessed Sacrament be removed and sequestered in private homes. After some urging, the bishop himself left his rectory and accepted the hospitality of a Protestant clergyman living nearby. This episode subsided, but another uprising broke out two months later resulting in the destruction by vandalism of St. Philip Neri Church. Not until martial law had been declared a second time did peace finally come to the City of Brotherly Love. As a result of the rioting, 40 people on both sides were killed, 60 more were injured, and 200 families were made homeless. Church property worth over $150,000 and public property worth about $100,000 was destroyed. In terms of fury and destructiveness, the Philadelphia anti-Catholic riots of 1844 were among the most notable civil disturbances of nineteenth-century America, on a par with the Haymarket Riot in Chicago and a couple of celebrated labor disputes of the 1890s.

In 1882, St. Joseph's was already commemorating its 150th anniversary. By that time, the conversion of many homes in the area into stores and the removal of many others had a serious adverse impact on the character of the area and of the parish. For many years St. Joseph's functioned as a downtown church that attracted visitors from other parts of the city and other parts of the nation. After World War II, the residential character of the area along the Delaware River began to revive. Condominium high-rise apartments and federal-period town houses began to proliferate and with them a number of exclusive shops and boutiques. As a result, Society Hill (named originally for the

Quaker Society of Friends) has once again become one of the more fashionable addresses in Philadelphia. With privately financed restoration came a determined effort to preserve the public buildings that make up historic Philadelphia. The Independence National Historical Park was created and enlarged and placed under the control of the U.S. Department of the Interior. The historic section of Philadelphia attracts many thousands of visitors each year from all over the United States who come to see the Liberty Bell and walk about and view the actual buildings that were in existence when the Declaration of Independence and the Constitution were written.

In 1959, Old St. Joseph's was designated as part of the historic district. This designation was bestowed because Old St. Joseph's was viewed as a symbol of religious liberty in the United States in light of its successful opposition to royal oppression, as demonstrated in 1733 when its right to exist was questioned by the British governor. Congress passed Public Law 86-273 of the Eighty-sixth Congress appropriating $46,200 to acquire 15,400 square feet of land immediately abutting the church along Walnut Street. The purpose of the acquisition was to demolish some old buildings on this site and create a park that would provide a view from St. Joseph's to the Bishop Todd House and the Bishop White House, across Walnut Street, and to Carpenters Hall a block away where the First Continental Congress met. The project was opposed by a group calling itself Protestants and Others United for the Separation of Church and State. They objected to the use of public funds to acquire land next to St. Joseph's because they felt that the purchase would indirectly enhance the value of church property. Their objection was not well taken, the land was acquired, and today a small, well-landscaped park can be found at Fourth and Walnut between the church and the rest of the historic district to the north.

St. Joseph's [**pictured above**] of course retains title to its old properties and they are still devoted to parochial use as they have been for more than two hundred fifty years. The aim of the parish today, as stated by its pastor in writing, is to be a people of God carrying out the mission of Christ as a structure of the Church according to the spirituality of St. Ignatius Loyola. More than five hundred people attend Mass each weekend. There is an active parish council to assist the pastor in his endeavor. Despite the upscale nature of the area, the parish is aware of many in the locality who have "fallen through the safety net" and who require immediate assistance. They can be found in garages and utility shacks and on top of grates in the winter. The parish has organized what it calls Care Walk, a program carried on by about 60 volunteers who distribute 20 to 30 bag lunches each evening to needy individuals and provide them with clothing and blankets. Each weekday afternoon, upwards of one hundred hot lunches are served to them in the church basement. Thus the "old chapel" on Willing's Alley continues in public the mission that Father Greaton started in private many years before the bell in Independence Hall proclaimed liberty throughout the land.

19
St. Mary

Philadelphia

PENNSYLVANIA

Old St. Mary's Church is located on South Fourth Street in the historic section of Philadelphia, less than a block south of Old St. Joseph's Church. The former dates back to 1763 and the latter to 1732. They have been neighbors for about two hundred fifty years. One might wonder why, when Catholic churches were so few in colonial America and Catholic resources were so scarce, two churches were built in such close proximity. Father Robert Harding, S.J., the pastor of Old St. Joseph's, was actually in need of more land for the parish cemetery when he purchased the land on which St. Mary's now stands. In a period of less than ten years, St. Joseph's cemetery had been the site of over two hundred burials, and it was running out of space. In 1759, Father Harding purchased for £328, a tract of land across Fourth Street some 63 feet in width by 396 feet in length, title to which was placed in the names of five laymen in trust for St. Joseph's Church. The land in question had once belonged to the Penn family. Four years later, a portion of this tract, measuring fifty feet by eighty feet, was conveyed to Father Harding and "his heirs," to use the words of the deed, for the sum of five shillings for the purpose of building a church. It was on this plot that a "new chapel," as the church was called, was soon erected.

At that time, the Catholic population of

Philadelphia exceeded four hundred people and began to outgrow the capacity of the "old chapel," St. Joseph's. It should be remembered that in those days a priest was only permitted to say one Mass a day without special permission, so everyone had to crowd into church on Sunday to attend the same Mass. The "new chapel," which was much larger, came to be used on Sundays while the "old chapel" was used during the week. However, St. Mary's was still considered to be a mission of the older church. Father Harding officiated at both places, assisted on occasion by Father Ferdinand Farmer, S.J., who ministered to German-speaking Catholics in Philadelphia when he was not away on mission trips to New Jersey or to central Pennsylvania. Both resided in the rectory at St. Joseph's.

During the years when the Continental Congress met in the Pennsylvania State House in Philadelphia, some of its members attended services from time to time at St. Mary's. This number occasionally included delegates who were not of the Catholic faith. John Adams wrote to his wife, Abigail, that he attended Sunday afternoon vespers on October 9, 1774. "Led by curiosity and good company [referring to George Washington], I strolled away to Mother Church, or rather grandmother Church; I mean the Romish chapel." He found the sermon, the ceremony, and the religious artifacts to be overwhelming. "The music consisting of an organ and a choir of singers, went all the afternoon except sermon time, and the assembly chanted most sweetly and exquisitely. Here is everything which can lay hold of the eye, ear, and imagination — everything which can charm and bewitch the simple and ignorant. I wonder how Luther ever broke the spell."

The British occupied Philadelphia from September 1777 until June 1778 while George Washington's troops were encamped at Valley Forge. Religious preferences played a role in both camps. On St. Patrick's Day, 1788, a small incident occurred in the colonial camp when Presbyterian troops taunted some of the Irish colonial soldiers on their feast day. In Philadelphia, the British attempted to recruit a regiment that would be called the Roman Catholic Volunteers. This was quite a change of heart on the part of British authorities and, like the enactment of the Quebec Act of 1774, was a policy dictated by military necessity. The British obtained the services of a member of St. Mary's Chapel, Alfred Clifton, as lieutenant colonel in its regiment and unsuccessfully attempted to recruit Father Farmer as regimental chaplain. They placed a newspaper ad seeking volunteers which stated that "during the present wanton and unnatural rebellion, and no longer, the sum of four pounds will be given above the usual bounty, a suit of new cloaths, and every other necessary to complete a gentleman soldier." When General William Howe evacuated Philadelphia in 1778, he marched out of town with three thousand inhabitants, including one hundred eighty members of the Roman Catholic Volunteers.

Once the British were gone, the Continental Congress returned, and with them came accredited representatives of those nations who were assisting the colonial cause. On July 4, 1779, at the invitation of the French minister to the United States, Alexander

Gerard, members of the Continental Congress, officials of the Commonwealth of Pennsylvania, and others attended a "Te Deum" sung at St. Mary's in honor of the third anniversary of the Declaration of Independence. Officiating at this ceremony was Father Séraphin Bandol, a Franciscan Recollect, who was the chaplain to the French minister. Shortly after Cornwallis's surrender in October 1781, Father Bandol celebrated a Mass of thanksgiving at St. Mary's attended by officials of the United States and the commonwealth. Father Bandol stayed in Philadelphia for several years until the French consulate was relocated to New York, during which time he assisted parish priests at St. Joseph's and at St. Mary's on Sundays.

In 1781, St. Mary's — with the approval of Father Robert Molyneaux, the new pastor of St. Joseph's — purchased for the sum of £400 a house on Walnut Street next to an old Quaker almshouse and converted it into a school. St. Mary's School was opened in 1782 and thus became the first Catholic school in the United States. It was called St. Mary's Free School and was supported by special collections that were made at the church. A few years later, when St. Augustine's Church was established by the Augustinians a few blocks north on Fourth Street, the school was made available by their parishioners as well. In 1782, St. Mary's collected the sum of £1,200 that it then spent to build a gallery inside the church building and to erect additional pews, which it could then rent to more pew holders. In 1784, Father Molyneaux reported to John Carroll, the prefect apostolic, that about one thousand Catholics in Philadelphia had made their Easter duty and he knew of about one thousand more who had not done so.

In 1788, the German-speaking members of St. Mary's Chapel formed their own community and erected Holy Trinity Church around the corner at Sixth and Spruce. They obtained a charter for this purpose from the Pennsylvania legislature and, in doing so, established the first Catholic nationality church in the United States. Their Flemish-bond brick structure built in 1789 is still standing at this location. A few years later, they asked Bishop Carroll to establish a separate German diocese under the control of a German-speaking bishop, but Bishop Carroll would not hear of it.

In the same year that Holy Trinity parish obtained a charter from the Pennsylvania legislature, St. Mary's did the same. The St. Mary's charter provided for the operation of a church under the control of eleven trustees, three of whom would be the priests of the parish and eight of whom would be elected annually by the pew holders. Trustees were empowered to administer church assets but could not sell the church building. This legislative act unwittingly laid the groundwork for an ongoing battle between the trustees of St. Mary's and successive bishops of Philadelphia that would last for more than forty years.

Disputes between lay trustees and the clergy were not uncommon in the early days of the Catholic Church in the United States, but the disputes that took place at St. Mary's and at the St. Louis Cathedral in New Orleans were widely publicized prototypes that fueled the fires of dissent elsewhere. At St. Mary's, the dispute escalated into formal schism. Unlike many internal disputes that have erupted in the late twentieth century, trusteeship fights did not involve any moral precepts or any theological questions other than those touching directly on church administration. In every case, the matter at issue was who was in charge. Trustees felt that they could control the "temporalities" of a parish without impinging upon its "spiritualities," which they conceded were the exclusive province of the clergy. It soon became evident that this was not possible. Trustees should not be compared to modern-day parish councils which are largely advisory in character. Trustees owned and administered church lands and assets in the name of the congregation which elected them much as Episcopal vestrymen are elected. Trustees hired and fired pastors, established and paid their salaries, and asserted the right to do so even in the face of contrary directions from the bishop of the diocese, whom they sometimes sought to control by the application of economic pressure. Trusteeship was essentially an adaptation to Catholic parishes of a Protestant view of church organization. It had no place in a Catholic setting, but it did great mischief until this fact gained general acceptance among Catholics.

In 1793, a yellow-fever epidemic broke out in Philadelphia that claimed the lives of a great many people, including three hundred sixty-seven who were buried in St. Mary's cemetery. Among that number were three priests who became victims of the epidemic when they ministered to others. In 1803, another epidemic occurred that resulted in two hundred fifty-one additional burials in the parish cemetery.

In 1801, when Father Matthew Carr, O.S.A., opened St. Augustine's Church, parish boundaries were drawn at Market Street. St. Augustine's was given everything north of Market Street as far as Trenton, New Jersey, while St. Mary's was assigned the territory south of Market Street as far as Wilmington, Delaware. Catholics in Philadelphia were eager to have a new diocese established in their city and petitioned Bishop Carroll for this purpose. Bishop Carroll wrote a letter to the trustees of all of the churches then operating in the city. He told them that it "was now indispensable to make provisions as well for the first expenses of the consecration of the new Prelate, as for his permanent support. . . . The established usage of the Holy See, when new Bishoprics are instituted, is to require solid assurances that the Bishops appointed for the purposes of preserving the integrity of faith, the purity of morals, and perpetuity of ministry as well as their successors, shall be above all inducements arising out of the narrowness of their circumstances, to relax their attention to those most essential duties of their charge, and consequently that their income, whatever it may be, shall be independent of the fluctuations of favor or public opinion." Little did he realize at that time the import of his words. St. Mary's pledged $400 a year toward the upkeep of the new bishop, while St. Augustine's and Holy Trinity pledged $200 apiece. St. Joseph's had closed temporarily in 1801, although its rectory was fully utilized, and it made no pledge.

Philadelphia's first bishop (as mentioned in the previous chapter) was Father Michael Egan, a Franciscan, who had come to the city in 1804 and had been stationed for a while at St. Mary's. He took up residence at St. Joseph's rectory and chose St. Mary's as his cathedral. This church remained the Philadelphia cathedral through all of the turmoil that was to come and did not cease to be so until 1839. Bishop Egan spent much of his time visiting outlying parishes in Pennsylvania. It was when he came home that troubles arose. In 1812, he had a head-on collision with the trustees of St. Mary's Church. They insisted that he fire an assistant pastor and replace him with Father William Harold, an Irish Dominican who had recently come to Philadelphia and who had gained favor with the trustees. The bishop refused so the trustees retaliated by declaring that they had no money to pay either the bishop or the priests at St. Mary's. Bishop Egan made a direct appeal for funds over the heads of the trustees to the parish pew holders. For this action he was criticized by the trustees in a pamphlet they published claiming that the bishop's actions were "riotous, disorderly, pernicious, and anti-christian." The trustees also requested the Pennsylvania legislature to amend the parish charter to exclude the three clerical members from the board. The legislature refused, but this was only the first of three occasions on which such a request was to be made in the next ten years.

Bishop Egan died in 1814, at which time Archbishop Carroll called upon Father Louis DeBarth in Conewago to come to Philadelphia on an interim basis to act as vicar general. Father DeBarth begged Archbishop Carroll on his knees not to be assigned to this job, but the archbishop commanded him to do so under holy obedience and he did, staying at Philadelphia until a new bishop was selected in 1820. During his tenure as vicar general, Father DeBarth made one notable mistake. He accepted into the diocese Father William Hogan, a native of Limerick, Ireland, who had been serving in the diocese of New York. Father Hogan wanted out of New York and told the bishop of that city that he was leaving. Apparently, Father DeBarth was not fully apprised of the circumstances or of Father Hogan's background when he assigned him to St. Mary's.

The trustees at St. Mary's petitioned the Holy See for the appointment of an Irishman as bishop of Philadelphia. They said that they were tired of administration by Frenchmen. (By that time, Archbishop Ambrose Marèchal had come to the see of Baltimore.) They recommended Father Harold for the position. The Holy See responded that they would get an Irishman but it was not to be Father Harold. To this position the pope appointed Father Henry Conwell who had been a priest in Ireland for nearly fifty years and vicar general of Armagh in Northern Ireland for twenty-five of those years. He was seventy-three years old when he arrived in Philadelphia in 1820.

Shortly after Bishop Conwell's arrival, Father Hogan preached sermons at St. Mary's in which he criticized Father DeBarth and mocked the bishop's manner of speaking. (The bishop had a slight lisp.) The bishop took personal umbrage at the remarks and from him came no soft answer to turn away wrath. He summoned Father Hogan before him in the presence of all of the priests of the city and denounced him as "a man not to be trusted with the care of souls." Father Hogan asked for a formal hearing on the latter charge, as it involved an allegation of personal immorality, but Bishop Conwell refused. He suspended Father Hogan's faculties, thus rendering him unable to perform priestly functions in Philadelphia with church approval. Throughout all of the battles to come, the bishop and the other priests then at St. Mary's continued to reside at the old St. Joseph's rectory on Willing's Alley, while Father Hogan resided in another apartment just next door, separated only by a party wall. The bishop had previously ordered Father Hogan to abandon his private residence and live at the rectory with the others but he had refused. Father Hogan continued to reside in his own apartment in the adjacent building until he eventually left Philadelphia. He was able to furnish the apartment in a suitable manner with funds voted by the St. Mary's trustees, while the bishop and the other priests lived in comparative penury next door. What would have happened had there been a little more prudence and charity on both sides we will never know. Everyone was spoiling for a fight and fight is what they did.

Father Hogan was very popular with the trustees and most of the congregation. He was a handsome man, a gifted orator, and was deferential to women and children in the congregation. He was a popular guest at private homes on social occasions. In another context, he would have made an outstanding candidate for public office. However, the campaign he conducted at St. Mary's against the bishop was doomed to failure, despite the support he had among most of the trustees. It should be remembered that the trustees had challenged clerical authority before Father Hogan arrived and they would continue to do so long after he left Philadelphia.

The trustees petitioned the bishop to restore Father Hogan's faculties, reminding the bishop that it was they and not he who owned St. Mary's and warning him of the "lamentable effects that will follow a refusal." Bishop Conwell persisted, telling the trustees in writing that he would not allow himself "to be led astray on this occasion" because to do so would "unhinge the hierarchy, undermine Church government, destroy subordination, and subvert all rule and order in the Church here. . . . Revolutionary movements tend always to disorder."

On February 2, 1821, about six weeks after his faculties had been removed, Father Hogan announced publicly that he would continue to preach and that he had rented a Methodist Church building for this purpose. On February 11, the bishop read a warning from the pulpit at St. Mary's, saying that if Father Hogan did so, he would be excommunicated and so would anyone who attended any of his services. The trustees then held a public meeting in which they announced their support of Father Hogan and criticized the bishop for depriving Father Hogan of due process in clearing his name of the charge that had been leveled against him. The accused priest appealed for support to two other bishops in the United States, John de Cheverus in Boston and John England in Charleston, South Carolina. Bishop Cheverus denounced Father Hogan and declined to become further involved. Bishop England came to Philadelphia some time later to act as a mediator but his efforts proved unavailing. The trustees once again asked the Pennsylvania legislature to amend the church charter to remove the clerical members from its board. The legislature did so but only conditionally, saying that any such change would also have to meet the approval of the state supreme court. The court refused the request, stating in its published opinion that the requested revision was not in keeping with the intent of the original incorporators. In that opinion, Chief Justice William Tilghman wrote: "... and if our Roman Catholic brethren do in their conscience believe that the power of conferring or withdrawing sacred rights of the clergy has been handed down in sure succession from the holy Apostle St. Peter to the Present Pontiff, Pius VII, the people of the United States of America have seen nothing in this belief either criminal or dangerous. Neither has it been remarked that during our revolutionary struggle or on any trying occasion since, the members of that Church have been less patriotic than their fellow Christians of other denominations. Their priests, therefore, are entitled and will receive the same protection as the other clergy." Sometime following the announcement of this decision, Bishop Conwell and the other priests loyal to him once again tried to occupy the pulpit at St. Mary's and were physically ejected from the premises by Father Hogan and the trustees in the course of a wild melee.

At the annual trustee election held on April 23, 1821, the Hogan-trustee faction won and voted to exclude Bishop Conwell from any of its future deliberations on the basis that the bishop was not a citizen of the United States. They invited Father Hogan, who was also not a citizen, to resume his former duties as pastor of St. Mary's. Bishop Conwell gave Father Hogan written notice that, if he did so, he would be excommunicated. Father Hogan ignored the warning and began to act as pastor. On May 27, 1821, Bishop Conwell read from the altar of St. Augustine's Church an order of excommunication, stating therein that "William has usurped and arrogated to himself the right of exercising priestly functions, not only without our approbation but in direct violation of our pastoral mandate" and "has not hesitated to rend and tear asunder the seamless garment of Christ, by causing confusion in the Church and endeavoring to establish a schism." Accordingly, the bishop felt impelled to "the disagreeable necessity of performing the most painful task ... in cutting off this incurable member by the sword of excommunication from the body of the Catholic Church," announcing that "in Virtue of our commission and authority of binding and loosing conferred on us ... we cut off, by the spiritual sword of excommunication the said William Hogan, a putrid member, lest any of our flock should be led into schism by error by attending the sacrilegious functions of his ministry, and thus treasure up for themselves wrath against the day of wrath." Bishop Conwell also placed St. Mary's Church under interdict. From that point forward, both Father Hogan and those who remained members of the congregation at St. Mary's were formally in schism.

Bishop Conwell immediately reopened St. Joseph's Chapel for the use of priests and laity who remained loyal to him and took up a collection to enlarge its seating capacity. He removed the altar vestments and sacred vessels from St. Mary's and took them to St. Joseph's rectory, whereupon the trustees went to court and obtained a writ of replevin to regain possession. Since technically they owned these items, the court ordered that the "utensils," as it called them, be returned to St. Mary's and they were. The trustees cut off Bishop Conwell's income from the parish, thus hampering his travels throughout the remainder of the diocese. A battle of pamphlets then ensued. Over the next five years, some seventy tracts and position papers, aggregating more than five hundred pages in all, were issued by both sides in support of their respective positions. Many were circulated throughout the United States. The trustees claimed that Father Hogan was a wronged man who had been treated unfairly. However, their basic claim was set forth in a document entitled "An Address of the Committee of St. Mary's Church in Philadelphia to their Brethren of the Roman Catholic Faith Throughout the United States." In this document, they stated flatly: "We claim the exclusive right, which always belonged to the Church, of electing our own pastors and bishops." For this position they solicited support from rather questionable sources, including a Spanish priest living in Philadelphia and calling himself the Right Reverend Dr. John Rico. Father Rico claimed to be the vicar general of all Catholics in the Spanish armed forces, but at the time the "vicar general" was engaged in operating a cigar store not far from the church. From his cigar-store chancery he issued an opinion on the canon law of the Church in support of the trustees which they printed and circulated to justify their activities.

In the fall of 1821, Bishop England came from Charleston to arrange a truce. He agreed to accept Father Hogan into his diocese if Father Hogan would leave Philadelphia and refrain from any more activities at St. Mary's. Bishop Conwell agreed to this solution and gave Bishop England faculties to remove any censure from Father Hogan once he left Philadelphia. After accepting this arrangement in writing, Father Hogan immediately reneged and said two Masses at St. Mary's the following Sunday in defiance of two bishops. Bishop England had no choice but to renew the excommunication and things remained essentially as they were.

The next trustee election took place during Easter week of 1822. Before election day, the trustees installed more pews at St. Mary's and sold them on a single-seat basis, thereby enlarging the voter rolls by more than one hundred persons. The charge was made that some of the new pew holders were not Catholics but were just ringers brought in to vote for the trustees. On election day, the bishop's supporters met at 3:00 A.M. at St. Joseph's Chapel and marched to St. Mary's in a body, occupying the cemetery portion of the premises. The trustee faction began to assemble on Fourth Street about 6:00 A.M., and a fight ensued during which about two hundred people were injured. Many required medical attention. The polls opened at 11:00 A.M. The incumbent trustees won by a small margin, but the election was protested. The results were submitted to an arbitrator who eventually decided in favor of the trustee faction, who were thereby assured of another year in office.

Father Hogan might have made a more sympathetic figure if his personal life had been above reproach. However, he became involved in a civil suit for assault and battery brought by one Mary Connell. Although he was acquitted, the fallout from the suit diminished his standing. He was also arrested in New York City in another well-publicized assault case. Both events hurt him personally. Then the battle got really nasty. Charles Bazeley, who operated a girls' school on Willing's Alley and was a member of the trustee faction, prevailed upon an unwed mother, Katharine Nevis, to file a paternity action against Bishop Conwell, who was then seventy-five years of age. The suit was ultimately dismissed and Ms. Nevis was prosecuted for perjury, but the matter was given such notoriety that Bishop Conwell felt compelled to discuss it in a detailed report of the schism which he submitted to the Propagation of the Faith in 1824. Viewed from a historical perspective of nearly one hundred seventy-five years, the incident seems both outrageous and slightly ludicrous but, at the time, Rome was not amused.

The trustees again tried to get the legislature to amend the charter of St. Mary's parish to exclude clergymen from the board. This time the legislature did so but the bill was vetoed by Governor Joseph Heister in March of 1823. His veto was sustained, but the bill in question, which came to be known as the "Catholic Bill," was widely discussed and even became an issue at the following election. It appeared that some Protestant state officials had greater respect for apostolic succession than did the trustees at St. Mary's.

Father Hogan saw that he was fighting a losing battle so he resigned and went to Europe. A year later, he returned briefly and offered his services again to the trustees as pastor of what he called an "American Catholic Church," which he said would be similar to the Greek Catholic Church. Both priestly celibacy and fasting would be eliminated. By that time, however, the trustees had obtained the services of another priest, Father Thaddeus O'Meally, who was also willing to officiate in defiance of the bishop. They declined Father Hogan's offer so he left Philadelphia for the last time. The trustees commissioned Father O'Meally to go to Rome on their behalf and to negotiate a settlement with the Holy See. However, they did not authorize him to concede their basic point, namely the right to appoint their own pastors. They wanted Father O'Meally to conclude a concordat with the pope, authorizing an arrangement similar to the right of appointment of bishops that had been enjoyed by various European princes in medieval times. When Father O'Meally got to Rome, he was chastised for his role in the schism but was given a chance to repudiate his role in the affair. He did so, eventually going back to Ireland, where he resumed his functions as a priest. This turnabout left the trustees without an emissary in Rome and without a priest to conduct services in Philadelphia. As a result, St. Mary's was closed for a year and a half because the trustees could not find another priest who was willing to serve them while under interdict. One result of closing the church was that the trustees could no longer collect pew rentals since those who were paying them were receiving nothing for their money.

Bishop Conwell continued to operate St. Joseph's Church for Catholics who observed the interdict at St. Mary's. One phase of this dispute that had been given surprisingly little attention was the question of legal title to the land on which St. Mary's had been erected. In 1811, Bishop Egan found a deed to the land that Father Harding had received in 1763. The deed had never been recorded so he saw to this formality. While the deed proved that the trustees did not own St. Mary's, it also established that Bishop Egan did not own it either. In accordance with the early custom, title was conveyed to Father Harding and "his heirs," but Father Harding had been dead for forty years. In order that a distant cousin or a niece or nephew might not be able to claim title by operation of law, Father Harding, like all of the Jesuit missioners in this position, made a will leaving all of his assets to a successor. His will left the property here in question to Father John Lewis, the Jesuit superior, and it was later devised in a similar fashion by Father Lewis and subsequently by Father Molyneaux. Whether any of these wills were ever admitted to probate is unknown. If so, all of the wills except for Father Harding's would have been probated in southern Maryland, although the lands involved might be scattered all over Maryland and Pennsylvania. It was a title searcher's nightmare. The present "heir" of Father Harding who was invested with legal title to St. Mary's Church was Father Francis Neale, who was residing at the Jesuits' provincial house in southern Maryland. It was not until 1825 that the diocese of Philadelphia took any steps to perfect legal title to its own cathedral. Bishop Conwell journeyed to St. Thomas Manor and obtained a deed from Father Neale. With a sense of history, the conveyance recited a purchase price of five shillings, the exact price Father Harding had paid for the land in colonial times. The Jesuits wanted no part of Bishop Conwell's troubles. They simply wanted to recoup their initial investment. Bishop Conwell waited six months after receiving the deed before he finally recorded it.

At long last, the aging bishop and the trustees came to a written understanding. The bishop wanted peace in his old age, and the trustees wanted the interdict removed and the church reopened. Bishop Conwell let the trustees retain their right to appoint and remove pastors. On November 5, 1826, St. Mary's was reopened. When the agreement was sent to Rome, it was immediately rejected, the diocese was placed in the hands of a temporary administrator, and Bishop Conwell was summoned to the Eternal City to explain why he had given away the ball game. His explanation was not accepted. The diocese was then permanently placed in the hands of Bishop Francis P. Kenrick and Bishop Conwell was told not to return. He did go back to Philadelphia and took up his old residence at St. Joseph's rectory but he was completely shorn of his powers. He lived out his days as bishop of Philadelphia in name only.

The trustees were soon given to understand that they were dealing with a younger and more vigorous man. Bishop Kenrick appointed himself as pastor of St. Mary's Cathedral. When the trustees refused to acknowledge in writing his right to do so, he placed the church under interdict and closed it for a period of five weeks until they came around. Six years later, he moved the cathedral to St. John the Evangelist Church at 13th and Chestnut, a church to which the diocese had title. In 1833, St. Joseph's parish became a separate parish for Catholics in the area who wanted no part of the St. Mary's trustees. At last, the fight was over.

In the ensuing years, St. Mary's necessarily became a smaller and smaller part of a rapidly expanding diocese. In the late 1800s, the area became increasingly commercialized, and the character of a locality that had been a well-to-do residential community was destroyed, not to be restored until long after World War II. In 1886, the entire church building was revamped. The old western entrance through the cemetery was closed off, and what was formerly the back of the church [**pictured above**] became the entrance on Fourth Street. At the same time, a new rectory was constructed next door.

Today, St. Mary's parish is in effect a small enclave in a large city. It has created for its three hundred fifty parishioners a small-town atmosphere in the restored historic section of Old Philadelphia. This upscale area is now made of new or reconstructed federal-period houses located along narrow, quiet, tree-lined brick streets and is largely insulated from the commercial hustle and bustle nearby. St. Mary's is a tourist attraction and can boast to visitors that its well-kept cemetery is the final resting place of such prominent early Americans as Commodore John Barry, the founder of the U.S. Navy; George Meade, grandfather and namesake of the Union Army's commanding general at Gettysburg; and Thomas FitzSimmons, a member of the parish who attended the Constitutional Convention that was held a few blocks away in 1787. With seven other downtown parishes, St. Mary's operates an interparochial school with about 240 elementary students; its longtime neighbor around the corner, Holy Trinity, now has only 27 registered family members and 60 individual members. While it functions as a separate parish, it is actually under the control of the pastor at St. Mary's.

Holy Trinity's cemetery also contains the remains of some French-speaking Catholics, as was the original burial site of Stephen Girard, the founder of Girard College. The membership at Holy Trinity increases when school is in session because many medical students and other personnel from nearby Jefferson Medical School attend services there. For this congregation a priest from St. Mary's says a noon Mass every Sunday at the old German chapel. While the Saturday evening Mass at St. Mary's is normally filled with tourists, the Sunday Masses, often followed by a small social hour, are attended by a stable complement of parishioners who are well known to their clergy, a phenomenon that does not always take place in a large city. The tranquillity of its present setting is a marked contrast to the turmoil of a stormy past long ago laid to rest with the remains of the trustees who lie buried in its ancient graveyard.

20
Sts. Peter and Paul Cathedral

Philadelphia
PENNSYLVANIA

When the 1844 riots (described in the previous chapter) finally subsided, Bishop Francis P. Kenrick returned to this procathedral at St. John the Evangelist Church and from there directed 50 priests in ministering to 100,000 Catholics in 60 churches of the diocese. St. John was referred to as a procathedral because it was used by the bishop as the seat of his administration without having been formally designated by the Holy See as the principal church of the diocese. It was his feeling that the Philadelphia diocese merited a larger and more ornate church for its cathedral but he lacked the resources to build such a structure. Bishop Kenrick was in the market to purchase a house at 18th and Race Streets next to a seminary operated by the Vincentian Fathers. The Vincentians had placed a contract on a large tract of land next to the seminary that was adjacent to a public square. When the Vincentians refused to go through with the purchase, the bishop reluctantly took over the contract. It was here, at what was to become Logan Circle, that he decided to erect Sts. Peter and Paul Cathedral.

On June 29, 1846, Bishop Kenrick sent a pastoral letter to all of the churches in the diocese, telling them of his plan and soliciting funds for this purpose. In his letter, he pointed out that "the cathedral is the common church of the whole diocese," hoping that this consideration would encourage the donations needed to bring it into existence. "It seems the order of Divine Providence, in any age, that works of piety and charity should depend on the concurrence of a great multitude of contributors, who, in offering the tokens of their zeal for the advancement of religion, secure to themselves a share of its blessings. In this way, the poor are on an equality with the rich, since merit is estimated not by the amount of the offering but by the cheerfulness of the giver." His request did not meet with an enthusiastic response. Many pastors who received the letter were burdened with debts incurred in constructing their own churches and felt that they could ill afford to assist in the construction of another one. His plan was criticized because the new cathedral was to be built three blocks northwest of city hall at a site that was simply too far west of the city. However, on July 26, 1846, the bishop called a meeting of eight hundred laymen and from this group a committee was formed in each parish of the diocese to raise money for the cathedral.

As a result of the criticisms that had been leveled at the project, Bishop Kenrick decided to move slowly. He resolved to let contracts for only so much construction that could be paid for immediately in cash. In September 1846, he laid the cornerstone for the cathedral before a crowd of eight thousand and took advantage of this occasion to collect an additional $4,100 for the building fund. However, the cathedral was not dedicated until 1864. By that time, Bishop Kenrick had moved to Baltimore, completed twelve years of service as archbishop of Baltimore, and passed away.

The cathedral, modeled after the Lombard Church of San Carlo al Corso in Rome, was designed by architect Napoleon Le Brun, who worked from sketches provided for him by two Vincentian priests. When Bishop Kenrick was transferred to Baltimore in 1851, only a shell of a building, with walls raised to a height of forty-five feet, had been completed. Work had ground to a halt on more than one occasion because of lack of funds.

St. John Neumann became bishop of Philadelphia in 1852 and took over the responsibility of moving the project forward. He continued Bishop Kenrick's pay-as-you-go policy. In 1854, he held a mass meeting that stimulated the collection of enough money to permit the work to be resumed. In 1857, Bishop James F. Wood became coadjutor bishop of Philadelphia and Bishop Neumann turned over to him the responsibility for completing the project. By 1859, the walls had been built, the keystone was placed, and a cross was raised to the top of the dome. The coming of the Civil War caused further interruptions in the work. In 1862, vesper services were held in the building and a papal blessing was read from the altar. It was on November 20, 1864, that the dedication ceremony took place.

The intention of the builders in erecting a permanent structure can best be derived by reflecting on the fact that the foundation walls are from five to ten feet thick and the walls of the building resting upon the foundation are four feet, six inches thick. The cathedral was constructed of Connecticut and New Jersey brownstone and is topped by a great copper dome that has acquired a green patina. The dome is 71 feet in diameter at its base and is 209 feet high at the top of the gold cross, making the entire height of the cathedral 413 feet above the pavement. The turmoil of the time in which it was built can be seen in the fact that the walls have no windows and that light is admitted only through the dome and through clerestory windows many feet above the ground. This precaution was taken so that future vandals could not smash stained-glass windows located at street level by an easy toss of a rock. The façade of the building [**pictured above**] has four sixty-foot Corinthian columns that are six feet thick. In the 1950s, cast-bronze doors and handrails were installed in the front of the church. The interior was originally 216 feet in length, 136 feet wide, and 100 feet high; in 1957, an apse was constructed in the rear of the church that extended its length to 261 feet. The walnut pews seat over twelve hundred people and this capacity can be increased to more than two thousand by the use of temporary chairs.

Attached to the main body of the cathedral is the Chapel of Our Lady of the Blessed Sacrament, which can be entered from the street. This chapel is used for daily Masses and for devotions that do not require the seating capacity of the entire cathedral. A portrait of St. John Neumann is prominently displayed in the chapel. It would not be possible to describe in detail the many architectural and artistic features that can be found within this building. It has eight side chapels, one of which was donated by the parents of Blessed Katharine Drexel, the Philadelphian who founded the Sisters of the Blessed Sacrament and who was beatified in 1988. Another chapel contains mosaic murals depicting the involvement of the Catholic Church in the history of Pennsylvania. A mosaic in another side chapel portrays events in the life of St. John Neumann. A carillon was recently installed that produces true bell music with the tonal equivalent of 100,000 pounds of cast bells. It is an electromechanical instrument that sounds the carillon both inside and outside the building. Beneath the main altar are the tombs of most of the bishops and archbishops of Philadelphia. One notable exception is St. John Neumann, who, in accordance with his wishes, was buried with his community at St. Peter's, the old Redemptorist church at Fifth and Girard.

In the years that have elapsed since its dedication, the cathedral has undergone several major renovations. An addition completed in 1877 was a high altar, which is now covered by a canopy, or baldachin, some thirty-eight feet high and containing a semicircular bronze dome. Another renovation in 1914 installed a new high altar made of white marble. At this time, the cathedral was repainted and the works of art that adorn the walls were rearranged. In 1975, additional murals and an enhanced lighting arrangement were installed and an overhaul of the main organ took place.

Sts. Peter and Paul is the principal church of an archdiocese that has been directly touched by the lives of two saints, one canonized and one beatified. Bishop Neumann was an immigrant from Bohemia. He spoke eight languages and made an effort to learn Gaelic so that he could hear confessions from Irish parishioners. He was bishop of Philadelphia and in that capacity took an active role in finishing the construction of the cathedral. He was an indefatigable traveler at a time when traveling about Pennsylvania and New Jersey was arduous work; in one year alone he visited fifty-two churches. He made a noteworthy contribution to the enlargement of the parochial school system. He still had time for his own parish, and his name appears repeatedly in the baptismal records of Sts. Peter and Paul as the officiating clergyman. His cause for canonization was begun in 1888, just twenty-eight years after his death, and was successfully concluded in 1977.

Mother Katharine Drexel was the daughter of a wealthy Philadelphia banker and financier, Francis A. Drexel. He was a convert and a devout Catholic. Emma Bouvier Drexel, the stepmother who raised her, was also a devout Catholic. The Drexel family home where Katharine was raised was only a few blocks from the cathedral at 1503 Walnut Street. Her particular interest was in missionary work throughout the United States among Indians and blacks. During a visit to Rome in 1887, she suggested to Pope Leo XIII that a religious order be formed in the United States that was particularly dedicated to working among groups whom she felt had been neglected, specifically blacks and Indians. Pope Leo threw the suggestion back to her and challenged her to form such an order and take up this work. She did so. She entered religious life in 1889 and founded the Sisters of the Blessed Sacrament in 1891. In 1920, she established a motherhouse for the new order at Cornwells Heights, near Philadelphia, to provide for the formation and education of nuns whose special work would be among Indians and blacks. Before entering religious life, she had spent about twelve million dollars of the fortune she inherited in this work. During her lifetime, she founded and maintained 47 black and 31 Indian churches and charitable institutions, as well as 23 rural schools. These establishments can be found in thirty-five states as well as in some foreign countries. They include Xavier University, established in New Orleans in 1915, the only black Catholic college in the United States. Mother Drexel became an invalid in her later years and lived out her life at Cornwells Heights, passing away in 1955 at the age of ninety-seven.

The fear that the new cathedral would be too far west of the city became muted in the 1860s as Philadelphia moved from the Delaware waterfront to the Schuylkill River and far beyond. In the late 1880s, this area was a favorable residential locality; but, later, industrial plants and municipal buildings began to replace private dwellings. This trend was accentuated in the 1920s when the Franklin Parkway was constructed and widened from city hall all the way to the Franklin Institute, another Philadelphia landmark. A large number of private homes were demolished to make way for this project. Thereafter, high-rise apartments began to replace private dwellings. More recently, large office buildings and hotels have come to dwarf the cathedral, which at one time was one of the most conspicuous landmarks in the entire city. During the first half of the twentieth century, Sts. Peter and Paul carried on the usual array of parish activities. As early as World War I, it began operating a day nursery for working mothers and carried on this activity for many years. In a nearby building, appropriately called Temperance Hall, it operated a recreational club for teenagers. The parish also provided a parochial school education for both boys and girls in the Cathedral School until the school closed in 1983 and its students transferred to another location.

Programs for youths have largely given way to programs for older Catholics as the demographics of the parish have changed. The parish now has about five hundred resident members, most of whom are elderly ladies living in nearby apartments, but a number of younger professional people have begun to move into old houses that are undergoing restoration. The northern portion of the parish contains a large number of Puerto Rican immigrants. For them the parish maintains a chapel on Spring Garden Street called the Chapel of the Miraculous Medal, or simply the Milagra. Mass is said in Spanish at the Milagra for about one thousand Hispanics living in its immediate locality.

A recitation of parish activities falls far short of describing the cathedral's present ministry. It is the principal church in an archdiocese that has 1,300 priests, 1.35 million Catholics, and 302 parishes. Because of its location and its unique status, many functions take place at the cathedral that are not purely parochial in nature. Each year some fifty to sixty couples from various parts of the city select the cathedral as the place where they want to be married. It is also the site of many high-school baccalaureate ceremonies. About six hundred Catholics working in downtown Philadelphia hear Mass each weekday at Sts. Peter and Paul, and this number more than doubles during Lent. Various organizations — Catholic police and firemen's associations, ethnic groups, alumni associations, professional and business groups, and others — have Masses said for their organizations each year at the cathedral. When the Eucharistic Congress came from all parts of the world in 1976 to meet in Philadelphia, three or four functions took place each day at this location. In October 1979, Pope John Paul II came to Philadelphia, visited the cathedral, and said Mass at a huge altar that was constructed out front on Logan Circle. About one million people attended this ceremony. Celebrations honoring Philadelphia's two local saints were conducted at the cathedral to coincide with beatification or canonization ceremonies taking place in Rome. Although more than one hundred forty years have elapsed since Bishop Kenrick circulated his pastoral letter inaugurating the drive to build Sts. Peter and Paul, the cathedral is still functioning as the 1846 prospectus said it would: "a splendid ornament to the chief city of this State, and a lasting monument to your zeal and generosity."

21
St. Mary Magdalen de Pazzi

Philadelphia

PENNSYLVANIA

St. Mary Magdalen de Pazzi parish, located in South Philadelphia about two miles from Independence Hall, is the oldest Italian Catholic parish in the United States. In the first half of the nineteenth century, there were but a handful of Italians in Philadelphia. They were members of various territorial Catholic parishes. About six hundred regularly attended services in the chapel at the cathedral. Some went to Mass at St. Augustine's, another of Philadelphia's original Catholic parishes founded by the Augustinians in 1796. Italian children were given catechetical instruction at St. Paul's Church every Sunday afternoon. This church, which is still in existence, is located about a mile west of St. Mary Magdalen de Pazzi.

On March 21, 1852, a meeting was held in a schoolroom at Old St. Joseph's Church on Willing's Alley for the purpose of organizing an Italian parish. A petition for this purpose was drawn up and submitted to Bishop John Neumann, and he approved the idea. On September 24, 1852, the bishop purchased a small Negro Methodist church and its adjacent cemetery on Marriott Street, now called Montrose Street, and thus began the "church for the Italians," as the diocesan newspaper called it. The building was enlarged by constructing walls around the existing structure and then removing the original walls. The cornerstone of the new church was laid by Bishop Neumann in 1854 and the church itself was dedicated in 1857. By that time, the framework of the original building was gone.

Bishop Neumann appointed Father Gaetano Mariani, a native of Florence, Italy, as the first pastor. Father Mariani had been teaching music at St. Charles Borromeo Seminary when he was summoned to take over the parish. The church was named in honor of a sixteenth-century Carmelite nun who had lived in Father Mariani's native city. A majority of its original parishioners were from northern Italy. Most were blue-collar workers, although there were also a few teachers, musicians, and small-businessmen. In the late 1860s, the church was closed briefly because of an internal dispute between the congregation and one of Father Mariani's successors, but it was reopened in 1870 under the pastorate of Father Antonio Isoleri, who served as pastor until 1926. During these fifty-six years, the parish grew enormously as the wave of immigration into South Philadelphia increased its Italian population many times over. Until 1900, St. Mary Magdalen de Pazzi was the only Italian national church in the city and had a membership approaching fifty thousand Catholics.

In 1870, Father Isoleri built a new rectory but it was destroyed by fire in 1873 along with some valuable early parish records. When the rectory was rebuilt, Father Isoleri found other quarters for himself and let the building be used as a school and then as a convent for the Missionary Sisters of St. Francis who had come to teach in the parish school. Later, when the parish began to operate an orphanage for Italian girls, the Sisters moved to that location, and Father Isoleri made his residence in the school building, despite the fact that school enrollment had increased to nearly four hundred students.

During this time, the church building itself was proving to be much too small to meet the needs of South Philadelphia's growing Italian population, so additional ground was purchased next door where an old lumberyard had been located and a new church was constructed. The cornerstone was laid in 1883, but the building itself **[pictured above]** was not completed until 1891, after which time a new rectory was built. While construction was in progress, Father Isoleri lived in the basement of the church, acting as his own sexton as well as pastor.

The present church building is the third that has served the parish. It was erected at a cost of $80,000 and, at this writing, is one hundred years old. It is adorned by various works of art that deserve particular notice. The building itself is sixty-five feet by one hundred ten feet and is designed in Renaissance style, its stucco interior richly ornamented. As might be expected, the church has undergone several renovations and interior improvements during the past century. On either side of the sanctuary in the upper, or main, church are paintings depicting episodes in the life of the parish patroness, St. Mary Magdalen de Pazzi. She was a mystic so these paintings portray her experiencing certain religious apparitions. In the center of the ceiling is a reproduction of Titian's Assumption, and on the walls are murals depicting the fifteen mysteries of the rosary. The walls, the altar rail, and other parts of the church are now made of Carrara marble.

Above the new altar is a mosaic portraying the Last Supper. These works of art were added from time to time as the financial posture of the parish improved.

If there was one thing that characterized St. Mary Magdalen de Pazzi parish during the first generations of its existence, it was grinding, widespread poverty that was a permanent resident in most homes and a daily visitor at the rectory door. While some of the original settlers who arrived in Philadelphia from Italy after the uprisings of 1848 might have been considered political refugees, the vast majority of Italian immigrants were economic refugees escaping from circumstances that provided little opportunity for employment and less hope for improvement. During the latter part of the nineteenth century, new parishioners formed a large number of small parish organizations, often naming their societies after the patron saints of their hometowns in Italy. These organizations had more than religious significance. When an individual arrived in South Philadelphia from an Italian town or village and was able to gain an economic foothold, he often served as the forerunner for the immigration of relatives and townspeople, who then clustered together after they arrived under the banner of one of these parish societies and worked to assist others from their locality in following the same path to South Philadelphia. At St. Mary Magdalen de Pazzi, they found both a religious and a cultural center in the company of others who spoke the same language.

In a large, highly structured, and diverse archdiocese such as Philadelphia, the basic organization of the Church was and continues to be parishes organized along territorial lines, as required by the First Plenary Council of 1852. Such lines were drawn on a map and Catholics living within those boundaries were expected to attend the parish church established in that area and contribute to the support of its pastor. Such parishes were almost invariably English-speaking parishes, so the pastor and his assistants were often unable to communicate with all of the immigrant groups who might be found in their neighborhood. Accordingly, there were superimposed upon this grid of so-called canonical or territorial parishes different national parishes or churches, which had no stated boundaries and which were administered by priests who spoke the language of the nationality for whom the parish was established. Pastors of national parishes were supposed to limit their ministry (and their collection baskets) to members of their own ethnic group who, but for this special dispensation, would be obligated to attend the nearest territorial church. Such rules could not be administered with a heavy hand and they were not, although friction occasionally arose between pastors of territorial churches and those in charge of national churches over just which Catholics were supposed to go where. In many instances, these churches were within blocks of each other.

St. Mary Magdalen de Pazzi was of course established as an Italian national parish, but it had a significant number of non-Italian parishioners. Father Mariani's entries on the very earliest parish records frequently contained the notation "Irlandesi," indicating that an Irishman had been baptized or married. Old documents, parish bulletins, and anniversary publications contain a sprinkling of Irish names. Father Isoleri was happy to have the Irish in his congregation, reasoning that, in those days, it was the Irish who had the good jobs and could best help him to meet parish expenses.

To solidify and improve the spiritual life of his parish, Father Isoleri wrote an Italian catechism and Italian devotional booklets and encouraged an ongoing devotion to the patroness of the parish. He published letters from devout parishioners and others who wrote to him claiming that their prayers had been answered through the intercession of St. Mary Magdalen de Pazzi. Sermons and parish functions were, for the most part, conducted in Italian, although Father Isoleri provided for English-speaking parishioners as well. In 1893, the Vatican began to send an apostolic delegate, usually an Italian bishop, to the United States to act as an overseer of the American Church. These delegates generally made it to St. Mary Magdalen de Pazzi from Washington on important ceremonial and anniversary occasions to participate in the festivities with their countrymen.

During the late 1800s and early 1900s, the parish grew at a remarkable rate. For instance, parish records indicate that in the year 1887 alone, some five hundred thirty-five baptisms were performed. A second Italian parish, Our Lady of Good Counsel, was eventually established a few blocks away to alleviate the overcrowding at its mother parish. However, it no longer exists, having been consolidated with another parish some thirty-five years later. St. Nicholas of Tolentine was established in 1912 and absorbed more parishioners from St. Mary Magdalen de Pazzi. The entire archdiocese of Philadelphia now has approximately twenty-three Italian parishes, some of which are organized as national parishes while others are territorial parishes whose boundaries happen to include a largely Italian population. St. Mary Magdalen de Pazzi has become a territorial parish.

This parish has experienced great stability by retaining pastors for long periods of time. Monsignor Vito Mazzone served as its pastor for forty-eight years beginning in 1937. At that time, the parish had over fifteen thousand members. During his pastorate, the character of the parish began to evolve into one made up of predominantly older people who were second- and third-generation Italians. A few years before Monsignor Mazzone came to the parish in 1937, a new parochial school had been completed that was eventually sold to the archdiocese for use as Southeast Catholic High School for boys. Later, it was transferred back to the parish but was eventually closed because of the demographics of the area, which showed intown parishes declining in size while suburban parishes were growing.

One neighborhood boy who caught Monsignor Mazzone's eye was Alfredo Cocozza. Although a bit on the wild side, Cocozza could really sing the "Ave Maria" and he often did, especially at funerals. He was encouraged to pursue a musical career and he did so, taking his mother's name, Lanza, as a stage name. After an unusually short but notable musical career, Mario Lanza died in Italy in 1959 at the age of thirty-four. His body was brought back to St. Mary Magdalen de Pazzi for a Mass of Christian Burial.

Monsignor Mazzone gained wide recognition and acclaim for his work among the elderly. One group that did not hold him in such high esteem were members of certain South Philadelphia "families" who gained their livelihoods from highly questionable activities. Monsignor Mazzone evidenced his disdain for their activities by simply refusing to permit them to be buried from his church.

Today, St. Mary Magdalen de Pazzi has about 1,800 members; this number includes about 125 children and about 600 to 650 older persons. It also has its first native American pastor, Father Donato Silveri. All Masses are now said in English. Anyone wishing to hear Mass in Italian must go a few blocks away to St. Nicholas of Tolentine where Italian Augustinians offer one Mass in Italian each weekend. While the parish is still ethnically Italian, only a few of its members can speak Italian. In fact, the parish now conducts classes in the Italian language for parishioners who want to use this medium to reestablish their roots in Italian culture. Like Society Hill, located a mile or so away, the neighborhood around the church is becoming gentrified as individuals buy up row houses located along South Philadelphia's narrow streets and remodel them into modernized town houses. Because South Philadelphia's large Italian market is only a few blocks away, the area has an economic attraction that also helps to preserve its ethnic character. Father Silveri encourages former members of the parish who have moved elsewhere to come back and settle where their grandparents once lived, and some have done so.

Many Italian parishes in Philadelphia conduct annual *festas*, which are festivals featuring Italian foods, games, and customs. This parish holds a large commemoration on the third Sunday of May in honor of the Blessed Mother. This date falls close in time to May 25, the Feast of St. Mary Magdalen de Pazzi. Following the noon Mass, parishioners and others who have returned for the celebration get out the statues of Italian saints that the old parish societies once used, place them on poles, and carry them through the streets of South Philadelphia — up Seventh Street to Fitzwater Street, over Fitzwater to Eighth Street, down Eighth Street to Federal Street, and over Federal and Seventh Streets to the church, where benediction then takes place. The procession is normally two blocks long and serves as an expression of identity both for Italians who still live in the area and for others whose parents and grandparents once resided there. It also establishes their identification with the impoverished immigrants who created this tradition as they sank their own roots into the land of their adoption.

22
Most Blessed Sacrament

Bally

PENNSYLVANIA

In 1741, Father Joseph Greaton, S.J., pastor of St. Joseph's Church in Philadelphia, was able to obtain the services of a German Jesuit, Father Thomas Schneider, as pastor for the German Catholic population that was beginning to migrate into the area near Reading. Father Schneider had been a rector of the university at Heidelberg but chose to abandon academic life and spend his remaining twenty-three years as a missionary in colonial Pennsylvania. Father Greaton purchased three hundred seventy-three acres of land at Goshenhoppen (now called Bally), near Perkiomen Creek in Berks County, from the descendants of William Penn. He sent Father Schneider to establish a mission church in this area. Additional land was later purchased from a disgruntled Mennonite, Ulrich Beidler. It contained both a Mennonite church and cemetery. Father Schneider struck a deal with the Mennonites. He offered to convey back to them their church and cemetery if they would lend him a hand in building a log chapel. They did so, and thus was constructed, in 1743 or thereabouts, the original St. Paul's Chapel. In the process, a long-standing friendship was also established between Catholics and Mennonites in the Perkiomen Creek area. The name of the area was later changed from Goshenhoppen to Churchville in recognition of the fact that the locality was large enough to boast two churches, one Catholic and one Mennonite.

Until the First Plenary Council of the American Catholic Church in Baltimore in 1852, both missions and parishes often had undetermined boundaries. A parish was, to some degree, the personal mission of the priest assigned to a general area. Father Schneider used St. Paul's Chapel as a base for missionary activities that took him to what are now Allentown and Bethlehem and beyond there to Bucks County and to Bound Brook, New Jersey. He also visited German Catholics in Philadelphia once a month. By 1757, Father Schneider had under his care about two hundred twenty-eight parishioners at Goshenhoppen and three hundred sixty-four more at his other regular mission stops.

In his spare time, Father Schneider hand-copied at least two Roman missals. Catholic publishing was forbidden in British colonies and none took place until Robert Bell printed a Catholic prayer book in Philadelphia in 1774. As a result, missals either had to be imported at great expense or copied by hand. Father Schneider also started a small school at Goshenhoppen and maintained it for a number of years. Details concerning the operation of the school are scant, but the parish claims it to be the first parochial school in the United States.

Father Schneider was succeeded by a series of pastors, some of whom were Jesuits and others of whom were either Franciscan or secular priests. Father Paul Ernsten completed the first enlargement of the original St. Paul's Chapel. In 1837, Father Boniface Curvin, S.J., completed the remaining addition just before his death. The church [**pictured above**] is the one that has been in existence since that time. Four early pastors, including Father Schneider, are buried under its main altar.

Father Schneider began a parish record of baptisms, deaths, and marriages that dates back to 1741. Recorded there are vital statistics concerning not only the Goshenhoppen area but other locations in the mission territory served from this church. Some of the entries in the death register reflect the pathos of life in the Pennsylvania colony that early missioners observed in making their rounds. For instance, there is a death recorded in 1765 of a woman who died "seven days after childbirth, her infant dying at birth or rather perishing through unskillful handling." Another entry records the death of a woman who "had been aiding Mary Hartman (above named) during her illness and having contracted the same ailment during her labor of charity, died of the same [dysentery] and was buried September 2, 1765 in the graveyard used by the Lutherans near her father's house." In the early 1800s, another graveyard was established across the road from the existing church. Many early grave markers were inscribed in German, since it was the prevailing language of the area until well into the nineteenth century. One notable exception is the grave of a black veteran of the American Revolution, Isaac Jones. A native of Ethiopia, he served in the Continental Army, lived out his life in eastern Pennsylvania, and was baptized a Catholic shortly before his death in 1847 at the age of ninety-four.

The principal source of income for the residents of Goshenhoppen was agriculture, although the area had, from time to time, a charcoal-manufacturing industry. It also supported foundries, called furnaces, for the smelting of iron ore. The Jesuits, who held title to about five hundred acres surrounding the church, farmed it with sharecroppers and used the income to support their missionary efforts, both at Goshenhoppen and elsewhere. It was standard procedure for Jesuit missionaries not to rely upon their congregations for contributions but to support themselves from independent sources. Another source of income for the colonial missions in the eighteenth century was the Sir John James Fund, created by the will of an English Catholic layman who died in London in 1741. Income from this fund was divided among Jesuit missionaries in certain poor London districts and those working in the American colonies, including the Goshenhoppen mission.

No reference to Most Blessed Sacrament parish is complete without mention of Father Augustin Bally, S.J., whose name was given to the town after his death in 1882. A German immigrant, he attended the Jesuit novitiate at St. Thomas Manor in southern Maryland and was assigned to this parish shortly after his ordination in 1837. There he spent the remaining forty-five years of his life as a country pastor, at first attending his parish on horseback and in later years by horse and buggy. It was he who changed the name of the church from St. Paul to Most Blessed Sacrament. Although more churches had been established by the time of his arrival in eastern Pennsylvania, his parish still extended over several counties.

During his tenure as pastor, Father Bally built a school in the developed portion of the town and operated it in conjunction with township officials as a "Church Public School." The parish furnished the building and paid teachers in the primary grades while the township paid for the teachers assigned to the higher grades. The township also certified the credentials of the teachers who were employed. Father Bally was quite insistent that all children speak English while on the school grounds and invented disciplinary measures to enforce this policy. He still used German while preaching Sunday sermons, introducing English during the later years of this tenure. One of the few times he left the parish during his pastorate was to journey to Fortress Monroe, Virginia, in the spring of 1863 to visit parishioners who were stationed in the Union Army near Richmond. Unfortunately, the Union Army was busily engaged at that time at Chancellorsville, so he was never able to proceed to their encampment for a personal visit.

As the Jesuit order began to transfer its attention and resources in the United States from missionary activity to education, the time eventually came when they would leave Bally and turn over the parish to the archdiocese of Philadelphia. During Father Bally's later years, he sold off small portions of parish land to individual parishioners with the intention of stimulating the growth of a community of Catholics living near the church. Not long after his death in 1882, the remaining property was sold to the archdiocese, and the parish has been staffed since that time by diocesan priests. It is now part of the diocese of Allentown.

Today, Most Blessed Sacrament is still essentially a country parish. It has a congregation of about six hundred families, many of whom have been in the Bally area for generations. It also operates a parochial school, although not in the same intimate relationship with the public school system that Father Bally maintained. A unique feature of the parish today is the fact that it maintains a museum and library to house and display books, vestments, artifacts, and other memorabilia of the parish dating back to its earliest days. In this museum, the story of two hundred fifty years of Catholic presence in Pennsylvania is available for anyone wishing to follow roots going back to the earliest days of American Catholic history.

23
St. George

Shenandoah

PENNSYLVANIA

The identity of the oldest Lithuanian Catholic church in America is, to a certain extent, a matter of defining the term "oldest." Certainly, any parish qualifying for that title would be located in the anthracite region of northeastern Pennsylvania. In 1862, the estate of Philadelphia financier Stephen Girard, operating through the Philadelphia Land Company, opened its first colliery in Shenandoah. After the construction of railroads permitted the shipment of large quantities of coal from this area, the region began to attract large numbers of Eastern Europeans of various nationalities who came to work in the mines. Shortly thereafter, the first all-Lithuanian parish was organized in Shenandoah, a town that also became the site of the oldest Eastern Rite Catholic parish in the United States. However, the Lithuanian parish in existence today in Shenandoah does not bear the same name nor is it the same parish as the one that was founded in 1872 by Lithuanian immigrants who had begun to flow into Schuylkill County from their czarist-dominated homeland. St. Joseph in nearby Mahanoy City, St. Casimir in Pittstown, near Scranton, and St. Casimir in Plymouth, Pennsylvania, were also founded by Lithuanian immigrants in the decades immediately preceding the turn of the twentieth century.

At one time, there were about seventy-five thousand Lithuanian Catholics living in the anthracite region, and Shenandoah was regarded as their unofficial capital. It was the focal point for Lithuanian parades, cultural celebrations, and conventions, as well as for fund-raising rallies for Old World religious and political causes ranging from a new seminary in Lithuania to the sale of Lithuanian war bonds during World War I. Shenandoah was also an important stop for Lithuanian religious and political dignitaries making trips to the United States.

The history of the Catholic Church in the homeland of these immigrants presents an ongoing saga of suppression and domination by one neighboring group after another. In 1987, Lithuanian Catholics celebrated the 600th anniversary of the conversion of Lithuania to Christianity, but the existence of Catholics in the area now called Lithuania dates back another century. There can be little doubt that Roman Catholicism helped to preserve Lithuanian cultural and national identity in the face of an assortment of German, Polish, and Russian invaders who, at one time or another, have occupied that country. Lithuanians are an Indo-European people whose ethnic origin and language set them completely apart from their Slavic and Germanic neighbors. While, in this country, they often settled near Polish and other Eastern European immigrants and frequently shared religious facilities with them, Lithuanians speak a language closely akin to Sanskrit but not to either Russian or Polish. Long ago, they adopted Latin Rite rather than Eastern Rite Catholicism and the Western alphabet rather than the Cyrillic alphabet of the Russians. From 1795 until 1919, Russia occupied Lithuania and tried to stamp out these distinctive features of Lithuanian culture, closing Catholic churches and schools and even forbidding the printing of books, including prayer books and missals, except by using Cyrillic letters. These efforts failed to achieve their purpose, but one of the results of Russian persecution was the emigration to the United States of a large number of people who were either illiterate or poorly educated.

No one knows how many Lithuanians came to these shores before 1898. Anyone who could scrape together the $35 to $65 which was the price of a ticket in steerage could immigrate to the United States, but when they arrived, they were simply listed on U.S. immigration records as Russians. Only after that date were separate statistics kept that identified Lithuanians by nationality. Between 1899 and the outbreak of World War I, between 10,000 and 15,000 Lithuanians entered the United States each year; in some years, that figure ran as high as 25,000. The 1910 census reported that there were 207,000 inhabitants of the United States of Lithuanian origin, of whom about a third were native Americans. More lived in Pennsylvania than in any other state.

The first Lithuanian families arrived in Shenandoah in 1869. They initially worshiped at Holy Family, a German Catholic church that was just being established. Shortly after their arrival, they formed the St. Casimir Beneficial Society and purchased two lots, some twenty feet by forty feet, on North Jardin Street where the Polish church of St. Casimir stands today. In 1872, they erected an unpainted, unplastered plank structure with a wooden roof and named it St. Casimir's Church. They invited Reverend Andrew Strupinskas, who had come to New York from Lithuania in 1866, to serve as their pastor. Upon arriving in Shenandoah, Father Strupinskas lived with his married sister who was already a resident of this growing mining town.

Father Strupinskas spoke both Lithuanian and Polish and was able to communicate with both groups of Catholics. Poles living in the town were invited to join St. Casimir's parish, and they did so in such numbers that they eventually took it over. In 1877, Father Strupinskas was replaced by a Polish priest who spoke no Lithuanian. The founders of the parish felt that they were being ousted from their spiritual home. They requested Archbishop Patrick J. Ryan in Philadelphia to send them a Lithuanian priest but he had none to send. In July of 1877, they blockaded the door of the church and tried to prevent the new pastor from entering, shouting to him to educate their children in the Lithuanian language. For this demonstration they were arrested, fined, and denounced in court as troublemakers. The Polish members of the parish were able to convince their Irish archbishop that the Lithuanian language was just another Polish dialect and that the protesters had no legitimate grievance, so Archbishop Ryan backed the Polish pastor and dismissed the complaint. At this time, it came to public attention that the deed to church property, which had been registered in the Schuylkill County courthouse, referred to St. Casimir's as a Polish church, so many Lithuanian members felt that they had been bilked out of property they had paid for.

Some Polish-speaking Lithuanians, especially those who had Polish wives, remained, but the others withdrew from St. Casimir's Church and formed a new organization called the St. George Beneficial Society. In the face of this disruption, the new Polish pastor tried to learn Lithuanian and, with the help of the church organist, prepared and read Lithuanian sermons from the altar. He also invited a German priest from the nearby town of Locust Gap to come to Shenandoah from time to time to hear confessions in Lithuanian. These efforts did not serve to heal the breach.

During the mid-1870s, a Lithuanian Franciscan Brother, Augustine Zeytz, came to Shenandoah and attempted to fill the spiritual void that had arisen in the Lithuanian community. He began to publish a Lithuanian paper and said the rosary and taught catechism in the homes of those who refused to attend what had come to be a Polish church. However, Brother Augustine eventually left the area. He had always wanted to found a monastery for Lithuanian Franciscans and eventually obtained a tract of land in Wisconsin for this purpose. Regrettably for his ambition, the monastery he established in Wisconsin suffered the same fate as St. Casimir's parish and eventually became a Polish foundation.

After about ten years, the members of the newly formed St. George Beneficial Society were able to obtain the services of another Lithuanian priest, Father Alexander Burba, who had just arrived in the United States in 1889. They were encouraged by the fact that a Lithuanian parish was being formed in nearby Mahanoy City and sought permission from the archbishop of Philadelphia to establish an all-Lithuanian parish in Shenandoah. Notwithstanding the objections of the Polish pastor at St. Casimir's, permission for a new parish was granted. Being without funds to proceed immediately, the members of the St. George Beneficial Society approached the pastor and asked him if he would establish a school where children could be instructed either in Polish or in Lithuanian. The pastor refused. He was also asked if Father Burba could come to St. Casimir's and serve, at least temporarily, as an assistant. The pastor's reply was, "Let your invited guest go dig coal."

In the face of this hostility, Father Burba had to conduct services in Latin and Lithuanian in a public hall that had been rented by the St. George Beneficial Society for this purpose. Not long after arriving in Shenandoah, he was transferred to a Lithuanian-Polish parish in Plymouth, so the society approached Father Peter Abromaitis to be their pastor. Father Abromaitis had just laid the cornerstone of a new Lithuanian parish at Mahanoy City, a church that took five years to complete. After his arrival in Pennsylvania from Lithuania, he had become acquainted with Lithuanians in Shenandoah, only four miles from Mahanoy City, and had visited that city from time to time to hear confessions. He agreed, subject to the approval of the archbishop.

On March 31, 1891, about fifteen hundred Lithuanian Catholics met in the hall where Father Burba had said Mass a few months earlier in order to discuss the establishment of the new church. In a month's time, they had raised $40,000 and purchased three lots on South Jardin Street, about six blocks away from St. Casimir. Title to the property was registered in the name of the archbishop of Philadelphia, despite minor grumbling about "giving our land to the Irish bishop." On October 26 of the same year, the Irish pastor of the local territorial parish, acting on behalf of the archbishop, laid the cornerstone of the present St. George Church **[pictured above]**. Over five thousand people attended this event. They came from every part of the anthracite region and from as far away as Baltimore. A huge parade, complete with marching bands and nearly two thousand participants carrying flags and banners, highlighted this occasion.

To finance church construction, parishioners were assessed the sum of $21.25 a year, but any man could work off all or part of this assessment at the rate of $1.25 a day. Many coal miners put in three or four hours' work in the late afternoon or early evening doing church construction after finishing a ten-hour stint in the mines. The original church had a seating capacity of 800 and was 120 feet long by 56 feet wide. As soon as the basement was completed, Father Abromaitis began to say Mass at the church. The entire building was completed in May of 1894 and was formally dedicated at that time.

A Pennsylvania statute enacted in 1855 governing the organization and administration of church property provided for the election of a church committee or trustees by the membership of the church to control the material aspects of the church operation while permitting clergymen the right to administer the spiritual aspects of the operation. The law was structured to reflect Protestant methods of church organization. Over the years, it led to serious internal difficulties at St. George and in many other Pennsylvania parishes, many of which were not of Eastern European origin. These difficulties endured until the law was amended in 1935. At St. George, the parishioners elected a committee to manage parish finances, as required by law. Father Abromaitis was elected treasurer and served in that position for twelve years. All went well so long as he was pastor, but after he was transferred, disputes between clergy and laity arose that consumed the energies of both priest and parishioners for nearly thirty years.

While most Lithuanian immigrants were and remain Roman Catholics, Lithuanian communities, both in Shenandoah and elsewhere, numbered among their members a significant and vocal group of dissidents who were generally regarded as either Communists, socialists, or atheists. In any community, the local Catholic church was the principal object of their enmity and they eagerly provided added impetus to any dissension that might arise in the ranks of regular churchgoers. In 1885, an avowed atheist, John Sliupas, came to Shenandoah and began to publish a newspaper called *Lietuwiszkas Balsas* (the *Lithuanian Voice*). He was able to divide the local Lithuanian community into factions, one supporting him and the other composed of practicing Catholics. Despite his pretension of championing Lithuanian ethnic interests against Polish control by St. Casimir's parish, he made common cause with Polish atheists in the locality, feeling that they made preferable allies to Lithuanian Catholics. He failed to gain a foothold on the local level in the Lithuanian community, but he assembled a convention in Shenandoah of Lithuanians from the eastern United States and formed an "Alliance for Lithuanians in America." This organization was led by Lithuanian clergy until the convention of 1901, when it split into two organizations, one clerical and the other national — the Lithuanian Roman Catholic Alliance and the Lithuanian Alliance of America. Following a pattern that also developed among Polish immigrants, one of these national organizations was made up of individuals who hewed closely to Catholic Church doctrines and the church organization while the other had a distinctly anticlerical cast to it. Today, these organizations content themselves with selling policies of fraternal life insurance and publishing periodic newspapers, but at the turn of the century they exercised significant political influence in Lithuanian communities that had come into being throughout Pennsylvania and elsewhere.

The history of the Lithuanian church in Shenandoah closely resembled the formation of other Lithuanian Catholic churches in the region. Most emanated from the organization of a beneficial society, often named after St. George or St. Casimir. For both social and economic reasons, Lithuanians and Poles often formed joint churches that later divided into separate nationality parishes after the two groups became sufficiently well settled that they could afford separate parishes. Often, these separations did not take place peaceably.

In Hazelton, about twenty miles away, both national factions in the joint Catholic church began to argue among themselves as to whether the title to the church should read "Polish-Lithuanian" or "Lithuanian-Polish." In November 1892, to resolve the issue, the Polish members of the parish devised a plan to fill the church at Sunday Mass and to snatch the collection baskets as they were being passed. After doing so, they walked out of the church, screaming at the Lithuanians in order to provoke an incident. When Lithuanian worshipers failed to rise to the bait and remained in their pews, the

Poles dispersed. Unable to prevail in a lawsuit that they filed, they withdrew from the parish and established their own church.

In Freeland, Pennsylvania, the Lithuanian faction tried to establish a joint parish as a "Lithuanian-Polish" church, giving themselves first billing. In reprisal, Polish members of the parish nailed the back door of the church shut and blocked the front entrance so that the Lithuanian pastor could not enter to say Sunday Mass. A fight ensued and the police were summoned. In a scuffle between the two factions, one Lithuanian parishioner was shot in the leg and five Polish parishioners and a policeman were hurt. The issue was settled when a majority of the Polish faction withdrew and set up their own parish. The bishop then intervened in the dispute in the original parish, requiring that two Masses be said each Sunday, one for the Poles and the other for the Lithuanians. He sent a Polish priest from Hazelton each Sunday to preach at the Mass attended by the Polish families who had remained in the parish.

At Plymouth, Father Burba, originally assigned to Shenandoah, was instructed by the bishop to give sermons in both Polish and Lithuanian. One Sunday, when he read the Gospel in Lithuanian, the Polish members of the congregation walked out of the church, locked the doors of the rectory, and forced Father Burba to live in a private home for three weeks. The Lithuanians received permission from the bishop to form a separate parish and did so but not before responding to a lawsuit litigating the ownership of the parish monstrance, several valuable chalices, and four vestments that they took with them when they left. They prevailed in the lawsuit; but, in reprisal for their loss in court, the Poles locked the gates of the parish cemetery to prevent the burial of two Lithuanian children. The priest officiating at the funeral removed the locks and proceeded with the burial ceremony; but, after it concluded, a few fanatics exhumed the two coffins and removed them from the cemetery. For their actions the individuals involved were prosecuted and imprisoned.

Despite these obstacles, Lithuanian parishes in general and St. George in particular grew and prospered. By 1900, there were thirty all-Lithuanian parishes in the United States, of which seventeen were located in Pennsylvania. By that date, the borough of Shenandoah had become a busy mining community. It is estimated that twenty different languages were spoken in the area. Lithuanians comprised the largest single nationality and were able to elect one of their number as mayor.

Even before the church had been completed, the St. George Beneficial Society had purchased a three-acre plot just outside the city limits for a cemetery. Over the years, this cemetery was enlarged and four other Lithuanian Catholic cemeteries were opened. Shortly after the church was completed, a three-story brick rectory was constructed next door, and it remains the church office and residence for the clergy. It should be noted that, in many Lithuanian parishes of that era, the most prominent person in the parish other than the pastor was the organist, who often had educational and cultural attainments considerably above those of most parishioners. At St. George, Professor John A. Zemaitis was retained as organist until his death in 1932. In addition to organizing the

St. Cecelia Choir, he taught reading, writing, and religion in classes that were held in the church basement. Some seventy children attended these classes at the outset. Later, adult-education courses were added. Professor Zemaitis, a noted musician and composer, wrote and published Lithuanian ballads drawn from Lithuanian folk songs.

Various physical improvements took place at St. George. Twin steeples were added to the original church and the exterior walls were faced with brick. Ten large bells, weighing a total of eight tons, were purchased and placed in the belfry. The parish retained the services of Francis Bogdan, a Lithuanian artist who had graduated from the Russian Academy of Fine Arts in St. Petersburg. He painted a large mural on the vaulted interior ceiling of the church depicting biblical scenes.

The parish sponsored a band, a marching society, a reading and writing society, and a grocery store, which eventually went out of business. Beginning as early as 1874, Lithuanians in Shenandoah began to publish pamphlets and books and continued this practice for a number of years. Many of these publications were smuggled into Lithuania to thwart the ban on books printed in Lithuanian or Western script which the Russians imposed from 1863 to 1904. A survey of Lithuanians in Shenandoah just before the turn of the twentieth century showed that they owned some one hundred nine places of business, of which fifty-nine were taverns. It is not surprising that among the many organizations sponsored by the parish there was a temperance society.

Labor troubles in the anthracite region at the turn of the century deeply involved thousands of Lithuanians and St. George parish. The Lithuanian Miners Union was formed. It eventually became part of the United Mine Workers of America. In Shenandoah alone, it had four thousand members. One of the first strikes that took place occurred in 1897 at Hazelton when five hundred miners marched toward the Lattimer Mine in a protest aimed at securing higher wages and improved working conditions. The Luzerne County sheriff and his deputies fired at the striking miners, killing twenty and wounding fifty-five. A mass protest meeting took place at St. George's Hall in Shenandoah that was attended by about three thousand people of various national origins. Father Abromaitis was one of the speakers who voiced a loud objection to the acts of public officials at the Lattimer Mine. They demanded that the sheriff and his deputies be prosecuted. A collection was taken up for the families of the victims and a requiem Mass for the dead miners was offered at St. George Church the following day. The sheriff and his deputies were indicted but were acquitted.

In 1900 and again in 1902, strikes took place in mines closer to Shenandoah to protest a cut in wages of ten percent. Strikebreakers were brought in from outside to keep the mines operating. Several incidents of violence occurred in confrontations between these individuals and striking miners. The strikers included many Lithuanian miners and hence many parishioners from St. George. To raise money for the strike fund, the St. George band gave concerts throughout the area. Eventually, the strikers prevailed and went back to work in the mines for wages ranging from $50 to $75 a month for a six-day workweek.

In 1908, the archbishop of Philadelphia transferred Father Abromaitis to the Lithuanian church in nearby Mahanoy City where he had formerly been stationed. In his place, he assigned Father Anthony Milukas. Father Abromaitis had been a popular figure in Shenandoah and his transfer was greeted with adamant opposition on the part of many parishioners. This event marked the beginning of an ongoing battle between the clergy and the trustees of St. George Church that continued for more than thirty years. When he asked the outgoing pastor for the keys to the church and for the parish records, Father Milukas was told that the trustees kept the keys and maintained all the books except for the sacramental records. The trustees then padlocked the church and the rectory, both of which were not opened until the pastor obtained the aid of the police. Upon entering the rectory, he found that every door had been padlocked and the rooms smelled of formaldehyde. Crowds jeered when Father Milukas took charge of the church premises. He insisted on his rights under canon law and began to take up the collection. The trustees countered by taking up their own collection.

Father Milukas was soon transferred and was replaced by Father Albin J. Kaminskas, who was able to pacify the trustees but not for long. Upon arriving at Mahanoy City, Father Abromaitis ran into similar difficulties with trustees in that city. A determined standoff took place between a succession of pastors and the trustees in Mahanoy City, who refused to allow the parochial school building to be used for school purposes and persisted in using it for several years as a pool hall and a cigar store. This situation continued until the pastor was able to obtain a court order restoring possession of the building to church authorities.

After settling in at St. George, Father Kaminskas told the trustees that all resolutions and decisions that they made would have to be submitted to him for approval. They disagreed. On Palm Sunday, 1910, he denounced them from the pulpit, at which point the trustees in the congregation interrupted his sermon and began to make fun of him. At Father Kaminskas' request, the archbishop sent Monsignor Peter Masson to St. George to address the congregation. He told the congregation, including the trustees, that the archbishop would insist on compliance with canon law and instructed the members of the parish to appoint two parishioners who, with the archbishop's representative, would inspect the financial records of the parish twice a year and would prepare reports to be read from the pulpit as to the condition of these records. Monsignor Masson warned that, without the pastor's permission, no collections could be taken up at the church, no graves could be opened in the parish cemetery, and no other church functions would be allowed to take place. The trustees responded to this warning by filing a lawsuit against church authorities. After a lengthy trial, the Court of Common Pleas, citing the old 1855 statute, ruled that the pastor could attend to spiritual matters at the parish but that the trustees still had the right to control church property. Encouraged by this ruling, the trustees padlocked the church so the archbishop countered with the unusual step of placing the church building under interdict. The pastor then rented space in the basement of Annunciation Church, the English-speaking territorial parish, and began to conduct services at that location. After the appointment of a fourth pastor, Father Simon Pautienius, St. George's was reopened and the fledgling Lithuanian parish in the basement of Annunciation Church was discontinued. However, this was not to be the end of trustee problems at St. George Church.

Father Pautienius tried to bring peace to the parish by allowing the trustees to administer church property. During his pastorate, he started a school, published at his own expense a translation of the New Testament, founded a commercial bank for Lithuanian immigrants, remodeled the church building by adding a granite facing, and purchased a second cemetery. However, the trustees became too much for him to bear. They asked each person coming to Mass for a ten-cent entry fee, making it appear that they were charging people for going to Mass. They conducted fund-raising events and parish socials on church property or at the church cemetery in derogation of good taste and the spiritual mission of the parish. Membership on the board of trustees of the parish was often a matter of prestige in the Lithuanian community, so individuals who had little or no interest in the religious mission of the parish sometimes aspired to these positions. In some instances, they may not have even been regular communicants but were interested principally in the money-making potential afforded them as parish trustees. Eventually, Father Pautienius left St. George and returned to Lithuania.

While Lithuanians in Shenandoah were rapidly improving their lot in life, positive changes were taking place in their original homeland. On February 16, 1918, as the czarist regime in Russia began to crumble from both internal and external pressures, the Lithuanian Council in Vilnius proclaimed Lithuanian independence. That event, Lithuanian Independence Day, is still commemorated each February at St. George and in many other Lithuanian communities. The declaration of independence was eventually supported by Allied military forces and postwar diplomats, who brought into existence a Lithuanian republic after one hundred twenty-five years of partition. For the Church, political independence of the nation meant an opportunity to grow and expand. In 1920, Polish armies entered the country but were content to seize a portion of it, the area that embraced the Lithuanian capital of Vilnius. In 1940, following a short-lived pact between Hitler and Stalin, the Russian Army entered Lithuania and annexed the country to the Soviet Union. Ironically, it was the Russian Army that restored Vilnius to the Lithuanian republic but only at the price of Soviet domination. During the twenty years of Lithuanian independence, two archdioceses and nearly one thousand parishes flourished. After Soviet occupation, many of these churches, including the cathedral at Vilnius, were closed, and many Catholics were deported to Siberia. Not until the Soviet empire crumbled in 1991 did Lithuania regain its independence and the Church its freedom.

During the 1920s, events abroad and restrictive immigration quotas imposed by a new American immigration law enacted in 1922 slowed new Lithuanian immigration to the United States to a trickle. In subsequent decades, a third factor served to limit the growth of St. George and other parishes as well. Coal mining reached its peak in

Shenandoah about 1930. Thereafter, mine after mine began to close or to limit production so that job opportunities diminished accordingly. These external events did not diminish the friction at St. George between the clergy and the trustees. To settle this problem with finality, it took both the appointment of an unyielding pastor and a change in Pennsylvania law.

In 1929, Father (and later Monsignor) Joseph A. Karalius became pastor of St. George, a post he held for forty years. After arriving in Shenandoah, he found that the parish trustees refused to give him the keys to the parish hall. In fact, they held the keys to all parish buildings. Trustees took it upon themselves to control the ringing of church bells and rang them when they felt it appropriate. They controlled the light and heat in the buildings, collected dues from parishioners, and managed parish finances. When Father Karalius objected, the trustees appealed to the parishioners to have him removed. At a meeting of the trustees, which took place in the parish hall, a dispute arose as to whether the pastor would even be allowed to open the meeting with a prayer. After he questioned the use of parish funds, one trustee spoke up to say that he had nothing to fear from priests, noting that "I haven't made my Easter duty for two years and nothing evil has happened to me." At another trustee meeting, a motion was made to withhold the pay of the pastor and to prevent him from officiating at funerals. The trustees requested parishioners to donate Mass stipends to them rather than to the pastor because they felt it was not necessary to pray for the dead. They also requested Cardinal Dennis Dougherty, the archbishop of Philadelphia, to transfer Father Karalius. Cardinal Dougherty rebuked the trustees and also demanded to know why they had not forwarded to the chancery the diocesan collections that had been made for the missions and the seminary fund.

The trustees conducted their own funeral services. Families of the deceased would bring the casket to the church door, a trustee would toll the church bells, and the procession would move to the cemetery for burial. In 1931, the trustees padlocked the organ and the door of the belfry, so church bells were not rung until the pastor obtained a court order permitting him to enter the belfry. Efforts at reconciliation took place. Committees representing both parties were formed and attorneys were retained, but committee members ended up fighting with one another. The pastor made efforts to have the trustees voted out of office, but he did not succeed.

About twenty different civil and criminal cases arose out of this dispute. Father Karalius preferred charges against the trustees; they, in turn, filed suits against him for illegal entry on church property. Occasionally, the pastor prevailed, but none of these individual cases was able to resolve the root problem, namely the legal right of trustees under Pennsylvania law to administer the financial affairs of the parish.

In 1935, Cardinal Dougherty asked the Pennsylvania legislature to amend the 1855 statute governing the control of church property. The legislature responded, changing Pennsylvania law to provide that church properties would henceforth be managed according to the laws and regulations of each religious group. To carry out the provisions of the amendment, Cardinal Dougherty then drew up a set of guidelines to apply to the management of Catholic churches in the archdiocese of Philadelphia. His decree provided that the pastor of each parish was entitled to administer church property and to retain all church collections. He was likewise obligated to maintain all churches and was forbidden from selling any land or buildings. He was also forbidden from contracting for any improvements in excess of $500 without the permission of the archbishop. Any laymen who might assist in these duties did so only as the assistants of the pastor. The trustees at St. George filed suit to declare the Pennsylvania statute unconstitutional and took their case to the state supreme court but the new law was upheld. Only then did peace come to the parish. One legacy of this dispute and the vindication of the right of the pastor to control parish assets was that the ousted trustees left Father Karalius with a debt of $114,000 that he had to pay.

Even while this litigation was in progress, Father Karalius was engaged in an effort to open a parochial school. Holy Family, the German parish, had seriously declined in membership and was closing because many German families had moved out of Shenandoah. Father Karalius wanted to acquire the property of the German church for St. George and to use it as a school. These efforts were complicated by the fact that tunnelling for coal under the church building had so weakened the structure that the church collapsed. After litigation with the owners of the coal company, the Girard Estate, over the damage to the property, the land was filled in and the school building was remodeled. The church itself was demolished and a playground was installed in its place. The new St. George school opened in 1936 with 134 students; at one time, the enrollment grew to about 350, with some 25 percent of the student body coming from Polish families. At the outset, German nuns taught in the school, but they were replaced by the Sisters of St. Casimir, an order of nuns of Lithuanian ancestry that was founded in the United States in 1907. The Sisters of St. Casimir remained until about 1985.

No sooner had Father Karalius settled the problems with the trustees and with the Girard Estate than a fire broke out at St. George. On March 1, 1938, a fire started in the boiler room and spread to the rest of the building. It did about $35,000 worth of damage. Renovation efforts took about two years to complete. New paintings and decorative glass portraying Lithuanian themes were installed. Two new windows contained, respectively, emblems of the United States and of Lithuania. Structural improvements were also made.

By 1960, almost all of the coal mines in Shenandoah had closed. As a result, the population of the city began to decline, and that decline has continued for decades as generations of younger residents have left the area to make a living. In 1923, the parish had ten thousand members. At its seventy-fifth anniversary in 1966, it had only about thirty-five hundred. A study compiled at that anniversary revealed that in 75 years there had been a total of 16,000 baptisms, 4,432 marriages, and 7,000 burials at St. George.

Today, St. George is one of about 105 Lithuanian nationality parishes in the United States; 50 of them are in Pennsylvania, with 10 of those in Schuylkill County alone.

Since there is little local industry, residents of the borough have to commute to Hazelton, Harrisburg, or elsewhere to find work. Both the borough and St. George parish have an inordinately large number of older residents, many of whom subsist on social security and private pensions. The borough has about six thousand residents, of whom nearly ninety percent are Catholics. St. George has eight hundred fifty families, most of whom claim some Lithuanian ancestry. However, few speak the language and, aside from occasional hymns, that language has not been used for church services for nearly a generation. In fact, parish records have been kept in English since 1924. In all of Schuylkill County, there is only one Lithuanian Mass said each month. Under the sponsorship of the Knights of Lithuania, it is offered at Our Lady of Siluva parish in Maizeville. Newer immigrants from Europe normally do not settle in the anthracite region as they once did but prefer the job opportunities offered in Chicago, where there is a Lithuanian community of nearly 100,000 people.

Since 1987, the two priests at St. George have taken over an additional responsibility: the management and administration of Our Lady of Mount Carmel parish, the Italian church located on the opposite side of the city. Our Lady of Mount Carmel has about two hundred seventy families and maintains a separate church building, along with separate records, but it has no priests, so priests from St. George say two Masses there each weekend and attend to other parish needs. All eight Catholic churches in the Shenandoah area now operate a single consolidated parochial school in a building formerly occupied by the school that Annunciation and St. George had operated together for several years. The present enrollment is three hundred eighty-five elementary students. The school is named after Shenandoah native Father Walter Ciszek, S.J., a former member of St. Casimir, the Polish parish. Father Ciszek surreptitiously entered the Soviet Union in the days when the Iron Curtain prevented the lawful entry of Catholic priests. He was captured and confined to a gulag in Siberia for nearly twenty-five years before being allowed to return to the United States. An effort to bring about his beatification has been undertaken.

Today, four Masses are offered each weekend at St. George. An estimated twenty-five baptisms and seventy funerals take place each year. This number is a dramatic contrast to the census of a generation ago. However, there is still an impressive vitality in the parish, notwithstanding its age and the economic condition of the borough it serves, which expresses itself in more constructive ways than did the energies of the trustees during the tumultuous days of the 1920s and 1930s. To prepare for the 100th anniversary of the parish, a massive structural renovation and redecoration of the church was undertaken by the present pastor, Father Robert J. Potts, and his assistant, Father Joseph J. Kweder. Both are natives of the parish. New stained-glass windows depicting various scenes in the life of Christ were installed. The interior was replastered, repainted, and gilded, and new murals were painted on the vaulted ceiling. The altar was decorated with a sculpture of the Last Supper, a large crucifix in the center of the church was redone, and all thirty-eight statues in the church were refinished. The massive organ was taken apart, renovated, and repainted, and new pews were installed. The exterior walls of the church are alternately wood, brick, and Belgian granite. The inside rain spouting was removed and placed on the church exterior, and the walls were replastered to remove water damage that had taken place over a period of many years. The entire effort cost nearly a million dollars, but no money had to be borrowed to meet the bills when they fell due. The old trustees would be impressed, and perhaps a bit embarrassed.

24
St. Michael (Byzantine Rite)

Shenandoah

PENNSYLVANIA

St. Michael's Church in Shenandoah, Pennsylvania, is the oldest Catholic parish of any of the Eastern Rites in the United States. Most Catholics in the United States belong to the Latin Rite, now called the Roman Rite, since Latin is no longer used in religious ceremonies. It is safe to say that most Roman Rite Catholics know very little about their Eastern brethren who are part of the same Roman Catholic Church and who, unlike Orthodox Christians, acknowledge the supremacy of the Holy Father. Each Eastern Catholic church, except for the Maronites, has an Orthodox counterpart that is larger in number and that, since 1054 or before, has been totally separate from the Bishop of Rome.

Beginning in the 1870s, a number of immigrants originating in western Ukraine and elsewhere in the Carpathian mountain region of what was then Austria-Hungary came to work in the anthracite mines of central Pennsylvania. In Shenandoah, they originally attended St. Casimir's Church, a Latin Rite Polish church, because there was no Ukrainian church available. In 1882, they wrote to Cardinal Sylvester Sembratovych, archbishop of Lvov (spelled Lviv in Ukrainian), and asked him to send them a priest of their own rite. Their plea was a plaintive one: "We have made it here, Valdyko (Master), although we feel deprived of sight. But we are not the same that we were in the Old Country because there is something lacking to that. We are in need of God. We pray thus: give us priests from the Old Country, give us blessing for the building of churches, in order that we would have in this foreign country all what stands for our holy Rus!"

In 1884, Cardinal Sembratovych sent Father John Wolanski to be their first pastor. He arrived in December of 1884 and celebrated vespers on the eve of St. Nicholas in Kern Hall, located a few blocks from where St. Michael's Church now stands. Services were held in rented premises because the eighty Ruthenian and Ukrainian families who made up the parish were not able to obtain the use of the Polish church they had been attending. This service was probably the first one conducted in any of the Eastern Rites in the United States.

St. Michael's is often described as a Greek church, although its members are not Greek any more than most Roman Rite Catholics are Roman. The reference is to the fact that one of the Eastern Rites, the Byzantine Rite, traces its origin to Byzantium (or Greece). The liturgy that originated in Byzantium was never said in a single language but historically was always offered in the language of the country in which the church was located. In the United States, there are Byzantine Rite churches of Ukrainian origin such as St. Michael's, where Old Slavonic was the original language of worship. There are also Ruthenian parishes where the prevailing language was Old Slavonic. Moreover, there are Byzantine Romanian and Byzantine Melkite parishes. The latter offer liturgies in Arabic and other Middle Eastern languages. The phrase "Eastern Rite" also includes Armenian, Maronite, and Chaldean Catholics, all of whom have liturgies performed in their own languages according to rites that did not originate in Byzantium but trace their roots to Alexandria, Jerusalem, and Antioch, the patriarchal cities of the early Church. When adherents of these various traditions first arrived in the United States, they too found themselves under the jurisdiction of Roman Rite bishops, who were not always sympathetic to their differences.

In 1907, acting on a request from Metropolitan (Archbishop) Andrew Sheptytsky of Lvov, Pope Pius X placed Byzantine Slavonic Catholics in the United States under their own bishop who established his see in Philadelphia. As other Eastern Catholics arrived in the United States in sufficient numbers to support a diocese, they were also given their own bishops. Today, there are four Byzantine Ukrainian and four Byzantine Ruthenian dioceses in the United States. Each has about 300,000 members. There are also Chaldean, Armenian, and Maronite dioceses, although they are much smaller than the Byzantine dioceses. A total of about 800,000 Eastern Catholics of all Eastern Rites now live in the United States.

Eastern churches not only use different prayers, different vestments, and employ different expressions of religious art, but many also use different alphabets to express their liturgies. At St. Michael's, prayer books were written in the Cyrillic alphabet. Most used the older Julian calendar, which placed Christmas on January 7 and Easter anywhere from one to four Sundays after Easter in the Gregorian calendar. However, the most striking difference between Eastern Catholics and their Latin Rite contemporaries was the fact that all of these rites had a long tradition of permitting a married priesthood. Some twenty-three of St. Michael's first twenty-four pastors were married. To be precise, Eastern bishops would accept married candidates for ordination. Once ordained, a priest could not thereafter marry, and no married priest could become a bishop. However, Eastern priests who entered religious orders, such as the Order of St. Basil, took vows of celibacy. To Western Catholics with a long history of a celibate priesthood, a married priesthood was culturally jarring. Because of this difficulty, the Holy See published an order in 1929 stating that Eastern Rite priests in the Western Hemisphere could no longer marry. However, this order did not extend to Europe or Asia Minor, so many Eastern priests in those areas still continue to follow the ancient practice of their churches.

In its own history, St. Michael's reflected some friction arising out of these differences. Father Wolanski, its founder, was not only a married pastor but an energetic leader who threw himself into various causes, including the incipient labor movement that was then trying to take hold in the anthracite region of Pennsylvania. He founded a Ukrainian-language newspaper. In the 1880s, the Church in America was still ambivalent regarding the Knights of Labor and other unions, such as the Molly Maguires, who were agitating in the coal-mining regions. Father Wolanski played a prominent role in a union march in Shenandoah and thus further estranged himself from other Catholics by his efforts. He was ultimately required to leave Pennsylvania and went temporarily to Brazil to minister to Ukrainian Catholics who had migrated there. He was replaced by a celibate priest but later returned to Shenandoah briefly.

Before he left, however, Father Wolanski was able to bless the first Ukrainian church in the United States. The original St. Michael's Church on West Centre Street was completed in 1886 and served as a parish church until it was replaced by a much larger one at the present site at Oak and Chestnut Streets, which was dedicated in 1907. In addition to religious services, the church organized cooperatives not only in Shenandoah but also in the nearby cities of Hazelton and Olyphant. It operated an evening school, a printing press, and a literary club. Some parishioners placed their savings in the parish treasury in what today would be called a credit union, but the management of this enterprise was called into question, and the church was put up for auction to satisfy unpaid depositors. Shortly after the sale, it was restored to parish use by the purchaser, a Ukrainian who lived in nearby Mahanoy City.

At one time, St. Michael's had one thousand families, but a parish of this size proved to be too large and too inconvenient to its members. Parishioners were known to walk many miles to liturgy on Sunday, often going barefoot and carrying their shoes around their necks to avoid soiling what they were going to wear to church. As a result, additional Byzantine parishes were founded in what is now the Shamokin deanery in order to accommodate growing numbers of new arrivals from the Carpathian mountain region.

The migration that gave rise to St. Michael's and many other churches founded in the late nineteenth century is often called the economic migration because it brought to this country large numbers of immigrants from Eastern Europe who were in search of economic betterment. A second migration, called a political migration, took place at the end of World War II and brought to this country large numbers of Eastern Catholics who were fleeing Soviet oppression. Most of western Ukraine, from which Eastern Catholics of another era had migrated, was absorbed either into the former Soviet Union or into other Soviet-bloc nations. In 1946, Stalin caused the state-supported Russian Orthodox Church to hold a synod with Eastern Catholics, in the course of which the Ukrainian Rite Catholic Church in the Soviet Union was dissolved and absorbed into the Orthodox Church. This was not only part of a campaign against organized religion but also against Ukrainian nationalism. Cardinal Josyf Slipyj, archbishop of the Ukrainian capital of Kiev, was imprisoned and later exiled. In 1948, Communist authorities in Romania engaged in the same activity, dissolving Byzantine Rite churches in five Romanian dioceses. With the coming of *glasnost* in the Soviet Union, efforts were undertaken to restore some of these properties and to permit Eastern Rite Catholics once again to worship in freedom. The dissolution of the Soviet Union completed this process.

Changes have taken place in the Eastern Churches as well as in the Western Church. In 1961, Byzantine churches adopted the Gregorian calendar and now celebrate religious holidays on the same day that Roman Rite Catholics do. In 1972, English was permitted in the Byzantine liturgy in the United States. The only married priests in these churches are those who have been ordained abroad and have migrated to the United States.

Tragedy struck St. Michael's on Easter Monday in 1980 when the nearly seventy-five-year-old church caught fire and burned to the ground. Parish life came full circle as services were transferred to the old Hall, now St. Michael's Hall, where they were held until a new church could be built. The families that now constitute the parish, as well as other friends and benefactors, demonstrated the present viability of the parish by constructing in a period of four years a modern building [**pictured above**].

In 1988, the Catholic Church celebrated the 1,000th anniversary of the establishment of Christianity in what until recently was the Soviet Union. The event in question was the conversion of St. Vladimir, prince of Kiev. Soviet authorities permitted the Russian Orthodox Church to commemorate this event in Moscow but little if anything was celebrated in the Ukrainian capital where St. Vladimir lived. Eastern Catholics were not a part of these observances. Accordingly, they held a series of commemorations not only in the United States but also in Rome with Pope John Paul II participating.

Today, St. Michael's is one of five Catholic churches that are located within five blocks of each other in Shenandoah. In addition to St. Michael's, there is the Irish church (Annunciation), the Polish churches (St. Stanislaus and St. Casimir), and the Lithuanian church (St. George). A generation ago, liturgy was offered in Old Slavonic at St. Michael's and in Latin at the other churches. Today, it is offered in English in all of these parishes, although one Ukrainian service is still offered at St. Michael's. Most younger residents leave Shenandoah after graduating from high school to seek employment elsewhere. St. Michael's now contains only about two hundred families, whereas it had several times that figure in more prosperous times.

Eastern Catholics who migrate to other areas may or may not continue their Eastern Rite affiliation, depending upon the degree of affinity with the church of their childhood and the availability of Eastern churches near their new homes. Attending an Eastern Catholic church in many areas often means driving many miles past Roman Rite churches. However, the comparative smallness of these parishes, in contrast to larger Roman Rite churches, is often an attraction that helps recent arrivals in a new city achieve the same kind of identity that immigrants from Eastern Europe sought years ago at St. Michael's "in order that we would have in this foreign country all what stands for our holy Rus!"

25
St. Mary

Lancaster

PENNSYLVANIA

William Penn encouraged German immigration into his colony. He also encouraged religious toleration. This policy was incorporated in the laws of England governing Pennsylvania, which provided "that all persons living in the province who confess and acknowledge the one almighty and eternal God to be the Creator, Upholder and Ruler of the World, and that hold themselves obliged in conscience to live peaceably and justly in civil society, shall in no way be molested or prejudiced for their religious persuasion or practice in matters of faith and worship, nor shall they be compelled at any time to frequent or maintain any religious worship, place of ministry whatever." Penn once published a tract in England urging repeal of the penal laws against Catholics, although this stated view had nothing to do with his basic attitude toward Catholicism. He had also written a book criticizing the Catholic religion itself. Penn was a friend of James II, the short-term Catholic monarch who was driven from the throne of England in 1688. At one time, Penn was accused of being a Jesuit, an allegation that he felt called upon to deny in writing. However, after the ascendancy to the throne of the Protestant William of Orange, Penn was not in a position to press his views on religious toleration with any great vigor, since he was in political and economic trouble himself. On one occasion, he was criticized for permitting "publick Mass in a scandalous manner" to take place in the Pennsylvania colony.

These twin policies, German immigration and religious tolerance, were followed by Penn's survivors after his death in 1718. They attracted many different groups from central Europe to Pennsylvania. Not only did German Lutherans come in considerable numbers, but members of other smaller religious groups — Dunkers, Mennonites, Amish, Schwenkfelders, and Moravians — also began to fill up the valleys of the Susquehanna, the Schuylkill, and the Lehigh Rivers. They set about farming its rich soil with skill and diligence. To give some idea of the extent of this influx, in the fall of 1749 alone, some twenty vessels bringing twelve thousand German immigrants to Pennsylvania arrived at the port of Philadelphia.

Among the new arrivals during the first part of the eighteenth century were a significant number of German Catholics. Father Joseph Wappeler, a German Jesuit who came to Pennsylvania to minister to the spiritual needs of German Catholics, wrote about religious toleration to his superiors in 1741: "The Judges did not require the usual oath from us nor from the German Catholics, who had lately arrived on four ships. The oath contained an abjuration of the Pope. The newly arrived were permitted to leave the court room when they came to this part in the usual formula of the oath." The fact that this portion of the Test Oath was omitted from naturalization ceremonies in Pennsylvania was of critical importance. In British colonies, only English citizens could own land. Insistence on the full oath could have been used as a means of precluding German Catholics from attaining English citizenship, thereby depriving them of the right to own their own farms.

After celebrating Mass in rented houses in Lancaster, Father Wappeler purchased some lots on what is now Prince Street and erected a log chapel in 1742 that he named for St. John Nepomucene. It was the first of three church buildings to be erected on this site. The land for the church was sold by James Hamilton, who is generally credited with being the founder of the city of Lancaster. In 1760, the log chapel burned to the ground, and arson was suspected. However, a reward of £20 was not sufficient to bring forth any information identifying the culprit. A second church built of stone was erected in its place and was known as St. Mary's. (The official name is actually Assumption of the Blessed Virgin Mary.) During colonial times, this parish became the second largest Catholic church in Pennsylvania, having some seven hundred members by 1785. It served as the mother church of all other Catholic parishes in Lancaster County. St. Mary's was also the seat of missionary activity extending throughout central Pennsylvania. One of its early pastors, Father John B. Cause, a Franciscan Recollect, was instrumental in getting the Pennsylvania legislature to establish a German school in Lancaster, and he was one of the founders of Franklin College, which later became Franklin and Marshall. Regrettably, Father Cause was later suspended as a priest by Bishop John Carroll after he left Lancaster and tried to start his own church in Philadelphia.

Some of the priests assigned to St. Mary's were French émigrés who came to the United States rather than submit to the control of leaders of the French Revolution who were trying to nationalize the Church and make it an agency of the French government. One such priest was Father Louis Barth, a French nobleman. Following an era when St. Mary's had received ten pastors in ten years, Father Barth settled in for an extended period of time and helped to stabilize the parish. One physical improvement that Father Barth made at St. Mary's was the addition of a twenty-five-foot steeple and belfry to the church building. One of his assistants in the early 1800s was Father Michael Egan, an Irish Franciscan, who had acquired a reputation as an orator. Father Egan, as mentioned elsewhere, was appointed the first bishop of Philadelphia when that diocese was established in 1808. Shortly thereafter, he named his former pastor as vicar general of the diocese.

Difficulties between English-speaking and German-speaking Catholics occasionally arose in various parts of Pennsylvania. However, in 1806, Irish parishioners at Lancaster wrote Bishop Carroll, with the concurrence of two individuals who styled themselves "German trustees" of the parish, asking that an English-speaking priest be sent to St. Mary's. Their argument was that German Catholics in the parish could understand English, but Irish Catholics could not understand German. German-speaking pastors, when available, were sent to Lancaster for many years, but this was not always possible.

During the first decade of the 1800s, Lancaster was the capital of Pennsylvania. Under this stimulus, the city began to grow and St. Mary's grew with it. Other Catholic churches came to be established in Lancaster County in areas that were formerly part of St. Mary's. This expansion was exceedingly important because, until parishes were established in outlying towns, Catholics had to walk many miles to St. Mary's to Sunday Mass, often doing so without breakfast if they wished to receive Holy Communion under the old fasting rules. During its first one hundred twenty-five years, St. Mary's had a great many pastors, some of whom stayed only a year or two. All but one of them were born abroad. In 1823, Father Bernard Keenan, a native of Northern Ireland, was appointed and served as pastor for fifty-four years until his death in 1877 at the age of ninety-seven. Two prominent political figures of the mid-1800s lived in Lancaster — President James Buchanan and abolitionist Congressman Thaddeus Stevens. Father Keenan was a close friend of President Buchanan and was occasionally his guest at the White House during the Buchanan Administration.

Title to St. Mary's property was originally placed in the name of individual Jesuit priests who bequeathed it to their successors in their wills. None of these documents was ever recorded or probated and were lost. In 1824, a faction in the parish sought to obtain a corporate charter and thereby to acquire legal title to church property. They failed in this endeavor because Father Keenan went to the newly revived Jesuits at Georgetown College and was able to obtain from them a power of attorney that named him as their successor in interest to the church property. Unlike a similar dispute that arose at the same time in Philadelphia, the matter subsided but title to church property was not formally conveyed to the diocese of Philadelphia by the Jesuits until about 1860.

As St. Mary's grew, the need for a second church right in the city became apparent. In 1850, St. Joseph's Church was dedicated and placed under the control of the Redemptorists. Thereafter, St. Joseph's became known as the German church while St. Mary's was regarded as the Irish church. In 1854, a new St. Mary's Church was constructed immediately to the west of the existing church. It was dedicated in that year by St. John Neumann, the bishop of Philadelphia.

Beginning in 1859, St. Mary's operated an orphanage. At first, orphans were placed in private homes. Later, in 1871, the parish leased a building for this purpose that had formerly housed the "Home for Friendless Children in the City of Lancaster." Sisters of Charity were brought to the city to operate what then came to be known as "St. Mary's Home." The first parochial school at St. Mary's was established in 1870.

About one hundred men from St. Mary's served in the Union Army, many of whom joined the 79th Regiment of the Pennsylvania Volunteers. A number of these men are buried at St. Mary's cemetery along with veterans of other Union Army regiments.

A serious fire in 1867 required a substantial reconstruction of the church, which included an increase in height, a new roof and tower, a new sanctuary, and a new altar. The building [pictured above] is the result of that reconstruction.

Today, St. Mary's parish has about seven hundred families. In recent years, the arrival of many Hispanic Catholics in Lancaster has given the parish a special mission. As it once served as a springboard for the establishment of German and other parishes in the Lancaster area, St. Mary's more recently has helped in the establishment of San Juan Bautista Church for Spanish-speaking Catholics. The parochial school now has about one hundred fifty students, of whom about eighty percent are Hispanic. St. Mary's has completed nearly two hundred fifty years of service in the Pennsylvania Dutch country. Catholics are now about twenty-five percent of the population of Lancaster County, a locality whose history has been characterized from the beginning by the idea of religious tolerance and cooperation.

26
Sacred Heart Basilica

Conewago Township

PENNSYLVANIA

Sacred Heart Basilica, constructed between 1785 and 1787, is located near McSherrytown, Pennsylvania, a few miles west of Hanover and about twelve miles east of Gettysburg. It was built on a hilltop overlooking Little Conewago Creek, a tributary of the Susquehanna River. The area in question is just north of the Maryland-Pennsylvania border and lies within territory that was disputed for nearly ninety years between the Calverts and the Penns. Until Mason and Dixon completed their survey in 1767, land titles, necessarily including the title to the church property, and the enforcement of criminal statutes was uncertain because Charles I and Charles II of England, being ignorant of colonial geography, made overlapping grants of land to the proprietors of the Maryland and Pennsylvania colonies.

By 1730, about twenty-five Catholic families had settled in the vicinity of what is now Conewago Township. English-speaking Catholics then began to arrive from Maryland while German-speaking Catholics crossed the Susquehanna to begin farming in this fertile agricultural area. About this time, Jesuit missionaries made occasional stops at the home of a surveyor, Robert Owings, to say Mass and dispense the sacraments. In 1741, Father Joseph Wappeler, who had started a church at Lancaster, erected a three-room log cabin on the hilltop where the present basilica [**pictured above**] stands in order to serve as a mission stop on the circuit he was riding. This spot was chosen because it was near a crossroad where an east-west trail from Philadelphia to the Monocacy River crossed a north-south trail leading from Baltimore to Carlisle. The cabin had no floor except near the altar and provided living quarters should such be required. Father Wappeler was unsure whether the area would ultimately be included within Pennsylvania, which evidenced a tolerant attitude toward Catholics, or whether it would become subject to the statutes of Maryland, whose penal laws forbade the construction of "publick Mass houses." Accordingly, he built the church so that it would appear to be a private dwelling in which chapels might lawfully be maintained under Maryland law. He named the church in honor of the Assumption, but it soon came to be known as Conewago Chapel.

In 1768, another German Jesuit, James Pellentz, was named the first resident pastor of the Conewago Chapel. This simply meant that it served as the headquarters for missionary journeys to other Catholic settlements in western Maryland, western Pennsylvania, and the Shenandoah Valley of Virginia. For years Father Pellentz and others made these journeys on horseback over crude mountain trails, often in disguise, to serve Catholics as far away as York, Carlisle, Hagerstown, and Loretto in the Allegheny Mountains. It is stretching the English language to suggest that the Conewago Chapel was then a parish. One writer described it as the center of a Catholic colony whose population included about five thousand Catholics. As more churches in this colony were constructed and were given resident pastors, the area served by the Conewago mission was reduced to a more conventional parish size.

In 1784, when Father John Carroll came to Conewago to administer confirmation, about one thousand Catholics lived in the immediate locality. He suggested to Father Pellentz that the old wooden cabin was too small and should be enlarged or replaced. Work on a new church, which was built of field stone, was undertaken shortly thereafter. Red sandstone was quarried from a spot on the Conewago River about 15 miles away and hauled to the present location where, over a period of two years, the nave of the church, some 60 by 80 feet and 40 feet high, was constructed. It was dedicated in 1787 and named in honor of the Sacred Heart. The new church had no floor, no transepts, and no steeple. These improvements were added periodically over the next eighty years. In addition to a church, a rectory was built, which Father Pellentz occupied until his death in 1800. During the latter years of his residence at Conewago, Father Pellentz served not only as pastor but as vicar general of the new diocese of Baltimore, which extended westward to the Mississippi River.

The parish then was agricultural in character and populated largely by Germans and a few Irish. All of its early pastors were German. Until the 1850s, sermons were preached alternately in English and in German. The first newspapers in the area were printed in German, not English, and German was a standard means of communication between all inhabitants of the area, regardless of religion. The Jesuits owned about five hundred acres of land and derived income from this property to support their various activities. About seven acres was set aside for the cemetery that presently surrounds the basilica. The earliest burial at the Conewago Chapel cemetery was that of Dudley Digges, heir to the original owner of Digges Choice, as the land patent from Lord Baltimore was called. He was shot to death in 1752 in a land title dispute with another claimant. The cemetery contains the remains of generations of Sacred Heart parishioners and includes the graves of fifteen veterans of the American Revolution. When the Jesuits relinquished the parish to the diocese of Harrisburg in 1901, they conveyed to the bishop the title to the church and the land immediately surrounding it, but they still retain title to about four hundred acres in that locality.

During the middle of the nineteenth century, several major architectural and artistic improvements were made in the basilica. Another noted pastor, Father Joseph Enders, S.J., built two transepts and obtained the services of an Austrian painter, Franz Stecher, to paint a ceiling mural of God the Son relinquishing the crown and accepting the cross. Another work, representing the Apparition of the Sacred Heart to St. Margaret Mary, was painted on canvas in a large ornate frame by Filippo Costaggini in 1887 as part of the 100th anniversary celebration and has been placed on the wall of the apse of the church behind the main altar. Stecher also painted fourteen stations of the cross and a picture showing the death of St. Francis Xavier. Another painting above the altar in the left transept depicted the Assumption and was painted at an earlier time by Monachesi. Early in the 1900s, the basilica was able to obtain a series of stained-glass windows manufactured in Munich.

Schooling at Conewago Chapel began as early as 1800 and two school buildings were constructed in the corners of the church yard about 1830. Another brick school was constructed in nearby Irishtown in 1868 and another in the town of Centennial in 1869. The parish now maintains a parochial school next to the church that for many years has been staffed by the Sisters of St. Joseph from Chestnut Hills. It has a current enrollment of one hundred seventy-five students.

The Civil War bypassed Conewago, but it did not bypass either Hanover or Gettysburg. In June of 1863, Jeb Stuart's Confederate cavalry and Judson Kilpatrick's Union cavalry rode through the area on their way to Gettysburg. A few days later, members of the parish could hear cannonfire from the historic battlefield, some twelve to fifteen miles away, during the momentous three-day battle that took place in July of 1863.

After one hundred sixty years, the Jesuits left Sacred Heart in 1901 and turned over the parish to the diocese of Harrisburg. In 1937, at its 150th anniversary celebration, some twenty thousand people came to Conewago to witness an outdoor Mass. In 1962, at its 175th anniversary celebration, Pope John XXIII conferred upon the church the status of a minor basilica. That basilica has now completed its 200th anniversary and remains an active parish of thirteen hundred members living in the predominantly Catholic subdivisions of Irishtown, Centennial, and Edgegrove. In 1987, nearly two dozen scheduled tours, both commercial undertakings and diocesan pilgrimages, visited Sacred Heart, while unnumbered individual tourists made visits to the basilica. The early Jesuit missionaries maintained personal diaries containing accounts of their travels, but most of these no longer exist. In 1790, the first council of the American Church at Baltimore decreed that such records be maintained at the rectory, so parish records date back to that year. When a former pastor, Monsignor Thomas J. McGeough, translated these records from their original Latin into English, they became a much-used source of genealogical research. After two centuries, Sacred Heart, its cemetery, and its landscaped parish grounds have become an attractive stop for anyone seeking Catholic roots in America.

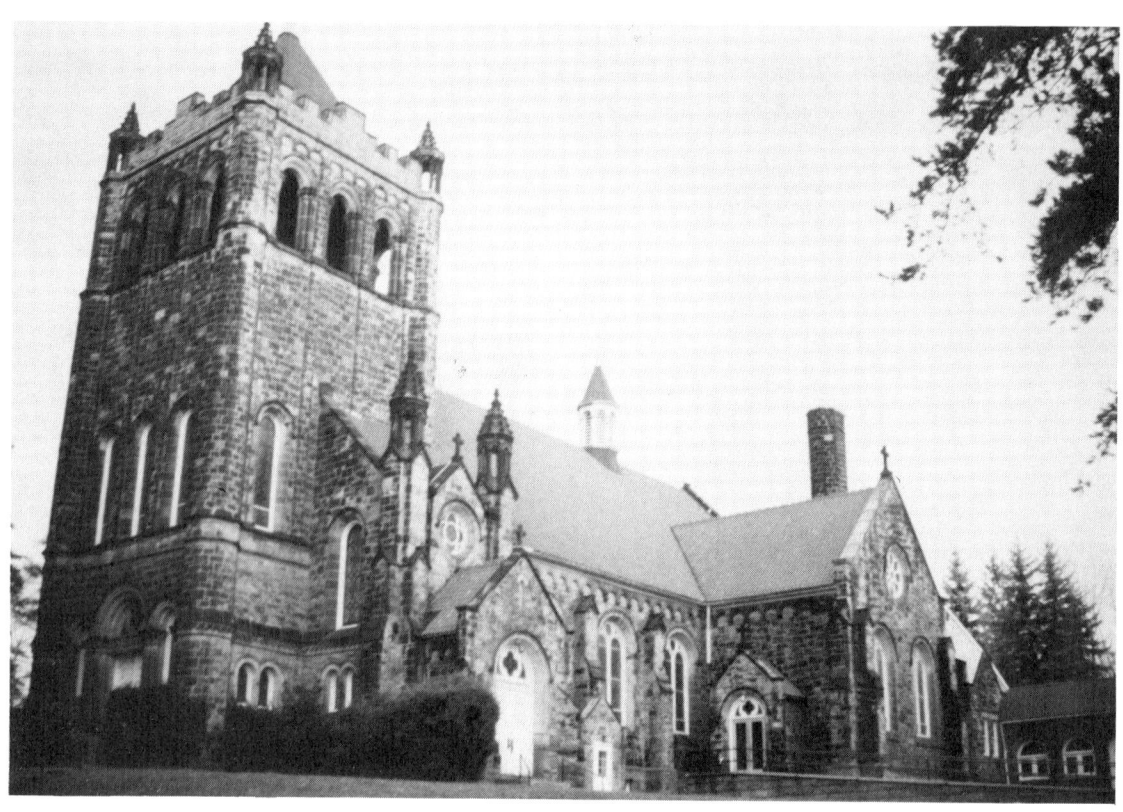

27
St. Michael

Loretto
PENNSYLVANIA

St. Michael's Church, located in Loretto, Pennsylvania, was for many years a solitary Catholic outpost in the Allegheny Mountains. At the time of its establishment as a parish in 1799, it was the only Catholic Church from western Pennsylvania to the French settlements along the Wabash and Mississippi Rivers. Since that date, the history of the parish has, in no small part, been bound up with the lives of three very different men — Captain Michael McGuire, Father Demetrius A. Gallitzin, and Charles M. Schwab, all of whom made memorable contributions to its foundation and continuation.

Loretto is located a few miles north of the old Kittanning Trail, parts of which are now U.S. Route 22. This old Indian trail led from central Pennsylvania to the town of Kittanning, on the banks of the Allegheny River, and connected this remote area to a river network that still leads to the Midwest and to the Gulf of Mexico. Following the Revolutionary War, the area caught the eye of Captain Michael McGuire, a resident of Pipe Creek Hundred near Taneytown in what was then Frederick County, Maryland. McGuire was the commander of a company made up of his Catholic neighbors who had served in the Continental Army. McGuire himself was present at Yorktown for the surrender of General Cornwallis. In 1785, he purchased several hundred acres of land in what was then Bedford

County, Pennsylvania. In 1788, at the age of seventy-one, he sold his Maryland farm and took his wife and seven children (one of whom was only three years old) to central Pennsylvania. Soon thereafter, some of his Maryland neighbors followed. McGuire assisted in the settlement of this area by making loans and grants to those who would join him in the new community, which he named McGuire's Settlement.

Beginning in 1791, missionaries from Sacred Heart Church at Conewago visited McGuire's Settlement periodically and said Mass in McGuire's log cabin. To encourage the establishment of a permanent church with a resident pastor, McGuire conveyed four hundred acres of land to church authorities. Part of this conveyance included the cemetery that today surrounds St. Michael's Church. In 1793, McGuire became the first person to be interred on this tract.

The founder of St. Michael's Church, Father Demetrius Gallitzin, was born of Russian nobility in The Hague where his father was serving as Russian ambassador to the Netherlands. His father, Prince Dimitri Gallitzin, owned estates surrounding Moscow that were larger in area than the Commonwealth of Pennsylvania. His mother was the daughter of a Prussian nobleman who had served under Frederick the Great of Prussia. The Gallitzins were not Catholics but freethinkers and admirers of Voltaire. As a result, the young Prince Gallitzin received an early education devoid of religious training. He held a commission in the Russian Army and was also a hereditary colonel in the Austrian Imperial Guard. He could have accepted either commission upon coming of age. While the young Gallitzin was nominally a Russian subject, he spent little, if any, time in Russia. The degree of his Russian acculturation can best be understood from the fact that he spoke English with a French accent.

From The Hague the Gallitzins moved to Geneva and then to Munster, Germany, where Princess Amalia Gallitzin and her family became acquainted with the Catholic Church through contact with Catholic friends and neighbors. After living in Munster several years, they joined the Church. The young Prince Gallitzin completed both university and military training in 1792. Instead of taking a grand tour of Europe, as was the custom of wealthy young men upon completing their education, Demetrius Gallitzin decided to visit the United States because the outbreak of the French Revolution made European travel uncertain at best. Traveling under the assumed name of Augustine Smith, he sailed from Rotterdam in 1792 for the New World. He never returned.

In Baltimore, he met Bishop John Carroll and became interested in the missionary activity of the Catholic Church then taking place in the United States. He enrolled at St. Mary's Seminary and was ordained in 1795, the first priest to receive both his seminary training and all of his holy orders in this country. Bishop Carroll assigned him to Sacred Heart Church in Conewago where he participated in the missionary activities, using that church as his base of operations. However, Father Gallitzin wanted to become a resident priest in a Catholic community rather than being constantly on the road, going from one mission stop to another. Upon visiting McGuire's Settlement, he determined that this was the kind of community he would like to serve permanently. The residents of the settlement were happy to have Father Gallitzin and petitioned Bishop Carroll to have him stationed permanently with them. The bishop granted their petition; so, in October of 1799, Father Gallitzin packed up a two-horse prairie schooner with an altar, sacred vessels, vestments, altar wine, coffee, a bed, and about one hundred books and left Taneytown, Maryland, for McGuire's Settlement. On Christmas Eve, 1799, he said midnight Mass in a log church, some forty-four feet by twenty-five feet, wearing vestments shipped from Europe that had been made from his mother's wedding dress. It was here that Father Gallitzin spent the next forty years of his life and acquired the title of Apostle of the Alleghenies.

Throughout his tenure as pastor, Father Gallitzin never accepted any compensation for his services. During the early years of his priesthood, he received a subsidy from his mother. With it he purchased three hundred twenty-eight acres of land next to the McGuire family holdings to be used for church purposes. Relying upon support from abroad, he contracted about $20,000 in debts to support church activities. However, in 1807, after his mother died, the Russian government revoked his citizenship because he had become a Roman Catholic and nullified his title to the family's hereditary properties. His family subsidy came to an end, so Father Gallitzin was left with the task of retiring all but about $2,000 of the debts that he had contracted. He spent the rest of his life in this effort. It proved to be a substantial drain on his vitality and energy during the declining years of his life.

In July of 1811, Bishop Michael Egan from Philadelphia visited Loretto and confirmed one hundred eighty-five children. A few months later, he wrote: "I have been indeed highly gratified with the rapid increase of religion in the different congregations I have visited, and this gratification would be greatly augmented had I ten more zealous priests to send to their assistance. The Rev. Mr. Gallitzin is scarcely any longer capable of attending to the spiritual necessities of the very numerous congregation committed to his care." In 1816, Father Gallitzin platted a town and laid out its two main streets, which he named in honor of St. Mary and St. Joseph. He also changed the name of the area from McGuire's Settlement to Loretto, the name of a Marian shrine located on the Adriatic Sea in northeast Italy. In 1817, he built the second of four church buildings to serve St. Michael's parish. In 1832, he built a chapel house that became his rectory. He also constructed a sawmill and put his engineering skills to work in diverting several streams into a current of sufficient force to operate a gristmill. He had a limited amount of medical training and sometimes acted as physician to members of his congregation. During the War of 1812, he employed his military training to drill recruits who had volunteered to fight the British. Father Gallitzin was vicar general for western Pennsylvania and was often mentioned as a candidate for bishop when vacancies arose in the Midwest. He turned down all such offers because he had no desire to relocate. He always insisted that Loretto should become the seat of a diocese. Western Pennsylvania was late in acquiring a bishop of its own. When a diocese was finally established, Pittsburgh understandably got the nod over Loretto. Father Gallitzin died in 1840 at the age of seventy and was buried in front of the church that he built. On the 100th anniversary of his death, a large marble monument, donated by Charles M. Schwab, was erected above his tomb.

The existence of Loretto as a Catholic enclave was enhanced in 1847 when a group of Irish Franciscan Brothers arrived to open a school for boys. They were not formally a part of the larger Franciscan order but lived under rules originally promulgated by St. Francis of Assisi. They had been invited to Loretto by Bishop Michael O'Connor of Pittsburgh and functioned under his supervision and control. While members of various branches of the Franciscan family had accompanied Spanish and French explorers to the New World in colonial times, the Brothers who arrived at Loretto formed the first permanent English-speaking community of Franciscans in the United States.

The Brothers' first home was an unclaimed log cabin. They leased a farm from Bishop O'Connor and set about building a brick building on the premises to serve as a school, dormitory, chapel, and motherhouse. This building became the central portion of the original Old Main Building at St. Francis College. It burned down in 1942 and was later replaced. Classes at St. Francis Academy opened in 1849. In the following year, some thirty Franciscan Brothers came to Loretto to operate the school. In 1850, St. Francis Academy advertised that it was providing "elementary and liberal education" with discipline that would be "exact, yet mild and parental."

In 1856, the Brothers sought to incorporate their order and asked that a bill for this purpose be introduced in the Pennsylvania legislature. When a measure was presented to the Pennsylvania House of Representatives granting the Franciscan Brothers the status of a nonprofit corporation, Representative Samuel McCalmont of Venango County denounced the Brothers with unrestrained fury: "Let us beware in time, lest we find when, too late, that we have created a monster to devour our children. Gentlemen may call it a school, a college, or an asylum, or what they will; but all their ingenuity and zeal have failed to hide the hideous fact that it is a bright-eyed, unprotected boy they will take home; they will feed and clothe him; they will educate him just as much as will answer their purposes and no more; and then doom him to a living death, to slavery more dark and hopeless than that in which the Southern master holds his helpless victim."

The bill passed the lower house, but when it came to the state senate, the Protestant Protective Association staged a demonstration of six thousand people in front of the state capitol at Harrisburg to defeat it. They submitted a petition in opposition, which, when unrolled, completely encircled the senate chamber. The bill was defeated and the Franciscan Brothers were not allowed to incorporate. Two years later, they were able to go to court to incorporate the academy itself under a general law providing corporate status for nonprofit educational institutions. The school continued to grow, to acquire additional faculty and improve its course offerings, and began to use the title St. Francis Academy and College.

In 1854, a third St. Michael's Church, a brick structure, was erected to replace the wooden building that Father Gallitzin had built. During the latter part of the 1800s, pastors of St. Michael's served on the board of the college. On one occasion, a pastor served as president for a short while. The pastor was also designated by the bishop as the ecclesiastical adviser to the Brothers.

The most famous alumnus of St. Francis College was Charles M. Schwab. Schwab grew up in Loretto, the son of pious German Catholics, and attended St. Francis College. He did not graduate but withdrew in 1879 and went to work for the J. Edgar Thompson Steel Works in Braddock, Pennsylvania. The mill was owned by Andrew Carnegie. By the time Schwab was twenty-five years of age, he was superintendent of Carnegie's Homestead Steel Works in Pittsburgh. He was not in charge during the famous Homestead strike of 1892 but returned shortly thereafter to manage the plant and its eight thousand employees. In 1897, at the age of thirty-five, Schwab was president of Carnegie Steel, earning $50,000 a year and annual bonuses of nearly a million dollars. By 1900, his base pay had reached the one-million-dollar mark. Schwab participated in the formation of the United States Steel Corporation, fell out with its leading director, Judge Elbert Gary, and resigned. He bought the Bethlehem Steel Corporation, then a small mill in eastern Pennsylvania that produced armor and ordnance for the U.S. Navy. It was at Bethlehem Steel that Schwab made most of his fortune, much of it on government contracts during World War I. Schwab was a knowledgeable and imaginative industrialist an accomplished union buster and strike-breaker, and the defendant in more than or fraud or antitrust suit.

Schwab lived high and spent big. He was also much more of a philanthropist than .e was ever given credit for. Throughout his entire career, he never forgot his roots. He was once quoted as saying that he was prouder of being president of the St. Francis Alumni Association than of being president of Bethlehem Steel. He owned a seventy-five-room mansion in New York City, another mansion in Bethlehem, and a home on the Riviera. He was a big gambler at Monte Carlo and a bigger gambler in the steel business. His private railroad cars, called the Loretto I and II, were each worth about $170,000. In 1898, he bought a tract of land in Loretto and built a summer home called Immergrun ("Evergreen"). He eventually acquired an estate of nearly one thousand acres at this location. He replaced his original summer retreat with a French Renaissance baronial mansion, four stories high with forty-four rooms and walls two feet thick. Immergrun acquired formal gardens, a 25,000-square-foot greenhouse, a Greek open-air theater, elaborate statuary, a nine-hole golf course, and many outbuildings and a cottage to house the employees who maintained the elaborate farm, gardens, and stock-raising activities that he underwrote. Schwab constructed a 1.5-million-gallon water tower that served both Immergrun and the town of Loretto. He built water and sewer lines for the town and paved its streets. The area had become a summer-vacation mecca, so Schwab invited to Immergrun many celebrated politicians, athletes, and theatrical stars to join him each summer. At the height of its activities, the estate employed one hundred seventy people.

Other changes of a more permanent character came about in Loretto as a result of Schwab money. The present St. Michael's Church **[pictured above]** was constructed on the 100th anniversary of the establishment of the parish in 1799. The new building cost $150,000, and Schwab paid for it all. A portrait of this church, painted by Marjorie Phillips, hangs in the Duncan Phillips Art Gallery in Washington, D.C. After Schwab's sister, Cecelia, joined the Carmelites and became a cloistered nun, he gave the Carmelites $250,000 to build their monastery at Loretto and disguised the gift as a donation from his mother. Schwab had no children. He had great affection for his wife and lived in awe of his mother, Pauline Schwab. Pauline Schwab never lived at Immergrun. She resided in a modest frame house on St. Mary's Street, a block from St. Michael's Church. Whenever Charlie came back to Loretto for a stay, Pauline saw to it that he attended Mass every Sunday at St. Michael's. When she learned that her son had made a large political contribution to the campaign of presidential aspirant Herbert Hoover, she promptly telegraphed him and insisted that he give an equal amount to her candidate, Al Smith.

During the years that Schwab was cutting a wide path both in the industrial world and at Loretto, his old school was undergoing significant changes, the most important of which was the arrival in 1908 of priests belonging to the Third Order Regular of St. Francis (TORs). The TORs are an ancient outgrowth of one of the three religious orders founded in the thirteenth century in Assisi by St. Francis. Historically, the Third Order of St. Francis has been composed of laymen. The TORs began as a group of priests whose purpose it was to minister to the lay members of the Third Order. When the TORs came to Loretto, many of the Franciscan Brothers who were already there joined and some eventually were ordained as priests. The college expanded and new buildings were constructed. Among the largest contributors to this expansion program was none other than Charles M. Schwab. The TORs opened a seminary for the education both of Franciscan seminarians and future diocesan priests who were sent to Loretto by their bishops for instruction in theology. While St. Michael's Church has always remained under diocesan control, a close relationship has developed over the years between the parish and the college. Some of the lay teachers and staff of the college are St. Michael's parishioners.

The development of Loretto as a Catholic enclave in western Pennsylvania was made complete by the arrival of the Sisters of Mercy, who were invited by Bishop O'Connor to establish a girls' school in the town. In May 1848, the Mercy nuns arrived from Ireland and established a convent in a little frame house on St. Mary's Street. They started teaching catechism in a tinner's shop next door. Their first classes of first Communion and confirmation candidates were ready for those sacraments in September of that year. In 1853, the Sisters opened St. Aloysius Academy for girls in Loretto. They could not afford to hire any janitors or maintenance men; so, in addition to teaching a wide range of courses, they maintained the convent yard and stable, carried coal and water to the school, and performed other hard manual labor. They also underwent such hardships as typhoid epidemics and the privation of long cold winters in the Allegheny highlands. As the academy grew, the Sisters expanded their services to teaching in the Loretto public school, where they conducted classes for both boys and girls. In 1897, the academy was relocated to nearby Cresson where it remains today as Mount Aloysius Junior College. In 1897, the Sisters established an orphanage at Loretto and later a home for the aged and infirm members of their order.

In 1921, St. Michael's parish opened a parochial school, so the Mercy nuns began to teach at this school. The effect of opening a parochial school in this community was to prompt public school authorities to close the public school, since most of its students had transferred to St. Michael's. The Sisters also took on the task of maintaining the Prince Gallitzin Chapel House in Father Gallitzin's old rectory and have continued to do so to this day so that the building and its contents can be displayed to pilgrims who regularly come to St. Michael's for a visit. Like so many other aspects of the St. Michael's parish complex, the restoration of the Gallitzin Chapel was accomplished with the assistance of Charles M. Schwab.

Schwab died in September of 1939 in New York City. After an elaborate funeral at St. Patrick's Cathedral, his remains were brought back for burial in St. Michael's old cemetery, not far from the grave of Captain McGuire. During the 1930s, Schwab suffered serious financial reverses that drastically reduced the value of his Bethlehem Steel holdings. The man who was once worth a hundred million dollars left an estate that was $338,000 in debt. Part of this debt included a $25,000 loan that the Franciscans had made to him on the promise that he would leave an endowment of two million dollars to the college in his will. The will contained no such provision. He had also borrowed $20,000 from the Carmelite nuns to meet a short-term cash-flow problem and had failed to repay it. It is doubtful that his estate could have met these debts even if he had made provision for them in his will. These loans were considered debts of honor that the Bethlehem Steel Corporation eventually repaid from corporate funds. Other creditors were not so lucky. In 1942, Immergrun was sold at auction and the Franciscans bought a large part of it at a very reasonable price. They renamed this large mansion Mount Assisi and installed their seminary in this building.

Today, St. Francis College has an enrollment of about thirteen hundred students. Its seminary has closed, and the land devoted to that purpose has been sold to the U.S. government for use as a minimum-security correctional institution. Loretto is still a Catholic enclave. Some ninety percent of the sixty hundred forty-two acres in the borough of Loretto is owned either by the college, the Sisters of Mercy, or the diocese of Altoona-Johnstown. St. Michael's parish now has about three hundred ninety families who derive their livelihood either from farming, from the college, from working for Conrail, or from the Bethlehem Steel mill in Johnstown. The parish school has slightly more than two hundred students. Loretto is still a few miles off the main thoroughfares that pass through this region, but it is not so far that it is not regularly visited by pilgrims and tourists who make their way through the hills to the stone church with the bright-orange tiled roof. There they are greeted by the large statue of Father Gallitzin presiding over the parish complex that he began to erect in the wilderness of the Alleghenies in the year that George Washington died.

28
St. Ignatius

Chapel Point
MARYLAND

If this volume seems heavily weighted with Maryland churches, it is because Maryland is heavily endowed with old Catholic churches. Southern Maryland, which includes Charles, Calvert, and St. Mary's Counties, has eleven parishes that were established before 1800 and six more that were established in the nineteenth century. The oldest of these is St. Ignatius at Chapel Point, founded by Father Andrew White, S.J., in 1641. It is the oldest English-speaking Catholic parish in continuous existence in the continental United States, having been founded only seven years after George Calvert (Lord Baltimore), sailing with a band of English Catholic refugees on the *Ark* and the *Dove*, landed at St. Clement's Island in St. Mary's County.

Chapel Point is a windswept hill located at the point where the Port Tobacco River flows into the Potomac. At this place, Father White began to give religious instructions to the Piscataway Indians, who maintained a village overlooking these two rivers. The Jesuits acquired indirectly from Lord Baltimore a four-thousand-acre tract of land along Port Tobacco River and began to operate it as a plantation in much the same manner as did other holders of land patents from the lord proprietor. Because of later penal laws and the general hostility of the English crown toward Catholics, the Jesuits often held title in the names of individual priests. This estate, known as St. Thomas Manor, was the headquarters for Jesuit missionary activities throughout the colonial era. Because the Catholic activity in the English colonies consisted of little more than the work of a Jesuit mission band of fifteen to twenty priests, St. Thomas Manor was in effect the headquarters for the Roman Catholic Church in the entire English-speaking portion of North America for several decades. The manor house was built in 1741 and served well into the nineteenth century as the headquarters for the Maryland province of the Society of Jesus.

Life was hard for the English Jesuits who maintained the parishes of southern Maryland in colonial times. Penal laws were not the only obstacles they faced. One of them, Father Joseph Mosley, was assigned to a parish at Newtown in Charles County, just a few miles from St. Ignatius. On September 8, 1758, and again the following year he wrote to his superior: "Our journeys are very long, our rides constant and extensive. We have many to attend and few to attend 'em. I often ride about 300 miles a week, and nary a week but I ride 150 or 200, and in our way of living, we ride almost as much by night as by day in all weathers, in heats, colds, rain, frost and snow.... I find here business enough in my way of Trade. I've the care of 1,500 souls.... I am daily on horseback, visiting ye sick, comforting the infirm, strengthening ye pusillanimous, etc."

The church **[pictured above]** dates from 1798 and is a brick Flemish bond structure. It was erected on a site formerly occupied by a chapel that dated back to 1662. As noted elsewhere, British law during the Reformation forbade the existence of Catholic churches open to the general public. They were disparagingly referred to as "publick Mass houses." However, another maxim of English law also came into play that permitted the existence of private chapels. A man's "home was his castle," so if a British subject chose, in the privacy of his own house, to engage in "popish practices" with the assistance of "Romish priests," authorities would normally leave him unmolested, although this was not always the case during Elizabethan times. In 1707, the Maryland General Assembly embodied this principle into a statute that permitted private Catholic chapels to exist in the colony. It was one of the few exceptions to the harsh anti-Catholic penal laws that were in effect or that were being enacted at that time. While Maryland was historically regarded as a Catholic colony, a census taken in 1708 showed that only about ten percent of its thirty-four thousand inhabitants were Catholics.

Thus, Catholic services were normally conducted in small chapels adjacent to or within private dwellings. The previous St. Ignatius Church and St. Thomas Manor house were built to comply with an early requirement that entrance to a Catholic chapel could be made only through a private residence, thus preserving the fiction that it was a place of worship designed not to serve the general public but only the owner of the dwelling. In 1963, when an empty well in the basement of an adjacent building was undergoing repairs, a parishioner uncovered the upper end of a tunnel that apparently ran several hundred feet from the church to the water and had been cemented over at some unknown earlier time. Apparently, the original inhabitants of St. Thomas Manor felt the need of an escape route to the river should authorities start to bear down upon them too heavily.

The parish cemetery has gravestones that bear entries made as long ago as the 1700s. These gravestones abound with such distinctly English names as Semmes, Digges, Mudd, Taney, and Jenkins. The cemetery would contain more of these markers except for the fact that during the Civil War, Union soldiers stationed at this strategic point along the Potomac River relieved the boredom of their assignment by using tombstones for target practice. The "Priests Plot," containing the graves of early Jesuits, dates back equally as far and includes a recently erected monument setting forth the names of English Jesuits who served as missionaries in Maryland but whose burial places are now unknown. One interesting gravestone marks the resting place of Olivia Floyd, from the nearby town of Port Tobacco, who was a Confederate mailcarrier (read "spy") during the Civil War. She is buried near the church building next to her parents in the Floyd family plot.

In 1866, fire destroyed the inside of the church and rectory, and both had to undergo extensive repairs and restoration. The same fire also destroyed parish records going back to colonial days. However, St. Ignatius continued to be the parish church for more generations of southern Maryland farmers and watermen down to the present time. For a long period it conducted a parochial school, but the school is now closed. One unusual enterprise sponsored by the parish was an amusement park located on the banks of the two rivers to provide a measure of local entertainment in this quiet community. The rides and other carnival paraphernalia have long since been removed.

Except for three priests at St. Ignatius and the staff of the Loyola Retreat House at nearby Pope's Creek, the Jesuits have withdrawn from southern Maryland and have turned their former parishes over to diocesan priests. They still own the twenty-one acres that constitute the St. Ignatius parish buildings and grounds and they occupy the St. Thomas Manor house, now a residence for priests who continue to serve the parish. Because they never abandoned this building even during the suppression of the order at the end of the eighteenth century, it is now the oldest Jesuit house of continuous residence anywhere in the entire world. The Jesuits also still own land at St. Inigoes and St. Francis Xavier, two manors in neighboring St. Mary's County, which date back to colonial times.

St. Ignatius Church now has about five hundred members and is in a state of transition from a rural parish to one made up of suburbanites and exurbanites from Washington and other nearby communities. About ten percent of its present members are Piscataway Indians, who still come to worship each week at the same place where Father White introduced their ancestors to Christianity over three hundred fifty years ago.

29
Sacred Heart

Bowie

MARYLAND

In 1728, James Carroll bequeathed two thousand acres of land along the Patuxent River in Prince George's County, Maryland, to his two Jesuit nephews in trust for the order to which they belonged. Because of English and Maryland penal laws, the Society of Jesus had no recognized legal existence and could not take title to the property in a collective or corporate name; so, like all holdings belonging to the Jesuit order, title was placed in the names of individual priests. The Jesuits began a tobacco plantation at this location, which they called White Marsh (sometimes spelled as a single word). Between 1729 and 1741, they erected a church named after a former Jesuit general, St. Francis Borgia. The rear of the chapel [**facing page**] is the original church. A front part was added in 1827 and, after a fire in 1853, was restored. The bell tower was added twenty years later, and additional renovations took place in 1916 and in the 1930s. A new parish church, operated by the archdiocese of Washington, was erected in 1969 after Sacred Heart was formally established as a parish. It is located a few hundred feet away on a major thoroughfare and serves a suburban congregation of about twelve hundred families.

Litigation arose over the original grant. One of the executors of the will of James Carroll was his cousin, Dr. Charles Carroll (not to be confused with the other four Charles Carrolls mentioned throughout this volume). Dr. Carroll had embezzled £1,000 from the estate and threatened to invoke the penal laws, which forbade priests from holding title to land, to protect himself from legal liability. This plan was eventually thwarted and Dr. Carroll abandoned his threat, but title to the land was not placed in corporate ownership until after the American Revolution when, in 1792, the Maryland General Assembly granted a charter to former Jesuit priests that permitted them to use this corporation to consolidate their holdings under one name. The Jesuits made improvements that permitted White Marsh to operate as a plantation. They also built a bridge across the Patuxent a mile or so north of the church to permit easy access to additional holdings they had acquired on the other side of the river. Moreover, the bridge facilitated monthly journeys to Annapolis and Baltimore where priests went to minister to small groups of Catholics. This bridge, now called Priest's Bridge, was replaced in 1925 by the state roads commission and became part of the Maryland highway system.

Not long after the American colonies signed a treaty of independence with Great Britain in 1783, the Catholic clergy of the former British colonies held a meeting at White Marsh to discuss the government of the Church in what would soon be the United States. Before the American Revolution, the Church in New England, such as it was, came under the responsibility of the diocese of Quebec. At least on paper, southern colonies were part of the diocese of Santiago, Cuba, a fiction that remained from the days when the king of Spain exercised power over a portion of the southern United States. The English-speaking colonies in the mid-Atlantic states, where most known Catholics resided, had been under the remote supervision of the vicar apostolic of the London district. When the colonies were separated from Great Britain, the vicar in London resigned his responsibilities for North America, so it was time for this area to have its own bishop. At first, the former colonies were designated a prefecture, not a diocese, and Father John Carroll was named prefect apostolic. In 1789, representatives of the American clergy, numbering fewer than thirty priests, met again at White Marsh. On May 18, after celebrating a Mass in honor of the Holy Spirit, they voted to recommend to the Propagation of the Faith in Rome that Father Carroll be named the first Catholic bishop of the United States. He was appointed to this post in the fall of that year, and Baltimore was designated to be the seat of his diocese. As noted elsewhere in this volume, he went to England to be consecrated bishop, a ceremony that took place in Lulworth Castle, near Dorset, on the Feast of the Assumption, 1790.

In the early 1800s, the Jesuits constructed a building next to the chapel capable of housing about twenty seminarians and lay Brothers. The facility became a novitiate, the name given to a seminary for those just beginning their studies for the priesthood. One prominent novice who studied there was Pierre De Smet, who was assigned to this facility in September of 1821 along with six other Belgian novices who had just arrived in America. Eighteen months later, De Smet and eleven others volunteered to go to Florissant, Missouri, where the Jesuits were establishing a second American province at the request of the newly appointed bishop of St. Louis, Joseph Rosati. De Smet completed his studies in Missouri and was ordained by Bishop Rosati in 1827, after which he began his celebrated career as explorer and peacemaker with the Indian tribes of the West.

The Jesuits were happy to reduce the size of their novitiate at White Marsh. They were unable to maintain a seminary of twenty students because the income from the plantation had diminished owing to the fact that they had failed to engage in proper crop rotation. Moreover, their title to the property was being questioned, and they were on bad terms with the archbishop of Baltimore. Eventually, they closed the novitiate entirely and moved their remaining students to Frederick, about forty miles away, and to Georgetown in the District of Columbia.

When, in 1773, the Holy See suppressed the Jesuit order, the pope required the society to turn over its properties to local bishops. The papal bull establishing the diocese of Baltimore required all religious orders in the diocese to transfer their properties to the new bishop. The first two archbishops, John Carroll and Leonard Neale, were former Jesuits and they did not question the right of their newly revived order to continue their ownership of White Marsh and the other Jesuit holdings in Maryland and elsewhere. Moreover, both archbishops had been paid an annual sum from the income derived from these properties to assist in their maintenance. However, the third archbishop of Baltimore, Ambrose Marèchal, appointed in 1817, was a Sulpician. Since he was not a former member of the Jesuits, the society informed him that it would no longer give him an annual maintenance for life from their revenues and would continue such payments only until his cathedral in Baltimore, due for completion in 1821, was finished.

Archbishop Marèchal was incensed at this action. Despite the fact that he was seriously embattled on several other fronts, he decided to lay claim to the Jesuit holdings for the archdiocese, citing as his authority the papal bulls suppressing the order and establishing the Baltimore diocese. At issue was not only White Marsh but Deer Creek, a 115-acre tract that the Jesuits had acquired in 1764 in the will of Thomas Shea. Deer Creek is about seventy-five miles from White Marsh on the other side of Baltimore in Harford County. There the Jesuits had established another mission, first called Priest Neale's Mass house, later St. Joseph's mission, and eventually St. Ignatius parish, Hickory, Maryland. The newly restored Jesuits resisted the claim, arguing that their order, as such, had never owned the properties in question because, in colonial America, a Catholic religious order was legally incapable of property ownership. They further argued that since the lands in question were entitled in the names of individual priests, the properties were not subject to the requirements of any of the papal bulls relied upon by the archbishop. They pointed out to Roman authorities that when a new corporation was established in 1792 that permitted them to own land under a corporate title, Bishop Carroll had relinquished any diocesan claims to Jesuit properties.

In 1821, Archbishop Marèchal went to Rome in order to press his claim. He was the first American prelate ever to visit the Eternal City in the capacity of an incumbent bishop. On July 23, 1822, a papal commission that had been specifically established to resolve this dispute ruled in his favor and directed the Jesuits to convey to the archdiocese of Baltimore two thousand acres of land, either at White Marsh, Deer Creek, or elsewhere at their discretion, in exchange for which they would be allowed to retain the balance of their Maryland holdings. The Jesuit general in Rome flatly refused to comply. The matter was referred to the president of the United States for mediation. The Monroe Administration, acting largely through Secretary of State John Quincy Adams, sided with the Jesuits to the extent that they faulted the archbishop for seeking the aid of a foreign power to resolve the dispute rather than litigating it in an American court. The matter still remained unresolved when, in 1826, the Jesuits proposed a compromise to the newly elected Pope Leo XII. They offered to pay Archbishop Marèchal an annual stipend equivalent to 800 Roman crowns ($800) for the balance of his life if they could keep all of their Maryland properties. The pope agreed. Archbishop Marèchal accepted the stipends during the remaining three years of his life. His next two successors in office insisted upon a continuation of the yearly fees, which the Jesuit general had been paying because the Maryland province was too impoverished to do so. Over objections, the Jesuits continued these payments for the next ten years when they arranged, for a sum of $8,000, to commute any additional amounts due and to terminate their obligation to the archdiocese. The lump-sum payment was derived from part of the proceeds which Father Thomas Mulledy, the Maryland provincial, derived from the sale and removal of slaves who had been working the White Marsh plantation. As a result, the Jesuits still own about seven hundred fifty acres of land surrounding Sacred Heart Church in the suburban fringes of Washington, D.C. The archdiocese of Washington owns about thirty-one acres, which comprise the buildings and grounds of the parish as it exists today.

In 1853, the old chapel, the novitiate building, and the rectory caught fire and burned. Left standing were the stone walls of the chapel, which served as a foundation for the rebuilding of the church, an effort that took the next three years. As noted above, additional construction and renovations have followed over the years. In 1972, an extensive effort was undertaken to shore up the walls of the chapel so that it could be preserved as it had existed in colonial and antebellum times. Parish records that were spared from the fire date back to 1819. The country churchyard surrounding the chapel contains markers dating back to the 1860s.

Because Sacred Heart was located in a relatively inaccessible corner of Prince George's County, it remained a small country mission for several generations. Its parishioners were mainly farmers, a large percentage of whom were black. When nearby Bowie became a rail junction and the site of a prominent race track, the center of population moved away from White Marsh toward the town where two parishes were established. Sacred Heart was operated first as a mission of Ascension, an older rural parish, and later of St. Pius X, a newer suburban church.

In the 1950s, Bowie experienced unprecedented growth. Instead of being a remote suburb of Washington D.C., it became a Levittown constructed on a large horse-breeding estate known as Belair. The city of Bowie now has forty thousand inhabitants and has become the second largest city in Maryland. Some of the development has taken place on land formerly owned by the Jesuits. With this expansion, Sacred Heart was established as a parish in its own right in 1965. Sunday Masses were held not only in the old chapel but also at a nearby movie theater. The main parish church, dedicated in 1969, now serves a congregation many times larger than the one that attended the old chapel during its period of greatest prominence.

Happily, the old chapel has been restored and is in active use. Daily Mass is celebrated at its altar and it is a popular site for weddings. The chapel sits on a hill and is somewhat removed from the suburban expansion that surrounds it. Recently, the Jesuits engaged the services of two major developers and have instructed them to attempt to rezone the seven hundred fifty acres of land that they still own for the maximum density obtainable so that their ancient holdings can be sold at the best possible price. The outcome of this effort will determine whether Sacred Heart will retain the tranquil setting it has enjoyed for more than two hundred fifty years.

30
St. John the Evangelist

Silver Spring

MARYLAND

This large suburban parish, located just north of Silver Spring, Maryland, can trace its roots to 1774 when Eleanor Carroll reputedly built a small wooden chapel on the family estate, often referred to as Rock Creek, so that her son, recently returned from theological studies and teaching duties in Belgium and France, could say Mass. Father John Carroll is also claimed by the parish as its first pastor, although there is some question as to whether the small chapel constituted a formal parish church as we know it today. Two years later, Father Carroll left his mission parish for three months and journeyed to Quebec with Benjamin Franklin to enlist French Catholic settlers in supporting the revolt against England. The effort, as mentioned earlier in this volume, was unsuccessful.

In 1790, Father Carroll was consecrated the first Catholic bishop of the United States and maintained his episcopal see at Baltimore, some forty miles away, from which point he supervised a diocese extending throughout all of the thirteen states and their western territories. In 1796, Eleanor Carroll was buried in a country churchyard just next to the old chapel, and her burial place is noted on a headstone marking that spot to this day. The cemetery is a two-acre tract that Daniel Carroll, the owner of Rock Creek Manor, conveyed to his brother John for this purpose. From 1813 to 1898,

St. John's at Rock Creek functioned as a mission of St. Mary's, a parish established in 1813 about ten miles away at the Montgomery County seat in Rockville.

Two chapels were built on this spot over the years, one in 1774 and the other in 1850. The red sandstone church **[pictured above]** was constructed adjacent to the site of the old chapels in 1893. It served as the parish church at Forest Glen, as this quiet residential area is known, until 1962 when the present church was erected about a mile away on a busy six-lane arterial road that leads to and from the city of Washington. The first resident pastor in modern times was Father Charles Rosensteel, who, at the turn of the twentieth century, used his horse and buggy to tend to the spiritual needs of Marylanders who worshiped at a series of missions extending from the District of Columbia all the way to Olney, about ten miles north. His mission territory now includes seven large suburban parishes. Father Rosensteel, who always thought of himself as a country pastor, died in 1940 and is buried just a few feet from the church where he labored for forty years. His name is commemorated in the Knights of Columbus Council Hall located just across the street. In 1906, a small wooden building was built toward the rear of the cemetery as a replica of the frame chapel that was erected in pre-Revolutionary times. It is maintained by the Rosensteel Council of the Knights of Columbus.

When Silver Spring grew northward and became the home of many Washington suburbanites, a new church was constructed, but the 1893 chapel was left intact. Today, St. John the Evangelist parish has about 1,450 families and operates a parochial school with three hundred students in its eight grades. The parish population has been stable for a number of years, but an increase may well be expected since the Metro line nearby has been extended and connects Forest Glen to downtown Washington by subway.

The old church is still in active use. In 1978, the archdiocese of Washington designated it as a church to serve Polish Catholics living in and about Washington. In 1983, a Polish ethnic parish was formally established and is called Our Lady of Poland and St. Maximilian Kolbe. It has about one hundred eighty families who live throughout the Washington area. Their pastor, recently arrived from Poland, resides at the old rectory next door and offers Mass in Polish each Sunday at the same location where John Carroll first said Mass over two hundred years ago.

31
Basilica of the Assumption

Baltimore

MARYLAND

The first Mass said in the city of Baltimore was offered by Father John Ashton, a Jesuit missionary from Doughoregan Manor, the ancient home of a branch of the Carroll family in Howard County. It was celebrated on Christmas Day, 1755, in a two-story brick house at Fayette and Calvert Streets where the state courthouse is now located. The first Catholics to come to Baltimore in any significant numbers were Acadian refugees from Nova Scotia, who were distributed by the British Navy in various port cities along the Eastern seaboard. A handful of Acadians, along with a few Irish immigrants, attended this service.

By 1770, the Catholic community in Baltimore had grown to about six hundred. For six pounds sterling the congregation purchased from Charles Carroll of Carrollton a plot of land located on a hillside at the corner of what are now Saratoga and Cathedral Streets, just a block from the present basilica. At that time, the property was just inside the corporate limits of the city of Baltimore. Under the penal laws, Catholics were not entitled to construct a public place of worship, so they built a two-story brick residence with a high-gabled brick roof designed to serve as a private "Mass house." A creditor of the contractor, John McNabb, had difficulty in finding assets to satisfy his debt. Instead of suing McNabb, who was bankrupt, McNabb's creditor brought suit in a colonial Maryland court for £200 against Pope Pius VI for the unpaid balance of McNabb's debt. History does not record if McNabb's creditor took judgment or even achieved service of process; but, by 1775, the Mass house was open for regular services and eventually became St. Peter Prince of Apostles Church. It was the first Catholic church in Baltimore.

During that time, Catholics in Baltimore were visited once a month by a priest coming from the Jesuit parish of White Marsh at Bowie, some thirty miles away. In 1782, Father Charles Sewall was appointed their first resident pastor. Father John Carroll became the second pastor about 1786. St. Peter's became the first Catholic parish in America to be supported by donations taken up from its parishioners, since the practice of Jesuit missionaries at that time was not to request donations from their missionary congregations but to support themselves from funds derived from other sources. These sources included donations from abroad and income from the manors or plantations that they operated.

As mentioned previously, Father Carroll was consecrated on the Feast of the Assumption in 1790 at Lulworth Castle in Dorset, England, as the first Catholic bishop of the United States. When he returned to Baltimore in December of that year, he was met at the Fells Point wharf by a greeting party and escorted up the hill to his old rectory at St. Peter's Church where he spent the remaining twenty-five years of his life. From this church, which then became his procathedral, Bishop Carroll administered his new diocese. It included the thirteen original states and all American territories stretching from the northern tip of Maine westward to the Mississippi River.

On December 2, 1790, Bishop Carroll delivered the first sermon in his procathedral. In it he outlined the task he faced as the first bishop in the United States: "But there are [other duties] still more burdensome to be borne by me, in this particular portion of Christ's church which is committed to my charge, and where everything is to be raised, as it were, from its foundation; to establish ecclesiastical discipline; to devise means for the religious education of Catholic youth — that precious portion of pastoral solicitude; to provide an establishment for training up members for the sanctuary and the services of religion, that we may no longer depend upon foreign and uncertain coadjutors; not to leave unassisted any of the faithful who were scattered through this immense continent; to preserve their faith untainted amidst the contagion of error surrounding them on all sides; to preserve in their hearts a warm charity and forbearance toward every other denomination of Christians, and at the same time to preserve therefrom that fatal and prevailing indifference which views all religions as equally acceptable to God and salutary to men. Ah! When I consider these additional duties, my heart sinks almost under the impression of terror which comes upon it. In God alone can I find any consolation."

On November 7, 1791, the first synod of the Catholic Church in the United States took place at St. Peter's. It was attended by Bishop Carroll and twenty-three priests. If a similarly structured meeting were held today in Baltimore, a large stadium would be taxed to its capacity. The synod devoted its attention to such basic matters as maintaining baptismal registries, the education of priests, the establishment of holy days of obligation, taking up collections, and the necessity for keeping churches clean.

The papal bull establishing the diocese of Baltimore in 1789 required that a suitable cathedral be erected as soon as possible. This task took thirty-two years. The original site that Bishop Carroll chose as a location for a cathedral was near the port at Pratt and Exeter Streets. A fund solicitation, including a public lottery (for which he had obtained special permission from the Maryland General Assembly), was unable to raise enough money to build the cathedral at this location. One problem with the lottery was that it set aside eighty-five percent of the proceeds for prizes. Apparently Catholics of that era were unfamiliar with a money-raising device known as the "50-50." Bishop Carroll drew one of the winning tickets, but he donated his prize to the building fund.

In 1805, the trustees sold this site and purchased land immediately north of St. Peter's, which was a small part of an estate owned by General John Eager Howard, a Revolutionary War hero. The Eager family had owned a two-hundred-acre tract in this area, known as "Lunn's Lot," for over a hundred years. General Howard sold the tract on which the basilica now stands for $20,000, a price the trustees felt was low enough so that the general should be regarded in a sense as a benefactor of the cathedral. The particular site, then known as Howard's Park, was a place where Mass had been celebrated many years earlier for the benefit of French troops who were passing through Baltimore on their way north from the British surrender at Yorktown. The trustees petitioned the city government to annex the land into the corporate limits of Baltimore but the city council did not get around to it until eleven years later.

It should be noted that at the same time that Bishop Carroll was soliciting funds for the erection of a cathedral he was also in the process of establishing a seminary and chapel a mile away on what is now North Paca Street. When Bishop Carroll took over his responsibilities in 1790, there was no seminary in the United States. Anyone wishing to study for the priesthood had to do as he had done and go abroad to France or Belgium for a seminary education. In 1790, Bishop Carroll prevailed upon the Sulpicians, a French order specializing in operating seminaries, to come to Baltimore for this purpose. At that time, the Sulpicians were being persecuted in their native land in the name of liberty, fraternity, and equality, so a number of them were happy to accept his invitation. In fact, more arrived in Baltimore than Bishop Carroll needed in his proposed seminary so he put some to work in various parts of his far-flung diocese as parish priests while attaching others to be part of the staff of the procathedral so that it might offer a full array of liturgical rites.

A tavern was purchased and converted into a school and residence for the Sulpicians. Called One Mile Tavern because it was located just a mile north of the city limits, it was actually a three-story building suitable for classrooms and residences. It served for several years both as a seminary and a school offering advanced academic courses for men who had no intention of entering the priesthood. In 1804, when French anticlerical fervor appeared to be waning, Father James Andrew Emery, the superior of the Sulpician Fathers in Paris, sought to close St. Mary's and to recall the Sulpicians to staff French seminaries that he was planning to reopen. Bishop Carroll regarded this decision as a real blow to the American Church and he protested the decision to Rome. When Pope Pius VII was in Paris in 1804 for the coronation of Napoleon Bonaparte as emperor of France, Father Emery brought the question of St. Mary's Seminary to the pope's personal attention. The Holy Father told Father Emery, "My son, let this seminary subsist. Let it. It will bear its fruit in time. To recall the directors in order to employ them in France, in other houses, would be stripping St. Paul to clothe St. Peter." Thus was St. Mary's Seminary spared, but the economics of its situation required that St. Mary's operate, in conjunction with its seminary, a school of general studies for laymen. Many of the latter were Protestant boys seeking higher education. It continued to operate a college of general studies until 1852. In 1824, Archbishop Ambrose Marèchal obtained from the Holy See the authority for St. Mary's to grant degrees in theology. He awarded such degrees at the cathedral to three instructors at St. Mary's.

The priests at St. Mary's Seminary constructed a chapel in 1808 that served both seminarians and Catholics living in the neighborhood. However, Bishop Carroll regarded them as priests of the cathedral parish. In 1808, Elizabeth Seton began an elementary school in a three-story house next to the seminary. In 1809, she took her vows as a nun in the basement chapel of the seminary church and then moved west to Emmitsburg where she founded a school and a motherhouse for an order later called the Daughters of Charity. St. Mary's Seminary chapel is an old church deserving of attention in its own right. It is still in existence, although the seminary long ago moved to more spacious quarters in Roland Park. The Sulpicians retain the property for use as a retreat house. Pius VII's vision of St. Mary's Seminary proved correct: it has borne fruit. During its long lifetime, it has produced over seven thousand priests, one hundred thirty bishops, and four cardinals.

While efforts to construct a new cathedral were still in their formative stages, the old Mass house that became a procathedral became the site of the first ordination in the United States (Father Stephen Badin, 1793) and the consecration of the first bishop (Bishop Leonard Neale, 1800). Bishop Neale continued to live at Georgetown where he served as president of Georgetown Academy for another eight years. In 1806, Bishop Carroll laid the cornerstone in Howard Park for the new cathedral but he did not live to see its completion. Shortages of funds and the outbreak of the War of 1812 delayed construction. Archbishop Carroll died in 1815, but it was not until 1821 that the Assumption Cathedral was completed and dedicated. He was reburied in the crypt beneath its altar in 1823.

The construction of a suitable cathedral for the premier see in America received a significant assist when Benjamin H. Latrobe agreed to serve as architect and to contribute his services free of charge. Latrobe had gained considerable prominence as the designer of the U.S. Capitol Building in Washington and was then engaged in the construction of the Chesapeake and Ohio Canal along the Potomac River from Washington to Cumberland. Latrobe wrote to Bishop Carroll in 1806 to explain why he was donating his services: "The principal motive which induced me to undertake the labor of the design at a time when neither my existing engagements nor the circumstances of my family permitted me to undertake it with convenience, were not entirely unselfish. They were motives of gratitude. To the disinterested benevolence and the pious sensibility of a clergyman of your Church I owe my existence, at all events an existence of which I have no reason to be ashamed, and I hope I have never since omitted an opportunity of honoring and serving the Church of which he was a splendid ornament."

Latrobe submitted four alternative plans to the trustees for their approval, one a Gothic structure and the other three of Roman design. Three of the plans were rejected because the churches were simply too costly to construct. The fourth was the Roman, or neoclassical, design, a cruciform church with a dome located at the junction of the nave and the transepts. It was approved by the trustees and construction began. Those who have compared the design to other buildings have suggested that Latrobe used as his models the Pantheon in Paris or Lulworth Castle in England where Bishop Carroll was consecrated bishop. A look closer to home would reveal a resemblance of the cathedral to the lower rotunda of the U.S. Capitol which Latrobe had also designed. Very recently, the Assumption Cathedral appeared on the face of U.S. postage stamps issued as a commemorative series honoring Latrobe and the most prominent buildings he designed during an illustrious career. The original church was 156 feet long and 75 feet wide at the transepts; its central dome was 72 feet in circumference and rose to an interior height of 95 feet.

In 1808, four additional dioceses were created in Boston, New York, Philadelphia, and Bardstown, Kentucky, so Baltimore became an archdiocese and John Carroll became the first archbishop in the United States as well as the first bishop. Construction of the cathedral was suspended for three years because the United States had been dragged into the concluding episodes of the Napoleonic wars. In 1814, a British warship, the *Saracen*, was causing considerable depredation in southern Maryland in the lower Chesapeake Bay. The Catholic chapel at St. Inigoes in St. Mary's County had been raided and British war parties had gone ashore in search of spoils of war. In particular, the British were looking for Irishmen, whom they could claim were British subjects and hence liable to impressment into the British Navy. British troops had just succeeded in leveling the major public buildings in Washington after which, in September 1814, they engaged in an all-out assault on Baltimore. They were repulsed a few miles east of the half-finished cathedral at a promontory called North Point. The bombardment of Fort McHenry in the port section of the city during that assault was easily visible from the cathedral, perhaps more so than from the British vessel on which Francis Scott Key was being held prisoner. In October 1814, after the British had withdrawn, Carroll directed that solemn services of thanksgiving be held in all Baltimore Catholic churches for the deliverance of the city.

When Archbishop Marèchal dedicated the cathedral in 1821, the total cost of construction had reached $225,000. This figure did not include the portico and pillars that were added forty years later. In 1821, the road in front of the cathedral was still unpaved and was lined with hitching posts and rails instead of a curb. The Catholic population of Baltimore, which was only six hundred when Bishop Carroll took office in 1790, had grown to ten thousand. By then, they were served by only four churches: the cathedral, St. Mary's Seminary chapel, St. Patrick's Church (which had been constructed in 1806 in the Fells Point section east of the port), and the old procathedral, which continued to be used until 1841 when it was razed to make way for Calvert Hall, a boys' school operated by the Christian Brothers. By 1830, the creation of other dioceses limited the archdiocese of Baltimore to the state of Maryland and the District of Columbia, although the archbishop of Baltimore continued to serve as administrator of the Richmond diocese for a number of years.

Baltimore during the Civil War was a sharply divided city in a sharply divided state. Early in the war, Union troops en route to Washington marched through the streets and were attacked by local mobs. They fired upon their attackers, killing several. The entire state of Maryland was placed under martial law. When Chief Justice Roger B. Taney, a Catholic and a Baltimore resident, issued a writ of habeas corpus directed to a military commander seeking the release of men held in military detention, the commander simply refused to honor the order because President Abraham Lincoln had suspended the writ of habeas corpus in Maryland.

It was the custom for many years at the cathedral to recite a prayer composed by Archbishop Carroll for civil and religious authorities. However, some priests assigned to the cathedral parish refused to continue this practice because the prayer included a sentence asking God to preserve the Union. When Archbishop Francis P. Kenrick, a Union supporter, decided to read the prayer himself, many members of the congregation simply walked out of church while others made rustling noises signaling their disapproval. Since the ecclesiastical province over which Archbishop Kenrick exercised supervisory responsibility as archbishop of Baltimore included most Southern dioceses, he felt the strain of the Civil War most acutely. He died just a few days after the Union victory of Gettysburg.

The anguish felt by many Baltimore Catholics during the war was well illustrated in the case of Cardinal James Gibbons, then a parish priest assigned to two churches at Baltimore Harbor that were located on either side of the Patapsco River. In this capacity, Father Gibbons came to serve as chaplain to Union soldiers stationed nearby at Fort McHenry and at Fort Marshall. However, his own family had relocated to New Orleans and was living under Union military occupation in that city. His younger brother, Thomas Gibbons, was a soldier in the Confederate Army.

The cathedral was the site of ten provincial councils held between 1849 and 1869. These were meetings of bishops of all of the dioceses in the ecclesiastical province of Baltimore. The cathedral was also the meeting place for three plenary councils of the

American hierarchy, held in 1852, 1866, and 1884. These meetings included all the American bishops and were the precursors of the semiannual meetings of the National Council of Catholic Bishops that now take place in Washington and elsewhere throughout the country. The first of these plenary councils formulated a policy that there should be a Catholic school in every parish, a policy followed with regularity until the ballooning cost of Catholic education made it impossible to carry out in every locality. The second council, held just after the end of the Civil War, was notable for both religious and secular reasons. At the time, it was the largest council of the Catholic Church to be held since the Council of Trent had recessed in 1570. President Andrew Johnson was in attendance at its final ceremony. The third council dealt with a variety of matters, including secret societies, marriage regulations, abstinence from the use of alcohol, Sunday observances, and missionary efforts among blacks and Indians. It established the six holy days of obligation now observed in the United States, decreed that priests should avoid engaging in politics both in and out of the pulpit, and told all priests in the United States that they had to wear Roman collars. Perhaps its most famous and most far-reaching effort was a formulation of the essentials of Catholic religious and moral teachings into a series of questions and answers for the purpose of providing instructional assistance to religion teachers. The Baltimore Catechism became a standard feature in Catholic schools and was looked upon by generations of American Catholics as the foundation of their religious education.

Cardinal Gibbons was installed at the Assumption Cathedral as archbishop of Baltimore in 1877 and served in that position for the next forty-four years. A native of the city, he was baptized in Old St. Peter's, served as parish priest in east Baltimore and in North Carolina, and then was appointed bishop of Richmond, Virginia. In 1886, he became the second American to enter the College of Cardinals. He was widely known as a liberal churchman, if that term can be understood in a nineteenth-century context, and, second only to John Carroll, is probably the most prominent clergyman in the history of the Catholic Church in America.

The details of his extensive career have been told elsewhere and told well. Cardinal Gibbons wrote a defense of Catholic teaching entitled *Faith of Our Fathers* that sold over 600,000 copies. He ordained more priests than any bishop in the history of the American hierarchy. He was instrumental in the founding of the Catholic University of America in Washington. Many controversies involving the Catholic Church in the late 1800s were resolved as they were because of his intervention or influence. Although many of those controversies seem relatively obscure or barely understandable to the twentieth-century mind, they were live and compelling issues in their day, and some involve matters of preeminent importance even now. He prevented Henry George's controversial economics treatise on the single tax on land from being placed on the *Index Librorum Prohibitorum* (*Index of Forbidden Books*). During the controversy over the Knights of Labor, he championed the right of workingmen to organize and engage in collective bargaining, thereby placing the Catholic Church solidly on the side of the

American labor movement during its critical formative years. He was frequently consulted by public officials on matters of state, especially on the relations of the United States with Catholic countries in South and Central America and our newly acquired territory, the Philippines.

Through it all, Cardinal Gibbons maintained a warmth and equilibrium that engendered widespread personal affection. He was always accessible to priests of the archdiocese who called without appointment, and this availability extended to neighborhood children who sometimes rang the bell at the door of the cardinal's residence on Charles Street asking to see him. He had a politician's memory for names and faces and kept an Irish sense of humor about him. When a stranger once asked him how far papal infallibility extended, he was heard to reply, "Well, the Pope always refers to me as 'Jibbons.' " When Cardinal Gibbons died in 1921 at the age of eighty-six, a lengthy period of mourning took place in Baltimore and over 200,000 persons visited the cathedral to pay their respects as he lay in state.

The basilica [**pictured above**] is no longer a cathedral but now bears the title of co-cathedral because of the posthumous meddling of one Thomas J. O'Neill. O'Neill came to Baltimore from Ireland at the age of sixteen, went into the dry-goods business, and opened a flourishing department store. He invested wisely in corporate stocks and in downtown Baltimore real estate. Among the clientele of his prominent department store were generations of Catholic students who regularly went to O'Neill's to buy their parochial school uniforms. He was an extraordinary businessman, a devout Catholic, a generous benefactor, and a poor judge of church needs. He and his wife were childless. When O'Neill died in 1919, he left a will providing that upon the death of his wife, two thirds of his estate should be given to the archdiocese of Baltimore for the express purpose of constructing a new cathedral. When Mrs. O'Neill died in 1936, the amount of the bequest approximated seven million dollars.

If there was one thing that Baltimore did not need in 1936 it was another cathedral. Latrobe's historic building, mother church of the United States and resting place of Carroll and Gibbons, was quite sufficient in the opinion of many Baltimoreans, including Archbishop Michael J. Curley, Gibbons' immediate successor. The archbishop did have great need for money to finance his expanding parochial school system and homes for the elderly, so he asked the executor of the O'Neill will to permit him to use the money for that purpose. Pointing to the explicit language in the will, the executor refused. Archbishop Curley sought legal advice as to whether the stipulations in the will could be set aside. He was told that the will could not be broken so he was forced to reconcile himself to its provisions. The original seven million dollars had grown to almost fourteen million dollars. In 1954, ground was finally broken at a twenty-three-acre tract located several miles north of the basilica for the Cathedral of Mary, Our Queen. It was completed in 1959. The new cathedral is Gothic in design, seats 1,900 people, and has two towers that are 134 feet high and support spires reaching upward another 29 feet. It is adorned with many artifacts, including a twenty-foot statue of Christ, the Risen King, sculpted by Theodore Barbarossa; a statue of Mary, Our Queen, done by Joseph Coletti; and three hundred fifty stained-glass panels. One of those stained-glass windows bears a likeness of Thomas J. O'Neill, with hands folded in prayer.

The old cathedral was designated a minor basilica by Pope Pius XI in 1937. A monograph about the cathedral prepared in 1951 estimated that, as of that time, it had been the site of more than two thousand ordinations and thirty-five episcopal consecrations. In 1889, it was the site of the formal celebration by the American bishops of the 100th anniversary of the establishment of the American hierarchy. They returned in 1989 to celebrate their 200th anniversary. When it was dedicated in 1821, Baltimore had about ten thousand Catholics. Today, the archdiocese of Baltimore, which now includes only about half the state of Maryland, has 443,000 Catholics.

Over the years, various enlargements and artistic decorations have been made to the original building. Nine large oil paintings were donated by Cardinal Joseph Fesch, uncle of Napoleon Bonaparte. The then recently restored Bourbon kings of France donated two huge canvases. Bell towers were added and bells made in France were installed in the south tower. After the portico was added in 1863, extensive repairs and renovations were undertaken in the interior. Brightly colored paintings of scenes from the Old Testament were placed on the walls. In 1879, the interior design was again altered by Cardinal Gibbons, who superimposed elaborate paintings and rococo artifacts upon the cathedral's neoclassical design. In 1890, the east wall was extended some thirty-three feet, thereby giving the effect of doubling the size of the sanctuary. From time to time down to the present, other redecoration, painting, and landscaping has been accomplished. In the 1940s, a series of stained-glass windows were installed, each of which has a three-part design depicting an Old Testament event, a New Testament event, and a scene from Maryland Catholic history, all illustrating a single theme in each window. In the 1960s, the interior of the cathedral was repainted, this time in muted tones that emphasize the original clean-cut design of the building. The cathedral seats nine hundred sixty comfortably and its capacity can be enlarged to seat three hundred more in the galleries. Recent improvements include the renovation of the cathedral organ containing the old organ case and some of the pipes installed by Thomas Hall in 1819.

The basilica's present pastorate is threefold: to the individuals living within or passing through its territorial boundaries, to the downtown Baltimore business and professional community, and to numerous others who have been attracted to the old cathedral because of its historical significance. The parish has about four hundred regular and associate parishioners but these figures are misleading. Between 1,200 and 1,500 people, including about 150 children, attend one of seven Masses said each weekend. Each year about fifty weddings are performed at the cathedral. Simple arithmetic demonstrates that this number could include only a handful of regular parishioners, many of whom are senior citizens. The same can be said for the significant number of baptisms of children brought to the cathedral from all over the Baltimore area for this purpose. The parish has a pastoral ministry, composed of two permanent deacons and one nun, who regularly visit the four hospitals and the several apartments for the elderly located in the neighborhood or elsewhere in the city. This number includes Basilica Place, a senior-citizen residence of about two hundred people operated by Associated Catholic Charities of the archdiocese. Mass is often said in those apartment units for older people who have difficulty in coming to church. The Basilica Guild sponsors both social and spiritual activities for its members. Very recently, the cathedral parish took over the operation of St. Alphonsus Parochial School, located about three blocks away. The school has about one hundred thirty students, most of whom are black. Upon coming to the cathedral, Monsignor Jeremiah F. Kenney, the present rector, instituted a parish council that has four active standing committees.

Because of its downtown location, the parish has long been called upon for years to provide food, rent, and utility payments to individuals who knock on the rectory door in considerable numbers. At one time during the Great Depression, local businessmen complained about the lines that formed each day on Charles Street in front of the rectory by individuals seeking help. In the past eight years, in conjunction with Catholic Charities, it has supported a soup kitchen on nearby Franklin Street where noon meals are distributed. This project, called Our Daily Bread, recently commemorated the fact that it had given out its one millionth meal. A notable feature of this activity is an effort to personalize a charitable outreach by calling upon parishioners to provide bread they have baked themselves and various entrées they have personally prepared. The parish also acts in conjunction with an interfaith association in downtown Baltimore with regard to other social welfare projects, such as a ministry to runaways.

The basilica is the site of high-school graduations and concerts of religious music, including concerts by choirs visiting Baltimore from abroad. Approximately ten thousand tourists make visits each year, many on organized tours and others simply on individual visits. Among these visitors are many classes in architecture that come to inspect Latrobe's handiwork up close.

Cardinal Gibbons loved the old cathedral and he expressed his affection effusively. To the congregation that gathered to celebrate the 100th anniversary of its dedication he stated: "What Mecca is to the Mohammedan, what the Temple of Jerusalem is to the Jew, what St. Peter's Basilica in Rome is to the faithful of the Church universal, this Cathedral is to American Catholics." What he said in 1906 is all the more meaningful, as additional generations have the opportunity of coming in contact with the mother church of Catholics in America.

32
St. Peter the Apostle

Baltimore

MARYLAND

In colonial times, the portion of Baltimore lying west of the port was known as Mount Clare, a 2,700-acre estate of Charles Carroll, the Barrister, not to be confused with Charles Carroll of Carrollton or other prominent Marylanders of that era who had the same name. Charles Carroll, the Barrister, was a member of the Church of England. He was a prominent lawyer, public figure, and plantation owner but made most of his money by mining iron on this property and operating a foundry. In the early 1800s, one of his descendants sold an acre of land to the B & O (Baltimore and Ohio) Railroad for a train station and, from that small start, railroading developed as the major occupation in the area. With the coming of the railroad came Irish railroad workers, who, after living in the locality for a few years, petitioned Archbishop Samuel Eccleston to establish a parish in their neighborhood. For this purpose a small tract of land was purchased at the intersection where St. Peter's **[facing page]** now stands. Coincidentally with this request came the demolition of the old St. Peter's procathedral, so when the new parish was established in west Baltimore, both the name and the altar relics from the old procathedral were transferred to the new church. At that time, it was the only Catholic church between downtown Baltimore and Ellicott City in far-off Howard County. At the same time the archbishop was building a new church for the Irish he also built another church near the cathedral named St. Alphonsus for German-speaking Catholics and placed it in the hands of German Redemptorists.

Before the construction of St. Peter's was completed in 1844, Archbishop Eccleston appointed Father Edward McColgan, then a newly ordained priest serving in southern Maryland, to be its first pastor. Father McColgan was suffering from typhoid, and many believed at the time that his pastorate would be a short one. He experienced a remarkable recovery and went on to serve for fifty-six years. During the latter part of his career, he became vicar general of the archdiocese and a close confidant of Cardinal James Gibbons.

Among Father McColgan's accomplishments was assisting the Xaverian Brothers in erecting a boys' orphanage near the parish called St. Mary's Industrial School. St. Mary's became the home of George Herman Ruth, who was born and lived a few blocks from St. Peter's. Ruth became a Catholic during his residence at St. Mary's. The "Babe" developed his remarkable athletic talent with the encouragement of the Xaverian Brothers and went on from there to one of the most remarkable careers in the history of baseball.

The church was built in considerable part by donations of "sweat equity," the personal labor of many in the congregation who lacked the means to make a financial contribution and instead dug foundations, hauled building materials, and performed many other chores incident to construction. What they built was a brick Grecian-style church, some seventy-three feet by one hundred twenty-three feet, with large Doric columns on the front portico. The church was dedicated in 1844 and enlarged about twenty-five years later. During the extension, more pews were added, the gallery was reconstructed, and stained-glass windows were installed.

Not long after the church was built, a school was opened and placed under the direction of the Daughters of Charity. In 1855, the Sisters of Mercy took over the operation of the girls' portion of the school and at one time maintained their provincial headquarters at the parish convent. From 1849 until 1891, the Christian Brothers operated a separate boys' school; but, in 1891, both schools were combined into a single elementary school under the supervision of the Mercy nuns, who remain at the parish to this day. St. Peter's was the first free Catholic school in Baltimore and at one time had about eight hundred students; however, demographic changes in the locality forced it to close its doors in 1967.

St. Peter's parish once included an area where eighteen Catholic parishes are now located. In recent years, its immediate environs have became commercialized and industrialized, and the housing stock has greatly deteriorated. The railroad yards, whose existence provided the initial impetus for the growth of the area and the establishment of the parish, are a thing of the past. A museum for railroad buffs is now located where freight trains were formerly serviced. Though the railroad is gone, the parish remains with a membership of four hundred fifty families and has every prospect of growing.

The present St. Peter the Apostle Church, like many inner-city parishes, serves a widely divergent population. It includes white-collar residents, some of whom are associated with nearby professional schools of the University of Maryland. It also includes a large number of the very poor. There is an ethnic mix of Irish, Lithuanians, Sicilians, Croatians, and blacks. However, as older houses become refurbished, younger families have been attracted to the area, as evidenced by the fact that in 1989 over one hundred baptisms were performed at the church. The former school is now a parish-life center. The religious order that formerly taught at the school is engaged at the parish-life center in a variety of different ministries that St. Peter's now maintains. It provides a preschool for four- and five-year-olds as well as a day-care center for retarded adults and a place where those adults can eat together. St. Peter's also participates in a program established nearby to teach adults in the area how to read and write.

33
St. Francis Xavier

Baltimore

MARYLAND

In colonial times, both black and white Catholics were the continuing subject of royal scrutiny. In 1745, Governor Thomas Bladen of Maryland wrote to a prominent Catholic in his colony counseling him that Catholics should not hold large meetings for public worship: "Nothing could give greater alarm to good subjects of King George than such frequent meetings of whites and Negroes under pretense of divine worship." This kind of message was directed especially at Catholics. The established church and many nonconformist churches simply refused to baptize blacks. They felt that baptism had an emancipating effect so blacks could not become a part of their regular congregations. With the coming of the American Revolution, this aspect of Catholic religious practice was no longer a matter of official concern.

In his report to Rome in 1785, Prefect Apostolic John Carroll estimated that there were about three thousand black Catholics in the United States, most of whom lived in Maryland, with a few residing in Pennsylvania. He also called the attention of the Holy See to their condition of servitude. The first detailed survey or census of black Catholics in the United States was not made by the hierarchy until 1928. It disclosed that there were, at that time, some 203,000 black Catholics in the United States, about half of whom lived in Louisiana. New York,

Maryland, and the District of Columbia ranked next, but their population figures were much smaller. Some 60 years later, the church census shows 1.2 million black Catholics in the United States, including 800 nuns, 350 priests, 12 bishops, and one archbishop.

In 1832, Archbishop James Whitfield of Baltimore wrote to the Society for the Propagation of the Faith in France: "How distressing it is to be unable to send missionaries to Virginia where there are 500,000 Negroes! It is undisputable that, had we missionaries and friends to support them, prodigies would be effected in this vast and untilled field. In Maryland, blacks are converted every day, and many of them are good Catholics and excellent Christians. At Baltimore, many are frequent communicants and three or four hundred receive the Blessed Sacrament every month. It is the same throughout Maryland where there are a great many Catholics among the Negroes."

His successor in Baltimore, Archbishop Samuel Eccleston, made a similar report to the Society for the Propagation of the Faith in 1838. He told them: "The slaves of these states also present a vast harvest for the apostolic workers. Their souls, redeemed by the same Savior, and destined to the same blessed immortality, are not, in the eyes of God, less precious than the souls of their masters; and often in their very simplicity they are better prepared to receive divine grace and make it bear fruit. I have done some special research on this subject, and I have constantly found that every time a Priest had given careful attention to these poor people, his zeal has soon been richly rewarded by their happy change of life, and by their edifying regularity in frequenting the sacraments. In our towns, many of the Protestant families prefer Catholic servants; in the country many of the Protestant planters who have in their neighborhoods some pious Catholic congregations, seeing how our Religion has influenced the slaves, have more than once sought to have them instructed in our salutary beliefs. I do not think that there is in this country, without excepting the Savages, any class of men among whom it would be possible to work more fruitfully. But, I repeat, far from being able to do what I should like to do for the salvation of unfortunate Negroes, I find myself unable to satisfy the thousands of whites who, equally deprived of the help of Religion, feel more keenly their spiritual abandonment."

St. Augustine's Church on Isle Brevelle in the Cane River area of southwestern Louisiana was founded before the Civil War as a black Catholic church, but priests could not conduct services without the presence of white people in the audience because of restrictions in the Louisiana Black Code against slave meetings. The oldest Catholic church in the United States with an all-black congregation is St. Francis Xavier, now located in east Baltimore. The original church was dedicated in 1864, a year following the Emancipation Proclamation. Ironically, that proclamation had no legal force or effect in Maryland, since, by its terms, it applied only to areas not under federal control. Maryland was subject to what amounted to military occupation throughout the Civil War. Slavery in the state boasting the oldest black Catholic church was actually abolished by a vote of the people, which took place in the fall of 1864 when voters of Maryland adopted a new state constitution containing an antislavery provision.

Black Catholics in Baltimore can trace their roots at least to 1793 when some 53 ships arrived from Santo Domingo bringing about 500 black and 1,000 white refugees from the slave uprisings that were then taking place on that island. Similar groups of refugees were arriving at this time in other ports along the Atlantic and Gulf Coasts. The Sulpicians at St. Mary's Seminary, who were also French, ministered to these new arrivals from the French Caribbean colony in the chapel at the seminary. In 1829, Father Nicholas Joubert of St. Mary's, himself a refugee from Santo Domingo, helped to organize the Oblates of Divine Providence, a religious order made up exclusively of black nuns. Two of the original members of the order were also French-speaking refugees from Santo Domingo. Elizabeth Lange, born in Cuba, was the first black American nun; she took her vows at St. Mary's in the same chapel where Mother Elizabeth Seton had taken her vows some twenty-one years earlier. In 1831, the Oblate Sisters were given formal recognition by the Holy See. Within a few years, they were operating a school for black children that had one hundred thirty-five girls and fifty boys.

While there were sporadic efforts during the antebellum years to minister to black Catholics in Baltimore, these efforts were essentially personal in character. When the priest, nun, or lay person involved in this work died or was transferred, the activity that person undertook came to an end. What was needed was an organized, ongoing ministry. The 1850 census shows that 29,075, or eighty percent of Baltimore's black population, were free. This figure meant that in Baltimore, unlike plantations in the rural South, most pre-Civil War blacks were accessible to the Church and were free to join if they chose.

In 1858, the Jesuits established St. Ignatius Church on Calvert Street in Baltimore. Its pastor, Father Peter L. Miller, S.J., had worked for thirty years among black Catholics in southern Maryland. He established a chapel in the new church for the use of black Catholics and named it in honor of Blessed Peter Claver (who, incidentally, was canonized in 1888). With the assistance of Bishop Michael J. O'Connor, who had just resigned as bishop of Pittsburgh in order to join the Jesuits, he was able to raise $6,000 to purchase a building a few blocks away on Calvert Street to become the first permanent parish home for St. Francis Xavier Church. The building in question had at one time been a Universalist church and later was used as a public meeting place. The Whig National Convention of 1844 and the Democratic National Convention of 1848 were held in this building. Just a couple of years before Father Miller purchased the building for the establishment of the first exclusively black Catholic Church in America, a secessionist rally had taken place at the same location. It was broken up by federal troops who arrested some of the participants.

The church was dedicated in February 1864 and remained at this location until 1933. Bishop O'Connor played a large role in the early development of the parish. By 1871, the parish had a convent, an academy for girls, and a parochial school. In 1880, the school was relocated to a nearby building vacated by the Christian Brothers, who had built a new and larger Calvert Hall Academy elsewhere. Between 1870 and 1881, St. Francis Xavier parish opened a lending library, a foundling home, and a home for widows. It also organized a burial society.

The establishment of St. Francis Xavier parish in Baltimore was soon followed by the establishment of other black Catholic churches in other cities — St. Peter in Charleston, South Carolina (1867); St. Augustine in Louisville (1869); St. Benedict the Moor in New York City (1883); St. Peter Claver in Philadelphia (1889); and St. Augustine in Washington (1874). A far-reaching pronouncement concerning blacks was made at the Second Plenary Council, which met in the Baltimore cathedral in 1866 just three blocks away from the new St. Francis Xavier Church. The bishops stated, ". . . we beg and implore priests, as far as they can, to consecrate their thoughts, their time and themselves, wholly and entirely if possible, to the service of the colored people." At this point, the entire American Church was itself administered by the Holy See as a missionary activity, and it remained as such until 1908. The quoted statement by the American hierarchy encouraged what was in fact a mission within a mission to a minority within a minority. At the Third Plenary Council in 1884, the bishops established an annual collection, to be taken up in every parish in the United States on the first Sunday of Lent each year, for the benefit of Indian and black missions. The plenary council also established a permanent commission to oversee the Church's ministry to blacks in the United States.

In 1871, another event directly affecting the Church's ministry to black Catholics occurred with the arrival in the United States of Father (later Cardinal) Herbert Vaughan and four members of the Missionary Society of St. Joseph. They were originally referred to as the Mill Hill Fathers and are now more widely known as the Josephites. The impetus for inviting the Mill Hill Fathers to the United States came from Bishop O'Connor. Father Vaughan offered to allow his companions to remain in Baltimore to work at St. Francis Xavier. The Josephites have been there ever since, eventually extending their ministry to four other black Catholic parishes in Baltimore.

The Josephites were founded at Mill Hill, a part of London, in 1865. Their original purpose was not specifically a ministry to blacks but to provide Catholic missions in all parts of the British Empire. However, when he came to the United States, Father Vaughn made an extensive personal survey of the spiritual condition of former slaves in the Reconstruction South. He was appalled by what he found, concluding that approximately half of the newly freed blacks had no religious affiliation at all. He decided to send missionaries to the United States to work among blacks insofar as his resources permitted. In 1893, American Josephites became a separate organization from the Josephites at Mill Hill. Each member of the Society of St. Joseph of the Sacred Heart, as the American Josephites are formally called, takes an oath to uphold the constitution of the society, which contains a specific provision dedicating their efforts to the evangelization of blacks.

One event leading to the creation of a separate branch of the society was the ordination in 1891 of a member of St. Francis Xavier parish, Reverend Charles R. Uncles. Father Uncles, the first black to graduate from St. Mary's Seminary, was also one of the first black priests to be ordained in the United States. He said his first Mass on Christmas Day, 1891, at St. Francis Xavier Church and became one of the organizers of the

American Josephites. Today, there are about one hundred sixty-five Josephites in the United States, fourteen of whom are black. Of the fourteen black members, three are bishops. At one time, they staffed one hundred twenty parishes in the South, but, because of reduced numbers of priests in recent years, they now staff only about seventy-five. One hallmark of Josephite ministry in the South has been the establishment of schools. They would often build a parochial school before building a church in order to devote scarce resources to what was perceived to be an immediate and critical need in their parishes.

Some parishes, such as St. Francis Xavier, are specifically designated as black parishes, much as a parish might be designated a Polish or a Lithuanian parish. Some territorial parishes become black parishes as the population of a neighborhood changes. In other places, blacks simply attend predominantly white churches as part of the regular parish congregation. St. Francis Xavier has remained a specifically black parish, notwithstanding two changes in location it has experienced in the past sixty years. In 1933, the construction of a freeway in downtown Baltimore made it imperative for the parish to move to another location. The church purchased the former Madison Square Methodist Church at Caroline and Eager Streets, about a mile east of the original location. In many respects, this relocation was a desirable step, since the original site was in an area that was rapidly becoming commercialized, whereas the Caroline Street location was in the middle of a residential area. A school was opened in 1943 and staffed by black nuns who were members of the Oblate Sisters of Providence. The school closed in 1968 when the parish was again relocated, this time to occupy the premises of the former St. Paul's Catholic Church a few blocks north on Caroline Street. The church [**pictured above**] is the present St. Francis Xavier Church at its third location.

St. Francis Xavier now has about seventeen hundred members and can accurately be described as a black middle-class parish, although much of the area nearby has low-income residents. The former school building next door houses a Head Start program for one hundred sixty children, ages three to five. In recent years, the parish has participated in various social-outreach programs, including Dismas House, a halfway house for former prisoners, as well as various drug-addiction programs and a current civic-action effort called BUILD, an advocacy group which was organized to stimulate government agencies in providing services for the immediate community.

In 1970, St. Francis Xavier organized one of the first Catholic gospel choirs. They have introduced gospel music into regular Catholic worship. As a result, "Go, Tell It on the Mountain" and "Swing Low, Sweet Chariot" have taken their places in Catholic liturgy alongside Gregorian chant and Masses by Bach and Mozart. The noon Mass each Sunday is a gospel liturgy. The parish choir has participated with other groups in concerts and in fact participated in a series of joint Catholic-Baptist revival meetings. At least five black Catholic churches in Baltimore can trace their roots to assistance and sponsorship by St. Francis Xavier, while every black Catholic church in America can properly claim this parish as its forerunner.

34
St. Mary

Annapolis
MARYLAND

St. Mary's Church and the Redemptorist rectory attached to it are located on a narrow street in the heart of old Annapolis where Duke of Gloucester Street meets Spa Creek. It was on the banks of Spa Creek, a tributary to Chesapeake Bay, that one of the Catholic branches of the Carroll family maintained its family home and estate throughout colonial times and until 1852. Charles Carroll, the Settler, his son Charles Carroll of Annapolis, and the most famous bearer of that name, Charles Carroll of Carrollton (sometimes known as the Signer), all owned this property. The latter, an agitator for American independence, celebrated signer of the Declaration of Independence, Maryland state senator, and later a United States Senator, was born at the Carroll home, known as Carroll House, in 1737. After going abroad with his cousin John to receive a Catholic education at St. Omer's in Belgium, he studied law in England. He returned to Annapolis, married, and took his bride, Molly Darnall, to live at Carroll House. There they had seven children, only three of whom lived to be adults. In this house, he lived to an advanced age and then moved to his daughter Mary's house, known as Caton House, located in Baltimore. There Charles Carroll of Carrollton, the last surviving signer of the Declaration of Independence, died in 1832 at the age of ninety-five. He is buried at the family's summer estate, Doughoregan Manor, about thirty miles from Annapolis. The old house in Annapolis is still standing on the St. Mary's parish grounds and at this writing is undergoing extensive restoration.

During the eighteenth century, Jesuit missionaries came to Annapolis from time to time and said Mass for Catholics in the area in the private chapel located on the top floor of the Carroll home. They worshiped together privately because of the existence of colonial penal laws forbidding public worship by Catholics. In 1822, Carroll built a small chapel on this site that served as the original St. Mary's Church.

In 1852, Carroll's descendants sold the property on Spa Creek to the Redemptorist Fathers, who had come to Maryland in 1840. They have occupied the premises ever since. One covenant attached to the deed was that the property should always be used for religion and that Masses should be said once a month for the repose of the souls of Charles Carroll of Carrollton, his daughter and son-in-law, and their children. At that time, Carroll House had fallen into a state of disrepair because the family had moved elsewhere and had leased it out. About twenty-five or thirty novices cleaned up the house and the premises and, soon thereafter, provided a great deal of manual labor that went into the building of the existing church and rectory. In 1853, the premises were inspected by civil authorities because the Redemptorists had been accused of keeping a prisoner in the basement of the church. This charge was part of the hysteria of the day that envisioned convent and rectory basements to be filled with hapless Catholics who were being held in servitude against their will. The inspection at St. Mary's disclosed that there was no prisoner and no basement. A new St. Mary's Church **[pictured above]** was completed in 1860. St. John Neumann, the Redemptorist bishop of Philadelphia, had blessed the church bell and cornerstone two years earlier. At one time, Bishop Neumann actually held title to a portion of this property but he deeded it to his congregation.

During the Civil War, the Annapolis area was occupied by federal troops to ensure that the Maryland General Assembly would not vote to secede and that the nation's capital would be accessible from the North. No battles were fought in the immediate area. However, the educational activities of the U.S. Naval Academy were transferred to Newport, Rhode Island, and the academy buildings were made over into a hospital for wounded Union soldiers. The Redemptorists from St. Mary's ministered to the sick and dying who were confined to this hospital. They also served as chaplains for Confederate prisoners of war who were kept at Camp Parole on the outskirts of Annapolis.

During its long history in the Maryland state capital, St. Mary's has served as a mission church for many parishes on both sides of the Chesapeake Bay. Redemptorist Fathers went from St. Mary's to Elkridge and West River and to Easton on Maryland's Eastern Shore to say Mass for small groups of Catholics located in these areas. Until 1907, the Redemptorists operated a novitiate in connection with the parish where they trained incoming members of the congregation. The parish and rectory were a base of operations from which priests were dispatched throughout the entire eastern portion of the United States to give retreats and to preach parish missions. These missions are distinctive Redemptorist activity, which involves going into a parish for a week or two at a time and conducting a special series of devotions in the nature of a revival. Priests from St. Mary's have also served as chaplains to both houses of the Maryland General Assembly.

Since 1862, the parish has conducted a parochial school at this location. Since 1867, it has been under the supervision of the School Sisters of Notre Dame. In 1874, when educational facilities for blacks were either scarce or nonexistent, they operated a public school for blacks on Chestnut Street in Annapolis. In 1903, it was moved to the parish grounds where it continued to be operated as a separate facility until 1949. St. Mary's parochial school now has about nine hundred students. Later, a high school was erected that now has approximately five hundred students.

The U.S. Naval Academy has played a preeminent role in the life of Annapolis for over one hundred forty years. Until 1947, when the academy appointed a full-time Catholic chaplain, the Redemptorist Fathers at St. Mary's served in that role on a de facto basis. In 1898, priests from St. Mary's were asked to minister to Spanish prisoners of war who were brought from Cuba and confined at the Naval Academy during the Spanish-American War. The parish boasts that it was Charles Adams Zimmerman, academy bandmaster and St. Mary's parish organist, who composed the famous U.S. Navy anthem, "Anchors Aweigh."

Today, Annapolis is an upscale gentrified city that relishes colonial- and federal-period architecture. In addition to being home to the Naval Academy and the Maryland state government, its port has become an attractive gathering place for vacationers, retirees, and sailing aficionados. A walk around City Dock, just a block from St. Mary's, is enjoyable and relaxing. Cabin cruisers and skipjacks are moored near the wharf where, in 1774, Annapolitans staged their own local version of the Boston Tea Party. In this setting, St. Mary's displays an energetic parish life that extends into many activities. About twelve Redemptorist priests and Brothers, some of them retired, still live at the rectory. Five are assigned to parish work.

The parish is a focal point for a variety of Catholic activities in Annapolis, as varied as a high-school basketball game or right-to-life activities focused on the Maryland State House nearby. Its optimism can be measured by the fact that St. Mary's has embarked upon an ambitious two-million-dollar capital program to expand school facilities and to establish an endowment for teachers' salaries and tuition assistance. About 3,900 attend 14 Masses that are offered each weekend, and about 10,000 attend Masses offered on major holy days. They worship publicly within a few feet of the upper room in Carroll House where a handful of early settlers gathered privately to hear Mass in colonial days.

35
U.S. Naval Academy Chapel

Annapolis

MARYLAND

The United States Naval Academy Chapel is the only interdenominational church or chapel profiled in this volume. Often called the Cathedral of the Navy, it is prominently located on the grounds of the Naval Academy at Annapolis immediately adjacent to the superintendent's quarters. In 1845, Fort Severn, constructed at the point where the Severn River empties into Chesapeake Bay, was transferred to the navy for the purpose of erecting a school to train members of its regular officer corps. In 1854, the first chapel was built on the academy grounds. It was Greek in style, with Ionic pillars, and was one of the first buildings to be constructed at the academy. Following the Civil War, the chapel was converted into a lyceum, or theater, and a second chapel made of brick was opened for worship in 1868. The second chapel served academy personnel and students until 1908 when the Main Chapel **[facing page]** was completed. The Main Chapel was designed by Ernest Flagg. The cornerstone was laid in 1904 by Admiral George Dewey, the hero of the Battle of Manila Bay. It was originally built in the shape of a Greek cross with four equal transepts, one wing of which housed the altar and the sanctuary. The other three wings contained seats for the congregation. The interior was essentially designed for the Episcopalian order of worship, and it is that order of worship that is still followed each Sunday at the main Protestant service conducted at 11:00 A.M.

Since the opening of the Main Chapel in 1908, many improvements and ornaments have been added. In 1912, some twelve thousand people, including Theodore Roosevelt, attended the reinterment of John Paul Jones. Captain Jones was originally buried in Paris in an obscure grave that had been covered over by the construction of a commercial building. A search for his remains uncovered his coffin and it was returned to Annapolis. He was finally laid to rest in a lead casket that was placed inside a large sarcophagus supported by statues of dolphins and surrounded by marble columns. An honor guard is posted at his gravesite daily when the chapel is open to the public.

In 1927, the large terra-cotta dome atop the Main Chapel was replaced by a metal one. In 1940, the chapel was enlarged by lengthening one of the wings so that the building took on the shape of a Latin cross. The result was an extension that permitted the chapel to seat twenty-five hundred people. Over the years, various academy classes and naval organizations have donated artifacts to decorate the chapel. In 1941, the Navy Construction Battalion, popularly known as the Seabees, donated a ten-and-a-half-foot votive ship that hangs from the ceiling. The Farragut Window on the right side of the nave, designed by Frederick Wilson, was presented by the Alumni Association. It depicts Admiral David Farragut, lashed to the rigging of his flagship while sailing into Mobile Bay. Two Tiffany windows are gifts of graduating classes. One is entitled "Commission Invisible" and the other, called the Sampson Window, portrays the "Angel of Peace." The large anchors at the main entrance of the Main Chapel come from the navy's first armored cruiser, the U.S.S. *New York*, which was Admiral William Sampson's flagship during the Spanish-American War. In the St. Andrew's Chapel in the basement of the Main Chapel is a baptismal font made of wood taken from the U.S.S. *Constitution* — "Old Ironsides."

For many years the chaplain service provided at the academy was exclusively Protestant. Since chapel attendance was mandatory until 1972, this fact presented problems for Catholic midshipmen. Until 1859, all midshipmen were required to attend Protestant services at the old chapel, regardless of their religious preference. In that year, a citizen named Jedediah V. Huntington protested this practice to the secretary of the navy and it was changed. In a letter to Mr. Huntington, dated January 18, 1859, Secretary Isaac Toucey wrote: "The Department has issued an order which will permit youths at the Academy of the Catholic persuasion to attend divine worship on Sundays at churches of their own faith."

Thereafter, Catholic members of the brigade were allowed to attend nearby St. Mary's Church, whose spire can easily be seen from the Naval Academy grounds. On Sundays, Catholic midshipmen formed into columns and marched from the academy grounds to Mass at St. Mary's. Jewish members also marched to a synagogue in downtown Annapolis. As noted earlier, Redemptorist priests at St. Mary's served as de facto chaplains for Catholic midshipmen until 1947 when the U.S. Navy began to assign

Catholic chaplains to the academy. At that time, the Naval Academy Chapel, like six hundred fifty other military and veterans' hospital chapels around the world, became an interdenominational house of worship. At present, three of the seven chaplains at the academy are Catholic priests. They have a busy schedule, since twenty-seven hundred midshipmen, some forty-seven percent of the entire brigade, are Catholics. This proportion far exceeds the Catholic percentage of the general population, and no one seems to be quite sure why this phenomenon has come to pass in recent years in Annapolis. In addition to midshipmen, the three Catholic chaplains have an additional nine hundred members in the congregation in the persons of academy staff, faculty, and their families.

Catholic chaplains at the U.S. Naval Academy, like all military service chaplains, are officers of their service department and are subject to the assignment, compensation, and other military orders as are any other officers. However, the spiritual aspects of their activities fall under the supervision of the Archdiocese for the Military Services, U.S.A., a worldwide ecclesiastical jurisdiction of the Catholic Church that now maintains its chancery in Silver Spring, Maryland, a suburb of Washington, D.C. Supported exclusively by private donations, it is the link between the Church and American Catholic chaplains throughout the world. Since a Catholic chaplain may not be commissioned or retained in service without the endorsement of the military ordinary, his control over Catholic chaplains is more than a purely moral influence. The military archdiocese is one of the largest American church jurisdictions, having about 2,290,000 members in all parts of the world; it has 776 full-time priests and another 1,000 priests who serve on an auxiliary or part-time basis. The jurisdiction of the archdiocese is a personal one, not a territorial one, in that it extends to all U.S. military personnel wherever they are located, to patients and personnel in hospitals operated by the Department of Veterans Affairs (VA), to members of the U.S. Diplomatic Corps and all U.S. government employees abroad, to military families everywhere, and to the families of U.S. Civil Service personnel overseas.

The widespread dispersion of Catholics and Catholic chaplains within the military archdiocese presents quite a communications problem. These chaplains are assigned to four hundred sixty-two military posts, to innumerable ships at sea, and to one hundred eighty-eight military and veterans' hospitals. Since chaplains are assigned at the pleasure of their military superiors, the archdiocese often does not learn about a new assignment or relocation until after a priest has assumed his new post. The archbishop sends out a monthly newsletter and chaplains are required to submit quarterly reports to him. These are the principal means used for routine communications.

The demographics of the military archdiocese are quite unique. Half of its members are between the ages of eighteen and twenty-five. This fact presents both a challenge and an opportunity. In a message sent by former Archbishop Joseph T. Ryan to all chaplains, he pointed out that "often, our Catholic people are either raw recruits with tenuous connection to the Church, or they are families constantly uprooted, or sick and aging veterans." One opportunity that regularly arises because of the closeness of many chaplains to their men is the recruitment of priests. About 300 military personnel have made serious current inquiries about entering the priesthood after completing their military service, and between 20 and 30 ex-servicemen are now studying for the priesthood as a result of the in-service recruitment program of the archdiocese.

The military archdiocese has the basic canonical functions of any other archdiocese. It has a marriage tribunal and it can grant dispensations from various church regulations. In a manner of speaking, it is also the world's largest parish, in that it maintains records at its Silver Spring chancery that under other circumstances would be found at a parish rectory. These include 1,133,000 baptismal records, 650,000 confirmation records, 430,000 first-Communion records, and 332,000 marriage records, all pertaining to Catholic personnel and their families who have received these sacraments from service chaplains in all parts of the world. Each year, the sacramental records department of the chancery receives and processes between 10,000 and 14,000 new baptismal records, 2,000 to 4,000 new marriage records, and 2,000 to 3,000 new confirmation and first-Communion records; each year it receives between 50,000 and 100,000 requests for copies of these records and certificates.

The history of Catholic priests in military chaplaincies goes back at least to Father Adam Marshall, S.J., who served aboard the U.S.S. *North Carolina* in 1824. Like many clergymen in the military service during that era, he was not given a formal classification as chaplain but held a commission for the position of schoolmaster. He is generally regarded as the first priest to be commissioned in any of the armed forces.

In 1846, President James Polk was attempting to avoid criticism that the war against Mexico was an anti-Catholic crusade against a Catholic nation, so he asked Bishop John Hughes in New York to recommend the names of priests who might serve as Catholic chaplains with the U.S. Army in Mexico. Indeed, a battle formation in that war might very well have looked like an assault on a Catholic position. A standard defensive tactic used by the Mexican Army was to line up soldiers in the face of an enemy advance and to place behind them priests dressed in full church robes, holding aloft the Blessed Sacrament in monstrances and urging the soldiers in front of them to do or die for God and country. Two Jesuits, Fathers John McElroy and Anthony Ray, accompanied the American Army in the field but served as civilians, not as commissioned officers.

Early on, American bishops were concerned about the spiritual welfare of Catholics in the American military and naval services. Their special concern was that Catholic soldiers and sailors were often required to attend Protestant religious services held on shipboard or in army camps. The plenary councils of the American Church held in Baltimore in 1852 and 1866 called attention to the plight of Catholics in the armed services and urged bishops and priests to diligence in providing Catholic religious services for military and naval personnel who might find themselves in their particular areas.

During the Civil War, about forty priests served in the Union Army, although not all of them served at the same time; twenty-eight priests served as chaplains in the Confederate Army. In view of the large number of troops in the field during that conflict, the ministry of Catholic chaplains was spread very thin. Pope Pius IX issued a papal rescript giving military chaplains in both armies faculties extending beyond their own dioceses and privileges not normally extended to priests, but this did not mean that they became part of separate military dioceses.

During World War I, a separate military ordinariate, or diocese, was established, and Archbishop (later Cardinal) Patrick Hayes was appointed to be in charge. American bishops formed what was called the National Catholic War Council and asked each diocese in the United States to supply priests to act as chaplains. A total of 1,026 priests served as chaplains but not all received commissions. Some one hundred sixty-five remained civilians and served as such. These priests were paid out of funds raised by the Knights of Columbus. A table showing the service of Catholic chaplains in our past four military conflicts is as follows:

War	Number of Catholic Chaplains	Number of Catholic Chaplains Who Died in Service
World War I	1,026	17
World War II	3,270	76
Korea	932	6
Vietnam	1,118	7

Perhaps the most famous of these chaplains was Father Joseph O'Callahan, a winner of the Congressional Medal of Honor, who died at sea in World War II in the company of two Protestant chaplains and a Jewish chaplain who were similarly honored. In addition to these priests, there were large numbers of auxiliary chaplains who served on a temporary or part-time basis.

During this period of time, the military vicar was the archbishop of New York, who was given this post as an ancillary assignment. The headquarters of the military vicariate was in New York City and it remained there until a separate archdiocese was established in 1986 when the chancery was relocated to the Washington, D.C., suburbs.

Since approximately eighty thousand people receive medical care each day, either as in-patients or as out-patients, at hospitals operated by the VA, the hospital ministry of the military archdiocese has taken on an important role. The VA employs 129 full-time Catholic chaplains and 600 part-time chaplains to staff its 172 hospitals throughout the United States.

Since midshipmen at the Naval Academy take between twenty-three and twenty-seven hours of classes each week, their schedules are very tight. They have only one hour of unassigned time each day, although weekends are less hectic. Such a routine leaves little time for extracurricular religious activities. However, Mass attendance is good and many midshipmen find the time to belong to the choir, the Catholic Midshipmen's Club, and various outreach programs. About one hundred eighty children from the families of faculty and staff members attend CCD classes which are regularly taught by midshipmen. Catholic chaplains attempt to provide graduating seniors with intensive training as lay readers and lay ministers, realizing that, when these men are commissioned and join the fleet, they will often be the only ones aboard ship to provide any kind of Catholic religious services. It is not possible to maintain chaplains aboard any but the largest naval vessels. Marriage-preparation courses are well attended. About fifty Catholic graduates are among the newly commissioned ensigns who are married each year after June Week and are seen emerging from the Main Chapel under a canopy of swords in picturesque and well-publicized ceremonies. However, it is a growing practice for graduates to wait a year or two and then return to the chapel to be married because most newly commissioned officers must immediately go to sea.

While no Masses at all were said on the U.S. Naval Academy grounds before 1947, two are now said each day and three are offered each Sunday. The Blessed Sacrament is reserved in three places — near St. Andrew's Chapel in the basement of the Main Chapel, at the all-faiths chapel in Mitcher Hall, and in a small chapel located to the right of the main entrance to Bancroft Hall, the enormous residence and dining facility in the middle of the academy grounds. The chapel in Bancroft Hall includes a Shrine to Our Lady of Perpetual Help and a plaque that reads:

> Commissioned as a Navy (Marine Corps) officer, I hereby inscribe my name and place my collar device on Our Lady of Perpetual Help Shrine in Bancroft Hall Rotunda Chapel in the United States Naval Academy.
>
> In so doing I dedicate my years of military service to the Honor and Glory of God. I pledge to serve with Christian loyalty, integrity, and nobility, consistent with the highest ideals of my Catholic faith. To this end, I ask God's blessing and strength through the intercession of Christ's Blessed Mother.

Surrounding this inscription are other plaques containing the names of Catholic midshipmen who, since this custom was inaugurated in 1975, have made this pledge publicly at the baccalaureate Masses preceding their graduations. Next to their names are the small collar devices or rank insignia that every midshipman wears as a part of his undergraduate uniform. Now, from naval bases, ships at sea, and vessels under the sea, Catholic roots reach back to U.S. Naval Academy chapels from all over the world.

36
Holy Trinity

Washington

D.C.

In 1751, the Maryland General Assembly authorized the subdividing of estates and the establishment of a sixty-acre town on highlands and bluffs overlooking the Potomac River. It was named Georgetown in honor of King George III. By 1790, this town, located at the upper reaches of the navigable portion of the Potomac, had grown to a population of about three thousand. It was here that the new prefect apostolic of the Catholic Church, Father John Carroll, decided to erect Georgetown Academy. It was designed to be a school of higher learning, whose presence in the United States would make it unnecessary for Catholic boys to go abroad to obtain a Catholic education as Father Carroll and many other sons of colonial Catholics had done for many decades. In 1787, a large landowner, John Threlkeld, deeded to Father Carroll a plot of ground, some sixty feet by one hundred twenty feet in dimension, as the cite for a Catholic chapel. The deed recited a nominal purchase price of five shillings. This parcel of land, located on the north side of Gay Street (now called N Street), became the site of the original Holy Trinity parish church erected there in 1794. That building remains intact to this day, although it has experienced a multitude of different uses since it was first constructed. In 1789, Threlkeld and William Deakins sold to Father Carroll an acre and a half of land nearby for

75 Maryland pounds as the site for an academy that later became Georgetown University.

The construction of Georgetown Academy was undertaken in 1789, but classes did not begin until the fall of 1791 because Bishop Carroll had difficulty in finding suitable instructors. The school did not achieve university status until some twenty-four years later, in 1815. One of the three original instructors, Father Francis Neale, was selected by Bishop Carroll in 1791 to be the first pastor of a new parish church designed to serve the entire Georgetown community. He was also given a secondary job as accountant-treasurer at Georgetown and later treasurer and vice-president of the academy. Father Neale was one of four Neale brothers from southern Maryland who had entered the priesthood in the 1770s. His brother Leonard eventually became the second archbishop of Baltimore. At first, Father Neale said Mass at a chapel in Old South Building on the Georgetown campus until the church was completed. Thereafter, he served not only Holy Trinity parish and the academy but acted as a missionary, saying Mass at other parishes in the area, including St. Mary's across the Potomac in Alexandria. He was designated missionary pastor at St. Mary's until 1818. In 1798, Father Neale spent 12 pounds, 10 shillings, of his own money for a strip of land along 36th Street (formerly Lingan Street), adjacent to the new church, to provide land for expansion. Since the Jesuit order was not formally functioning at this time, he was not bound by a vow of poverty and hence had assets of his own. On this land the church was erected between 1849 and 1851. In 1806, Father Neale served as novice master when the first Jesuit novitiate in the United States was opened in a house across the street from Holy Trinity Church. When Father Neale was transferred to other duties in 1817, he had served Holy Trinity longer than any of the forty-five pastors who would succeed him.

What Bishop Carroll began to develop on the "Hilltop" overlooking the Potomac was not merely a school or a church but a total Catholic complex. It was similar to what a Holy Cross missionary, Father Edward Sorin, was to establish some fifty years later in northern Indiana at the south bend of the St. Joseph River, near a small body of water called Notre Dame du Lac. Georgetown Academy was not only a school of higher education for laymen; until 1869, when the Jesuits opened a seminary at Woodstock just outside Baltimore, it also served as a seminary for future Jesuit priests. College undergraduates mingled with seminarians on the same campus. In 1808, Holy Trinity served as the site of the ordination of four Jesuit seminarians. Ordinations of Jesuits continued to be held at the parish church from time to time until 1892.

In 1799, the Poor Clares opened a small school for girls in Georgetown. They had to abandon it when they returned to France at the end of the French Revolution's Reign of Terror. Archbishop Leonard Neale was able to prevail upon three laywomen, described in records of the day as "pious ladies," to carry on the school. In 1808, he acquired a tract of land on 35th Street (then Fayette Street), just north of the present Visitation Convent, where they could erect a school building. In 1814, he assisted these "pious ladies" in forming a religious community and, as second archbishop of Baltimore, was instrumental in obtaining approval for them to continue permanently under the rules of the Order of the Visitation, a cloistered order in which they made their solemn professions. When he succeeded John Carroll as archbishop of Baltimore, Leonard Neale was too ill to travel to his episcopal city. He lived in a small house near the college and governed the archdiocese from that location. Bishop Cheverus came from Boston to confer upon Archbishop Neale the pallium, the symbol of his metropolitan rank. However, he had to perform the ceremony at Holy Trinity rather than in the cathedral at Baltimore. Archbishop Neale died at Georgetown and he and the first president of Georgetown College, Father Robert Plunkett, are buried in the crypt beneath the Visitation Convent chapel.

Both Georgetown and Visitation have continued to this day to exercise their educational ministries, although Visitation, once both a high school and a junior college, is now exclusively a high school. Both of these institutions are still separated by a high gray stone wall that encloses the cloister. During the nineteenth century, both schools provided higher education in an area where such services were rare. They enrolled the sons and daughters of many Protestant families, especially from the South. Charles Dickens recognized this fact in his *American Notes*, which he published after his visit to the United States in 1842: "At Georgetown, in the suburbs, there is a Jesuit College; delightfully situated, and, so far as I have had an opportunity of seeing, well managed. Many persons who are not members of the Romish Church avail themselves, I believe, of these institutions, and of the advantageous opportunities they afford for the education of their children. The heights of this neighborhood, above the Potomac River, are very picturesque and are free, I should conceive, from some of the insalubrities of Washington." Until about 1840, the viability of Georgetown College was continually in doubt because, in compliance with the rules of the Society of Jesus, it could not charge its students any tuition. A relaxation of that rule was finally achieved when Maryland Jesuits were able to convince their superiors in Rome that American colleges could not subsist as European schools did, on benefices and donations from wealthy patrons.

Early accounts of Holy Trinity parish indicate that the congregation soon began to exceed the capacity of the church, so overflow crowds were often accommodated at the Visitation Convent chapel. The parish was supported in those days by pew rentals. Those who did not pay these annual rents were required to hear Mass in a central portion of the church where they could either stand or could sit on chairs brought from home. Being without a regular pew could result in considerable discomfort, since priests in those days were accustomed to reading their Sunday sermons while seated at the altar, and it was not uncommon for such sermons to go on for an hour or two.

In 1818, a parochial school for boys was established by the next pastor, Father Benedict Fenwick, S.J., the future bishop of Boston. Called the Free School for Boys, it was taught originally by a layman and later by Jesuit Brothers. It moved from its original location across N Street into the old church in 1877. Beginning in 1818, the Visitation nuns taught the "Benevolent School" for poor girls, called St. Joseph's School. In 1824, the parish started a "seminary for colored girls," a free elementary school for blacks who were then migrating to the Georgetown area in great numbers from the South. It closed a few years later. In 1918, a fund-raising drive for new schools was conducted, which garnered $75,000. This money was used to erect a parochial school for boys and girls and a high school for girls that was taught by the Sisters of Mercy. The parochial school is still in operation and has about three hundred students. The high school closed several years ago.

In 1851, the second Holy Trinity Church **[pictured above]** was dedicated by Bishop Armand François Charbonnel of Toronto. It has a simple neoclassical design with a Greek portico in front supporting four Ionic columns. A steeple originally erected over the narthex of the church was removed when its weight caused the roof to leak. With some alterations the building continues to be the parish church today. The former church around the corner has been preserved and has been used since that time as a school, a parish hall, and, most recently, a rectory.

War has been no stranger to Holy Trinity parish. The parish barely escaped the British sacking of Washington in 1812. Whether the British were dissuaded from coming to Georgetown out of fear of the stalwart Georgetown militia, which had erected breastworks along the west bank of Rock Creek, or whether they simply felt that burning the Capitol and the White House was a sufficient day's work, we will never know. However, forty-nine years later, when the Union Army was routed at Bull Run during what Washingtonians thought would be an interesting Sunday afternoon outing, casualties were brought to Holy Trinity. In the following year, on the Sunday after the Battle of Antietam, which took place in western Maryland in September 1862, the entire church was given over to the Union Army as a hospital. (The same use was made of several Protestant churches in Washington.) After Sunday vespers and benediction, the men of the parish removed the carpeting and the cushions from the pews. The following Tuesday, carpenters arrived to erect planks over the tops of the pews and over the sanctuary. The new construction formed the floor of the temporary hospital. The new church was then abandoned by the parish and services resumed in the old building around the corner on N Street.

St. Aloysius, the Jesuit church located near the Capitol Building, was much nearer the Seventh Street Wharf where wounded soldiers regularly disembarked upon arriving from Southern battlefields. It avoided the same fate when its pastor agreed to construct, within a period of seven days, a makeshift building called St. Aloysius Hospital which served the same purpose and avoided the necessity of using the church itself.

Holy Trinity was paid for the use of the church by the government and used the proceeds to buy a new organ. During the Civil War, the government also used dormitories on the college campus to house Union troops who were hastily summoned to the nation's capital to prevent its capture by Southern forces. In many instances, these soldiers took the rooms of Georgetown students from the South who had withdrawn from the college to wear the gray of the Confederate Army. The involvement by Georgetown students on both sides of this conflict resulted in the adoption years later of blue and gray as the university's colors.

Following the Civil War, Holy Trinity had as a pastor a Confederate Army chaplain who had been assigned to a Louisiana regiment. Later, one of its assistant pastors was a former Union Army drummer boy in an Ohio regiment. Happily, they were not assigned to the parish at the same time.

Georgetown was an incorporated city within the sixty-four square miles that the state of Maryland ceded to the United States for the seat of government. After the District of Columbia came into existence in 1800, it retained its municipal status and, with the city of Washington and the city of Alexandria, became one of three municipalities located within the newly established federal territory. This status lasted until 1871 when Congress revoked the town charter that the Maryland General Assembly had conferred in colonial times. Slavery was permitted in the District of Columbia until 1862. It was abolished in that year by an act of Congress passed shortly before Lincoln issued the Emancipation Proclamation. At that time, a vast majority of blacks, both in Georgetown and in the entire federal district, were free people, not slaves. The Georgetown area continued to have a large black population until the end of World War II when private urban renewal and skyrocketing real-estate prices had the effect of inducing them to move to other parts of the city.

From its inception, there have been a significant number of black Catholics in Holy Trinity parish. The first entry in parish records on January 1, 1795, recorded the marriage of two slaves, "David Thomas and Philis." Baptismal records contain many names of children born to slaves. There is little doubt that, in those years, the parish engaged in segregation in accordance with the rigid practice of the times. Separate Masses were once said for blacks in the old church. Later, a balcony, long since removed, was placed in the new church for black parishioners. Parish groups, such as the St. Peter Claver Society, were organized for blacks. In 1925, Epiphany parish was formed from Holy Trinity parish territory in the eastern part of the Georgetown area and was placed under the direction of the Josephite Fathers, whose special ministry is to black Catholics. Epiphany parish grew to a membership of six hundred persons, but as the demographics of Georgetown changed, Epiphany eventually changed into a white parish so the Josephites were transferred to the other parishes they now staff in the Washington area.

Because of its location, Holy Trinity and Georgetown have been host to prominent Americans. On two occasions in 1796, George Washington, whose grandnephew attended the academy, addressed Georgetown students from the porch of the Old North Building on the college campus about a block away. Abraham Lincoln attended a requiem Mass at the church in honor of a deceased Union Army general. Perhaps Holy Trinity's most prominent parishioner was John F. Kennedy, who attended Mass frequently with his family after moving into a nearby house on "O" Street. He continued this practice after relocating to other quarters on Pennsylvania Avenue.

Moviegoers everywhere were introduced to the environs of Holy Trinity parish when Hollywood decided to film "on location" in Georgetown a story about the devil. *The Exorcist*, a novel written by Georgetown College graduate William Blatty, is a fictionalized version of an actual event that occurred in the Washington area in the late 1940s; however, the actual event took place in Mount Rainier, a Washington suburb, not in Georgetown. He preferred to make the setting for his book in the part of the city he knew best, so extensive filming was made not only of the college campus but also of the area's tightly packed and restored federal-period houses, tree-lined streets, brick sidewalks, and cobblestones that are among its unique features.

In 1979, the church was closed for nine months and services were held in the Holy Trinity theater next door. The 130-year-old building needed extensive renovation to "bring it up to Code." At this time, the fund-raising that was accomplished for this renovation was challenged by a widely publicized activist who engaged in confrontational hunger strikes. His purpose was to embarrass the parish into diverting renovation funds from the purposes for which they were solicited to a soup kitchen under his supervision and direction. The parish refused to be intimidated or embarrassed.

Holy Trinity is one of the largest and most active parishes in the metropolitan Washington area. Its membership is now drawn not only from its territorial boundaries in Georgetown but from Maryland and Virginia as well. A new parishioner is handed a directory that contains eight pages of parish activities, ranging from Meals on Wheels for feeding the elderly to the Jesuit Center for Spirituality, which has an office in the school building. For many years dramatics has played an active role in the cultural life of the parish. Trinity Theatre has long been the site of a wide variety of performances staged not only by parish and university groups but by Washington-area dramatic societies as well. Washington has a large number of transient and unattached persons, so Holy Trinity has adapted its programs to such people. It has adult social groups for various ages, a society for separated, divorced, and remarried Christians, and a marriage-preparation course of seven weeks' duration, which usually has one or two classes in progress throughout the year. Interestingly enough, the marriage-preparation courses are conducted by a pastoral team that includes a priest, a married couple, and a divorced person.

Holy Trinity still maintains a close relationship with the university, although it goes without saying that a parish of thirty-one hundred families cannot be on the same intimate terms with a university of twelve thousand students that Father Neale and Father Plunkett maintained when they both lived in Old North Building on the campus and ate each day in the same refectory. Vestments, Mass book, cruets, and other altar articles are no longer carried back and forth between the parish church and the college chapel, as they were in the 1790s, when only one of each item existed in the area and the college and the parish were forced to share them. Commencement exercises for the college are no longer conducted in the parish church, and the president of the university can no longer take time out from his duties, as Father Plunkett did, to assist the pastor in making parish rounds. Priests from the parish do not teach college courses on the side, as they formerly did. In 1942, the university conveyed to the archdiocese its legal title to parish property, although it retains the title to the old parish cemetery located about a mile away on Wisconsin Avenue. However, the parish CCD program, providing religious instruction for children attending public and non-Catholic private schools, has seven hundred students, so university classrooms are placed in service to house some of these classes. Prominent theologians from the campus preach regularly at the parish, and Georgetown students attend services at Holy Trinity, although the campus ministry at the university conducts a large number of programs and services adapted to students that follow the tempo of college life. These activities center on Dahlgren Chapel, located just two blocks away in the quadrangle of the Georgetown "Yard." Dahlgren Chapel is an old church in its own right, dating back to 1893, and, along with the other campus chapels, is a place where students and others can attend Mass as late as 10:30 P.M. on weekdays and 11:15 P.M. each Sunday night.

Georgetown University celebrated its 200th anniversary in 1989. The parish had already celebrated its 200th birthday, choosing to date its beginning from the year Father Carroll obtained a deed to church property rather than from the time the first church was opened for services. No matter, for whatever date it uses to mark its beginning, Holy Trinity can demonstrate a considerable return on Father Carroll's original five-shilling investment.

37
St. Matthew's Cathedral

Washington D.C.

As far as anyone knows, the first Mass ever said in the territory now known as the District of Columbia was celebrated about 1760 at a chapel located in the west wing of a manor house belonging to Notley Young, whose home overlooked the Potomac River at what is now 10th and G Streets, Southwest. The Mass was celebrated by Young's brother-in-law, Father Thomas Digges, one of many Jesuit missionaries who ministered to Catholics in colonial Maryland. Several plantations located in what is now the District of Columbia were owned by Catholic settlers, and it is quite probable that other priests from southern Maryland made their rounds in the area, saying Mass not only at the Young manor house but at other places as well.

In 1794, some six years before Maryland transferred jurisdiction over this territory to the United States government, Father Anthony Caffrey came across the Potomac River from Alexandria where he had been assisting Father Francis Neale at St. Mary's and purchased land in what is now the heart of downtown Washington. There he erected the original St. Patrick's Church. Twenty-five years later, another church in the central portion of the District of Columbia (then referred to as the city of Washington, to distinguish it from Alexandria and Georgetown) was started three blocks from the Capitol Building. It was named in honor of St. Peter.

By the late 1830s, these two parishes numbered several thousand members. In a report made in 1838, Archbishop Eccleston of Baltimore recounted that the District of Columbia contained 100 square miles (it still had its northern Virginia component) and 40,000 inhabitants, of whom 10,000 were Catholics. Existing church facilities were taxed to capacity, so Father William Matthews, who was to serve St. Patrick's as its pastor for fifty years, purchased a small plot of land at 15th and H Streets, about two blocks from the President's House, in a tract subdivided from an old plantation known as Jamaica. He formed a committee, which included the mayor of the city of Washington, and began a public drive for subscriptions collecting about $30,000. By 1840, he had completed the construction of a church of Grecian Doric design, some fifty-seven feet by one hundred two. Later, a large steeple was added. The new church was named St. Matthew's to honor the priest who founded the parish.

The Christian Brothers opened a school for boys at St. Matthew's in 1852, calling it St. Matthew's Institute. This school eventually became St. John's High School. It had one hundred seventy pupils and charged $100 a year for board and tuition. In the 1840s, the Daughters of Charity opened St. Matthew's Female Parish School. One of the sites occupied by this school was the historic Octagon House where the Treaty of Ghent was signed concluding the War of 1812. It was also the place where James and Dolly Madison sought temporary shelter after their regular quarters had been torched by the British. The students at the parish school were principally interested in the fact that the gardens behind Octagon House were suitable for games at recess. The Daughters of Charity ultimately closed this school but returned to St. Matthew's years later to teach in a reorganized parish school, to operate an evening school for working men, and eventually to start an infant asylum that took the name St. Ann's. In the interim, Holy Cross Sisters from Notre Dame, Indiana, opened another St. Matthew's School for Girls, which was conducted on the Massachusetts Avenue site occupied for many years by the United States Catholic Conference. Later, they moved to a then-suburban location and opened both a high school and Dunbarton College. Eventually, they closed the college and relocated their high school in the Maryland suburbs. A parish history notes that, by 1887, St. Matthew's parish had thirty-five hundred members and a school enrollment of five hundred seventy-nine.

At its inception, St. Matthew's parish had a significant number of black parishioners. A chapel in the basement of the church, named for Blessed Martin de Porres, was opened for the special benefit and use of black parishioners. In 1858, the School for Colored Children was also opened by members of the St. Vincent de Paul Society, some of whom were black. It lasted until the Civil War when lack of funds forced it to close. In 1863, Father Charles I. White, the pastor, held a fair on the White House grounds to raise money for a new church for black Catholics. President Lincoln attended the event briefly. The fair raised about $1,200, and construction began on a church about two blocks from the White House. However, the church, still bearing the name of Blessed Martin de Porres (named a saint in 1962), was ultimately housed in the building next door where the school had been located. In 1876, the chapel developed into St. Augustine's Church, the first independent parish for black Catholics in Washington.

In 1852, as the result of a decree of the First Plenary Council of the Catholic Church in the United States, parishes in this country other than ethnic parishes were first required to have defined boundaries. The territory assigned to St. Matthew's ran from "the Canal," now Constitution Avenue, to the northern border of the District of Columbia, about eight miles away. Five other parishes now serve all or part of this area. In the early 1890s, a decision was made to construct a newer and larger St. Matthew's Church. For this task Cardinal James Gibbons, then archbishop of Baltimore, selected Monsignor Thomas Sim Lee, then rector of the basilica cathedral in Baltimore, and appointed him pastor of St. Matthew's. Monsignor Lee was a Marylander whose Catholic ancestor was governor of the state during the Revolutionary War. He served as pastor for thirty-one years. Immediately upon assuming his new responsibilities, he undertook a European trip to visit cathedrals and obtain ideas to be used in constructing the new St. Matthew's.

The new church [**pictured above**] was located at its present site on Rhode Island Avenue, near what even then was the booming Connecticut Avenue area. A New York architect, Grant LaFarge, was retained to design and supervise the building of the new church. The cornerstone was laid in 1893. By 1895, a transept and crossings were completed, and the church was opened for services, although it was not formally dedicated until 1913. Meanwhile, the old St. Matthew's continued to function as a chapel until 1909 when the property was sold and became the site of an office building.

St. Matthew's Cathedral has a Byzantine Romanesque design. It is constructed of red brick and sandstone and is 155 feet by 137 feet, topped off by a dome some 190 feet high made of copper that has been oxidized to a green patina. Monsignor Lee envisioned that the church might someday became a cathedral; so, at the outset, he placed near the altar a chair appropriate for a bishop's chair. It has served that purpose since St. Matthew's became a cathedral in 1940. A verbal description cannot adequately depict the various artistic improvements that have been made over the years to the interior of the cathedral. A white marble altar with insets of floral decorations, together with a baptistry of matching design, were given to the cathedral by the archbishop of Agra, India. Above the altar is a mosaic of the cathedral patron, St. Matthew. The interior dome, about two hundred feet from the floor, is supported by four interior pillars containing large mosaics of the four evangelists. The main aisle is flanked on either side by Our Lady's Chapel on the left and an extensive chapel in honor of St. Anthony of Padua on the right. In the front of the cathedral, to the left of the main altar, is the Blessed Sacrament Chapel. The Wedding Chapel is located to the right of the main altar. Near the entrance to the church are the St. Francis Chapel and the baptistry.

The parish boundaries include both the White House and approximately fifty-five foreign embassies, legations, and consulates. They also include a growing number of large downtown office buildings that have had the effect over the years of displacing a portion of the area's residential population. As a result of this unique constituency, St. Matthew's Cathedral has been the scene of many official celebrations and commemorations, many of which were prompted by foreign dignitaries from Catholic countries. Each year, the John Carroll Society renews a custom dating back to the Inns of Court in medieval England and sponsors a Red Mass in honor of the Holy Spirit asking the blessing of God upon the courts during their coming term. It is usually attended by several Supreme Court justices. As might be expected, large public celebrations or commemorations have taken place upon the coronations and the deaths of several popes. St. Matthew's has been the site of American obsequies conducted in honor of King Alfonso of Spain, King Humberto of Italy, Empress Elizabeth of Austria-Hungary, and four presidents of France, including General Charles de Gaulle. It has also conducted large public celebrations of the anniversary jubilees of several popes, the fiftieth jubilee of Emperor Franz Joseph of Austria, the end of the Civil War, the American victory in the Battle of Manila Bay, and a memorial service attended by the U.S. Joint Chiefs of Staff in honor of American marines killed at the Beirut airport.

It is not possible to discuss the cathedral parish in the nation's capital at any length without dropping names. In 1855, Senator Thomas Hart Benton's daughter Susan was married at the old St. Matthew's to the French chargé d'affaires in the United States. (No emissaries with the rank of ambassador were sent to the U.S. in those days.) Dolly Madison's niece, Adele Cutts, was a member of the parish, but since her husband, Senator Stephen A. Douglas, was not a Catholic, they were married in 1856 by the pastor at her father's house. Five years later, the "Little Giant" became a Catholic as he lay dying at his home in Chicago. St. Matthew's has been the site of the baptisms of John Tyler's sister and Lyndon Johnson's daughter as well as the wedding of Senator Joseph McCarthy. It has also conducted funerals for AFL-CIO President George Meany, singer Kate Smith, TV anchorman Frank Reynolds, Washington lawyer and New Deal "brain truster" Thomas Corcoran, and former Philippine President Manuel Quezon.

Almost every president of the United States in the twentieth century has come to St. Matthew's on one or more occasions. President Kennedy was buried from there on November 25, 1963, and the spot where his casket rested is prominently marked. This event was the occasion of one of the largest gatherings of heads of state in recent world history and is reminiscent of the notable gathering of heads of state that took place in Westminster Hall in 1910 to pay last respects to Edward VII. Pope John Paul II addressed the clergy of the archdiocese of Washington from the pulpit of St. Matthew's when he visited Washington in October of 1979. Many visiting cardinals and other church dignitaries from all over the world have enjoyed the hospitality of St. Matthew's and have usually offered a public Mass during their stay. St. Matthew's has also welcomed such world figures as Chancellor Konrad Adenauer, General Charles de Gaulle, and Haile Selassie, emperor of Ethiopia.

In the days when pew rentals were still a standard practice in Catholic churches, Chief Justice Edward Douglass White held pew number 4. The chief justice lived only four doors away and was buried from St. Matthew's in 1921. His home was later purchased by the cathedral and was for many years used as its parochial school. Justice Joseph McKenna and Civil War Cavalry General Philip Sheridan were also pew holders.

St. Matthew's became a cathedral in 1940 after the District of Columbia was designated as the archdiocese of Washington in 1939. At the time, this title had more technical than real significance, since Archbishop Michael J. Curley of Baltimore was also designated archbishop of Washington and continued to administer these two jurisdictions from Baltimore. Upon his death in 1947, the archdiocese of Washington was expanded to include five Maryland counties, and Monsignor Patrick A. O'Boyle, who was then head of Catholic Charities in New York, was named archbishop. In 1967, he became a member of the College of Cardinals.

Archbishop O'Boyle came to Washington just as the city was emerging from a medium-size, slow-moving Southern city into a booming world capital. His principal ongoing task for the next twenty-five years was to keep up with the growth of the area, particularly in the city's Maryland suburbs. During this quarter of a century, he built 44 parishes, 30 schools, and a total of about 300 buildings of all kinds and descriptions. Immediately upon coming to Washington, Archbishop O'Boyle issued an order desegregating the Catholic schools of the archdiocese, an order that preceded by several years the Supreme Court's public school desegregation decision. In the late 1960s, he was challenged by a number of priests who dissented from the teaching on contraception contained in the papal encyclical *Humanae Vitae*. It was a personally distressing decision for Archbishop O'Boyle to expel a number of priests who had publicly dissented from this doctrine. He did so because he felt obligated to uphold the Church's teaching but he still referred to the dissidents affectionately as "my boys." Cardinal O'Boyle lived to the age of ninety-one and became the first prelate to be buried in the Archbishops' Crypt located at the entrance of the St. Francis Chapel.

Over the years, St. Matthew's Cathedral and its parishioners have generated a number of social service and cultural activities. Not all of these are still in existence. Perhaps the best known are a series of settlement houses sponsored by the Christ Child Society, an organization founded in 1896 by parishioner Mary Virginia Merrick, who, in spite of a crippling accident in her youth, became a leader in the development of these centers and several boys' and girls' clubs that bear her name. At one time or another, the parish has operated a Catholic home for elderly women, a halfway house for recently released prisoners, a social hall to serve the large number of single younger people who come to Washington to work in government and related activities, and a playhouse for the performance of amateur theatrical productions. Within its boundaries the Anchor Mental Health Association, founded by a priest with a legacy left to him by his parents, has maintained a halfway house for mental patients who have been released from hospitalization. Today, the Young Adults Club and the Cathedral Club have an active social schedule. There are not many children in the parish. The Calvert School, its parochial school, was closed about twenty years ago. However, St. Matthew's has a

Spanish-language CCD program and regular first-Communion classes, mostly for Hispanic children.

The parish now has only about eight hundred members, of whom approximately half live beyond its boundaries because the area near St. Matthew's Cathedral has lost much of its residential character. However, more than six hundred people attend Mass every business day, and this number doubles during Lent. On Ash Wednesday and holy days of obligation, the nine-hundred-seat capacity of the church is exceeded by about one half at the noon Mass. The cathedral is open throughout the day and, for that reason, receives many additional visitors daily. A large percentage of each Sunday's congregation is composed of persons visiting Washington from abroad. It maintains a twenty-six-member choir, some of whom are associated with the Catholic University School of Music, and is evidencing its commitment to full liturgical presentations by the purchase and installation of a new $400,000 pipe organ. Every Sunday there is a folk Mass, a Spanish Mass, and both an English and a Latin sung Mass. Occasionally, the choir is called upon to assist in a liturgy in another language, such as a Polish Mass or an Armenian Rite Mass celebrated in Arabic. The archdiocesan chancery is no longer next door, having been moved by Cardinal James A. Hickey to a former seminary in the suburbs, so additional changes in the parish complex are in the offing, principally the construction of an office building on part of the parish property to provide revenue both for parish and archdiocesan activities.

Both the nation and its capital are vastly different places from what they were on the Feast of St. Matthew in 1838. On that day, Baltimore Archbishop Samuel Eccleston and a solemn procession, accompanied by the U.S. Marine Corps Band, marched up G Street from St. Patrick's Church and northward past the President's House and the newly constructed Treasury Building in order to lay the cornerstone at the old St. Matthew's Church. After one hundred fifty years, St. Matthew's remains a notable fixture with a diverse ministry in a city that is given over to rapid and myriad changes. That diversity may include religion classes for Hispanic youngsters, a Mass in Arabic, or a requiem for a president, and it must respond to these calls, now that the world has become its parish.

38
St. Mary

Alexandria

VIRGINIA

The first Catholic settlement in Virginia took place in 1687 near Aquia Creek, a wide place in the Potomac River about fifty miles south of Washington. The penal laws of the colony made Virginia an inhospitable place for Catholics, and there is no permanent memorial dating from that period which marks this settlement. In all probability, Catholics living there were attended by priests from Charles County, Maryland, who came across the Potomac from time to time to minister to their spiritual needs.

Virginia was one of four American colonies where Catholics could be found in any numbers before the Revolutionary War. Most were in northern Virginia. They were not welcome. Over a period of more than one hundred years, the House of Burgesses at Williamsburg enacted a series of penal laws aimed at discouraging Catholic settlement in Virginia. Catholics were disqualified as witnesses in any court litigation. Any priest found at a Virginia port was given five days to leave or be subject to execution. All Virginians were required to attend services of the established church or pay a fine of £20. Catholics were disqualified from voting and, if caught doing so, were subject to a fine of five hundred pounds of tobacco. In 1746, William Gooch, lieutenant governor of Virginia, issued a proclamation that read: "Whereas, it has been presented to me in Council, that several Roman Catholic priests are lately come from Maryland to Fairfax County in this Colony, and are endeavoring, by crafty insinuations, to seduce His Majesty's good subjects from their fidelity and loyalty to His Majesty, King George, and his royal house; I have therefore thought fit, with the advice of His Majesty's Council, to issue this proclamation requiring all magistrates, sheriffs, constables, and others of His Majesty's liege people within this Colony, to be diligent in apprehending and bringing to justice the said Romish priests, or any of them, so that they may be prosecuted according to law."

The first Catholic church constructed in Virginia was St. Mary's Church, located in Alexandria. Parish histories maintain that the building of this church was first discussed at a St. Patrick's Day party given by Colonel John Fitzgerald, a prominent local businessman and aide-de-camp to George Washington during the Revolutionary War. Colonel Fitzgerald lived in Alexandria and occasionally invited missionary priests to say Mass at his home. In attendance at this historic party was General Washington himself, who lived only five miles south at Mount Vernon. Reportedly, Washington made a donation to get the project moving.

Whatever Washington's role might have been in helping to found St. Mary's Church, it is well established that he was a friend of Catholics, notwithstanding his own membership in the Episcopal Church and in a Masonic lodge that now bears his name. An exchange of correspondence between himself and Bishop John Carroll and other prominent Catholics of the time indicated their esteem for him and his high regard for them. President Washington wrote to American Catholics on March 12, 1790: "As Mankind becomes more liberal, they will be more apt to allow, that all those who conduct themselves worthy members of the Community, are equally entitled to the protection of Civil Government. I hope ever to see America among the foremost Nations in examples of Justice and Liberality. And I presume that your fellow-citizens will not forget the patriotic part, which you took in accomplishment of their Revolution, and the establishment of their Government — or the important assistance, which they received from a Nation, in which the Roman Catholic Faith is professed."

The tract of land on which the original St. Mary's Church was built in 1796 was donated to the church by a Quaker, Robert T. Hooe. The area in which the church building was located is called Jones Point, a promontory extending into the Potomac where Hunting Creek flows into the larger river. The old brick church was about a quarter of a mile from this point. At that time, the city of Washington, now just across the water, was little more than one hundred milestones laid out in a square by the surveyor of the federal city, Daniel Carroll, brother of the new bishop of Baltimore. The boundary line between what Virginia ceded for the District of Columbia (and later received back) ran just south of the church and its cemetery. The old cemetery contains one gravestone dating back to 1798 and a great many that were placed there in the early nineteenth century.

Originally, St. Mary's was served by missionary pastors, all Jesuits, who came to

Alexandria each week from Georgetown College just up the river in order to say Mass and administer the sacraments. The first resident pastor was assigned to the parish in 1818. Most of the priests who served at St. Mary's until 1891 were Jesuits. At that time, the diocese of Richmond took over the responsibility for its staffing.

Members of the parish began to feel that the original church site was too far from the center of the city so they bought land at Duke and Royal Streets, in the center of Alexandria, and built the present church at that location, while retaining title to the cemetery and to adjacent land that is now used for a parochial school building. The new church was opened in 1826, although the building **[pictured above]** is a considerable revision of what was originally erected at this location. In 1856, the original church was considerably enlarged and given a façade of imitation stone in the Gothic style with large stained-glass windows. A 133-foot steeple was erected and later torn down to be replaced by the present bell tower. An entire new front was constructed with Indiana limestone. In 1877, a Revolutionary-era parsonage was torn down and replaced by another rectory. Several churches in downtown Washington were later built that bear a striking resemblance to the building that eventually emerged as St. Mary's Church. A fire in 1929 caused considerable damage, but the main portions of the old church remain.

St. Mary's was another parish in which the problem of lay trusteeship arose. Originally, title to the newly acquired church site was placed in the name of Father Francis Neale, its first missionary pastor. After he was replaced, the property somehow came under the control of a lay board of trustees, who supported the new pastor in some disagreements that he had with the archbishop of Baltimore. After the archbishop removed the pastor, he had to bring a lawsuit in federal court in order to evict him from the rectory.

During the Civil War, federal troops occupied Alexandria as soon as Virginia seceded from the Union, and martial law was imposed throughout the area. Most of the parishioners were Southern sympathizers, and this fact caused considerable difficulty for the pastor who served during that era, a Dutch Jesuit named Peter Kroes. Father Kroes incurred the enmity of federal troops on more than one occasion but was able to keep the parish in operation despite the tensions that existed in the locality. No Civil War battles were fought in Alexandria, but two major battles took place at Bull Run and another one was fought at Chantilly, all just a few miles west. Alexandria remained part of the defense perimeter of the nation's capital throughout the war. The old cemetery contains a couple of tombstones on which are engraved the fateful letters "CSA," indicating that the deceased went off to fight for the "Lost Cause" of the Confederacy and returned to live through the Reconstruction in St. Mary's parish.

Alexandria had a small port that generated a few factories and shops. It was also a railroad town, so the population of St. Mary's parish reflected this fact for many years. Before the Civil War and until the 1950s, St. Mary's maintained mission churches throughout northern Virginia. Many of these are now large suburban parishes.

At the outset of World War II, the government built the "world's largest office building" just four miles north of the church. The Pentagon employed and still employs between forty thousand and fifty thousand civilian and military personnel. Their presence has been a pervasive fact throughout northern Virginia. By 1945, before additional parishes could be erected, St. Mary's grew to have an enrollment of about twelve thousand parishioners. The rapid population growth of northern Virginia has continued. In 1974, the Holy See erected the diocese of Arlington and included within it all of the Washington suburbs in Virginia and much of the Shenandoah Valley. At that time, the Arlington diocese had 150,000 Catholics; 15 years later, it had grown to more than 215,000 Catholics.

In the 1960s, a massive private renovation and reconstruction effort began to take place in the area surrounding the church. Known as Old Town, it revitalized Alexandria and turned the locality into a gentrified federal-period community of expensive, upscale homes, offices, and boutiques similar to Annapolis and Georgetown. This too has affected the parish, which, despite its appearance of affluence, still has pockets of poverty.

St. Mary's operates a parochial school at the site of the original church having an enrollment of four hundred children. The old cemetery now abuts the Capital Beltway, a major circumferential thoroughfare that brings more than a quarter of a million cars a day past the ancient graveyard. Some one hundred ninety years after its establishment, St. Mary's now offers seven Masses each weekend to accommodate a parish of five thousand people, a number equal to the population of the entire city of Alexandria at the time the parish was founded.

39
St. Peter

Harpers Ferry

WEST VIRGINIA

The Shenandoah and Potomac Rivers come together in a picturesque setting about fifty-five miles northwest of Washington and form a peninsula that has been the site of more than a small share of American history. From this vantage point one can see the states of Maryland, Virginia, and West Virginia. In the center of the peninsula is a huge mass of stone, called Jefferson's Rock because tradition has it that Thomas Jefferson sat atop these stones when he wrote his "Notes on Virginia." In the 1790s, the War Department decided to build and operate a factory along the Potomac River side of the peninsula for the manufacture of muskets. For that purpose it purchased a 125-acre tract of land from the heirs of Robert Harper, the original settler in the area. Some say that George Washington had a hand in selecting this site. In any event, an armory was constructed and opened for business in 1796. As the years went on, it was enlarged, and houses for workmen were constructed nearby. When the B & O Railroad to the west was completed, its tracks crossed the Potomac River at this point. The armory expanded as military technology advanced. Eventually, it was producing rifles as well as muskets.

A Father Dubois used Harpers Ferry as a mission stop as early as 1790. However, no permanent Catholic church or chapel was constructed at that time. In 1823, a small Catholic chapel was built to serve the increasingly large population of Irish who were coming to Harpers Ferry to work at the armory. However, it was washed away by floodwaters. To ensure against any such repetition, a permanent church was erected part way up the hill formed by Jefferson's Rock, on the south side of what was known as Cemetery Hill. It was completed in 1833. This church and its successor, completed in 1896, have been in continuous operation at this location since that date. One local historian, writing in 1903, described St. Peter's as follows: "There can be no doubt that this church, at least, is 'built on a rock,' for there is not soil enough anywhere near it to plant a few flowers around the House of Worship or the parsonage, and the worthy Fathers have been obliged to haul a scanty supply from a considerable distance to nourish two or three rosebushes. If 'the Gates of Hell' try to prevail against this institution they had better assault from above. There will be no chance for attacking the foundation, for it is solid rock, extending, no one knows how far, into the bowels of the earth or through them, perhaps all the way to the supposed location of those terrible gates themselves."

As St. Peter's parish grew, it eventually generated a mission church, St. James, located a few miles away in the county seat at Charles Town. The stability of the population of the area was enhanced in 1852 when the War Department decided to sell the housing accommodations it had constructed for armory employees to the employees themselves.

In 1859, Harpers Ferry was still a part of the Commonwealth of Virginia. It had about three thousand inhabitants, about ten percent of whom were black. The pastor of St. Peter's at that time was Father Michael A. Costello, a native of Ireland, who was serving his first parish assignment after graduating from the Irish seminary at All Hallows. On Sunday night, October 16 of that year, John Brown and a group of about twenty abolitionists crossed the Potomac River railroad bridge from Maryland, seized the armory and the arsenal, and began what they hoped would be an armed uprising of slaves, aided by weapons seized from the federal installation. The initial defenders of the town and its government facilities were a disorganized group of civilian militiamen drawn hurriedly from the surrounding area. One of them, Thomas Boerly, a Catholic, was shot and killed during a crossfire. The insurgents allowed Father Costello to pass through their barricade to administer last rites to Boerly, and Father Costello did so as Boerly lay dying in the street. On the following day, Colonel Robert E. Lee arrived with ninety U.S. Marines, stormed the engine house where Brown and his followers were holed up, and put an end to the raid. During the final charge, Marine Private Luke Quinn received a fatal musket wound. Father Costello again entered the hostilities to administer last rites to Quinn and to another marine who had been less severely wounded.

"Old Brown," as he was often called at the time, was taken to the jail at Charles Town, along with several of his followers. He was tried in the Circuit Court for Jefferson County, Virginia, convicted, and hanged within a period of three weeks. While Brown was awaiting execution, Father Costello visited him in jail, as did ministers of other denominations. None were cordially received. Father Costello recorded the visit in a letter written the following spring to his seminary professor back in Ireland: "I visited 'Old Brown,' who was the commanding general of the invaders, some time previous to his execution, and he informed me that he was a Congregationalist. He said that he would not receive the services of any minister of religion, for he believed that they, as apologists for slavery, had violated the laws of nature and of God, and that they ought first sanctify themselves by becoming abolitionists, and then they might be worthy to minister unto him. Let them follow St. Paul's advice, he said, and go and break the chains of slaves, then they might preach to others. I told him that I was not aware of St. Paul ever giving such advice, but that I remembered an epistle of St. Paul to Philemon where we are informed that he sent back a fugitive slave Onesimus from Rome to his master. I then asked him what he thought of that, and he said that he did not care what St. Paul did, but what he said, and not even what he said if it was in favor of slavery."

On December 2, 1858, Brown was taken from jail, placed in a furniture-hauling wagon, and seated atop the casket he ultimately occupied. He was driven to a gallows two blocks away. There he was hanged in the presence of one thousand Virginia militiamen who had been sent to keep the peace, and before the eyes of a shocked nation that eventually decided to go to war.

Virginia seceded from the Union in May of 1861, about six weeks after the firing on Fort Sumter. Harpers Ferry was occupied by Confederate troops several weeks before formal secession took place. Union forces attempted to burn down the armory to keep it from falling into Southern hands but were not able to do so. The machinery inside the armory was dismantled and removed to North Carolina for use by the Confederate government. Thus began four years of turmoil that saw Harpers Ferry change hands several times and serve as a no-man's-land between successive occupations. During those times, troops stationed on high hills across both rivers used the town as a shooting gallery, and they were not always particular about whom they shot. Over a period of four years, several shells pierced the roof of St. Peter's, which sat in a very prominent position on a high hill right in the middle of the target area.

With the dismantling of the armory there was no local manufacturing and many people left town. One writer commented that the principal industries in Harpers Ferry during the Civil War were pie baking, whiskey smuggling, and spying. During this four-year period, the railroad bridge across the Potomac was destroyed and rebuilt nine different times.

The junction of the Shenandoah and Potomac Rivers was a strategic location for controlling the entire Shenandoah Valley. For this reason federal troops endeavored to control the town and, for the most part, they did so. In September 1862, when General Lee was marching north into Maryland, he dispatched Generals Stonewall Jackson and Ambrose P. Hill to capture Harpers Ferry and its Union garrison. They occupied the town, taking over twelve thousand Union troops as their prisoners. They had no way of maintaining their captives, so they paroled them, a procedure used by both sides during the Civil War. They simply released the prisoners to go home on their promise that they would never again take up arms. Any paroled soldier caught violating his promise was hanged.

The day following the taking of Harpers Ferry, paroled Union prisoners were marched out of town, and Jackson and Hill departed immediately to Antietam Creek, about fifteen miles north on the Maryland side of the Potomac, in an effort to keep General Lee's bloody defense of a small town called Sharpsburg from turning into a rout. For most of the remainder of the war the federal presence predominated in Harpers Ferry, although Lee came through the next year on his way to Gettysburg and Jubal Early rode through with his cavalry in 1864 on his way to Washington.

St. Peter's survived this turmoil, notwithstanding the strategic position it held commanding a view of both river valleys for a distance of several miles. It was the only church in the Richmond diocese to escape damage or destruction during the Civil War. One factor that helped to ensure its survival was the presence in the area of Union troops having large Catholic units, such as Colonel James A. Mulligan's Irish Brigade, the 23rd Illinois Volunteers. They looked with disfavor on any suggestion that the church be closed or destroyed. (Regrettably, Colonel Mulligan met his death in a battle fought in nearby Winchester in July of 1864.) Father Costello, a native of Ireland and perforce a British subject, hit upon the idea of flying the British flag to proclaim the neutrality of St. Peter's, so he prominently displayed the Union Jack over the church throughout the war. Perhaps the best explanation as to why St. Peter's remained intact while other churches were destroyed was the fact that Father Costello was the only local clergyman to remain in Harpers Ferry during the hostilities. All the others left town shortly after the Civil War began.

Shortly after the war, Father Costello returned to Ireland. He died not long thereafter at an unusually youthful age. One of his successors was Father John J. Kain, later bishop of Wheeling and archbishop of St. Louis. Father Kain reopened the parochial school that had been started in 1854 but was closed because of hostilities. During his tenure as pastor, he mounted a large bell in the church steeple that regularly rang out the Angelus each day loud enough that it could be heard for several miles up and down the Shenandoah and Potomac River valleys.

During the Civil War, the state of West Virginia was carved out of the seceding commonwealth. Harpers Ferry is located at what became the easternmost tip of the new jurisdiction. In 1869, the government auctioned off what was left of the old armory, so the town settled back permanently into a much more tranquil and much less prosperous existence. One of St. Peter's pastors in the late nineteenth century was Father Augustine Van de Vyver, who went on to serve for twenty years as bishop of Richmond. In 1896, what years of cannonading and sharpshooting had failed to accomplish took place in a single day. St. Peter's Church burned and had to be replaced. A new church **[pictured above]**, seating about two hundred people, was constructed and still occupies the same site about halfway up Jefferson's Rock.

St. Peter's, which had generated a mission church in nearby Charles Town, actually became a mission of that parish from 1962 through 1981 when both churches were operated under the auspices of the Trinitarian Fathers. Today, it has its own resident pastor once again. The population of the town has declined from what it once was. Its current residents include a substantial number of people who work in Washington. About fifteen hundred acres in and about the town are now owned by the National Park Service, which has developed an extensive historical program that regularly attracts a large number of tourists. If you look down from St. Peter's to the place where Fouts Hotel was located and where victims of the 1859 insurgency were taken for medical care, you will see a railroad station and a parking lot that is filled each weekday morning with the cars of commuters who have caught the Amtrak to Washington. The parish itself now has less than two hundred resident members. It would have more, except for the fact that some older Catholics prefer to attend Mass at other nearby churches where they do not have to climb the one hundred or so steps that lead up the side of Jefferson's Rock to St. Peter's. Its two Masses each weekend are attended by large numbers of tourists who come to Harpers Ferry to see if John Brown's "soul goes marching on," as the old ballad says it does. They can see that St. Peter's continues, performing the same functions it did long before "Old Brown" and his followers walked across the Potomac River bridge late one Sunday evening and set a nation on fire.

40
St. Mary

Charleston
SOUTH CAROLINA

Santa Elena Island, located on the South Carolina coast near the present Parris Island U.S. Marine Corps Base, was discovered by Lucas Vásquez de Ayllón, a Spanish explorer, in 1520, presumably on the Feast of St. Helen in that year. In 1566, Don Pedro Menéndez de Avilés, the founder of St. Augustine in Florida, established a small military fort on that island which he called San Felipe. Three years later, he sent two Jesuits, Fathers Juan de la Carrera and Juan Rogel, to Fort San Felipe, both to minister to soldiers at this encampment and to Christianize nearby Indians. Father Rogel went inland to the Indian village of Orista and attempted to instruct the Indians who were living there. They were not receptive to his message and gradually abandoned the village. When he began to preach against the devil, the remaining Indians revolted against him so he returned to the fort. Soon thereafter, the Jesuits returned to Cuba. Later, Franciscans established a *visita* (mission) at Santa Elena Island and maintained it well into the sixteenth century as an outpost for evangelizing the Indians. However, when the British took control of the area, they abandoned this effort entirely.

The Carolinas, north and south, came under British control and were designated a proprietary colony in 1663 when King Charles II gave the area to eight lords proprietary. The colony was not separated into north and south until 1729. Most of the early settlers in the English colony were Protestant Englishmen and French Huguenots, although a few individual Catholics migrated to the area. Originally, religious tolerance was practiced. Later, a test oath, obliging individuals to abjure the pope, was required of anyone who wished to vote. In 1696, the Church of England became the established church in the Carolinas. Shortly thereafter, at the request of Governor Joseph Blake, an act was passed providing "that all Christians which now are or hereafter may be in that Province (Papists only excepted) shall enjoy the full, free, and undisturbed liberty of conscience."

Warfare between Carolina forces and Spanish forces broke out from time to time. As a part of these ongoing hostilities, Carolina soldiers raided Spanish settlements along the Florida coast. This English versus Spanish confrontation was also a Protestant versus Catholic fight. In raiding the Florida coast, Carolina soldiers focused on Catholic chapels, which were usually burned to the ground and their contents confiscated. If religious artifacts were found to have any value, they were brought back to Carolina as booty. John Gilmary Shea compares the attack by Governor James Moore and his Carolina militiamen on a Spanish settlement in Florida in 1703, which resulted in the deaths of several Franciscan friars, with the massacre of several Jesuits in Upstate New York by the Iroquois.

A steady stream of immigrants began to arrive in the Carolinas in the beginning of the eighteenth century. In 1716, the Carolina State Assembly enacted a law requiring the master of any vessel who wished to enter a Carolina port to take an oath declaring "to the best of their knowledge none of the servants imported to be either, what is commonly called native Irish, or persons of whom scandalous characters were predominant, or Roman Catholics."

The largest group of Catholics to arrive in Charleston in the eighteenth century were French Acadians who had been driven from their homes by English forces and scattered in cities up and down the Atlantic seaboard. At first, ships bearing Acadians were forbidden to land in Charleston Harbor. Later, they were permitted to disembark at Sullivan Island a few miles away. Most became servants. As they merged with the rest of the population, many lost their faith because of the absence of priests. In 1767, a report of the legislature complained that "many Romish priests pass unnoticed to visit the covert Papists under disguise of Quakers and New Lights. . . ." If they did, they were unknown to Bishop Richard Challoner, vicar general of the London district, under whose ecclesiastical jurisdiction the English colonies in America had been placed. He wrote at the time that he had no knowledge of any Catholics in the Carolinas or in Georgia. During the agitation surrounding the American Revolution, there were instances when figures representing the pope, the devil, and the British governor were publicly hanged in effigy in Charleston. In 1776, the newly independent South Carolina colony adopted a constitution making the "Christian Protestant religion" its established religion. This provision was eliminated from the constitution in 1790.

After American independence had been secured from Great Britain, some Charleston Catholics wrote to Father John Carroll, then prefect apostolic, and asked him to send a priest to Charleston. He replied by telling them that he had no one to send. There is a recorded instance of a Mass being offered secretly in Charleston in 1785 at the home of an Irish Catholic family by an Italian priest, en route to South America, whose ship was detained in port because of bad weather. In 1787, two Charleston Catholics wrote to the Spanish consul in New York requesting that the king of Spain assist them in building a Catholic church in their city as he had in New York. There is no evidence that King Carlos III ever provided any assistance. In 1788, a Father Paulin came to Charleston to start a school. He told Catholics that he would offer Mass whenever a suitable room was provided. On July l, 1788, he said the first announced Mass in Charleston at City Tavern and preached a sermon in French. However, he left Charleston when he learned that Father Carroll was able to obtain the services of another priest. The man in question was Father Matthew Ryan, who had just come to Philadelphia from Ireland. Father Carroll prevailed upon him to go to Charleston. Father Ryan arrived in September 1788 and remained for two years, after which he was reassigned to Emmitsburg, Maryland, because of ill health. He is generally regarded as the first pastor of St. Mary's Church, although the congregation that he organized did not adopt that name until many years later.

In the year following Father Ryan's arrival, Catholics of Charleston were able to obtain title to a tract of land, ninety feet by one hundred fifty feet, on Hasell Street together with a building that was sold at a sheriff's auction. The price was £460. The building on this site was a ramshackle house, some seventy-five feet by fifty feet, which had formerly been used as a Methodist church. Title to the property was conveyed by the sheriff to five named individuals in trust for the Roman Catholic community of the city of Charleston. In two years, Father Ryan did a diligent job in locating Catholics who were living in Charleston. When he left, his replacement, Father Thomas Keating, took charge of an established congregation numbering more than two hundred persons. Like his predecessor, Father Keating was in poor health and was soon transferred to Philadelphia where he died in 1793 of yellow fever.

In 1791, at the request of Father Keating and sixteen members of the parish, the South Carolina legislature passed an act incorporating the members of the congregation and permitting them to hold title to church property in a corporate name. In 1799, this act was revised to place the control of the corporation in a board of trustees elected by the Catholic congregation. The trustees referred to themselves as a vestry, a title used by the controlling body of an Episcopal church. It is in this act that the seeds of internal dissension were sown. In 1793, the Marquis de Grasse, a French nobleman, arrived in Charleston with about one hundred French Catholics and their black servants. They were refugees from a slave uprising in the Caribbean. The Marquis' father, the famous Admiral François de Grasse, had been an officer in the French Navy and had participated in naval actions supporting colonial troops who had brought about the British surrender at Yorktown. These French émigrés settled in Charleston and became the core of the

French faction in a parish made up principally of Irish. Other refugees from Santo Domingo followed. The descendants of some of these French settlers still reside in St. Mary's parish today.

Like the rest of the United States, the Carolinas and Georgia were part of the Baltimore diocese and remained directly subject to the bishop of Baltimore until Charleston became a diocese in 1820. Even then, the area was part of the ecclesiastical province of Baltimore and remained under the general oversight of the archbishop of that city until recent times. In 1790, Baltimore was a nine-day boat trip from Charleston. This meant that the turnaround time on any correspondence between Charleston Catholics and their bishop was nearly a month, even under the best navigational circumstances. It took between six weeks and three months to get a letter to Rome and much longer during the Napoleonic wars, when most of Europe was under blockade by the British fleet. An exchange of correspondence between American Catholics and the Holy See might take six months or more. The sheer remoteness of Catholics in Charleston and elsewhere meant that they were truly on their own. This fact of geography played a large role in the difficulties that the American Church and in particular the Church in Charleston experienced during the first part of the nineteenth century.

In 1793, Bishop Carroll appointed Reverend Simon Felix Gallagher, who came from Dublin, to be the pastor of the Charleston parish. He remained in this position until 1818, at which time he was removed. Father Gallagher was reputed to be a learned and eloquent man. In fact, after arriving in Charleston, he taught at the College of Charleston, giving classes in math and several other secular subjects. His bishop in Dublin warned Bishop Carroll that Father Gallagher had a "weakness of character" but Bishop Carroll was desperate for assistance and welcomed him to the Baltimore diocese. Father Gallagher's problem was intemperance, sometimes leading to public profanity and drunken public displays. Later on, this problem played a role in making Father Gallagher what early writers referred to as a "refractory priest."

Between 1801 and 1806, the Charleston congregation erected a brick church on Hasell Street. It replaced the old wooden building they had purchased in 1790 which had become dilapidated beyond repair. The new church was sixty feet by forty feet and, like many Southern churches, had a small gallery. Later, a front porch was added along with four Tuscan columns that stood about twenty-five feet high. The parish also acquired a rectory when Mary Watson, a parishioner, bequeathed her home to the church upon her death in 1796.

Father Gallagher's alcoholism brought complaints by several vestrymen to Bishop Carroll. The bishop wrote to Father Gallagher and demanded that he resign. The latter refused so Bishop Carroll suspended him. The deposed pastor appealed the suspension to the Propagation of the Faith in Rome. A little later, Bishop Carroll transferred a French priest, Father Oliver Le Mercier, from Savannah to Charleston. The predominantly Irish vestrymen refused to accept him on a permanent basis but allowed him to stay on during Father Gallagher's absence. In 1805, Father Gallagher returned to

Charleston, notwithstanding the fact that he was still under suspension. Bishop Carroll permitted him to say Mass privately in his home but refused to permit him to exercise any pastoral functions. Father Gallagher took advantage of this exception by saying public Masses attended by his supporters. At the request of the trustees, who had complained about Father Gallagher in the first instance, Bishop Carroll permitted him to resume his pastorate at St. Mary's, whereupon Father Le Mercier left Charleston and returned to France. Shortly thereafter, Bishop Carroll offered to transfer Father Gallagher to another assignment, either in Washington, D.C., or New York City, but Father Gallagher declined, saying that he preferred to remain in Charleston.

In 1810, the vestry adopted what they called a vestry rule, according to which clergymen were prohibited from voting or being present at vestry meetings. They also required all communications from clergymen (meaning of course Father Gallagher) to be in writing. Father Gallagher denounced this rule as schismatic. Upon learning about it, Archbishop Carroll wrote the trustees, also denouncing what they had done. In 1812, Archbishop Carroll appointed Father Joseph de la Clorivière, a French refugee, to be the assistant pastor at St. Mary's. Father Clorivière had royalist sympathies and, while a young man in Paris, was involved in a plot to assassinate Napoleon. He barely escaped with his life to the United States. Upon coming to this country, he abandoned his political activities, entered St. Mary's Seminary in Baltimore, and was ordained at the age of forty-four. When he arrived in Charleston, he was informed by Father Gallagher that he would not be accepted as assistant pastor. The vestry also refused to accept him because they opposed the appointment of a French priest in their parish. Notwithstanding this opposition, Father Clorivière remained and went about his duties as best he could. He was successful in increasing the number of parishioners who received Holy Communion from six to one hundred thirty and began giving catechism lessons to black children. In 1814, at the end of the Napoleonic wars, he returned to France but came back to Charleston after only a brief stay.

Meanwhile, Archbishop Carroll had died in 1815 and was succeeded in office by Leonard Neale, a former Jesuit, former president of Georgetown College, and Carroll's coadjutor, or deputy bishop. Archbishop Neale was a member of a large Catholic family of English origin that had resided in southern Maryland since the beginning of that colony. He lived only two years following his appointment. His successor in Baltimore was Ambrose Maréchal, a Frenchman and a Sulpician. Archbishop Neale's relationship with Charleston Catholics, both lay and cleric, was disastrous. The affairs of the Church in that city did not improve under his successor.

Problems began to arise when Father Clorivière returned to Charleston from France. The vestry again refused to accept him as an assistant pastor so he was temporarily transferred to Savannah to keep the peace and to avoid a schism. Father Gallagher was still the pastor at Charleston and had become quite close with another Irishman, Father Robert Browne, an Augustinian who was assigned to be pastor at Augusta, Georgia. Father Browne came to Charleston to assist Father Gallagher. Upon learning of these events, Archbishop Neale reprimanded the vestry for their obstinacy, removed both Fathers Gallagher and Browne, and, in January of 1816, transferred Father Clorivière back to Charleston as pastor. While the latter was in the sacristy vesting for Mass, he was confronted by Father Browne, who refused to accept him as pastor. They quarreled over who would say Mass. Father Browne publicly insulted Father Clorivière and wrote a letter to the archbishop requesting that Father Clorivière be excluded from St. Mary's Church and permitted to say Mass only in a private oratory.

Father Gallagher was absent from Charleston at this time. Upon his return, he also wrote to the archbishop and asked him to fire Father Clorivière. Archbishop Neale responded by revoking the faculties of both Fathers Browne and Gallagher. He also suspended Father Gallagher for excessive use of liquor and began to assemble a dossier of affidavits from people in Baltimore, Charleston, and elsewhere to support his removal action. Notwithstanding the archbishop's action, both priests continued to act as co-pastors. Father Clorivière had private means with which he purchased property at a place called Cannon's Bridge, located at the corner of Cannon and Thomas Streets (now Ashley Avenue). Following a suggestion made to him by Archbishop Neale, he opened a private chapel on this property in the spring of 1816 to serve Catholics who were remaining faithful to the church establishment. The chapel, known as St. Mary's Chapel, was eventually surrounded by a small cemetery. The chapel was used by Father Clorivière for nearly three years.

Father Gallagher appealed his suspension by Archbishop Neale to the Propagation of the Faith in Rome. The archbishop wrote a letter to Father Gallagher in which he told the latter that "if you mean to meet with employment, you may go elsewhere without testimonials of good behavior from me, for refractory spirits I never did and never will recommend." In one of his exchanges with Father Gallagher, the archbishop made an unusual statement reflecting on the canonical status of St. Mary's parish. To Father Gallagher's charge that his rights as the pastor of a parish had been violated, Archbishop Neale replied that, inasmuch as the United States was a missionary country, it had no parishes, only congregations, so pastors of those congregations did not have the canonical status they might enjoy elsewhere. He also told Father Gallagher, "As you stand, you cannot celebrate Mass without a glaring sacrilege, nor perform any pastoral function. Your absolutions are null and unavailable. If you proceed to influence others to follow you, you will involve them in the same desperate ruin with yourself and render your case more desperate."

The archbishop repeated the same thing in a letter he dispatched to Father Clorivière, a letter that he intended to be brought to the attention of Charleston Catholics. He stated that both priests had "incurred the great and formidable ecclesiastical censure of irregularity which renders the celebration of holy Mass, administration of the sacraments, and performance of pastoral duties sacrilegious and their absolutions perfectly null and void." St. Mary's Church itself was placed under interdict, meaning that Catholics were not permitted by church authorities to enter it for the purpose of performing their religious duties. For the most part, St. Mary's on Hasell Street stood empty during the period of the interdict.

Father Gallagher traveled to Georgetown (D.C.) to see Archbishop Neale in an effort to regain his standing in the Church. The archbishop instructed him to go to New York, place himself under the jurisdiction of the bishop of that city, make a retreat, and acknowledge his misconduct publicly. He further instructed Father Gallagher to apply to the bishop of New York for reinstatement, which would be granted only upon condition that he would never return to Charleston. Father Gallagher complied in part. He obtained reinstatement; but, after promising never to return to Charleston, he reneged on that promise and returned.

At this point, the Propagation of the Faith muddied the waters in an incredible fashion. It actually reversed Archbishop Neale's censures of both priests pending final resolution of their formal appeals in Rome. Archbishop Neale still refused to permit them to exercise any priestly functions at St. Mary's. The action of the Propagation hit the American hierarchy like a bombshell. Charleston was not the only place where schism was being threatened or was actually taking place. Similar difficulties were breaking out between trustees and their bishops in New York, Philadelphia, and Norfolk. Trustees in those cities were in frequent communication with each other. They actually began to lay plans for the establishment of what they called the "Independent Catholick Church of the United States," a church that would be free from the control of local bishops appointed by the Holy See. At the time, a majority of American bishops were French while a majority of these restive congregations were Irish. They complained to Rome at various times about the "Sulpician faction" and "avaricious foreigners." One communication stated that the Roman Catholic religion in the United States was "blighted by the breath of Sulpicians and Jesuits, who are now swarming like locusts among us to consume the fruits of our religious zeal."

Archbishop Neale wrote to Propagation officials expressing his dismay at their action. He asked them point-blank how they expected him or any other missionary bishop in the United States to maintain discipline in the Church if they were going to be undermined by the Holy See. Other bishops joined in the clamor. After a dossier had been assembled and sent to Rome documenting the misconduct of Fathers Gallagher and Browne, the Holy Father personally intervened. He reversed the action of the Propagation and sustained the actions of Archbishop Neale. Regrettably, Archbishop Neale did not live to see this happen. In a rescript, dated July 9, 1817, Pope Pius VII stated that the archbishop of Baltimore was at liberty to proceed against both priests because their appeals were at an end. The Holy Father denounced "the public scandal given by Father Simon Felix Gallagher, and the insupportable obstinacy with which he has not only shown himself incorrigible for many years, but by means of which he has twice attempted to deceive the said Congregation [for the Propagation of the Faith]."

When a copy of the rescript was forwarded to Charleston, the two priests and their supporters among the vestrymen of St. Mary's claimed that it was a forgery. The vestry wrote to Archbishop Marèchal, who had just replaced Archbishop Neale, telling him that under no circumstances would they accept Father Clorivière as their pastor. They also claimed the right to nominate their own pastors, or at least to veto the appointment of any priest sent to them by the archbishop whom they did not like. In a move aimed at eventually lifting the interdict at St. Mary's, Archbishop Marèchal sent a list of questions to the vestry dealing with the administration of the parish and requested a reply. They wrote back that "in the administration of the temporal concerns of our church, we admit no superior to direct or control; being vested with that trust as well by the laws of the state as by the will of the congregation for which we act." In light of this response, the interdict remained.

In 1819, the promoters of the "Independent Catholick Church," including several members of the St. Mary's vestry, made contact with Father Richard Hayes, an Irish Franciscan. Father Hayes had gained considerable recognition because he had irritated prominent members of the Roman Curia in trying to defend the rights of the Irish hierarchy in a controversy generally known as "vetoism." The British government had proposed to the Holy See that it would remove English penal laws aimed at Catholics if the Holy See would give the government a veto over the selection of Catholic bishops. Such a right of patronage was occasionally accorded during the Middle Ages to Catholic monarchs but never to a Protestant government. The Irish bishops were outraged at the proposal, but it had supporters among Roman officials who would not have to live with the consequences of a British government veto over episcopal appointments. Father Hayes became so persistent in his efforts to thwart such an agreement that he was expelled from Rome and sent back to Ireland. The dissident trustees felt that, in a priest who had so antagonized the Roman Curia, they might find someone who would champion their fight as well. They seriously miscalculated.

The trustee committee went to Ireland and met with Father Hayes. They proposed that he go to Holland and seek to be consecrated a bishop by a schismatic Jansenist archbishop who was living in Utrecht. According to their plan, he would then come to the United States and consecrate other bishops who would be selected by the trustees. These clergymen could then operate a Catholic Church composed of validly ordained priests and bishops but free from Roman interference. Father Hayes would have none of it and sent them packing.

Meanwhile, Archbishop Marèchal felt that peace might be brought to St. Mary's by appointing another pastor in place of Father Clorivière. He appointed Father Benedict Fenwick, S.J., a former president of Georgetown University, and sent him to Charleston along with Father James Wallace, S.J., who was both a priest and an astronomer. Father Clorivière was content to leave and to live out the balance of his days as chaplain at the Visitation Convent in Washington. Father Fenwick was empowered to lift the interdict that had closed St. Mary's Church and met with the trustees for this purpose. The vestry agreed that they would accept any pastor appointed by the archbishop of Baltimore except Father Clorivière. With this understanding, the interdict was lifted.

Rome came to the conclusion that the only way to deal with trustee problems in Virginia and in Charleston was to create new dioceses and place bishops in those locations who could deal immediately and directly with restive congregations. It created the diocese of Richmond without even consulting Archbishop Marèchal, from whose diocese the new suffragan see was created. The archbishop had long known of the proposal for a bishop in Charleston, but when it came to selecting the first bishop, he was also rebuffed. He recommended the pastor who was then in place in Charleston. Father Fenwick was not appointed, although, a few years later, he was named the second bishop of Boston. The new bishop sent to Virginia proved to be a mild disaster. He soon resigned and returned to his native Ireland. The new bishop sent to Charleston proved to be an extraordinary choice and, in the opinion of some, the most outstanding figure in the American hierarchy from the death of John Carroll until the appointment of James Gibbons sixty years later.

Bishop John England was consecrated in Cork, Ireland, and arrived in Charleston on December 30, 1820. At that time, Charleston had about thirty-five thousand inhabitants, of whom only two thousand were Catholics. It had only one Catholic church, St. Mary's. A majority of the city's population was black. The new diocese, comprising both Carolinas and Georgia, had over one and a half million inhabitants, of whom only about five thousand were Catholics. Outside of Charleston, Catholic churches existed in only three other cities. Bishop England described his new diocese as follows:

> The whites were composed of the descendants of English and Irish Protestant settlers and of many Huguenot families who came hither upon revocation of the Edict of Nantes. These were blended with settlers from Virginia and the Northern States and several from New England; the great bulk was of some Protestant denomination. Along with those were Catholics, refugees from Santo Domingo, a few who fled from the sufferings in France, many Irish emigrants, and some few from Maryland. The peculiar circumstances of Catholics caused them to be without property; and great prejudice existed against them. They scarcely had a ministry. A considerable number of slaves were Catholics but they were chiefly those who accompanied the French, and were altogether confined to Charleston, Savannah, and Augusta.
>
> * * *
>
> Two of the priests I brought from Ireland died; the two I procured left me because of the great labor and small means; I procured three others, who I had to send away for misconduct; two others are now serving in Georgia. Another went away through fear of the climate, another dissatisfied with my mode of appointing.

Bishop England became the pastor of St. Mary's parish. He met with the antagonists of his predecessors in Baltimore — Fathers Browne and Gallagher and the vestrymen. Within two weeks, he began a tour of his entire diocese. The tour actually meant scouting out Catholics who were thought to be living in various localities. When he found them, he administered the sacraments, said Mass, and asked them to band together in small, informal congregations. He appointed laymen to read the Mass prayers to these groups on Sundays because he had no priests to send them to say Mass. This request meant supplying them with English missals, a scarce commodity. He arranged to have an English-language missal then in use in Ireland and England reprinted in New York and sent to Charleston. This effort aroused some consternation in Rome because the Propagation had received erroneous information that Bishop England was embarking on an unauthorized translation of the Bible. He wrote and circulated a lengthy pastoral letter to all of the members, lay and clerical, of his new diocese whom he could locate, urging them to hold fast to their religious convictions and fulfill their religious duties as best they could.

Bishop England made peace with both priests who had made life difficult for Archbishops Neale and Marèchal. He restored their faculties and offered Father Gallagher a post in the seminary he was trying to establish. Father Gallagher declined and moved to Natchez, Mississippi, where he died in 1825. Father Browne was sent back to Augusta as pastor and was eventually appointed pastor at St. Mary's, a post he held until his death in 1839.

Bishop England wrote and proclaimed a new constitution for his diocese that provided for annual conventions of both the clergy and the laity. They met in two separate groups, similar to the Congress and Parliament, and worked on resolutions addressing many of the social and charitable activities of the diocese. They were not allowed to legislate on basic questions of church discipline or administration but they could address other problems affecting the diocese and the region. These meetings took place annually for a period of fifteen years. The bishop established a seminary that educated more than twenty priests during his tenure of office. He also founded a newspaper, the *United States Catholic Miscellany*; during the forty years of its existence, the *Miscellany*, the first Catholic newspaper in the country, gained a circulation throughout the United States.

St. Mary's Church served as his cathedral when Bishop England first arrived in Charleston simply because it was the only Catholic church in the city. However, he soon realized that he would have ongoing problems with the vestry if he continued to occupy it as the principal church of his diocese. To use his words, "It is folly to raise the edifice of Catholicity upon Calvinist foundations." He met with the vestry and told them that their bylaws were illegal. He appointed a committee to revise these rules to bring them into harmony with canon law and Catholic practices. When an impasse arose over the proposed revisions, he denounced the vestry for making "uncanonical claims" and spoke of its board as being composed of two factions, "Catholics and infidels." When the vestry refused to comply with his wishes, he warned them that the church would again be closed again until they complied.

Like Catholic church trustees in other cities, the St. Mary's vestry resorted to the state legislature for help. They asked that body to amend the church charter to thwart the bishop, but Bishop England went to the state capital at Columbia and was able to prevent this legislation from being enacted. Finally, the bishop moved out of the church rectory to another house nearby and, like Father Clorivière before him, opened a small chapel for the Catholic faithful who elected to observe church discipline. At this point, St. Mary's Church ceased to be the Charleston cathedral and was again closed for religious services for another two years. It was not reopened until the vestry agreed to comply with the bishop's request concerning their bylaws.

Bishop England purchased land, whose title was vested in him in his official capacity, and began to build another permanent church that became the Charleston cathedral. The first church was a wooden building, about eighty feet by forty feet. It was erected at Vauxhall Gardens for the sum of $2,200. He named it after St. Finbar, the patron of the cathedral in Cork where he had been consecrated a bishop. St. Finbar's Cathedral and the land surrounding it, not St. Mary's, became the center for Catholic activities and Catholic institutions in Charleston.

Bishop England was beginning to acquire a reputation that extended well beyond the diocese of Charleston. The extent of this reputation can be gauged by the fact that he was the first Catholic clergyman ever invited to address the United States House of Representatives. He delivered this address before he had even been sworn in as a citizen. It happened that President John Quincy Adams, while serving as secretary of state in the Monroe Administration, had made a Fourth of July speech in which he denounced the Catholic Church as "a pretentious system of despotism and superstition." In preaching a Christmas sermon at St. Patrick's Church in Washington some years after Adams had made these remarks, Bishop England referred to them as the text for his sermon and proceeded to refute them.

His sermon was so widely publicized that he received an invitation to address the House about two weeks later. On January 8, 1826, he spoke to a crowded chamber. President Adams arranged to attend and was barely able to find a seat. Bishop England spoke for two hours without a prepared text or notes. In his speech, he gave his audience an outline of Catholic apologetics in which he explained the origins of the Church, its sacraments and worship, and defended its teachings and activities against certain popular claims that were then being made against them. Interestingly enough, he took the position that the pope was not infallible in matters of faith and morals, a position widely held by Catholics in good standing until papal infallibility was defined years later at the Vatican Council in 1870. The speech was well received, so later he took great pains to reconstruct it, with the help of the official reporter of House debates, in order that it could be published and circulated.

The slavery question became highly sensitive in South Carolina in the 1830s with the growth of abolitionism in the North. Since blacks constituted nearly fifty percent of its population, the slightest overtures toward emancipation were met with fierce popular outcries. South Carolina's Black Code prohibited the education of slaves but it did permit free blacks to attend school. In 1831, three Irish immigrant women organized a diocesan religious congregation known as the Sisters of Our Lady of Mercy. With Bishop England's support, they opened a school for free blacks that eventually had eighty students. In 1835, the Ursuline nuns came to Charleston and opened a second convent for religious women. The arrival of a second religious order gave rise to an intensification of anti-Catholic feeling in the city. In that same year, abolitionist tracts from the North began to arrive at the Charleston post office. When local pro-slavery activists learned of their presence, they raided the post office and seized the literature. They also made overtures toward attacking schools for free blacks being operated by the Sisters of Mercy and by certain Protestant denominations. A group calling itself the Irish Volunteers assembled at Bishop England's request at the school and at a nearby convent and seminary to ward off any attack. None came.

Bishop England was appointed by the Holy See to be apostolic delegate to Haiti. He visited Haiti to attend to certain church problems that had arisen on that island. When he returned to Charleston, he became associated in the public mind with abolitionism because he had acted as a Catholic Church envoy to a black nation. He publicly denied any connection with abolitionism. His position on the slavery issue became more difficult in 1839 when Pope Gregory XVI issued an apostolic letter condemning the international slave trade. Congress had outlawed the importation of slaves into the United States many years earlier, but scant distinction existed in the popular mind between the importation of slaves and the domestic continuation of the practice, so the Church in the South continued to be painted with an abolitionist brush, especially by people who were hostile to its existence on other grounds. Bishop England set forth his personal position on the subject in the *Miscellany* in 1841, not long before his death. It read: "I have been asked by many . . . whether I am friendly to the existence or continuation of slavery? I am not, but I also see the impossibility of now abolishing it here."

Bishop England died in 1842 at the age of fifty-six. At his death, the Charleston diocese had grown to a population of seven thousand. It had a total of sixty-five congregations in three states who were served by twenty-one priests. The city itself had three Catholic churches: the cathedral that Bishop England had built, St. Mary's, and a new church, St. Patrick's.

St. Mary's Church was destroyed in April of 1838 by a fire that consumed about a third of Charleston. Within a month, parishioners met at St. Finbar's Cathedral to plan for a new building. A solicitation for funds was made throughout the United States. By August, the cornerstone of the new church was laid. In June of the following year, Bishop England dedicated the church **[pictured above]**, which was constructed in Classic Revival style. Over a period of one hundred fifty years, it has survived military and naval bombardments, several hurricanes, and an earthquake. In 1989, it was the site of the 200th anniversary celebration observed by the parish.

In 1845, St. Mary's received another pastor who was destined to have a colorful and unusual career. Father Patrick N. Lynch, a native of South Carolina, was assigned to take charge of the parish and remained for two years. Over a period of time, he was also given other tasks. He and two colleagues collaborated in editing the collected works of Bishop England, a publication that included sermons, pastoral letters, correspondence, and various other writings. It came to five volumes. Father Lynch was also assigned by the new bishop the tasks of superintending the construction of a new cathedral as well as the job of editing the *Miscellany*, which continued to be published despite the death of its founder. In 1858, he was appointed the third bishop of Charleston.

During the Civil War, the Confederate government was anxious to achieve diplomatic recognition from the Papal States. Jefferson Davis was under the illusion that his government could achieve such status because Pope Pius IX had written to Archbishop John Hughes in New York and to Archbishop John Odin in New Orleans suggesting that the Church might use its good offices as a mediator in the conflict between North and South. Bishop Lynch was called to Richmond, given diplomatic papers and expense money, and sent to Rome on this mission. He boarded a blockade runner to the Bahamas and transferred to a foreign vessel bound for Europe. Upon arriving in Rome, he presented his credentials to the pope and asked for recognition for the Confederate States of America. The pope said he would consider the request and get back to Bishop Lynch. The reply never came, and Bishop Lynch stayed in Rome for over a year. At the end of the Civil War, he was afraid to return to the United States and delayed doing so until August of 1865, when President Andrew Johnson gave him a pardon. He then went to the American embassy in Paris, took an oath of allegiance to the United States, and returned to Charleston. For the next seventeen years he labored to support an impoverished diocese in the face of a harsh Reconstruction.

During the war, St. Mary's Church was closed for a considerable period of time. Beginning in April of 1863, Union troops and naval forces blockaded the port and stationed large artillery pieces around its perimeter. These guns were capable of propelling huge shells great distances and were often fired at will on downtown Charleston. Several shells struck St. Mary's Church. A mark made by one of the shells still remains on the south wall. One shell knocked down a huge canvas containing a painting of the Crucifixion. Shells also destroyed the organ and many tombstones in the cemetery surrounding the church. During this period of time, Mass was said in the drawing room of the Robinson home, located on Ashley Street. Charleston was not put to the torch by Sherman, as was Columbia, but it was occupied by Union troops in the spring of 1865. They remained another twelve years. Shortly after Confederate troops abandoned the city in February of 1865, an effort to repair the damage caused by shelling was promptly undertaken, and the church was reopened for services during Lent of that year.

St. Mary's has been victimized by several natural disasters that have taken place over the years, including an earthquake in 1886 and a hurricane in 1893. Most recently, Hurricane Hugo visited destruction on Charleston in September of 1989. On none of these occasions was serious damage done to the church. In 1897, the final chapter was written in the bitter dispute between the vestry and the bishops of Baltimore and Charleston when the vestry gave the bishop a deed conveying to the diocese of Charleston legal title to the church and to the parish grounds that surround it. There is no record that the vestry ever held a meeting thereafter. Since title had been secured, which was free and clear of any liens, the church was consecrated in 1901.

Today, St. Mary's is a well-to-do parish of more than seven hundred members and serves the central section of downtown Charleston. Some of its members live in the suburbs and travel considerable distances to come to Mass. The area served by St. Mary's was formerly quite dilapidated, but it has been revived as Charleston has restored its old houses and developed a thriving tourist industry. The parish has not had a parochial school for many decades but has a functioning CCD program that provides religious education to over one hundred children. The city is about six percent Catholic, while the diocese is less than three percent Catholic. The relative size of the Catholic population is not greatly different from what it was in the days of Bishop England. However, the number of Catholics is growing rapidly as new businesses and industry bring with them Catholics from the North. Relations with the Protestant majority have vastly improved since the early days of the parish. The recent bicentennial celebration of St. Mary's parish included an ecumenical Mass at which Protestants and Jews assisted with Scripture readings, singing in the choir, and reading the prayers of the faithful during the liturgy. The visit of Pope John Paul II in 1987 brought the pontiff to Columbia, not to Charleston, but his presence in the diocese proved to be a great morale booster. Such a visit to an overwhelmingly Protestant state would have been unthinkable not many years ago. It is no secret that his itinerary was influenced by Cardinal Joseph Bernardin of Chicago, a native of Columbia and former chancellor of the Charleston diocese.

The terrible destruction that Hurricane Hugo visited upon Charleston in September 1989 left St. Mary's Church largely unscathed because a large hotel and a parking garage that had been constructed to the rear and to the east of the property buffered it from the ocean. However, buildings as close as a block away were leveled. St. Mary's is an integral part of historic Charleston, but its solid and tranquil appearance gives few hints that its history is marked with conflict and controversy as well as the regular practice of religion.

41
St. John the Baptist Cathedral

Savannah
GEORGIA

The first Catholics who came to Georgia were the Spanish. As early as 1592, Spanish Franciscans were operating a mission at St. Peter's Island, now called Cumberland Island, which is located just off the Georgia coast. Their mission was unsuccessful in no small measure because they objected to the Indian practice of polygamy. As a result of this opposition, several priests were killed by the Indians during a brief uprising in 1597. Spanish priests persisted in their efforts to win converts among the Indians, especially those who were living on the coastal islands. When the British began to extend their sphere of influence southward, they often enlisted the aid of Indian tribes to drive out the Spanish, including Spanish missionaries. One such incident occurred in 1685 at St. Catherine's Island when an entire Indian village established by Spanish priests was destroyed and its Indian Catholic inhabitants carried off into slavery by the British.

Georgia was regarded by the British as a buffer between their principal colonies to the north and Florida, an area from which they were repeatedly unable to dislodge the Spanish. In 1732, Governor James Oglethorpe obtained a charter from the king to establish a debtor colony in this buffer zone. The colony was to extend from south of the Savannah River westward to the Mississippi. Its charter granted religious freedom to all groups except "Papists." Originally, slavery was forbidden, but eventually the restrictions against both Catholics and slaves were removed. As in the case of other coastal cities, the first Catholics to come to Savannah were Acadian refugees who were distributed along the Atlantic seaboard by the British after their forced evacuation from Nova Scotia in 1755. About four hundred landed in Georgia. At first, they were allowed only to stay the winter. Many were then separated from their children and sent inland, while their children were distributed among Protestant families to be raised as Protestants.

It was not until 1790 that another group of Catholics arrived in Georgia. These were native Americans of English ancestry who migrated from southern Maryland to Locust Grove, a town that no longer exists. The community was located in Lownes County, about one hundred miles up the Savannah River from the city of Savannah and not far from Augusta. These native Catholics were soon joined by Irish and by Royalist French immigrants. Many of the latter were aristocrats who had fled the Revolution in France or slave uprisings in Santo Domingo, or both. They were attended briefly by a refugee priest, Abbé John LeMoine from Morley le Roi in France. Father LeMoine died penniless and alone in Savannah in 1794.

In 1796, Bishop John Carroll sent Father Oliver Le Mercier to the Catholics who were living in Locust Grove and Augusta. While in Savannah, he found Father LeMoine's grave and, on October 15, 1796, recited the funeral prayers at the gravesite some two years after the burial. Father Le Mercier reported this event to Carroll in his broken English, adding also: "[Locust Grove] is distant 50 miles from Augusta, and Augusta is 120 miles from Savannah. We shall be two days and a half going. I do believe I have no money enough. My board in Savannah ruins me entirely. I have no more than a pocket piece I have shewn to you. More than a half of it will pay my seat to Augusta, then my baggage, then my staying in Augusta. I am afraid I will be obliged to pawn my watch."

In the 1790s, Savannah was beginning to flourish as a coastal seaport. It was located on a sandy island and was surrounded by rice fields that were often malarial. The city had been the subject of a fierce Revolutionary War battle in 1779 in which the Catholic commander of revolutionary forces, Count Casimir Pulaski, was killed, as were six hundred French Catholic troops under Count Henri D'Estaing. Between 1796 and 1801, Father Le Mercier journeyed from time to time to Savannah and said Mass at the home of Pierre Michel Mirault, a retired French Army officer and former planter in Santo Domingo. Mirault was one of many French aristocrats living in Savannah in reduced circumstances. He listed his current occupation as "baker." At that time, there were about one hundred Catholics in the city.

Father Le Mercier eventually decided to make his headquarters at Savannah. His congregation was able to obtain from the city a subdivided lot for the construction of a church. The board of aldermen were donating parcels of land to various religious groups for this purpose and gave to the Catholics a small tract on the west side of Liberty

Square, sometimes referred to as 123 Montgomery Street. On May 30, 1800, Father Le Mercier laid the cornerstone for a small frame chapel that he named in honor of St. John the Baptist. The church that was thereafter constructed had a steeple, a belfry, and a cross atop the belfry. The surrounding area was planted with trees. This church served the Catholic congregation of Savannah for the next thirty-nine years.

In 1801, the Georgia legislature granted a charter to several lay "trustees of the Roman Catholic Church of the City of Savannah." The trustees listed in the charter had both French and Irish names. Happily, none of the problems associated with lay trusteeship in other cities arose in Savannah.

Father Le Mercier left Savannah in 1803 to serve in other parishes in the Southeast. He was lost at sea in 1811 during a voyage to the West Indies. Father Anthony Carles, another French priest, was in Savannah for several years thereafter but left in 1819. St. John the Baptist Church often functioned as a mission stop visited by priests from Charleston or Augusta. One such visitor was Father Samuel S. Cooper, who was assigned to Holy Trinity parish in Augusta. Father Cooper, a native of Norfolk, Virginia, was born and raised a Protestant. After a lengthy study of the Scriptures and various doctrinal books that he purchased on a trip to England, he became a Catholic and entered St. Mary's Seminary in Baltimore. There he met another convert to the Church, Elizabeth Bayley Seton. Impressed with her devotion and her desire to establish a Catholic school, he made a donation from his personal fortune that enabled her to begin her work at Emmitsburg, Maryland.

At that time, Georgia was still part of the archdiocese of Baltimore. Following his ordination, Father Cooper was assigned to Augusta by the archbishop of Baltimore. That city had been without a priest for some time as a result of the internal problems at St. Mary's parish in Charleston and the desire of the Augusta pastor, Father Robert Browne, to remain in Charleston to support his colleague. From Augusta, Father Cooper also visited Catholics at Locust Grove and Savannah. He was a polished, well-educated individual and was readily accepted both by aristocratic French émigrés and less-educated natives. He traveled extensively throughout the South, giving sermons and missions. In 1828, he became ill and was forced to retire. He spent much of his retirement in France where he became confessor to Cardinal John de Cheverus in Bordeaux after Cheverus, a missionary bishop in New England, had been summoned back to his homeland.

In 1811, the board of aldermen of the city of Savannah granted the Catholic trustees of St. John the Baptist Church legal title to two lots on Elbert Square for the construction of a second church. The resolution they passed on August 11 of that year said: "[The original Catholic church in Savannah was] erected from liberal subscriptions among themselves [Catholics] and other citizens of Savannah; that owing to continued emigrations from Europe and the West Indies, settling on these hospitable shores to avoid death and persecution, the said congregation has grown numerous and respectable, and formed of citizens and inhabitants of Savannah; but, from the troubles and ruin in the West Indies and Ireland, those whose consolation is placed in the practice of the Roman Catholic religion are mostly unable to provide that assistance which other churches receive from their congregations so the repairs of the church and other incidental expenses fall heavily upon a few; that as your honorable body has ever been anxious and solicitous to promote the cause of religion and the propagation of every religious sect. . . ."

The aldermen were thus persuaded to provide additional land to assist the Catholic congregation. The lots were sold with city permission in 1819 and the proceeds used to purchase other property at Drayton and Perry Streets where a second church was eventually built to replace the one that was falling into disrepair. The congregation in 1820 numbered about five hundred. Because of the restoration of the Bourbon monarchy in France, a number of its supporters who had always regarded themselves as living in exile returned to reclaim their ancestral estates. Others remained.

In 1820, Savannah became part of the diocese of Charleston and was visited from time to time by Bishop John England. In 1832, Bishop England appointed Father Jeremiah F. O'Neill as the pastor in Savannah. (He is sometimes referred to as Father O'Neill "Sr." to distinguish him from his nephew, Father Jeremiah F. O'Neill "Jr." who, twenty years later, became the first Catholic pastor in Atlanta.) For a while Father O'Neill "Sr." continued to administer the Savannah church from Charleston as a mission. After coming to Savannah as a permanent resident, he was able to secure the assistance of two Irish laymen to open a small school for boys. It should be remembered that no public schools existed in the city at that time. Father O'Neill also secured funds for construction of the second church, which was erected on a pay-as-you-go basis. As money became available, construction continued; when funds dried up, construction was halted until more was collected. The new church, a plain brick building seating nearly one thousand people, was built in what was then the outskirts of the city and dedicated in 1839. It was free of debt at the time of its dedication.

Father O'Neill's parish included about one third of Georgia's fifty-eight thousand square miles. In the 1840s, there were about four thousand Catholics in all of Georgia, of whom about one thousand resided in Savannah. Father O'Neill visited the outlying parts of this parish on horseback and later in a horse-drawn sulky. When he obtained an assistant, Father John Kirby, the latter continued these visitations, extending them to certain Atlantic coastal islands, to East Florida, and even to the Florida Keys. In 1845, several Sisters of Mercy arrived in Savannah from Charleston to open a convent, a girls' school, and an orphan asylum. Among their students some years later were Jefferson Davis, Jr., and his sister Varina Anne (nicknamed Winnie), two of the Confederate president's six children.

Father O'Neill gained the gratitude of the city when he headed off a possible riot by Irish railroad workers who had come to Georgia to construct a portion of the Okmulgee and Flint River Railroad. The railroad went bankrupt, and its employees felt that they had been bilked out of their pay by the owner, A. H. Brisbane. They were not particular about whom they should collect their wages from, and Father O'Neill was instrumental in seeing to it that their justifiable anger did not result in violence.

In 1850, Savannah became a diocese that included all of Georgia. As St. John the Baptist was the only church in the city, it became the cathedral. The first bishop was Francis X. Gartland, an Irishman from Dublin. He served only four years, during which time the Catholic population of his diocese doubled. He built two new churches, a residence for the Sisters of Mercy, and restored the roof of his cathedral after it blew away during a hurricane. During this period of time, the Irish population of Savannah had increased to the point that a second parish, named in honor of St. Patrick, was established. Moreover, the beginning of the annual St. Patrick's Day parade dates back to this era. It is still a major spring event in Savannah. The celebration begins with Mass at the cathedral, but the ensuing activities take on a distinctly secular flavor.

In 1854, a yellow-fever epidemic struck Savannah, during which forty to fifty people per day died. An inordinately large percentage of these deaths took place among Catholics, whose impoverished condition rendered them particularly vulnerable to disease. The cathedral rectory was receiving eighty to a hundred sick-call requests each day, many of which were handled personally by Bishop Gartland. Priests were often called upon to administer the last sacraments under extreme circumstances. Sometimes, Bishop Gartland had to hear the final confessions of a husband and wife as they lay dying together in the same bed. Finally, the bishop himself succumbed and was buried in the cathedral cemetery, southeast of the city, along with Bishop Edward Barron, the vicar apostolic of Africa, who came to Savannah to help Bishop Gartland during the epidemic and died from the same disease.

On September 15, 1861, St. John the Baptist parish and the diocese of Savannah received their most controversial and colorful bishop, the Most Reverend Augustin Verot, S.S. As noted elsewhere in this volume, Bishop Verot, during his brief tenure as vicar apostolic in St. Augustine, Florida, had acquired the title of "rebel bishop" because of his outspoken support of the Confederacy and his public justification for the South's "peculiar institution" of slavery. Bishop Verot was born at Le Puy in south central France. After his ordination in 1828 in France, he joined the Sulpician Fathers and was assigned to their seminary, St. Mary's in Baltimore. There he taught mathematics, astronomy, chemistry, and physics for more than twenty years. In the five years immediately preceding his consecration as bishop, he was pastor of St. Paul's parish in what was then called Ellicott Mills, Maryland. Upon becoming a bishop, he was sent to the newly created vicariate that embraced all of Florida. Two years later, he was named the third bishop of Savannah.

Bishop Verot did not want the appointment to Savannah. He was in Baltimore when he was notified of the selection and was pressured by Archbishop Francis Kenrick to accept it. The Civil War was well under way at this time, so he had to make his way south by going first to the federal post at Fortress Monroe, Virginia, and thence under a flag of truce to Savannah. The appointment to Savannah was not in lieu of his responsibilities to the St. Augustine vicariate but in addition to them. In Georgia, he was responsible for eight thousand Catholics and ten churches. To assist him there were only eleven priests in the diocese, four of whom were stationed at the cathedral. In Florida, there were three thousand Catholics, six churches and chapels, and only three priests. The city in which Bishop Verot was to live for the next nine years had a population of twenty-two thousand, of whom eight thousand were black. Its white residents were strongly in favor of the Confederacy and were supplying men and money to the cause. To their efforts Bishop Verot added his prayers. Each time a Southern victory occurred, he ordered a "Te Deum" to be sung in all of the churches of the diocese.

Shortly after his arrival, federal troops took Port Royal, about twenty-five miles away. In April of 1862, they captured Fort Pulaski just outside the city. However, it was left to General William Tecumseh Sherman to occupy the city itself, something that did not happen for another two and a half years. To visit most of his diocese, the rebel bishop had to pass through military lines on both sides, something he could usually (but not always) do without difficulty.

Despite the burdens he carried, Bishop Verot wrote prolifically. Because of the difficulty in importing written materials from New York during the Civil War, he composed a catechism for his diocese and arranged to have it printed locally. In February 1862, he sent a Lenten pastoral letter in which he urged Georgia Catholics to accept with good grace "the many privations, sufferings, and calamities entailed upon us by the war in which we are now engaged for the preservation of our just liberties and legitimate possessions." In 1863, he engaged in a widely published dispute with Archbishop John Hughes of New York over the right of the South to secede. In what he called a peace pastoral, issued in that same year, he urged the parties to the Civil War to negotiate a settlement. This is something that the Lincoln Administration steadfastly refused to do, taking the position that there was no legitimate political authority in the South with which to negotiate. In the last days of the war, the bishop wrote many columns for a Catholic publication called the *Pacificator*. It was published by two laymen in Augusta with his approval and championed the Southern cause until it became a lost cause.

There were many Catholics among the Confederate troops stationed in Georgia, and he attempted to provide them with religious services. Two chaplains were stationed at the military post at Dalton, Georgia. There were also many Catholic soldiers to attend to among General Joseph E. Johnston's Army of Tennessee. This effort and his own personal feelings did not prevent Bishop Verot from crossing military lines and visiting Union installations along the Georgia and Florida coast (including the city of St. Augustine where he had previously lived), saying Mass, hearing confessions, and administering confirmation to Union troops.

The most trying experience during the Civil War, both for Bishop Verot and the priests from the cathedral, took place in the course of a ministry they conducted in the summer and fall of 1864 some one hundred seventy-five miles due west of Savannah. There an ongoing atrocity, referred to down through the years simply as Andersonville, was committed under the supervision of Confederate military forces. The Confederate high command decided that Union prisoners of war should be moved south, as far from rescue as possible. In November 1863, a crew of Confederate soldiers and slaves cleared a pine forest near the village of Andersonville and erected a double stockade, about 1,540 feet long and 750 feet wide, where, during the following year, about 50,000 Union enlisted men were relocated, at one time or another. During 1864, some 10,187 of them died at the camp as a result of their experience.

Eighteen feet from the inner wall of the stockade was a deadline marked by poles. Any prisoner entering the deadline area was shot on sight. The stockade was completely uncovered. During the heat of a subtropical summer, about thirty-three thousand Union soldiers were confined in this space at one time. Sweetwater Creek, which ran through the stockade grounds, served as a running sewer. Prisoners suffered from malnutrition, scurvy, and dysentery. Many went mad. Some walked about half naked and others entirely naked. Lice and other vermin were prevalent. The camp was closed in October of 1864 after the fall of Atlanta to the Union Army. All able-bodied prisoners were transferred to camps farther south because Confederate officials feared they would be freed and form the nucleus of an effective army to complete the occupation of Georgia. Following the war, the commandant of the prison camp, Captain Henry Wirz, was court-martialed, convicted, and hanged as a war criminal. He was the only Southern official, civilian or military, to be treated in this manner.

Father William J. Hamilton, pastor of the Catholic church at Macon, some sixty-two miles way, first brought to Bishop Verot's attention the conditions at this prison camp when he visited the compound in the spring of 1864. It is estimated that about six thousand Catholics were confined at Andersonville. This was close to the total number of Catholics living in the entire state of Georgia. Father Hamilton described his visit as follows in testimony given at Captain Wirz's trial: "I found the place extremely crowded, with a great deal of sickness and suffering among the men. I was kept so busy administering the sacrament of the dying that I had to curtail a great deal of the service that Catholic priests administer to the dying, for the reason that they were so numerous — they died so fast."

Bishop Verot sent Father Peter Whelan from Savannah to Andersonville to serve, in effect, as a full-time chaplain. When Father Whelan was overwhelmed with the assignment, Bishop Verot detailed Father Henry P. Clavreul from the cathedral staff to help. Later, Father John Kirby was sent from Augusta. When this effort was still not enough, the rebel bishop left his cathedral and came himself. Throughout the summer, Bishop Verot maintained these priests at Andersonville at his own expense.

Father Whelan was a veteran priest in rural Georgia. He had been stationed for eighteen years at Locust Grove and later at other parishes. He was an independent and self-reliant Southerner. He once told Archbishop Kenrick of Baltimore that he would never accept an appointment as bishop. While at Locust Grove, Father Whelan lived in a log cabin and farmed the land around the cabin with a plow horse that he also rode on parish visitations. He was acting as chaplain to Confederate forces at Fort Pulaski when it was taken by Union troops in 1862 and became a prisoner of war himself. He was sent to a Union prison at Fort Lafayette in New York and was later paroled and allowed to return to Savannah.

It was well that federal forces released Father Whelan. While at Andersonville, he provided both spiritual and material assistance to Union prisoners. He testified later at the Wirz court-martial that the quality of the daily diet was so poor that many sick prisoners could not eat it. He personally raised $10,000 in Confederate money (the equivalent of $500 in federal greenbacks) and bought ten thousand bushels of wheat to be used to feed starving Union prisoners. Bread made from this donation was referred to by prisoners as "Father Whelan's bread."

After the war, Bishop Verot wrote to a friend in France:

> The prisoners, more than thirty thousand of them, were packed together pell mell. . . . Inside this bizarre prison they had to spend the hottest months of the year, June to September, without any kind of shelter to shade them from the tropical sun. Some of these unfortunates sought shelter by hanging their rags on the end of a stick.
>
> As the sicknesses mounted, an appalling mortality quickly followed. Men became accustomed to heaping one on top of another, victims condemned to a death as horrible as it was premature. I felt obliged to go there on two occasions. These two priests [Fathers Whelan and Clavreul] spent all day in camp hearing the confessions of the dying and administering extreme unction, for the Catholics there were numerous. A number of Protestants and non-believers had the good fortune of conversion to our holy religion and received baptism. This was a new kind of ministry: we had to hear the confessions of the sick as they lay on the ground in the middle of the crowd; but the imminence of death did not leave time for human niceties.
>
> What most revolted our human nature during the exercise of this ministry was the horrible stench that rose from this vast agglomeration of men packed together so closely. It took a superhuman effort to cross the thin stream of water that passed through the middle of the camp and served as a receptacle of all the filth.

Father Hamilton later testified at the court martial: "I did not keep an account of the dying men I used to attend per day to administer the last sacrament, but judging from the hours I was engaged and what I know to be the length of the service, I suppose I must have attended from twenty to thirty every day. . . . I would frequently have to creep on my hands and knees into the holes that the men had burrowed into the ground and stretch myself out along side of them to hear their confessions."

Father Anselm Usannaz, S.J., interrupted his academic pursuits at Spring Hill College in Mobile to assist the diocesan priests at Andersonville. Later on, one Latinist described his service in the college records as follows: *meritis aeque ac pediculis coopertus* — he returned "covered with merits and lice." A repeated complaint heard from Union prisoners both during and after their ordeal was summarized by an Andersonville veteran many years later in a letter to Father Clavreul: "I never saw or heard of a

Protestant minister entering Andersonville." The only one who ever came was Reverend E. B. Duncan, a Methodist circuit rider who visited Andersonville on two different occasions to conduct services for Confederate prison guards and took advantage of the opportunity to preach to federal prisoners in the stockade.

In November 1864, Sherman and his sixty thousand troops made their famous march to the sea from Atlanta to Savannah. In sharp contrast to the siege of Atlanta, the taking of Savannah occurred without incident. On the evening of December 20, General William Hardee's Confederate troops left town quietly across hastily constructed bridges made from eighty-foot rice flats that had been lashed together. On the following morning, Union forces marched in. Bishop Verot was saying Mass at the cathedral when Union troops arrived. He wrote in his memoirs that "I heard their yells and hurrahs." Sherman telegraphed Lincoln that he was presenting Savannah to him as a Christmas gift. Sherman's troops who attended Mass at the cathedral on Christmas Day made a present of $400 in the Christmas collection for the support of orphans in Savannah.

Verot was able to travel about his diocese without military interference, once receiving a pass written out by Sherman himself. In the spring of 1865, after the bulk of Sherman's troops had departed in order to pursue the Confederates northward, Union Army engineers began to lay out a defense line that went through the cathedral cemetery, disturbing the graves of Bishop Gartland and others who had died in the 1854 epidemic. Bishop Verot wrote a stinging letter to Secretary of War Edwin M. Stanton, protesting this desecration and insisting that there was no possible military necessity for it inasmuch as all Confederate forces were gone and the war was almost over. Stanton did not like the tone of the bishop's letter but gave orders that the cemetery was not to be disturbed unless absolutely necessary. Work on the defense line abated, and Union troops restored the grounds and the mortuary chapel.

With the emancipation of slaves, the Church in Savannah and elsewhere was presented with a new challenge. Before the war, Catholic priests had no access to blacks, except for freedmen living in cities. As noted elsewhere in this volume, it has been estimated that only 100,000 out of four million blacks were Catholics at the end of the war. Georgia had a pre-Civil War statute forbidding the education of blacks. To fill this educational void, abolitionists from the North were sending teachers to the South to set up schools for emancipated slaves. In this effort, they had the support of the newly established Freedmen's Bureau of the U.S. government. Bishop Verot had a particular dislike for abolitionists, whom he regarded as hypocritical philanthropists. He was not the only one to point out that many of the same people who were championing the cause of abolition of slavery were, at the same time, promoting limitations on immigration and advocating other restrictions aimed at Catholics. The bishop went back to his hometown in France and recruited Sisters to come to Savannah to open a school for blacks. The Sisters of St. Joseph, an order having as its principal function the establishment of missions in Africa, were located in Le Puy, France. They responded to the bishop's request to supply teachers in Savannah and elsewhere in the Savannah diocese. Four arrived in

1867, and, with their arrival, Bishop Verot established in Savannah the first school for blacks that had been opened under Southern white sponsorship. About sixty children were enrolled when the school opened.

Bishop Verot also sought assistance from the city council and the board of education to operate what he called Catholic public schools in Savannah. In 1860, Father Jeremiah O'Neill had opened a school for boys at the cathedral but its duration was short-lived. In the 1850s, the city had begun a practice of subsidizing certain private academies, but a formally organized public school system did not take shape until after the Civil War. The bishop's first efforts to secure public assistance for Catholic schools was turned down. However, a petition to the city council signed by parishioners succeeded in revising that position. At that time, about eight thousand of the city's forty-five thousand inhabitants were Catholics, a higher percentage than in almost any city in the South except New Orleans and Baltimore. City fathers were happy to be able to accommodate a significant number of their constituents.

In the agreement between the board of education and the trustees of the Catholic Church of Savannah, the board would occupy, control, and maintain church-owned buildings used for Catholic public schools. The board would hire and pay teachers, control the curriculum, and select and purchase schoolbooks. Catholic applicants would be given preference for teaching jobs in Catholic schools. All texts to be selected would be those used throughout the entire public school system, except for the history books. History books to be used in Catholic schools would be standard texts generally used in Catholic schools. Opening exercises, including Bible readings and prayers, would be those selected by Catholic schoolteachers. Catholic public schools would observe Catholic holy days of obligation. Under this arrangement, Cathedral Public School and St. Patrick's Public School opened in 1870 with eight hundred eleven pupils. Fourteen additional teachers were hired by the board of education to provide instruction. The total operating cost to the board during the first year was $2,500. The Savannah Plan, as it came to be known, was adopted in Macon and Augusta. When news of it became nationally known, it was adopted in other cities outside Georgia. The two Savannah Catholic public schools continued to operate under public control and assistance for the next thirty-five years. In 1916, a local lawyer wrote to the Georgia attorney general to ask his opinion whether the plan was constitutional. The attorney general ruled that it was not, so the board of education discontinued a working arrangement that in a generation and a half had educated several thousand Catholic children.

Despite the turmoil and destruction of the war, the Catholic Church in Georgia and throughout the United States grew tremendously in the decade of the 1860s. The overall United States Catholic population grew about 1,500,000; in Georgia, it grew from 8,000 to 20,000. Instead of ten churches there were thirty churches and chapels in the Savannah diocese. Much of the financial support for this expansion in Georgia came from elsewhere, especially from the French Society for the Propagation of the Faith. The Civil War brought about the permanent separation of various Protestant denominations into

Northern and Southern factions. At the 1866 plenary council of the Catholic Church in Baltimore, bishops from all eleven dioceses in the eleven former Confederate States attended and participated along with Catholic clergy from elsewhere in the United States. One of those in attendance was Bishop Verot.

To improve the spiritual life of his congregations, Bishop Verot, like many Southern bishops and pastors, invited the Redemptorists to preach missions throughout the diocese. At missions conducted in 1868 at the cathedral and at St. Patrick's, about twenty-five or thirty converts entered the Church. Some four thousand confessions were heard at the cathedral. Special missions were preached to blacks. One critical minister wrote in 1870 in a Presbyterian newspaper published in North Carolina that "the shrewdness with which the Roman Catholic Church became all things to all men during the late war is now an element of influence with many of our people."

Bishop Verot left Savannah in 1870 and returned to St. Augustine as bishop of a newly created diocese that embraced almost all of Florida. Three years later, Bishop William Gross laid the cornerstone of the third St. John the Baptist Church at Lafayette Square. The restored version of that church is **pictured above**. The 1873 church was in French Gothic style, with a high nave and transepts and a triple row of arches supported by bronze columns. The main altar and four side altars were Italian white marble. The church took twenty years to build. In 1896, the twin spires were completed. Bishop Gross, a Redemptorist, renamed the cathedral in honor of Our Lady of Perpetual Help, but he was later required by the Vatican to restore the original name. In February 1898, the cathedral was nearly destroyed by fire. Only the walls, part of the twin spires, and one stained-glass window depicting Our Lady of Perpetual Help remained. It was rebuilt in a period of two years. Among the cathedral's more prominent parishioners during that era was Admiral Raphael Semmes, commander of the Confederate cruiser *Alabama* and, after the cruiser was sunk in Cherbourg Harbor, commander of a flotilla known as the James River squadron.

In 1912, the spires were restored. Murals depicting the communion of saints were painted in New York and installed under the direction of Christopher Murphy, a Savannah artist. In 1959, another major renovation took place. In the early 1980s, the foundation began to settle because timbers that had been sunk in the soil as supports began to decay as the water table lowered, causing the wooden beams to decay. Cracks began to appear in the walls and in the steeples, so the cathedral was closed for a period of two years to permit substantial structural repairs to be performed. Catholics in the entire Savannah diocese, which now includes ninety south Georgia counties, contributed more than two million dollars to finance the repairs. The fund drive was so successful that there was sufficient money left over to purchase a new organ. The restored cathedral was rededicated in 1985 by the apostolic pro-nuncio.

Among the principal artifacts in the restored cathedral are the original high altar, stations of the cross that were imported from Munich, transept windows depicting several Marian themes, and a great rose window in the choir loft portraying St. Cecelia, patroness of music. A new altar required by the liturgical changes from Vatican II was constructed with wood from old confessionals. The interior of the cathedral is now painted to resemble the motif of the church as it existed before the 1898 fire.

In 1937, all of Georgia became what was then called the diocese of Savannah-Atlanta. In 1956, after Atlanta became a separate diocese, St. John the Baptist Cathedral remained the principal church in a smaller diocese that now has sixty thousand Catholics. The parish itself has about four hundred registered members but over one thousand people attend Mass each weekend. Many of them are tourists. These visitors are often invited to raise their hands during Mass to indicate to fellow worshipers that they have come from some distance to attend Mass. The parish supports an elementary school of about two hundred seventy students who are taught by the Franciscan Sisters. A majority of the students are black, and some are from St. Benedict the Moor parish nearby, which is predominantly black. Next to the cathedral stands St. Vincent's Academy, a private girls' school that has remained in approximately the same location since the Sisters of Mercy opened it in 1845.

The area in downtown Savannah near the cathedral is slowly becoming gentrified. There is a mix of inhabitants, which include younger professionals, a large number of students attending the School of Art and Design, and many elderly, some of whom live in homes for the aged that are located within the parish boundaries. The cathedral sponsors a Renew program and discussion groups whose membership cuts across various age-groups. A historic feature of a history-laden city, the church is visited during the tourist season by an average of three hundred visitors each day who find in the tranquillity of Lafayette Square an institution rooted in both the gentility and the turbulence of the Old South.

42
Shrine of the Immaculate Conception

Atlanta

GEORGIA

Atlanta, capital of Georgia and commercial hub of the southeastern United States, developed comparatively late in Georgia history. There is no mention of it until about 1837 when a town called Terminus (and later Marthasville) came into being as a railroad junction. With the coming of railroads to the area came Irish railroad workers and German immigrants. By 1850, Atlanta had a population of about twenty-five hundred, of whom ten percent were immigrants to the United States. During its early days, priests such as Father Thomas F. Shanahan visited Atlanta from Macon and Augusta to say Mass in the homes of railroad workers. In 1848, Father John Barry built a small wooden church on the site of the present Immaculate Conception Church. This church was dedicated in 1849 and served Catholics in Atlanta until it was replaced in 1873. In 1851, Immaculate Conception parish received its first permanent pastor, the younger Father Jeremiah F. O'Neill (mentioned in the previous chapter), who used the church not only to minister to Catholics in Atlanta but as a base for missionary visits to such Georgia towns as Dalton, Marietta, and Albany and to communities in eastern Tennessee. The state capital at the time was about 75 miles away in Milledgeville, a city of 3,000 inhabitants, of whom only 12 were Catholics.

At the start of the Civil War in 1860, Atlanta had grown to ten thousand residents who were employed in railroad yards and shops and in foundries and mills that had sprung up in the preceding decade. The city played a pivotal role in the outcome of the war. In 1861, Father Thomas O'Reilly, a thirty-year-old native of County Cavan, Ireland, was appointed pastor of Immaculate Conception Church. His eleven-year pastorate in the critical years of the Civil War and the Reconstruction played a notable part in the history not only of the parish but of the city it served.

In the summer of 1864, the Union Army of Tennessee, under the command of General William Tecumseh Sherman, laid siege to the city. There is conflicting evidence as to whether Sherman himself was a Catholic. He was raised by the Ewings, a Catholic family living in Lancaster, Ohio. One account states that Sherman was baptized a Catholic when he was five years old. Another points out that he attended Mass at the cathedral in Charleston, South Carolina, long before the war, while he was stationed at Fort Sumter. A third states that he was a deathbed Catholic and was not baptized until shortly before he died. Sherman married Ellen Ewing, the daughter of the family that raised him. She was a devout Catholic, and their children were educated in Catholic schools. Long after the war, Sherman's son, Thomas Ewing Sherman, entered the Society of Jesus and was ordained a priest. Sherman reportedly said of his son's calling that he was "some sort of Catholic divine."

The question of Sherman's Catholicity gave rise to public controversy even after his death. Sherman died on February 13, 1891, at the family home that he established on West 71st Street in New York City. The cause of death was listed in contemporaneous accounts as erysipelas. He had caught a cold and it developed into a fatal illness. Priests from nearby Blessed Sacrament Church were summoned by the family during the final days of the general's life. They gave conflicting published accounts as to whether they had administered extreme unction, as the anointing of the sick used to be called. On the day following the general's death, his brother, Senator John Sherman of Ohio, felt constrained to write a letter to the *New York Times*, which was published on its front page. Instead of commenting on his brother's celebrated accomplishments, he concentrated on his last hours, stating that "it is well known that Gen. Sherman and myself, as well as all of my mother's family, are by inheritance, education, and conviction Christians but not Catholics, and this has been openly avowed on all proper occasions by Gen. Sherman, but he is too good a Christian and too human a man to deny his children the consolation of their religion."

Sherman's son and three other priests conducted a private funeral ceremony at the family home, which was followed by a mammoth procession to the railroad station where Sherman's remains were placed aboard a train to St. Louis. At Calvary cemetery in St. Louis, Father Sherman conducted a public burial ceremony for his father as the general was laid to rest next to his wife. In a statement made on the day of the funeral, also carried on the front page of the *New York Times*, Father Sherman was quoted as saying: "The [private funeral] service was Catholic. My father was baptized in the Catholic Church, married in the Catholic Church, and attended the Catholic Church until the outbreak of the Civil War. Since that time, he has not been a communicant of any church, but he repeatedly told me that if he had any regular religious ideas they were Catholic. A week ago today, my father received absolution and Extreme Unction at the hands of Fr. Taylor [pastor of Blessed Sacrament parish in Manhattan]. He was unconscious at the time but that has no important bearing, for the sacrament can properly be administered to any person whose mind can be interpreted as desirous of receiving them."

Whether or not Sherman was a practicing Catholic as he was poised to take Atlanta, he was perceived as such. Beleaguered Southerners, looking for some kind of relief from the threatened devastation by an avenging army, were not inclined to quibble over details in searching for some way to prevail upon him to spare their city. It is a fact that a large percentage of Sherman's army was made up of Irish Catholic immigrants.

After defeating three attempts by Confederate General John Bell Hood to destroy the much larger Union Army that stood at the gates of the city, Sherman surrounded Atlanta, cut off its railroad connections with the outside, and waited while his artillery fired at will into the besieged defenders. When Hood's troops slipped out of town to avoid capture, Sherman's marched in and took control on September 2, 1864. He immediately ordered the evacuation of all civilians and gave them ten days to comply. Mayor James C. Calhoun went to Sherman and protested, calling the order "studied and ingenious cruelty." He drew Sherman's particular attention to the hardship that would be visited upon the sick and the aged who would be forced to leave and asked him to exempt them from the order "in the name of God and humanity." Sherman simply replied that war was cruelty and proceeded to enforce the evacuation order. One person who refused to comply was Father O'Reilly. He also refused to evacuate the Immaculate Conception rectory and continued to say Mass at the church, often for members of Sherman's army.

In mid-November, Sherman finally received from Ulysses S. Grant, commander in chief of all Union armies, the permission he needed to make his famous 250-mile march to the sea. Before leaving Atlanta, Sherman ordered his troops to burn anything and everything that could be of use to the Confederates. Townspeople then turned to Father O'Reilly to see if he could use his standing as a priest to prevail upon Sherman to spare the city. Father O'Reilly did not speak to Sherman personally but approached one of his corps commanders, General Henry W. Slocum. Instead of appealing to General Slocum in the name of God and humanity, Father O'Reilly reminded the general that a large number of his troops were Catholics and warned him that they would mutiny if he ordered them to burn a Catholic church. Slocum and Sherman took the hint. Guards were posted in front of Immaculate Conception Church, four Protestant churches, and the city hall to prevent them from being torched by Union soldiers. As Sherman's army left town, most of it was being consumed by fire but these buildings were spared. The Episcopal church became a horse stable, the Methodist church became a storehouse, and the Presbyterian church was used as a slaughterhouse for hogs. Immaculate Conception Church was transformed into a hospital. The only church in Atlanta available for public worship on Christmas, 1864, was the Second Baptist Church. Many years later, Father

O'Reilly's role in protecting these buildings was commemorated in a public monument that stands in downtown Atlanta today.

After the Civil War, the old frame church that had served Immaculate Conception parish for more than fifteen years was badly in need of repair. There was blood on the floor, stemming from the use of the building to care for wounded Union troops. Parishioners decided to build a new church. After consulting an architect, they learned that a brick church could be built for about $75,000, and they went ahead with the project. However, the new Immaculate Conception Church took a long time to build. In the meantime, repairs had to be made to the spiritual and moral life of the parish that had suffered during the war and the evacuation of the city. As pointed out earlier in this volume, the bishop of Savannah invited Redemptorists to Georgia in 1868 to give a series of missions designed to revive the religious life of Catholics in the state. When the Redemptorists came to Atlanta, their presence was criticized by several Protestant ministers. Nevertheless, during a week-long mission at Immaculate Conception Church, they heard fifty-five hundred confessions and brought twenty-three converts into the Church.

In 1866, four Sisters of Mercy from Savannah arrived in Atlanta to open a parish school. They began both a day school and a boarding school. The boarding school continued until 1924 and the day school lasted until 1967, at which time the residential character of downtown Atlanta had diminished to the point that a parochial school was no longer needed.

The old wooden church that Father Barry built was lifted from its foundation and moved to a corner of the property while the new church **[pictured above]** was under construction. The cornerstone of the new church was laid in September 1869, but its dedication did not take place until 1873. Construction was not entirely completed until 1880. During this period, the city began to take on additional significance in Reconstruction Georgia. In 1868, the capital was relocated from Milledgeville to Atlanta. Ultimately, the state constructed its capitol building, modeled after the U.S. Capitol in Washington, just a block away from the new Immaculate Conception Church.

Father O'Reilly, who had inaugurated the effort to build a new church, never lived to see its completion. In 1872, his funeral was held in the old frame church and he was laid to rest in the basement of the new church, just under its main altar. One of his successors, Father Thomas Cleary, was buried next to this grave in 1884. Apparently, their graves were bricked over and the whereabouts of their remains was unknown for many years. After considerable research and excavation, these coffins were recently rediscovered and now repose beneath the altar in a fitting and secure mausoleum.

Until 1898, Immaculate Conception was the only Catholic church in Atlanta. In the next decade, three more were built. In 1956, when Atlanta became one of the two principal cities of the newly designated diocese of Savannah-Atlanta, Christ the King, a church in the northern part of the city, became the co-cathedral. Just before this occurred, extensive renovations took place at Immaculate Conception, including new stained-glass windows and a new organ. In 1954, the old church was given the title of "shrine" and this title remains today.

In 1958, the Franciscans, who in recent decades have undertaken a specialized ministry of operating downtown parishes, took charge of Immaculate Conception Church. They remained until 1987 when the archdiocese of Atlanta again assumed the responsibility for staffing the parish. On August 6, 1982, a fire caused by defective electrical wiring broke out in the roof of the church and spread throughout the building. It gutted the entire church. Only the brick exterior remained. The restoration of the church took nearly two years, during which time one Mass was said each Sunday at a nearby Presbyterian church.

The roof was entirely replaced and the original wooden trusses were replaced by steel beams. About half of the present altar contains pieces of marble from the original altar, which were joined together and then repolished. Much of the original brick was reused but with cement mortar instead of the original sand-and-lime masonry. The new ceiling is decorated by paintings, made in cloverleaf design, which represent each of the twelve apostles. A new pipe organ was installed, as were new stained-glass windows. There are about 50 windows that have between 13,000 and 14,000 individual glass segments. The windows depict Marian themes, including titles derived from the Litany of the Blessed Virgin.

The archdiocese of Atlanta, which had only 30,000 Catholics in its 69 counties when it became a separate diocese in 1962, now has 160,000 Catholics. Many are transplanted Northerners holding middle-management positions, who have moved to the Atlanta area with their families in the past three decades. Over twenty new parishes have been established in Atlanta during this period of time to meet the burgeoning demand. Catholics today constitute the third largest religious denomination in Atlanta but are still only about ten percent of the population.

Immaculate Conception, the mother church of the Atlanta archdiocese, numbers about two hundred seventy-five households among its own regular parishioners. Most live outside the parish boundaries. Its noon Mass each weekday is well attended by Catholics working in nearby private offices and state and county buildings. Because of its central location, the church is often used by various groups for religious meetings. Right-to-Life supporters often conduct prayer meetings at the church before undertaking demonstrations at the capitol building nearby.

The parish operates a soup kitchen that feeds five hundred people each week. In conjunction with neighboring Protestant churches, it provides shelter for homeless men throughout the winter months. About thirty-five stay at Immaculate Conception and about seventy-five are accommodated at the Presbyterian church. The archdiocese maintains a priest at Immaculate Conception on a full-time basis to provide a ministry to AIDS carriers. Each Tuesday evening, the parish serves dinner in the church basement to between one hundred and one hundred twenty men who have AIDS. It is a difficult ministry in a parish whose history has been marked with difficult challenges from its very outset.

43
St. Augustine Cathedral

St. Augustine

FLORIDA

The oldest Catholic parish in the oldest city in the continental United States is the St. Augustine Cathedral-Basilica, located in a city that can trace its beginnings to 1565, some forty years before the English settlement at Jamestown and an equal number of years before the French first settled in Quebec. After at least six unsuccessful efforts to explore and to colonize the southeastern coast of what is now the United States, the Spanish sent an expedition of fifteen hundred people to Pascua Florida, as it called the Florida peninsula, principally to thwart the southern encroachment of the French. The expedition, made up of soldiers and priests, men and women, was under the command of Don Pedro Menéndez de Avilés who was designated by King Philip II as *adelantado* (governor-general) and the king's personal representative. Fierce Indians, poor soil, and the absence of any precious metals had discouraged previous overtures to settlement. However, the Atlantic channel between Florida and the Bahamas was regularly used by Spanish convoys going back and forth from the Caribbean to the mother country twice a year. In the mind of King Philip, it was being threatened by a foreign power. In 1564, René de Goulaine de Laudonnière, a French Huguenot, had established a French military base, Fort Caroline, on the St. John's River, near the place where Jacksonville is now located. In the following year, French Admiral Jean Ribault assembled a fleet to reinforce the fort. These actions prompted King Philip to renew Spanish interest in what had been a forbidding peninsula.

After selecting Menéndez, the king assigned to him a religious as well as a military mission. Part of his cedula (or contract) read: "As we have in mind the good of the salvation of those [Indian] souls, we have decided to give the order to send religious persons to instruct the said Indians, and those people who are Christians and our subjects, so that they may live among and talk to the natives so that by association and conversation with them, [they] might more easily be taught our Holy Catholic Faith and be led to good practices and to perfect behavior." It was a tall order and one which the Indians resisted for many years.

After making supply stops at two Caribbean islands, Menéndez and his nineteen ships sailed up the Florida coast. On August 28, 1565, they spotted a small village the Indians called Seloy, located on the river the French had called the River of Dolphins. The expedition sailed a few miles northward to the St. John's River, encountered the French fleet, and engaged in a brief skirmish. They returned to the earlier sited location, which Menéndez named in honor of St. Augustine because he had first passed it on the Feast of St. Augustine. At a place a mile or so north of where the cathedral is now located, he went ashore on September 8, 1565, knelt, and kissed a large ceremonial cross held by Father Francisco López de Mendoza. In the company of his expedition, Menéndez attended a Mass of thanksgiving offered by Father Mendoza and three other priests who were with him. This event marked the beginning of the settlement of St. Augustine, as well as the parish that assumed the name of the city it has served for well over four hundred years. Father Mendoza was its first pastor. The parish continued with many difficulties but without interruption for one hundred ninety-nine years, until the Spanish surrendered Florida to the English in 1764. It resumed its parochial life in 1784 when the Spanish returned and has continued to function as a parish church since that time.

The place where the first Mass was said eventually came to be an Indian mission known as Nombre de Dios. A few days after landing there, Menéndez wrote back to the king: "As for myself, Your Majesty may be assured that, if I had a million [ducats] more or less, I would spend it all upon this undertaking, because it is of such great service to God, Our Lord, for the increase of our Holy Catholic Faith, and for the service of Your Majesty. I have offered to Our Lord all that He may give men in this world, all that I may acquire and possess, in order to plant the Gospel in this land for the enlightenment of its natives, and in like manner I pledge myself to Your Majesty." While these lofty sentiments bespoke the mind of a dedicated missionary, his deeds a few weeks later betrayed the attitude of a religious fanatic in the service of a political cause.

Menéndez assembled his soldiers, marched northward, and destroyed the French fort. In doing so, he spared only women, children, and French soldiers who claimed to be Catholics rather than Huguenots. The rest were killed. Upon his return to St. Augustine, he found Admiral Ribault and two hundred French sailors shipwrecked at the Matanzas River, just south of Nombre de Dios. Not governed by the rules of war as we know them today, Menéndez took them prisoner and killed all of them except a few who professed to be Catholics. Thus, he carried on, if indeed he did not set in motion, a series of scorched-earth, take-no-prisoners reprisals and counter-reprisals between the Spanish and the French and later between the Spanish and the English, which punctuated the settlement of Florida and the Caribbean for the next two centuries.

Menéndez set about establishing a chain of Spanish forts along the Atlantic south to Cape Canaveral, north to Santa Elena in South Carolina, and west as far as Tampa and Charlotte Harbor. More diocesan priests arrived, sent by the bishop of Santiago, Cuba, and they were stationed at different locations. In 1566, Jesuits, under the leadership of Father Pedro Martínez, S.J., arrived at St. Augustine. Within two weeks after his arrival, Father Martínez was killed in an Indian massacre near the St. John's River. Other Jesuits were slain during the next six years. In light of these difficulties, the Jesuits reassigned their remaining priests in Florida to Mexico in 1573.

When he returned to Spain in 1572, Menéndez had not established any successful settlement other than St. Augustine. One obstacle to the evangelization of the Indians, which the Jesuits recognized immediately, was the migratory habits of the tribes. Unless they could be induced to live in permanent or semipermanent settlements, there was little hope that any missionary efforts would be successful.

In a personal letter to Menéndez written in 1569, Pope Pius V wrote: "You understand, we know well, that those Indians should be ruled and governed with good judgment and prudence, that those who are still weak in the Faith may be encouraged and fortified, and that the idolaters may be converted and receive the faith of Christ that the converts, who know the benefits of divine mercy may praise God, and those who are still unbelievers, guided by the example of those who have been rescued from their blindness, may follow them and be brought to a knowledge of the truth. But there is nothing more important for the conversion of these idolatrous Indians than to make every effort to keep them from being scandalized by the vices and bad habits of those who go to those lands from Europe. This is the keystone of the arch of this Holy undertaking and in it is contained the very essence of your pious aim." It was left to later Spanish governors of Florida to pursue the "pious aim" of Pedro Menéndez de Avilés. They did so principally with the assistance of the Franciscans, whose efforts over the following one hundred seventy-five years rivaled their more publicized undertakings in California in the late eighteenth century.

A few Franciscans arrived at Santa Elena as early as 1573. A group of thirteen came to St. Augustine in 1587 and established their headquarters. Thus the city was not only the capital of the Spanish province but of the Franciscan missionary effort as well. In 1595, a large-scale Franciscan effort began with the backing of King Philip. He promised each friar three reales a day for maintenance and directed the royal governor to provide this stipend as well as other support to each missionary. Franciscans were not in the habit of accepting salaries so they referred to their stipends as "His Majesty's alms." Payments by local governors were not always forthcoming as directed. The entire colony was under a severe financial strain and it was not always possible for colonial governors to carry out the king's wishes, even if they were personally disposed to do so.

The original Franciscan headquarters burned down in 1599, so the friars moved into a hospital called Our Lady of Solitude (Nuestra Señora de la Soledad). A few years later they constructed a new *convento*, as they called their residence, so La Soledad, a landmark in St. Augustine for the next one hundred sixty years, resumed its original function. It was the first hospital in the United States. The seminary established by the Franciscans at their *convento* was the first school in this country. Nombre de Dios, just outside the city walls, had become a successful Franciscan mission to the Timucuan Indians. They were sufficiently advanced in their religious training that they could sing high Mass and vespers in the stone chapel at the mission. In 1620, a shrine or hermitage was erected at Nombre de Dios called Our Lady of Nursing Mothers and Safe Delivery (familiarly La Leche or "the milk"), to foster prayers for expectant mothers. It was a devotion that had originated in Madrid in 1598 and had become quite popular in a short time among Spanish Catholics.

During the next sixty years, the Franciscans built and maintained a chain of thirty-eight missions along the Atlantic Coast and inland as far west as what is now Tallahassee. Major missions having a resident priest were called *doctrinas*; smaller mission stops visited occasionally by a priest were referred to as *visitas*. At the peak of missionary activity, these missions served about twenty-six thousand Christianized Indians, most of them Timucuan or Apalachee. Both residences and chapels at these missions were primitive. They were constructed with the aid of pine trees whose trunks were used to hold up roofs and walls. Roofs were made of palmetto thatching placed over a latticework of horizontal wattles woven between the walls. At each mission outpost, the Franciscans taught the Indians elementary arts and crafts as well as the fundamentals of the Catholic religion. All Indian *catecúmenos* were given long and thorough indoctrination before being baptized.

Missions were not established without considerable personal sacrifice. During the mission era, a total of seventeen Franciscan priests and Brothers were killed in Florida and Georgia in the course of Indian massacres. One such event occurred at Tupiqui in 1597 during a Guale Indian uprising. Father Blas Rodríguez was taken prisoner by Indian insurgents, some of whom had received religious instruction. He was told that he was going to be put to death, so he asked for time to say Mass before being executed. The Indians granted his request and sat around on the floor watching him as he said his last Mass. After Mass, he disposed of his possessions to the Indians of the village, urged them to observe the law of God, and knelt before them while they clubbed him over the head with a weapon called a *macana*.

The parish church at St. Augustine was maintained by secular priests to serve the Spanish inhabitants of the village. Along with the rest of the settlement, it was burned down in 1586 during a raid by Sir Francis Drake, a British privateer. Existing parish records go back to 1594. The first entry records the baptism of María, "legitimate daughter of S. Ximénez de la Queva and María Meléndez, his wife," by Father Diego de Sambrana. The date was June 25, 1594. These registers are the oldest written records of any kind kept anywhere in the United States. The whereabouts of earlier parish records is unknown. Presumably, they were burned during Drake's raid.

Father Francisco Marrón, the Franciscan superior, was pastor for a short while in addition to his other duties. However, here as elsewhere, the Franciscans were reluctant to serve as parish priests and insisted that their function was to evangelize the Indians. His successor, an Irishman named Father Ricardo Artur (Richard Arthur), was also appointed vicar of Florida and ecclesiastical judge by the bishop of Santiago. This meant that he was the bishop's deputy and in control of all church activities in Florida. Investing such powers in a diocesan priest did not sit well with the Franciscans, who claimed faculties from their superiors and independence from the bishop and his vicar. However, no serious difficulties arose between seculars and Franciscans because each had different functions and each had all that they could handle.

In 1606, the first bishop to set foot in the territory of the future United States came to St. Augustine for an official visit. He was the Most Reverend Juan de las Cabezas Altamirano, bishop of Santiago (although he resided in Havana). His diocese included Florida. His arrival on March 15, 1606, was the occasion for an enormous celebration. On Holy Thursday, he consecrated holy oils for use in chapels throughout Florida. On Holy Saturday, he ordained twenty men (although it is not clear whether they received minor or major orders). On Easter Sunday, he confirmed three hundred fifty adults and children. He then began a visit to missions throughout the peninsula, traveling westward as far as what is now Gainesville. In the course of his visit, Bishop Altamirano confirmed nearly one thousand people, both Spaniards and Indians. The visit served to energize Catholic activity throughout the province. Regrettably, Florida did not receive another episcopal visitation for nearly seventy years.

The harshness with which Spanish civil and military authorities often treated the Indians brought about tribal resentment and occasional revolt. However, these uprisings were directed at civil, not religious, authorities. Mistreatment of the Indians also engendered ongoing friction between the Franciscans and the Spanish civil administration. Franciscans sometimes took complaints against local governors to Spanish authorities in Cuba or Santo Domingo and sometimes were able to bring about temporary improvements.

The parish at St. Augustine continued to be staffed by secular priests, who experienced the widespread poverty that characterized this remote outpost of the Spanish Empire. The parish had a wooden church and did not possess a single candle when Bishop Altamirano arrived in 1606. Periodically, petitions were sent to Spanish authorities to repair the building because it was beginning to crumble but nothing was ever done. In 1668, Robert Searles, a British pirate, raided St. Augustine and robbed the church of what little it had in the way of furnishings. In 1673, a priest complained that the parish was so poor that he could not say Mass because there were no Communion hosts and no wine.

In 1674, Bishop Gabriel Díaz Vara Calderón made the second episcopal visit to Florida. Among the "firsts" of this visit was the first definitely established ordination of priests to take place in the United States. The ceremony occurred at St. Augustine Church. Bishop Calderón made a detailed report to the queen of Spain concerning the condition of the Church in Florida. He gave the specific locations of twenty-four Timucuan and Apalachee missions and wrote that the city of St. Augustine was, in his opinion, virtually uninhabitable because of poverty, hunger, and unhealthy conditions. He reported confirming 13,152 Indians and described their religious practices as follows:

> As to their religion, they are not idolaters, and they embrace with devotion the mysteries of our holy Faith. They attend Mass with regularity at eleven o'clock on the Holy Days they observe, namely Sunday, and the feasts of Christmas, the Circumcision, Epiphany, the Purification of Our Lady, and the feast days of St. Peter, St. Paul, and All Saints' Day, and before entering the church each one brings to the house of the priest a log of wood as a contribution.
>
> They do not talk in church, and the women are separated from the men. . . .
>
> They are devoted to the Virgin, and on Saturdays, they attend [church] when her Mass is sung. On Sundays they attend the Rosary and the *Salve* in the afternoon. They celebrate with rejoicing and devotion the Birth of Our Lord, all attending the midnight Mass with offerings of loaves, eggs, and other food. They subject themselves to extraordinary penances during Holy Week and during the twenty-four hours of Holy Thursday and Friday . . . they attend standing, praying the rosary in complete silence — 24 men, 24 women, and 24 children — with hourly changes. The children, both male and female, go to church on weekdays and to a religious school where they are taught by a teacher whom they call the interpreter.

Within a few years, many of these Indian Catholic communities were to disappear, largely because of invasions from Carolina by English settlers who wished to extend British influence southward. One tactic employed by the British to rouse the Indians against Spanish authorities was to use Indian grievances against the Spanish civil administration as a basis for forming military alliances. A standard military tactic of British hit-and-run incursions into Spanish areas was to burn Indian Catholic villages to the ground, including their religious establishments. The British were not reluctant to murder Catholic Indians or to carry them off to Carolina as slaves.

In the year 1700, if one were to look about St. Augustine for places of worship, one could find of course the old parish church. There was the military chapel at Castillo San Marcos (originally Fort San Juan), a short distance to the north. There was also a chapel at La Soledad Hospital, one at the Franciscan friary, and one at the Indian mission at

Nombre de Dios. In 1702, during the War of Spanish Succession (called Queen Anne's War in the colonies), Governor James Moore of Carolina and a raiding party burned three churches and convents on the island of San Marcos, took three Franciscans captive, and dispersed a large number of Christian Indians. Then they laid siege to St. Augustine for fifty days while the inhabitants of the city took refuge within Castillo San Marcos. Before leaving the city, they burned to the ground the old parish church, the chapel at Nombre de Dios, and the Franciscan friary. In 1704, Moore returned to central Florida and destroyed the Indian mission village at La Concepcíon de Ayubale not far from Tallahassee. During this raid, he killed and dismembered three Franciscans. In the course of the next three years, he burned eight of the 14 *doctrinas* (principal missions) in the Apalachee country of north central Florida and took between 10,000 and 12,000 Indians back to Carolina as slaves. The net effect of these raids was to bring about the beginning of the end of more than a hundred years of Franciscan missionary effort in Florida and south Georgia. A few missions lingered on until the Spanish quit the peninsula in 1764; but, after 1708, they never regained the size or the vigor they enjoyed a generation earlier.

In St. Augustine, the Spanish never rebuilt the parish church. In the 1740s, they began to erect the walls of a new church but it was never completed. The parish used the chapel at La Soledad Hospital from 1702 until 1764, although the hospital continued to keep its wards open for medical treatment. For a while the Franciscans used a small rock chapel and wooden huts for living quarters. Eventually, they built a new monastery at the south end of the settlement on the banks of the Matanzas River. Begun in 1724, it was completed in 1737 and is still standing. After the cession of Florida to the United States, it was used for military housing and is now the headquarters of the Florida National Guard.

The chapel at Nombre de Dios was rebuilt from coquina rock, a shell conglomerate mined on nearby Anastasia Island, which had been used to construct the fort and was later used to build a new St. Augustine Church. In 1728, the Carolinians attacked the city again, burned the chapel at Nombre de Dios, and carried off some religious statues.

The effect of this warfare on parish administration can be gleaned from the fact that, just after the Moore invasions, the bishop of Santiago decided to station an auxiliary bishop at St. Augustine. When the bishop arrived in 1709 after narrowly escaping capture by British warships, he became so disheartened by what he saw that he sailed back to Cuba. It was not until 1735 that another auxiliary bishop, Francisco de San Buenaventura, arrived at St. Augustine.

He found the city in a state of physical and moral decay. In reference to the chapel at La Soledad, he wrote that "when it rains it is the same as being outside." He repaired the roof, started catechism classes, and voiced public criticism of immoral activities he observed in the city. He opened a classical school for boys. In 1737, he confirmed nearly eight hundred people. This regeneration took place in time for the next English siege, which was conducted in 1740 by Governor James Oglethorpe and two thousand men from his newly founded debtor colony in Georgia. During this ordeal, Bishop San

Buenaventura was able to rally the spirits of the townspeople who gathered for safety once again at Castillo San Marcos. Oglethorpe was eventually driven off when Spanish relief ships arrived with supplies and lifted the siege. In 1745, the bishop was transferred to Yucatán in Mexico and was not replaced.

In 1763, the British captured Cuba for the express purpose of trading it off for Florida. For many years Spanish authorities had regarded this colony as a dubious asset. They were not unhappy to exchange it for an island that was key to their Caribbean holdings. The British promised religious freedom to any Spanish Catholics who chose to remain. Remembering a series of raids, sieges, and church burnings dating back to the time of Sir Francis Drake, few were prepared to take the British at their word. By March of 1764, some thirty-one hundred had sailed to Havana. At that time, there were only eight priests in the city, and all of them left.

Before the British took possession of Florida, Juan Elixio de la Puente, the Spanish royal auditor, conveyed title to the bishop's house, the Franciscan monastery, and the hermitage chapel of La Leche to John Gordon, a wealthy Carolina Catholic. The pastor of the parish conveyed the land and the unfinished walls of the new church to an agent of the same individual. The purpose of these conveyances was to prevent church properties from falling into the hands of the British crown. Great Britain had a law stating that only British subjects could own land within the British Empire and Gordon was willing to take the holdings to protect the Catholic Church. However, the British regarded the transfer deeds as spurious and refused to record them. As Spanish title to these properties was held by the king of Spain, upon the cession of Florida they became the properties of the king of England. The bishop's house was assigned to the Anglican bishop who came to St. Augustine, and the chapel at La Soledad became the site of St. Peter's Anglican Church. Before the Spanish left, the bishop of Santiago ordered an inventory of all movable Catholic Church property. He sent a boat to transport statues, vestments, sacred vessels, and other items to Havana. Among the parish properties removed to Cuba were the historic registers in which baptisms, marriages, and deaths had been recorded since 1594. After two centuries, the Spanish left nothing behind them in Florida except a few footprints in the sand.

After the British occupied the former capital of the Spanish province, no Catholic activity took place in St. Augustine for the next thirteen years. In this interim, a settlement of Minorcans, Greeks, and Italians took root seventy-five miles to the south at a place called Mosquito Inlet, where a Scottish physician and land speculator, Andrew Turnbull, had obtained a grant of 100,000 acres to grow cotton, indigo, silkworms, olives, and other subtropical crops. To work this land he and his partners were able to bring to Florida 1,225 indentured servants and their families from Minorca, a Mediterranean island in the Balearic chain off the east coast of Spain. The new arrivals at the Turnbull plantation, called New Smyrna, began life in a world frequented by lack of food and clothing, poor housing, cruel punishment from overseers, disease, and overwork in the fields. About four hundred fifty died during the first year.

The Minorcan settlement was attended by two priests, Father Peter Camps, a secular, and Father Bartolomé Casanovas, an Augustinian. Both spoke Minorcan, a language quite different from Spanish. They built a chapel and named it for St. Peter. They also ministered to the Greeks who came to New Smyrna. The Greeks were Orthodox rather than Roman Catholic but they attended Roman Catholic services. They were the first group of Greek Orthodox settlers ever to come to the United States. Their presence at New Smyrna and later at St. Augustine is commemorated at the Greek Orthodox shrine of St. Photious located just a few blocks from the present Roman Catholic cathedral [**pictured above**].

In 1781, Spain retook by force an area referred to as West Florida — a strip of land along the Gulf of Mexico stretching from the Apalachicola River in Florida westward to the Mississippi. In 1784, they regained by treaty East Florida, that is, the remainder of the Florida peninsula. St. Augustine once again became the capital of a far-flung province with fourteen hundred inhabitants, a third of whom lived in or about the city. The pervasiveness and oppressiveness of the tightly controlled mercantile economy that the Spanish reinstituted was well described by Charles B. Reynolds, a local historian:

> The Minorcans, who still remained on lands given to them by the British, fished and hunted; but the town's chief dependence was upon supply ships that came from Spain, and the game and beeves brought in by the Indians. . . .
>
> * * *
>
> The town was a great military station; and beyond this, nothing. In one way or another, the people were all engaged in the service of the King. They kept the King's accounts, labored at the King's fort, wrought in the King's forge, manned the King's pilot boats, bought their bread at the King's bakery and their meat at the King's market. The barracks were filled to overflowing with a garrison, for which it taxed the Governor's ingenuity to find employment.

Such a situation proved particularly critical in 1788 when the Spanish government ran out of money and could not pay its employees in St. Augustine for six months.

St. Augustine parish was restored in 1784, but there was no church in existence. The chapel at La Soledad had been gutted by the departing British; La Leche Chapel at Nombre de Dios was in ruins. Spanish priests began to occupy the bishop's house on the plaza and offered Mass on the second floor of the building. This makeshift arrangement was quite inconvenient and eventually became unsafe, but it was all the parish could provide for the next thirteen years.

As English-speaking frontiersmen were beginning to settle in north Florida, the king of Spain thought it expedient to station English-speaking priests in St. Augustine. Since the outset of the Reformation — a period of over one hundred fifty years — the kings of Spain had provided a seminary education for exiled Irish clergy at the Royal Irish College in Salamanca. A few graduates of this seminary were requested to come to

Florida and to Louisiana; several did so. Fathers Thomas Hassett and Michael O'Reilly were sent to St. Augustine. They were placed under the jurisdiction of an auxiliary bishop whom the bishop of Santiago had stationed at New Orleans. Father Hassett became pastor of St. Augustine parish and vicar of East Florida.

In 1788, Bishop Cyril de Barcelona came from New Orleans to St. Augustine on an official visit. As was the custom of the times, he published an *edicto de pecados públicos* — an edict of public sins. This was a solemn command to Catholics in St. Augustine to appear before him and to report any abuses that had arisen in the area. The bishop's call was not limited to reports on the shortcomings of priests; it included complaints against doctors, slaveholders, and anyone who might exercise any kind of authority. The *edicto* extended to the administration of the sacraments, whether church bells were rung on a regular schedule, whether priests were engaging in private commercial activities, whether couples were "living in sin," and if doctors were telling their patients how sick they really were so that patients could prepare to receive extreme unction. Bishop Barcelona also inquired into the treatment of slaves. He threatened excommunication to any slaveholder who failed to provide religious instruction for his slaves.

In 1786, the king ordered the construction of a new St. Augustine Church; but, with the slowness of the Spanish bureaucracy, it was 1793 before construction began and 1797 before it was completed. The parish had received title to some rental properties in Cuba, so the income from these houses was applied to the construction cost. The royal treasury supplied the rest. The church was built on land located on the north side of the main plaza, which was purchased for this purpose in 1793. The building plans were prepared by Mariano de la Rocque, the royal engineer. The original plan was rejected as being too costly, but eventually he came up with a design for an affordable church that was personally approved in Madrid by the king himself. The eventual cost was 16,000 pesos ($25,000), far above the original estimate. One saving was effected by using coquina rock taken from the ruins of La Leche Chapel and from other ruins as well. The balance of the construction material came from the king's quarry on Anastasia Island, about three miles away.

The church built by the Spaniards appears much as the cathedral does today. Its front swept upward in ogee curves to a Moorish belfry topped by a cross. The façade had simple moldings, recesses, and cornices, and pairs of windows on either side of the front door. On a pediment in a niche over the door was a statue of St. Augustine. The exterior of the building was finished with lime stucco. By the time the church was ready for occupancy, Father Hassett had moved on to New Orleans where he became vicar of the entire Louisiana Territory and in charge of the fortunes of the Church in that immense territory during the early years of transition from Spanish and French rule to the United States. The church at St. Augustine was dedicated by Father O'Reilly, who remained as its pastor until his death in 1812.

The last twenty years of Spanish rule in Florida is a story of economic privation and general decline, both in the fortunes of the city and of the parish of St. Augustine.

European wars had drained the Spanish treasury, and the Napoleonic conquest of Spain had disastrous consequences throughout all Spanish colonies in the New World. A unique local problem addressed by the Church in Florida during this period was the question of marriages of American settlers who were pouring into Florida. Many were Protestants, but there were no provisions in Spanish law for marriages of non-Catholics. All marriages had to be performed before a priest who acted in both a religious and a civil capacity. While church law and practice made provision for a mixed marriage between a Protestant and a Catholic, it made none for a church ceremony in which both parties were not Catholic. In such circumstances, Protestant couples either had to leave the territory and be married in Georgia or live together without any publicly recognized status. The local Catholic clergy and the bishops in Cuba finally devised a formula to accommodate this situation. Catholic priests in Florida were given permission to preside at all-Protestant weddings simply as civil witnesses, thereby giving official sanction to such marriages in the eyes of civil authorities.

The impoverished Spanish government sold Florida to the United States in 1819, and two years later the American flag was raised over the capital city of East Florida. The western boundary of the new American territory became the Perdido River. At that time, there were about three hundred or four hundred Catholics in St. Augustine. The entire territory had only two churches, one at St. Augustine and the other at Pensacola. In 1822, the sole remaining Spanish priest in St. Augustine was forced to leave because of ill health, so the city was left without any Catholic clergy. Moreover, the territory was without a bishop. The bishop of Havana wrote to Bishop John England in Charleston and asked if the latter would please "look after" the area. Bishop England had just taken over a diocese containing three Southern states and had very little with which to "look after" all of Florida; but, for several years, he did what he could.

Another question soon arose after the American assumption of authority in Florida as to who actually owned St. Augustine Church and the other Catholic Church properties in the city after the king of Spain had relinquished control. American authorities took the position that the church, the bishop's house, the Tolemato cemetery, the Franciscan friary, El Soledad Hospital, and the Indian mission at Nombre de Dios had been the property of the king of Spain; so, as government property, it became the property of the United States government. Legal title to the bishop's house was given to the new American Episcopal bishop of Florida. Congress soon recognized the anomaly of a nation that professed to have a separation of Church and State retaining title to a Catholic church and a Catholic cemetery; therefore, in 1823 and again in 1827, it passed laws divesting itself of ownership, though retaining title to other Catholic lands and buildings. Unfortunately, in doing so, Congress unwittingly laid the groundwork for a bitter future controversy. Instead of transferring title to the church and the cemetery to a bishop or some other Catholic Church official, the government deeded the properties to the Catholic congregation of St. Augustine. It was not long before another trustee battle was in full swing.

In 1825, both Florida and Alabama were placed in a vicariate headed by Bishop Michael Portier, who made his headquarters at Mobile. Bishop Portier appointed Bishop John England of Charleston as his vicar for Florida, and the latter continued to send priests to St. Augustine. In 1825, a six-member board of wardens became incorporated and took possession of the church at St. Augustine. At first, they were happy to have the priests whom Bishop England sent to them. However, money problems arose. The wardens refused to permit Father Timothy McCarthy, whom they had received as pastor, to accept so-called "stole fees" for performing marriages and funerals. They also refused to provide him a salary sufficient for his needs. Father McCarthy tried to take up collections at Mass but no one contributed. The wardens failed to pay certain parish bills so Father McCarthy was arrested by civil authorities because of the nonpayment of those debts. He finally had enough so he packed up and sailed back to Charleston.

In 1828, Bishop England sent Father Edward F. Mayne, an Irishman, to St. Augustine. Shortly after he arrived, Father Mayne conducted a funeral service for Joseph Sánchez, a former treasurer of the board of wardens. Gerónimo Álvarez, a member of the board, objected. Álvarez was a former mayor of the city and Sánchez was his political enemy. Álvarez claimed Sánchez was a Mason and not entitled to a Catholic burial. Father Mayne persisted, so Álvarez locked the doors of the church and forced Father Mayne to hold the funeral at the cemetery. Father Mayne then informed the wardens that he would not enter the church thereafter for any purpose until they assured him that he would not be molested again in the performance of his duties. The wardens removed Álvarez from the board, but the congregation reelected him to fill the vacancy caused by his removal.

Because of confusion over the appointment of a new pastor, Bishop Portier sent other priests to St. Augustine to take charge. They left shortly after arriving, but Father Mayne remained. Bishop Portier confirmed Father Mayne's appointment as pastor, but the wardens, acting under the influence of Álvarez, refused to permit him to resume his functions and locked the church. Father Mayne went to court and sought judicial process to permit him to enter and once again take charge of the church. After a long and unsuccessful attempt to mediate the controversy, the local circuit judge refused Father Mayne's request, holding, as American authorities had done since the outset of the Florida territorial government, that Catholic Church property had passed from the hands of the king of Spain to the U.S. government and that the government could give it to whom it pleased. Having given title to St. Augustine Church to the congregation rather than the bishop, the government had vested the congregation with the lawful right to act as it did. Years later, an arbitrator appointed to decide a dispute as to other church properties in the city came to the same conclusion.

Faced with this situation, Bishop Portier took the long trip from Mobile across north Florida to St. Augustine once again. Upon arriving in St. Augustine, he asked the congregation for a bill of particulars detailing their complaint against Father Mayne. Their only reply was that they did not like him, so Bishop Portier threatened to place the church under interdict if they did not relent. When the wardens promised to permit Father Mayne to resume his duties and to accept any pastor appointed by the bishop, Bishop Portier permitted the church to reopen, and a public Mass of reconciliation followed. Years later, Álvarez made his own personal reconciliation by donating a bell that still hangs in the church belfry.

As Florida grew, St. Augustine became a Catholic enclave in an increasingly Protestant state. By 1850, there were only five Catholic churches or chapels in the entire state, as compared with one hundred seventy Protestant churches. A notable name associated with the parish during this era was that of Father José Varela. He grew up in the city while the Spanish were still in control. After ordination, he moved to Cuba and was elected to the Spanish parliament. A strong supporter of Cuban independence, he was expelled from Spain, whereupon he went to New York, became pastor of a parish, and later vicar general of the New York diocese. He was a noted writer and won widespread recognition for his works. After retirement to St. Augustine on account of ill health, he died in 1853. Forty years after his burial at the Tolemato cemetery, his remains were taken to Havana, where they were reinterred near a monument proclaiming him to be a Cuban national hero.

In 1857, all of Florida except its westernmost tip was placed in a vicariate separate and apart from Mobile. Its new bishop was Augustin Verot (who, as described earlier in the chapter on St. John the Baptist Cathedral, Savannah, Georgia, was later transferred to St. John from St. Augustine). He was a most colorful and controversial figure. When he arrived in St. Augustine in 1858, there were only two parishes in the entire vicariate and no Catholic educational institutions. The city had about fourteen hundred Catholics, one third of whom were black. Florida had just begun to realize the value of growing oranges and inviting Northerners to spend the winter. The city was still as poor as it had been for many decades. Shortly after arriving, Bishop Verot wrote back to Archbishop Kenrick in Baltimore to tell him that "the country is very poor and the people are not like [those in] the North, fond of giving to the Church even out of their poverty." To forestall any resurgence of the old trustee problem, Bishop Verot convened a meeting of both the church wardens and the congregation and insisted that they execute a perpetual lease of the church and the cemetery to the bishop and his successors. He also insisted that they renounce any right to control the appointment or removal of pastors. The wardens and the congregation quietly complied.

As war clouds gathered, President Buchanan designated January 4, 1861, as a national day of prayer and fasting. Bishop Verot took advantage of this occasion to mount the pulpit at St. Augustine Church and deliver a sermon that was to earn him the title of "rebel bishop." He denounced federal interference with Southern customs and practices and supported the secession movement, which was then well under way. He went on to justify the institution of slavery and to denounce abolitionists, while at the same time denouncing abuses that had characterized the Southern slave system. He called for the enactment of a slave code or "bill or rights" similar to slave codes that existed in Spanish countries. As envisioned by Bishop Verot, a slave code would accord certain rights to slaves while preserving the system intact. His support for reform instead of abolition was a unique idea at the time but had few supporters, either in the North or the South. However, it placed Bishop Verot solidly in the Confederate camp. Whatever might be said concerning the merits of his sermon, it was politics, not theology, and was recognized as such later on. He published his remarks in a document he styled *A Tract for Our Times* and circulated it widely. *Le Propagateur Catholique*, a French publication in New Orleans, translated it into French and distributed it throughout Louisiana. The secular press in the South hailed it. Bishop John B. Purcell in Cincinnati denounced it, while Archbishop Kenrick tried to have it suppressed in Baltimore.

Bishop Verot was transferred to Savannah at the beginning of the Civil War but continued to administer the Florida vicariate from that city. In the spring of 1862, St. Augustine was occupied by federal troops and remained under Union control during the remainder of the war. A great many residents fled the city to areas under Confederate authority. About fourteen thousand Floridians joined the Confederate Army, while some twenty-five hundred, half of them black, enlisted in the Union forces. Upon coming to St. Augustine, Bishop Verot had prevailed upon the Sisters of Mercy from Charleston to establish a girls' school in the city called St. Mary's Academy. With the evacuation of the city, the school lost its enrollment and was closed. Bishop Verot decided to transfer the Sisters to Columbus, Georgia, and came to St. Augustine to escort them personally. They made it as far as Savannah. Their trip by rail and tent wagon, through swamps and deserted countryside, past Union sentinels and Confederate guerrilla bands, is an absorbing saga in and of itself. After the war, the Mercy Sisters returned to St. Augustine and reopened their academy.

Widespread poverty marked both the civic and religious life of St. Augustine and the Florida vicariate during the Reconstruction. On one occasion, a Palm Sunday procession in St. Augustine had an escort of Union troops from the 7th Infantry Regiment, which had been assigned to occupy the city. In 1868, the Redemptorists came to St. Augustine, as they did in other cities in Florida and Georgia, to preach parish missions. One missioner wrote of his experience that "our mission was a perfect jubilee. The Protestants even attended in such glee that balls and parties were deferred until after the mission." The St. Augustine *Examiner* reported large crowds in attendance and expressed the hope "that our city will long remember the present occurrence, and that the mission will banish many vices from our midst, and will give a tone of morality, honesty, and industry to our city that will be more creditable than the empty privilege of being the oldest city in the country."

By 1870, Florida had 19 Catholic churches and chapels, 12 priests, and about 10,000 Catholics. St. Augustine became the seat of a full-fledged diocese and Bishop Verot returned as its bishop. He was given the choice of staying in Savannah or of returning to St. Augustine. He opted for the latter choice, explaining: "I have chosen St. Augustine in preference to Savannah principally because St. Augustine and Florida are the place where I was first sent, and also because in Florida there is more holy poverty as well as more good to be done in building churches and founding schools."

On two occasions, first upon coming to St. Augustine and later as bishop of Savannah at the end of the Civil War, Bishop Verot had gone back to France to recruit both priests and nuns and to raise money to build and support the churches in his jurisdiction. He was successful in bringing several French priests to Florida and in persuading the Sisters of St. Joseph to come both to Savannah and to St. Augustine to start schools for newly freed blacks. He also raised about $40,000 for his diocese.

When the Sisters of St. Joseph came to St. Augustine in 1867 and opened a school for black children, their initial enrollment was sixty pupils. They also conducted classes at night for adults. Not long thereafter they opened schools for blacks in Jacksonville and Fernandina. It should be recalled that, until 1869, there were no public schools in Florida for any students, so these schools for blacks were an innovation of some consequence. The nuns' school at St. Augustine remained open until 1964 when the federal Civil Rights Act put an end to segregated private schools. In 1867, a Catholic school for white boys was opened by the Christian Brothers, and the Sisters of Mercy returned to operate a school for white girls.

In his six years as bishop of the new St. Augustine diocese, Bishop Verot built a gallery in the old Spanish church, which was now his cathedral. He placed a new tin roof on the building, redecorated its sanctuary, and replaced the woodwork in the interior. For the sum of one dollar he purchased from a farmer named John McGuire the property on which the Nombre de Dios mission had stood, restored the site, and built a new chapel in honor of Our Lady of Nursing Mothers. Bishop Verot traveled to Havana and located in the diocesan archives in that city the old St. Augustine parish registers. They contained some 1,340 pages. In 1906, after long negotiations, they were returned to St. Augustine; in 1939, another volume was discovered and returned. At that time, the St. Augustine diocese, in cooperation with the Carnegie Institute and the National Archives, caused these pages to be laminated in protective shields of cellulose acetate foil. They are now located in the diocesan archives in Jacksonville.

In 1882, Henry M. Flagler, who had made a fortune in oil with John D. Rockefeller, moved to St. Augustine and opened a resort hotel two blocks away from the cathedral. In the next fifteen years, he was to remake not only the city of St. Augustine but also all of south Florida by providing easier access to these areas along his Florida East Coast Railroad. In 1887, fire broke out at the St. Augustine Hotel, a vacation resort, and spread to the cathedral. It destroyed everything at the cathedral except the walls and the façade. The story goes that Flagler tried to comfort the pastor as he watched his church go up in flames by saying that he would help with the rebuilding effort. James Renwick, Jr., the architect of St. Patrick's Cathedral in New York, happened to be staying at the demolished St. Augustine Hotel and promised the pastor he would help in the restoration. To raise funds for the rebuilding project, Bishop John Moore did what other bishops had done in the past: he went begging for funds in Northern cities and was remarkably successful in obtaining them. Renwick proposed that the cathedral be lengthened twelve feet and that a transept be added. These improvements were included in the restored building, which opened a year later. Flagler made good his promise and donated a bell tower, designed by Renwick, which is located to the west of the main building.

In 1911, another parish, St. Benedict the Moor, was opened, principally at the request of black Catholics who wanted their own church. During that era, Florida enacted a school segregation law that, among other things, forbade white teachers from instructing black children. The St. Joseph Sisters, who taught at the school for blacks, refused to comply. At the instigation of Governor Park Trammell, the local sheriff arrested three Sisters for violating the law. One of them, Sister Mary Thomasina, refused to request a release from jail and remained in confinement until she was released in the custody of the cathedral rector. When their case came to trial, Circuit Judge George C. Gibbs dismissed the charge, holding that the statute in question applied only to public schools, not to private schools.

As late as 1958, St. Augustine was the seat of a diocese that included all of Florida except its westernmost tip. There were 193,000 Catholics in 110 parishes; today, Florida has a total of seven dioceses that in a period of slightly more than 30 years have grown to more than 1.5 million Catholics. In 1965, to commemorate the 400th anniversary of the parish, Archbishop Joseph T. Hurley completely renovated the cathedral and added many of the artifacts that can be seen today. Murals were painted that depict scenes from Florida's Catholic history. The 1790 bells, which were beginning to lose their timbre, were recast in Holland and put back in the old belfry. Twelve large stained-glass windows depicting the life of St. Augustine were installed, as were oil paintings of the stations of the cross that were painted in Rome. A host of other pictures, statuary, and objets d'art were acquired that lend a distinctively modern look to an aged house of worship.

The parish today has about seventeen hundred households. Its population is mixed but is made up in substantial part by retired people who have moved to the city from the North. Depending on the season of the year, from one third to one half of those attending Mass each Sunday are vacationers. Anyone moving into the parish is handed a brochure containing about forty different activities and outreach programs that are operated by parishioners. The parish has a preschool with forty students and a parochial school with two hundred fifty students. Each year the cathedral is visited by nearly 250,000 people who come to the city to witness where America began and to the cathedral to see where the Catholic Church in America started.

44
St. Mary, Star of the Sea

Key West
FLORIDA

It is difficult to believe that in the 1890 census Key West was the largest city in Florida. Ten years later, at the turn of the twentieth century, it boasted sixteen thousand inhabitants while its fledgling neighbor to the north, Miami, had a population of only 1,681. Because of these historical facts, Catholic roots in south Florida extend ultimately to Key West, not to Miami, and to St. Mary, Star of the Sea parish, the third oldest church in Florida.

Key West is the last of a 120-mile chain of coral reefs extending southwestward from the Florida mainland into the Gulf of Mexico. The name is an English version of Cayo Hueso, "island of bones," the name given to it by Spanish explorers who navigated about these islands in the sixteenth century. As early as 1567, a Catholic mission was established by Spanish priests on Upper Matecumbe Key, halfway up the island chain between Key West and the mainland, but the mission did not endure. The Los Kayos Indians, the object of this effort, became decimated by smallpox and measles, so the mission came to an end.

From 1724 to 1727 there was a church at Key West. In the early eighteenth century, English raiders from the Carolinas attacked Spanish settlements on the Keys on three different occasions. These depredations as well as Indian attacks forced the few remaining Cuban residents to return to their homeland. In 1743, two Italian Jesuit missionaries came from Havana and opened a mission chapel for Indians at Key West. They also built a chapel at Biscayne Bay, near what is now Miami. However, the Spanish governor was unable to erect any kind of a fortification to protect them, so he ordered them to return to Cuba and they did. For the next few decades south Florida was under British control, so Catholic activity was almost nonexistent.

Development on Key West did not occur until after the United States acquired Florida from Spain. Shortly before American annexation in 1819, the Spanish governor granted to Juan Pablo Salas legal title to the island but soon thereafter Salas sold it for $2,000 to John Simonton, a New Orleans real-estate speculator, in a deal consummated at a bar in Havana. In 1828, the town of Key West obtained a charter from the Florida territorial legislature and began its existence as an organized community.

The sea and the remoteness of Key West from other settlements were controlling factors that influenced growth in its early years. The island was visited once a month by a steamer from Charleston and four or five times a year by a mail packet. Then, as now, the nearest major city was Havana, only ninety miles away across open water. Key West Catholics have been the successive responsibility of bishops living in Santiago (in Cuba), New Orleans, Mobile, Savannah, St. Augustine, and, since 1958, Miami. The remoteness of the island and the smallness of its population made it difficult for bishops to provide Catholics on the island very much in the way of church services or religious activities until the middle of the nineteenth century. In the 1830s and 1840s, priests came twice a year by ship from Savannah to administer the sacraments. There was no resident pastor and no church.

In its early years, life in Key West had a laconic Spanish pace to it. Tropical heat discouraged much activity. Ever since Florida became a part of the United States, the United States Navy and now the U.S. Coast Guard have been a continuing presence and a continuing source of support for the local economy. Navy Lieutenant Matthew C. Perry took control of the island in 1822 in the name of the United States. Beginning in 1829, Commodore David D. Porter used the island as a base for a "mosquito fleet" of small schooners that patrolled the Gulf of Mexico and the Atlantic Ocean looking for pirates and slave traders. More recently, the objects of these searches have been drug smugglers. During the Civil War, Key West was completely under Union control and was used as a base for enforcing a Union blockade of Southern ports and for capturing Confederate blockade runners. The presence of naval and military forces in Key West has continued to date and has provided an ongoing source of membership in St. Mary's parish over the years.

A Catholic community has existed at Key West since the Mallory family came to the island in 1820. The origins of St. Mary's parish and its religious ministrations to a widely divergent group of people is generally set in 1846 when a Spanish priest from Havana came to say Mass on the second floor of a fish market located at the pier. The building also served as city hall. Technically, the area was part of the diocese of Mobile until 1850, but Bishop Michael Portier had difficulty in providing any assistance to the Catholic community. Early residents included Spanish Catholics, Bahamians, and blacks, both free and slave, who had come to the island from St. Augustine. In 1852, the city had 650 houses and a population of 3,000, of whom about 300 were Catholics. They constructed a small wooden chapel on Duval Street, now one of the principal commercial areas of the city. Bishop Francis X. Gartland came from Savannah to dedicate the church and to give the parish its present name. He appointed Father J. N. Brozard to be its first resident pastor. A former slave quarters next door was transformed into a rectory. Bishop Gartland purchased from the city for the sum of one dollar a plot of land that now forms the Catholic portion of the city cemetery.

Existing sacramental records relating to the Catholic community at Key West date back to 1842. Earlier records of baptisms and marriages were destroyed by fire. The boundaries of the parish were set at the Atlantic Ocean and the Gulf of Mexico, two bodies of water that meet at Key West. In a city that lays claim to the title of "southernmost" for a variety of buildings and geographical points, St. Mary's became and remains the southernmost Catholic church in the continental United States. The small church on Duval Street, sometimes described only as a chapel, served Key West Catholics for the next fifty years.

The history of the Church is not exclusively the story of its clergy and sometimes involves the accomplishments of the laity as well. The most prominent Catholic in Key West during its early years was not a clergyman but a layman, Stephen R. Mallory, whose name is memorialized in a public square located near the pier. The Mallory family name appears frequently in the sacramental records at St. Mary's Church. It is safe to say that Mallory was one of the more prominent Catholic laymen in the United States during his lifetime and certainly one of the most prominent in the South. Mallory's father, a construction engineer, brought his family of four to Key West in 1820. He died not long thereafter, and his Irish wife, Ellen, was forced to open a boardinghouse to support herself and her two small children. Stephen Mallory attributed his Catholic upbringing to her, since there was no Catholic church or school and only an occasional visiting priest to contribute to his religious formation. The first church constructed on the island was an Episcopalian church, built in 1834, and Mallory's biographer states that he attended that church for a while, not because he adhered to its tenets but simply because there was no other place of worship around.

Mallory "read law" in the office of the federal district judge who had been assigned to Key West to hear maritime claims. After entering practice, he became an admiralty lawyer and handled a number of maritime-prize cases. These were disputes between salvage crews over a division of the spoils from shipwrecks that regularly occurred near the Florida Keys. Mallory was appointed arbitrator in a dispute between the Franciscans at St. Augustine and the U.S. government over the old Franciscan friary that the government claimed as the successor in title to the king of Spain. Mallory decided in favor of the government.

Mallory married Angela Moreno, the daughter of a Spanish family from Pensacola. Mrs. Mallory was an ardent Catholic, and there is little doubt that her faith proved to be a guiding light to her husband throughout his life. In 1850, he was appointed by the Florida legislature to the United States Senate and represented his state in Washington until a fateful day in 1861 when he and other Southern senators arose in the Senate chamber to make brief speeches announcing their resignations in order to support the Confederate cause.

During his eleven years as a senator, Mallory put through a number of measures designed for the benefit of Key West, including appropriations for a naval base and for the construction of a massive brick fortress called Fort Jefferson, located on the island of Dry Tortugas in the Gulf of Mexico some seventy-five miles west of the city. Ironically, as chairman of the Senate Naval Affairs Committee, he also sponsored a measure that improved Fort Lafayette in New York Harbor, a place where he would later be held a prisoner immediately following the Civil War. He took the Senate floor in 1854 to speak at length to defend his fellow Catholics from charges of disloyalty that had been circulated throughout the country by the incipient Know-Nothing Party.

Shortly after the establishment of the Confederate government, Jefferson Davis appointed Mallory to be the Confederate secretary of the navy. Mallory was the only member of Davis's cabinet to serve in the same post throughout the entire Civil War. Confederate ships were active in raiding Union merchantmen and were effective in several engagements against Union naval vessels. Unfortunately for Mallory, the United States never recognized the legitimacy of the Confederate government nor the belligerent status of its navy. In its view, the Confederate Navy was simply guilty of piracy and Mallory was the chief pirate.

During the last days of the Confederacy, Mallory left Richmond and accompanied Jefferson Davis on his flight south. Davis was arrested in Georgia and sent to a Union prison in Virginia to await trial for treason, a trial that never took place. Mallory was also arrested by Union soldiers and transported to Fort Lafayette, New York, where he spent the next ten months of his life in solitary confinement. Alone of all Confederate cabinet officers or major military commanders, Mallory was singled out for trial and punishment. The charges were treason and piracy against the United States. Both were hanging offenses.

During his stay at Fort Lafayette, Mallory underwent a remarkable spiritual transformation. Throughout his life he kept a minutely detailed diary and he was allowed to follow this practice during confinement. The diary contains notations indicating that he began and ended each day in prayer. It also contains some touching prayers that he composed, asking the protection of God, the Blessed Mother, and the angels over his wife and his four children. While at Fort Lafayette, Mallory also wrote a lengthy letter to his son, Buddy, then a student at Georgetown College. The letter provides some interesting insights into Mallory's religious sentiments:

> Cling to your religion, my son, as the sheet anchor of life here and to come. Never permit yourself to . . . question its great truths, or mysteries. Faith must save you or nothing can; and faith implies mystery. The rationalist who believes only what he can understand . . . has led away ardent minds of youth from the days of the Grecian philosophers. . . . He cannot be a Christian.
>
> * * *
>
> I frankly say to you — and not without regret and humiliation — that I too long neglected this, and that I did not give you the proper example. Learn by my present feeling . . . to do your duty. Before I left Richmond, I visited the Confessional, made a clean breast of it to Almighty God, and partook of the B. Sacrament at Charlotte and at Atlanta. [These were stops made on the flight from Richmond before his capture at Lagrange, Georgia.] You have ever had the example of your mother, whose noble, wife-like devotion I owe my confession and Communion, after years of neglect.

Mallory was released from Fort Lafayette in March of 1866 in response to requests for a pardon made by his wife and many friends to President Andrew Johnson. His release was called a partial parole, but it amounted to a complete termination of all charges against him by federal authorities. He eventually returned to Florida but not to Key West. Before the war he built a mansion at Pensacola so that his wife could be near her relatives during his absences in Washington. It was to Pensacola that he went and where he lived the remainder of his life. He died in 1873 and was buried from St. Michael's Church in that city.

In the three decades that followed the opening of St. Mary's Church in 1852, the parish had a rapid succession of pastors, few of whom stayed more than a year or two. Bishop Augustin Verot tried to get Spanish Jesuits from Havana to come to Key West, but his request was met with only occasional success. Jesuits came for short periods of time but did not remain. Three priests assigned to the parish during this era died during yellow-fever epidemics. The first to do so, Father Sylvanus Hunincq, contracted the disease in 1862, shortly after coming to the parish and after having ministered to many in the city who were suffering from the epidemic. A marble slab was placed in the church commemorating his efforts. Others who succumbed to the same disease during these decades were Fathers J. B. Allard and J. E. McDonald and a Father Foucard. All are buried in the Catholic cemetery nearby. In 1880, Father Felix Ghione, an Italian, was appointed pastor and remained in that post for seventeen years until he returned to Italy. This was the first time that the parish enjoyed a continuity of leadership over an extended period of time.

For many years St. Mary's was the only church in south Florida. Priests from the parish occasionally visited Tampa, Fort Myers, and the military installation at Dry Tortugas. Parish records indicate that in March of 1872 several baptisms and marriages were performed by a Father DuFau "in a place generally known as Miami." Priests from the parish also acted as de facto chaplains for U.S. Army and Navy personnel stationed at

Key West as well as for the crews of naval vessels that docked at the port. In later years, the navy provided chaplains to handle this responsibility.

Following the Civil War, the massive fort on Dry Tortugas was used as a federal penitentiary, a forerunner of Alcatraz but on a much more remote island. Bishop Verot made three episcopal visits to St. Mary's — in 1865, 1867, and 1875 — either as bishop of Savannah or as bishop of St. Augustine. During his second visit, he sailed to Dry Tortugas and said Mass for the prisoners. He also heard the confession of Dr. Samuel A. Mudd, who had been imprisoned at Fort Jefferson for complicity in the assassination of Abraham Lincoln. Mudd's crime was that he had set the broken leg of John Wilkes Booth as the latter was making a midnight ride through southern Maryland to escape apprehension.

During the nineteenth century, the principal industries at Key West were salvaging shipwrecks, sponge fishing, and cigar making. The abolition of slavery in Cuba in 1868 and the outbreak of a civil war that lasted ten years prompted thousands of Cubans to take refuge in Key West. Many of them became employed in cigar manufacturing. At one time, the island had about ninety cigar factories. This industry helped the island grow to a population of twenty-five thousand. Strikes and other factors, such as the growth of Tampa, prompted many cigar makers to relocate their factories to that city, a development that measurably reduced the size of Key West and its major industry. Most Cuban immigrants regarded themselves as Catholics, but many were merely nominal or cultural Catholics. They did not support or attend the church and looked to the priests at St. Mary's only to baptize their children, perform marriage rites, and bury the dead. A parish record from 1885 shows that it had seven thousand Cuban parishioners. There were one hundred twenty-seven baptisms of Cuban children, but none were in the school or in the religious-education program. No Cubans made their Easter duty that year. During this period of time, they often insisted that baptisms and marriage ceremonies be performed in their homes rather that at the church. Bishop Verot gave permission for such marriages to take place. He was afraid that if Catholic priests did not perform such ceremonies, they would be performed by Cuban Protestant ministers in the area who were advertising themselves as Catholic priests and who were happy to perform marriages in private dwellings, since they did not have any church. From 1879 to 1898, St. Mary's operated a special chapel for Cuban Catholics. Its use was discontinued after the Jesuits came to Key West but the building is still standing.

St. Mary's parish was not entirely self-supporting during the latter half of the nineteenth century. Parish records indicate an annual income ranging from $1,500 to $4,000 a year, the figure usually being in the lower range. Successive bishops of St. Augustine, in whose diocese St. Mary's was located, made repeated fund solicitations and visits to Northern cities for the purpose of raising money to support mission churches throughout Florida. That designation included St. Mary's.

Both stability and improvement in the quality of Catholic life in Key West occurred with the coming of the Sisters of the Holy Names of Jesus and Mary. A contingent of five nuns arrived in 1868 after a harrowing sea voyage from Montreal. They took up residence in some abandoned barracks Union soldiers had occupied during the Civil War. The buildings were actually owned by Stephen Mallory, who let the Sisters use them rent-free. Later, he deeded the property to Bishop Verot who in turn transferred it to the Sisters. Within a month after their arrival, the nuns opened the first School of Mary Immaculate to twelve students. One of the island's many yellow-fever epidemics broke out the following year and the school was closed until the epidemic passed. The school closed again three years later when a smallpox epidemic struck the city. The Sisters volunteered their services to nurse smallpox victims, so three of them were housed in a building ten feet square which had been constructed in a remote part of the city next to the pest house where the smallpox victims were being quarantined. The whole area was patrolled by a U.S. Marine Corps guard to prevent any violation of the quarantine.

In 1872, the Sisters purchased an old home near the port and used it to house the St. Francis Xavier school for black children. This school remained in operation until 1961 when it was integrated into the parish school system. The Sisters also started a school for Cuban girls, but it remained open only for a short while. Schools for blacks and Cubans were always tuition-free and were supported by income derived from other Catholic schools. The pastor of St. Mary's, a Father La Rocque, wrote to Bishop Verot in 1875 concerning the free school: "The present generation is irrevocably lost to the faith and all our effort toward saving the rising generation should receive a stronger impulse than ever — free schools for Cuban boys and girls should no doubt go far to achieve this end."

These schools for girls were soon complemented by a boys' school, St. Joseph's, which was opened in 1881. There was an effort to expand the school into a college during the early 1900s, but there was insufficient demand for such an institution so the college portion was discontinued in 1916. The boys' school ultimately merged with another school operated by the Holy Names Sisters.

In 1875, the Sisters began the construction of a large Convent of Mary Immaculate, about a mile from the parish church. It was constructed from rock quarried from the coral deposits on and around the island and was completed in 1878. There they conducted a large girls' school, called the Convent of Mary Immaculate. By the turn of the century, it had grown to an enrollment of nearly six hundred, of whom three quarters were Protestants. The Protestant patrons were impressed by the discipline and the academic quality of the school and the nuns were happy to have their financial support. When the Spanish-American War broke out, the Sisters volunteered the use of the convent school to the United States Navy for use as a hospital. The offer was gratefully accepted, especially since the Sisters made no request for compensation other than that the premises be returned to them after the war in good condition. School was closed and students were sent home for the duration of hostilities.

After the U.S.S. *Maine* blew up in Havana Harbor in February 1898, several victims were brought from Havana to the convent-hospital for treatment and recuperation. In May, after hostilities began in earnest, wounded soldiers began to arrive in large numbers. They were treated by a team of nine doctors and four trained nurses employed by the military services, but the Sisters volunteered their services to assist the nurses. The Spanish-American War lasted only about four months. During that time, some six hundred sick and wounded soldiers were brought to the Convent of Mary Immaculate for treatment and occupied either the convent buildings or tents that were pitched on the convent grounds.

In 1889, the bishop of St. Augustine entered into a contract with the Jesuits of the New Orleans province in accordance with which the Jesuits were given the "exclusive and perpetual right" to operate all Catholic parishes in central and south Florida. Bishop John Moore, who entered into this contract, told his chancellor that he had taken the extraordinary step of turning over half of his diocese to a religious order because he needed help in caring for the Cuban population that had immigrated to the area and was unable to obtain the services of any Spanish diocesan priests. The Jesuits began to build churches in Tampa and Miami, which they still maintain, and they began to serve at St. Mary's in 1898.

The first Jesuit pastor at Key West, Father Anthony B. Friend, found that he had a large task at hand. Key West then had 18,000 inhabitants, of whom 8,000 were Cubans, 4,000 were black, and 6,000 were white Americans. His assistant, a Father Faget, wrote: "The practice of religion among men is not encouraging but women are better disposed. Our only hope of improving their religious state lies in the efforts made by the zealous Sisters of the Holy Names. Even the American portion of the parish is largely made up of lukewarm Catholics. A great deal of hard work is before us."

In 1904, one priest of the parish described his difficulty in reaching Cuban parishioners as follows: "I never once asked for money, on the contrary I always explicitly said to them that I would baptize, marry, and bury them *gratis*. . . . We cannot visit them socially; if we try, as I have tried it hundreds of times, we are misjudged, sinister intentions are attributed to us. We should not dare go when the husbands are not at home and when these are home, the women are relegated to the back rooms of the house. . . . Nothing but a miracle of grace will save them."

The hard work of which Father Faget wrote became even harder on September 20, 1901, when an arsonist set fire to the church on Duval Street during broad daylight. Firefighting techniques were hopelessly inadequate, so the church burned to the ground. For the next four years Sunday Masses were celebrated at the chapel of the Mary Immaculate Convent, located about a mile away.

Father Friend decided to abandon the central city location for the parish church and to reconstruct St. Mary's next to the convent. He acquired a nearby lot, arranged with the city to trade the lot for a relocation of Windsor Street, and began the building of the church **[pictured above]** on land immediately adjacent to the convent and its school. The church was built from coral rock extracted on the church property and cost $25,000.

It was dedicated in 1905. It was not until after World War I that the old rectory was completed. For about sixteen years the parish had maintained a Cuban chapel near the old church, but it was closed and the building relocated to the new parish grounds.

In 1912, Key West ceased to depend entirely on the sea for transportation and access. In that year, Henry Flagler, the oilman turned railroad and hotel builder, completed a 150-mile railroad from the Florida mainland to Key West. It was built on trestles constructed over the water that lay between the islands making up the Keys. The railroad lasted until 1935 when it was destroyed by another of the ferocious hurricanes that strike the region from time to time. It was replaced by a causeway that brought automobile traffic to the city from the mainland for the first time. These improvements gave Key West its principal and most lucrative industry — tourism — and brought to St. Mary's parish the responsibility for providing religious services to a large number of winter visitors as well as a permanent retirement community.

Key West was originally only a small coral island. It was greatly enlarged when the government dredged a large amount of coral rock from the sea and filled in the area surrounding the original island. The distinction between the old town and the new town is essentially a division between buildings constructed on the original island and those built on filled land. Environmental concerns have put an end to this practice, so the present island, and hence the parish, will not have any more geographical expansion. St. Mary's was originally an elongated parish that included all of the Keys; but, in recent years, additional parishes have been established on other Keys to accommodate growing retirement communities.

Over the years, improvements to the church and its grounds have been made from time to time. In 1922, the Holy Names Sisters completed the building of a Lourdes grotto on the lawn to the rear of the church. Made of coral rock, it was constructed at the urging of Sister Louise Gabriel, who had lived and taught at the convent for more than twenty years. At her request, the grotto was dedicated as a prayer "to prevent the eye of the hurricane from passing over Key West again." In 1940, a new sanctuary and altar of Italian marble were installed in the church. In 1958, the interior of the building was revised so that its seating capacity could be increased from four hundred to six hundred. The following year, a new rectory was completed. In 1961, the Convent of Mary Immaculate became a coeducational school for grades 7 through 12, and its name was changed to Mary Immaculate High School. In 1970, the Jesuits turned the parish over to the archdiocese of Miami, which has staffed it since that date with diocesan priests. Three years later, the Holy Names Sisters left the parish, so the high school and the grammar school were operated thereafter by the parish with the use of lay teachers.

In the spring of 1980, proximity to Cuba once again brought to Key West and to St. Mary's parish a large number of refugees. Unlike previous Cuban immigration, this influx did not take place over a few years but over a few weeks. After Fidel Castro terminated an airlift to the United States for Cubans who wished to leave his Communist state, he opened the port of Mariel on the north coast of Cuba to anyone who wished to leave by boat. The boatlift, or freedom flotilla as it was sometimes called, soon brought 125,000 exiles to Florida. Despite the efforts of the U.S. Coast Guard to intercept them and to turn them back, they kept on coming until Castro once again denied them exit visas. Almost all of them landed at Key West, less than two miles from St. Mary's Church.

This sudden inundation of people was complicated by the fact that many public agencies were slow to lend any assistance to their plight. This event did not have any direct impact on St. Mary's parish, but it had great impact on south Florida and on the archdiocese of Miami. Most new arrivals were eventually bussed to Miami to be processed by the Immigration Service. However, a large number had to be temporarily billeted and fed at Key West. Many were placed in a hangar at the Naval Air Station. On May 7, 1980, Archbishop Edward McCarthy of Miami visited the hangar and, from an altar erected on an army cot, said Mass for over four thousand people who were housed in the building. In a public statement made later that day, he stated: "This is America. We have a tradition of welcoming refugees. To turn them away is to turn the Gospel away. This is the Kingdom of God, helping the hungry, the needy. The refugee problem affects not only the south Florida area but the whole United States. This is a national responsibility. The entire nation should take its share."

About half of the Cuban refugees had relatives in Miami and could be placed in their care and custody. The other half were taken to resettlement centers as far away as Arkansas, Alabama, and Pennsylvania. Some stayed in these centers for more than a year. Several church groups assisted in the resettlement effort, but the bulk of the responsibility fell to the Catholic Charities for the archdiocese of Miami and the U.S. Catholic Conference. Castro continually referred to the refugees as "antisocial elements" and tried to lend credence to his description by allowing inmates from Cuban prisons and insane asylums to leave his island on the boatlift. However, a detailed study of the immigrants established clearly that most of them had skills, trades, and professions that equipped them to make a living both in Cuba and in the United States.

Until 1958, St. Mary's was the only parish on the Keys. Today, there are five. In 1960, a second parish, St. Bede, was established at Key West, but it was discontinued in 1985. Its parish buildings now house an AIDS hospice operated by the parish and a private organization that specializes in maintaining such facilities. In its first five years, the AIDS hospice has served more than two hundred patients.

Today, the parish population of St. Mary's is mixed. About twenty-five percent are retirees, most of whom are comparative newcomers, and there are military families as well. The rest are longtime residents who have made their livelihood on the island for many years. About fifteen percent of the parish is black, and another significant percentage have Cuban antecedents. Many black and Cuban parishioners are descendants of original settlers of Key West; some Cuban parishioners arrived in 1960 when Castro assumed power ninety miles away. The parish formerly had a Spanish Mass each weekend, but now it has become a bilingual Spanish-English Mass. Most Cuban parishioners are sufficiently acculturated that they can attend English services without difficulty. The high school was closed in 1985 because of financial difficulties. The parish sold the land on which it was located and invested one million dollars from the sale into a trust fund for the benefit of the grammar school. The latter now has one hundred eighty-five students and has derived great benefit from the concentration of available funds on primary education.

45
Immaculate Conception Cathedral

Mobile

ALABAMA

A sharp distinction between Florida and southern Alabama did not exist until after Spain ceded Florida to the United States in 1819. While Mobile and Pensacola are today in different states and different dioceses, during the first two hundred years or more of the development of the Gulf Coast area, the entire territory that included these cities was known as West Florida and was included in one diocese — first Quebec, then Santiago, Cuba. It extended from the Apalachicola River in Florida to the Mississippi. During the Spanish period, its capital was Pensacola.

The first Catholics to attempt a settlement in this area came in 1559 when Don Tristán de Luna, with an army of five hundred men and one thousand colonists, landed on August 14 at what is now known as Santa Rosa Island at the mouth of Pensacola Bay. Upon their arrival, the colonists knelt in the sand to say a rosary of thanksgiving for their safe arrival. On the following day, the Feast of the Assumption, Dominican priests who accompanied the expedition offered the first Mass to be said in western Florida on a seashore that has now become a tourist and vacation resort. A plain white cross has been placed by the Knights of Columbus to mark the spot where this occurred.

The Spanish erected a small wooden chapel that

they dedicated to St. Michael, the Archangel, the same name used today by Pensacola's oldest parish. Within two years, the expedition was recalled. Dissension had broken out among the settlers; they had great difficulty in making a livelihood from the surrounding territory and they had failed to find the gold they were seeking when the expedition was formed. The Spanish left and did not return for nearly a century and a half.

In 1698, another expedition under Admiral Andrés de Arriola arrived at Pensacola Bay and established what proved to be a permanent settlement. They called it St. Michael's mission and constructed a small church with the same name.

In the same year, Pierre Le Moyne D'Aberville and his brother, Jean Le Moyne de Bienville (the latter is the founder of New Orleans), came to Pensacola in hopes of making a French settlement. Finding the Spanish in place, they went westward instead to Mobile Bay and established a French village about twenty-five miles upriver from the coastline. Bienville built a small church to serve the settlement and put Jesuit Father Paul du Rhu in charge.

In 1703, the bishop of Quebec, who exercised church jurisdiction over all French territory in North America, canonically erected a parish at this location. In place of a Jesuit missionary, he appointed a diocesan priest from the Seminary of Foreign Missions in Quebec, Father Henri Roulleaux de la Vente, to be the first pastor. The foundation of Immaculate Conception parish and entries in its parochial records date back to 1704, although the church did not acquire its present name until later.

In 1711, Mobile was moved downriver to the location near the coast the city occupies today. In that year, a new church was constructed and French Capuchins were placed in charge. For a while the French at Mobile and the Spanish at Pensacola coexisted amicably. However, as an offshoot of one of the many European wars in which these nations were then engaging, the French captured Pensacola in 1718 and then relinquished it to the Spanish four years later under the terms of a peace treaty concluded in Europe. Before they left, the French burned the entire village, including the church dedicated to St. Michael. The Spanish later constructed an octagonal church at Santa Rosa Island, not far from where Tristán de Luna and his party had landed in 1559. This church was destroyed by a hurricane in 1752; so, in 1757, a third Pensacola church was built on the mainland near where the Pensacola City Hall now stands.

Mobile began to grow as a French town. The Catholic church, which was originally built in 1711, was rebuilt in 1741 and named in honor of Our Lady of Mobile. In addition to serving as a parish church for Mobile, it was also the headquarters for Jesuits and other missionaries who went inland from Mobile to evangelize the Indians. The British took control of West Florida in 1763 by virtue of the Treaty of Paris, an agreement that ended Spanish political control along the eastern Gulf of Mexico and French control everywhere in North America. When this occurred, some seven hundred seventy-five Spanish and Yemassee Indians living in Pensacola simply packed up and went to Cuba, as the Spanish settlers at St. Augustine had done. This left St. Michael's Chapel without a congregation to serve so it closed. The French in Mobile remained. They asked British authorities to be allowed to continue to practice their religion, and the British consented, imposing only one restriction. No public religious processions, except for funerals, were allowed. After the French left, Capuchin Father John Francis and Augustinian Father Ferdinand ministered to the Mobile parish until 1769. During the ensuing ten years, Father Paul, a Spanish Capuchin from New Orleans, visited Mobile from time to time to attend the French Catholics living there under British rule.

In 1780, the Spanish regained control of Mobile and retained it until the territory was ceded to the United States forty years later. Don José Espeleta, commander of the Spanish garrison, directed that the local church be called La Iglesia de Purísima Concepción. It has borne this title, either in Spanish or in English, since that date. Regular Catholic worship was restored under a Mercedarian priest, Father Salvador de la Esperanza, and parish records, previously kept in French, began to be kept in Spanish. The church building itself had suffered serious deterioration and was restored by the Spanish Army. In the next few years, a rapid succession of priests, both Capuchins and Dominicans, served the new Immaculate Conception Church under the supervision of the bishop of Santiago, Cuba, whose diocese included Mobile. At Pensacola, the commander of the Spanish garrison restored Catholic worship by placing the chaplain of the Spanish troops in charge of the local parish church. However, the only place available for public worship was a converted warehouse near the port. It served as St. Michael's Church until well into the nineteenth century. As a concession to the English-speaking communities that existed in both cities, the king of Spain sent English-speaking priests to the area, three to Pensacola and two to Mobile. Most were Irish and graduates of the Royal Irish College in Salamanca.

In 1791, the old Mobile church was abandoned and a new one built at Royal and Conti Streets. It stood at this location until it burned down in 1827, just after the first American bishop arrived to take charge of a new vicariate. In 1791, both Pensacola and Mobile were visited by the auxiliary bishop of the Cuban diocese. At that time, about six hundred people lived in Pensacola and a slightly larger number resided in Mobile. A majority in both cities, both black and white, were Catholics.

In 1795, all of West Florida was placed by the Holy See in a new diocese consisting of Louisiana and the Floridas, which had its headquarters at New Orleans. The Spanish bishop in charge of that diocese was transferred to Guatemala in 1801, just as Spain and France were getting ready to relinquish possession of these areas. For the next twenty years the Church in Louisiana was without a bishop. In the early 1800s in West Florida, the bishop of Santiago appointed Father James Coleman, a Spanish-trained Irish priest, to serve as vicar. He was in charge of the Church in the Mobile-Pensacola area until after this territory came under military control of the United States in 1813. After the Spanish vacated the area, Immaculate Conception Church received no further government aid, so its parishioners were forced to support it from private donations.

Following the annexation of East and West Florida to the United States, the Holy See first decided that Mississippi and Alabama should all become part of a new vicariate under the supervision of Bishop Joseph Rosati in St. Louis. Bishop Rosati declined the assignment. At that time, churches existed only in Natchez, Mobile, Pensacola, and St. Augustine. The plan was criticized, especially by Archbishop Ambrose Marèchal in Baltimore, in whose diocese most of these territories were located. Eventually, only Alabama and Florida were placed in the same church jurisdiction. It included only three Catholic parishes at the time it was created in 1823. All of them were located in coastal cities. No Catholic churches existed inland to serve the newcomers who were flocking into this region from the east.

The Holy See appointed Father Michael Portier, a French-born priest of the New Orleans diocese, to be the first bishop of the new vicariate. Later, it designated Mobile as the principal city of this new see when the vicariate became a diocese because Mobile had grown larger than Pensacola and gave promise of growing even more as its port facilities expanded. Illustrative of the problems generated by distance and poor communications, the preparation of the papal brief making the appointment of Bishop Portier was delayed several months because church officials in Rome had trouble finding out his first name. When the document finally arrived in New Orleans, a familiar scenario took place. Father Portier did not want the assignment. At the suggestion of his own bishop in New Orleans, he sent the brief back to Rome. Pope Leo XII forwarded it to New Orleans a second time, commanding Father Portier to accept under holy obedience. He complied and was ordained a bishop in the St. Louis Cathedral in 1826. His new vicariate contained six thousand Catholics who were spread over all of Alabama and Florida. It had three churches and two priests, both of whom belonged to the diocese of New Orleans and who eventually left him.

While these changes were taking place at the hierarchial level, the congregation at Immaculate Conception Church, now deprived of royal patronage, took advantage of a new Alabama territorial law relating to the organization of churches by drawing up articles of government and a constitution for the parish. The document established a five-member board of trustees, one of whom would be the pastor serving *ex officio*. The lay trustees were to be elected annually. They had difficulty in filling the position of pastor. The trustees had voted the pastor an annual salary of $800, but there was rarely enough money on hand to pay him more than $200.

The church building itself was in a state of disrepair. One visitor to Mobile wrote that it resembled a barn. He also reported that its sacred altar vessels were made of tin. (Mobile Archbishop Oscar Lipscomb, in his dissertation on Bishop Portier, disputes the latter assertion.) The parish rectory had been sold at public auction in 1807, and a lawsuit to recover it from the purchaser ultimately failed. The only asset owned by the parish that had any value was a plot of land, some three hundred feet by four hundred feet, located on Dauphin Street. Since 1790, it had been used as a cemetery. The land eventually became the site of the cathedral **[pictured above]**.

In 1827, shortly after his arrival in Mobile, Bishop Portier entered into a strange contract with the trustees. They leased to the bishop the cemetery property for a fee of

$250 a year on condition that he build a church at that site. The lease further provided that the trustees could repossess the land and the church if the bishop fell behind in the rent more than sixty days. No one ever attempted to repossess the Immaculate Conception Cathedral, but it was not until 1940 that a suit in equity was filed by the bishop of Mobile to preclude any title disputes to the premises.

During his first year in Mobile, Bishop Portier wrote to his friend Bishop Joseph Rosati in St. Louis that "if Catholics [in Mobile] were counted by their number, [there would be] 2,000 faithful, a very bad church, some considerable properties, a people buried in speculations, a pastor who is a good preacher but as inconstant as a weather vane, and an almost incurable base of indifference." Pensacola presented a somewhat brighter picture. In that city, about fifteen hundred Catholics had been worshiping in a converted warehouse for about forty years. However, Bishop Portier felt that Pensacola had a more Christian population and a better pastor than Mobile. Pensacola was beset with haphazard public administration, was extremely hot in the summer, and suffered repeatedly from yellow-fever epidemics. Bishop Portier decided to live temporarily in Pensacola and was asked by local officials to stay on permanently. However, since Pensacola was a smaller town than Mobile, he eventually moved back to Alabama.

Bishop Portier's decision to reside for a while in Pensacola was also prompted by the fact that on October 20, 1827, a fire destroyed nine blocks in the central part of Mobile. It consumed two hundred twenty buildings and inflicted an estimated two million dollars in damage. Immaculate Conception Church, located close to the hotel where the fire began, was totally destroyed. Its pastor said Mass in a private home for the next month but then sent word to Bishop Portier that his situation had become impossible so he was returning to New Orleans, the diocese to which he actually belonged. His departure left Mobile without a resident priest and with no church. For more than six months Bishop Portier was the only priest in his entire vicariate, so he had to shuttle back and forth from Pensacola to Mobile to attend to the Catholic congregations in both cities.

To replace the demolished church, Bishop Portier hastily constructed a wooden shed, twenty feet by thirty feet, next to the old graveyard, which at that time was still outside the city limits. It was adorned only with six candlesticks and a picture of the Blessed Virgin. He referred to it as a "poor barn." There was always the possibility that it would blow away in a heavy wind. During a rainstorm, it was impossible to say Mass inside. Later, the building was lengthened some twenty feet. It served as the cathedral church for the diocese of Mobile until 1836.

Bishop Portier supervised a vicariate of 108,000 square miles, an area larger than the entire Italian peninsula. He was able to impress this fact upon church officials in Rome when he made requests for funds and personnel. Of his immense responsibility he once wrote that "of all the pains of the ministry, the greatest, the most bitter, is to see the good and not be able to perform it." To visit the territory assigned to him, he set out in 1827 to travel across the swamps and the piney woods of north Florida to St. Augustine at the other end of his vicariate. St. Augustine had the only other church under his supervision.

In describing the trip, he wrote: "I was obliged to spend the night in a swamp next to a large bayou, with only foul water to drink, among all the beasts and all the insects of creation. I could see, ten feet away from me, crocodiles playing in the river, and I knew from reports that bears, panthers, and wolves abounded in these parts. I had luggers, rattlesnakes, and moccasins to fear; mosquitoes had already announced a disagreeable visit. Add to this accumulation of human miseries the fact that I had not eaten but two corn biscuits in twenty four hours; that, though my clothes were wet, I did not have the strength to change them, and that my horse, badly off as I, might be ruined by this hard ordeal. How was I to sleep in this awful haunt? The muffled growling of the crocodiles, the sharp cries that filled the forest, to which darkness and solitude added something sinister; a huge fish which sprung from the water, then fell back with the whole length of his enormous body; this was enough to cause fear. The crocodiles never left my mind. . . . I admit my fears with frankness, but I must also add, in truth, that they were shortlived, and that I soon recovered my heart as a bishop. Remembering that Jesus Christ assured us that not one hair of our head would fall without permission, I gathered my cloak around me, placed my saddle for a pillow, and stretched out on the ground to await daylight."

The experience was made more harrowing by virtue of the fact that Bishop Portier caught a fever in St. Augustine and, for a while, was afraid he might die unattended by another priest. As a result of this illness, he always tried to send priests on the mission in pairs so they would not be placed in the position of facing death without someone available to administer the last sacraments. Mission work was high on his list of priorities. He once stated that the way to plant Catholicism in the South was "to be campaigning always in the field."

Like many other bishops, especially those of French ancestry, Bishop Portier turned frequently to the Society for the Propagation of the Faith in Lyons, France, for financial assistance. In 1829, he made a trip to France and to Rome to recruit priests and to obtain funds for his vicariate. During the trip, he obtained money from the society and asked the Holy See for $23,000 to be used for the education and transportation of eight priests from Europe. He received most of his request, which was destined also for a rectory at Mobile, repairs to the church at Pensacola, and for building a seminary and a cathedral at Mobile. He enlisted priests at Lyons and at Montauban and while in Rome was able to bring about the reclassification of his vicariate to the status of a full-fledged diocese.

After returning to Mobile in 1830, Bishop Portier bought a small house to be used as a rectory. There he personally taught catechism, performed baptisms, and heard confessions. He devoted the limited assets of the diocese into education. At first, he rented a hotel large enough to accommodate thirty students and opened a boys' school of general studies. It was attended by Protestants as well as Catholics and was a welcome addition in a city that had few educational facilities. His ultimate goal was establishing a college of general studies that would also graduate the priests he needed to administer his diocese. In 1833, he invited the Visitation nuns from Georgetown in the District of

Columbia to come to Mobile to start an academy for girls and assisted them financially in setting it up. He then bought a house and twenty-seven acres of land for a seminary. The dwelling was large enough to house himself, one other priest, and six seminarians. To clear the land and make improvements, the bishop put the seminarians to work doing physical labor and assisted them with his own efforts. One priest wrote that "our good bishop, with axe in hand, was always in the lead."

Bishop Portier acquired six hundred acres about seven miles from the city. It was located on the highest point in the area, a place where people would be relatively free from mosquitoes and the dreaded yellow fever that devastated Mobile on repeated occasions. On this point he constructed a college known today as Spring Hill. Opening its doors in 1830 to fifty lay students and twenty seminarians, the school grew rapidly. Bishop Portier taught some classes of seminarians and, in 1835, he conducted the first diocesan synod at the college. This meeting addressed such questions as proper attire for priests, the hearing of confessions of women in circumstances that would ensure privacy but prevent the giving of scandal, the proper ceremony to be used for adult baptisms, and the keeping of parish records. These were questions that were then of concern to the bishop and the diocese and were made part of the diocesan statutes that resulted from the meeting. The school chapel served as the site for other synods as the years went by.

Until 1847, Bishop Portier experienced great difficulty in staffing the college. He obtained the services of the Eudist Fathers for a short while, but they left. The Fathers of Mercy took over the college, but they too did not remain long. Ultimately, he was able to induce Jesuits from a French province to come to Mobile to take charge. They did so and have been at St. Joseph's College, now called Spring Hill, since that time, operating the oldest educational institution of higher learning in the South.

In 1835, the cornerstone was laid for the cathedral church [**pictured above**]. Fifteen years elapsed before the dedication could take place. The Mobile cathedral resembles, on a larger scale, the old St. Louis Cathedral on the banks of the Mississippi next to the Gateway Arch. The diocese was fortunate in obtaining the services of Claude Beroujon, an ex-seminarian from France. He assisted in the design of the cathedral and supervised its construction. He was also the architect who designed buildings at Spring Hill and a convent for the Visitation Sisters. As soon as the cornerstone of the permanent cathedral was laid, the temporary wooden church built just after the 1827 fire was demolished and immediately replaced by a brick structure on Conti Street. It served as the second Mobile cathedral for about fifteen years and eventually came to be used by the Daughters of Charity as an orphan asylum.

Immaculate Conception Cathedral was the focal point for mission efforts in the Mobile area. Priests were regularly sent from the church to Bayou La Batre, an old French fishing village about thirty-five miles south of the city on Mobile Bay, to Blakely, and to other outlying communities. Priests were also sent from Mobile east into Florida and north into all parts of Alabama. By the 1840s, permanent churches had been established at Montgomery and Tuscaloosa in Alabama and at Apalachicola and Tallahassee in Florida. Mission priests from Mobile went as far as Huntsville in northern Alabama, but they reached this area only on rare occasions. The few Catholics who resided in northern Alabama were sometimes visited by priests from Tennessee sent by Bishop Richard P. Miles in Nashville.

While Mobile began its existence as a largely Catholic community, it did not remain so. Today, the population of the city is only about fifteen percent Catholic while the remainder of Alabama is about three percent Catholic. A few Irish and German immigrants came to Mobile before the Civil War, but their numbers were nothing compared to the immigration occurring in Northern cities. It was from this source that the Church in America grew during the antebellum era.

The factor that more than anything else discouraged foreign immigration into the South was the institution of slavery. It depressed wage scales so drastically that newcomers could barely survive on what they were able to earn as laborers and craftsmen. However, Alabama experienced great immigration by Protestant Americans and became a predominantly Methodist and Baptist state. In 1845, Bishop Portier wrote to the Society for the Propagation of the Faith that the Catholic population of his diocese was being "absorbed by the immense population that presses it on all sides."

Anti-Catholic sentiment broke out from time to time. Occasionally, Irish voters were assaulted when they went to the polls. Bishop Portier himself experienced a few confrontations with zealots. However, he was disposed to write to the Holy See that, despite occasional incidents, "the actual state of Protestantism is very favorable to the growth of our Holy Religion. They are no longer animated with that spirit of bitterness which made them look upon Catholics with horror. They are beginning to respect them and have the highest regard for priests. Prejudices remain as always, but are no longer deep rooted as in the past. They need only to see the light to follow it."

One instance where antebellum prejudice did arise was in 1854. The Daughters of Charity were operating a municipal hospital at the request of the city council. Anti-Catholic and anti-immigrant Know-Nothing sentiment, then on the rise throughout the United States, influenced the council to remove the nuns from control of the hospital. Upon being expelled, the Sisters opened their own hospital, which they called the Providence Infirmary. Just before the outbreak of the Civil War, they were invited to come back and once again took charge of the municipal facility.

Work on the new cathedral was slowed by economic considerations. Construction proceeded on a pay-as-you-go basis and once came to a standstill when the walls had reached a height of nine feet because there was no money available to continue. Meanwhile, three Masses were being said each Sunday before capacity crowds in a commercial building on Conti Street that later became a parish hall and then an orphanage. To complete the cathedral, the Society for the Propagation of the Faith contributed 1,000 French francs ($2,000). This was only a small part of the $50,000 the society sent to Mobile for the work of the diocese during the 1840s. A number of Protestants were among the donors who assisted in completing the building. A crowd of twenty-five hundred persons attended the dedication, which took place on the Feast of the Immaculate Conception in 1850.

The cathedral sits on a hardpan of red clay. It was built, in large part, with locally manufactured brick and with granite. It is 60 feet high, 164 feet long, and 88 feet wide in the front, with its 12 windows measuring 7.5 feet by 23 feet. All but the front walls are ten feet thick at ground level. The walls that support the steeples and the pillars on the portico are eleven feet thick. Plainly, this cathedral was built to last but it was not completed at the time of its dedication. Its only interior adornment was the marble altar. It took another thirty years to finish the steeples and to enlarge the portico. During the era in which the cathedral was being dedicated, two other churches, St. Francis de Sales and St. Vincent de Paul, were also built in order to accommodate a Catholic population that had grown to about five thousand.

Bishop Portier died in 1859 and became the first of five bishops to be buried in the crypt beneath the altar. At the time of his death, the cathedral parish was staffed by three priests. There were about sixteen Jesuits, most of them French, at Spring Hill who performed pastoral duties in addition to their teaching assignments. The city also had about forty nuns, mostly Visitandines and Daughters of Charity. By the time the Civil War began, the Church had become well established in Mobile.

When he arrived in Mobile on December 11, 1859, Bishop John Quinlan, the second bishop of Mobile, was welcomed with a large parade that escorted him to the bishop's residence on Conti Street. He took possession of his cathedral, still not entirely finished, and spoke of it as being "chaste and elegant." Not long thereafter, the outbreak of the Civil War forced a suspension of further improvements, although the bishop established a building society to solicit contributions to complete the work. The most that he could do immediately was to build a fence to surround the building. In contrast to his predecessor, Bishop Quinlan was Irish, not French. Most of his congregation was one or the other. There was occasionally some friction between the two groups but nothing of any great consequence. Like his predecessor, he immediately went to Europe to recruit priests. Instead of going to France, he went to All Hallows Seminary near Dublin and to a seminary at Queenstown (Cobh) in County Cork. He was successful in this effort and was also able to recruit a few priests from France.

War broke out shortly after he returned, and Alabama seceded from the Union. Most Catholics in the Mobile diocese sided with the Confederacy and so did their bishop. In a pastoral letter circulated in 1861, Bishop Quinlan stated: "While regretting the dismemberment of this great republic — and heaven knows we would do all we legitimately could to prevent it — we would not purchase union at the expense of justice." In a ceremony held at the cathedral in the summer of 1861, Bishop Quinlan blessed the flag of the Emerald Guard — Company One of the 8th Alabama Regiment — before it went off to war. Some one hundred four of its one hundred nine members were born in Ireland.

In September of the following year, he offered a requiem Mass at the cathedral for the Confederate troops who had fallen in the defense of New Orleans. At another service conducted at the Sisters' chapel in the Visitation Convent, he sang a "Te Deum" in thanksgiving for a Confederate naval victory. During the war, when Jefferson Davis proclaimed various days of fasting and prayer, Bishop Quinlan urged Catholics to keep them rigorously.

Three Jesuits from Spring Hill and several diocesan priests entered the Confederate Army as chaplains. Other priests followed Confederate troops from place to place without having any formal military status and were able to minister to Catholics in gray in this fashion. After the Confederate defeat at Shiloh in Tennessee in the spring of 1862, Bishop Quinlan went himself to the army camp south of Shiloh to attend sick and wounded soldiers and comfort the bereaved.

A priest in military service during the Civil War faced certain problems imposed by canon law. At that time, a priest could not function in any diocese other than his own without specific permission of the bishop in the locality he was visiting. Traveling with a military unit from place to place also meant moving rapidly from one diocese to another. Today, Catholics in military or naval service are part of one worldwide diocese, so the necessity of obtaining faculties — permission to say Mass and hear confessions — from local bishops presents no problem. This arrangement did not exist in the United States in the 1860s.

During the Civil War, the Holy See issued to Archbishop John Odin in New Orleans special faculties so he could extend to Confederate chaplains in the field permission to travel with troops from place to place without obtaining special local faculties until the priest had been in a particular area for two months. These faculties also allowed chaplains to dispense soldiers from church regulations governing fasts and abstinence and to impart plenary indulgences in battle to those who had been unable to go to confession or receive extreme unction.

Bishop Quinlan was sometimes hampered in traveling from Mobile to parts of his diocese by military movements and federal occupation. Pensacola had been occupied by federal troops early in the war. To reach this city Bishop Quinlan had to pass through federal lines. To obtain a pass from the federal commander at Pensacola, he had to swear an oath of allegiance to the United States. He steadfastly refused to do so and was prevented on that account from going to Pensacola for an extended period. On one occasion, while traveling in Mississippi, his own Confederate passport was not in order, so he was arrested by a Confederate captain and locked in a makeshift jail overnight while his identity was being verified.

Before the federal occupation of Pensacola had been completed, Union troops occupied Santa Rosa Island at the mouth of Pensacola Bay opposite the village of Warrington. The Daughters of Charity in Mobile were asked by Confederate General Braxton Bragg to come to Warrington to operate a military hospital. They did so and ministered to eight hundred patients within two miles of actual fighting. The hospital itself was little more than a shed; many patients were left to lie in the open and often succumbed to yellow fever and other diseases while being treated for battle wounds. From time to time, the hospital was fired upon by federal guns at Santa Rosa Island. A few nuns were also assigned to St. Mary's Hospital in Montgomery, Alabama, where more Confederate wounded were being treated. At first, the surgeon in charge refused to permit the nuns to enter the hospital, saying that he did not want any Catholics around. However, he was soon overruled. Soldiers occasionally regarded the nuns with fear or embarrassment and would turn their backs or cover their heads when the Sisters entered the room. Their attitude changed dramatically as they came to experience the care and attention the nuns provided.

While Pensacola was occupied by Union troops, Mobile was under Confederate control throughout the Civil War. In August of 1864, Admiral David Farragut "damned the torpedoes and sailed full speed ahead" into Mobile Bay but he preferred to wait for infantry support before entering the city itself. The fall of Mobile itself did not come until April 1865, just as the war was ending, so Immaculate Conception Cathedral and other churches in the city were spared the depredations that befell many churches located in combat zones. To guard against seizure or confiscation, the French Jesuits who owned and operated St. Joseph's Church in Mobile had placed their property under the special protection of the French consul at Mobile and even flew the French flag as a sign of their neutrality in the North-South conflict. The precaution proved to be unnecessary. However, churches in other places were not so fortunate. At Warrington, near Pensacola, St. John's Church was first used by federal troops as a stable and then was burned down. At Selma, marauding soldiers vandalized the Catholic church and robbed its pastor.

During federal military occupation, the Union Army used as its headquarters the old mansion that now serves as the rectory for the Immaculate Conception Cathedral. Within six weeks after the end of hostilities, an enormous explosion took place at a warehouse in downtown Mobile where two hundred tons of explosives were being stored. The explosion damaged most of the central city and blew the windows out of the cathedral some fourteen blocks away. About two hundred fifty people were injured and were treated by the Daughters of Charity at their infirmary.

During Reconstruction, cotton was no longer king in Alabama, and widespread poverty took its place. Like many Southern bishops, Bishop Quinlan made a fund-raising tour of Northern cities to obtain money to restore the damaged churches of his diocese. He also revived the cathedral-building society. He took great pride in the fact that he was able to finish the portico in front of the church and to erect the mammoth pillars that are its dominant feature. The front of the building was constructed to resemble the Church of the Madeleine in Paris. The overall cost of the cathedral has been placed at $88,000. Today, it is insured for six million dollars. It was Bishop Quinlan's desire to be buried beneath the portico he completed rather than in the crypt beneath the altar. His gravestone can be seen near the front door by anyone entering or leaving the church.

After Alabama reentered the Union in 1868, Bishop Quinlan avoided any confrontations with federal authorities. The Episcopal bishop in Alabama had run afoul of the local military commander by removing from the order of worship at his church certain prayers for the president of the United States. He was actually suspended by the commander from his ministry until these prayers were restored. No such problem arose with the Catholic bishop. The efforts of the Mobile diocese turned to its own reconstruction. Shortly after the end of the Civil War, another church, St. Patrick's, was built in downtown Mobile to accommodate the increasing number of Irish immigrants. It eventually became a defunct parish as the residents of the center city moved to the suburbs. In 1871, a huge parade was staged in Mobile to celebrate the twenty-fifth anniversary of the pontificate of Pope Pius IX. Some five thousand participants, coming from the seven parishes in the Mobile area, formed at the cathedral, marched through the streets, and returned for benediction and the singing of a "Te Deum." The Mobile *Register* commented that "the whole affair was the finest Mobile has ever seen and reflects the highest praise on the zeal and piety of our Catholic fellow citizens." The paper noted that Pope Pius IX was the only foreign prince or potentate that had offered the Confederate government and its president "the respectful consideration to which they were entitled."

On February 4, 1869, Catholics in Mobile and in the South suffered a blow when Spring Hill College burned to the ground. The loss amounted to $300,000, and there was only $30,000 in insurance to cover it. The school was temporarily relocated to a Jesuit establishment at Grand Couteau, Louisiana, while the rebuilding effort began. The school was reopened in the fall of the year on a reduced scale while the Jesuits continued the slow and expensive process of constructing the campus anew.

During the postwar era, a number of notable clergymen served at the cathedral. One of them was Father Abram J. Ryan, the so-called poet-priest of the Confederacy. Father Ryan, a native of Maryland, originally joined the Vincentians. He did not remain long in that congregation but continued to serve as a priest at various places throughout the South. He was a Confederate Army chaplain during the war. Afterward, he wrote widely for newspapers and other periodicals and published several volumes of poetry, including "The Sword of Robert E. Lee" and "The Conquered Banner." In 1877, he was transferred to St. Mary's parish in Mobile. The latter part of his life was devoted not to parish work but to speaking and giving retreats.

In the early 1870s, Father Anthony D. Pellicer was the rector of the cathedral. He was the grandson of Andrew Pellicer, the man who led a band of six hundred starving Minorcans from New Smyrna to a new home at St. Augustine during the British era in Florida. In 1874, Father Pellicer and his first cousin were consecrated bishops at the cathedral. He then left Mobile to serve as bishop of Galveston.

By 1880, there were 20 churches and chapels in the entire Mobile diocese; among the clergy there were 15 diocesan priests, 16 Jesuits, and four Benedictines. One third of them were native-born. The year 1887 produced a small milestone in the history of the parish. Father James P. McCaffrey, the first native of the parish to become a priest, was ordained at the cathedral. By this time, several Catholic schools were functioning in Mobile. The Holy Cross Sisters and the Sisters of Mercy conducted schools for girls, and the Sacred Heart Brothers operated a school for boys. However, out of 1.2 million inhabitants of Alabama, there were only eighteen thousand Catholics. Most lived in or about Mobile.

The bell towers atop the cathedral were added in the 1890s. The stained-glass windows, which were manufactured in Germany, were installed in 1910. The windows all portray Marian themes. The interior of the church is replete with polished marble and carved wood and features a burnished bronze baldachin that covers the altar.

A more recent improvement has been made in order to enhance the setting in which the church is located. The property in front of the church has belonged to the diocese and its predecessors since French and Spanish colonial days. Over the years, a number of small commercial buildings were erected that provided the church with some rental income. When they deteriorated, Bishop John L. May had them removed and donated the land to the city as a park. The result is a large open plaza that has greatly improved the setting in which the cathedral is located.

In 1954, the interior of the church was gutted by a fire set in the basement by a drunk who was trying to warm himself. Extensive damage was done, including injury to panels of stained-glass windows. Fortunately, the original designs from which the windows had been manufactured were still in existence, so replacement windows were obtained that are identical to the original ones. In 1962, the Vatican designated the cathedral as a minor basilica. When Mobile became an archdiocese in 1980, the cathedral achieved the status of being not only the principal church in a jurisdiction of twenty-eight Alabama counties but the principal church for an ecclesiastical province that includes all of Mississippi and Alabama.

Today, the cathedral is an intown parish that has only about one hundred registered parishioners, most of whom are senior citizens. However, its five weekend Masses attract about one thousand worshipers and its daily Mass is well attended. In conjunction with the U.S. Department of Housing and Urban Development, the archdiocese built and operates Cathedral Place, a building near the church containing one hundred ninety-two apartments for the elderly, of whom only a few are Catholics. Downtown Mobile long ago ceased to have substantial numbers of residents with small children, so the schools operated by the cathedral parish closed in the 1950s and the buildings eventually removed.

Immaculate Conception has all of the liturgies normally performed at a cathedral, including ordinations and the chrism Mass on Holy Thursday. To assist in all of its liturgies, it maintains a choir that is enlarged when it performs at concerts or liturgical events. It is also the site of two public concerts each year. Since it is one of the principal historic sites in Mobile, it is regularly visited by a large number of tourists, many of whom attend one of its Sunday Masses. It calls itself the mother church of all Catholic churches in the Gulf Coast, and its 290-year history fully justifies the claim.

46
St. Patrick

Cleveland

OHIO

The first Catholic church in Cleveland was called Our Lady of the Lake. Built in an area called "The Flats," near where the Cuyahoga River empties into Lake Erie, it was erected to serve both English- and German-speaking Catholics and was dedicated by Bishop John Purcell of Cincinnati on his way home from a conference of bishops in the East. At that time, Catholics in northern Ohio were served by a variety of missionaries who rode circuit on horseback to a number of communities such as Sandusky, Doylestown, Elyria, New Riegel, and Glendale to say Mass and administer the sacraments. The area was then a remote part of the Cincinnati diocese.

St. Patrick's parish in West Park was founded the year after the Cleveland diocese was established. It is one of the two oldest Catholic churches in Cleveland. It was established in response to a request made to the new bishop, Louis Amadeus Rappe, by about forty Irish settlers living in what was then called Rockport, an area located along the Rocky River a few miles south of Lake Erie. West Park is now within the Cleveland city limits. The first Mass in this parish was said on St. Patrick's Day, 1848, at the home of an early settler, Morgan Watters.

A wooden frame church was erected in 1852 on the site where the present church is located. In that year, the newly formed Cleveland diocese reported to the First Plenary Council of the American Church in Baltimore that it had 55 churches that were either built or were under construction and that it included 42 priests serving an estimated 30,000 Catholics in northern Ohio.

Once a country crossroad, the location of St. Patrick's Church is now a busy corner intersected by two arterial roads. The small country cemetery next to the church building stands out in sharp contrast to its present crowded suburban setting and is immediately across Puritas Avenue from a shopping center parking lot.

The first priests at St. Patrick's were missionaries who traveled from church to church on horseback and used this church as their way station. Later, St. Patrick's became a point of origin for priests dispatched to other mission sites in Cuyahoga County. In 1875, the first school building was erected behind the wooden frame church. It was a two-story wooden building, the top floor of which was used as a convent by the Notre Dame Sisters who were brought in to teach at the school.

Its first permanent resident pastor was assigned in 1892. Shortly thereafter, a newer and larger church building [**pictured above**] was constructed. Built from stone quarried at nearby Berea, Ohio, it was dedicated in 1898. In 1953, in the midst of the post-World War II expansion of West Park, an extension to the rear of the church was completed. In 1930, the old four-room school building was replaced by a large school building, and another building, now used as a primary school, was added in 1960. At one time during the baby boom of the 1960s and 1970s, the school enrollment was nearly twelve hundred; it is down to about seven hundred now. Like many parochial schools, St. Patrick's is now staffed largely by laymen. However, three Irish nuns, members of the Incarnate Word Sisters, still supervise and teach there.

After leaving behind its agricultural beginning, West Park was, for many years, a sparsely settled suburb connected to downtown Cleveland by the New York Central Railroad, whose main line from Cleveland to Detroit ran through the area. After World War II, the area mushroomed into rows of small detached homes along dozens of neatly kept streets. It retains this character today. In many instances, these houses have served as starter homes for young families who moved to larger quarters. This sociological fact has, over the years, provided a steady stream of students for St. Patrick's School. West Park is a heavily Catholic area, but it is no longer predominantly Irish. Like most of northern Ohio, many of its residents can trace their ancestries to a variety of Eastern European countries. West Park is, for the most part, a blue-collar suburb of a large industrial city whose residents are employed in the mills and factories that still predominate the Cleveland economy. In recent years, its population has declined. Some neighborhoods adjacent to the nearby Cleveland-Hopkins Airport were demolished and converted into green space because their proximity to the expanded airport made these localities inappropriate for residential use.

At one time in the 1960s, St. Patrick's had over thirty-three hundred families on its parish rolls. The basement of the church was converted into a chapel seating seven hundred fifty people. Ten Masses took place each Sunday, three of which required the congregation to "double up," Mass upstairs being celebrated before seven hundred fifty while another Mass was taking place downstairs before an equal number. Church facilities are no longer taxed as stringently as they were during the baby-boomer years. The lower portion of the church is now given over to a variety of parish activities, and six Masses each weekend are sufficient to accommodate its three thousand members.

When the parish commemorated its 140th anniversary on St. Patrick's Day, 1988, former parishioners and priests from all parts of the Cleveland area who had been assigned to the parish returned to join current parishioners in a historic celebration. Like any large suburban parish, life at St. Patrick's is now characterized by a variety of activities of both a social and religious nature. A current resident of the rectory is a missionary priest from India who uses St. Patrick's as a base of operations for collecting funds to support Catholic missions in Patna. Instead of dispatching missionaries on horseback to Brook Park or Berea, St. Patrick's is now redirecting its missionary effort from the Rocky River to the banks of the Ganges some twelve thousand miles away.

47
St. Joseph

Somerset

OHIO

St. Joseph's Church, located about two miles southwest of Somerset, Ohio, was founded in 1818 and is the oldest Catholic parish in Ohio. There are indications that Catholic priests attended the spiritual needs of Ohio residents living at both ends of the state at earlier dates — as early as 1794 at Fort Recovery, near Toledo, and at Gallipolis, on the Ohio River. However, their visits were of short duration, and no permanent churches or chapels remain to mark their brief efforts. In the late 1790s and early 1800s, Father Stephen Badin spent a great deal of time in Ohio seeking out Catholic families who were scattered throughout the state. He was a missionary whose name often appears in this volume and in the annals of early Catholic history in the Northwest Territory.

The town of Somerset was founded in east central Ohio in 1805, just two years after Ohio achieved statehood. It is located on a national highway called the Lancaster-Zanesville Road, another of the early Midwestern turnpikes that promised to be major thoroughfares but whose development fell far short of expectations. In the late 1790s, Jacob Dittoe, an Alsatian who had lived near Frederick, Maryland, migrated to this area with his family and the families of his brother and his brother-in-law, Joseph Finck. In January of 1805, he wrote to Archbishop John Carroll in Baltimore asking that the archbishop apply for title to some preempted government land that was being offered for sale near Somerset. Dittoe informed the archbishop that he expected about thirty Catholic families to be migrating to the area from Conewago, the mission church in southern Pennsylvania that the Jesuits had established some fifty years earlier.

Apparently, the archbishop made a claim for the property but was unable to make any payments necessary to complete the purchase. Again, in 1808, Dittoe wrote Carroll, asking him for $480 to complete the purchase and warning that if the money were not forthcoming the land would be forfeited to the government. In a letter dated February 1, 1808, he also told the archbishop: "We will exert ourselves in making improvements on the land. If you have any prospect of sending a priest, we will have a good house for him to go in, with a tenant." He added that any priest assigned to the Somerset area would not be lonesome, inasmuch as the land envisioned for a church site was located only two miles from a national highway. Apparently, Dittoe bought the land himself, as title to a half section (three hundred twenty acres) was entered in his name and the names of Joseph and Anthony Dittoe and Joseph Finck in the records at the Chillicothe land office.

While the exact date is in dispute, in either 1808 or 1810, Somerset was visited by Father Edward D. Fenwick, a Dominican missionary from the newly formed priory of St. Rose of Lima at Springfield, Kentucky. Father Fenwick is often referred to as the founder of the Dominican order in the United States. He had come to Kentucky at the request of Archbishop Carroll and, in all probability, went on to Ohio at the archbishop's direction as well. According to tradition, Father Fenwick was traveling through this locality when he heard a sharp crackling noise made by a woodsman swinging an axe. As he approached the sound, he found Jacob Dittoe working in the woods near his log cabin. Father Fenwick was greeted by the Dittoes; the following day, he offered the first Mass ever said in central Ohio. He did not stay but continued his missionary journey into other parts of the state. Early missionary activity in Ohio differed somewhat from missionary work in eastern states. Catholics along the Atlantic Coast settled in particular spots that were generally known to church authorities; they could be reached by priests traveling regular routes to mission stops from a central location. Catholics migrating into Ohio came in small groups and were scattered all over a large area. Their whereabouts were often unknown, so missionary priests spent much of their time searching for them. Such was the task of Father Fenwick and other Dominicans in Ohio during the first decades of the nineteenth century. Ohio was a large wilderness, so the job of a priest was a particularly hard one. Father Fenwick once wrote: "It often happens that I am compelled to traverse vast and inhospitable forests wherein not a trace of road is to be seen. Not infrequently, overtaken by night in the midst of these, I am obliged to hitch my horse to a tree and, making a pillow of my saddle, recommend myself to God and go to sleep with bears on all sides."

In 1808, Bardstown, Kentucky, was designated as the seat of the first Midwestern diocese. Bishop Benedict Flaget was named its first bishop. However, it was more than two years before he was consecrated because he was quite reluctant to accept the appointment. In a letter written by Jacob Dittoe to Archbishop Carroll in 1810, Dittoe asked Carroll to be sure to tell Bishop Flaget about the small Catholic settlement near Somerset "which will be a place of rest and refreshment" for any clergyman who should come into the area. He went on to inform the archbishop: "There are some Catholics in this place that wish to join in marriage . . . that are waiting upon the head of his coming, as it is a point of some importance. And should he not come now, we will thank you to write us whether they will be allowed to be joined together by an Esquire who is a Roman Catholic. . . ."

It was sometime before Bishop Flaget reached Somerset. However, Father Fenwick resigned as prior at St. Rose so that he could devote all of his time and attention to missionary work in Ohio. He lived with the Dittoes from time to time and used their house as the starting point for travels that took him throughout the entire state.

Bishop Flaget visited Somerset in 1812 en route to a provincial council in Baltimore. During his visit, he urged Dittoe to build a chapel and a house for a priest on the land that had been acquired for church purposes, but he was unable at that time to provide them with a priest on a regular basis. Three years later, Bishop Flaget wrote to the Propagation of the Faith in Rome that there were about fifty Catholic families in Ohio and added: "I hear there are others but those who have migrated to Ohio have never seen a priest since leaving their former homes. Many have almost forgotten their religion and are bringing up their children in complete ignorance. . . . I can scarcely send a missionary to them even once a year."

In the fall of 1818, Bishop Flaget was finally able to establish a parish church near Somerset. He appointed Father Fenwick to be its first pastor. Dittoe transferred title to the property he had acquired for a church to "Fr. Fenwick of St. Thomas College, in Washington County, Kentucky, for the benefit of the Roman Catholic Church in Perry County, Ohio." On December 6, 1818, a log cabin, which measured twenty-two feet by eighteen feet and had openings in the walls for windows, was dedicated as a church under the title of St. Joseph. Nearby was a priest's house that had a kitchen, a living room, and two bedrooms. It became a Dominican convent, a term normally associated with residences of religious women but which technically applies to all religious houses, whether their inhabitants are male or female. Immediately adjacent to the church was a small area where hot coals could be kept burning in the winter so that parishioners could warm themselves on their way to and from Mass. It was necessary in cold weather to keep a brazier burning near the altar so that altar wine would not freeze.

St. Joseph's Church continued to be a mission center and was used as a base of missionary operations by Father Fenwick and by its second pastor, Father Nicholas Young, O.P. Father Young was Father Fenwick's nephew and had recently come to the Midwest following ordination. From Somerset both priests traveled to Lancaster, Zanesville, and elsewhere in central Ohio. As a result of the early efforts of these and other Dominican missionaries, many parishes that were founded in this area are Dominican parishes.

When Father Fenwick opened the parish registry on Christmas Eve, 1818, to record the first baptism, he noted that he had baptized one hundred sixty-two people in Ohio during 1817 and 1818 "whose names and sponsors cannot be recalled as I was then an itinerant missioner — and such persons were generally discovered and brought to me accidentally." Father Young later noted that he had baptized thirty people during a journey that he had made from Somerset back to Baltimore.

In 1821, Father Fenwick left St. Joseph's to accept an appointment as the first bishop of Cincinnati, a post that he held until his death in 1832. Father Young replaced him. By this time, the area had begun to receive many Catholic settlers, so the original church had to be enlarged. A stone addition was attached to the back of the log cabin for this purpose. In 1822, another parish was established nearby and assigned to the Dominicans. The cornerstone was laid for Holy Trinity Church, located two and a half miles away in the middle of the village of Somerset. It was a brick church, some seventy-five feet by forty feet, and was built, in large measure, from the proceeds of a gift from Peter Dittoe, a relative of the principal benefactor of St. Joseph's. Holy Trinity was dedicated in 1827 and grew as the town of Somerset grew. In 1830, Dominican Sisters arrived in Somerset and established a girls' academy near the church. Some one hundred sixty years later, in 1987, the two parishes were consolidated and now have the same Dominican pastor.

In 1829, the second St. Joseph's Church was built. Made of brick, it was eighty-two feet long and replaced the log cabin that Jacob Dittoe had constructed. Five years later, St. Joseph's was designated by the Dominicans as a priory. This meant that in addition to fulfilling parish duties the Dominicans were establishing a residence for priests who would serve other purposes as well. In this instance, St. Joseph's Priory became a novitiate — a school for students beginning to study for the priesthood —and a house of studies for advanced seminarians studying either philosophy or theology. In 1836, a priory building was dedicated at a Mass that had an overflow attendance made up mostly of farm families living in the vicinity of the church.

During this era, other improvements continued to be made. In 1827, the cemetery that is still located on church property was established. In addition to the grave of Jacob Dittoe, it contains the remains of two veterans of the American Revolution, nine from the War of 1812, two from the war with Mexico, and twenty-three from the Civil War. Most of the names on the tombstones are either English, Irish, or German, reflecting the character of the population that settled in and about Somerset over the years. After its foundation, the priory was the center for Dominican missionary activity throughout central Ohio. In 1836, the first Catholic church in Columbus was established by priests from Somerset.

Between 1839 and 1843, a third church was erected to serve both the parish and the Dominican community, replacing the 1829 brick church. Money available for the third church was in short supply, so a simple wooden altar was its only artifact or adornment, except for a large crucifix that was placed in the center of the sanctuary. The crucifix was brought to St. Joseph's from Cuba by one of the priests then in residence, Father Joseph Sadoc Alemany, the first archbishop of San Francisco. The "Alemany Cross," as it has come to be known, still hangs in the present St. Joseph's Church near the altar.

During the years immediately before the Civil War, the Dominicans expanded their educational establishment at St. Joseph's far beyond anything that Jacob Dittoe had ever envisioned. In 1849, a new priory was constructed south of the church containing classrooms, a library, and larger quarters for the monks. In 1850, they opened a general school of higher education called St. Joseph's College. In 1853, they built a dormitory for the lay students who attended this college. Tuition ranged from $120 to $140 a year, and students came from all over Ohio and the upper South to attend. The college boasted that Stephen A. Douglas, the noted senator from Illinois and Democratic candidate for president against Abraham Lincoln, spoke at one of its commencement exercises. At the outbreak of the Civil War, a large number of Southern students withdrew and the school was forced to close. It never reopened.

In 1864, the third St. Joseph's Church was destroyed by fire. Only the walls were left standing. The new priory building also burned down. Some of the members of the priory were in favor of abandoning the entire undertaking at Somerset and asked permission of their master general in Rome to do so. He refused, saying that the order had an obligation to keep faith with the people who had founded the parish and who had made grants of land and money to establish the church. The seminary carried on, being housed in the old priory and college buildings while a new church was under construction using the remnants of its predecessor. In 1866, the building **[pictured above]** was completed. It has served both the parish and the Dominican community since that time. It has one steeple, in contrast to the two that stood atop the former building. No sooner had this improvement been completed than the seminary was temporarily relocated to Kentucky to permit its buildings to be occupied by St. Mary of the Springs, the girls' academy in Somerset. The buildings belonging to the academy had burned down, and the nuns were in immediate need of a place to house their students. A year later, the Sisters decided to leave the area and to transfer the academy to Columbus. Thereafter, the seminarians in Kentucky returned to their former home.

A number of different changes took place in the ensuing years at St. Joseph's Seminary. In 1879, the novitiate was transferred to Kentucky. In 1882, a third priory building was erected. Some years later, the Dominicans felt that it would be more advantageous to their advanced students to be educated in more cosmopolitan surroundings. The Catholic University in Washington was beginning to assemble in the vicinity of its campus several houses of studies maintained by various religious orders whose members were attending classes at the university, so the Dominicans established a house of studies next to the university and transferred their theology students to that house in 1905. In 1925, another group of novices who had come to reside at St. Joseph's were transferred to River Forest, Illinois. In 1929, the seminary at Somerset was again reopened for theology students; but, in 1939, it closed, and the last ordinations to take place at St. Joseph's were held. Between 1846 and that date a total of one hundred fifty Dominican priests had been ordained at this church. Thereafter, philosophy students — those in their middle years of seminary training — continued to be educated at this location until the 1950s.

The church itself has seen many improvements over the years. As noted, the "Alemany Cross" was rescued from the fire of 1864 and was given a prominent place in the new building. In 1886, handcarved oak stalls were placed on one side of the altar and adjacent to the novitiate entrance to accommodate the monks as they came to pray in chapter. In that position, they served to isolate the monks from the lay congregation. Later, the stalls were placed on each side of the altar near the pews occupied by parishioners. In 1918, to commemorate the 100th anniversary of the parish, stained-glass windows manufactured in Munich for St. Vincent Ferrer Church, the large Dominican parish in uptown Manhattan, were removed and brought to St. Joseph's. Other artifacts include a stained-glass window containing the coats of arms of Dominican bishops in the United States who had lived at St. Joseph's. Parts of the old organ in the choir loft are reputedly an heirloom of the Dittoe family.

Toward the end of 1957, the old convent was made into a novitiate for lay Brothers. It ceased to serve this purpose in 1968. In the same year, clerical novices were transferred to another Dominican house in Massachusetts. Since that time, St. Joseph's has returned to its original character as a quiet rural parish. The buildings that served as a priory and as a college were removed. What remains today is the 1866 church and, across the road, an old farmhouse now used as a rectory for the combined parishes. St. Joseph's has about one hundred families, while Holy Trinity in town has about four hundred. The parochial school across the street from Holy Trinity has about one hundred sixty students. The three hundred twenty acres donated by the original settlers has been enlarged to five hundred acres, most of which is leased to a tenant farmer. From its inauspicious beginning in Somerset, the Catholic Church in Ohio has, in a period of one hundred seventy-five years, grown into two Roman Rite archdioceses and five Roman Rite dioceses. St. Joseph's has become a place of pilgrimage for many Ohio Catholics who have signed its visitor's book when they come to see the place where Jacob Dittoe and Father Fenwick established a mission outpost for an area that now has more than three million Catholics.

48
St. Peter in Chains Cathedral

Cincinnati
OHIO

St. Peter in Chains Cathedral in Cincinnati has often been called the mother church of the Midwest because of the prominent role it played during the nineteenth century in the development of Catholicism in the Ohio Valley. When Cincinnati was incorporated in 1803, the town had fewer than one thousand inhabitants and not many of them were Catholics. In 1811, an advertised meeting was held at the home of William Dabler for the purpose of organizing a Catholic church but nothing came of the meeting. Between 1816 and 1820, Catholic communities were becoming organized in such Ohio villages as Somerset, Zanesville, Lancaster, and Dungannon. For the most part they were served by Dominican missionaries from Kentucky. It was at this time that Catholics in Cincinnati purchased a plot of ground at Vine and Liberty Streets for the purpose of erecting a church in a section called Northern Liberties located outside the city limits. At this location, they erected as their church a plain barnlike structure that for some time went unplastered and had no ceiling. This group became incorporated as Christ Church, but there is some evidence that the church itself was named in honor of St. Patrick. It was this meager building of which Edward D. Fenwick "took possession" when he arrived in Cincinnati in January 1822 as its first bishop.

As noted in the preceding chapter, Bishop

Fenwick is credited with being the founder of the Dominican order in the United States. He served as a missionary in Ohio for several years before being appointed the founding bishop of the nation's ninth Catholic diocese, a jurisdiction that originally encompassed not only Ohio but Michigan and the Northwest Territory extending into Wisconsin and Minnesota. At that time, only four percent of Ohio's population were Catholics, and they were scattered throughout the entire state. In a letter to the Society for the Propagation of the Faith in Paris begging for funds, Bishop Fenwick described himself as "beyond contradiction, the poorest of all bishops in the Catholic world." Upon coming to Cincinnati, he rented two rooms, one for himself and the other for the two priests he brought with him from Kentucky. From this address he began to function as the bishop of the diocese. He normally preached at the Cincinnati Catholic church four times on Sunday, either at Mass or at catechistic meetings, and took up collections ranging from one to three dollars each week.

The Cincinnati *Gazette* greeted Bishop Fenwick rather warmly: "We congratulate the Roman Catholics of this city and environs on the arrival of the Rt. Rev. Dr. Fenwick, lately consecrated Bishop of Cincinnati and the State of Ohio. This circumstance interests not only the Catholics but all the friends of literature and useful knowledge, as we understand that his intention is ultimately to open a school, aided by the members of his order, long distinguished for their piety and learning." These sentiments were not universally shared. Bishop Fenwick soon decided to remove the small church that served as his procathedral and to relocate the building on Sycamore Street. As it was being carried through the streets of the city, it collapsed and the relocation effort was met with hoots and derision from anti-Catholic onlookers. The building was reassembled on Sycamore Street, where it stood for another three years. In 1826, it was replaced by another, sturdier building named in honor of St. Peter.

Bishop Fenwick borrowed a small sum of money and went to Europe to seek funds and priests with which to operate his far-flung diocese. While in Rome, he conferred with Pope Leo XII and offered to submit his resignation so that the pope could appoint someone else who might be more suited to the task of being bishop of Cincinnati. The Holy Father would hear none of it but lent a sympathetic ear to the bishop's plea for help. So did others throughout Europe. Bishop Fenwick returned with about $10,000 and a work of art that still hangs in the cathedral, a painting of the Annunciation given to him by Napoleon's uncle, Cardinal Joseph Fesch. He also brought back to Cincinnati a fine gold tabernacle, a gift of Pope Leo, which now reposes on the marble altar in the archbishop's chapel in the cathedral. Bishop Fenwick was appointed commissary general of the Dominican order in Ohio, a post that entitled him to control not only diocesan properties but several parishes in the state using land owned by the Dominican order.

The new brick cathedral that Bishop Fenwick built in 1826 was 110 feet long, 50 feet wide, and 30 feet high. It cost between $10,000 and $12,000. Next to it he built the bishop's residence and a school, called the Atheneum, which eventually served both as a seminary and as a liberal-arts school for boys. When it opened in 1829, the school, named in honor of St. Francis, had four seminarians and six other students in the preparatory class. A few years later, Bishop John B. Purcell, the second bishop of Cincinnati, conducted classes at the seminary in theology, in addition to administering his diocese. In 1827, the Poor Clares arrived in Cincinnati and opened a Catholic school for girls that soon had an enrollment of seventy students.

In 1832, Bishop Fenwick died of exhaustion during the cholera epidemic that had plagued the city. He was buried in the original St. Peter's Cathedral. Before his successor could be appointed, the diocese of Detroit was created, so the Cincinnati diocese taken over by Bishop Purcell was limited to the state of Ohio. It had grown remarkably during Bishop Fenwick's tenure to 30,000 Catholics, 17 priests, and 17 churches.

Catholicism in Cincinnati has had a distinctly German flavor, although St. Peter's parish itself was always regarded as an Irish parish. In 1825, Father Frederic Résé, who would become the first bishop of Detroit, arrived from Germany and was joined shortly thereafter by another German priest. They were assigned to travel throughout Ohio and to prepare a roster of all German Catholics living in the state. They found German Catholics living everywhere in the state who responded favorably to the ministry of priests who spoke their own language. Unlike the Irish, who tended to migrate to the cities, German Catholic immigrants frequently went to rural areas and began to farm. In the mid-1830s, a German Catholic newspaper, *Der Wahrheitsfreund (The Truth's Friend)*, was founded in Cincinnati for the benefit of German Catholics. It continued to be published for seventy years. In 1834, the second church in Cincinnati, Holy Trinity, was founded as a German nationality church because there was opposition among the Irish to the continued use of St. Peter's by a German congregation.

Between 1830 and 1860, Catholics in Ohio of all ethnic origins had to contend with outspoken anti-Catholicism that erupted from time to time. It was largely of nativist origin and came as a reaction to immigration that was taking place in considerable numbers, both in Cincinnati and in other areas. In 1831, the *Catholic Telegraph*, one of the first Catholic newspapers in the West, was founded in part for the purpose of answering attacks on the Church that were repeatedly being made by Protestant ministers. It was one of thirteen Catholic newspapers and magazines founded at that time throughout the United States for the express purpose of answering Protestant attacks on the Church. In 1836, the Young Men's Bible Society in Cincinnati accused Catholics of suppressing the use of the Bible. Bishop Purcell responded by issuing a challenge that, if the society would supply him with copies of the Douay Bible in English and Allioti's German Bible, he would personally deliver them door to door throughout the city. The challenge was not taken up. On two occasions, the bishop engaged in public disputations on religious topics with ministers from the pulpits of Protestant churches, but he personally disliked such confrontations and tried to avoid them whenever possible.

The 1850s saw the destruction of Catholic churches in Ohio as in other states. Churches were either dynamited or burned to the ground in East Liverpool, Masillon, and Sidney, Ohio. No physical harm ever came to St. Peter's; but, in December 1853, an incident (previously touched on in this volume) occurred that threatened the existence of the church and the life of the papal nuncio who was then visiting Cincinnati. Archbishop Gaetano Bedini had come to the United States to survey the development of the Church in this country and to attempt to resolve certain disputes that had arisen in parishes in other cities. While he was in Cincinnati, the *Hochwächter*, the organ of an anticlerical German group, suggested the desirability of the assassination of Archbishop Bedini during his visit. This event did not take place. However, a mob of about eight hundred German immigrants gathered at Freeman's Hall and, armed with weapons, began to march on the cathedral carrying anti-Catholic banners. They were confronted by the police about a block from the church and shooting ensued, in the course of which one of the rioters was killed, fifteen were wounded, and about sixty were arrested. This show of force by public authorities was sufficient to quell the disturbance and to safeguard both the life of the nuncio and the property of the cathedral.

By 1840, Cincinnati was clearly the principal city in Ohio. It was experiencing the annual arrival and departure of five thousand steamboats that were navigating the Ohio River. Bishop Purcell decided that the time had come to build a larger cathedral, so he purchased land for this purpose at Eighth and Plum Streets where the church **[pictured above]** is located. He engaged the services of Henry Walter, a student of Greek Revival architecture, who had designed the Ohio capitol building at Columbus. Walter drew up plans for the Cincinnati cathedral according to some general guidelines laid down by the bishop. What emerged was a cathedral modeled after the ancient Tower of the Winds in Athens. It was 200 feet by 80 feet and 55 feet high, surrounded on three sides by a colonnade of 12 pillars and topped by a steeple some 220 feet high. The cathedral was given the name of "White Angel" because it was constructed of white marble quarried at Dayton and shipped by canal to Cincinnati. Following a visit to Cincinnati, Charles Dickens wrote that the new St. Peter in Chains was the finest example of Greek Revival architecture in the United States.

Estimates of cost ranged from $120,000 to $300,000. Construction took four years and was periodically halted because funds occasionally ran low and the bishop insisted that the church be built only on a pay-as-you-go basis. The cathedral was financed by the sale of a ten-acre plot of ground that had originally been set aside for a cemetery, as well as by a campaign to collect $1.50 a year from every Catholic wage earner in Ohio. At its dedication in 1845, parishioners gathered at the old cathedral, received Holy Communion, and then marched to the new building in a procession that included the largest assembly of Catholic prelates that had ever gathered in the Midwest. While many were still observing the eucharistic fast, they witnessed a dedication ceremony that took four hours to complete. By 1845, the Cincinnati diocese numbered 75,000 Catholics, who were served by 66 priests in 70 churches and chapels.

When he began the construction of the new cathedral, Bishop Purcell entrusted the Athenaeum to the Jesuits of the Missouri province, who began to operate it as St. Xavier's College, the predecessor of Xavier University. Upon the dedication of the new cathedral, the old cathedral continued to function as a parish church for fifteen years, when it was torn down to make way for St. Xavier, the Jesuit church that still functions in downtown Cincinnati.

The prestige of St. Peter's Cathedral was enhanced in 1853 when Cincinnati was designated the third archdiocese in the United States and the cathedral became the center of an ecclesiastical province that included dioceses in Kentucky, Indiana, Michigan, and elsewhere in Ohio. During the next twenty years, St. Peter's was the site of five provincial councils and four diocesan synods. These conferences brought together within its walls the principal Catholic leaders of the Midwest, who met for the purpose of determining church policies and practices for an entire region. One of the more noteworthy statements of policy made at St. Peter's emerged from the provincial council of 1861, a gathering that included bishops from both Northern and border states. Purcell, who was by then an archbishop, was an enthusiastic supporter of the Union cause. He had ordered the American flag to be flown from the top of the cathedral steeple throughout the Civil War where it could easily be seen from the Kentucky side of the Ohio River, where secessionist sentiment was strong. The bishops of the provincial council were not so pronounced in their sentiments. In reference to the causes of the oncoming hostilities, they stated: "This inquiry more belongs to those who are directly concerned in the affairs of the republic. The spirit of the Catholic Church is eminently conservative, and while her ministers rightfully feel a deep and abiding interest in all that concerns the welfare of the country, they do not think it their province to enter into the political arena. They leave to the ministers of the human sects to discuss from their pulpits and in their ecclesiastical assemblies the very exciting questions which lie at the basis of our present and prospective difficulties. Thus, while many of the sects have divided into hostile parties on an exciting political issue, the Catholic Church has preserved her unity of spirit in the bond of peace, literally knowing no North, no South, no East and no West."

Over the years, St. Peter's gained its reputation as the mother church of the Midwest because it was the scene of the consecration of twenty-three bishops, a majority of whom were Cincinnati natives, who were assigned to head dioceses both in the Midwest and in mission territories. It has also been the scene of the ordination of more than two hundred priests.

In 1871, the first of several renovations of the cathedral took place. The sanctuary was enlarged, balconies were added, and stained-glass windows were installed. During this era, a prominent benefactor, Reuben Springer, contributed about $150,000 both to the improvement of the church building and to the construction of other Catholic facilities, including a school located across the street that was named in his honor. For many years the cathedral operated both St. Peter's Academy and Springer Institute. The academy no longer exists, but the Springer Institute, not now connected with St. Peter's, continues to provide an educational program for students who have learning disabilities.

The commercialization of downtown Cincinnati and the consequent decline of a residential community worked the same effect on St. Peter's parish as this phenomenon has in many other cities. While Cincinnati grew rapidly as an archdiocese, St. Peter's declined in numbers and activity. In 1938, when a large new church, St. Monica's, was constructed in the suburbs, the cathedral for the archdiocese was removed to that location while St. Peter's continued to function as one of several downtown parishes.

When Archbishop Karl Alter took office in 1950, he decided that the seat of his episcopal see would "come home" to St. Peter's. He was influenced in his decision by the adoption of a city master plan for the development of downtown Cincinnati and a desire to promote that development. One facet of the master plan that appealed to him involved proposed freeways that were designed to bring people into the central city from the suburbs and that would, in his estimation, serve to revive the fortunes of downtown churches such as St. Peter's. One incidental effect of his decision to refurbish St. Peter's was that the city decided to retain its principal offices in the old city hall, a building located just across the street and shown in the background of the photo of the cathedral [see above]. To raise funds for this project Archbishop Alter did as Bishop Purcell had done more than a hundred years before, sending an appeal to all of the parishes of the archdiocese for the means to provide the entire Catholic community of Greater Cincinnati with a fitting building for their principal church. He collected more than five million dollars. In 1953, St. Peter's was closed for four years, and services each Sunday were held in a small building on West Seventh Street.

The reconstruction that took place during those four years was no ordinary renovation. The building was gutted, the floor was removed, and the entire west wall was torn out and replaced. The ground on the south and west sides was found to be soft and so it received extensive shoring. The original cathedral was a rectangular building. It was lengthened by the construction of a transept that now houses the Blessed Sacrament Chapel and the baptistry. The steeple was rebuilt because iron clamps that had held the old steeple in place had rusted over the years. New flooring was installed for three quarters of the present floor space. A new outside wall on the west side was built from white marble obtained from the original Dayton quarries that had provided the marble for the church in 1845. These quarries had been closed for many years and had to be reopened so that the reconstruction could be made from stone of the same quality and color found in the original building.

Doors of polished bronze were hung in both the outer and one of the inner doorways. New steps leading to the front door were constructed, and extensive landscaping and new shrubbery were placed about the front and sides of the building. Twelve new bells, named in honor of the apostles, were anointed at a public ceremony and installed in the belfry along with St. Peter, the 3,400-pound bell that was retained from the original carillon.

The interior nave of the reconstructed cathedral is quite dramatic. The walls of the atrium, the wainscoting in the narthex and the nave, and the columns leading to the baptistry and the Blessed Sacrament Chapel are lustrous black marble that set off a large mural of Christ behind the main altar. The mural is a mosaic made from thousands of pieces of Venetian glass infused with twenty-four-carat gold. The mosaic bears a legend in Latin that reads: "And Peter was imprisoned, bound with chains." The borders of the mosaic are large chain links while two pictures at the bottom portray St. Peter being delivered from imprisonment in Jerusalem and being visited by St. Paul in the Mamartine prison in Rome. The high altar, set on a sanctuary floor of green and white marble, is also marble. Portraits of the Evangelists can be found in the crystal windows between the narthex and the nave.

The cathedral houses several works of art. One of the most noteworthy is a gilded bronze figure of Christ sculpted by Benvenuto Cellini, the most noted Italian goldsmith of the sixteenth century. It is mounted as the corpus of a processional cross. There is also on display a fifteenth- or sixteenth-century missal stand that was handcarved in Spain as well as several old paintings. The latter include a Madonna painted in the seventeenth century by the Rubens school and possibly by Rubens himself, a restored seventeenth-century Italian portrait of the Pietà, and a seventeenth-century study of Mary Magdalen attributed to the Murillo school.

Sacramental records at St. Peter's date back to 1839. A publication issued by the parish in 1987 states that, during the century and a half that the cathedral has been in existence, more than ten thousand weddings and over twenty-one thousand baptisms have taken place within its walls. Most of these took place before the parish lost its residential character. Now there are about 35 to 40 weddings and about 20 baptisms each year. Unfortunately for St. Peter's, the highways on the master plan that Archbishop Alter envisioned as bringing people from the suburbs into downtown Cincinnati also bring them out of downtown and back to the suburbs at the end of each business day. The parish now has about two hundred fifty registered parishioners, a majority of whom are either single or are couples without children. Half of these parishioners are residents of downtown Cincinnati and the other half live outside the parish boundaries. The parish offers three Masses each weekday that are attended by an estimated seventy-five people and Masses each weekend attended by about seven hundred. The cathedral receives a subsidy from the archdiocese it serves. This archdiocese has grown to include some 540,000 Catholics living in 247 parishes in 19 counties. The city in which St. Peter's is located is about thirty-five percent Catholic, who still regard this refurbished ornament as the mother church of Catholicism in the Midwest.

49
St. Joseph

Bardstown

KENTUCKY

St. Joseph's Protocathedral (proto meaning first) in Bardstown is the focal point of the history of Catholicism in Kentucky. It celebrated the 175th anniversary of its dedication in 1819 although it is by no means the oldest Catholic church in the state. For several decades St. Joseph's — and the "Holy Land" of central Kentucky, where it is located — was the focal point of the Catholic Church in the entire Midwest.

The first Catholics to venture west of the Allegheny Mountains were Marylanders, all of English stock. Beginning in 1785, they sold their tobacco farms and plantations in St. Mary's County and elsewhere in southern Maryland and headed West. Not many years before this migration began, a break had been discovered in the Allegheny mountain chain along the Tennessee-Kentucky line, known as the Cumberland Gap, through which Daniel Boone had mapped out the Wilderness Trail from the Carolinas into the Blue Grass country of north central Kentucky. Settlers were pouring into this region from all parts of the eastern seaboard. The route of choice for travelers bound for Kentucky from southern Maryland was first overland to Pittsburgh. Then came a three-hundred-mile ride on a flatboat down the Ohio River to Limestone (now Maysville), Kentucky, and overland again for one hundred thirty miles to the area around Bardstown, where most of them relocated.

In 1785, the first group of Maryland Catholic émigrés took this route and arrived at Pottinger's Creek, about nine miles south of Bardstown. Later groups settled at Hardin's Creek, ten miles east, and at Cartwright's Creek, about twenty miles east. They bore such English names as Mattingly, Lancaster, Spalding, Hagan, Edelin, Nalley, Mudd, Montgomery, and Abell. The localities settled by these Catholic pioneers now comprise Nelson, Washington, and Marion Counties.

The first settlers at Pottinger's Creek conducted their own religious services without the aid of a priest in the home of a Maryland émigré, Basil Hayden. In 1787, Father Charles Whelan was sent to Kentucky by Father John Carroll and organized the first Catholic congregation in the state. After being involved in a dispute with the congregation, he left. His replacement, Father William de Rohan, built a small wooden church at Pottinger's Creek in 1792 and called the new parish Holy Cross. This was the first Catholic church constructed in Kentucky. Thirty years later, Father Charles Nerinckx, a Belgian missionary and one of the most prominent names in the early days of the Catholic Church in Kentucky, replaced this log-cabin church with the brick edifice that still stands today. It is now located in the midst of a large country churchyard at a quiet country crossroad named Holy Cross, Kentucky, where it serves an active rural parish.

Bardstown began to develop as a commercial center in the 1780s. Located along the Louisville-Nashville Turnpike, it was a frequent stop for stagecoaches and travelers. Later, it became a county seat, thereby attracting a number of prominent lawyers who made it a site of active litigation. Among those coming to Bardstown to sue for the vindication of his rights was Thomas Lincoln, father of the sixteenth president. His farm at Knob Hill, some twenty miles south, was the subject of a title dispute with Kentucky authorities, and he wished to secure a clear title to it before settling permanently in southern Indiana.

As early as 1798, a small Catholic congregation existed at Bardstown. A log-cabin church, built at what is now a cemetery on the outskirts of the town, served this fledgling congregation. In 1807, Father Nerinckx built a larger and more substantial church, but religious services were often conducted in private homes until the cathedral was completed.

In 1793, Father Stephen Badin, the most prominent figure in the early days of the Church in Kentucky, arrived at Pottinger's Creek. Immediately after his ordination, he was sent to Kentucky along with Father Michael Barrières, whom Bishop John Carroll designated simply as vicar general of the West.

Like other frontiersmen, the two priests walked from Baltimore to Pittsburgh, took a flatboat to Limestone, and walked the rest of the way. Three miles from Pottinger's Creek, Father Badin built a small log cabin and then a church he named in honor of his patron, St. Stephen. The area is now Loretto, Kentucky. From St. Stephen's Church he assumed the responsibility for the affairs of the Church in Kentucky during its early formative period. What was Kentucky County, Virginia, had just became the second new jurisdiction to join the original Thirteen Colonies as a full-fledged state. This occurred in

1792. Father Badin estimated that among Kentucky's 70,000 residents there were about 300 Catholic families, numbering 1,500 people, who were served at five mission stops.

Throughout his sixty years as a priest, Father Badin had the reputation of being controversial. As one person put it, he was respected by all but loved by few. The source of the difficulty was his harsh view of Catholic morality. It is sometimes described as Jansenism, a form of Catholic Puritanism. He roundly criticized public dancing, one of the principal forms of recreation on the American frontier. He was known to have refused absolution to young men unless they promised to refrain from attending dances, and he told married men that it was wrong to have relations with their wives more than once a week.

In an age when public penances were not unheard of, he required one penitent to dig a shallow grave and lie in it once a week. He defined the obligation of attending Sunday Mass as falling upon any Catholic who walked to Mass and lived less than five miles from church and upon any Catholic coming by horseback who lived less than ten miles from church. In the matter of moral severity, Father Badin had a kindred spirit in his friend, Father Nerinckx, although the latter was much better able to communicate with parishioners than was Father Badin. Father Nerinckx once wrote in his notebook a catechism question that read: "Q. What harm do the easy confessors do? A. They fill the earth with sinners and hell with the damned."

Father Badin ultimately left Kentucky in 1819 after a dispute with the bishop over title to church property. In the early days of the Church in Kentucky, Father Badin often took title to church property in his own name, at the same time incurring personal responsibility for church debts to be satisfied out of the property he had acquired. No one ascribed greedy intentions to him, but the problem was sufficiently complicated and vexing that Bishop Benedict J. Flaget, Bardstown's first bishop and Father Badin's longtime friend and fellow countryman, took up the question specifically in a report made in 1815 to Pope Pius VII.

Bishop Carroll liked Father Badin and relied heavily upon him. It was largely due to Father Badin's recommendation that a new diocese was established west of the Alleghenies and that Bardstown was selected as its headquarters. Father Badin wrote the first book of Catholic doctrine published west of the Alleghenies. Called *Principles of Roman Catholics*, it was written in response to attacks upon church doctrine and practices that were being leveled by an assortment of Protestant ministers. He had a regular habit of visiting parishes and mission stops by horseback five days out of each week. There were occasions when he was the only priest to minister to six thousand Kentucky Catholics spread over an area of eight hundred square miles. Constant efforts were being made to send him help, but some priests who came West proved unsuitable while others simply came and left. Two died, one from disease and the other from exposure suffered after being thrown from a horse. In 1806, Father Badin wrote that "no clergyman could form to himself a true image of Kentucky unless he had gone through a million of hardships above ordinary imagination." In a report to the Propagation of the Faith in

Rome, he observed: "Pretty nearly half the settlers do not affiliate with any religion but believe in general in a confused manner in revelation, and they die without having made choice of any sect. There are heretical German and English bibles in almost every house ... even among ... skeptics, who are much multiplied here in the last ten years. The men in office and almost all the people of education are of this party."

Help came to Father Badin and to the Catholic population of north central Kentucky in several ways. Bishop Carroll prevailed upon the Dominicans to place their first establishment in the United States in this area. In 1806, Fathers Edward D. Fenwick, Samuel Wilson, and William Tuite acquired about six hundred acres at Cartwright's Creek, near the present city of Springfield, with money derived from a bequest that Father Fenwick received from his father. Here they established the parish of St. Rose of Lima and a school called St. Thomas College.

The term "college" was loosely applied in that era to any school whose curriculum was more advanced than the education received in a one-room schoolhouse. As an illustration, Jefferson Davis, its most prominent alumnus, was enrolled at St. Thomas College when he was only eight years old and remained about two years. The college existed only a few years and was replaced by a Dominican seminary, which, many years later, was transferred to another location.

In 1809, the Dominicans completed the construction of St. Rose of Lima Church. At the time, it was the largest and most elaborate Catholic church in the West. Part of the original building forms the apse of the parish church that still exists at this location. In 1811, it was the site of the first ordination west of the Alleghenies. Catholics in the area welcomed Dominican confessors, whose attitude in applying the provisions of the moral law, sometimes referred to as "Springfield spirituality," differed sharply from the harsh approach of Fathers Badin and Nerinckx.

In 1808, the Holy See created four new dioceses in the United States, locating their headquarters respectively at Boston, Philadelphia, New York, and Bardstown. In defining the boundaries of the Bardstown diocese, the Holy See displayed its characteristic vagueness in dealing with North American geography. The papal bull signed by Pope Pius VII recited the boundaries of the other three dioceses and then stated: "4th, Bardstown, that is, in the town or city of Bardstown, and thereto we assign as a diocese the states of Kentucky and Tennessee, and until otherwise provided by this Apostolic See, the territories lying northwest of the Ohio, and extending to the great lakes and which lie between them and the diocese of Canada, and extending along them to the boundary of Pennsylvania."

The area so described now contains nine states and thirty-five dioceses. In 1808, it contained twenty-four churches and mission stops in Kentucky as well as Catholic settlements at five other locations — western Illinois at Cahokia, Prairie du Rocher, and Kaskaskia, Vincennes in southwestern Indiana, and Detroit. There were half a dozen priests in Kentucky (including those Dominicans at St. Rose who were available for parish work) and one each at the three churches located outside the state of Kentucky. A few years later, Bishop Flaget wrote that he could not understand why Boston had been included among the four new dioceses. As late as 1822, Kentucky had twenty thousand Catholics, while Boston had only about thirty-five hundred.

At the time of his episcopal consecration in Baltimore in 1810, Benedict J. Flaget had been in the United States for eighteen years. Like his great friend, Father John B. David (who would later be his coadjutor, or assistant bishop), and like Fathers Nerinckx and Badin, Bishop Flaget was a refugee from the French Revolution. Before he came to America, he had joined the Sulpician order and was a seminary professor at Nantes. After arriving in this country, he was sent to be a missionary at Vincennes, served as a chaplain to the troops of General Anthony Wayne, and taught several years at Georgetown College. Like many other prelates in the early days of this country, he initially declined his appointment and took it only after being told by the superior general of the Sulpicians that he had to accept.

Bishop Flaget had to borrow money to make the trip to Kentucky. When he arrived at Bardstown, he lingered only long enough to say Mass and proceeded directly to Father Badin's church, St. Stephen, where he was formally received by the priests of the diocese. There he "took possession" of his episcopal see, which he described as being two or three times as large as France. Both he and the seminarians who had accompanied him to Kentucky stayed with Father Badin a few months before moving to a three-hundred-acre tract near Bardstown that Thomas Howard had left to the church. Bishop Flaget called it the Plantation. He built a house and a church and made his episcopal residence at St. Thomas until a new home was completed at Bardstown seven years later.

Building a cathedral was only second on Bishop Flaget's list of priorities. A former seminary professor, his first priority was to establish a school for the training of priests. He shared the fear of many churchmen of his day that many Catholics would simply fall away from the Church because of a lack of priests. In 1813, he wrote in his diary: "It is almost impossible to form an idea of the Catholics who forget their religion on account of lack of priests, or the lack of zeal of priests who have charge of these congregations. Not a day passes that we do not find great numbers of these strayed sheep who, because they do not see a real shepherd, become Baptists, Methodists, etc., or at least nothingists. To remedy this great evil it would be necessary that a priest, filled with the spirit of God, and convinced of the value of souls, should often get away from the accustomed route, and going out into the country ask if there are not Catholics in this region. The discovery of a single one will lead to the discovery of ten others. If he found only one family he could say Mass there, preach, catechise, and pray. Let him show a great desire for the salvation of souls and a contempt for their money. With such dispositions a priest would have the consolation of bringing to the bosom of the Church millions of his children who will never enter it unless we go after them."

He named his seminary on the Howard tract in honor of St. Thomas and later gave the same name to the parish that was erected there. He taught the seminarians when he could but placed Father David in full charge of the school. During its first year, St.

Thomas Seminary had only six students, two of whom had not yet made their first Communion.

However, it began to prosper. Seminarians had to work their way through school. A portion of each day was set aside for manual labor on the Plantation, which included the construction or repair of buildings and farming the land. Before the Bardstown diocese had a cathedral, it had two seminaries, one conducted by the bishop and the other by the Dominicans. During the next fifty years, these two seminaries produced an imposing array of priests and bishops to serve the Church in the Middle West.

The key to the success of St. Thomas Seminary was Father David, a Sulpician and a shy, academic figure in contrast to the more outgoing personality of Bishop Flaget. When the Sulpicians threatened to transfer Father David to another seminary and the Holy See gave some indication that it was considering him to head another diocese, Bishop Flaget, with Father David's wholehearted concurrence, was able to keep him in Kentucky as the head of St. Thomas Seminary by the stratagem of having him appointed coadjutor bishop of the Bardstown diocese. Upon the dedication of the cathedral, the seminary moved to Bardstown. Bishop David remained its rector but also became the rector of the cathedral parish and vicar general of the diocese. St. Thomas became and remains today a parish on the outskirts of the city.

In 1812, the Bardstown diocese was the site of the establishment of two religious orders of women, the Sisters of Loretto at the Foot of the Cross and the Sisters of Charity of Nazareth. The Loretto Sisters were placed under the spiritual direction of Father Nerinckx. However, the rule proposed by Father Nerinckx for the Loretto Sisters was modified when it was submitted to Rome for approval because church authorities regarded it as too severe. Within ten years, the new order had over one hundred members. It purchased a large tract of land at St. Stephen's where its motherhouse now stands.

The Sisters of Charity originated at St. Thomas and were first housed in a building adjacent to the seminary. They adopted the rule of the Sisters of Charity founded by Mother Elizabeth Seton at Emmitsburg, Maryland, although they never formally affiliated with that establishment. Bishop David became their spiritual director and served in that capacity until his death. They acquired a tract of land just north of Bardstown, where their motherhouse is now located and until 1971 operated Nazareth Academy (later Nazareth College) at that location.

In 1822, the Dominican Fathers at St. Rose founded a community of Dominican Sisters that grew rapidly. They founded, among other establishments, a school of higher education, which is now St. Catharine's Junior College.

In 1816, Bishop Flaget and Father David staked out the dimensions for the Bardstown cathedral. Bishop Flaget wrote that the ground itself cost what turned out to be the equivalent of $700. In July, he blessed the cornerstone in a ceremony that he claimed was attended by more Protestants than Catholics. During a recent renovation of the cathedral, the cornerstone was rediscovered under a pilaster on the front portico. It bore an inscription attributed to Bishop Flaget that reads: "I pray you to ask God that I may be myself the cornerstone and holiest ornament of the cathedral, the first in these vast lands."

Bishop Flaget's initial estimate of the construction cost was $20,000, most of which he raised himself. Cash was scarce in the Kentucky wilderness, so most of it came from European sources because such contributions were difficult to obtain from Bardstown residents. He set up a building committee composed of three Protestants and three Catholics. A substantial amount of financial support came from Protestants. There were disquieting rumors that the seat of the diocese might be removed from Bardstown to Lexington or some other city in the region, a move that would undermine the efforts of city fathers to develop an important and thriving community, so boosterism as well as ecumenism explained some of the interest of Protestants in the success of the project.

Bishop Flaget originally contracted with Maximilian Godefroy to be the architect of the building. Godefroy had built the chapel of the Sulpician College, St. Mary's, at Baltimore. However, a great deal of time passed and Godefroy did not present any plans, so the bishop retained John Rogers, a local architect. It was Rogers who designed and supervised the construction of the federal-period building that was actually constructed. A great deal of local support came in the form of in-kind contributions — a pledge of labor, of lumber and building materials, or simply of produce that could be sold to purchase necessary supplies. Rogers received much of his architect's fee in produce rather than in cash. Foundation stones were quarried nearby. Brick was manufactured at a kiln located on the premises. The walls that were constructed are thirty-four inches thick. The columns in front were made from large yellow poplar logs obtained locally. The nails used in the original carpentry were all wooden, as metal nails were not used until about 1840.

On August 8, 1819, the cathedral **[pictured above]** was consecrated and put into use, although several interior and exterior features were yet to be finished. The selection of the preacher at the dedication ceremony was a native of Kentucky, Father Robert Abell, who was born in Washington County in 1792, educated at St. Thomas Seminary, and ordained by Bishop Flaget the previous year. The week following the dedication ceremony Bishop Flaget ordained his close friend John David to be a bishop. It was the first episcopal consecration west of the Alleghenies.

Behind the cathedral the bishop constructed what is now called Spalding Hall, a building designed to house both the seminarians and laymen enrolled at St. Joseph's College. The latter became one of the early Catholic institutions of higher learning in the entire Midwest. Not long after it opened, the original building was enlarged. The Sisters of Nazareth had already opened a school for girls, so St. Joseph's was designed to fill the same role for boys. When a Catholic boys' school in New Orleans was closed in the early 1820s, a number of its students transferred to St. Joseph's. By 1825, the college had ninety boarding students and one hundred local day students. The boarders from the South occasionally caused disciplinary problems because, according to their preceptors, they simply were not accustomed to academic and personal discipline.

The seminary was eventually relocated to Louisville in 1871. The college remained in existence until 1892. During its seventy years, it graduated many prominent figures in the early public life of Kentucky. Like other Catholic schools of that era, both St. Joseph's College and Nazareth Academy included a large number of Protestants in their student bodies.

In 1821, Father William Byrne opened a school in a former distillery a few miles south of Bardstown in Marion County. It evolved into St. Mary's College. During the 1840s, the Jesuits briefly operated St. Mary's but withdrew to take charge of a small school that was then being opened in the village of Fordham, New York. St. Mary's College continued under diocesan sponsorship until 1869 and thereafter was operated as a seminary by the Resurrectionist Fathers until it closed in 1976.

The year 1825 was designated by the Holy See to be a jubilee year. Catholics who were able to do so were encouraged to make a pilgrimage to Rome. By this time, the Bardstown diocese, which twenty years before had been little more than a collection of widely dispersed log-cabin churches, possessed a cathedral of noteworthy proportions, two major seminaries and a minor seminary, the motherhouses of three flourishing orders of nuns, two schools of higher education, two bishops, 17 diocesan priests, six Dominicans, 19 seminaries, 10 frame churches, and nine brick churches.

Encouraged by the idea of a jubilee year, Bishop Flaget thought it was time to try to improve the quality of spiritual life in his own diocese by proclaiming a diocesan jubilee. In the fall of 1826, the priests of the diocese were called to St. Joseph's Cathedral for a week of prayer that preceded the jubilee. The parish then provided a pilot program for jubilee activities that were to follow at other churches during the following year. The jubilee was essentially an eight-day retreat. Each session lasted all day, so parishioners brought their lunches and picnicked on the front lawn of the church. The exercises included Mass, confessions, and conferences. Invalid marriages were solemnized, and confirmation was administered at the end of each weekly event. Attendance was large and included both Protestants and Catholics.

The most popular part of the mission was a question-and-answer session devoted to points of religious doctrine. It was conducted by two priests, one of whom acted as interrogator posing questions and objections to the Catholic faith. The other responded to the issues that were raised. Religious disputations, like other debates, frequently occurred on the frontier and were usually well attended.

Some years earlier, Bishop Flaget had engaged a preacher named Tapscott in a well-attended open-air debate that lasted two hours. The principal subjects debated were the Real Presence of Christ in the Blessed Sacrament and the historical basis for the existence of the Catholic Church. Doctrinal questions were also debated at length in print in such frontier publications as *The Western Protestant* and the *Catholic Advocate*. It was no surprise that such discussions had an attentive audience when they mere made a part of the jubilee exercises.

The team of priests, accompanied by Bishop Flaget, traveled from parish to parish to conduct the jubilee. It was fortunate to have among its number Father Francis P. Kenrick, the rector of the cathedral and, in later years, bishop of Philadelphia and archbishop of Baltimore. It was he who normally provided responses during the question-and-answer period. During one such session, a Protestant minister appeared and took over the questioning. Encouraged by the fact that a large audience had gathered, the minister went on for half an hour with a series of hostile remarks, during which Father Kenrick pretended to have fallen asleep. After his questioner had run out of verbal ammunition, Father Kenrick then arose and responded point by point to each objection that had been raised. Statistics that were kept attested to the success of the jubilee. There were 6,000 confessions, 4,345 Communions, and 1,216 confirmations administered throughout the state.

Before coming to Kentucky, Bishop Flaget had made the acquaintance of Louis Philippe, claimant to the French throne and an exile for many years during the Revolution. After becoming king of France in 1830, Louis Philippe (known as the Citizen King) made a gift of a number of books, paintings, vestments, and other religious articles that are still retained by the cathedral. King Francis I of Naples and Pope Leo XII donated several paintings to the cathedral, including several attributable to the schools or the families of Van Eyck, Murillo, and Van Dyck. They hang today along the walls on either side of the church. In 1952, three of these paintings, including the "Flaying of St. Bartholomew," were cut from their frames by burglars and removed. Six years later, the FBI recovered them in Detroit in the trunk of an automobile.

St. Joseph's still has in its possession one of the first pipe organs installed west of the Alleghenies. It was brought to Bardstown in 1819 and used until the 1840s when it was replaced by another organ that is still used today. The outside of the church contains artifacts that might be regarded as period pieces. They are each of the Ten Commandments, printed in early nineteenth-century type design and placed at intervals along the outside walls. Inside, the protocathedral has undergone several renovations over the years — in the 1840s, in 1890, in the 1950s, and again in 1984. Stained-glass windows dating from the 1840s appear in the original windows. The marble altar rail dates from 1890. Recently, the interior of the church was repainted. Thereafter, a local artist, James Cantrell, painted portraits of each of the twelve apostles, together with a representation of how each of them died, at the top of each of the interior columns.

As the Midwest grew, it was inevitable that significant portions of the oversize Bardstown diocese would be taken to form new dioceses. Bishop Flaget expressed relief each time this occurred. The first new diocese was Cincinnati (1821), and then Detroit (1833), Vincennes (1834), and Nashville (1837). When Bishop Richard P. Miles, O.P., a graduate of the Dominican seminary at St. Rose, was appointed bishop of Nashville, the Bardstown diocese became limited exclusively to the state of Kentucky. This growth happened within a thirty-year period. Soon thereafter, the seat of the Kentucky diocese was moved to Louisville, about thirty-five miles north of Bardstown. Since Louisville was a thriving port of commerce on the Ohio River, its growth had far outstripped that of any other Kentucky city. Bishop Flaget once expressed the opinion that the headquarters of the Kentucky diocese should have been located at Louisville from the outset. However, he liked Bardstown, and it was with mixed emotions that he left in 1841 to take up residence in the city that has remained the seat of the diocese (and later an archdiocese) since that time. Bishop Flaget lived long enough to bless the new Louisville Cathedral of the Assumption but not long enough to see it completed. He died in 1850 in his eighty-seventh year and was buried at the Louisville cathedral.

Know-Nothing bigotry and the Civil War were to plague the Church in Kentucky and in Bardstown during the next fifteen years. One event of note that sent shock waves far beyond its city limits was Louisville's Bloody Monday riot of August 6, 1855. Bloody Monday was an election-day massacre, an uprising aimed at German and Irish Catholics who had migrated to the city during the preceding twenty years and who were making their weight felt at the ballot box. Most of the newcomers were Democrats, while the mayor and city council were Know-Nothings, a short-lived political party that was, in part, the fallout from the disintegrated Whig Party.

Feeling against Catholics had been building for sometime. It was fanned by articles and speeches, including editorials in the Louisville *Journal*, which denounced Democratic candidates for city office as representing "every faction, ism, and sect from the foreign pesthouses . . . and the grasping priests, bishops, and archbishops." The paper claimed that "the hierarchy is yet drunk on the blood of saints" and urged Louisville citizens to "rally to put down an organization of Jesuit bishops, priests, and other papists, who aim by secret oaths and horrid midnight plottings to sap the foundation of our political edifices."

During that summer, the school board had fired every Catholic teacher in the public school system and a controversy was still brewing concerning the use of the King James Version of the Bible in public schools. On election day, mobs tried to prevent Irish and German voters from having access to polling places. One group stole a cannon from the courthouse lawn, loaded it, dragged it to an Irish tenement district known as Quinn's Row, and fired it into a tenement house. Instead of providing police protection, Mayor John Barbee and a committee of the council entered the cathedral to search for a hidden cache of arms and ammunition. They found none. When the day was over, the Know-Nothings had won the election but twenty residents of the city were dead.

During the ensuing week, both the city council and the Louisville *Journal* issued statements blaming the victims for the riots. The Bardstown *Gazette*, commenting on these events that occurred just a few miles away, denounced the Know-Nothings as a "government within a government." While a repetition of Bloody Monday never occurred in Kentucky, the religious affiliation of Catholic candidates for public office continued to be a matter of frequent controversy throughout the state for many years.

Like other border states, Kentucky was split during the Civil War. It contributed more troops to the Union than to the Confederacy, but there was substantial pro-Southern sentiment in and about Bardstown. The division of public opinion was reflected in the hierarchy. Louisville's second bishop, Martin J. Spalding, was a native of the Catholic "Holy Land" area around Bardstown. He opposed abolition and had distinct Southern leanings. His immediate superior, Archbishop John B. Purcell of Cincinnati, was a Union supporter, as was the auxiliary bishop of Cincinnati, Sylvester Rosecrans. Bishop Rosecrans's brother, William, was the commander of the Union Army of the Cumberland, which controlled northern Kentucky during much of the war, and made his headquarters close to Bishop Spalding's cathedral.

In October 1862, at a spot thirty-five miles east of Bardstown, a battle took place, mostly by chance, near the town of Perryville. While this engagement did not reach the scale of Antietam or Gettysburg, its results determined the fate of the Bardstown area for the balance of the conflict. After Confederate General Braxton Bragg withdrew his troops from Perryville to Tennessee, northern Kentucky became secure for Union forces, except for an occasional cavalry incursion by Morgan's Raiders.

St. Joseph's College closed during the Civil War and enrollment dropped perceptibly at Nazareth Academy. Union troops occupied the Bardstown cathedral briefly to use it as a hospital. They also used St. Joseph's College for the same purpose. Thirty Sisters of Charity from Nazareth volunteered to staff Union army hospitals in Louisville, Paducah, and elsewhere. One of them, Sister Lucy Dosh, died while nursing Union Army fever victims and was given a full military funeral.

Toward the end of the war, the Sisters of Charity were afraid that their property might be confiscated by Union forces because of the distinctly pro-Southern sentiment of many members of the student body, so they sought the protection of Abraham Lincoln. Lincoln sent the Sisters of Charity a handwritten note in which he said "let no depredation" take place at their motherhouse in Nazareth.

In 1908, the Bardstown protocathedral was the site of the 100th anniversary celebration of the founding of the Bardstown diocese. Not long thereafter, the Sisters of Charity and the Sisters of Loretto observed their own centennial anniversaries.

Bardstown is now a deanery in the Louisville archdiocese. The counties that make up this area are still largely Catholic. Bardstown's own county, Nelson, is one-third Catholic, as is Washington County. Marion County to the south is over fifty percent Catholic. A map of the area contains such biblical place names as Gethsemane and Nazareth as well as other titles like St. Catherine, Holy Cross, Loretto, St. Francis, and St. Mary, so writers have often referred to it as Kentucky's Holy Land.

Bardstown is supported by tobacco, tourism, distilleries, and several small factories. It is close enough to Louisville to be a bedroom community for an increasing number of commuters. St. Joseph's parish now has about 1,750 families, most of whom are descendants of the original English settlers from southern Maryland.

The parish has a grade school of three hundred seventy students and a CCD program that educates three hundred more. Across the street is a consolidated coed Catholic high school, Bethlehem High School, which is conducted under the supervision of the Sisters of Charity. It has about one hundred sixty students. St. Joseph's publishes a thirty-one-page booklet of religious ministries that are carried on by its parishioners.

    The protocathedral remains the focal point of Kentucky's Holy Land and is visited each year by more than ten thousand people, who come to view what Bishop Flaget described one hundred seventy-five years ago as an ornament "in these vast lands."

50
Abbey of Our Lady of Gethsemani

Trappist

KENTUCKY

For more than one hundred forty years a noteworthy feature of Kentucky's Holy Land has been the oldest monastery of contemplative monks in the United States. Sometimes referred to as America's proto-abbey, the monastery of Our Lady of Gethsemani, located about twelve miles south of Bardstown, was carved out of the wilderness by priests and Brothers of the Order of Cistercians of the Strict Observance — the Trappists — who arrived at this spot just before Christmas of 1848 after a two-month journey from Normandy in France. Here they hoped to plant in the New World a cloistered house of prayer and self-denial where the ancient Rule of St. Benedict could be observed in silence and austerity. They succeeded in founding the first of twelve Trappist monasteries for men that now exist in all parts of the United States.

The roots of this order stretch back to 1098 when a group of monks gathered together at Cîteaux, near Dijon in the wilderness of Burgundy in eastern France, to construct a monastery where men who were repelled by the laxity they had found in other monasteries could observe the Rule of St. Benedict with the strictness they felt it required. From Cîteaux, the Cistercians developed other monasteries in France throughout the Middle Ages. Centuries later, the order itself was the subject of an internal reform movement aimed at purging a perceived laxity that had crept into the observance of the Benedictine rule. In 1664, a French nobleman, Armand-Jean de Rancé, founded the monastery of La Grande Trappe in Normandy (hence the name Trappists) where a strict observance of the rule would once again prevail. The monks at Gethsemani trace their roots to this monastery as well as to Cîteaux.

The first Trappists who came to Kentucky were not the forty-three men who arrived at Gethsemani in 1848. Forty years earlier, a group of thirty-seven Trappists under the direction of Dom Urbain Guillet were forced to leave the monastery of Our Lady of Melleray near Nantes in western France as a result of persecutions that had occurred during the French Revolution and its Napoleonic aftermath. During this political upheaval, the Trappists had refused to take an oath of allegiance to the anticlerical constitution the revolutionary government had proclaimed in 1793. As a result, some were imprisoned in France. Others were sent to French Guiana and put in chain gangs in a penal colony that was the forerunner of Devil's Island. Still others escaped to Switzerland and elsewhere in Europe, while a few found refuge in Great Britain.

The monks from Melleray sailed to Baltimore and from there went to Pidgeon Hill, near Hanover, Pennsylvania, to start a foundation. They soon left Pennsylvania and headed for Kentucky, arriving at Holy Cross, near Rohan's Knob, in 1805. There they opened a school for boys and maintained a mission church for seven Catholic families who lived at Casey Creek. Even on the Kentucky frontier, they did not abandon the austerity of their rule. They did not break their fast until noon each day and lived off vegetables and black bread. However, when their log-cabin monastery burned down, they left Kentucky for Cahokia, Illinois, near East St. Louis. Before leaving Kentucky, they had buried eight of their members in the cemetery that surrounds Holy Cross Church. Those who went to Illinois fared no better. They built several cabins at a place that came to be known as Monks Mound because it was located near some ancient Indian burial grounds. An outbreak of typhoid claimed fourteen members of the congregation. After the downfall of Napoleon, they were recalled to France and were happy to return. Neither education, parish work, nor missionary activities are part of the calling of the Trappists, and, back at Melleray, they were able to resume the contemplative life, which is the basic purpose of the order.

Forty years later, the same abbey at Melleray was filled to capacity, an indication to the Trappists that the time was ripe to establish a new foundation. Moreover, they anticipated more political upheavals in France and felt it would be wise to have an abbey in the United States that could serve as a refuge in the event of another exile. This time they scouted a prospective site for a monastery before sending another group of monks into the wilderness. They had been asked by Bishop Benedict Flaget in Louisville to come to Kentucky and felt that the presence of a large number of Catholics in the area around Bardstown would guarantee a friendly environment for cloistered monks. With these considerations in mind, they bought, on credit, fifteen hundred acres of land from the Sisters of Loretto and made plans to send a group to Gethsemani.

The land in question had belonged to the Dants, one of the early Maryland Catholic families who had come to the area in 1785. James Dant had donated a large tract to the Sisters of Loretto in 1818 and asked that they name it Gethsemani — the biblical name (now usually spelled "Gethsemane") of "the dark and bloody land" where Christ was betrayed by Judas. The Sisters did so and built several log cabins where they conducted an orphanage. Their order prospered, and they were able to construct a motherhouse nearby, so they were in a position to dispose of "the dark and bloody land" to the Trappists. The acreage consisted of many knobs, a Kentucky phrase for small hills normally covered by trees. Much of what the Trappists acquired was forested. While arable, it was not prime farmland and had to be cleared before any planting could take place.

A group of forty-three monks made the trip from Melleray to Gethsemani in 1848. The sea voyage took two months and brought them through the free port of New Orleans and up the Mississippi and the Ohio to Louisville. One monk died en route. During this voyage, they set up what might be termed a mini-monastery. They attempted to maintain their strict regime on shipboard, rising early to say the Divine Office together and to celebrate Mass. They were welcomed by Bishop Flaget in Louisville and by the Jesuits at St. Joseph's College at Bardstown. However, upon reaching Gethsemani, they found only a few log cabins that the Sisters of Loretto had vacated and some corn left standing in the field. They picked the corn and went about adapting the cabins, as best they could, to suit their immediate needs. Three of their members defected during the first month, and their prior, Dom Eutropius Proust, became seriously ill and was thought to be dying. However, he recovered in the following spring.

The monks began to clear the fields for spring planting, which they devoted to corn and potatoes. They made two thousand bricks and set about building their first permanent structure. However, they had almost no funds and it was money they needed in order to erect a stone abbey. Dom Eutropius went back to Melleray to ask for money but received none. He then asked for permission to beg for funds. A fund-raising effort to obtain construction money might seem today like a commonplace undertaking, but in 1850, both the order and the Holy See did not favor such activities on the part of monastic orders, insisting that they support themselves from working their own lands rather than from receiving what was regarded as alms. However, the Trappists in America had no wealthy benefactors, as did many abbeys in France, so the chapter at Melleray drew a distinction between capital and operating expenses and allowed Dom Eutropius to beg for the money needed to build an American monastery.

Dom Eutropius visited several parishes in France but came away with only 38,000 francs. During his travels, he made the acquaintance of Bishop Guy Chabrat, who had lived for many years in Bardstown and returned to France when his eyesight failed and he was no longer able to fulfill his duties. Bishop Chabrat initiated a movement that resulted in the immediate designation of Gethsemani as a full-fledged abbey, even before it had a church or any but the barest living quarters for its monks. Such a precipitous action would not have taken place today; but, in 1850, Pope Pius IX was anxious to see the establishment of a contemplative monastery in the United States so he approved the request in July of 1850. Dom Eutropius was able to bring this news back to Gethsemani when he returned, but he was not able to secure permission for Gethsemani's monks to wear cotton habits during the summer months. Rules governing monastic clothing were drawn up in France in light of continental weather conditions. They prescribed woolen habits year-round. Lay Brothers wore them while working in the fields and all monks wore them at night while sleeping. Such fashions in monastic attire took no account of the scorching heat of Kentucky summers. Eventually, these habits were modified in Kentucky, as they were in South Africa and South America, where Trappists were in the process of establishing other monasteries.

The designation of Gethsemani as an abbey meant that those who were stabilized at the abbey — that is, who had taken a vow to remain at the abbey for life — would be called upon to elect an abbot for life. The monastery still remained under the general supervision of Melleray, whose abbot was the Father Immediate (direct supervisor) of the abbot of Gethsemani, but such supervision was indeed remote. In 1851, the monks of Gethsemani elected Dom Eutropius to be their first abbot. In October of that year, he went to St. Joseph's Cathedral in Bardstown where he received from Bishop Martin Spalding the first abbatial blessing ever given in the United States. The ceremony took place in Bardstown because there was no church at Gethsemani where it could properly be performed.

Dom Eutropius immediately began the slow work of constructing both the Church of Our Lady of Gethsemani and the permanent buildings of the monastery. He hired an architect named William Kelly and outlined for Kelly his desire for a massive quadrangle looking very much like Melleray, except that Dom Eutropius wanted a three-story residence building instead of the two-story building that existed at the motherhouse in France. In 1852, monks began digging trenches for the foundation of the abbatial church that exists on this site today. A Protestant neighbor, George Pottinger, donated the foundation stones. However, cash was needed to complete these projects and Dom Eutropius did not have any. Bishop Spalding promised his assistance in raising funds. However, he made certain requests that Dom Eutropius felt obligated to fulfill. The bishop appointed Dom Eutropius as his vicar for that part of the Louisville diocese near the abbey. This was a distinctly un-Trappist assignment. He also asked the abbot to operate a parish church at Gethsemani for Catholics living in the neighborhood. The bishop went on to suggest that the monks might consider opening schools for boys and girls in the area because there was a pressing need for such facilities. Dom Eutropius looked upon the school as an eventual source of needed revenue. He went as far as promising Catholics in the neighborhood free tuition for their children if they would help in the construction.

The abbot had no difficulty finding monks to staff these facilities. Most Trappist monasteries have within their communities priests who served as parish curates or who were members of other religious orders before attempting the more demanding life of a Cistercian. His problem was in taking them away from the life they thought they were going to live when they became Trappists. He assigned a former curate of a French parish who was living in the community to be the pastor of the abbey parish. Later, the abbey was able to find a diocesan priest for this function, a man who lived at the abbey but was not a part of the community. The parish was so successful that later the bishop was able to prevail upon the abbey to take over the responsibility for a second parish, St. Vincent de Paul. However, in 1870, these functions were returned to the bishop, who was then in a better position to take them over. A lasting memento of the abbey parish is the cemetery located in front of the present monastery just outside its enclosure walls. It contains the remains of many former parishioners as well as several Sisters of Loretto who were buried there before they sold the property to the Trappists. One noted parishioner buried there in 1859 was Zachariah Riney, a native of Hardin's Creek. Riney was a schoolmaster who operated a one-room school a few miles south at Knob Creek. His most famous pupil was Abraham Lincoln.

The cornerstone of Our Lady of Gethsemani Church was laid on March 25, 1853, but the project took more than ten years to complete. To finance construction, Dom Eutropius and two other monks went on extensive fund-raising tours. The abbot traveled in eastern Canada and along the Atlantic seaboard in the United States. The other monks went all the way to South America, raising money for Gethsemani in places as remote as Argentina and Uruguay. In the course of his travels, Dom Eutropius compiled a list of more than six thousand individual contributors. Once again he was impeded in his effort by superiors at Melleray, who feared repercussions in Rome if the Holy See found out about the extent of his monastic "begging." The abbot was able to contact the papal nuncio while the latter was in Cincinnati and obtained from him approval to continue, which superseded the instructions he had received from France.

The Civil War broke out a few years later and interrupted both construction and fund-raising efforts. One problem that had to be addressed was how to use one building both for a parish church and for a monastic choir in a cloistered abbey. Several times each day more than sixty Trappists gathered to chant their Office together. Normally, monks occupy choir stalls located in the sanctuary for these exercises. Gethsemani's second abbot, Dom Benedict Berger, solved the problem by dividing the church in half, constructing a large partition from the roof to the floor, which separated the parish church in front from the monastic chapel to the rear. The parish church, named Sacred Heart of Jesus, was dedicated in 1864 in an elaborate ceremony that featured, as the principal speaker, the same Kentucky native, Father Robert Abell, who delivered the principal sermon at the dedication of the Bardstown cathedral forty-five years later. The monastic chapel was dedicated two years later at a six-hour ceremony attended both by parishioners and ecclesiastical dignitaries from all parts of the East and Midwest.

The boys' school, later called Gethsemani College, was staffed by both Trappists and laymen. It was located a few hundred feet from the monastery so that the presence of a large number of high-school and college students would not unduly disturb the silence of the cloister. The girls' school never flourished. The abbot was able to hire a woman to conduct a small girls' school at Mount Olivet, a building located about a mile or so from the abbey. She resigned when her husband found employment elsewhere. A group of Franciscan nuns operated the school for a while, but eventually they also relocated so it was closed. Fifteen years later, an additional effort was made to revive the school but this effort was short-lived. The Trappists had always felt that they had no calling to be in the field of education at all and even less to be in the field of educating women.

The Civil War passed Gethsemani by with little direct impact. The community was largely French plus a smattering of other European nationalities, so the war was simply not regarded as their fight. The only depredation suffered at the abbey was the loss of a few horses and mules that were taken by General Braxton Bragg's Confederate troops before they withdrew to Tennessee.

The abbey did not receive its first American postulant (applicant) until 1868 and he did not remain. In fact, for the first thirty years of its existence, the community had no permanent American members. Any additional members were men who came from Europe, usually from another Trappist abbey. The reasons for this lack of local vocations were varied. The abbey was not well known and monasticism was not a popular way of life in the minds of gregarious and materialistic Americans. The austerity of the particular regime followed by the Trappists was also enough to discourage many who might otherwise have seriously considered a monastic vocation. Moreover, Dom Benedict, the second abbot, was reputed to be an unusually strict and inflexible superior. As one writer put it, life at Gethsemani resembled the life of a French peasant, not an American frontiersman.

Gethsemani's first permanent American member was a Kentuckian named John Green Hanning, whose life as a lay Brother was detailed in a biography entitled *The Man Who Got Even With God*. Brother Joachim, as he was called, was a former cowboy who was attracted to monastic life after spending many years on the range in Texas. He entered at the age of thirty-six and eventually became the abbey's cellarer, the title given to the individual who superintends the farms and acts as purchasing agent. However, the spiritual trials he underwent under the tutelage of Dom Benedict were a case study in the curbing of an unruly will by the application of Trappist discipline. By 1889, Gethsemani had only thirty-four members. The fact that it was so slow in attracting Americans gave Trappists in France reason to feel that their experiment in Kentucky might be a failure and that the monks at Gethsemani should either be recalled or sent to other abbeys.

A prevalent suspicion existed throughout the United States during the nineteenth century, at least among many Protestants, that there must be something awry when groups of men or women would retreat from the world and go off to live secluded lives in convents and monasteries. This suspicion was fed by an occasional lurid but fictional account of convent life. These suspicions erupted into violent hostility in a few instances. They were reinforced by the fact that, from time to time, bishops sent erring priests to the monastery to serve ecclesiastical penances before being restored to duty. The charge was made that Gethsemani was a priest's prison. In fact, anyone, including any Trappist, was always free to leave at any time and some did. One former member of the community wrote a book in which he claimed that he had been held against his will. The individual in question died in an insane asylum. A blow to the abbey, one that nearly resulted in closing the college, came in the early 1890s when the headmaster of the college, a layman, was found guilty of embezzling school funds. He too wrote a book "unmasking the Trappists," but a careful reader would have learned that the "unmasking" emanated from a prison cell in Louisville where the author was serving time for larceny.

A revival of the fortunes of Gethsemani occurred in 1898 with the election of Dom Edmond Obrecht as the monastery's fourth abbot. An Alsatian by birth, he learned English when he was sent to work at a home for newsboys operated by a priest in New York City. He always claimed that he did not speak English, only American. Upon being elected, he moved to dispel the image of the monastery as a French refuge in the Kentucky hills. He directed that all communications within the monastery be made only in English. He appointed a native American to be the prior and left much of the running of the abbey to him because Dom Edmond was frequently sent elsewhere by his superiors to attend to the business of the order. Thirty-five years later, his stand-in, Reverend Frederic Dunne, became its first American abbot.

For its fiftieth anniversary celebration in 1898, Dom Edmond staged a large jubilee for the purpose of advertising the abbey's existence. Pursuing this technique further, in 1901 he invited the governor of Kentucky, J.C.W. Beckham, and an entourage of state officials to tour the monastery. Governor Beckham was not the first Kentucky governor to come to Gethsemani but his official visit established a precedent followed by many of his successors. Then, as now, the cloistered portion was off-limits to women. A large sign over its entrance read: "Women may not pass beyond here under pain of excommunication." To avoid possible embarrassment to the wives of invited officials, Dom Edmond obtained from the apostolic delegate in Washington permission to permit women to enter these restricted precincts, a privilege granted in medieval times only to European royalty. Inside the abbey the visitors heard Gregorian chant while outside they were serenaded by the college band playing both marches and "My Old Kentucky Home." It was Dom Edmond's desire that the state anthem should come to apply to Gethsemani as well.

Dom Edmond established a post office at the gatehouse and had his prior appointed postmaster. The address is now Trappist, Kentucky 40051. He prevailed upon the Louisville and Nashville Railroad to erect a station on a spur line about a mile away called Gethsemane (spelled with a final "e"). It was there that visitors to the monastery, which included many church and public dignitaries, got off the train when coming to the monastery.

The abbot disliked the garish red brick of the monastery buildings and felt that it presented a jarring sight against the landscape, so he had them covered by a façade of imitation cut stone. New barns and shops were built, and a new cloister was constructed. In the past, the monks had been accustomed to put white paint on the church windows each spring to protect worshipers inside from the heat of the summer sun. Dom Edmond discontinued this practice and installed stained-glass windows, one of which was donated by a longtime friend and supporter of the monastery, Cardinal Dennis Dougherty of Philadelphia. In 1915, he brought about a real innovation in traditional monastic construction: the installation of steam heat in the buildings.

Political persecution of the Trappists continued in France well into the twentieth century. In 1903, the Radical Party controlling the general assembly put through a measure expelling most Catholic religious orders from the country. Some Trappist monasteries were spared, but the abbey at Fontgombault in the Loire country was closed and seventeen of its monks sought refuge in the United States. Gethsemani welcomed them. In fact, Dom Edmond went to New York to greet the exiles as they disembarked at the port.

In 1912, the college buildings caught fire and burned to the ground. During its final twenty years, Gethsemani College had issued baccalaureate degrees under a charter granted by the Kentucky legislature and had developed a body of loyal alumni. Many sent in unsolicited donations earmarked for the rebuilding of their alma mater but Dom Edmond returned them. It was his feeling that adequate educational facilities had developed in the Midwest since the time the college was founded and it was now time for Trappists to leave the field of education and return to their original calling. The land was cleared of the charred ruins of the college buildings. In their place, Dom Edmond erected a statue of St. Joseph, the patron saint of the contemplative life.

While the abbey was able to withdraw from education and parish activities, one religious function it has continued to provide to the general public is retreats. For years individuals had visited the abbey for this purpose, staying at the guesthouse for various lengths of time and consulting priests of the community concerning their spiritual problems. In 1921, at the request of the Knights of Columbus in Louisville, the abbey undertook an ongoing program of weekend retreats. This program now includes weekday retreats as well. The community had, among its members, a former Jesuit who was experienced in giving retreats, so he was assigned to this activity. The motherhouses of the Loretto and Charity Sisters nearby soon began to open their doors to retreats for women. While the program at Gethsemani was originally open only to men, retreats for women are now conducted from time to time in the abbey's vastly expanded guest facilities.

When the abbey celebrated its seventy-fifth anniversary in 1924, the Church of Our Lady of Gethsemani was completely renovated. The most important change was the removal of the partition that divided the church into a public area and a monastic chapel. For the first time in over fifty years the complete length of its two-hundred-foot nave could be viewed in its entirety. Oak flooring was laid and the masonry was refaced. The last major physical improvement made by Dom Edmond took place beginning in 1930 when a six-thousand-foot brick wall of enclosure was erected. The Rule of St. Benedict requires such an enclosure, so Dom Edmond put the monks to work building it. This task took about two years. The church can still be entered without violating the enclosure, but the public is permitted inside only in a limited area in the rear. Beyond that point, the choir stalls of the monks line both sides of the sanctuary. They come together in these stalls seven times each day to chant their Office, a series of prayers based upon the one hundred fifty Psalms of David.

Two events occurring a dozen years apart provided silent testimony to how well situated the monastery had become since the turn of the century when its continued existence was being called into serious question. In 1932, at the annual general chapter meeting of all of the Cistercian abbots in Rome, the abbot general announced that the Roman headquarters of the order had been taken under eminent domain for the purpose of building a road so the order had to find a new office. He had his eye on a large house that was for sale for 700,000 lire and asked the abbots if they could provide the purchase money. None of the other Trappist abbeys were in a position to contribute. Dom Edmond told his fellow abbots that Gethsemani would be happy to underwrite the purchase, whereupon he wrote the abbot general a check for 700,000 lire.

In 1944, the monastery was filled to capacity, so it inaugurated the first of five foundations that have sprung from Gethsemani. Abbot Frederic Dunne bought a large tract of land at Conyers, Georgia, about thirty-five miles southeast of Atlanta, and relocated twenty monks from Gethsemani to this new home. Leaving Kentucky was a wrenching experience for many who had spent their entire adult lives at Gethsemani. In a repetition of an event that had occurred at Melleray nearly a hundred years earlier, he called the community together in the abbey church and read off the names of those who were being sent to Georgia. Three days later, the existing Gethsemani community gathered for the last time to chant their Office together and to sing the traditional prayer of the Trappists for monks who are going on a journey. Those assigned to the new foundation then departed for the railroad station in Louisville where they boarded a coach that had been chartered for this purpose from the Louisville and Nashville Railroad.

On the overnight trip to Atlanta, they did as their predecessors had done on shipboard, creating a mini-monastery on the nightcoach. They awoke early, chanted the Divine Office at the appointed hours, and continued as best they could to observe the Benedictine rule while in transit. During their first three months in Georgia, they slept dormitory-style in the loft of a barn until their first housing was completed. Their new neighbors greeted them with more curiosity than hostility. However, a deputation from the Rockland County, Georgia, grand jury visited the premises to assure themselves that the new arrivals did not include any fugitives from justice and that no one was being held against his will. They went away satisfied on both counts. Father James Fox, the superior of this new priory, returned to Gethsemani a few years later as its abbot.

No reference to the Abbey of Our Lady of Gethsemani would be quite complete without mention of its most celebrated inhabitant, Thomas Merton, who lived there for twenty-seven years as Father M. Louis. Merton was a graduate of Columbia University and a convert to the Catholic Church. After teaching English briefly at St. Bonaventure

College, he applied for admission to Gethsemani and was admitted in December of 1941. Thereafter he underwent training in the Trappist novitiate, studied for the priesthood, and was ordained at the abbey church in 1950. During his studies, he wrote *The Seven Storey Mountain*, an account of the spiritual odyssey that brought him to Gethsemani, and *The Waters of Siloe* (Shiloh in the King James Version of the Bible), a history of the Trappists and of the abbey. Later books included *Seeds of Contemplation* and *The Sign of Jonas*. These were efforts to explain to the world the contemplative life that he had embraced. All were best sellers, but it was *The Seven Storey Mountain* that made him a literary figure of great prominence for the next two decades. In the process, these books also made both the contemplative life and the monastery at Gethsemani more widely known than either had ever become in the previous one hundred years.

While most members of the Gethsemani community live as cenobites — monks who spend each day in close contact with other monks as they work, pray, and eat together — Merton was allowed, toward the end of his life, to live as a hermit in an individual cottage located some distance from the main buildings. There he could work and pray alone, visiting the abbey only on Sundays and major feast days. During the 1960s, Merton wrote on peace and social-justice issues as well as on the contemplative life. He acquired an interest in the monasticism of oriental religions and was allowed to attend a conference in 1968 of representatives of various faiths who gathered in Bangkok, Thailand, to discuss common features of their contemplative experiences. It was there that he was electrocuted in a bizarre accident. His body was brought back to Gethsemani where, like any other monk, he was laid to rest next to the abbey church in a grave marked only by one of the many iron crosses serving as tombstones in the abbey cemetery.

Merton once told a questioner that the reason he became a Trappist was that he believed in the power of intercessory prayer. By prayer, he did not mean only the chanting of the priest's Office in the abbey church but the total life of austerity, self-denial, and sublimation of the will to higher purposes that are the ingredients of the contemplative life. A common thread running through all of his writings is the continual difficulty experienced by contemplative monks down through the ages in avoiding the temptation to abandon or to modify their basic mode of living, even to perform laudable works of religion or charity that are the function of other religious orders as well as individual priests and laymen. He continued to insist that the role of the Trappist is to pray and do penance so that, in the economy of grace, their efforts will redound to the benefit of others engaged in more active and public ministries. This is the intercessory prayer to which he had reference. His explanation was not a popular one or even an understandable one to many who are totally immersed in a world of programs, causes, and political and social activism.

In the late 1960s, following the conclusion of Vatican Council II, the abbey church was again renovated. Many Gothic decorations and older religious artifacts were removed. As a result, the interior of the building was almost stripped bare and remains a reflection of the austere life that is supposed to be lived at the monastery. So many changes had been made that, when the abbey tried to place the old church on the National Register of Historic Places, permission was refused because the alterations had radically changed the decor of the original building.

Today, the Gethsemani community numbers about seventy-five members, down considerably from the one hundred seventy-five or so who were there during the years immediately following World War II. About one third are priests, and the rest are Brothers. There is no longer a seminary at the abbey. Those who study for the priesthood are sent to a Benedictine college in Rome for philosophy and theology. The abbey **[pictured above]** owns about two thousand acres of land, some six hundred of which are being farmed. The principal crops are alfalfa and soybeans. The monks still have a large herd of beef cattle. The cheese and fruitcakes made on the premises are sold nationwide and constitute the abbey's principal "cash crop."

The Trappists still follow the strict dietary regime of their predecessors, the central feature of which is that they abstain totally from eating meat except when it is required for medical reasons. Eggs, bread, cheese, and, on major feast days, fish constitute the staples in their refectory, along with a variety of vegetables. These restrictions of course are not imposed on retreatants during their stay in the guesthouse. The monks rise each day at 3:15 A.M. After both individual and common prayer, Mass, and a light breakfast, they begin their workday at 8:00. Work includes a variety of manual and intellectual tasks, depending on the assignment and the talent of each monk. They gather at noon for common prayer and their main meal, rest a while, and go back to work until vespers at 5:30. After supper is the last of the common prayers — compline — and then to bed. Silence prevails throughout the day, although the monks have abandoned the hand signals they used to employ. They speak whenever charity or job requirements demand until the monastery bell sounds at eight in the evening. Then the great silence descends over the monastery until eight o'clock the next morning.

The world still presses in on the Trappists and in ways that never bothered the early founders of the abbey. Each week about thirty-five people make a retreat at Gethsemani. They are encouraged to come, to share the quiet, and to attend religious services in the portion of the abbey church set aside for the public. Contemplation can be interrupted by correspondence, the news of the day, a phone call that can be put through the switchboard from any place in the world, or a trip to town, possibly to pick up a supply of locally distilled Kentucky bourbon used in making fruitcakes. Each age brings its encroachments on the strict observance of the Rule of St. Benedict, and each has to be addressed and dealt with. Merton compared the way of contemplation to the waters of Siloe. As he reminded us, they flow in silence.

51
Ste. Anne

Detroit
MICHIGAN

What some believe to be the second oldest parish in continuous existence in the United States, Ste. Anne de Detroit (as it was originally called) traces its origin to a small chapel established on the Feast of Ste. Anne in 1701, by Antoine de la Mothe Cadillac. He had been sent by the Comte de Frontenac, governor general of New France, to establish a trading post and military fort along the river that connects Lake Huron with Lake Erie. Cadillac's daughter Marie Thérèse was the first child to be baptized at Ste. Anne at a ceremony recorded on February 2, 1704.

This straw-thatched log chapel was formally dedicated in 1701 by French Recollect priests and was the first of seven church buildings to occupy a site at Fort Pontchartrain or a nearby site near Larned and Bates Streets, both of which are now part of the financial district in downtown Detroit. The eighth and present Ste. Anne's Church [**facing page**] was built in 1886 at a location some three miles from the original parish churches that bore this name. The first church was burned in an Indian raid. The third church was destroyed in 1805 when all but one of Detroit's three hundred buildings burned to the ground.

For many years Ste. Anne was the only parish church in what is now Michigan and, in 1738, generated an Indian mission across the Detroit River that became Assumption parish in Windsor, Ontario. Parish records from 1701 through about 1830 are now in the custody of the archdiocese of Detroit and are a valuable historical record of an area that has been under three different flags — those of France, Great Britain, and the United States. Current parish records on file at the church date back to the 1830s.

Both fire and the need for bigger, more permanent structures accounted for the construction of several church buildings at the original downtown site. In 1822, Michigan became part of the Cincinnati diocese and had six thousand Catholics at that time. In 1833, a diocese was established at Detroit covering Michigan and the Northwest Territory, which then included Wisconsin. Ste. Anne was the only church in the city and served briefly as the first Detroit cathedral.

As the spelling of its name and its origin suggests, Ste. Anne was originally a French-speaking parish. An internal dispute arose when a second French-speaking parish, St. Joachim, was established by the bishop of Detroit in the 1880s. It had overtones of the age-old problem of lay investiture, since church holdings were in the hands of a lay board of trustees. Eventually, the property was sold, the old church demolished, and the proceeds divided between the two French-speaking parishes.

One of the relics removed to Ste. Anne's present location were the remains of Father Gabriel Richard, a Sulpician who was its pastor during the early 1800s. He had been ordained in Paris just after the French Revolution and began his ministry in America at Prairie du Rocher and Kaskaskia, two early French settlements on the banks of the Mississippi River in Illinois. Father Richard gained considerable fame upon being elected territorial delegate from Michigan to the U.S. House of Representatives, the first priest ever to have sat in that body. He was also one of the founders of the University of Michigan. He died in 1832 while attending cholera victims in a plague that claimed the lives of one fifth of Detroit's five thousand inhabitants. Father Richard's remains are entombed in a small chapel in the present parish church.

The present Gothic Revival church, dating from 1886, was designed by a parishioner. The bishop of Detroit was able to have it staffed by French-speaking Canadian priests who were members of the Congregation of St. Basil. The Basilian Fathers have remained to this day. For many years the parish sponsored separate elementary schools for boys and girls that were bilingual. Those schools are now closed.

As in the case of many downtown or intown parishes, the neighborhood and the parish that Ste. Anne served changed markedly over the years. The École Ste. Anne is closed, and the last French sermon was preached in 1942 as French-speaking residents of the area dispersed.

In 1967, there was considerable doubt that the present church could remain open because of serious structural flaws that had developed. The entire right aisle was roped off and placed off limits because of physical deterioration. Archdiocesan architects and engineers estimated that between $350,000 and $500,000 would be required to make the necessary repairs. The pastor, Father Roger de Billy, stated that if Ste. Anne were any other church, it would have been destroyed because its continued use would be impossible. However, the funds were raised and the required repairs were made, so Ste. Anne's was rescued from age and the elements by its parishioners and others who contributed to the fund raised by a group called Friends of Ste. Anne.

Ste. Anne now has approximately eight hundred families, about five hundred of whom are Hispanic. Many are drawn to the parish from areas outside its parish boundaries. Some Masses and other services are conducted in Spanish, and these are well attended. Banners and displays about the church testify to the fact that what was once a French-English parish is now a Spanish-English parish.

A look at the area surrounding Ste. Anne today makes it plain that the neighborhood has seen better days. Nearby is the Ambassador Bridge, which forms a major port of entry into the United States from Windsor, Ontario. Heavy truck traffic to and from Canada runs through the parish at all hours of the day and night. Many of the older frame houses are in a state of decline and some have been demolished. Since it is close to downtown Detroit, the parish will predictably undergo a major revival. However, that proximity poses a problem as well as a solution, since there are economic forces that want to enlarge the Ambassador Bridge port of entry, the Bureau of Customs facility, and truck terminals and garages. The purchaser of the old Michigan Central Railroad depot also has commercial and industrial plans for the area. The parish, acting through the Hubbard-Richard Neighborhood Council, is insistent that the area retain its residential character and that any older residents who have been displaced by development are enabled to find affordable housing in their old neighborhood. Once plans are final, the question of financing redevelopment still remains.

Reconstruction of the central portions of Detroit will eventually extend into the parish boundaries and, when it does, the 285-year-old church will be there to greet it, as it has greeted many earlier changes, to ensure that the parish remains a place in which to live and worship, not just an area to drive through.

52
Sts. Peter and Paul

Detroit

MICHIGAN

The oldest church building in the city of Detroit still in use by any denomination is Sts. Peter and Paul Church, located on East Jefferson Street across from the renowned office and shopping complex known as the Renaissance Center. In an earlier day, before roadways and skyscrapers obscured the view, Sts. Peter and Paul Church overlooked the Detroit River and the Windsor skyline on the Canadian side.

This church was constructed at the insistence of Peter P. Lefevere, Detroit's second bishop, who was appointed in 1841. Bishop Lefevere was a rigorist clergyman, a stern and unbending pastor. He was also a missionary at heart and spent much time and energy traveling to Indian villages and white settlements in a far-flung diocese that extended all the way to St. Paul in the Minnesota Territory. He was particularly concerned about alcoholism, which he saw as a serious threat to the people of his jurisdiction, and he frequently led congregations in "taking the pledge." His first Mass in Detroit was said on Christmas Eve, 1841, at Ste. Anne de Detroit Church, after which he asked his congregation to take an oath swearing off the use of alcoholic beverages.

From the outset of his tenure Bishop Lefevere was plagued by financial difficulties. His predecessor and others had bought, in the name of the Church, several tracts of public land in the Michigan Territory. They found that they could not make local tax payments on some of its properties and were being foreclosed upon. One such property was a completed church building having an outstanding $3,000 mortgage. Bishop Lefevere found that he had to direct much of his effort in meeting this financial problem before addressing the other problems associated with the growth and development of his diocese.

In light of these circumstances, it was not surprising that he moved cautiously in building his own cathedral. Sts. Peter and Paul [**pictured above**] was designed in Italian Renaissance style by Francis Letourno. It is 80 feet by 160 feet and 72 feet high, and was constructed to seat 1,000 people. The original plans called for the erection of a steeple in the front, but this feature was never undertaken. The church was built on a pay-as-you-go basis. No contracts were let for brick or labor until there was money in the bank to pay the bill. Upon completion, the church cost about $30,000 to construct.

Sts. Peter and Paul was started in 1844 and consecrated in 1848, just as Detroit was beginning to experience a large influx of Catholic immigrants. It was designated as the cathedral parish because Bishop Lefevere was having difficulties with the trustees who actually owned the property of Ste. Anne's Church. He moved out of Ste. Anne's and relocated the seat of his diocese in the new church. When this occurred, he temporarily closed Most Holy Trinity, the Irish church that had been established in 1835, to make sure that his new church would have a sufficient congregation to support its activities. When he found that there were enough Irishmen to go around, Bishop Lefevere then reopened Most Holy Trinity. For the next seventy-five years Sts. Peter and Paul was generally regarded as an Irish parish. In fact, it was once necessary for its pastor to publish an announcement reminding his congregation that in the United States St. Patrick's Day was not a holy day of obligation.

In 1852, Bishop Lefevere reported to the First Plenary Council of the American Church in Baltimore that his diocese included 40 existing churches, 13 more under construction, and had 32 priests serving approximately 85,000 Catholics. As for the cathedral parish, it flourished. In 1857, the pulpit, originally constructed in the middle of the building because of poor acoustics, was placed near the altar. The altar, the confessionals, and a chapel were adorned with wood carvings, and an artist, Angelo Paldi, was retained to paint an altar fresco, which he spent a year completing. It was also the site of an occasional ordination, since Bishop Lefevere operated a seminary in his residence to educate priests for his expanding diocese. Parish records indicate that during its first 21 years the parish conducted 5,000 baptisms, approximately 1,200 marriages, and 2,300 funerals.

When Bishop Caspar Borgess came to Detroit in 1869 upon the death of Bishop Lefevere, one of his principal ambitions was to start a Catholic college in the city. In the 1840s, the Missouri province of the Society of Jesus, headquartered in St. Louis, was asked to start colleges in both Cincinnati and Detroit. It had insufficient personnel for two colleges and opted to open Xavier University in Cincinnati. Bishop Borgess renewed the invitation to the Jesuits to come to Detroit and offered to transfer to the society the title to Sts. Peter and Paul Church and the property surrounding it as an inducement. They agreed and, on April 5, 1877, the society took title to the church property. The parish was also given definite territorial boundaries and has been operated as a Jesuit parish since that time. Bishop Borgess then transferred the seat of his diocese to the newly erected St. Aloysius Church on Washington Boulevard.

The Jesuits began their educational mission at this location almost immediately. In the following year, there were ninety-five students in the college that the Jesuits had named after the city in which it was located. Originally, the rector of the college also served as pastor of the parish, but eventually the two positions grew to be too burdensome for one individual, so the responsibilities were divided. By 1887, there were nineteen Jesuits in residence at the college and parish.

A parochial school had been established at Sts. Peter and Paul before the coming of the Jesuits but did not last long. In 1856, the Christian Brothers established another school, which was then taken over by lay teachers in 1859. In 1864, the Immaculate Heart of Mary Sisters from Monroe, Michigan, arrived. They were eventually superseded by the Madames of the Sacred Heart, who in turn were replaced in 1889 by the Sisters of Charity. The latter remained with the parish until the school was closed in the 1950s.

During the late 1800s and early 1900s, the area surrounding Sts. Peter and Paul Church was one of the most attractive and prosperous parts of Detroit. Jefferson Avenue was a wide, tree-shaded boulevard leading from the downtown area along the Detroit River to the Belle Isle Bridge, which was about two miles "up river." In this setting, Sts. Peter and Paul parish, flanked by a growing college of higher learning, flourished. In 1890, a new building for Detroit College, as it was then called, was constructed at a cost of $60,000. In 1892, the church itself was extensively renovated, enlarged, and landscaped. The parish was large and active. An 1894 parish diary, reporting on the Lenten retreat, or mission for men and women, stated: "March 11 — close of women's parish retreat. Church packed, jam-packed! 9 confessors hearing all day. At least 1,000 confessions heard." An entry for the men's retreat the following week was equally upbeat but with a different emphasis: "1,000 communions — heavy confessions — immense crowds."

By the turn of the century, certain social divisions began to grow within the parish and its ethnic character began to change. Along the banks of the Detroit River a series of shacks came into existence that were occupied by a large number of poor families. Father Ferdinand Wineman, S.J., an assistant pastor, founded what was then called a settlement house on Woodbridge Street to provide social and educational services for these residents. The house took on his name after he died in 1907. It lasted at this address until 1946 when the commercialization of the area eliminated most of the residents, both poor and otherwise. The League of Catholic Women, who had operated Wineman House for a number of years, relocated it to Avery Street to serve two other parishes that had retained their residential character.

In 1911, Detroit College became the University of Detroit. In 1916, it opened a law school right next to the parish church. In 1922, the university purchased property on Six Mile Road, in what was then a suburb, and by 1927 it had relocated many of its activities. By 1931, the University of Detroit High School, which had also been at the Jefferson Avenue location many years, moved even further out in the suburbs. Still remaining next to the parish church, in an area now given over to the courts, to local government, and to business and finance, are the university's School of Business and Finance and the Law School. The entire university, which had only ninety-five students in 1878, now has more than six thousand in all of its various colleges and is one of the largest Catholic universities in the United States.

Ironically enough, the automobile, which brought most of the prosperity and expansion to Detroit, contributed in no small way to the decline in the size and activity of Sts. Peter and Paul. Not only did parishioners move farther and farther away from the central city when new office and store construction moved in the direction of the church, but the character of Jefferson Avenue changed from a tree-shaded boulevard to a busy throughway shunting large numbers of cars past the church into downtown Detroit at high rates of speed. Today, the church advertises itself as a metro parish. It has only about two hundred regular parishioners, many of whom live well beyond its territorial boundaries. It regularly serves a large number of Catholics employed in downtown Detroit. Its prominent neighbor, the "Ren Cen," has yet to generate a significant renaissance in residential development, and this is the foundation of any parochial existence. However, additional apartment complexes continue to be built from time to time along East Jefferson, taking the place of residences, and, as this trend continues, Sts. Peter and Paul expects to experience a similar improvement in the renewal of its parish life.

53
Holy Name of Mary

Sault Ste. Marie
MICHIGAN

The roots of the Catholic Church in Upper Michigan extend into the histories of three existing parishes. Holy Name of Mary, the first cathedral of the Marquette diocese, is located a block from the St. Mary's River, which divides the United States from Canada. In so doing, the river unites Lake Superior to Lake Huron through what was originally a waterfall and is now a series of five canal locks. The "Soo" (the pronunciation of the Old French word *sault* for "rapids" or "falls"), as it is familiarly called, is an hour by car and two and a half days by dogsled from St. Ignace, formerly referred to as Pointe St. Ignace. That city overlooks the Mackinac Straits, which divide Lake Huron from Lake Michigan. Its parish is St. Ignatius Loyola. About ten miles offshore at this point is Mackinac Island, originally an Indian settlement and now an upscale vacation resort, where Ste. Anne's Church has been located for more than two centuries.

The mission effort of the Catholic Church in this region was undertaken by French Jesuits. They made their headquarters originally at what is now Midland, Ontario, at a spot on Georgian Bay they called Huronia. The major thrust of their mission effort was directed to the Hurons, the Ottawas, and the Chippewas. In the summer of 1641, Father Isaac Jogues and Father Charles Raymbaut sailed to the Soo from Huronia and erected a large cross on the banks of the St. Mary's River. At this place, nearly two thousand Indians regularly gathered during the summer months to avail themselves of the excellent fishing in Whitefish Bay near the Lake Superior end of the river. There the two missionaries said the first Mass offered in this region about a block from where Holy Name of Mary Church is now located. Coincidentally, this event occurred in the same year that English Jesuits were beginning to evangelize the Piscataway Indians on the banks of the Potomac River in southern Maryland. Fathers Jogues and Raymbaut departed shortly thereafter. They intended to return and establish a mission on the St. Mary's River, but their plans came to naught because, in the following year, Father Raymbaut died of tuberculosis and, five years later, Father Jogues was martyred at the hands of the Mohawks in Upstate New York.

It was another nineteen years before the Jesuits returned to the Upper Peninsula of Michigan. In October 1660, Father René Ménard said Mass on the banks of Lake Superior about two hundred twenty-five miles west of Sault Ste. Marie at L'Anse. Little is known of what became of Father Ménard, except that he went south into Wisconsin where he met his death at the rapids of the Wisconsin River. Years later, his personal effects were recovered in a Sioux village hundreds of miles west of this location.

In 1665, Father Claude Allouez, S.J., came to the Upper Peninsula carrying with him the rank of vicar general of the diocese of Quebec. He was en route to Wisconsin and decided that a mission should be established at the place Father Jogues had visited two decades earlier. It was left to Father Jacques Marquette, S.J., to establish that mission. He did so in the summer of 1668. At a place that is now a public park, he and a Jesuit Brother erected a stockaded house and a chapel next to a trading post that was already there. They began the work of evangelizing the Indians who lived or assembled at this location. A later missionary, Father Claude Dablon, S.J., described the river in a letter to his Jesuit superior:

> What is commonly called the Sault is not properly a sault, or a very high waterfall, but a very violent current of waters from Lake Superior which, finding themselves checked by a great number of rocks that dispute their passage, form a dangerous cascade of half a league in width, all of these waters descending and plunging headlong together, as if a flight of stairs, over the rocks which bar the whole river.
>
> It is three leagues below Lake Superior and twelve leagues above Lake of the Hurons, this entire extent making a beautiful river, cut up by many islands, which divide it and increase its width in some places so that the eye cannot reach across. It flows very gently through most of its entire course, being difficult of passage only at the Sault.
>
> It is at the foot of these rapids, and even amid these boiling waters, that extensive fishing is carried on, from spring until winter, of a kind of fish found only in Lake Superior and Lake Huron. It is called in the native language Atticameg, and in ours "whitefish," because in truth it is very white, and it is most excellent, so that it furnishes food, almost by itself, to the greater part of these people.

Father Marquette's chapel was destroyed by fire not long after it was built but his successor, Father Dablon, built a bigger one in its place. In 1671, a representative of the French government convoked a large council of Indian tribes at this location for the purpose of establishing the sovereignty of the king of France over this region. The Jesuits participated in the meeting and supported the effort of public authorities to exercise control over the Indians. The Hurons and the Chippewas were quite content to subordinate themselves to French rule so long as the French could protect them from their ancient enemies, the Iroquois and the Sioux.

Shortly thereafter, Father Gabriel Druillettes, S.J., wrote to his superiors that "Christianity has generally become established here, despite all obstacles." One obstacle was the promiscuous lifestyle of the Indians. It sharply conflicted with Catholic standards of family life. Another obstacle, which arose as soon as French soldiers and traders came into the area, was the liquor traffic. Generations of missionaries, beginning with the French Jesuits, preached against the menace of alcohol among Indian tribes. Soldiers and trappers were happy to use it for barter and for influencing Indians to submit to their orders. The issue of liquor traffic brought the Jesuits into disfavor with the French colonial government as well as with local governors and military commanders such as Cadillac. It also brought Bishop François Laval in Quebec into an ongoing dispute with Governor General Frontenac, who looked with a tolerant eye on giving liquor to the Indians.

In 1674, the French held another Indian council at the mission and trading post of Sault Ste. Marie, during which an incident of treachery and internal feuding broke out into a serious civil disturbance that threatened the existence of the mission. During the 1680s, the mission declined in importance and finally came to an end. Thereafter, the handful of Indians left at this fishing spot were visited occasionally by missionaries who passed through the area.

In 1670, Father Marquette left Sault Ste. Marie and took over another mission on the southern side of the Upper Peninsula at St. Ignace. Two years thereafter, Frontenac sent Louis Jolliet (also spelled Joliet) on an exploratory journey "to the country of the Mascoutens, to discover the South Sea [the Pacific Ocean] and the Great River called the Mississippi, which is believed to empty into the Gulf of California." Jolliet came to St. Ignace and enlisted the help of Father Marquette, who was eager to go to the country of the Illinois to evangelize the Indians who lived in that area. With a party of Indian guides, they set off from St. Ignace on their celebrated exploration that took them as far south along the Mississippi as the Arkansas River.

Father Marquette never saw St. Ignace again. In the spring of 1675, as he was attempting to return to his point of origin, he died of typhoid on the shores of Lake Michigan near Ludington and was buried by his companions. Two years later, his grave was discovered by Indians. They placed his remains in a birch-bark coffin and brought them back to the mission chapel where he was interred beneath the altar. Father Philip Pierson, S.J., wrote to his superiors that "the savages often come to pray at his tomb."

The St. Ignace mission on the southern side of the peninsula grew as the one on the northern side declined. However, in 1701, Cadillac indirectly caused the demise of all of the Upper Peninsula missions operated by the Jesuits, including the one they had established in 1695 at Mackinac Island. He founded a military post and village at Fort Pontchartrain, now Detroit. At this fort, he erected a church which he placed in the hands of Franciscan Recollects. Most of the Indians from the St. Mary's River and St. Ignace missions migrated to Fort Pontchartrain, leaving the Jesuits with only a small band of resident Indians.

In 1702, Father Étienne de Carheil, S.J., explained the plight of the Jesuit missions to the governor general of Canada as being "reduced to such an extremity that we can no longer maintain them against an infinite multitude of evil acts — acts of brutality and violence; of injustice and impiety; of lewd and shameless conduct; of contempt and insult. To such acts the infamous and baleful trade in brandy gives rise everywhere, among all the nations, up here — where it is carried on by going from village to village, and by rowing over the lakes with a prodigious quantity of brandy in barrels, without any restraint. Had His Majesty but once seen what passes, both here and at Montreal, during the whole time this wretched traffic goes on, I am sure he would not for a moment hesitate, and at the very first sight of it, to forbid it under the severest penalties."

Continuing, he said: "In our despair, there is no other step to take than to leave our missions and abandon them to the brandy traders, so that they may establish therein the domain of their trade, of drunkenness, and of immorality. This what we shall propose to our superiors in Canada and in France, being compelled thereto by the state of uselessness to which we have been reduced by the permission given to carry on that deplorable trade."

In summing up his problems, Father Carheil wrote: "The first is the commerce in brandy; the second is the commerce of the savage women with the French. Both are carried on in an equally public manner, without our being able to remedy the evil because we are not supported by the commandant. They, far from attempting when we undertake to remonstrate with them to direct these traders, themselves carry them on with greater freedom than do their subordinates."

In 1706, the Jesuits left St. Ignace. Before leaving, they burned their chapel to the ground so that it could not be desecrated after they left. In 1712, they attempted to revive the mission at the request of the governor general, but there were few Indians and fewer French in the area to warrant a continuing ministry. During the next several decades, the presence of priests at this location was sporadic. In 1760, the French lost Canada to the English. The French had withdrawn the Jesuits a few years earlier.

From the time British rule began in 1763 until British troops actually left in 1796, religious freedom was granted to Catholics but there were only a few around to enjoy it. The St. Ignace mission was relocated to the Lower Peninsula and the only remaining place of Catholic worship in Upper Michigan was on Mackinac Island. Father Du Jaunay, a Jesuit missionary, lived on the island from 1742 until 1765 or thereabouts.

However, the first permanent church was not constructed until 1780. In fact, the building in question was the chapel located on the mainland at St. Ignace, which was dragged across the ice during the winter and placed on a lot known as the old graveyard. Trustees were elected to maintain the church, and, beginning in 1785, it was visited from time to time by Father Louis Payet. He stayed only a short while but made many entries in the sacramental records of Ste. Anne's parish during his visits. In 1799, Father Gabriel Richard visited Mackinac Island shortly after coming to Michigan. He found a very distressing situation that arose from abuse of alcohol, lack of religious instruction, and the absence of a priest for many years. However, for the next several decades, the only religious ministrations were by visiting priests who came from time to time, usually in the summer months.

In 1820, there were only half a dozen English and French families living at the Soo. In 1822, the U.S. government established a military post, Fort Brady, in the midst of what was the ancient village. The fort remained until 1971. As a result of this military establishment, a number of Irish Catholics came to Sault Ste. Marie. Henry Rowe Schoolcraft, a geologist and writer, lived in the area for many years. In 1820, he wrote that the village "has the marks of an ancient settlement fallen to decay." He noted that there were about forty Chippewa lodges in the vicinity.

In 1828, the Michigan territorial government established Chippewa County. It included all of the Upper Peninsula and extended into Wisconsin and eastern Minnesota. Sault Ste. Marie was named the county seat. About 1830, Father Samuel Mazzuchelli, an Italian Dominican, heard there were Catholics living along the St. Mary's River and visited the location twice a year for the next few years. At that time, the Upper Peninsula was part of the diocese of Cincinnati, so Bishop Edward D. Fenwick, the first bishop of Cincinnati, came to Sault Ste. Marie in 1830 during a canonical visitation of the area. Since there was no church in existence, Mass was celebrated in a private home on Water Street.

The first pastor of St. Mary's Church, as it was originally called, was Father Francis Haetscher, a Redemptorist, who was assigned to the area just after the creation of the diocese of Detroit. Immediately after his arrival in 1834, he built a small log chapel, the third Catholic church to be constructed in the area. The church was built on a tract of land near the river that had been quitclaimed to Catholic authorities in 1823 by a French settler, Jean Baptiste Du Bois, for the sum of 450 livres. Du Bois retained the right to reside on the property in his log cabin for the remainder of his life. Bishop Frederic Résé, the first bishop of Detroit, visited Sault Ste. Marie the same summer and confirmed nearly one hundred people. Records of St. Mary's parish date back to 1837 but contain entries, made many years after the events, of baptisms that took place as early as 1815. These entries sometimes contained the notation "stray baptism."

Father Haetscher was recalled in 1836 by the Redemptorists and sent to one of their missions in Ohio. His replacement, Father Francis Pierz, built another church, some forty-five feet by seventy-five feet, made of boards and logs. The crevices between the logs were packed with mud, the inside was plastered, and the outside was clapboard.

This construction was financed in part by the Leopoldine Society, the Austrian missionary society located in Vienna. The church was located just in front of where the present Holy Name of Mary Procathedral stands.

Father Pierz was not a resident pastor. He came to Sault Ste. Marie from time to time as his schedule permitted before he moved on to a mission at La Pointe. The parish then was attended by a series of diocesan priests until 1845 when the Jesuits agreed to accept it as a mission and returned to the Soo after an absence of one hundred forty years. In the same year, the village of Sault Ste. Marie was granted a municipal charter. By this time, there were about four hundred Catholics in the city, most of whom were Frenchmen who supported themselves from the fur trade or from logging operations. Because the parish had not been regularly served by resident priests, Catholics in the area were not accustomed to attending Mass every Sunday, so the Jesuits had to reeducate them in their obligation of regular Sunday observance. With a brief hiatus of about five years, the Jesuits remained at the parish until 1954.

During this era, Sault Ste. Marie and the entire diocese of which it is now a part came to know the most celebrated figure in the Catholic Church in Upper Michigan, Father (and later Bishop) Frederic Baraga. Baraga was born in Slovenia, until recently a part of Yugoslavia but then a part of the Austro-Hungarian Empire. The son of well-to-do parents, he studied law in Vienna where he met Clement Hofbauer, a Redemptorist priest and renowned spiritual adviser, who was canonized in 1888. St. Clement pointed Baraga in the direction of the priesthood. After graduating from law school, Baraga said good-bye to his fiancé and entered the seminary at Laibach. After being ordained in 1823, he was assigned to a series of parishes in Slovenia but felt a call to be a missionary to the Indians of North America.

His interest in the Indian missions was stimulated by a booklet written by Father Gabriel Richard, then vicar general of the Cincinnati diocese in Michigan. In this booklet, Father Richard quoted an Indian chief as saying to him, "We hope you will send us a priest who will teach us how to live on earth." Father Richard's published reaction to the request was: "If only my voice could be heard over Catholic Europe, I would cry out and I would not stop repeating: 'The poor Indians are famished for spiritual food, they are languishing and they beg your charity: Give it to them or they will perish . . . no . . . they will not perish because there are still 3,000 priests and religious in Rome.' "

Father Baraga volunteered for the Cincinnati diocese and was accepted by Bishop Fenwick. When he arrived in the United States in 1830, only four percent of its thirteen million inhabitants were Catholics; in Ohio, only one percent of its 581,000 residents were members of the Church. In 1831, Father Baraga accompanied Bishop Fenwick on a tour of Lower Michigan. On May 28, 1831, they arrived at what became Father Baraga's first Indian mission, L'Arbre Croche (Crooked Tree), now Harbor Springs. It is located on the northwest tip of Michigan's Lower Peninsula. A church, mission house, and school building had already been built in the Indian village by a French secular priest who had to return to his native country, so Father Baraga took them over. He visited each wigwam, heard confessions, burned pagan idols found in the village, and, in a year's time, had learned enough of the Ottawa language to write a prayer book and a hymnal in the native tongue. He published these books. They became the first of thirty-two religious tracts that he wrote in Indian languages. Father Baraga spoke seven European languages and put his talent to use by writing a dictionary and a grammar in the Chippewa and Ottawa languages. They remain today the principal sources of information about these primitive tongues, both of which have largely disappeared.

In describing his first mission in a letter to the Leopoldine Society, he wrote: "Our church, the school house, and my house are all of wood, roofed with tree bark. All of this the Indians have made themselves. One can imagine how they look. When it rains, I must spread my overcoat over the table on which I have my books and papers in order to protect them from inundation; over my bed I spread my umbrella, and I save myself as well as I can in a corner of my small room where it drips the least. Nevertheless, I am happier here in my little room than all the employers and kings in their golden palaces." He added, "It is unspeakably joyful and consoling for me to be here."

In 1833, Father Baraga was transferred to another Indian village at Grand River where he built another log church and school with funds supplied by the Viennese mission society. He looked upon his function in Michigan as one of building new mission churches that others would then take over as he moved on to yet another mission area. In addition to the church at Grand River, he also founded a church at Grand Rapids. Like the Jesuits one hundred fifty years earlier, he preached constantly against alcohol and warned of its dire consequences. He met with little success and, on one occasion, was attacked by a mob who took exception to his remarks about liquor.

Father Baraga was able to convince the Indians to go to Mass at least on major feast days such as Christmas. Some would travel three or four days in order to attend such celebrations. He was confronted by many unexpected obstacles that were unique to the Indian missions. One seventeen-year-old girl came to Grand River from Muskegon and requested to be baptized despite the fact that her father had threatened to cut off her ears if she ever became a Christian.

In 1835, Father Baraga was transferred to Upper Michigan. There he spent the rest of his life in a mission effort centered on and around Lake Superior, the lake that Longfellow's *Song of Hiawatha* referred to as Gitche Gumee, "the shining Big-Sea-Water." He built a mission on Madeline Island, located in Lake Superior, at a village called La Pointe. He remained at this post until 1843 when he was transferred one hundred miles east to L'Anse, an area on the lake shore that Father Ménard had visited two hundred years before. There he built another Indian mission church.

At this time, the Upper Peninsula was beginning to see an influx of white settlers who came to work in the lumber industry and in iron and copper mines that were being opened. Their presence placed more burdens on church authorities in providing religious services. It shifted their focus from missionary work among Indians to the establishment of parishes in new white settlements. For Father Baraga and other priests this meant, among other things, preaching and hearing confessions in several languages. It was not uncommon for him to preach three sermons on Sunday, one in French, one in English, and the third in either Ottawa or Chippewa.

Two physical factors seriously impeded the work of Father Baraga and other priests in the Upper Peninsula. One was the remoteness of settlements and the other was weather. Shipping on the Great Lakes takes place only between May and November. During the rest of the year, the lakes are frozen solid and the only means of travel available in pioneer days was by dogsled or on foot. Snows frequently accumulated to depths of three feet or more; roads were few and little more than trails. Any missionary who wished to get about had to do so on foot with the use of giant, awkward snowshoes, the kind that were among Father Baraga's most valuable possessions.

His daily routine called for rising at 3:00 A.M. in the summer and 4:00 A.M. in the winter and spending an hour in prayer before beginning the day's work. Then he began his missionary rounds. He often stayed in the confessional until 11:00 P.M. to accommodate penitents.

Stories abound concerning both his charity and his physical stamina in the face of natural obstacles. On one occasion, he was met by a traveler while walking from La Pointe to Fond du Lac, a distance of two hundred fifty miles, to bring medicine to a village where he had heard there was great suffering. He was traveling on foot when his snowshoes gave out, so he had to be assisted by a traveler he met in order to keep from perishing in the deep snow. Traveling often meant sleeping in the open in blizzards when the temperature was 20° or 30° below zero. On one trip in 1852, he walked through a snowstorm for twenty-four consecutive hours with only a piece of bread in his pocket in order to make a sick call. He did not stop to rest because, in doing so, he might have fallen asleep and died from exposure. On yet another occasion, he awoke one morning to find himself marooned on an ice floe that had become detached and was floating free in a body of cold water. Even after the annual spring thaw, traveling by boat could be perilous, since storms often arose that required voyagers to come ashore and wait out the fury of the gale.

In 1853, Upper Michigan was designated a vicariate, and Sault Ste. Marie was named its principal city. The old clapboard church Father Pierz built in 1837 became its cathedral. The vicariate was called Marianopolis. After twenty years in the missions throughout this area, Father Baraga was appointed the first bishop and was consecrated on November 1, 1853, at St. Peter in Chains Cathedral in Cincinnati. Immediately thereafter, he left for Europe to seek both funds and priests with which to operate the vicariate. While in Rome, he presented Pope Pius IX a Chippewa and Ottawa dictionary. The Holy Father gave him a silver chalice that now reposes in the cathedral at Marquette. One thorny question Bishop Baraga had to take up with church authorities was the application of the Pauline Privilege on divorce and remarriage to newly converted Indians, many of whom had lived in a polygamous state before being baptized, so they could be lawfully united in a sacramental marriage.

Bishop Baraga arrived by boat in Sault Ste. Marie in August of 1854 and carried his carpetbag from the dock to St. Mary's rectory. He made his principal residence in the city for the next eleven years, building an unimpressive two-story clapboard house a block from the cathedral to serve as his episcopal palace. It is still standing. He was not interested in technicalities concerning either diocesan boundaries or parish lines. Neighboring bishops were happy to let him support missions that could be supervised from Sault Ste. Marie, even though they might be located outside the boundaries of the vicariate. As a result, Bishop Baraga assumed responsibility for a series of Indian missions ringing Lake Superior on both its Canadian and American shores. He also supervised a number of missions along the coast of Lower Michigan that were in the Detroit diocese. Instead of calling his churches parishes, he referred to them as missions and did not draw any parish lines. He made determined and repeated efforts to visit all of these missions.

Weather dictated his schedule. For five months of each year the only way to travel in or out of Sault Ste. Marie was on foot. The lakes were frozen solid. During the winter months, he remained in Sault Ste. Marie and served as the actual functioning pastor of the cathedral parish, since the Jesuits had left St. Mary's parish shortly after the vicariate was established and did not return until about 1864. During the summer months, he was always able to find another priest to take over his parish duties so that he could travel throughout the vicariate. In 1857, the vicariate was elevated to the status of a diocese, but this fact did not materially affect Bishop Baraga's routine.

This procedure had its drawbacks. For instance, the Indians who lived at Mackinac Island usually left the island early in the spring to work at logging operations, so they had to be reached by the bishop during the winter months in order to administer confirmation. This meant a two- or three-day walk on snowshoes from Sault Ste. Marie to St. Ignace and then a trip across the ice to the island. This difficulty did not deter the bishop.

Most of the parishioners at St. Mary's were French so Bishop Baraga had to deliver sermons on Sunday both in French and in English. The only source of parish income was the pew rental, and often it was not paid. In 1856, Bishop Baraga built a new altar and enlarged the building that was being used for a school. For a brief period the Ursuline nuns taught at the school, but they left, so the bishop tried to continue the school with the use of laymen. This proved unsatisfactory. Later, the Sisters of St. Joseph came to teach the girls. The bishop was finally able to prevail upon the Jesuits to take over the parish once more. When Father John B. Menet arrived at the Soo, his boat was given a six-gun salute by the soldiers at Fort Brady. He brought with him a Brother LaCoste, who once again began to teach the boys as he had done years before.

Bishop Baraga made an effort to provide for the security of the parish by requesting the United States government to recognize an ancient title to church property that antedated the deed the church had received from Du Bois. The claim in question involved a strip of land seventy-nine feet wide stretching inland from the river for more than a mile. Fort Brady was located on a small portion of the claimed property near the river and disputed the church's title. The effort to obtain a clear title took twenty-five years and was not completed until long after Bishop Baraga's death. The government certificate, issued in 1880, excluded Fort Brady from recognized church title and limited it to a tract of twenty-six acres. It was not until the government recognized this title that the parish undertook to build a larger and more elaborate church.

The designation of Sault Ste. Marie as the cathedral city for the vicariate coincided with significant development in and around the city. Between 1853 and 1855, canal locks were built to permit shipping between Lake Superior and Lake Huron, which is twenty-two feet below the level of the larger body of water. Before that time, Sault Ste. Marie was a portage. Ships were actually dragged on greased rails through its streets from one lake to the other. The canal generated widespread commercial activity, but the Soo still lacked rail transportation and was not connected to a railroad until 1887. Meanwhile, another Upper Peninsula city, Marquette, some one hundred sixty-five miles west, became a railhead as copper and iron mining were coming into full operation. Communication remained difficult between the bishop at Sault Ste. Marie and missionaries in other parts of the diocese, especially in the winter; so, in 1865, at Bishop Baraga's request, the seat of the diocese was moved to Marquette and has remained there ever since. St. Mary's then was deemed to be a procathedral.

Bishop Baraga suffered a stroke in 1866 at the Second Plenary Council in Baltimore but was able to return to Marquette. He died there in 1868 and was buried in his new cathedral. Some sixty-five years later, Slovenian Catholics in his native diocese began a beatification cause that is still in progress. It is supported not only in Europe but also by an organized effort by the diocese of Marquette and Catholics generally in the Upper Peninsula. The memory of the old bishop has been perpetuated by public authorities in the name of a Michigan county and several townships and other political subdivisions.

The brick church [**pictured above**] was completed in 1881 and has served the parish since that date. It was the only Catholic church in the city until about 1940. Now there are four. At its dedication, the church acquired the present title of Holy Name of Mary, although it is still referred to as St. Mary's. In 1967, the parish constructed next to the church a large concrete tower, some two hundred ten feet high, for the benefit of tourists and others who come to the Soo in large numbers. From the top of the tower one can see the five locks of the Sault Ste. Marie canal and a few of the seventeen thousand ships that pass through these locks each year. During the summer months, the parish, in cooperation with local Protestant churches, has sponsored a Pathway Program designed to provide tour guides to all of the old churches and points of interest in the city.

Today, Sault Ste. Marie, Michigan, has only about fifteen thousand inhabitants, while its neighbor with the same name across the river in Ontario has about eighty thousand. The Canadian side is relatively prosperous, thanks to the Algoma Steel Mill located at the Lake Superior end of the canal locks. On the American side, the Michigan city has suffered economic problems with the closing of Fort Brady, a nearby U.S. Air

Force base, and two major factories. While shipping through the locks is brisk, few if any ships stop at the Michigan city. The decision of the state of Michigan to place a large prison complex at the Soo has recently boosted chances for economic recovery.

A substantial portion of the city is made up of senior citizens, as is St. Mary's parish. The parish has about six hundred families, but its own parochial school and one operated by a neighboring parish have closed. As a result, St. Mary's has an active CCD program at all grade levels. Mass was said in French until about 1970 but this practice has been discontinued. The parish has substantial numbers of Irish, French, Italian, and Chippewa parishioners. Some of the latter live in town in preference to their reservation, which is only a few miles away. The parish has just completed a $200,000 renovation on the century-old building, and it was rededicated in 1987. Among the artifacts that the church retains are memorabilia of Bishop Baraga — a chest, some prayer books, and of course his snowshoes.

On the other side of the peninsula, St. Ignatius Loyola parish at St. Ignace has about four hundred fifty Catholic families who live year-round in a city that is about forty-five percent Catholic. St. Anne's on Mackinac Island has about six hundred fifty permanent parishioners; but, at the height of the tourist season, about ten thousand people come to the island, so the church must arrange to meet their spiritual needs. In the center of the town of St. Ignace is a monument next to the former parish church, now a museum, which marks the burial place of Father Marquette who, as mentioned earlier, died near Ludington in 1675. In 1877, a birch-bark box containing what are believed to be his remains was discovered by Patrick Murray, a local resident, who was clearing a spot near his home for a garden. The site of the discovery was the location of the early Jesuit mission church. The best scientific opinion asserts that what Murray found were actually the remains of the famed Jesuit explorer, whose body was brought back to St. Ignace from Ludington some two hundred years before the discovery was made. These relics are only a small memento of an extraordinary individual whose efforts as a missionary and pathfinder in the Northwest Territory laid the groundwork for the settlement of an entire region.

54
Basilica of St. Francis Xavier

Vincennes
INDIANA

The Basilica of St. Francis Xavier is located on the banks of the Wabash River on a route French voyageurs used in the sixteenth and seventeenth centuries to reach the Mississippi River from the Great Lakes. Originally called the St. Jerome River, the Ouabache (Wabash) was regarded by the French as the principal river in the region. In their mind, the Ohio was but a tributary. There is historical support for the belief that a French Jesuit missionary said Mass in the Vincennes area as early as 1702. These missionaries, including Father Pierre Mermet, S.J., were principally concerned with evangelizing the Indians, not with ministering to French inhabitants. Vincennes took its name from François Morgan, Sieur de Vincennes, who built a small fort at the present site of the city sometime around 1732. He was later burned at the stake in Louisiana by the Chickasaw Indians, together with members of a party that included Father Senat, a Jesuit missionary.

Post Vincennes, as the French fort came to be known, was one of three principal settlements in Indiana in pre-Revolutionary times. The others were Lafayette (Fort Ouiatenon) and Fort Wayne (known earlier as Fort Miami). Church records at Vincennes date back to 1749 when Father Sébastien Meurin, S.J., built a crude log building, some twenty feet by sixty feet, which became the first St. Francis Xavier

Church. It was made of timbers, with adobe mud used to fill in the cracks between the logs. This church was one of several mission posts that French Jesuits tried to establish in the Illinois-Indiana area. The original parish records were kept in French but later entries were made in Latin.

Father Meurin was not a resident pastor. Along with other missionaries in the area, he visited the community from time to time. When the French government expelled the Jesuits from North America about 1753, Father Meurin obtained special permission to remain and was the only priest left in the region. As a result, missionary activity, both among the Indians and French settlers, came to a halt. In 1763, the British took nominal control of the region, but the presence of civil authority was so limited that the territory existed in a state of near anarchy.

Despite changes in political control, about seven hundred French settlers remained in and about Post Vincennes. In 1767, they wrote Jean Olivier Briand, the bishop of Quebec, in whose diocese Vincennes was located, and asked him to send them a priest. Bishop Briand passed the request along to Father Pierre Gibault, his vicar general in the West, who lived at the French settlement on the Mississippi at Cahokia. Father Gibault came to Vincennes in the fall of 1769 and wrote the following to the bishop after staying in the village for three months: "After nearly seven years that it has been deprived of priests, everything is lax, and free thinking and irreverence have come in; nevertheless, upon my arrival all the people came in crowds to receive me at the shore of the Wabash River. Some threw themselves on their knees without being able to speak, others spoke only with sobs: some cried, 'My father, save us, we are at the edge of hell'; others said, 'God has not forsaken us yet, for it is He who sends you to us to make us repent of our sins.' Some said, 'Oh, sir, why did you not come a month ago? Then my poor wife, my dear father, my dear mother, my poor child would not have died without the sacrament.' "

After leaving Vincennes in February 1770, Father Gibault did not return until July of 1775. During his absence, a layman, listed in the records only as Phillibert, performed lay baptisms and recorded them in parish registers. He held a minor civil post called notary and evidently felt that it was incumbent upon him as notary to maintain church records as well as government ones. After Father Gibault's brief visit in 1775, no priests, other than an occasional missionary from Detroit, came to Vincennes until 1784. Again it was Phillibert who continued to function at the church as he had in the past.

In 1778 and 1779, events of controlling significance in the West occurred, centering, in large part, on Father Gibault and St. Francis Xavier Church. In the spring of 1778, General George Rogers Clark was commissioned by Patrick Henry, the governor of Virginia, to organize a contingent of Kentucky militiamen and to attack British forts along the Mississippi and the Wabash in order to secure the region for the American colonists. General Clark and his men captured Kaskaskia on the Mississippi where he met Father Gibault and Colonel Francis Vigo, a merchant. Colonel Vigo, who was born in Italy and had joined the Spanish Army, provided financing to General Clark that enabled Clark to continue his expedition. Father Gibault was convinced that the British should be expelled and agreed to help the Kentucky militia. With a physician by the name of Jean Laffont and several others, he traveled to Vincennes for the purpose of inducing French Canadians living in the area to support the American cause. This was no small undertaking. Father Gibault always felt that as a clergyman he should ordinarily stand aloof from political or military disputes. Moreover, he was technically a British subject, so his actions could have been interpreted by British authorities as treasonable.

Upon arriving at Vincennes, he rang the bell atop the old log cabin church and summoned the French inhabitants to a meeting. He convinced them to support the colonial cause, whereupon they took an oath of allegiance to the Commonwealth of Virginia. The British had maintained a military presence at Post Vincennes, which they called Fort Sackville. However, they had retreated to Detroit, leaving it in the hands of the local French militia. These soldiers surrendered the fort and raised the colonial flag. The commander in Detroit was Colonel Henry Hamilton, known as the "hair buyer" because he had encouraged Indian tribes to present him with the scalps of insurrectionary American settlers. When he learned of the surrender of Fort Sackville, he returned to Vincennes with a detachment of British Army regulars and Indian allies and regained the fort.

In the following February, General Clark made his celebrated march through the swamps of southern Illinois from Kaskaskia to Vincennes and surprised the British. After a brief battle in which he was supported by French settlers, he obtained Colonel Hamilton's surrender and forced the British to make a permanent retreat to Detroit. From this point forward, the Ohio and Wabash Valleys were secured to the American cause. Father Gibault was given a great deal of credit for General Clark's success. In later years, he tried to get the American government to redeem some paper money it had given him and to reaffirm the French title he held to two small tracts of land in Cahokia. When his requests were denied, he left and went west to Missouri, then under Spanish control, with the feeling that he had been the victim of rank ingratitude on the part of the American government.

Before leaving the Northwest Territory, Father Gibault lived four years at Vincennes. By this time, the few Catholic churches that could be found in the Northwest Territory had come under the control of American Church authorities, principally Father John Carroll, who was functioning under the title of prefect apostolic. During his final residence in Vincennes, Father Gibault constructed a second St. Francis Xavier Church, a building ninety feet by forty-two feet, and converted the original church into a presbytère, or rectory. Church records indicate that in 1788 he performed fifty-three baptisms. By this time, English names began to show up on a register that formerly had included only French or Indian names. Father Gibault held catechism classes twice a day to instruct children of the parish in the rudiments of the Catholic religion. It was his hope that through them he could raise the spiritual and moral level of their elders. It was a large task. In 1786, he had written to the bishop of Quebec: "Everybody is in poverty, which engenders theft and rapine. Wantonness and drunkenness pass here as elegance and amusements quite in style. . . . No commandant, no troops, no prison, no hangman, always, as in small places, a crowd of relatives or allies who sustain each other; in a word, absolute impunity for these and ill luck for the stranger."

In 1788, the American government appointed Colonel John Hamtramck, a Catholic, to take charge of Post Vincennes. It was renamed Fort Knox. He could do little to bring about law and order. A continuing problem during this era were repeated Indian raids. When the French predominated in the area, there was little friction between white and Indian residents. They frequently intermarried. Upon the arrival of America settlers, hostility increased and often resulted in bloodshed.

After Father Gibault departed, Colonel Vigo, who had become a member of St. Francis Xavier parish, journeyed east to visit the newly consecrated bishop of Baltimore, John Carroll, and to ask him to send a priest to Vincennes. As was so often the case when such requests were made, Bishop Carroll had no one to send. During this period, two laymen, Antoine Gamelin and Pierre Mallet, performed the duties formerly undertaken by Phillibert.

In 1792, a former French seminary professor, Father Benedict J. Flaget, arrived in Baltimore with several other refugees from the French Revolution. Bishop Carroll immediately sent him to Vincennes where he remained for more than two years as resident pastor. During his stay, he lived at the home of Colonel Vigo. Father Flaget was popular. In fact, many years later when he returned to the city as bishop of Bardstown, he was enthusiastically greeted by old parishioners who had remembered him after an absence of twenty years. Upon arriving in Vincennes on December 13, 1792, he found the church dilapidated and its altar nothing but boards. At Christmas, only twelve of an estimated seven hundred members of the parish received Holy Communion. Like Father Gibault, he tried to reach the adults in his congregation through their children. He opened a school of religion where he taught catechism, prayers, and singing. He trained a few altar boys. Both Indian and black slaves lived in the locality, and he made an effort to care for them. There were instances when he even dug graves for some of these slaves whom he had baptized during their final illnesses.

Slowly, adults began to come to confession and to attend Mass. Many looked upon Father Flaget as an adviser and arbitrator, even in business and domestic matters. He had brought with him a few books that he had used as a seminary professor in France. Regrettably, only a few members of the congregation were literate. As a Sulpician, he was subject to the orders of his Sulpician superiors as well as Bishop Carroll. In 1795, his Sulpician superior ordered him to leave Vincennes in order to undertake an assignment in Cuba. He did so, and once again St. Francis Xavier was without a priest.

In June 1796, Father John Francis Rivet arrived in Vincennes. Like clergymen of several denominations, he was employed by the American Army to go among the Indian tribes of the Northwest Territory to attempt to pacify them. For these efforts they were promised $200 a year, a sum that was often not paid. At the outset, his ministry to the white settlers at Vincennes was incidental to his duties toward the Indians. The records of the parish indicate that at that time many Indian baptisms took place. In addition to the older French inhabitants of the area, there were also a number of Irish Catholic soldiers at Fort Knox who required his attention.

Father Rivet was born on the French island of Martinique and was another clerical refugee from the French Revolution. He was ill prepared for work among the Indians and often signed himself "Le Pauvre Missionnaire" — the poor missionary. He found it difficult to explain basic religious doctrines such as the Trinity and the Incarnation to Indian converts and often wondered if he had imparted to them sufficient instructions to justify the adult baptism he had performed. In 1800, the interpreter whom the government had furnished died, and he had to hire another from his own funds. In 1801, he wrote to Bishop Carroll: "In effect, I employ all my strength for the spiritual and temporal happiness of these poor Indians. I enlighten them in their fears. I settle, when I can, their quarrels. I visit them assiduously in their sicknesses, employ at my own expense an interpreter for these various duties, and finally I give them the last succor of religion and aid them to die well. This is all the present state of things allows me to do for them, and, it seems to me the greatest service that the United States can render to these poor unfortunates."

In 1800, there were an estimated one hundred Catholic families in Vincennes. Father Rivet gradually settled in to become their pastor. Like his predecessors, he found his parishioners lax in their religious observances and unduly attached to wild, all-night dancing. He also attempted to discourage the liquor traffic with the Indians. He solemnized marriages that had been contracted by Catholics before civil authorities as well as other unions that had not been formally contracted before anyone. He refused the sacraments to any Catholics who declined to have their marriages validated in accordance with church law. In 1804, he baptized Simon Petit Lalumière, who was born into an old Vincennes family. Years later, Lalumière entered the seminary at Bardstown and became the first native of Indiana to be ordained a priest. He returned to Indiana to serve the Vincennes diocese throughout his lifetime.

The financial support received by Father Rivet from the parish was almost nonexistent. In one six-month period, he received a total of $10 for performing a large number of baptisms and marriage ceremonies. He was able to earn a little extra money by teaching Latin in a boys' school that Territorial Governor William Henry Harrison had established at Vincennes. (Harrison would later become the ninth president of the United States.)

Father Rivet was named vicar general of the West by Bishop Carroll. He remained at St. Francis Xavier until he died of tuberculosis in 1804. At that time, the nearest priest was Father Donatien Olivier, who was located nearly two hundred miles away at Cahokia. Father Rivet sent for him during his final illness, but Father Olivier did not arrive until three days after Father Rivet died. In anticipation of this possibility, Father Rivet wrote out his final confession and placed it in a sealed envelope to be delivered to Father Olivier upon his arrival.

During the period of time that elapsed between Father Meurin's first baptisms in

1749 and the arrival of Bishop Simon Bruté in Vincennes in 1834, some thirty priests signed the register at St. Francis Xavier to indicate that they performed religious services at the parish. Of this number, Father Rivet alone remained until death. His service is commemorated by a large cross that was placed many years later in the old cemetery next to the church. In light of the transient nature of the clergy during this eighty-year period, the continuity of the parish depended largely upon the laymen who resided permanently in the city. It is little wonder that a trustee problem arose when a resident pastor arrived in the 1820s and began to assert his authority.

Following Father Rivet's death, St. Francis Xavier was without a permanent resident pastor for the next twenty years, although missionaries visited Vincennes with greater regularity than they had during similar periods in the past. The city began to grow in size and prestige. Before Indiana became a territory, Vincennes was the county seat of Knox County in the Northwest Territory, a county that embraced what is now three states. After Indiana achieved individual territorial status, Vincennes was designated as its capital and the home of its governor, William Henry Harrison. He constructed an imposing residence called Grouseland about a mile from St. Francis Xavier. From this mansion he conducted both the civil and military affairs of the territory and embarked upon extensive military campaigns, both against the Indians and later against the British after the outbreak of the War of 1812.

In 1808, Vincennes and most of the West was included in the newly created diocese of Bardstown, Kentucky. After Bishop Flaget arrived in his new diocese, a petition was sent by the Catholics of Vincennes requesting the assignment of a resident priest to St. Francis Xavier. The petition was endorsed by Governor Harrison, although he was not a Catholic. Like Bishop Carroll before him, Bishop Flaget had no one to send; but, in 1814, he came himself. It was the first of seven visits that he made to the parish as bishop and the first visit ever made by a bishop to Vincennes. He was graciously received and stayed two weeks, during which time he administered the sacraments, including the confirmation of eighty-six individuals. He later wrote that he heard the confessions "of some sinners who had grown old in their iniquities."

In 1810, the trustees of St. Francis Xavier Church obtained a charter from the Indiana legislature that gave them a recognized corporate existence. The charter was renewed by a second act of the legislature passed in 1819. The charter lay at the root of certain difficulties that soon arose. Colonel Vigo was briefly a member of the board of trustees and lent a note of restraint and common sense to their deliberations. After he left the board, problems began to arise between the other members and Father John Leo Champomier, whom Bishop Flaget sent to Vincennes as pastor in 1823 shortly after he graduated from the seminary at Bardstown. Father Champomier had been a soldier in Napoleon's army and was used to military discipline and obedience. Simply put, his parishioners were unaccustomed to military or any other kind of discipline. He immediately ran afoul of many members of the congregation. They even sued him in a civil court to enforce their asserted prerogatives.

In this dispute, Father Champomier had the complete backing of Bishop Flaget. The latter described the trustees in most unflattering terms: "[They] are in general nothing but nominal Catholics. They visit their church on Sundays through curiosity and care nothing or very little for the instructions they hear. They never or very seldom appear in the tribunal of penance and do not partake of the sacred body and blood of Jesus Christ. These people, because they are checked by their priest for their irregular conduct, for their improper discourses, for their laziness, for their fondness for pleasures and dissipations, not being able to impeach his character, wishing at the same time to hurt his feelings and turn him out of the congregation if they can; they pretend the greatest zeal for the rules and statutes of the charter, for the temporalities of the church; but to a reflecting man, resentment and revenge are the groundwork of all their steps and their clamors, and they care for the glory of God and the good of their church no more than I care for the dust on my shoes." The lawsuit and the underlying disputes were settled but only after the personal intervention of Bishop Flaget.

In his dissertation on the Catholic Church in Indiana, a Father McEvoy states that Father Champomier "often passed the meal time without a thing to eat. The clothes he had brought from France were in tatters, and he had no means of getting new ones. His presbytery was open to the winds, and he lived in fear that it would soon come tumbling down about him. The church was not a proper lodging for an animal. . . . He had sixteen hundred people who did not know how to read and, yet, had no rosaries with which to pray. To teach them to pray he needed a school, rosaries, and other aids of Catholic instruction and prayer." Father Champomier was able to obtain the services of Sister Harriet Gardiner from the Sisters of Charity at Nazareth, Kentucky. She came to Vincennes in 1824 and opened a school. She died three years later, but the school was able to survive her death.

Father Champomier began the effort that led to the construction of the church [**pictured above**]. He envisioned a structure sixty feet by one hundred fifteen feet, crossed by a transept. Beyond the transept he planned to place a sanctuary having side chapels. The parish then owned one hundred thirty acres of land. Father Champomier asked the parishioners to farm it and to apply the profits to the building fund. He appealed for support from non-Catholics as well as from members of the parish and traveled as far as Missouri and Kentucky to raise money. On March 30, 1826, the cornerstone was laid in the course of a well-attended public ceremony.

Thereafter, Father Champomier went to the East Coast and to Canada on fund-raising trips. During his first trip, the beginnings of the new structure caught fire; during his second trip, it was hit by a hurricane. By 1828, the walls had been completed, and the building was enclosed and painted. However, the parish was saddled with debts and little or no prospect of paying them. By 1831, the task of being pastor at St. Francis Xavier became too much, so Father Champomier resigned and left the United States.

During the 1820s, a second parish was founded in the area about twenty-five miles east of Vincennes. It was located in Daviess County at Black Oak Ridge, now

Montgomery, Indiana, and is the second oldest parish in the state. Called St. Peter's, it was organized to meet the needs of Kentucky Catholics who were beginning to move into southwestern Indiana. St. Peter's was originally visited only by missionaries coming to Vincennes from Louisville, but the responsibility was eventually transferred to the pastor at Vincennes. In the early 1830s, it received its first resident pastor, Father Lalumière, a native of the area, and one of three priests in the diocese when Bishop Bruté arrived a few years later.

At the urging of Bishop Flaget and many others, Vincennes became a diocese in 1834 and St. Francis Xavier, though not yet complete, became its cathedral. Vincennes was the thirteenth diocese to be established in the United States in a period of forty-five years. It extended throughout Indiana and included a strip of territory in eastern Illinois running to Chicago. The first bishop, Simon Bruté, was a French native and a friend of Bishop Flaget. He had studied medicine early in life and was a physician as well as a priest. Most of his life in this country had been spent at Emmitsburg, Maryland, as president of Mount St. Mary's College.

When he arrived in Vincennes in November of 1834, he assumed the leadership of a diocese comprising about thirty thousand Catholics, of whom three thousand lived in or near the city. The only other priests in the diocese were Father Simon Lalumière, Father John Irenaeus St. Cyr in Chicago, a Father Picot at St. Francis Xavier, and a fourth who ministered to German Catholics in eastern Indiana. The state had about 400,000 inhabitants. The *Catholic Directory* for 1834 indicated that, in all of Indiana at that time, there was only one regularly scheduled Sunday Mass, namely the 10:00 A.M. Mass at St. Francis Xavier. The exterior of the cathedral had been completed, but it was neither plastered nor whitewashed. The church had a wooden altar, a gilded tabernacle, and six candlesticks. It was surrounded by a small garden, a stable, and a cemetery. The mission house next door became Bishop Bruté's episcopal residence. Pew rental at St. Francis Xavier was then set at $100 a year. Those who paid it normally did so in grain since money was scarce.

In his first year, Bishop Bruté confirmed 90 Catholics, most of whom were in the age-group of 17 to 20. Many had made their first Communions only weeks before. Like many other pioneer bishops, he returned to France shortly after taking office to seek both money and men with which to operate his diocese. In five years, he established a small seminary, a free school, and an orphans' asylum at Vincennes. With respect to the cathedral, he wrote in 1838: "We are completely upside down with our church repairs. The sanctuary unroofed, the nave and the aisles a forest of scaffolding for the plastering, then the steeple is to be got up — the wood already cut at St. Francisville, and soon to sail up our proud Wabash, and go and tell the skies, not a lie, as the tall column in London, but the true love of Vincennes for the honor of God."

Upon returning from a sick call one day, Bishop Bruté was caught in a terrible storm and prayed for survival. After the storm lifted, he blessed the city and prayed that it be forever spared from any natural disasters. In the past one hundred fifty years, Vincennes has never experienced an earthquake or a tornado because, as some believe, of the blessing of the old bishop.

Bishop Bruté never lived to see his cathedral completed. In the year following the writing of the above statement, he caught a cold during a mission trip and died shortly after returning to Vincennes. His final hours were spent penning letters to Catholics who had ceased practicing their religion. He was making a dying appeal to them to save their souls. In the year following his death, he was buried beneath the sanctuary of the cathedral where his tomb can be found today. His three successors are buried next to him.

During this period, St. Gabriel's College was founded nearby, and the Eudist Fathers came briefly to Vincennes to take over the operation of the seminary. St. Rose's Academy for girls was established next to the cathedral by the Sisters of Providence, who had just opened their motherhouse at Terre Haute. In 1843, all of Illinois was taken from the Vincennes diocese and given to the new diocese of Chicago. The next division took place in 1857 when Fort Wayne received its first bishop and the eighty thousand Catholics then in Indiana were equally divided between Fort Wayne and Vincennes.

In the 1850s, the French influence in the Catholic Church in Indiana began to decline as English and German Catholics moved into the state. In 1851, a German Catholic Church, St. John Baptist, was established in Vincennes. Two generations later, new immigration caused St. Francis Xavier to change into a Belgian parish. German influence among Indiana Catholics increased when German Benedictines founded a monastery in 1853 at St. Meinrad. Later, they opened a seminary at the monastery. During the twenty-eight-year reign of Bishop Jacques Saint-Palais in Vincennes, which extended from 1849 to 1877, he ordained ninety priests, only six of whom were natives of Indiana. Most had come from Germany.

During the 1850s, the influx of new immigrant Catholics gave rise to the growth of the Know-Nothing movement in the state. It had an estimated membership of between thirty thousand and fifty thousand. While it never elected any statewide officials, it did elect local candidates in Vincennes and in other towns and cities. The Vincennes *Gazette*, which supported the Know-Nothing Party, stated that it was organized "to resist the insidious policy of the Church of Rome and other foreign influences in our country by placing in all offices the gift of the people, or by appointment, none but native-born Protestant citizens." Outbreaks of anti-Catholic violence took place in several southern Indiana cities, including New Albany, then the largest city in the state. However, nothing of this sort occurred in Vincennes.

No Civil War battles were fought in Indiana. The state was solidly in the Union camp, but there was pro-slavery sentiment in southern portions near Vincennes. Bishop Saint-Palais permitted the Union Army to use St. Gabriel's College as a hospital for wounded soldiers and asked the Sisters of Providence to assist in caring for them. The nuns came to Vincennes and took care of about two hundred men. The rector of the cathedral, Father Ernest Audran, was a native of France and not inclined to take a strong position on either side of the conflict. His principal concern was that the war end quickly. However, he saw service briefly in the spring of 1862 when battles were fought in northern Kentucky at Fort Henry and Fort Donaldson. He went to these battlefields to care for wounded Union soldiers and recorded that he spent the entire day on Palm Sunday hearing the confessions of Catholic soldiers.

One telling indication of the change that had come about in St. Francis Xavier parish was that services in 1866 began to be held in English rather than in French. Most of the old Creole families had died off. Their places were being taken by English-speaking newcomers. When, in 1877, Bishop Saint-Palais was laid to rest in the cathedral, Vincennes lost its last resident bishop. His replacement, Bishop Francis S. Chatard, was instructed to make his home in Indianapolis. He still referred to himself as bishop of Vincennes, a title that did not change until 1898, but the focal point of church activities moved to the principal city in Indiana. Today, Vincennes is in the diocese of Evansville, which was created in 1944.

In 1968, the Lilly Endowment (the Eli Lilly and Company Foundation) made a grant of $180,000 to St. Francis Xavier Church to enable it to construct a library and courtyard behind the old church building. The library houses a collection of eleven thousand books and various art treasures that have come into possession of the parish over the past one hundred fifty years. These include twelfth- and thirteenth-century psalters, a letter signed by Pope John XXII in 1319, the original of a letter written in 1644 by St. Isaac Jogues, a letter written in 1660 by St. Vincent de Paul, and Mother Elizabeth Seton's Bible, which her spiritual adviser, Bishop Bruté, brought with him from Emmitsburg. The Bible contains various annotations written in the margins by the saint herself. The library has oil paintings by fifteenth- and sixteenth-century French and Spanish painters as well as vestments and altar vessels dating from 1780. Also preserved are the buildings in which the schools and seminaries founded by early bishops were located. In 1970, Pope Paul VI bestowed the title of basilica on the church in recognition of its historical importance to the religious life of the Middle West.

Today, St. Francis Xavier is a growing parish of five hundred twenty-five families. It no longer has any ethnic identification. Parishioners live in nearby Illinois towns as well as in Vincennes. The church is one of three Catholic churches in Vincennes and one of five in Knox County. Children from this and other parishes attend a consolidated parochial elementary school, Flaget School, which has about two hundred thirty students. Father Rivet High School, located a block from the old cathedral, has more than one hundred fifty students. The parish CCD program includes about sixty public school students.

The present setting of the basilica is enhanced by the fact that it is immediately adjacent to the George Rogers Clark Memorial, a monument located on land formerly occupied by the old fort and part of the old French cemetery. Most of the graves in the old cemetery are not marked, but it is estimated that about five thousand early settlers were buried there before Bishop Celestine de la Hailandière opened another Catholic cemetery elsewhere in the city in 1846. Among the gravestones that are still preserved are those of several Revolutionary War veterans, most of whom have French names.

The niches above the doors in the façade of the basilica house the statues of the parish patron, St. Francis Xavier, and St. Patrick and St. Joan of Arc, patrons of the two nations whose immigrants played an important role in the early life of the parish. The belfry houses a bell brought to the colonies from France in 1742 and used in the original church building. It is the same bell that Father Gibault rang to summon the townspeople to the meeting at which they decided to support the Revolutionary cause and is referred to as the Northwest Liberty Bell. Another bell, named Marie Françoise, was given to the parish in 1785 by a parishioner who named it after his daughter. A larger bell, Mary Anne, sits on the porch of the old seminary behind the basilica. The legend on the bell recites that it was blessed and placed in service by Bishop Bruté.

While the Clark Memorial is maintained and operated by the U.S. Department of the Interior, the seven buildings that make up the present parish complex — the 1826 church, the 1840 rectory, and the old seminary and school buildings — are the responsibility of the parish. Their maintenance poses endless problems. However, their continued presence after more than one hundred fifty years lends substance to Bishop Bruté's prediction that his cathedral would "go and tell the skies . . . the true love of Vincennes for the glory of God."

55
Sacred Heart

Notre Dame

INDIANA

Sacred Heart Church, a prominent feature of the campus of the University of Notre Dame, is both a college chapel and a canonically erected parish church in the diocese of Fort Wayne-South Bend. The original chapel of St. Mary of the Lake was established at this site by Jesuit missionaries in 1686 and was served on an occasional basis by visiting priests until 1759, when the Jesuits were expelled from France and from all French territories. Many members of Indian tribes whom they instructed remained faithful to their Catholic teachings. There are recorded instances in which Indians from northern Indiana went to Detroit, recited the Lord's Prayer and the Apostles' Creed before the bishop, and asked him to send a "black robe" — their name for the Jesuits — to return with them to the area.

More recent roots can be found in the log chapel built a few miles from the south bend of the St. Joseph River in 1831 by previously mentioned Reverend Stephen Badin. He served as a missionary in the Ohio-Indiana area for a period of nearly sixty years. He located his chapel at this point as a mission to the Potawatomi Indians, many of whom were in the process of being evacuated to Iowa. They had been forced to relinquish their lands to the federal government in a series of treaties from 1805 to 1833. A few Potawatomi, belonging to a band headed by Chief Pokagon, maintained a village just over the

Indiana line from Father Badin's mission in an area known as Bertrand, Michigan. They were living on forty-nine sections of land reserved to them in an 1821 Indian treaty. When all of the Potawatomi were forced to move westward after the Treaty of 1833, Pokagon's band requested permission, "on account of their religious creed," to remain in Michigan. They were allowed to do so. This band of Potawatomi, together with a handful of French settlers on both sides of the Indiana-Michigan line, formed the bulk of Father Badin's mission parish. When soldiers eventually drove the other Potawatomi westward along what has been called the Trail of Tears, Father Badin's successor, Father Benjamin Petit, went with them and died en route.

Father Badin erected his log chapel on land that he had purchased from the government. When he left the area on another assignment, he deeded the property to the bishop of Vincennes. The diocese of Vincennes at that time covered all of Indiana and eastern Illinois. In 1834, Bishop Simon Bruté, during his first visit to northern Indiana, recorded in his diary: "Crossing the [St. Joseph's] River, we visited 'St. Mary of the Lake,' the mission house of the excellent M. Badin, who has lately removed to Cincinnati. He had a school there kept by two Sisters who have also gone away, leaving the place vacant. The 625 acres of land attached to it, and the small lake named St. Mary's, make it a most desirable spot, and one soon I hope to be occupied by some prosperous institution. M. Badin has transferred it to the Bishop on condition of his assuming the debts, a trifling consideration compared with the importance of the place."

In 1842, Father Edward Sorin, a priest from LeMans, France, arrived in Indiana with several other members of a religious group called the LeMans Auxiliaries. This group eventually became the Congregation of the Holy Cross. Bishop Celestine de la Hailandière gave him the land on which Father Badin had started a mission so that Father Sorin could continue the mission and start a school. On November 26, 1842, Father Sorin and three companions arrived at Father Badin's log cabin, located on the edge of two lakes that he then named in honor of St. Mary and St. Joseph. From this beginning Father Sorin erected what eventually became the University of Notre Dame du Lac — Our Lady of the Lake. His lifework, which ended in 1893, is a portrait of one of the most extraordinary entrepreneurs in the history of the Catholic Church in the United States.

At first, the old log cabin served as a residence as well as a place of worship. Father Sorin and his companions set about cutting trees to construct an additional building, which was completed the following spring. It was the first of thirty-four buildings that Father Sorin put up on the Notre Dame campus. Since the school also owned considerable acreage, the priests and Brothers began to farm it for support. During the first one hundred years of its existence, Notre Dame engaged in extensive agricultural activities, both at the campus and on other farms that it later purchased. In 1843, the university was incorporated. In 1844, it was able to advertise the opening of a new school under the direction of the priests of the Holy Cross, in association with the Brothers of St. Joseph, "having all the advantages of convenience" that "combine here to form not only a healthful abode, but also an agreeable solitude, which facilitates so effectually the intellectual improvement of youth." Tuition, room, and board came to $100 a year.

Father Sorin was also determined to bring Holy Cross nuns from France in order to establish a girls' school. Although Father Sorin had the full cooperation of the bishop of Vincennes in starting a boys' school, the bishop forbade him to open a Catholic school for girls because such a school was already being started at Terre Haute and the bishop was afraid that there was insufficient demand to support two girls' academies. Father Sorin was not the kind to be thwarted by any such opposition. He was able to find Sisters willing to come from France and a few American postulants who would assist in his plan for a girls' school. He obtained a house for them from his friend Joseph Bertrand, who operated a trading post and tavern on the Detroit-Chicago Military Road, some five miles north of Notre Dame just over the state line in Michigan. The house was beyond the jurisdiction of the Indiana bishop and within the diocese of Detroit. He obtained permission for this school from the bishop of Detroit and started St. Mary's Academy. When the bishop of Vincennes heard about this "trick," he was outraged and protested to the bishop of Detroit that Father Sorin had flaunted his order. The protest was to no avail. In 1855, after Bishop Hailandière resigned as bishop and had returned to France, Father Sorin moved the academy from Bertrand, Michigan, to a site adjacent to the Notre Dame campus where it grew into the College of St. Mary's of the Lake, today one of the largest Catholic women's colleges in the United States.

The first of two Sacred Heart Church buildings was constructed between 1848 and 1852. Then, as now, it occupied a spot on the campus immediately adjacent to the main administration building. The first church was a wooden structure, ninety feet by thirty feet, and had two large spires. One of the steeples was constructed by a local carpenter in exchange for a year's tuition for his son at Notre Dame. Among the noteworthy features of the original church were a rose window made by Carmelite nuns in France and an organ having 1,527 pipes. In 1854, a twenty-four-bell carillon was imported from France. It was too heavy to be placed in the church steeple so it was housed in a separate building. The carillon is still in use and is the oldest one in North America. In addition to his other duties, Father Sorin was the first pastor of Sacred Heart parish; but, as his other duties increased, he turned this position over to Father Alexis Granger. This was one of the few posts that Father Sorin ever relinquished.

In the 1850s, the campus was plagued by epidemics of malaria and cholera. By 1855, some twenty-three persons associated with the university had died from these diseases, which were attributed to the fact that the marshlands that separated St. Mary's Lake from St. Joseph's Lake did not drain and were rife with mosquitoes. Father Sorin set about to drain them but ran into obstacles because the farmer who owned the creek running from the lakes to the St. Joseph's River maintained a dam blocking the drainage. He refused to sell. When Father Sorin was finally able to negotiate the purchase of the property, he personally assisted in destroying the dam even before title to the property had passed. As the infected marshlands dried up, more rich marl deposits, which had been noted and used as early as 1843, became available and were mined extensively for brick. They produced a yellow-buff "Notre Dame brick," which was sold commercially and used for construction of campus buildings, including the present Sacred Heart Church.

During the Civil War, the Holy Cross Fathers provided eight chaplains for the Union Army, including Reverend William J. Corby, who later became president of the university. Holy Cross Sisters from Notre Dame and from St. Mary's College supplied the army and navy with eighty-nine nuns to staff their hospitals. It was at Notre Dame that the wife and children of General William Tecumseh Sherman received word that Atlanta had fallen to Union troops.

By 1870, the first Sacred Heart Church had become much too small for its congregation. Father Sorin solicited an architectural rendering from Patrick C. Keely, the noted Catholic church architect. Keely submitted a plan calling for a building two hundred feet long, having three naves and large enough to seat two thousand people in its transept. When Keely quoted a construction price in excess of $100,000, Father Sorin backed away from the proposal and assigned the job of designing a new church to its pastor, Father Granger, and to Brother Charles Harding, a Holy Cross Brother who is generally given credit for the plan that was used. The new church [**pictured above**] greatly resembled the parish church in Father Sorin's hometown in France. It is 275 feet by 114 feet and has a single tower, 218 feet high, that is strong enough to accommodate the carillon that had been imported from France in 1854. The cornerstone was laid in 1871. The church was put into use in 1875 but was not dedicated until 1888.

The present Sacred Heart Church has many prominent features and religious artifacts. It has forty-two stained-glass windows containing one hundred fourteen life-size figures. The window patterns were painted by Carmelite nuns in France. Because of damage done during World War II to stained-glass windows in various churches in France, the windows at Sacred Heart are now ranked among the largest and best-preserved examples of nineteenth-century French windows to be found anywhere in the world.

Over the years, the university has often had an artist in residence. From 1874 to 1891, its artist in residence was Luigi Gregori, formerly a painter in the papal household of Pope Pius IX. During his stay at Notre Dame, he painted several frescoes in the church as well as the stations of the cross. They were removed in the 1960s, following Vatican Council II, but were later restored. During his years on campus, Gregori was involved in an ongoing feud with Brother Amadeus, the Holy Cross Brother who served as sacristan at Sacred Heart. Invoking a practice common among medieval painters, Gregori scored a lasting point in this long-standing dispute as he painted the stations of the cross. He painted Brother Amadeus's face on certain figures representing hostile bystanders who were present during the procession to Calvary.

Another artist in residence during a later era was the Croatian sculptor Ivan Mestrovic, who lived at Notre Dame from 1955 to 1962. Some fourteen of his works can be found at different places throughout the campus. His Pietà, carved in Carrara marble, was brought to Sacred Heart from the Metropolitan Museum of Art in New York because Mestrovic strongly believed that religious sculpture should be placed in churches, not in museums. In order to permit installation, part of the side wall of the church had to be removed temporarily.

During his lifetime, Father Sorin made fifty-two trans-Atlantic crossings, thus establishing the precedent for much-traveled university presidents. During one such trip, he purchased an altar built in Rome by students of Vatican architect Giovanni Bernini, the sculptor of the permanent canopy above the main altar at St. Peter's Basilica. The altar purchased by Father Sorin was one of eleven known Bernini altars and was installed in 1886 in the apse of Sacred Heart Church in a chapel dedicated to Our Lady. This chapel is used most frequently for weddings and for Sunday afternoon vespers. The main altar was built in France and brought to the United States in 1876 for the Philadelphia Exposition. Soon after the exposition had closed, Father Sorin bought it duty-free and moved it to Notre Dame. Successive renovations have taken place, the latest in 1967 to conform to liturgical changes introduced by Vatican II. Another renovation, which would require the closing of the main church for an extended period time, is being contemplated.

On April 23, 1879, most of the Notre Dame campus burned to the ground in a fire that broke out on a coal-tar roof on the east wing of the main building. Sacred Heart Church and the presbytery behind it were spared. The fire did several hundred thousand dollars' worth of damage, only a fraction of which was covered by insurance. Immediately after the fire was extinguished, Father Sorin called the entire university community together in the church. He was then sixty-nine years of age and had a long, white beard, giving him the appearance of an Old Testament prophet. From the steps of the altar in the apse of the church he delivered the most important pep talk ever heard on the Notre Dame campus. He told the assembled audience that "if it were all gone, I should not give up." He promised that he would build a new administration building and place on its top a golden dome and a statue of Our Lady. Immediately, he set about building the "new Notre Dame." By May of that year, ground had been broken for new buildings, and foundations were in place. In the fall, classes resumed. The golden dome and the statue above it exist today as the most prominent and well-known landmarks on the entire campus.

In focusing on Sacred Heart Church, it is clear that today, as for the past one hundred fifty years, it enjoys an unusual "town and gown" existence. The upper portion of the church is reserved for student devotions. The crypt, or lower chapel, is for the parish. One of Father Sorin's many enterprises was that of real-estate developer. He platted and recorded a large subdivision of private homes on land located to the south of the campus. He envisioned that a town would grow up and become a community of academics and workmen associated with the university. Not surprisingly, he called his development Sorinville. It is now an area of detached single-family homes located within the city limits of South Bend. However, the university itself lies in an unincorporated portion of St. Joseph County and is served by a post office called Notre Dame. This name was given to the campus post office by its first postmaster, who just happened to be Father Sorin.

Today, the territorial boundaries of Sacred Heart parish encompass little more than the campus itself. The parish is the oldest in northern Indiana and oldest of some nine parishes in South Bend that are staffed by the Holy Cross Fathers. It currently serves six hundred families, most of whom technically live outside its boundaries. It is a growing parish and offers its parishioners, many of whom have no connection with the university, a full range of parish activities. Some activities take place in university buildings while others do not. Campus-parking restrictions are relaxed on Sunday mornings to permit parishioners to drive from all parts of South Bend to park right in front of the church.

Father Sorin envisioned that prominent Catholics from all parts of the United States would wish to be buried at Notre Dame and designed the crypt church for that purpose. His vision did not materialize. However, Father Badin and two early priests of the parish were buried in the crypt and were recently reinterred in a replica of the log-cabin church that was constructed a few hundred feet away. Notre Dame professor Orestes Brownson, a prominent nineteenth-century author and social reformer, is still buried in the crypt church. The lower church itself seats about two hundred thirty people and is now used exclusively for parish services. The presbytery, which was once Father Sorin's office and later a community residence for Holy Cross priests, is now the parish rectory. Two priests live at the rectory and are assigned exclusively to parish work.

Sacred Heart parish has a CCD program for about fifty children but it has no parochial school. In 1854, Holy Cross Sisters began to teach in a grade school located on campus. Then, in 1882, a boarding school called St. Edward's Hall was started on campus for what the university then called its Minim Department, a preparatory school for young boys who were referred to as "minims." For nearly fifty years it was possible for a so-called "lifer" to begin his education at Notre Dame at the age of six and continue on to receive a bachelor's degree without ever leaving campus. The Minim Department was discontinued in 1929 when the university decided to concentrate its resources on collegiate and postgraduate education. The same is true of the former Manual Labor School that was begun in 1844 to provide training in various trades and crafts to boys whose talents did not fit them for academic pursuits. Now any parishioners who wish their children to attend parochial schools must send them to one that is operated by a nearby parish. Two parochial functions that are fully utilized are marriages and baptisms. Between one hundred to one hundred twenty-five weddings take place each year at Sacred Heart. Many of them involve Notre Dame graduates who come from all over the country to be married next to the golden dome. The same patronage explains the approximately seventy-five baptisms that take place each year. Many Notre Dame grads bring their children to Sacred Heart to be baptized, often by a member of the faculty whom they knew particularly well during their undergraduate years.

The upper church is used exclusively for religious activities designed for the nearly ten thousand students on campus, more than ninety percent of whom are Catholics. In addition to the upper church, there are forty chapels on campus in its twenty-six residence halls. Members of the Campus Ministry sometimes refer expansively to Sacred Heart as the campus "cathedral" and the residence-hall chapels as "parishes." About one hundred seventy scheduled public Masses are said each week in these chapels in addition to innumerable private Masses. Sacred Heart Church became familiar to moviegoers in 1940 when the cinema classic *Knute Rockne, All American* was filmed in part on location. Rockne's funeral in 1931 was reenacted in the upper church with the assistance of the Notre Dame choir. Recently, the upper church was closed to permit a seven-million-dollar renovation to take place. In addition to structural improvements, such as repairing the roof and the plaster on the ceiling, a great many of the spartan revisions stemming from the post-Vatican II era were removed and earlier painting and ornamentation re-emphasized.

It is not possible to talk about the collegiate portion of the Sacred Heart community without mentioning football. Since the days of Rockne and "The Gipper," neither of whom started life as Catholics, football prowess has been an integral part of the Notre Dame mystique. When a victorious team returned to campus in the 1980s after winning the mythical national collegiate championship, they were greeted with signs that modestly proclaimed: "God Made Us No. 1." The same spirit and conviction seems to have carried over into other years when God evidently had other designs. A chaplain has always been assigned to major varsity athletic teams. Before each football and basketball game, home or away, Mass is said, and each player is individually blessed. When Notre Dame plays football at home, the team is cloistered after the Friday evening pep rally at the Holy Cross Seminary across the lake until game time so that team members will not have their concentration disturbed by extraneous matters.

The football spirit has also given rise to a certain amount of campus humor. Adjacent to the Sacred Heart Church is the statue of Father Corby blessing the troops of the Irish Brigade as they marched into battle at Gettysburg. His right hand is held high in the posture of a priest dispensing general absolution. This statue is called "Fair Catch Corby." Joseph Turkalj's statue of Moses on the west side of the Memorial Library shows the prophet with the index finger of his hand pointed upward. This statue has become "No. 1 Moses." Millard Sheets' mosaic of Christ the Teacher is a portrait, some six stories high, that adorns the front façade of the library facing the football stadium. The mosaic shows Christ with both hands held high above his head. It is known as "Touchdown Jesus." And of course on football weekends, the ancient French carillon in the Sacred Heart steeple peals out the "Notre Dame Victory March" along with the other music in the carillonneur's repertoire.

Between Sacred Heart Church and St. Mary's Lake a grotto was constructed of large rocks resembling the grotto at Lourdes where the Blessed Virgin appeared to St. Bernadette. It was built by alumni donations and completed in 1896. Over the past ninety years, it has become a campus landmark. At the end of a noted career of bringing medical and hospital care to the people of Southeast Asia, Dr. Thomas A. "Tom" Dooley wrote to Notre Dame president Father Theodore Hesburgh referring affectionately to the grotto. In a letter dated December 2, 1960, written as he lay dying of cancer in a British hospital in Hong Kong, Tom Dooley stated: "Cold prayers from a hospital bed are just as pleasing to God as more youthful prayers from a grotto on the lid of night. . . . If I could go to the Grotto I think I could sing inside. Notre Dame is twice on my mind . . . and always in my heart. That Grotto is the rock to which my life is anchored. Do the students ever appreciate what they have while they have it. . . ? I must return to the states very soon and I hope to sneak into that Grotto . . . before the snow has melted."

Tom Dooley never made it back to the grotto, but an informal group does each evening at 6:45, winter or summer, rain or shine, gathering at this spot to recite the rosary. In bad weather, they simply stand under its arched roof. Perhaps the best way to appreciate Sacred Heart Church and its surroundings is to visit the grotto after supper on a summer night. Most of the student body has gone and quiet has descended over the campus. As the rosary is being said, the cadence of the prayers blends in with the buzz of insects and the evensong of the meadowlarks. If, in the hush of a summer twilight, you stand nearby on the edge of a lake named in honor of Our Lady and listen carefully enough, you will also hear generations of Notre Dame students as they join with this gathering to wake up the echoes cheering her name.

56
St. Mary

Chicago

ILLINOIS

The first Catholics, and perhaps the first white men of any religious denomination, to visit the Chicago area were Father Jacques Marquette, the Jesuit explorer, and his companion, Louis Jolliet. Both men passed through the area on the return trip from their exploration of the Mississippi River in 1673. Father Marquette returned the following fall. He camped temporarily near Lake Michigan and, on December 13, 1674, said the first Mass to be offered in the Chicago area. He spent the rest of the winter about two miles away, near what is now 26th and Damen Streets, trying to recuperate from what proved to be his final illness. On Easter Sunday, 1675, Father Marquette said Mass at his winter quarters and began the trip back to his mission at St. Ignace, in Upper Michigan. He made it only as far as Ludington, on the eastern shoreline of Lake Michigan, where, as noted before, he died in April of 1675.

Two years later, Father Louis Allouez, another Jesuit missionary, arrived at the mouth of the Chicago River and set up a temporary mission for Indians and French trappers. In 1696, Father Francisco Piret, a third French Jesuit, established the Guardian Angel mission at this location. Two Miami Indian villages were built along the Chicago River and grew to have about one hundred fifty cabins. Father Piret constructed a log-cabin church that during the next six years attracted trappers as well as Indians. In 1702, Father Jean Mermet, the last of the missionaries at the Guardian Angel mission, left to attend to another mission at Cahokia, on the Mississippi River south of St. Louis, so the mission at Chicago closed. Coincidentally, this was one year after the French had established a permanent fort and church at Detroit.

There is little evidence of Catholic activity or of any activity in the Chicago area for the next one hundred years. In 1795, the United States obtained from various Indian tribes at the historic Greenville Treaty the cession of a six-square-mile tract along Lake Michigan at the mouth of the Chicago River. In 1803, the government began to erect Fort Dearborn at this location. There are recorded instances of priests passing through the Chicago area during this period but none of them remained.

The city of Chicago was incorporated in 1833. At that time, its Catholic inhabitants, who numbered about half of the population of two hundred, felt that the time had come for the establishment of a permanent church. The area was then in the diocese of Bardstown, Kentucky, but in a section of that diocese that was being administered by Bishop Joseph Rosati of St. Louis. In March 1833, a petition written in French was sent to Bishop Rosati. It read: "We, the Catholics of Chicago, Cook Co., Ill., lay before you the necessity there exists to have a pastor in this new and flourishing city. There are here several families of French descent, born and brought up in the Roman Catholic faith, and others quite willing to aid us in supporting a pastor, who ought to be sent here before other sects obtain the upper hand, which they very likely will try to do. We have heard several persons say were there a priest they would join our religion in preference to any other. We count about one hundred Catholics in this town. We will not cease to pray till you have taken our important request in consideration." The petition was signed by thirty persons, including the commandant at Fort Dearborn, the postmaster, several businessmen, the president of the city board of trustees, and several Potawatomi chieftains and headmen.

Bishop Rosati replied almost immediately. He had just ordained Father John Irenaeus St. Cyr, a native of France, who had come to St. Louis to complete his seminary studies. Bishop Rosati sent Father St. Cyr to Chicago a few days after his ordination to establish a church. On May 5, 1833, Father St. Cyr arrived in the city and said Mass in a twelve-foot log cabin. He made his residence at the Sauganash Hotel, a prominent establishment owned by Mark Beaubein, and lived there largely on the charity of its owner. Later in the same year, he baptized his host's son, also named Mark, the first Catholic to be baptized in Chicago. Parish records at St. Mary's date back to this event. The abject poverty of the parish and its pastor can be sensed from communications from Father St. Cyr to his bishop, in which he complained that he had to borrow $2.50 to pay the freight for the shipment of his trunk from St. Louis and that he would not be able to pay the postage on letters sent from the bishop to Chicago. (In those days, the recipient of a letter, not the sender, paid the postage.)

Since the parishioners were unable to raise enough money to purchase a site for a church, Father St. Cyr was able to obtain permission to build on a canal lot at Lake and

State Streets (State Street had not yet been cut through). However, this proved to be risky, since the lot had been donated by the government to the Michigan and Illinois Canal Commission to help finance a canal from the Chicago River to Des Plaines. Father St. Cyr went to St. Louis to seek financial aid in constructing this church and obtained some assistance. Augustine and Anson Taylor purchased sawed lumber that had been shipped to Chicago from St. Joseph, Michigan, and constructed a temporary church on the canal lot. The first St. Mary's Church was also the first building in Chicago to be constructed from sawed lumber. It was 36 feet by 24 feet and was 12 feet high, with six windows on each side. It cost $400 and was a so-called balloon frame building, an architectural innovation at the time.

In the fall of 1833, a large number of Potawatomi Indians had come to Fort Dearborn to collect their annuities and to participate in the last large Potawatomi treaty cession east of the Mississippi. Many of the Potawatomi were Catholics. When the new church was completed, Potawatomi women cleaned the inside in preparation for the first Mass, which was said in October 1833. At that time, the church was still unpainted and unplastered and had no steeple or bell tower. Its only furnishings were a rough table and benches. The first Mass was attended by about four hundred Indians as well as a large number of Chicagoans, both Catholic and Protestant. St. Mary's was the first church of any denomination to be opened in the new city. Father St. Cyr wrote to his bishop: "We have Mass and vespers every Sunday with all the solemnity possible under the circumstances."

The new pastor continued to live with the Beaubeins. In fact, he often heard confessions in the Beaubein family parlor. In 1836, it became necessary to relocate the original church building because the land under it had been auctioned off by the canal commission and the parish could not raise sufficient money to participate in the auction. A lot at the corner of Michigan Avenue and Madison, then a part of Fort Dearborn, was purchased from the government. The small frame church was physically transported to this location, some six blocks away.

During this period of time, Chicago was placed under the newly created diocese of Vincennes, Indiana. Its new bishop, Simon Bruté, was shorthanded and asked Bishop Rosati to leave Father St. Cyr in Chicago for a while. Father St. Cyr remained for three years, at the end of which he returned to St. Louis. Bishop Bruté had great plans for Chicago, which he once referred to in a letter to a newspaper as the "Cincinnati of the North." However, few of these plans were realized. He sent Father Bernard Schaeffer to the city along with a Father O'Meara. Father Schaeffer's task was to minister to a large number of German Catholics who were arriving in great numbers, but the fledgling St. Mary's parish was unable to support two priests. Bishop Bruté visited Chicago in 1838 and wrote to his mother back in France:

> Chicago, 150 miles north of Vincennes, on Lake Michigan, southwest corner, a city of seven or eight thousand, largest in the Diocese. Alas, so small a wooden church

where I have just celebrated the Divine Sacrifice, though we have near a thousand Catholics, they tell me. One Priest, Mr. O'Meara. I had a second, Mr. Schaeffer. Our Lord called him to heaven, I hope.

A small wooden church not sufficient for a fourth part, and yet most, as usual, of our Catholics are of the poorest and few better off (as usual, too, in the west) so eagerly busy at the great business of this west, growing rich, richer, richest — too little ready, when the talk is only of lots, interest, and estate in Heaven, or of placing in its bank on earth, by the hands of the Church, and that poor bishop, the cashier of said bank in this part of the world who could sign bills of millions of eternal acquittal, etc. Well, Mother, tell me how I will succeed to spirit our busy Chicago to build a large brick church. Another man — yes — some proper man might succeed, but not this unworthy Simon. But enough. Must go to meet Mr. [Father] O'Meara and draw plans.

In some accounts, Father O'Meara was described as a "refractory priest," since he purchased property in his own name and began to minister to Catholics at this site without regard to the bishop or the new pastor, Father Maurice de St. Pallais, whom Bishop Bruté had sent to take charge of St. Mary's. Father O'Meara eventually left the city to avoid further difficulty, leaving Father St. Pallais alone to enlarge the old frame church and to carry out the bishop's plans for a much larger brick church, which he began to construct a block away at the corner of Madison and Wabash.

In 1843, the Holy See created the diocese of Chicago and included within its jurisdiction the entire state of Illinois. At that time, there was only one church — St. Mary's — in Chicago and about fifty thousand Catholics scattered throughout Illinois. Father William Quarter, a native of Ireland and pastor of a parish in New York City, was appointed bishop. When he arrived in Chicago in May of 1844, he found that the brick church that had been started by Father St. Pallais had not been completed, so he continued to say Mass in the old frame church that he described as "a long, low, frame building having a small steeple and surmounted by a cross." He also found that a debt of $3,000 had already been incurred on the new church, and there was no money available either to pay the debt or to finish the job that had been undertaken. Bishop Quarter brought his brother, Father Walter Quarter, with him to Chicago. The two paid off the existing debt on the brick church, now a cathedral, with their private funds and arranged for the completion of the building. Their generosity served as an example that sparked Catholics in Chicago to come forward with additional money. On October 5, 1845, St. Mary's Cathedral was dedicated. It faced eastward on Wabash, was one hundred feet by fifty-five feet, and supported a spire and a golden cross. Its steeple was the first to be constructed in Chicago and could be seen from great distances, both on Lake Michigan and by land to the west. At the time of the dedication, Chicago had about three thousand Catholics, of whom some one thousand were German-speaking.

Bishop Quarter was not only hard-pressed for funds, he was also short of help in ministering to his large and sparsely settled diocese. When the new diocese was created, bishops who previously had responsibility for the territory withdrew some of their priests to serve in their own shorthanded dioceses, leaving Bishop Quarter in considerable difficulty. When he arrived in Chicago, there were only two priests in the entire city, himself and his brother. Within two years he opened a college that he hoped would provide education both for laymen and seminary students. He went to New York to beg for funds to complete St. Mary's. He also visited Pittsburgh and prevailed upon the newly formed Sisters of Mercy to send a group of nuns to Chicago. When they arrived in 1846, he gave them his home next to the church and moved into a small cottage on Michigan Avenue, which was described in a contemporary newspaper account as a shanty. The old frame church was sawed in half. A portion of it was located behind the new brick cathedral and was used by the Sisters as a parochial school for girls. The rest was converted into a school for boys that the Mercy nuns opened the following year. These Sisters also started a so-called select school (supported by tuition) for girls in the former home of the proprietor of the Sauganash Hotel, Mark Beaubein. They called it St. Francis Xavier Female Academy. The select school and their convent were located in a large brick building that was constructed on Wabash Avenue immediately adjacent to the cathedral.

Bishop Quarter was able to avoid the trustee problem that plagued the Church in other areas by obtaining an act of the Illinois legislature designating successive bishops of Chicago a corporation sole. This was an old English legal device, now widely used by the Church in the United States, under which the bishop is regarded in law as a one-man corporation. All diocesan property was placed in Bishop Quarter's name as corporation sole, meaning that both he and future bishops could develop and administer it without interference from others. Bishop Quarter's expenditure of time and energy in Chicago and throughout Illinois over a period of four years was so prodigious that he literally wore himself out. In 1848, at the age of forty-two, he died unexpectedly and was buried in the cathedral that he had completed only three years earlier.

In the ensuing decades, Catholics came to Chicago in great numbers. Establishment of new parishes, both territorial and national, also continued apace in Chicago and throughout Illinois in general. The headquarters for this activity was St. Mary's Cathedral and the new bishop's "palace," as it was called, a house constructed a few blocks away to replace the shanty that Bishop Quarter had occupied. Over a period of twenty-five years, St. Mary's was the cathedral church for five bishops. This fact is commemorated on a plaque affixed to an office building at Wabash and Madison Streets, the site of the old church. Several noteworthy events took place during this period. Illinois Senator Stephen A. Douglas, a deathbed convert to Catholicism, was buried from the cathedral. Ceremonies were held during the Civil War sending Colonel James Mulligan and his Irish Brigade off to battle for the Union cause. In 1864, when Colonel Mulligan was killed in action in Virginia, his body was returned to St. Mary's for burial.

St. Mary's Cathedral and all of the buildings surrounding it were totally destroyed in the 1871 fire. At that time, there were twenty-four Catholic parishes in and about

Chicago, a remarkable increase from the solitary church that stood in downtown Chicago when Bishop Quarter arrived in 1844. Seven of these churches were completely destroyed, as were many other Catholic establishments. Bishop Thomas Foley immediately purchased an abandoned Congregational church several blocks south on Wabash to be used as his procathedral. This church had survived the fire, as had other buildings in outlying areas. Originally the Plymouth Congregational Church, it was a limestone building with the spartan interior design of an old New England Protestant church. It served St. Mary's parish for the next ninety-eight years. Located south of the Loop, Chicago's main business district, the church was not so far from the center of commercial activity that it could avoid both the benefits and difficulties of a downtown parish. In 1876, when Holy Name Church was reconstructed north of the Chicago River, Holy Name became the cathedral for the new Chicago archdiocese and St. Mary's reverted to its original status as the territorial parish for downtown Chicago. It has retained that status to this day.

The area served by Old St. Mary's, as this parish has come to be known, was and is a study in contrasts. During the latter part of the 1800s and well into the 1900s, the church was near the railroad yards and was frequented by railroad workers and by transients. In an age when anticipated Saturday Masses and Sunday evening Masses were unknown, its 3:00 A.M. Mass on Sunday morning was quite popular. Known as the printer's Mass, it could also be correctly called the night owl's Mass, serving the convenience of partygoers who wished to go to church before turning in for the evening. As many as fifteen hundred persons might attend on a Saturday night. In the 1880s, a black congregation began to hear Mass regularly in the basement of the church. In 1893, this congregation grew into St. Monica's Church, the first black parish in Chicago. Father Augustus Tolton, the pastor of this congregation, was one of the first black priests to be ordained in the United States. He became a priest in 1886. In later decades, when other immigration patterns brought large numbers of Mexicans and Filipinos to Chicago, the parish also organized missions to serve these groups. Today, a large number of Filipinos still attend Mass at Old St. Mary's, though many do not actually live in the parish.

In 1903, the parish was assigned to the care of the Paulist Fathers. They have staffed it since that time. The Paulists are the first native American religious order, founded in 1858 by Father Isaac Hecker, a former Redemptorist and himself a convert to the Church. One of the principal functions envisioned for the order by its founder was the making of converts. In recent years, one of its specialties has come to be communications — evangelization through radio and television as well as through the printed word. The Paulists own one of the largest Catholic publishing houses in America. St. Mary's was one of the first parishes that this congregation began to operate.

The Paulists used Old St. Mary's not only as an opportunity to perform missionary work in Chicago but to do so throughout the Midwest. Its rectory served as the headquarters for a Paulist mission band that traveled throughout the entire region. In downtown Chicago, they opened a day nursery for working mothers, an unusual parish activity in the early 1900s. Not many years after Jane Addams opened the first settlement house in the United States on South Halstead Street in Chicago, the Paulists opened one on South Wabash Street that served several hundred foreign-born children and their parents living in that locality. Perhaps their best-known activity was the formation of the Paulist Choristers, a group of about one hundred men and boys who not only sang at religious services in the former Congregational church but who also traveled throughout the United States and Europe giving concerts and engaging in choral competitions. The group was made up of volunteers coming from all parts of the city. It was begun in 1903 by Father William J. Finn, C.S.P., and continued on after 1928 under the direction of Father Eugene O'Malley, C.S.P. Father O'Malley was a professional musician before becoming a priest. He gained fame not only as a musician but as a strict taskmaster. One former member was quoted recently as saying that being in the choir was like going through a U.S. Marine Corps boot camp. Referring to Father O'Malley, the same alumnus said, "You feared him until you got to know him better. He could do more with a look than most people can do with a club."

One of Father O'Malley's strictest rules was that choir members could not yell when they played. This was a serious handicap to active teenagers, who were required to communicate with each other while at play by whistling. Father O'Malley's purpose for imposing this rule was to preserve their voices for singing. In the 1940s, when the story of Father O'Malley's traveling choir was featured in a newspaper article, Paramount Pictures seized upon it as the basis for two motion-picture classics, *Going My Way* and *The Bells of St. Mary's*. Both pictures starred Bing Crosby as a musically inclined parish priest and even retained in their story lines the names of Father O'Malley and St. Mary's. Following World War II, the choir discontinued its principal activities, but its alumni still gather occasionally to provide Old St. Mary's with a musical setting for Sunday Mass at its present location.

In 1954, the Paulists established a chapel several blocks north of the main parish church in order to be closer to office workers in downtown Chicago. This chapel eventually became the main parish church and the fifth location of Old St. Mary's. The chapel was originally located in an office building just to the side of the elevated railroad tracks at Wabash and Van Buren. In 1961, the chapel was completely redesigned and turned into the church that has served the parish for more than thirty years. It seats more than seven hundred fifty people on the ground floor and its balconies. In 1970, the old church, which had served the parish and downtown Chicago for nearly a century, was closed and the property sold to the Standard Oil Company to permit the construction of an office building. All parish activities were conducted in the converted chapel thereafter. The rectory was now located in a building immediately adjacent to the church on Van Buren Street.

As the territorial parish for downtown Chicago, Old St. Mary's has about five hundred resident parishioners. Some live in hotels and others in new condominiums that have been built along the lakefront. Recently, Dearborn Park, a complex of homes for middle-income residents, was opened nearby. These residences provide Old St. Mary's with a parochial base that is supplemented by a large number of office workers who attend Mass during the week. The church now offers three Masses each day that are attended by about 200 people, five Masses on Sunday attended by more than 1,000, and 10 Masses on holy days of obligation that draw more than 2,500. Many resident parishioners were members of other Chicago parishes before they retired and moved downtown. The parish provides bus transportation from major senior-citizen residences to the principal Sunday Masses.

In 1990, Old St. Mary's entered into a joint agreement with a downtown developer to construct a twelve-story combination church and parking garage on the site of the chapel at Wabash and Van Buren. The architect's rendering [pictured above] shows a church on the street floor that is designed to seat four hundred twenty-five people and a garage above it that can house eight hundred vehicles. The bell tower with a cross on top is actually the elevator for the parking garage. According to the agreement, the parish retains title to the land while the developer has title to the air rights. From this project Old St. Mary's hopes to derive an annual income of about $75,000, or 2.5 percent of the net receipts from the garage. Parishioners get free parking on Sundays and holy days of obligation. Because of the developer's recent financial difficulties, the project has been placed on hold but the parish is hopeful that it can and will be completed.

The bulk of the parish is work-oriented so parochial life is not what it is in a large suburban parish. However, the church is open throughout the day and maintains a bookstore and information center that is staffed during normal business hours. Old St. Mary's conducts classes in Scripture, a convert class for adults, and catechism classes for the children of families residing nearby. Perhaps the most important religious event to have occurred within the parish boundaries in recent years took place in October of 1979 when Pope John Paul II said Mass at Grant Park on the lakefront. It was attended by more than a million Chicagoans, who were a dramatic contrast to the small impoverished group of Catholics for whom Father St. Cyr said Mass in a twelve-foot log cabin when Old St. Mary's began its parochial existence a few blocks away in 1833.

57
Holy Name Cathedral

Chicago
ILLINOIS

Holy Name Cathedral, located on Chicago's near north side, is the fifth oldest church in the second largest archdiocese in America. It has been Chicago's cathedral parish since about 1874. Holy Name Church grew from a college chapel on the campus of a school established by Chicago's first bishop, William Quarter, who obtained a charter from the Illinois legislature a few months after coming to Chicago in 1844. In the following year, construction began north of the Chicago River on Bishop Quarter's university. He raised most of the construction money in New York where he had served as a pastor before becoming bishop and also from French and German missionary societies. A three-story wooden building was dedicated in 1846 and opened its doors in that year to a small student body. Room and board was $150 a year, a figure that also included tuition. Washing and mending was extra. Father Jeremiah Kinsella, an Irish missionary who had served as an assistant at Chicago's new St. Mary's Cathedral, was appointed by the bishop as president of the university.

At that time, there were about two thousand English-speaking Catholics (mostly Irish) and about one thousand German-speaking Catholics in Chicago. A German church, St. Joseph's, had been opened at the corner of what is now Chicago and Wabash Streets, but English-speaking Catholics living north of the Chicago River had to walk several blocks to go to Mass at St. Mary's Cathedral, which was then at Wabash and Madison. When the chapel of the Holy Name was installed on the first floor of the college building, they began to attend Mass at this location. Father Kinsella, the university president, also became their pastor. The congregation was formally recognized as a parish in 1849.

In the same year, the Illinois-Michigan Canal, linking Lake Michigan to the Illinois River, was completed. Not long thereafter, railroads began to reach the city and it started to boom. Many new Catholic arrivals were desperately poor. They also had to contend with a resurgence of anti-Catholic sentiment that broke out following the conclusion of the war with Mexico. In 1849, Holy Name parishioners erected a wooden frame church at the corner of State and Superior Streets, which soon proved to be inadequate to their needs. Four years later, they began to build a much larger church on the south side of Superior Street. It was made of Milwaukee brick, was 196 feet long and 82 feet wide, and boasted a spire that stood 248 feet high. The new Holy Name Church was Gothic in style, contained many stained-glass windows, and cost over $100,000. Dedicated on Christmas Eve, 1854, it remained at this location until the famous Chicago fire of 1871. The old frame church across the street where the present cathedral now stands housed what was called the Male Free School. Because the new brick church was far and away the largest Catholic church in Chicago and one of the largest buildings of any kind in the city, it was often used for functions normally reserved to a cathedral. In fact, there are references to Holy Name as a cathedral as early as 1861, but it did not achieve this status until the new church **[pictured above]** was completed following the great fire.

During the first twenty-five years of its existence, the Chicago diocese had a rapid succession of bishops. As pointed out in the preceding chapter, Bishop Quarter died at an unusually early age after serving only four years. His two immediate successors resigned after short tenures in office and the fourth Chicago bishop was removed because he went insane. Both Bishops James Van de Velde and Anthony O'Regan got into disputes with Father Kinsella concerning the use of a legacy in Bishop Quarter's will. Bishop Quarter left all of his estate to St. Mary of the Lake University, but his successors wanted to use the money for general diocesan purposes. Bishop O'Regan eventually fired Father Kinsella and three other priests who taught at the university. All of them left the diocese, but they had little difficulty finding responsible posts elsewhere. In 1856, Bishop James Duggan was able to prevail upon the Holy Cross congregation at Notre Dame to take charge of the school, but they agreed to operate it only as a high school. When the congregation withdrew in 1861, Bishop Duggan was able to get Father John McMullen, the chancellor of the diocese, to take charge. Father McMullen erected additional buildings and opened schools of law, medicine, and divinity, but he too got into a dispute with the bishop and was transferred to a remote parish, whereupon the university was closed. Some sixty years later, it was revived, using the charter that Bishop Quarter had obtained from the Illinois legislature in 1844. However, the new school, St.

Mary of the Lake, was relocated to a distant suburb named in honor of Cardinal George Mundelein and has been operated since that time strictly as a seminary.

An early and noteworthy spiritual exercise that took place at Holy Name was a series of missions given in 1856 by Father Arnold Damen, a noted Jesuit preacher. People came from all parts of the city to listen to his sermons. At this time, Bishop Duggan offered to let the Jesuits take charge of the parish, but they declined, doubtless because they did not want to be drawn into controversies relating to the nearby university. Eventually, the Jesuits started Holy Family, a parish on Roosevelt Road on Chicago's near west side, which grew into one of the largest parishes in the United States.

Following the establishment in Holy Name parish of the Boys' Free School, St. James' Free School for Girls was established on North Clark Street by three Sisters of Mercy. It continued until 1856. Then Holy Cross communities of Brothers and nuns took over the boys' and girls' schools. By 1860, nearly two hundred fifty students were attending each institution. After the Holy Cross Brothers withdrew, the parish school was turned over to the Christian Brothers. The Sisters of Charity took over the girls' school after it was merged with another school called the Academy of the Holy Name. In addition, at least three hundred or four hundred children who attended public schools received Sunday afternoon instruction from both laymen and members of religious orders.

Other Catholic institutions began to emerge in Holy Name parish. In 1850, the Sisters of Mercy opened St. Mary's Female Orphan Asylum; the following year they opened the first Catholic hospital in Chicago. In 1866, the Sisters of St. Joseph began to use the vacant university buildings for an orphanage, housing both girls and boys. They were caring for about two hundred eighty children at the time of the 1871 fire, when the entire institution burned to the ground. St. Vincent's Infant Asylum (conducted by the Sisters of Charity) and a home for wayward women (conducted by the Sisters of the Good Shepherd) were also opened in the parish.

After the rector, Father McMullen, was removed from the university and transferred to a distant parish, he went to Rome to make a critical report to the Propagation of the Faith about the condition of the diocese under Bishop Duggan, who had gone insane. After Bishop Duggan was replaced by Bishop Thomas Foley, Father McMullen was recalled to Chicago in 1870 and designated pastor of Holy Name, where he remained until he was appointed bishop of Dubuque, Iowa, in 1880. By that time, the parish had grown to twenty-three hundred families.

The celebrated fire that demolished downtown Chicago in 1871 broke out on Sunday evening, October 9, and lasted throughout the night. An eyewitness quoted in a history prepared by Holy Name parish for its 100th anniversary described the scene as follows: "I went to the corner of State Street and Chicago Avenue to see how the fire seemed across the bridge. As I stood there the great unfinished spire on the Church of the Holy Name began to lurch eastward in the terrible heat, and, as I watched, it went down with a great crash on the roof of the church. In an instant, the roof was ablaze. The building seemed to melt down in from three to five minutes." Only the brick walls remained.

Father McMullen had been visiting a friend in the city and returned to the church when the fire broke out. He was quoted as saying: "We heard a great noise in the street and, on looking out the window for the cause, I was startled at witnessing an illumination as if the whole city was on fire. I heard the roaring of the flames and saw a multitude of people carrying household goods and rushing toward the Rush Street bridge. I started on the run with the others and, by the time we reached the bridge, it was burning."

Father McMullen was able to reach Holy Name Church and to retrieve the Blessed Sacrament from the tabernacle just before the church was completely consumed by the conflagration. There was pandemonium in the streets. The Sisters of St. Joseph were able to remove the children from their orphanage nearby and fled with them from the entire area. When the fire subsided, the entire Holy Name property as well as St. Joseph, the nearby German church, and the property formerly occupied by the university were all destroyed. All in all, the diocese of Chicago suffered the loss of over a million dollars.

Father McMullen erected a temporary wood church that was dubbed the "shanty cathedral." Many parishioners were burned out of their homes and were so impoverished by the fire that only about thirty percent of them were able to contribute toward the rebuilding of Holy Name. Three years elapsed before work began on the present church, which faces west on State Street just north of Superior. It was designed by the seemingly omnipresent Catholic architect, Patrick C. Keely, and is made of stone, not brick. The church originally was two hundred eighteen feet long and supported a spire two hundred ten feet high. Because construction funds were scarce, Father McMullen and other priests went on speaking tours throughout the United States to raise money. In November 1875, the present church was dedicated in a day-long ceremony that included a parade of fifty-five hundred men and eighteen bands. At this time, it formally became a cathedral — the seat of an archbishop — as Chicago had become an archdiocese following the establishment of Peoria as a diocese.

The new cathedral had been opened only seventeen years when extensive renovation work was required. The steeple began to sag and there was considerable doubt that the walls of the church could support it. To remedy this situation, large metal cylinders were sunk into the sand beneath the church to a distance of eighty feet where they reached the hardpan below. Sand was then removed from the cylinders, and concrete was poured to form pillars to shore up the building and the spire on top of it. At the same time, interior improvements were also undertaken. Intricate wooden paneling was placed in the ceiling and some fifteen hundred electric lights were installed — a real innovation in those days. Twenty years later, another major structural change took place. The area around the altar had proved to be much too small to accommodate the large number of priests and acolytes who were frequently present during important ceremonies. To enlarge the area, the apse was physically severed from the rest of the building, moved back thirty feet, and placed on a new foundation. Then additional walls were constructed to fill in the space between the relocated apse and the principal parts of the building.

Until 1904, the Holy Name rectory also served as the chancery for the entire archdiocese. During that year, another building was constructed to provide space for archdiocesan offices, but priests assigned to that office continued to reside at the rectory. In 1929, a new rectory was built that housed eighteen priests — both parish and chancery staff members as well as seminary professors who taught at Quigley Preparatory School. The latter was a minor seminary — a high school for prospective seminarians — which Archbishop James Quigley had opened in an old mansion nearby that was formerly the consulate of the Austrian government.

Until 1904, the Viatorian Fathers operated a parish high school for boys and the Madames of the Sacred Heart conducted the girls' high school. In that year, the Sisters of the Blessed Virgin Mary from Dubuque, Iowa, were brought to Holy Name to take charge of the parochial school. They also established a high school for girls. This order has staffed parish schools since that date. In 1937, Cathedral High School was opened under their supervision and has provided secondary education for both boys and girls for more than fifty years.

The church has welcomed enormous crowds on many noteworthy occasions. In 1926, the International Eucharistic Congress was held in Chicago and was attended by over 250,000 Catholics from all parts of the world. The opening ceremonies were held at the cathedral, as were other liturgical exercises that took place during the next four days. In 1934, some eighty thousand Chicagoans visited the cathedral to pay their respects to Cardinal George Mundelein on the occasion of his twenty-fifth anniversary as a bishop. Five years later, over a million people came to pay their last respects to the cardinal as he lay in state in front of the altar. On October 4, 1979, Pope John Paul II drew a huge throng, both inside and outside the cathedral, when he made his historic visit to Chicago.

Holy Name parish is a study in contrasts. Its eastern border is Lake Michigan. Along Lake Shore Drive are a large number of apartment houses inhabited by wealthy Chicagoans who desire a prestigious intown address. In the days when large Victorian mansions were in style, many were built in the area served by this church, although most of their owners were not Catholics. As one moved westward from the lake, one could find a large number of tenements occupied by recent immigrants. This area was known in the 1920s as Little Hell. Some of these buildings are still there, although most have been replaced over the years by warehouses, stores, and high-rise office buildings that are now spotted throughout the near north side.

This wide variation in the character of the locality meant that Holy Name parish was not to be spared the turmoil that beset Chicago during the Prohibition Era and thereafter. Immediately across State Street from the church were a series of stores and small apartments where parking lots can now be found. It was here that Dion O'Banion, one of Chicago's famed gangland leaders in the early 1920s, maintained his legitimate business front. O'Banion was involved in the sale of illegal liquor, hijacking, extortion, and related criminal activities. At the time of his death, Chicago Police Chief Morgan Collins stated for publication that O'Banion had been responsible for twenty-five murders in the city of Chicago. He was also a former choirboy at the cathedral and he loved flowers. For that reason he opened a florist shop. It is said that he derived much of his legitimate income from supplying large floral displays to gangland funerals.

On November 10, 1924, O'Banion was gunned down by rival mobsters in a scenario that sounded like a Hollywood movie. The reputed culprits, who were never caught, were thought to be members of the Al Capone gang. The dispute pitted Irish gangsters against Italian gangsters, southside Chicago against northside. O'Banion's assassins phoned the florist shop for a bouquet of flowers, saying that they could come by to pick them up. When they entered the State Street establishment, they took O'Banion by surprise, shot him, and drove away.

Cardinal Mundelein refused permission for O'Banion to be buried from the cathedral, notwithstanding the fact that the deceased had once been a member of the parish. The cardinal stated that a notorious criminal should not be given a Christian burial. His decision provided only a slight hitch in the funeral arrangements. A $10,000 casket was hurriedly shipped in from Philadelphia. A crowd of fifteen thousand mourners, marching in a mile-long procession. Led by trucks carrying an estimated $50,000 worth of flowers, it followed O'Banion's casket to Mount Calvary cemetery, where he was laid to rest in unconsecrated ground. The only public prayers offered during this ceremony were said at the graveside by a priest who had grown up with O'Banion in Holy Name parish. Sometime later, O'Banion's wife was able to have her husband's remains removed to consecrated ground, where they rest today just a few feet from the tombs of three of Chicago's archbishops.

O'Banion's State Street store was then taken over by one of his northside colleagues, Hymie Weiss, who was engaged in various illegal enterprises. Weiss did not share O'Banion's penchant for flowers so he closed the florist shop. Weiss and his gang were on equally bad terms with Capone, who had once tried unsuccessfully to eliminate Weiss in a public shootout. Not to be outdone, Capone's men rented the upstairs rooms of the buildings adjacent to the former florist shop and sat waiting for Weiss to appear. On October 11, 1926, Weiss attended a trial in the Cook County courthouse of two of his gang members who were being charged with first-degree murder. His purpose in attending the trial was to make sure that the $100,000 legal defense fund he had collected reached the hands of the jurors who were sitting in that case. After the acquittals, Weiss returned to the State Street premises where he was met with a fusillade of machine-gun fire from Capone's hit men, who were waiting in the upstairs rooms next door. The assailants used State Street as their field of fire, pouring more than fifty bullets in the direction of their victim. They reached their mark. No pedestrians were killed in the melee, but the gunmen poured fifteen bullets into Paddy Murray, Weiss's bodyguard and part-time beer salesman. He died instantly. Three other companions were seriously injured but lived. When his remains were removed from the street, Weiss was found to have been carrying a set of rosary beads in his pocket.

Many of the machine-gun bullets that were aimed at Weiss struck the cathedral across the street. They nearly obliterated the legend on its cornerstone, a quotation from St. Paul's Epistle to the Philippians that read: "To the Name of Jesus, every knee should bend, of those that are in heaven and on earth." At that time, separate stairways led to each of the doors of the cathedral. Later, the front and south doorways of the church were joined by a single continuous set of stairs that, in effect, form a portico in front of the church. As a result, the damaged cornerstone is now almost entirely obscured by new construction. However, a careful examination of the area above the cornerstone reveals bullet holes that have been plugged up.

A third notorious northside gangster of the Prohibition Era who met a more conventional end was George "Bugs" Moran. Moran's legitimate front was the cleaning and dyeing association that he headed. He was better known for an assortment of criminal activities that brought him into confrontations not only with the police but with the Capone gang as well. He missed a celebrated gangland execution of seven of his followers that took place in 1929. Capone gang members, dressed as policemen, "arrested" Moran's followers, lined them up against a wall in a garage, and machine-gunned them to death. The St. Valentine's Day Massacre still stands as a notable benchmark in the history of criminal warfare. However, Moran did not go free forever. Several years later, he robbed a national bank of $10,000, was apprehended, convicted, and sent to Leavenworth Federal Penitentiary where he died in 1957 at the age of sixty-four from lung cancer.

A few weeks before he died, Moran made his peace with the Church and received the last rites from Father John W. O'Connor, the prison chaplain at Leavenworth. In contrast with his friend O'Banion, Moran was carried to his grave in a simple procession, led by Father O'Connor and consisting of six inmates dressed in prison denims who acted as pallbearers. A few weeks later, an inquirer wrote to Father O'Connor to ask whether it was actually true that the aging gangster had returned to the Church during his final days. Father O'Connor replied that, in fact, he had done so and expressed in writing the opinion that God would be good to "Bugs" Moran.

Holy Name Cathedral has been the episcopal church of eight archbishops, five of whom have been elevated to the College of Cardinals. In addition to Cardinal George Mundelein, Cardinals Samuel Stritch, Albert Meyer, John Cody, and Joseph Bernardin have presided at this cathedral. However, none of them has had a more widespread or lasting impact on the city or the nation than the Most Reverend Bernard J. Sheil, who served as auxiliary bishop of Chicago for forty-one years. Bishop Sheil was ordained a priest and consecrated a bishop at Holy Name. Between 1919 and 1922 he served as an assistant pastor at the parish and continued to live at its rectory after being named chancellor of the archdiocese. Even after being appointed pastor of a nearby parish, Bishop Sheil stated in writing that he considered himself still to be a part of what was called the "Holy Name family."

Benny Sheil's boyhood is a scenario that could find its way into a movie script. He attended St. Columbkille's Church, a parish to the west of Holy Name that no longer exists. His childhood hero was Christy Mathewson, the New York Giants pitcher. Sheil's father sent him to high school and college at St. Viator's College, a school operated by the Viatorian Fathers at Bourbonnais, Illinois. There he pitched on the college baseball team, gaining fame and respect when he pitched a victory over the University of Illinois. During summer vacations, he pitched for a Chicago sandlot team known as the Logan Squares. After he graduated, Sheil was offered a major league contract by Charles Comiskey, the owner of the Chicago Black Sox. He turned it down and went back to St. Viator's to study for the priesthood. He was graduated and ordained in 1910.

In the early 1920s, inmates at the Cook County jail were served by priests from Holy Name parish. In this jail, the state of Illinois carried out capital punishment, which at that time meant death by hanging. As a curate at Holy Name, Father Sheil was assigned to be the prison chaplain. In this capacity, he walked the so-called "last mile" with more than twenty prisoners, mounted the gallows, and stood beside them to offer consolation and encouragement before the trapdoor was sprung. Most of the men who were hanged at the Cook County jail were either in their late teens or early twenties. It was then that Father Sheil made a private vow that he would try to do something that would reclaim the young people of the city before the streets and the gangs captured them. It was a vow that took a while to carry out.

In 1922, he was promoted from his duties as an assistant at Holy Name to vice-chancellor and then to chancellor of the archdiocese. In 1924, he accompanied Archbishop Mundelein to Rome when the latter received his "red hat" and became the "cardinal of the west," the first American to be named to the College of Cardinals from west of the Atlantic seaboard. During this visit, Father Sheil made the acquaintance of Pope Pius XI, himself an athlete in his youth (mountain climbing, not baseball). In 1928, Father Sheil was consecrated bishop.

In his new position, he was able to prevail upon his friend and mentor, Cardinal Mundelein, to permit him to organize the Catholic Youth Organization (CYO) as a means of combating juvenile delinquency by giving underprivileged boys athletic activities as an alternative to the lure of the streets and the petty criminal activity that he knew could lead only to disastrous consequences. His first proposal was a boxing tournament. Later, he sought and obtained permission to extend the reach of the CYO into other sports through the unheard-of device of using the elaborate parish network that the church had painstakingly established for spiritual purposes as the framework for athletic leagues composed of competing teams from various parishes. Cardinal Mundelein was skeptical of these proposals but permitted Bishop Sheil to go ahead because of his confidence in the man he had selected to be his chancellor.

Boxing tournaments involving eight different weight classifications were organized in various parts of the city. Some two thousand applicants participated. The sixteen top fighters competed in the finals where winners would receive not only gold medals but four-year scholarships to college. The finals of the first CYO boxing tournament were held at the Chicago Stadium on December 4, 1931, before a capacity crowd of eighteen thousand. Among those in attendance was Al Capone, who came over from the "Bloody Twentieth" Ward — Chicago's Little Italy — to enjoy the evening. He also wanted to scout out prospects for his own organization, which was made up in large part of former street fighters. Bishop Sheil climbed into the ring, recited the CYO pledge, and set in motion a program that grew with rapid strides throughout Chicago. The annual boxing tournament was the CYO's principal fund-raiser; later came the annual CYO track meet. The bishop was also quite adept at tapping wealthy Catholics for additional donations to support the program. He established a headquarters and gym at the south end of the Loop on East Congress Street and later opened other gyms in Little Italy and on Chicago's south side, where large numbers of blacks were arriving from the South. It was estimated that, in its first ten years of existence, some 250,000 Chicago youths participated in CYO programs. These were expanded to include most major sports, band competition, social activities, dramatics, and athletic leagues for girls.

The success of the CYO in Chicago prompted Bishop Sheil to undertake other enterprises. He founded a home for working boys, a home for parolees (a halfway house), a CYO radio station, a school of aeronautics (Lewis College of Science and Technology), and an adult continuing education program (Sheil School of Social Studies). In 1939, he helped to organize the Chicago Back of the Yards Neighborhood Council in the areas along South Halstead Street where large numbers of packinghouse workers and their families resided. He also assisted John L. Lewis and the CIO in organizing the employees of the four major packinghouses in South Chicago. In this later endeavor, Bishop Sheil incurred the enmity of many of his wealthy Catholic backers, some of whom threatened to get rid of him. They never did. His standard reply to their criticisms was that he had never said anything in the area of social justice and labor relations that the popes had not said many years before.

After World War II, CYO programs were established in many other dioceses. Recently, the CYO has broadened the scope of its activities from athletic and social programs to youth ministry, which includes leadership training, retreats, and other religious functions. It is reliably estimated that today a majority of the nation's 19,600 parishes have put in place a CYO or related youth-ministry program and that between 2.1 million and 2.3 million youngsters participate. There are no estimates of how many millions of Catholics, many well past their physical prime, have participated in CYO activities since that winter evening in 1931 when Bishop Sheil stepped into the ring at the Chicago Stadium, recited the CYO pledge, and sounded the opening gong on what is now an elaborate national effort to provide for the special needs of the Church's young people.

The years have been kinder to Holy Name parish than they have been to many downtown and intown parishes. The arrival of the subway on State Street in 1943 ensured ready accessibility to the parochial school and to Cathedral High School for interested students living far beyond parish boundaries. In 1968, the cathedral was again found to be structurally unsafe, so it was completely closed for a period of sixteen months in order that repairs might be made. The inside was gutted, and a stronger foundation of steel and concrete was placed under the building. Several significant artistic improvements were also made, including new stained-glass windows, new stations of the cross, and a new main altar weighing about six tons that was carved from a single block of red-black Argentine granite. While the repairs were in progress, Mass was said for parishioners at six different locations throughout the parish, including apartment buildings, a prominent social club, and a funeral home.

Slums remain in certain parts of the parish, but Chicago's famous Gold Coast, a mixture of high-fashion boutiques and expensive condominiums, still borders the lake. Many old families have moved out, but Holy Name parish still has about four thousand to five thousand parishioners, including large numbers of elderly Catholics and a group of younger professionals who have not yet started their families. The grammar school has enrolled one hundred seventy students and Cathedral High about four hundred fifty. This wide mix of parishioners provides the parish with an annual operating budget in excess of one million dollars. As a result, the parish can support many programs that might otherwise suffer. A full repertoire of liturgical music is available at the wide variety of religious services that a cathedral is expected to hold. Each year, Christmas dinner is served in the school cafeteria for three hundred or more poor people. Parish priests act as chaplains for nine nursing homes and hospitals located nearby. These include some of the largest and busiest medical facilities in Chicago. Holy Name remains the principal church in an archdiocese that numbers more than 400 parishes, over 2,000 priests, and 2,350,000 Catholics, who can find in the history of this parish a significant revelation of their own Catholic roots.

58
St. Stanislaus Kostka

Chicago
ILLINOIS

The oldest Polish Catholic church in the United States is not to be found in one of the large Eastern or Middle Western cities where Poles settled in large numbers following the Civil War. It is located in the small Texas town of Panna Maria (Blessed Virgin Mary), some seventy-five miles southeast of San Antonio. In 1851, Father Leopold Moczygemba, a Polish Franciscan, came to Texas at the request of Bishop John Odin, the first bishop of Galveston, in order to minister to German Catholics. Father Moczygemba was a native of Silesia, a section of Poland then under the control of the Imperial German government. He felt that Texas would be a suitable place for fellow Poles, so he wrote to friends in Silesia and urged them to come to Texas. In the fall of 1854, some one hundred Polish families living in Silesia sold most of their possessions, boarded a transport at Bremen, and took a nine-week voyage to Galveston. Having rented carts in which to carry their remaining belongings, they walked more than one hundred miles inland to a place in Karnes County where the San Antonio River meets Cibolo Creek. There, on Christmas Eve, 1854, Father Moczygemba said midnight Mass for them under an oak tree. At this spot, Polish immigrants later erected Immaculate Conception Church, the first Polish Catholic church in the United States. Many Polish families still reside either in Panna Maria or in other portions of south central Texas.

Life was exceedingly hard for these immigrants. Some died on the way and others perished shortly after arriving in Texas. Harsh winters, hot summers, lack of food and shelter, grasshoppers, and hostile neighbors combined to make life in the *Nowy Swiat* (the New World) barely endurable. Some blamed Father Moczygemba for enticing them to immigrate by painting such rosy pictures of what they might expect to find upon their arrival. Father Moczygemba did not remain long in Texas but eventually moved to large cities that were beginning to experience growing Polish immigration. He served as pastor of churches in Louisville, Syracuse, and Detroit.

At the outbreak of the Civil War, only seven thousand Poles lived in the United States. Slightly more than one hundred resided in Chicago. In February 1864, Father Moczygemba came to the West Town section of Chicago, located on the near northwest side along the north branch of the Chicago River. He visited the Polish settlement that was starting to take shape there and that had been served by the nearby Bohemian church (St. Wenceslaus) and by two German parishes (St. Michael and St. Joseph). However, the Poles very much wanted a church of their own where they would have a priest who spoke their own language. Father Moczygemba heard their Easter confessions and stayed a few months. During that time, the St. Stanislaus Benevolent Society was formed and bought land on Noble Street where, three years later, it erected St. Stanislaus Kostka Church, the oldest Polish parish in Chicago. The society was organized by Peter Kiolbassa, a city policeman who had moved to Chicago from Texas after serving in both the Confederate and Union Armies.

Contemporaneous with these events was the arrival of the Resurrectionist Fathers in the United States. They came first to Texas and then to Detroit. This order was founded in Paris in 1842 by Father Bogdan Janski and two other Polish émigré priests. The founders of the order feared that the spiritual welfare of working-class families, especially Poles, would be undermined and eventually destroyed by socialism, liberalism, secularism, and other antireligious forces that were making inroads in Catholic communities throughout central Europe. They planned to combat these perceived spiritual evils by forming a network of community parishes in which the church would be not only a place of worship but the focal point for community activity extending to such institutions as Catholic schools, hospitals, orphanages, homes for the aged, and other welfare agencies. In a community parish, as envisioned by the Resurrectionists, there would be sufficient educational and welfare agencies to attend to the basic needs of parishioners so that they could live in a totally Catholic environment, undisturbed by any outside forces which might offer in addition to social services an alien ideology to go with them. St. Stanislaus Kostka parish, *Stanislawowo,* came to be one of the first and probably the largest effort that the Resurrectionists made in establishing a community parish in the United States. From this base they were able to expand their influence and the community parish idea into a great many other parishes in Chicago that were assigned to their care by the archdiocese.

The plight of Polish immigrants to the United States following the Civil War cannot be completely understood without referring to the fact of Polish partition. Between 1796 and 1920 there was no Poland. *Stave kraj* (the old country), which existed under Polish kings throughout the Middle Ages, had been divided and taken over by three countries — Prussia, Russia, and Austria-Hungary. Poles were literally men and women without a country. The two unifying forces that maintained their identity were language and the Catholic Church. Those living in Prussia and Russia lived under a Protestant government or an Orthodox government that cared little for their Roman Catholicism. Poles living in Austria-Hungary were subject to a Catholic monarch and could practice their religion freely. However, their economic plight was the worst of all three regions. Most Poles *w stavem kraju* (in the old country) were either peasants or unskilled workers, intensely Catholic, uneducated, and poor. When they came to the United States, they remained at the bottom of the social and economic ladder. Thus the attitude, outlook, and value system of Poles at *Stanislawowo* and elsewhere in Chicago's *Polonia* (Polish community) were rooted in conditions existing in the world from which they came and to which they still felt great personal and emotional ties. In many instances, the motivating factor that brought them to Chicago and other large cities was to earn enough money to return to Poland to buy a farm, something they could never aspire to if they remained in Europe.

In September 1869, the St. Stanislaus Benevolent Society began the construction of a two-story frame church near the site where the present church is located. During this period of time, factionalism began to arise in the Polish community in West Town, which eventually would spread far beyond St. Stanislaus Kostka parish, reaching into Polish communities throughout the United States. Kiolbassa and his followers viewed the benevolent society as a means of preserving the Catholic religion among Polish immigrants. Another group of recent arrivals, led by Ladislaus Dyniewicz, felt that the principal function of Polish organizations should be the support of Polish national aspirations and the reestablishment of their homeland as a separate nation. This ambition was similar to those held by organizations formed in Irish, Greek, and other ethnic communities that over the years provided substantial financial assistance to oppressed compatriots in Europe. The Dyniewicz faction in Chicago formed a faction they called the *gmina Polska* (Polish commune). They tried to infiltrate the benevolent society and to take control of it but failed. Within the next few years, Kiolbassa and those who emphasized the religious character of Polish organizations formed the Polish Roman Catholic Union (PRCU). Its first meeting was held at the St. Stanislaus parish hall in 1874. It was clerical in outlook and orientation. The stated purpose in its charter was "to serve God and Country with a pure Catholic heart."

Dyniewicz and his followers first formed a group calling itself the St. Joseph Society. Ultimately, those who believed in the more nationalistic approach formed another group called the Polish National Alliance (PNA). Soon the PRCU and the PNA grew to have national dimensions in the United States. Its opponents in the PRCU denounced the PNA as an anticlerical movement. If that were so, it was anticlericalism Polish-style, since the PNA grew out of an organization naming itself after a saint, included in its membership a large number of priests, and emerged from the St. Joseph Society whose initial goal was the foundation of a Catholic parish on Noble Street, just two blocks away from St. Stanislaus Kostka. Holy Trinity Church was opened in 1872 supposedly to relieve the overcrowding that was already occurring at St. Stanislaus because of rapid Polish immigration. However, for many years, Holy Trinity remained a bastion of anti-*Stanislawowo* sentiment and activity.

Bishop Thomas Foley of Chicago dedicated the first St. Stanislaus Kostka Church in June of 1871. The event was delayed because of the reluctance of the benevolent society to deed the title to the property to the diocese. Because of trustee problems that had existed all over the United States, the bishop refused to dedicate any church until title had been transferred to diocesan authorities. At this time, St. Stanislaus Kostka parish had fifteen hundred families. Four months after the dedication, the entire central portion of the city of Chicago was destroyed by the famous fire of October 1871, but St. Stanislaus Kostka, lying beyond the Chicago River, was spared. One immediate effect of the fire on its parishioners was that, with the rest of the city lying in ruins, there was abundant work for any craftsman who sought employment in the rebuilding effort.

The first pastor of St. Stanislaus Kostka parish was Father Joseph Juszkiewicz, a diocesan priest, whose presence was resented by some parishioners because he was Lithuanian, not Polish. One night, six masked men entered the parish rectory under the pretext that they were summoning a priest for a sick call and assaulted Father Juszkiewicz, threatening him with much worse if he did not resign. He took their advice and moved to Pennsylvania. His successor received numerous death threats and was often observed carrying a revolver when he left the rectory to make parish rounds.

In 1871, the year that the church was dedicated, Father Jerome Kajsiewicz, Father General of the Resurrectionist order, visited Chicago and concluded with Bishop Foley an agreement according to which the Resurrectionists were given the exclusive right for the next ninety-nine years to staff all Polish parishes in Chicago. This agreement was supported by the clerical faction in Chicago's *Polonia* but was deeply resented by the *gmina Polska*, who now saw as their enemies St. Stanislaus parish, the Resurrection priests, and the Irish hierarchy "downtown" to whom the Resurrectionists, in their opinion, had "sold out." When Holy Trinity parish was opened in the following year, the bishop assigned a Resurrectionist pastor, but the parish committee voted to oust him. Bishop Foley countered by closing the church for a short while, refusing to reopen it until Holy Trinity parishioners agreed to accept the pastor assigned to them by the bishop. This was the first of five occasions in the next twenty years during which this church would be closed by church authorities because of a dispute with its neighbor or with diocesan officials. Despite overtures of friendship from the new pastor of St. Stanislaus Kostka, parishioners at Holy Trinity voted to form a "committee of public safety" to guard their church from the Resurrectionists.

Two events of note occurred in 1874. The School Sisters of Notre Dame arrived at St. Stanislaus Kostka to open the first parish school. At first, they were accused by some members of the parish of trying to "Germanize" the school. Notwithstanding this hostile beginning, they began an attachment with the parish that was to last well over a hundred years. Their school had one hundred fifty students when it first opened and grew to an enrollment of three hundred fifty the following September. The second event of consequence was the arrival of Father Vincent Barzynski, who had served in Polish mission churches in Texas for eight years before being requested by the Resurrectionists to come to Chicago. He was appointed pastor of St. Stanislaus Kostka by Bishop Foley and remained in that post until his death in 1899.

Father Barzynski came to be far more than the pastor of a single parish. He was one of the founders of the PRCU and served for years as a national officer. Bishop Foley, and later Archbishop Patrick Feehan (originally Feighan), came to look to Father Barzynski for advice concerning all of the Polish parishes in Chicago. He became the de facto vicar of Chicago's *Polonia*. No Polish parish was established without his approval; no Polish pastor or assistant was appointed anywhere in Chicago without his consent. When Polish parishes wished to get the bishop's ear in an effective way, they went through Father Barzynski. He recruited not only Polish priests for the archdiocese, principally from members of his own religious congregation, but also secular priests. He built schools, orphanages, homes for the aged, and other welfare institutions for Polish immigrants. He started a Polish-language newspaper, the *Dziennik Chicagoski*, which continued to be published and circulated in Chicago and nationally until 1971. This paper gave the Resurrectionist-Stanislawian-PRCU faction a vehicle for promoting their point of view and was soon countered by the *Gazeta Polska,* which the nationalist faction started for the same reason. Father Barzynski often used the columns of the *Dziennik Chicagoski* to denounce his opponents, such as the PNA, the Holy Trinity parish committee, and assorted socialists, Freemasons, and freethinkers whom he felt were in league with his principal opponents.

Father Barzynski was a classic example of a generation of builders who served the Church during this era. In 1877, he completed the lower portion of the church building **[pictured above]**. Four years later, the upper church was completed; ten years later, its twin towers were installed. One tower was struck by lightning in 1964 and was never replaced because the insurance money was used to pay off part of the debt on the new high school. In 1890, St. Stanislaus College, a high school, was started in the old frame building that had originally housed the church. Because of the influx of Polish residents into this area, the parish grew to the point where, in the 1890s, it had between forty thousand and fifty thousand parishioners. At that time, it was the largest parish in the United States and, some claim, in the entire world. The parochial school had, for many years, about forty-five hundred students who were taught by seventy-five nuns and a few lay persons. In size alone, St. Stanislaus Kostka parish was, at the turn of the century, larger than any city in the state of Illinois except the one in which it was located. At the time of his death in 1899, Father Barzynski was the most prominent figure in Chicago's *Polonia*, which then numbered some 250,000 persons living in twenty-three parishes.

The importance of this parish as a power center came to be appreciated by others far removed from its parish boundaries. Perennial candidate William Jennings Bryan once spoke at St. Stanislaus Hall. When the parish opened a new twenty-four-room addition to its school in 1908, the notables on the platform at the dedication ceremony included Charles W. Fairbanks, the vice-president of the United States.

Along with the phenomenal growth of the area in the latter part of the nineteenth century came increased factionalism between St. Stanislaus Kostka and Holy Trinity, the latter having twenty-five thousand parishioners of its own. When he came to West Town in the mid-1870s, Father Barzynski tried to transform Holy Trinity Church into an overflow chapel for St. Stanislaus and to deprive it of any independent parochial existence. In this effort, he was quite unsuccessful. When the bishop closed Holy Trinity Church at Father Barzynski's request, its parishioners appealed to the Vatican and were able to have their parish church reopened. They pointed to the size of Holy Trinity parish and prevailed with the argument that always had telling effect in Rome, namely that if their church remained closed, the Polish community would suffer a large exodus from the Church and souls would be lost to heretical sects or to religious indifference.

After Holy Trinity was reopened, Father Adalbert Mielcuszny, a diocesan priest, was appointed pastor. His presence did not please the parishioners of Holy Trinity. From time to time, riots broke out on Noble Street involving members of the two rival parishes. Father Mielcuszny was once assaulted in the street. Eventually, he was suspended by the archbishop because, among other things, he refused to transfer title to the church property to the archdiocese of Chicago. After the suspension, he refused to vacate the rectory. Regrettably, he met his end under very mysterious circumstances. His housekeeper returned from some midday errands to find him lying face down in a pool of blood. An autopsy determined that apoplexy was the cause of death. Members of both parishes blamed each other for foul play resulting in his death but the identity of his alleged assailants was never determined.

The Resurrectionists under Father Barzynski were able to regain control of Holy Trinity by decree of the archbishop but their tenure was not long. When Father Simon Kobrzynski, the new Resurrectionist pastor, announced to Holy Trinity parishioners that collections taken up at the church would be given to the pastor at St. Stanislaus to be administered by him and that only low Masses would be said at Holy Trinity on Sunday, he was met with an uprising. As described by Dr. Joseph J. Parot in his scholarly and detailed study of Polish Catholics in Chicago: "This rather mild form of rebuke, however, was the cause for a wild demonstration within the sanctuary itself. Worshippers began stamping their feet and throwing their hymnals about the church; women groaned hysterically; children were sent running up and down the church aisles, while other adults climbed over the pews in an effort to leave the church as a sign of protest. The shaken Kobrzynski, who believed that Trinitarians in particular were prone to such forms of anarchy, returned to the altar in an attempt to finish Mass. During the Offertory, [two trustees] moved to the front of the church to take up the usual collection. Whether they did so in a particularly aggressive or threatening fashion is not known; however, when Kobrzynski saw them coming, he took the approach as a threat and fled."

The feud was serious enough that it brought the newly appointed apostolic delegate, Archbishop Francesco Satolli, to Chicago to act as moderator. Peace — or even a cessation of open hostilities — did not come to Noble Street until Archbishop Feehan withdrew the Resurrectionists from Holy Trinity parish in 1893 and appointed a young Polish-speaking Holy Cross Father from Notre Dame, Father Casimir Sztuczko, as pastor. Father Sztuczko was able to ingratiate himself with his unruly congregation. He even joined the PNA, an act that demonstrated his independence from the PRCU and the Resurrectionists. His talents clearly filled the leadership vacuum that existed at Holy Trinity, where he remained as pastor until his death fifty-five years later.

The animosity generated along Noble Street in Chicago between these two mammoth parishes spread to the rest of Chicago and to Polish parishes throughout the United States. The first major long-term schism to take place in the United States arose in neighboring St. Hedwig's parish with what was called the "independent movement" headed up by a layman named Jacob Tamillo and a popular but erratic priest, Father Anthony Kozlowski. Father Kozlowski, an assistant at St. Hedwig, was serving in the same parish in which Father Vincent Barzynski's brother Joseph was pastor. They did not get along. The Old Catholic Church was a schismatic group that originated in Europe in 1871 as a reaction to Vatican Council I and especially to the adoption by that council of the doctrine of papal infallibility. It took an interest in the schism in Chicago. Father Kozlowski asked a bishop of the Old Catholic Church to ordain him and to bless St. Hedwig's Church. After this occurred, Father Kozlowski was suspended from his functions by the archbishop of Chicago and was ordered to leave St. Hedwig's rectory. Again riots occurred. Parishioners seized the church and drove Father Joseph Barzynski from the rectory. He was forced to take refuge at his brother's church. Irish policemen summoned to the scene were initially unable to cope with the situation, which included mobs of irate women entering the church wielding pots and pans. Eventually, the archbishop had to resort to a civil court to oust the trespassers. Similar "independent movements" broke out elsewhere in the United States. In Omaha, for instance, when an Old Catholic pastor gained control of the Polish Roman Catholic church in that city, he was confronted by a mob of Roman Catholic parishioners who wanted to regain possession of the premises. A pitched gun battle ensued inside the church, in the course of which the schismatic pastor shot two of his opponents.

Father Kozlowski was eventually excommunicated and was then ordained a bishop in the Old Catholic Church. He was able to organize a following of seventeen thousand in a group calling itself the Polish Old Catholic Church. Most of its membership returned to the Roman Catholic Church in 1908 when the Holy See appointed the first Polish bishop in the United States. Others joined with another schismatic church, the Polish National Catholic Church, which originated in Scranton and which has about 250,000 members in the United States today.

A recitation of the disputes that arose in Chicago's *Polonia* has the tendency to divert attention from the very real and very substantial success that Father Vincent Barzynski and his Resurrectionist successors achieved at St. Stanislaus Kostka and at other parishes that sprang from this beginning. St. Stanislaus Kostka is located in what was the heart of Chicago's *Polonia*, a triangle formed by Milwaukee Avenue, Ashland Avenue, and Division Street. The Polish tenements in this area at one time had a population density of fifty thousand people per square mile. Milwaukee Avenue, called the "Polish corridor," extends from Chicago's Loop northwesterly to St. Adalbert's cemetery in Niles, Illinois, just beyond the city limits. Division Street was "Polish Broadway," an area lined with stores and a large number of taverns. "Polish Downtown" was located on Milwaukee Avenue between Ashland and Damen. Many Polish Jews helped to develop the "Downtown" as a business district. Being the largest parish in the United States (and possibly in the world) imposed great burdens on parish priests at St. Stanislaus Kostka. An early Resurrectionist at the parish wrote to his superior in Rome that "we have as much to do here in one day as you have back in Rome in a month." Some of the difficulties experienced at the parish can be attributed to a ratio of several thousand parishioners to one priest and a school with sixty or more students per classroom. At one time, this parish had nearly seventy-five organizations — cultural, spiritual, social, economic, and charitable. It was a showcase for the Resurrectionist idea of a community parish. These groups were always active. For instance, in 1908, the Living Rosary Society was composed of four thousand young women, a figure that equaled the entire population of most of Chicago's Catholic parishes. The Society of the Virgins of the Most Holy Rosary encouraged Polish girls to make a public pledge of their virginity as "roses." This event usually took place during ceremonies held in May. In 1917, more than fifteen hundred young women who were members of this society publicly professed their chastity during Marian devotions as "roses" of the Society of Virgins.

Every parish organization was designed to shore up the Polish Catholic family, uprooted as most of them were from the *ojczyzna* (the homeland), and to enhance its ties to the Church. On a Sunday in the early 1900s, a typical family at St. Stanislaus Kostka would attend a crowded Mass at the church. After breakfast, they might take a bus ride out Milwaukee Avenue to St. Adalbert's cemetery in Niles, which the parish had acquired early in its existence. There they would give expression to the strong Polish reverence for the dead by visiting the graves of family members and friends, after which they would proceed to the local picnic groves and forest preserves. In these recreational areas, Polish bands played all Sunday afternoon and beer and kielbasa could be obtained inexpensively. The whole family had a chance to socialize with friends, fellow parishioners, and acquaintances from all parts of Chicago's *Polonia*. Then came the long trolley ride back to a tenement in the city following a sufficient respite to permit one to face another sixty-hour week of backbreaking toil in a factory, a sweatshop, or the stockyards.

Chicago's *Polonia* spread from the Milwaukee Avenue corridor to other parts of the city. Large numbers of Poles who worked in the stockyards settled on the south side near Halstead Street in an area that came to be known as "Back of the Yards." Another enclave grew up in southeast Chicago not far from the Indiana line and the city of Gary, where new steel mills were being constructed. One might look at this immense crush of people who filled enormous parishes and wonder why "they" did not erect more Polish parishes. "They" did. The Resurrectionists and two generations of Irish bishops — Thomas Foley, Patrick Feehan, and James Quigley — built fifty-two Polish parishes in Chicago and its suburbs over a period of half a century. They were among five hundred Polish parishes then in existence in the United States. However, there never seemed to be enough money or manpower to fill the need, especially in communities that were desperately poor and lacked any middle-class or professional members. During his reign as pastor of St. Stanislaus Kostka, provincial of the Resurrectionists, and vicar for more than 250,000 Polish Catholics in Chicago, Father Barzynski created the *Bank Parifialny*, an early version of a credit union, or neighborhood savings and loan association. Thousands of Poles invested their meager savings in the *Bank*, whose deposits Father Barzynski used to finance the construction of new Polish parishes. Its loan portfolio became overextended and the bank failed. There was never any suggestion of wrongdoing, just poor business judgment, but the distinction was cold comfort to uninsured depositors who lost their savings. This failure contributed to the unrest in Chicago's *Polonia* and to hostility toward Father Barzynski and the Resurrectionists at a time when opposition from other sources was rising.

Tension in Chicago's *Polonia* was materially reduced in 1908 when the Holy See appointed the first Polish bishop in the United States. He was Father Paul Rhode, who had grown up in St. Stanislaus Kostka parish and who was then pastor of a southside Polish church. Polish Catholics in the United States had been pressing the Holy See for fifteen years to appoint a Polish bishop. In 1904, a delegation from Chicago went to Rome and personally delivered this request to Pope Pius X, who, incidentally, was canonized in 1954. The Holy Father assured them that this would eventually occur but it took Rome four years to act. When asked to submit the name of a suitable candidate, Archbishop Quigley called together the pastors of all of the Polish parishes and asked them to select one name. Father Rhode won the balloting, his name was submitted to Rome, and he was appointed. When he was consecrated in 1908, a daylong celebration took place throughout Chicago. Some 200,000 people lined a parade route to greet the new bishop. He was accompanied by 20,000 uniformed men serving as an honor guard, as well as 700 Polish priests, hundreds of nuns, 20 bishops, and a large contingent of priests from other ethnic groups. They marched down Noble Street past St. Stanislaus Kostka Church and past thousands of homes that had been decorated for the occasion. After a generation or more of internal fighting, a degree of unity had finally emerged in Chicago's Polish community.

To Polish Catholics in Chicago and elsewhere, World War I meant not only defeating Prussian imperialism but also a chance to restore the Polish nation. Poles supported

Woodrow Wilson by overwhelming majorities. Determined efforts were made to get Polish residents registered to vote, an effort that had the incidental effect of encouraging them to become naturalized citizens, since only citizens could vote. Polish parishes in Chicago sent over ten thousand men to fight in the war. Most of them joined the U.S. Army, but many fought in an émigré army organized in Europe to fight under the Polish flag. Some seven hundred fifty parishioners from St. Stanislaus Kostka parish joined the U.S. Army while ninety others enlisted in the Polish Army. Large sums of money were contributed by parishioners not only to U.S. war bond drives but also to Polish relief agencies operating in Europe. Following the war, Poland gained independence after one hundred twenty-five years. About one percent of the Polish population of the United States sailed from the port of New York in 1920 to return to their recently liberated homeland. For the rest, it was clear at that time, if indeed it was not always clear, that they were here to stay.

Polish Catholics had enjoyed an uneasy but generally harmonious relationship with Chicago's Irish hierarchy. Whatever misgivings they may have had about their Irish bishops were supposedly set to rest when a prelate of German origin, Bishop George Mundelein, was appointed archbishop of Chicago in 1915. At the same time, Chicago's own Polish auxiliary bishop, Paul Rhode, was sent to Green Bay, Wisconsin, where he served as bishop until his death twenty years later. Mundelein, who became a cardinal in 1924, was enormously popular with every ethnic group in Chicago except the Poles. They were the largest ethnic group in his archdiocese, numbering 340,000 at that time and having over 50 parishes and 140 priests. The Polish clergy, including but by no means limited to Father Francis Gordon, the pastor of St. Stanislaus Kostka, drew up a lengthy memorial of grievances and requests and forwarded it to Rome. Among other things, they asked that Bishop Rhode be assigned to an archdiocese having a large number of Polish Catholics, that Polish auxiliary bishops be assigned to several named cities that had large Polish populations, that courses in Polish literature and culture be included in the curricula of seminaries in dioceses having large Polish populations, and that only limited application be given to provisions found in the new Code of Canon Law which required that most parishes be territorial in character while national parishes had to be severely limited in number. Despite their old rivalry, both the PRCU and the PNA joined to support this petition.

These requests ran strictly contrary to a determined and long-standing policy called Americanism, which many bishops, including Mundelein, strongly supported. It was a policy designed to bring about the integration of immigrant Catholics into the mainstream of American life. What the Polish clergy were proposing was to protect the faith of their parishioners by what amounted to cultural isolation. Their petition to Rome was denied. The policies they proposed might have achieved some short-term success in protecting the Catholic faith of Polish immigrants. In the long run, such cultural isolation could not possibly have been maintained, even in a city like Chicago whose Polish residents exceed in number the population of any Polish city in the world except Warsaw.

Like many other central city parishes, St. Stanislaus Kostka began to experience the outmigration of its younger members who, over the years, left the deteriorating housing stock in West Town for the suburbs. However, the highly developed network of Resurrectionist parish organizations had sufficient pull on these parishioners to delay this outmigration many years after similar changes had begun to occur in other Chicago parishes. When it did come to pass after the end of World War II, younger families moved northwest along the corridor staked out by Milwaukee Avenue and relocated in newer parishes farther out along the Polish Corridor. A major physical change in the area took place in 1957 when the Kennedy Expressway (Interstate 94) was completed from the Loop in downtown Chicago to O'Hare Airport. As originally planned, it would have run straight through church property. Poles throughout Chicago mounted a campaign to save the "mother church" of Chicago's *Polonia* and were able to prevail upon public authorities to redesign the right of way to avoid most of the church property and bring it through coal yards and a rail line to the east. The parish was spared, except for its heating plant, the gym, and a few classrooms in the high school, while the taxpayers reportedly saved three million dollars from the relocation of the roadway. Travelers from the nation's busiest airport to the nation's third largest city now pass immediately behind the old church and within a block of its ancient rival, Holy Trinity.

Changes in the neighborhood have resulted in uprooting the families of most of the original founders of St. Stanislaus Kostka parish with another ethnic group. The same holds true of Holy Trinity. Between 1950 and 1960, large numbers of Puerto Ricans and Mexicans moved into West Town and now reside there. The parish today has about 680 older Polish families and about 200 to 250 Hispanic families. The latter figure is an estimate, since newer Hispanics are often reluctant to register formally in a parish. In 1975, the Holy Cross Fathers could no longer supply a priest to serve at Holy Trinity, so the Resurrectionists were asked by Cardinal John Cody to take over the administration of the parish after an absence of eighty-two years. They agreed to come for a year but stayed on for eleven years, leaving only because a shortage of Polish-speaking priests prevented them from continuing. Today, Holy Trinity is operated as a Polish mission of the archdiocese.

Masses at St. Stanislaus Kostka are now said in English, Polish, and Spanish. The parish bulletin is trilingual. Devotions to Our Lady of Guadalupe are conducted where years ago devotions to Our Lady of Czestochowa were more popular. The parochial school of two hundred students is predominantly Hispanic. When the first Polish pope, John Paul II, visited Chicago in 1979, his visit excited great enthusiasm in St. Stanislaus parish and throughout Chicago's *Polonia*.

The parish is a study in contrasts. Land values are rising rapidly and a portion of the parish is becoming gentrified. On the other hand, St. Stanislaus Kostka operates a soup kitchen that feeds two hundred people each day. Doubtless the area is "coming back," but it still remains to be seen what "coming back" means in terms of commercialization versus a residential community and what kind of residential community will emerge.

When Father Barzynski celebrated the first Mass in the present church on Christmas Eve in 1875, he told the congregation that had assembled in the church basement: "Let us do something constructive — as a group — and begin to build a church for the honor and glory of God and for the nourishment of souls. This church will be a testimony not only to . . . unbelievers but also an everlasting heritage to your beloved children, grandchildren, and great grandchildren."

The passage of time has quieted the strife that once beset this parish and plagued Father Barzynski; indeed, it has even obscured the reasons for it. However, the passage of time has brought about more than fifty Polish parishes in Chicago that do exist today and constitute the heritage of which Father Barzynski spoke over a hundred years ago.

59
St. John Cathedral

Milwaukee
WISCONSIN

The first Mass said in Wisconsin was offered in August of 1661 by Father René Menárd, a Jesuit missionary, at a portage to the Wisconsin River near what is now the city of Merrill. Father Menárd had come to Wisconsin from Keweenaw Bay in northern Michigan in search of some Catholic Huron Indians who were fleeing from their historic enemy, the Iroquois. He disappeared mysteriously. Years later, his cassock and breviary were discovered many hundreds of miles away among the Sioux, a tribe that ventured eastward from time to time into Wisconsin from the Dakotas. In 1669, Father Claude Allouez, another Jesuit, established the St. Francis Xavier mission at Green Bay and the St. James mission near Portage as well as several other mission stops in Menominee and Potawatomi villages. In the course of his journey from Upper Michigan to the Mississippi, Father Jacques Marquette passed through Wisconsin to reach the Father of Waters, as did Father Louis Hennepin, the Capuchin missionary, who traveled with the La Salle expedition some years later. The Jesuits built a mission house and church at De Pere, in the central part of the state, but it was burned to the ground during a Fox Indian uprising in 1687. Jesuit missionaries were also known to have visited Potawatomi and Kickapoo villages located along the Milwaukee River. After the Jesuits abandoned their mission at Green Bay in 1738, there was no Catholic activity in Wisconsin for more than eighty years.

The first Catholic parish established in Wisconsin in modern times was St. John's, located at Menomineeville near Green Bay. It was founded in 1831, just a few years before priests began to visit Catholics in the locality where the Milwaukee River empties into Lake Michigan. In 1835, Indian title was cleared to the Milwaukee area and the Potawatomi and their neighbors were moved westward by the U.S. Army. In that year, Solomon Juneau, a native of Canada who came there in 1818, bought land along the lakefront from the U.S. Land Office and subdivided it into lots for resale. Juneau, the first mayor of Milwaukee, is generally credited with being the founder of the city.

There is some question among historians as to where the first Mass was said in Milwaukee. The prevailing opinion is that Father Florimond J. Bonduel offered it at the Juneau home, located at what is now North Water Street and East Michigan Avenue. The date is put at August 1837, although some feel the event took place a year or two earlier. At that time, Milwaukee was part of the diocese of Detroit. The Wisconsin Territory was in the process of being organized as a jurisdiction separate and apart from the state of Michigan. Juneau gave two of his subdivided lots to the bishop of Detroit for the purpose of erecting a church, which was begun two years later by Father Patrick O'Kelly, the first resident priest in Milwaukee. It was named in honor of St. Peter and was completed in 1842, at which time Father O'Kelly was transferred back to Michigan. In 1842, the first entry was made in the baptismal records of St. Peter's parish. The church was a small frame building, originally twenty-eight feet by forty-two feet, and was lengthened two or three years later to accommodate the growing parish. When Bishop John Martin Henni arrived in Milwaukee in 1844, this building became the first cathedral of the Milwaukee diocese. A few years later, as other churches came to be built, the use of this building for regular parish worship was discontinued. It became in turn a seminary chapel, a children's chapel, a chapel for a new Bohemian parish, and later a Sunday school. After being dismantled and relocated on two occasions, it was eventually placed on the grounds of St. Francis Seminary, where it stands today as a memento of the early days of the Catholic Church in Milwaukee.

In 1842, Father Martin Kundig, one of the most prominent figures in the history of the Church in Milwaukee, was appointed pastor of St. Peter's by the bishop of Detroit. At that time, there were only five other priests in all of Wisconsin — two at Green Bay, two at Prairie du Chien along the Mississippi River, and one near Lake Superior. Father Kundig was born and raised in a German canton in Switzerland. He was educated abroad and in the United States and was ordained in Cincinnati in 1829. He organized various German parishes both in Cincinnati and Detroit. Immediately before coming to Milwaukee he had been active in aiding cholera victims during one of several massive epidemics that struck Detroit and was the first superintendent of the Wayne County, Michigan, Poor Farm. He spoke four languages. Upon coming to Milwaukee, he took over a parish composed of French, Irish, and German Catholics.

Father Kundig was an enterprising individual whose interests and activities extended beyond the building of a new parish. Milwaukee had no public schools until about 1849. He was instrumental in securing public support, both in Milwaukee and Racine, for the establishment of a public school system. There was opposition among wealthier citizens to being taxed "to educate the Dutch and the Irish," but Father Kundig was effective in convincing the community that new immigrants would become better citizens if they and their children had the benefit of an education. In the meanwhile, he established small schools for boys and girls in the basement of St. Peter's Church. At first, they were taught by laymen. For a short while these schools were supported, in part, by public funds until Milwaukee was able to get a tax-funded system on its feet. As late as 1859, only half of the school-age children in the city attended any school, either public or private. Father Kundig also promoted the dredging of Milwaukee Harbor, a public works project that was necessary to permit the city to grow as a port.

Not long after Father Kundig arrived in Milwaukee, church authorities began to discuss the possibility of forming Wisconsin into a diocese separate from Detroit. Three cities were in the running as the seat of the new episcopal see. To promote the interest of Milwaukee, Father Kundig organized a mammoth St. Patrick's Day parade, involving some three thousand participants. Its purpose was to convince church officials that Milwaukee was a strongly Catholic city that deserved to be selected. It must have been an unusual St. Patrick's Day observance, since it was conducted under the sponsorship of the Catholic Temperance Society of Wisconsin, a group that Father Kundig had organized the previous year. The celebration achieved its purpose, and Milwaukee was selected in 1843 to be the seat of the new diocese. Its first bishop was Father Kundig's seminary classmate, a Swiss German named John M. Henni. He came to Milwaukee in 1844 and served as bishop and later as archbishop until his death in 1881.

When Bishop Henni arrived in Milwaukee, there were only four priests in his diocese, which included the entire Wisconsin Territory. Milwaukee was growing at the rate of two hundred to three hundred immigrants per week, and it became difficult to serve both German and Irish congregations in the same small church, since separate Masses, having sermons either in English or in German, had to be celebrated. In 1846, Bishop Henni founded St. Mary's parish nearby, and it grew to become the German Catholic church for East Milwaukee. Many more German churches were soon constructed throughout the state. In the same year, Bishop Henni was able to prevail upon the Daughters of Charity at Emmitsburg, Maryland, to send a contingent of nuns to Milwaukee to teach in the girls' school he was establishing in the basement of St. Mary's Church. Shortly after they arrived, the nuns also opened an orphan asylum and St. John's Infirmary. The first major challenge for the new hospital was caring for victims of a smallpox epidemic that swept the city in 1848.

During his tenure as the leader of the Milwaukee diocese, Bishop Henni acquired a reputation for shrewdness in the acquisition of real estate. His first major effort in this regard was the assembling of several lots from various purchasers to build a cathedral.

He acquired most of the block across the street from the county court house, now called Juneau Square, including a strip of land located between the future church and rectory that was given by Juneau to secure the dedication of two pews in the cathedral to the permanent use of the Juneau family.

In 1847, Bishop Henni began the construction on this site of the cathedral, which he named in honor of St. John the Evangelist. The bishop was sometimes criticized for the ambitious nature of this undertaking; however, he insisted that he was going to build a church that would last a hundred years. But for a devastating fire that occurred in 1935, this ambition would have been realized. In fact, the walls and the lower part of the tower he originally built remain intact today. The cost of this project was originally estimated at $20,000 to $30,000. Upon completion the figure was nearer to $70,000. It was and is located on a high plateau. Before the construction of office buildings and apartment houses that now surround it, the tower of the cathedral could be seen from Lake Michigan. The cathedral was designed and built under the supervision of Victor Schulte, a local architect. Its style has been variously described as Roman, Grecian, and Spanish Renaissance. It is probably a mixture of all three. Bishop Henni traveled to Europe, Canada, and Mexico to raise funds for this undertaking.

Upon completion the cathedral (which was dedicated on July 31, 1853) stood 154 feet by 74 feet, and had ceilings that were 36 feet high; the lower portion of the tower stood 120 feet and was surmounted originally by a wooden portion bringing its overall height to 186 feet.

One notable feature of the new cathedral that put it in into contact with the daily lives of all Milwaukeeans was the tower clock that was imported from Munich. The clock has a ten-foot pendulum, weighted at the end with a 130-pound disk, and it is said that most of its parts were handmade. In 1858, the city council made an agreement with Bishop Henni to pay a small fee for the operation and maintenance of the clock and designated it to be the official city clock, replacing two others located at either end of the city that had served as unofficial city clocks but had never kept the same time. The cathedral clock is no longer an official municipal timepiece but it still keeps accurate time.

When the cathedral was dedicated in 1853, the Milwaukee *Sentinel* wrote: "We congratulate our Catholic friends upon the possession of so commodious and elegant a place of worship and, above all, upon the flourishing condition of their charitable institutions, which have accomplished and are accomplishing much good for this community."

The dedication ceremony was a liturgical extravaganza. It was conducted by the papal nuncio to Brazil, who was then on an inspection tour of the United States for the Holy See. There was some question that the ceremonies might prove to be too exhausting for him, especially in light of the eucharistic fast that was observed at the time, but he held up well. The dedication began at 7:00 A.M. and lasted until 11:00 A.M., followed by a solemn high Mass. Mass was over at 2:00 P.M., but the participants were back in the church at three o'clock for benediction and a sermon in German. Then, at 5:00 P.M., came vespers, during which Archbishop John Purcell of Cincinnati preached for an hour and twenty minutes, followed by a second benediction and a grand "Te Deum."

Despite the achievement of Milwaukee Catholics in erecting a large cathedral to the plaudits of many in the community, they were not held in universal esteem or affection. The rise of the Know-Nothing Party throughout the United States had anti-Catholic overtones, as did the residual effects of the Mexican War. The Mexican War did not start nor was it fought on account of religious considerations, but the fact that American troops were repeatedly arrayed in battle against Catholic soldiers of a Catholic nation resulted in a certain amount of religious hostility. Father Peter Leo Johnson, late professor of church history at St. Francis Seminary, once wrote: "Suffice it to say that in the early '50s no priest could appear on the streets of Milwaukee without exposing himself to indignities and insults. The external violences of the '30s and '40s, symbolized by the burning of churches, had given way to a more subtle attack but one which was much more disastrous to winning recruits for the front line, or keeping those already here."

One of Bishop Henni's most vexing problems was finding German-speaking priests for German-speaking parishes. The supply of foreign-born priests was wholly insufficient to meet the demand. As one German parish put it to him in requesting a priest: "We have bread. Send us priests." He found it necessary to build a diocesan seminary that would attempt to provide for this need not only in Wisconsin but for other dioceses throughout the Midwest. The first Milwaukee seminary, called Bishop's College, consisted of four seminarians who occupied the house in which Bishop Henni lived when he first arrived in the city. It was plainly inadequate to the need, so the bishop began to build St. Francis Seminary at St. Francis, Wisconsin. The site was then four miles from Milwaukee. Now it is a suburb along the south shore of Lake Michigan that abuts the city limits. Ten thousand parishioners in German parishes throughout the state contributed to its construction, which began in 1856. Classes were taught in English as well as German, and many English-speaking seminarians were enrolled. Today, it is not only a seminary but also provides offices for the archdiocese of Milwaukee, called the Archbishop Cousins Catholic Center.

Bishop Henni opposed slavery and supported the Union cause during the Civil War, as did most of the 400,000 German immigrants of all religious denominations who had come to the United States in the preceding thirty years. German immigrants throughout Wisconsin and the Middle West provided many regiments to the Union Army. Bishop Henni encouraged enlistments in sermons preached at the cathedral and flew the American flag from its clock tower. In 1864, the Daughters of Charity, who were teaching at the parish girls' school, suspended classes early in May so that they could leave the city and join other members of their order who were performing nursing chores for the Union Army. President Lincoln had made a request to the provincial house at Emmitsburg, Maryland, for nuns to start a hospital in Washington to care for wounded soldiers. The Sisters complied. The summer of 1864 was a particularly bloody one. Ulysses S. Grant was marching on Richmond and William Tecumseh Sherman was marching on

Atlanta, so the casualty rate was high. After spending their summer vacation caring for wounded soldiers on battlefields and in convalescent hospitals, the Sisters at St. John's School returned to Milwaukee in September to resume their classroom duties for another school year.

In 1867, Green Bay and La Crosse became dioceses and, in 1875, Milwaukee became an archdiocese. In 1868, when Bishop Henni celebrated his twenty-fifth anniversary as a bishop, there were nearly a million inhabitants in Wisconsin. Approximately one half of them were Catholics. The rest were principally Lutherans. Father Kundig became not only the rector of the cathedral parish but vicar general of the archdiocese and retained these posts until his death in 1879. He kept the financial accounts for both entities. Parishioners at St. John's complained from time to time that they were paying for parish facilities that were actually being devoted to diocesan functions and felt that other parishes should contribute to those activities, so Father Kundig had to be careful to establish separate accounts and make separate expenditures that would reflect an equitable apportionment of costs. In 1874, he constructed a building behind the cathedral, which he called Bishop's Hall. It housed both the "boys' department" and the "girls' department" of the parish school. After 1884, both schools became free schools. Before that date, tuition was five dollars a year. They were the first free parochial schools in Wisconsin. The yearly operating cost to the parish was about $4,000.

From 1846 to 1895, the Daughters of Charity taught in the parish school for girls. Laymen and later the Holy Cross Brothers from Notre Dame operated the school for boys. For nearly twenty years, Father Kundig's sisters conducted what might be called a quasi-parochial school in their home, located just across the street from the cathedral, and in a conference room located in the rear of the church building. In 1895, all schools were taken over by the Dominican Sisters from Sinsinawa, Wisconsin, who continued to operate an elementary school and a high school until the 1960s when demographic changes in East Milwaukee forced a closing of both schools. By then, there were very few families with school-age children left in the area.

Every history of St. John's parish devotes considerable attention to three major disasters occurring between 1860 and 1892 that had a devastating effect on the parish. On September 6, 1860, a large excursion boat, the *Lady Elgin*, which was returning from Chicago to Milwaukee, sank in the middle of the night with nearly five hundred passengers aboard. It struck a schooner loaded with lumber not far from the Milwaukee port, but rescue efforts were ineffective because of the darkness and the choppiness of the water. It took eight weeks to determine just how many lives were lost; bodies of victims continued to be washed ashore on a daily basis. Nearly three hundred of the deceased passengers were members of St. John's parish. Bishop Henni offered a funeral Mass at the cathedral for the deceased. About eight thousand people stood outside the crowded cathedral for the requiem Mass and then joined a mile-long procession to the cemetery. Mass is still offered at the cathedral some one hundred forty years later for the victims of the *Lady Elgin* disaster.

In 1883, a six-story hotel, the Newhall House, burned to the ground. Sixty-four people perished in the fire, half of whom were Catholics. Twenty-one victims were buried from the cathedral at a single requiem Mass. Nine years later, a fire broke out at a nearby business house and spread throughout the parish, demolishing sixteen square blocks of homes and businesses. The cathedral was spared and was opened to provide temporary housing for the dispossessed. This fire, known as the "Third Ward Fire," had a long-term effect on the parish because, as rebuilding efforts took shape, many parishioners simply decided to move out of the area and start anew in other parts of the city.

Ward Three in East Milwaukee was the Irish ward. During the latter part of the nineteenth century, St. John's, which was located in Ward Three, came to be known as the Irish parish, while St. Mary's served as the German parish. During this period, friction arose from time to time, both in Wisconsin and elsewhere, between English-speaking and German-speaking Catholics (and others). In 1890, the Wisconsin legislature enacted the so-called Bennett Law, named after its sponsor, a Catholic assemblyman from Iowa County named Michael John Bennett. Among other things, this law compelled the use of English in all schools, both public and private. Its sponsors regarded it as an effort to integrate foreign-born citizens into an English-speaking culture. Germans, both Catholic and Lutheran, looked upon it as an invasion of parental rights and an attempt to destroy religious schools. Milwaukee Archbishop Michael Heiss and his successor, Archbishop Frederick F. X. Katzer, both German, agreed and they pressed for its repeal. The American Catholic hierarchy was far from unanimous on this subject. Men like Cardinal James Gibbons, Archbishop John Ireland of St. Paul, and Bishop John Lancaster Spalding of Peoria felt that the Catholic Church should promote the Americanization of foreign-born Catholics and that Catholic schools should be used as an instrument of this policy. The teaching of classes in Catholic schools in a language other than English was wholly at odds with their concept of Americanization. Both Lutherans and Catholics combined forces to bring about the repeal of the Bennett Law but not without active intervention by the clergy in the 1890 election campaign. Years later, the U.S. Supreme Court put an end to this controversy in a case involving a German-language parochial school in Nebraska. It declared a Nebraska statute similar to the Bennett Law unconstitutional.

In 1887, eighty-four German-speaking priests in St. Louis organized an association called the *Priesterverein*. The movement spread to Cincinnati, Milwaukee, and other cities having large German Catholic populations. The program of the *Priesterverein* included much more than the establishment and maintenance of German-language parochial schools. It also called for the establishment of nationality parishes to be treated on a par with territorial parishes (most of which were Irish), the appointment of more German bishops, and the establishment of separate German dioceses. The emergence of the *Priesterverein* generated the formation in Milwaukee of another organization of English-speaking priests, the American Catholic Clerical Union, whose views were diametrically opposed to the program of the German organization. Adding fuel to this fire was an international organization known as the St. Raphael's Society for the Care of German Catholic Emigrants, headed by a wealthy German Catholic, Peter Paul Cahensly. In 1883, Cahensly toured the United States and found that the treatment by the Catholic Church of German Catholic immigrants was unacceptable from his point of view. His major complaint was that large numbers of German Catholic immigrants in the United States were in danger of losing their faith and that this matter required greater attention than was being given to it by the American hierarchy. In 1890, the St. Raphael's Society held a convention in Lucerne, Switzerland, at which it adopted most of the program of the *Priesterverein* (except for separate German dioceses) and had an audience in Rome with Pope Leo XIII to press its views.

This action enraged many members of the American hierarchy, especially the so-called Americanizer faction, a name given to those who objected to the Balkanization of foreign-born Catholics, both Germans and others, into permanent national enclaves. They also were incensed by the effrontery of a European organization in going directly to the Holy See to influence the practices and policies of the Church in this country. Cahenslyism, as this activity was sometimes called, was also viewed with alarm by public authorities, even though it was an internal church matter. President Benjamin Harrison once expressed to Cardinal Gibbons his unofficial but real concern about the implications of Cahenslyism and was relieved to learn, as were members of the American hierarchy, that Pope Leo had rejected Cahensly's overture.

When Archbishop Katzer arrived at St. John's Cathedral in 1891, he invited Cardinal Gibbons, the acknowledged leader of the American hierarchy, to come to Milwaukee to confer upon him the pallium, the symbol of his rank and authority as the head of a metropolitan see. Gibbons accepted the invitation. The pallium is a small band of white wool that an archbishop — but not a suffragan bishop — wears about his shoulders at official ceremonies. It is made from the wool of lambs brought annually to the Basilica of St. Agnes in Rome and blessed by the Holy Father. Traditionally, each pallium is laid overnight on the tomb of St. Peter before being sent by the pope to a new archbishop.

When he mounted the pulpit at the Milwaukee cathedral, Cardinal Gibbons denounced Cahenslyism with uncharacteristic ire. He warned: "Woe to him, my brethren, who would destroy or impair this blessed harmony that reigns among us! . . . Woe to him who would breed dissension among the leaders of Israel by introducing a spirit of nationalism into the camps of the Lord! Brothers we are, whatever may be our nationality, and brothers we shall remain. We will prove to our countrymen that the ties formed by grace and faith are stronger than flesh and blood."

As time went on, the ethnic friction that came into focus by the efforts of Cahensly subsided. When he made another trip to the United States in 1910, Cahensly was given a cordial reception, not only in Milwaukee but by Americanizer bishops as well. When he passed through Baltimore, Cardinal Gibbons invited him out to dinner.

On January 29, 1935, an early morning fire destroyed the entire cathedral except for the walls and the clock tower. The fire started in the basement; the actual cause was never discovered. No one was killed, but $300,000 in property damage occurred. Among the items that were completely destroyed were a 3,100-pipe organ that had been donated to the cathedral in 1923 by the Cudahy family, many works of art (including paintings donated by King Ludwig of Bavaria), and the stained-glass windows (all of which melted and burst as a result of the heat). The reconstruction effort took eight years, in the course of which Bishop's Hall to the rear of the building was removed so that the cathedral could be lengthened about fifty feet. The result of this enlargement was to increase the seating capacity from one thousand to fourteen hundred. The new improvements include rows of twin pillars running the length of the nave on either side, a forty-foot bronze baldachin covering the altar, and new stained-glass windows depicting St. Paul and the twelve apostles. The cathedral was reopened at midnight Mass on Christmas Eve, 1943. Thirty years later, it was designated by the U.S. Department of the Interior as a national landmark.

Today, St. John's Cathedral **[pictured above]** has one thousand registered parishioners, a large percentage of whom are single. Its residential component lives largely in apartment houses. While there are few families with small children, the parish had twenty-five baptisms in 1989 and participates in a consolidated parochial school with seven other parishes to educate children who do reside in its boundaries. About one thousand people attend Mass each weekend, of whom some twenty-five percent are tourists. The number of visitors increases dramatically in the summer when ethnic celebrations take place at nearby Juneau Park. A regular feature is the 8:00 A.M. radio Mass celebrated each Sunday by Archbishop Rembert G. Weakland. Archbishop Weakland resides at the rectory and uses this means of staying in personal contact both with the parish and his archdiocese.

Buildings that were formerly devoted to parochial schools have, at one time or another, been occupied by the Archdiocesan Hispanic Ministry, a school for licensed practical nurses, a Montessori school, and now the Milwaukee School of Engineering. The former convent is now a pre-release center operated by Wisconsin correctional authorities. There are a number of poor and elderly living in the area as well as street people who depend upon the parish for assistance. St. John's participates with Protestant churches in the area in a program known as Interchange that at one time operated a food pantry at the church. It now serves sandwiches each noon to as many as a hundred individuals who appear at the door.

Ever since the extraordinary celebration that took place at the dedication of the cathedral in 1853, St. John's has emphasized the importance of church music to enhance Catholic worship. It has a fine-arts committee that organizes annual musical programs, using the cathedral as an auditorium. These productions employ paid performers and are subsidized, in part, by the parish as its contribution to the cultural life of the city. They attract to the cathedral people from throughout the area who otherwise would have no occasion to set foot inside the building. This effort receives a substantial assist from Archbishop Weakland, a Benedictine and an internationally known liturgist who holds two graduate degrees in music from Columbia University. In the course of his academic research, the archbishop came across a twelfth-century mystery play, the *Play of Daniel*, and translated the musical portion of the manuscript from medieval to modern musical symbols. Poet W. H. Auden, who died in 1973, translated the text, and it was first presented at the Cloisters in New York about thirty-five years ago. The St. John's Fine Arts Committee began its activities by presenting the *Play of Daniel* for several years as a Christmas program. It received an enthusiastic reception. Recently, it produced another medieval mystery play, *St. Nicholas*, as well as a modern play by Benjamin Britten. The Fine Arts Committee also presents choral programs, organ recitals, and performances of the Milwaukee Symphony and the Wisconsin Conservatory of Music. The cathedral has a thirty-member volunteer choir. Before the beginning of Lent each year, the organist and the choir director meet with the archbishop and together they plan the music for Holy Week services.

Today, St. John the Evangelist Cathedral is the principal church in a state having a million and a half Catholics. They live in nine hundred forty-one parishes, in five dioceses, and are served by over eighteen hundred priests. The faith that took root in east Milwaukee has, in one hundred seventy years, spread with remarkable vigor among people of many national origins who have fashioned an American Church that can only dimly remember the divisions of the past.

✳ ✳ ✳

I was going to call this page an epilogue but it isn't. It is just a needed rest stop on a journey that follows the sun westward across America. In looking at the life stories of fifty-nine Catholic churches, we have found many living examples illustrating Walt Whitman's famous line: "I hear America singing. Its varied carols I hear."

The Church in America belongs to a variety of ethnic groups and to people having no particular ethnic identification. It is the product of the old gentry in Maryland and the tenements of Boston and New York. Its growth in a brief two hundred years — replacing a wilderness with an elaborate infrastructure of parishes, schools, colleges, hospitals, monasteries, convents, retreat houses, and other institutions — can only be described as spectacular. If ever the Parable of the Mustard Seed found a practical illustration, it is on these shores.

In the East we have seen the Church embrace canonized saints from Philadelphia and Baltimore as well as something less, both there and elsewhere. We have seen it extend its ministry and its aid to Civil War prisoners, youngsters in the slums, pioneers in the wilderness, striking miners, and immigrants in search of a new home. It has extended this assistance despite repeated epidemics, ridicule, mob violence, grinding poverty, political oppression, bitter internal wrangling, and, worst of all, indifference and neglect. The Church has prospered enormously, notwithstanding these obstacles, starting with next to nothing and growing quickly in every corner of the nation. It has done so largely through the generosity of an economically disadvantaged membership. No king or potentate paid the way.

But we are nowhere near the end of our journey. Beyond the Mississippi River, which the French originally named in honor of the Immaculate Conception, there is much ahead. We have yet to traverse the Santa Fe Trail and the Oregon Trail and to meet up with such colorful figures in the Old West as Archbishop John Lamy and Father Pierre De Smet. We have still not examined the contributions of Archbishop Joseph Alemany, who performed on the Pacific Coast a task similar, if not equal, to what Archbishop John Carroll undertook along the Atlantic seaboard. California will introduce us to such people as Bishop Patrick Manogue, who worked his way through the seminary by panning for gold during the Gold Rush and who returned to Moore's Flat after ordination to say Mass for old friends in the mining camp. As for antiquity, the cathedral at Santa Fe dates back to 1610, just three years after the English foundation at Jamestown, while Father Jacques Marquette's parish at Kaskaskia, whose original site now lies at the bottom of the ever-changing Mississippi River, was founded in 1675. And of course there's still Hawaii, whose cathedral can trace its roots back to 1833. Most important, we have not yet made contact with the saints of the West — Father Junípero Serra, Father Damien de Veuster, and Mother Rose Philippine Duchesne — whose lives were so intimately bound up with churches that are still alive and functioning.

So it is well to rest up now before we cross the River of the Immaculate Conception.

Bibliography

Abell, William S., *Patrick Cardinal O'Boyle As His Friends Know Him*, Carroll Publishing Co. (1986).

Alive and Well and Living in New York, monthly magazine published by St. Patrick's Cathedral, New York, N.Y., May 1990 and February 1991.

Allsop, Kenneth, *The Bootleggers — The Story of Chicago's Prohibition Era*, Arlington House (1961).

Amadeus, Rev. M., O.C.S.O., *The Rt. Rev. M. Edmond Obrecht, O.C.S.O., Fourth Abbot of Our Lady of Gethsemani*, Abbey of Our Lady of Gethsemani (1937).

Anderson v. Laird, 406 F. 2d. 283, United States Court of Appeals for the District of Columbia (1972).

Alerding, Rev. H., *A History of the Catholic Church in the Diocese of Vincennes*, Carlon and Hollenbeck (1883).

The Archdiocese of Chicago — Antecedents and Development, author unknown, St. Mary's Training School Press (1920).

Baa, Enid, Rev. Joseph G. Daly, Rev. Stephen McKenna, and Rev. John Gauci, C.SS.R., *Praise God — Two Hundred Years (1773-1973) — History of St. Peter and Paul Parish, St. Thomas, U.S.V.I.*, published by the parish (1973).

Baker, Rev. Robert J., Charles Coombes, and Albina Davis, *The Cathedral Basilica of St. Augustine and its History*, Bell Tower Religious Shop (1987).

Bentivenga, Dr. Joseph J., editor of *Bicentennial Commemorative — History of Loretto, Penna.*, Damin Printing Co. (1976).

Blied, Rev. Benjamin J., *Three Archbishops of Milwaukee*, published by the author (1955).

Bolton, Harry, *St. John's Cathedral (1847-1947)*, Wetzel Brothers (1947).

Brennan, Rev. Robert E., O.P., *Cradle of the Faith in Ohio (1818-1968)*, Spenser-Walker Press, Inc. (1968).

Browne, Jefferson B., *Key West — The Old and the New*, University of Florida Press (reprinted, 1973).

Burden, Shirley, *God in My Life*, Reynal Co. (1960).

Burns, C. A., S.J., *The Glory of Sts. Peter and Paul (Detroit) A Centennial Sketch*, the Graphic Arts Process Co. (1948).

Burtenshaw, Msgr. Noel G., *A History of the Immaculate Conception Shrine (Atlanta)*, published by the parish (1984).

Byrne, Rev. John F., C.SS.R., *The Redemptorist Centenaries*, The Dolphin Press (1932).

Cabral, Stephen L., *Portuguese Feasting in New Bedford*, AMS Press (1989).

Campo Lacasa, Cristina, *Notas Generales Sobre La Historia Eclesiástica de Puerto Rico en el Siglo XVIII*, Escuela de Estudios Hispano-Americanos de Sevilla (1963).

Cardozo, Manoel da Silvera, *The Portuguese in America (590 B.C.-1974)*. Oceana Publications, Inc. (1976).

Carthy, Sister Margaret, O.S U., *A Cathedral of Suitable Magnificence*, Michael Glazier, Inc. (1984).

Carthy, Mother Mary Peter, O.S.U., *Old St. Patrick's — New York's Oldest Cathedral*, Master's Thesis, Catholic University of America, unpublished (1948).

Castner, Harold W., *The Barnburners* (unpublished), in Castner Collection, Damriscotta Library, Damriscotta, Me.

The Cathedral of St. John the Baptist, Savannah, Ga., author unknown, published by the cathedral (1985).

The Catholic Church in Wisconsin, authors unknown, Catholic Historical Publishing Company of Milwaukee, Wisc. (c. 1900).

Cathedral of St. Peter in Chains, published by the cathedral (1987).

Cathedral of St. Peter in Chains, Cincinnati, Dedication Program, author unknown, published by the archdiocese of Cincinnati (1957).

Cathedral of San Juan Bautista of Puerto Rico, author unknown, Caribe Tourist Promotions, Inc. (1980).

The Catholic Standard, newspaper of archdiocese of Washington, May 2, 1985.

Catholic Red Book of Baltimore, Kohn and Pollock (1908).

The Chapels — United States Military Academy, West Point, N.Y., C. Harrison Conroy Co. (date unknown).

Church of Ste. Anne de Detroit, 1701-1976, Custombook, Inc. (1976).

Columbia magazine, October 1988 issue, published by the Knights of Columbus.

Congressional Record, June 29, 1898, pp. 6496-6505.

Congressional Record, July 7, 1898, pp. 6735-6736.

Conley, Rev. Patrick T., and Rev. Matthew J. Smith, *Catholicism In Rhode Island — The Formative Era*, published by the diocese of Providence (1976).

Conley, Patrick F., *Rhode Island Catholicism — A Historical Guide*, published by the author (1984).

The Connecticut Catholic Yearbook (1876-1877), author or authors unknown, Connecticut Catholic Publishing Co. (1877).

Crews, Rev. Clyde F., *An American Holy Land — A History of the Archdiocese of Louisville*, Iconographics, Inc. (1987).

Cusick, Rev. Msgr. William J., *A Century in the Life of a Parish — Saint Michael's Church (Pensacola, Fla.) — 1886-1986*, Pfeiffer Printing Co. (1986).

Cuyler, Rev. Cornelius M., S.S., *The Baltimore Cathedral, Its History and Description*, published by the author (1951).

Daley, John M., S.J., *St. Joseph's Church, Willing's Alley (Philadelphia)*, published by the parish (date unknown).

Daly, Rev. Joseph G., C.SS.R., *Conflict in Paradise — Beginning of the Redemptorist Mission to the Virgin Islands (1855-1860)*, published by the Congregation of the Most Holy Redeemer (date unknown).

De Hostos, Adolfo, *The Cathedral of San Juan*, extract from *San Juan — Walled City*, reprinted in *El Mundo*, March 1, 1990, p. S-25; March 8, 1990, p. S-27; March 15, 1990, p. S-32.

Dever, Joseph, *Cushing of Boston, A Candid Portrait*, Bruce Humphries (1965).

Drummond, Rev. Robert T., O.S.A., "Catholics at West Point," *Assembly*, published by the West Point Alumni Association, December issue, 1979.

Dugan, Dr. Virginia, *A History of the Cathedral Basilica of Saints Peter and Paul (Philadelphia)*, published by the parish (1979).

Durkin, Rev. Joseph T., S.J., *Stephen R. Mallory, Confederate Navy Chief*, University of North Carolina Press (1954).

Eckert, Rev. John C., *The History of Old St. Mary's (Phila.)*, Blaetz Brothers, Inc. (1976).

Ellis, Msgr. John Tracy, *Documents of American Catholic History*, Vols. I, II, and III. Michael Glazer, Inc. (1987).

Ellis, Msgr. John Tracy, *The Life of James Cardinal Gibbons*, Bruce Publishing Co. (1952).

Evening Herald of Shenandoah, Penna., Commemorative Section — St. George's parish, February 23, 1989.

Farley, Cardinal John M., *History of St. Patrick's Cathedral*, published by the Society for the Propagation of the Faith (1908).

Fenning, Rev. Hugh, O.P., *The Irish Dominican Mission to the Danish West Indies*, Archivium Hibernicum XXV, No. 16, pp. 75-122 (1962).

Fereira, Rev. Manuel P., *St. John the Baptist Church (New Bedford, Mass.) Church History*, published by the parish (1972).

Flynn, Rev. Joseph M., *The Catholic Church in New Jersey*, The Publisher's Printing Co. (1904).

Fuller, Florence, *A History of St. Mary, Star of the Sea, Key West, Florida*, prepared for the parish (unpublished).

Gannon, Rev. Michael V., *The Cross in the Sand — The Early History of the Catholic Church in Florida*, University of Florida Press (1967).

Gannon, Rev. Michael V., *Rebel Bishop — The Life and Era of Augustin Verot*, The Bruce Publishing Co. (1964).

Garraghan, Rev. Gilbert J., S.J., *The Catholic Church in Chicago (1671-1871)*, Loyola University Press (1921).

Garraghan, Rev. Gilbert J., S.J., *The History of Old St. Mary's (Chicago)*, a centenary history published by the parish (1933).

The Georgia Bulletin, newspaper of the archdiocese of Atlanta, November 12, 1981, issue, p. 4.

Gillard, Rev. John T., S.S.J., *The Catholic Church and the American Negro*, St. Joseph's Society Press (1930).

Gregorich, Joseph, *The Apostle of the Chippewa — Life Story of The Most Rev. Frederick Baraga*, Bishop Baraga Association (1932).

Griffin, Martin I. J., *A History of Old St. Joseph's — Philadelphia*, Irish Catholic Benevolent Union (1883).

Guilday, Msgr. Peter, *The Life and Times of John England* (Vols. I and II), The America Press (1925).

Gurney, W. J., *A Short History of the St. Augustine Cemetery, South Boston, Mass.* (publisher unknown) (1952).

Hartley, Most Rev. James J., *Diocese of Columbus, Ohio (1868-1918)*, published by the diocese of Columbus (1918).

Haymen, Rev. Robert W., *Catholicism in Rhode Island and the Diocese of Providence (1780-1886)*, published by the diocese of Providence (1982).

Hennessey, Frances Marie, *In the Beginning — St. Mary's Church, Charleston, S.C. (1789-1889)*, published by subscription (1989).

Historical Highlights of the Mobile Cathedral, author unknown, published by Immaculate Conception Cathedral, Mobile, Ala. (date unknown).

A History and Guide Book of the Old Cathedral and the City of Vincennes, published by St. Francis Xavier parish (date unknown).

History — St. Mary's Parish, Newport (R. I.), author unknown, published by the parish (1978).

Holy Cross Cathedral (Boston), Parish Visitation Report, prepared by the parish (1987).

Jezernik, Maksimiljan, *Frederick Baraga*, Studia Slovenica (1968).

Johnson, Rev. Peter Leo, *Centennial Essays for the Milwaukee Archdiocese (1843-1943)*, Husting Printing Co. (1943).

Kelly, Rev. Laurence J., S.J., *Holy Trinity Church — Washington, D.C.*, John D. Lucas Printing Co. (1945).

Kenny, Rev. T. J., *Historical Sketch of St. Peter, The Apostle, Church, Baltimore*, The Metropolitan Printing and Publishing Co. (1917).

Kirlin, Rev. Joseph L. J., *Catholicity in Philadelphia*, John J. McVey (1909).

Koenig, Msgr. Harry C., editor, *A History of the Parishes of the Archdiocese of Chicago*, The New World Publishing Co. (1980).

Kosak, Rev. Michael F., *St. Ann's Church, A History of the Barrenspot Chapel from its Beginning in 1825 to the Present*, published by the parish (1975).

Kucas, Dr. Antanas, *Lithuanians in America*, Encyclopedia Lituanica (1975).

Kucas, Dr. Antanas, *St. George's Parish, Shenandoah, Penna.*, published by the parish (1968).

Kraybill, Eugene, Lancaster *Intelligencer Journal — 700 Churches*, March 1985.

Kupke, Rev. Raymond J., *Living Stones: History of the Catholic Church in the Diocese of Paterson (N.J.)*, diocese of Paterson (1987).

La Montagne, Hector O., *St. Mary's Church — Claremont, N.H. (1823-1973) — 150 Years of Faith*, published by the author (1973).

Lamott, Rev. John L., *History of the Archdiocese of Cincinnati*, Frederick Pusted Co. (1921).

Langley, Harold D., and John Cain, *Holy Trinity Church, Washington, D.C.*, published by the parish (1979).

Lauriola, Msgr. Francis J., and Sister M. Felicitas Powers, R.S.M., *St. John the Evangelist Parish, Silver Spring, Maryland (1774-1984)*, published by the parish (1984).

Lipscomb, Most Rev. Oscar Hugh, D.D., Ph.D., *The Administration of John Quinlan, Second Bishop of Mobile*, Master's Thesis, Catholic University of America, unpublished (1959).

Lipscomb, Most Rev. Oscar Hugh, D.D., Ph.D., *The Administration of Michael Portier (1825-1859)*, Doctoral Dissertation, Catholic University of America, unpublished (1963).

Lord, Rev. Robert H., and Rev. John H. Sexton, *History of the Archdiocese of Boston*, Sheed and Ward (1944).

Lucey, William L., S.J., *The Catholic Church in Maine*, Marshall Jones Co. (1957).

Lyle, John H., *The Dry and Lawless Years*, Prentice Hall, Inc. (1960).

Madden, Rev. Richard C., *Catholics in South Carolina — A Record*, University Press of America (1985).

Mantz, E. Philip, and Rev. Michael J. Roach, *St. Peter's — The Mother Church of N.Y. State*, republished by the parish (1985).

Martin, Rev. Paul R., *The First Cardinal of the West — The Story of the Church in the Archdiocese of Chicago Under the Administration of His Eminence George Cardinal Mundelein*, The New World Publishing Co. (1934).

McAvoy, Rev. Thomas T., C.S.C., *The Catholic Church in Indiana (1789-1834)*, Columbia University Press (1940).

McCoy, Clyde B., and Diana H. Gonzales, *Cuban Immigration and Immigrants in Florida and the United States: Implications for Immigration Policy*, Bureau of Economics and Business Research, University of Florida Press (1985).

McNally, Rev. Michael J., *Catholicism in South Florida (1868-1968)*, University of Florida Press (1982).

Merton, Thomas, *The Waters of Siloe*, Harcourt, Brace & Co. (1949).

Miami *Herald*, May 8, 1980.

Mitchell, Very Rev. Joseph D., *Historical Sketch of the Parish of St. John the Baptist of Savannah*, Bulletins of the Catholic Laymen's Association, December 1920 through August 1922.

Morrison, Ross I., Sr., *It Happened in Lancaster County*, Rimien Echoes (1984).

Mulrenan, Patrick, *A Brief Historical Sketch of the Catholic Church on Long Island*, P. O'Shea (1871).

Musser, Edgar A., *St. Mary's Church, Lancaster, Penna., 1785-1877*, Journal of the Lancaster County Historical Society (1971).

New Bedford *Standard-Times*, June 16, 1979.
New Bedford *Standard-Times*, October 28, 1972.
New York *Times*, February 14, 1891, p. 1.
New York *Times*, February 20, 1891, p. 1.
Nolan, Rev. Hugh J., *Most Rev. Francis P. Kenrick, Third Bishop of Philadelphia*, American Catholic Historical Society Review (1948).

O'Connell, Rev. Jeremiah J., O.S.B., *Catholicity in the Carolinas and Georgia*, D. & J. Sadlier and Co. (1879).

O'Daniel, Rev. Victor F., O.P., *Rt. Rev. Edward D. Fenwick, O.P., Founder of the Dominicans in the United States*, New Era Printing Co. (1920).

O'Donnell, Rev. James H., *History of the Diocese of Hartford*, D. Hurd Co. (1900).

The Official Catholic Directory, P. J. Kenedy & Sons, 1987, 1989, 1990.

O'Hearn, Rev. David J., *Fifty Years at St. John's Cathedral (Milwaukee)*, Burdick and Allen (1897).

One Hundred Years — The History of Church of the Holy Name (Chicago), author unknown, published by the Cathedral of the Holy Name (1949).

Parish magazine — "The Catholic Chapel of the Most Holy Trinity," West Point, N.Y., Spring, 1988, and Summer, 1988.

Pap, Leo, *The Portuguese Americans*, Twayne Publishers, Div. of G. K. Hall Co. (1981).

Parot, Dr. John Joseph, *Polish Catholics in Chicago — 1850-1920*, Northern Illinois University Press (1981).

Petras, Very Rev. David M., *Eastern Catholic Churches in America*, published by the Office of Religious Education, diocese of Parma, Ohio (1987).

Philibert, Misses Helene, Estelle, and Imogene, *St. Matthew's of Washington (1840-1940)*, A. Hoen and Co. (1940).

Quinter, Edward H., and Msgr. Charles L. Allwein, *Most Blessed Sacrament Church (Bally, Penna.)*, published by the parish (1976).

Raymond, Rev. M., O.C.S.O., *The Man Who Got Even With God*, Abbey of Gethsemani (1941).

Raymond, Rev. M., O.C.S.O., *Burnt Out Incense*, P. J. Kenedy & Sons (1949).

Reilly, John T., *Conewago — A Collection of Local Catholic History*, published by the author (1885).

Reynolds, Charles B., *Old St. Augustine — A Story of Three Centuries*, 5th ed., published by the author (1891).

Rezek, Rev. Antoine Ivan, *History of the Diocese of Sault Sainte Marie and Marquette*, Vols. I and II, M. A. Donohue & Co. (1907).

Rice, Edward, *The Man in the Sycamore Tree*, Doubleday & Co., Inc. (1970).

Rost, Msgr. George W., *Basilica of the Sacred Heart of Jesus (Conewago, Penna.), 1787-1987*, published by the parish (1987).

Rush, Rev. Alfred C., C.SS.R., introduction to and translation of *The Autobiography of St. John Neumann*, Daughters of St. Paul (1977).

Ryan, Rev. Leo Raymond, *Old St. Peter's — The Mother Church of Catholic New York (1785-1935)*, The United States Catholic Historical Society (1935).

St. Bruno's Parish, Van Buren, Maine — Sesquicentennial (1838-1988), author unknown, published by the parish (1988).

Saint Mary, Star of the Sea, Key West, Florida, Souvenir Program, published by the parish (1940).

Saint Michael's Ukrainian Catholic Church, Shenandoah, Pennsylvania, 100th Anniversary Commemorative Booklet, published by the parish (1984).

St. Patrick's Church, Cleveland, Ohio, 125th Anniversary Album, published by the parish (1973).

St. Patrick's Old Cathedral — New York, Souvenir of Centennial Celebration (1809-1909), published by the parish (1909).

Schauinger, J. Herman, *Cathedrals in the Wilderness*, Bruce Publishing Co. (1952).

Schlereth, Dr. Thomas P., *The University of Notre Dame — A Portrait of Its History and Campus*, University of Notre Dame Press (1976).

Schroeder, Sister Mary Carol, O.S.F., *The Catholic Church in the Diocese of Vincennes (1847-1877)*, Catholic University of America Press (1946).

Schuefer, William Bishop, *Memoirs of the Rev. Augustin Bally, S.J.*, Records of the American Catholic Historical Society, September 1909.

Sharp, Msgr. John K., *History of the Diocese of Brooklyn (1853-1953)*, Vols. I and II, Fordham University Press (1954).

Shea, John Gilmary, *A History of the Catholic Church in America* (four volumes), The Mershon Company Press (1886, 1890, 1892).

Simmons, Agatha Aimar, *Brief History of St. Mary's Roman Catholic Church, Charleston, S.C.*, John J. Furlong & Sons (1961).

Sister Marie Edith, *St. John's Parish (Paterson, N.J.) — 150 Years*, published by the parish (1971).

Skabeikis, Philip, *Catholic Lithuania — 600 Years*, published by the Lithuanian Roman Catholic Priests' League (1987).

Smith, Hubbard Madison, M.D., *Historical Sketch of Old Vincennes*, published by the author (1902).

South Boston, published by The Boston 200 Corp. (1976).

The Southern Cross, newspaper of the diocese of Savannah, March 15, 1984, issue, pp. 1, 7.

Stephens, Msgr. Edward L., *150 Years for Christ — St. Mary's Church, Alexandria, Virginia*, published by the parish (1945).

Taney, Ellen, *The Other Toussaint*, Daughters of St. Paul (1981).

Tourscher, Rev. Francis A., O.S.A., *The Hogan Schism and Trustee Troubles in St. Mary's Church (Phila.)*, The Peter Reilly Co. (1930).

Treat, Roger C., *Bishop Sheil and the CYO*, Julian Messner, Inc. (1951).

Triple Celebration of the 10th Anniversary, Rededication of Holy Cross Church Triumph of the Cross, and the 10th Anniversary of the Establishment of the Diocese of St. Thomas, author unknown, ABS Printing Co. (1987).

Usalis, John E., *A Church History — St. George's, Shenandoah, Pa.*, published in *Bridges*, a Lithuanian-American news journal, June 1991.

Usalis, John E., *St. George's 100th Anniversary Book*, published by the parish (1991).

USA Today, November 15, 1990, p. 3A.

The West Point Guide Book, published by the Public Affairs Office, U.S. Military Academy, West Point, N.Y. (author and date unknown).

Index

(NOTE: The main entries — that is, the subject matter of this volume — are listed first.)

Abbey of Our Lady of Gethsemani, Trappist, Kentucky 463-473
Basilica of St. Francis Xavier, Vincennes, Indiana 497-507
Basilica of the Assumption, Baltimore, Maryland 287-296
Holy Cross, Christiansted, St. Croix, U.S. Virgin Islands 33-43
Holy Cross Cathedral, Boston, Massachusetts 55-60; *also* 63, 69, 76, 91
Holy Name Cathedral, Chicago, Illinois 529-538
Holy Name of Mary, Sault Ste. Marie, Michigan 485-495
Holy Trinity, Washington, D.C. 321-327
Immaculate Conception, Salem, Massachusetts 69-73
Immaculate Conception Cathedral, Mobile, Alabama 415-427
Immaculate Conception Cathedral, Portland, Maine 83-86
Most Blessed Sacrament, Bally, Pennsylvania 227-230
Most Holy Trinity Chapel, West Point, New York 179-185
Sacred Heart, Bowie, Maryland 277-281
Sacred Heart, Notre Dame, Indiana 509-516
Sacred Heart Basilica, Conewago Township, Pennsylvania 259-262
Shrine of the Immaculate Conception, Atlanta, Georgia 379-383
St. Augustine, Boston, Massachusetts 63-66
St. Augustine Cathedral, St. Augustine, Florida 385-400
St. Bruno, Van Buren, Maine 97-101
St. Francis Xavier, Baltimore, Maryland 303-307
St. George, Shenandoah, Pennsylvania 233-245
St. Ignatius, Chapel Point, Maryland 273-275
St. James Cathedral, Brooklyn, New York 165-176
St. John Baptist Cathedral, San Juan, Puerto Rico 45-53
St. John Cathedral, Milwaukee, Wisconsin 555-564
St. John the Baptist Cathedral, Paterson, New Jersey 187-192
St. John the Baptist Cathedral, Savannah, Georgia 365-376
St. John the Baptist, New Bedford, Massachusetts 75-81
St. John the Evangelist, Silver Spring, Maryland 283-284
St. Joseph, Bardstown, Kentucky 449-460
St. Joseph, Philadelphia, Pennsylvania 195-200
St. Joseph, Somerset, Ohio 433-438
St. Mary, Alexandria, Virginia 337-340
St. Mary, Annapolis, Maryland 309-311
St. Mary, Charleston, South Carolina 349-362
St. Mary, Chicago, Illinois 519-526; *also* 529, 530
St. Mary, Claremont, New Hampshire 103-106
St. Mary, Lancaster, Pennsylvania 253-256
St. Mary, New Haven, Connecticut 117-123
St. Mary Magdalen de Pazzi, Philadelphia, Pennsylvania 221-225
St. Mary, Newport, Rhode Island 109-114
St. Mary, Philadelphia, Pennsylvania 203-213
St. Mary, Star of the Sea, Key West, Florida 403-413
St. Matthew's Cathedral, Washington, D.C. 329-334
St. Michael (Byzantine Rite), Shenandoah, Pennsylvania 247-251
St. Michael, Loretto, Pennsylvania 265-271
St. Patrick, Cleveland, Ohio 429-431
St. Patrick, Newcastle, Maine 89-94
St. Patrick's Cathedral, New York, New York 143-162; *also* 131, 134, 135, 138, 155-157, 166, 168, 171, 271, 399
St. Peter, Harpers Ferry, West Virginia 343-347
St. Peter in Chains Cathedral, Cincinnati, Ohio 441-447; *also* 492
St. Peter, New York, New York 125-141; *also* 143, 144, 146, 147, 151, 153, 165, 166
St. Peter the Apostle, Baltimore, Maryland 299-301
St. Stanislaus Kostka, Chicago, Illinois 541-552
Ste. Anne, Detroit, Michigan 475-477; *also* 479, 480
Sts. Peter and Paul Cathedral, Philadelphia, Pennsylvania 215-219
Sts. Peter and Paul, Detroit, Michigan 479-482
U.S. Naval Academy Chapel, Annapolis, Maryland 313-318

A

Abell, Robert 450, 455, 467
Abnaki Indians 90
abolitionism; *also* abolitionist, abolitionists 113, 173, 255, 344, 345, 359, 360, 373, 397
abortion 43

Abromaitis, Peter 236, 239, 240
Acadia 22, 118
act of Congress 179, 325
Act of Supremacy 45
Act of Toleration 20
Acushnet River 78
Adams, Abigail 204
Adams, John 56, 204
Adams, John Quincy 280, 359
Addams, Jane 525
Adenauer, Konrad 159, 332
Africa 24, 64, 76, 117, 369, 373, 466
African Free School 151
AIDS 383, 412, 503
Alaska 25, 41
Albanians 65
Albany 134, 150, 152, 156, 171, 379, 505
Albertus Magnus College 123
alcohol; *also* alcoholism 72, 73, 293, 352, 479, 487, 489, 491
Alemany, Joseph Sadoc 437, 565
Alencastre, Stephen 77
Alexandria, Egypt 248
Alexandria, Virginia 322, 325, 329, 337-340
Alfonso (king) 332
Allen, Dominic 35, 36
All Hallows' Seminary 23, 344, 423
Allard, J. B. 407
Allegheny Mountains 23, 260, 265, 449
Allegheny River 265
Allioti's German Bible 443
Allouez, Claude 18, 486, 555
Allouez, Louis 519
Alter, Karl 128, 446, 447
Álvarez, Gerónimo 396, 397
American Protective Association (APA) 181
American Revolution 20, 25, 27, 28, 64, 66, 97, 98, 110, 127, 131, 189, 228, 261, 278, 303, 350, 436
Amish 254
Anchor Mental Health Association 333
Ancient Order of Hibernians 149

Anderson v. *Laird* 184
Andersonville 370-373
Andreotti, Giulio 159
Anglican Church 19, 20, 392
Annapolis 21, 22, 113, 184, 278, 309-311, 313-315, 340
Anne (queen) 20, 391
anthracite region 233, 234, 236, 239, 244, 249
anti-Catholic 21, 22, 64, 131, 132, 147, 151, 152, 153, 168, 169, 172, 173, 198, 199, 274, 316, 360, 422, 442, 444, 505, 530, 559
anti-Catholic bias 121
anti-Catholic mob; *also* anti-Catholic mobs 138, 148
Antietam 156, 324, 346, 459
Apache Indians 15
Apalachee Indians 388, 390, 391
Apalachicola River 393, 415
apostolic delegate 42, 224, 360, 469, 547
apostolic pro-nuncio 375
Appalachian Mountains 18, 27, 179
Aquidneck Island 111
Arce, Martín Vásquez de 49
Arizona 17
Arkansas River 22, 487
Armenian 248, 334
Arnold, Benedict 179, 196
Aroostook War 98
Arouet, François-Marie — *see* Voltaire
Arriola, Andrés de 416
arson 84, 119, 254
Artur, Ricardo (Richard Arthur) 389
Arundell, Thomas 89
Ashton, John 287
Associated Catholic Charities 296
Astor, John Jacob 146
Atlanta 368, 371, 373, 376, 379-383, 407, 471, 512, 560
Aubry, Nicholas 90
Auden, W. H. 564
Audran, Ernest 505
Augusta 353, 357, 358, 366, 367, 370, 371, 374, 379

Augustinian; *also* Augustinians 63, 76, 169, 188, 189, 205, 221, 225, 353, 393, 417
Ayllón, Lucas Vásquez de 349
Azores 75-80

B

Back Bay 58
Bacon, David W. 83-86, 99, 100
Badin, Stephen 290, 433, 450-453, 509, 510, 514
Bahamas 361, 385
Balboa, Bernardo de 49
Bally, Augustin 229
Baltimore 12, 22, 24, 25, 29, 30, 38, 39, 56, 90, 91, 98, 110, 129-131, 133, 154, 167, 207, 216, 228, 236, 260-262, 266, 273, 278-280, 283, 309, 316, 322, 323, 330, 331, 333, 334, 338, 339, 352-357, 361, 367, 369, 371, 374, 375, 397, 398, 418, 430, 433, 435, 436, 450, 453, 455, 457, 464, 480, 494, 500, 562, 565
Baltimore Catechism 293
Bandol, Séraphin 29, 205
Baraga, Frederic 490-495
Barbee, John 458
Barbelin, Felix 197, 198
Barber, Daniel 103, 104
Barber, Jerusha 104
Barber, Mary Josephine 105
Barber, Samuel 104
Barber, Virgil 104, 105
Barcelona, Cyril de 394
Bardstown 291, 434, 449-459, 463-467, 500-502, 520
Bardstown *Gazette* 458
Barnburners 93
Barrières, Michael 450
Barron, Edward 369
Barry, John 213, 379, 382
Barth, Louis 255
Barzynski, Joseph 547
Barzynski, Vincent 545, 546, 547, 548
Bath 84
Battery Park City 140, 141

Battle of the Boyne 117
Bazeley, Charles 210
Beaubein, Mark 520, 523
Beckham, J.C.W. 469
Bedini, Gaetano 153, 172, 444
Beecher, Henry Ward 173
Beidler, Ulrich 227
Belair 281
Belgian 41, 42, 136, 245, 278, 450, 505
Belgium 26, 136, 283, 289, 309
Bell, Robert 228
Benedictine; *also* Benedictines 23, 426, 464, 471, 473, 505, 564
Bennett, Michael John 561
Bennett Law 561
Bentley, William 70
Berger, Benedict 467
Bernardin, Joseph 362, 535
Bernini, Giovanni 513
Beroujon, Claude 421
Bertrand, Joseph 511
Bethlehem Steel Corporation 269, 271
Bienville, Jean Le Moyne de 416
Billy, Roger de 476
Biscayne Bay 404
Bishop Todd House 200
Bishop White House 200
black; *also* blacks 22, 35, 36, 42, 58, 59, 78, 117, 134, 172, 188, 189, 192, 198, 218, 228, 280, 293, 296, 301, 303-307, 311, 324, 325, 330, 331, 344, 351, 353, 357, 359, 360, 370, 373-376, 397-400, 405, 409, 410, 412, 417, 446, 464, 500, 503, 509, 524, 536-538
black Catholics 303-306, 325, 330, 331, 400
Black Code 304, 359
Bladen, Thomas 21, 303
Blake, Joseph 350
Blatty, William 326
Bloody Monday 458
Boerly, Thomas 344
Bogdan, Francis 239
Bohemian church 542

Bonaparte, Joseph 197
Bonaparte, Napoleon 27, 135, 290, 295
Bonduel, Florimond J. 556
Bonnie Prince Charlie 21
Book of Common Prayer 19, 20
Boone, Daniel 449
Booth, John Wilkes 408
Borgess, Caspar 480, 481
Boston 25, 55-59, 63-66, 69, 70, 73, 76-78, 81, 83, 85, 91, 92, 99, 103, 104, 110, 111, 113, 118, 133, 134, 137, 144, 150, 154, 162, 173, 198, 208, 291, 311, 323, 357, 452, 453, 565
Boston College 66, 100
Bouis, Pascal Vincent 180
Bourbonnais 536
Bourbons 25
Bouvier, Jacqueline 114
Bowie 29, 277, 280, 281, 288
Bragg, Braxton 424, 459, 468
Brazil; *also* Brazilians 26, 37, 81, 153, 249, 558
Briand, Jean Olivier 498
Brisbane, A. H. 368
British 18-20, 22, 23, 27-29, 34, 38, 39, 45, 48, 52, 66, 69, 72, 97, 98, 110, 117, 118, 126-128, 144, 148, 155, 195, 196, 200, 204, 228, 254, 267, 274, 278, 287, 289, 291, 306, 324, 330, 346, 349-352, 356, 365, 366, 389-393, 404, 416, 417, 426, 488, 498, 502, 516
British Army 20, 55, 179, 499
Britten, Benjamin 564
Brooklyn 58, 84, 134, 146, 150, 156, 165-176
Brooklyn Bridge 174
Brooklyn Common Council 168
Brooklyn Lyceum 168
Brooks, Erastus 151
Brown, John 344, 345, 347
Browne, Robert 353-355, 357, 358, 367
Brownson, Orestes 514
Brozard, J. N. 405

Bruté, Simon 30, 502, 504-507, 510, 521, 522
Bryan, William Jennings 546
Buchanan Administration 255
Buchanan, James 255
Buffalo 150, 151, 153
Bulfinch, Charles 56
Bulger, Richard 166, 189
Bull Run 324, 339
Bunker Hill Tavern 198
Burba, Alexander 235, 236, 238
Burgundy 463
Burlington convention 188
Butler, Thomas E. 38
Byrne, John 166
Byrne, Patrick 76, 111, 112
Byrne, William 456
Byzantine Rite 247, 248, 250
Byzantine Romanesque 331
Byzantine style 78

C

Cabezas Altamirano, Juan de las 389
Cabrini, Frances 12
Caddington, William 109
Cadillac, Antoine de la Mothe 18, 475, 487, 488
Cadillac, Marie Thérèse 475
Caffrey, Anthony 329
Cahensly, Peter Paul 562
Cahokia 18, 452, 464, 498, 499, 501, 520
Calderón, Gabriel Díaz Vara 390
Calhoun, James C. 381
California 12, 16, 17, 24, 28, 76, 77, 81, 387, 487, 565
Calvert, George (Lord Baltimore) 90, 261, 273, 287, 292, 305, 333
Camps, Peter 393
Canada 10, 14, 27, 28, 84, 85, 99, 101, 104, 105, 118, 121, 452, 467, 477, 485, 488, 503, 556, 558
Canary Islands 76
Cane River 304
canon law 15, 210, 240, 358, 424, 550
Canonesses of St. Augustine 42

Cantrell, James 457
Cape Canaveral 387
Cape Cod 77, 81, 90
Cape Verde 76
Capone, Al 534, 535, 537
Capuchin; *also* Capuchins 23, 90, 128, 129, 135, 416, 417, 555
Carder, Christopher 55
Care Walk 200
Carheil, Étienne de 488
Carib Indians 46
Caribou 100
carillon 161, 217, 446, 511, 512, 515
Carles, Anthony 367
Carlisle 260
Carlos III 17, 26, 127, 351
Carlos V 46
Carmelite; *also* Carmelites 23, 222, 270, 271, 511, 512
Carnegie, Andrew 269
Carnegie Institute 399
Carnegie Steel 269
Carolinas 349, 350, 352, 357, 403, 449
Carr, Matthew 206
Carrera, Juan de la 349
Carreras, José 159
Carroll, Charles
 of Annapolis 22, 309
 of Carrollton (the Signer) 27, 112, 287, 299, 309
 the Barrister 299
 the Settler 309
Carroll, Dr. Charles 277
Carroll, Daniel 283, 338
Carroll, Eleanor 283
Carroll, James 277
Carroll, John 10, 24, 26, 27, 29, 38, 55, 56, 70, 91, 92, 98, 110, 127, 129, 130, 133, 134, 143, 144, 189, 197, 205-207, 254, 255, 260, 266, 267, 277-279, 283, 284, 288-294, 303, 321-323, 338, 351-353, 357, 366, 433-435, 450-452, 499, 500-502, 565
Carroll House 309-311
Cartwright's Creek 450, 452

Casanovas, Bartolomé 393
Castro, Fidel 65, 411, 412
catechism 53, 131, 136, 146, 152, 224, 235, 270, 293, 353, 370, 391, 420, 451, 499, 500, 526
Cathedral of the Assumption 458
Catherine the Great 25
Catholic Advocate 456
Catholic Daughters 159
Catholic Directory 504
Catholic Emancipation Act 19, 148
Catholic history 10-12, 230, 295, 400, 433
Catholic paper 147
Catholic public schools 374
Catholic publishing 228, 524
Catholic School for the Blind 158
Catholic Telegraph 443
Catholic University of America 158, 293
Catholic Youth Organization (CYO) 536
Cause, John B. 254
CCD (Confraternity of Christian Doctrine) 93, 184, 192, 318, 327, 334, 362, 459, 495, 506, 514
Cellini, Benvenuto 447
Cengotiti, Juan Bautista 52
Chabrat, Guy 465
Challoner, Richard 26, 127, 187, 350
Champlain, Samuel de 17, 90
Champomier, John Leo 502, 503
Chapel Point 273
chaplain; *also* chaplains 17, 21, 28, 29, 55, 76, 81, 123, 127-129, 132, 180, 183, 184, 204, 205, 292, 310, 311, 314-317, 325, 356, 370, 371, 407, 408, 417, 424, 426, 453, 512, 515, 535, 536, 538
Charbonnel, Armand François 324
Charles I 259, 330
Charles II 109, 259, 349
Charles III 52
Charles River 58, 70
Charleston 208, 210, 306, 349-362, 367, 368, 380, 395, 396, 398, 404
Charles Town 344, 347

Charlestown 198, 199
Charlestown convent 173
Chatard, Francis S. 506
Chesapeake Bay 291, 309, 310, 313
Cheverus, John de 30, 56, 57, 63, 70, 71, 76, 91, 92, 103, 104, 110, 118, 133, 134, 144, 208, 323, 367
Chicago; *also* Chicago River 25, 149, 161, 174, 199, 244, 332, 362, 504, 505, 511, 519-526, 529-538, 541-552, 560
Chicago Back of the Yards Neighborhood Council 537
Chickasaw Indians 497
Chief Pokagon 509
Chippewa Indians 485, 487, 489, 491, 492, 495
cholera 64, 168, 443, 476, 511, 556
chrism Mass 176, 427
Christian Brothers 139, 147, 149, 157, 170, 191, 292, 300, 305, 330, 399, 481, 531
Christiansted 33-39, 42
Christ's Church 288
Churchill, Winston 159
Church of England 18, 19, 45, 299, 350
Cincinnati 24, 398, 429, 436, 441-447, 457, 459, 467, 476, 480, 481, 489, 490, 492, 510, 521, 556, 559, 561
Cincinnati *Gazette* 442
Ciquart, Francis 98
Cistercian; *also* Cistercians 463, 466, 471
Ciszek, Walter 244
Civil War 10, 24, 37, 41, 57, 64, 72, 75, 76, 84, 85, 93, 99, 113, 119, 155, 156, 173, 175, 190, 216, 261, 275, 292, 293, 304, 305, 310, 313, 316, 324, 325, 330, 332, 333, 339, 345, 346, 361, 369, 370, 373, 374, 380, 381, 382, 398, 399, 404, 406, 408, 409, 422, 423, 424-426, 436, 437, 445, 458, 459, 467, 468, 505, 512, 523, 541, 542, 559, 565
Claremont 103-106

Clark, George Rogers 498, 499
Clark, James 184
Classic Revival style 180, 360
Clavreul, Henry P. 371, 372
Cleary, Thomas 382
Clement XIV 25
Cleveland 429-431
Cleveland Administration 181
Clifton, Alfred 204
Clinton, DeWitt 132, 144
Clorivière, Joseph de la 353, 354, 356, 359
Cobh 423
Cocozza, Alfredo (Mario Lanza) 224
Cody, John 535, 551
Coleman, James 417
College of Cardinals 56, 78, 293, 333, 535, 536
Collins, J. Lawton 183
Collins, Morgan 534
Colt Manufacturing Company 191
Colt, Roswell C. 189, 190
Columbia College 145, 154
Columbus, Christopher 14, 33, 34, 42, 45, 46, 53, 76, 158, 398, 436, 437, 444
Comiskey, Charles 536
Common School Fund 131, 146, 151, 152
Company of the West 18
Concanen, Richard L. 135
Conewago 105, 207, 259-261, 266, 434
Conewago River 260
Connecticut River valley 103
Confederate Army 292, 324, 325, 398, 424, 426
Confederate States 155, 361, 375
Confraternity of Christian Doctrine — *see* CCD
Confraternity of the Blessed Sacrament 147
Congregation of St. Basil 476
Congregation of the Holy Cross 510
Congregational 91, 119, 173, 524, 525

Congregationalist; *also* Congregationalists 126, 345
Congressional Medal of Honor 317
Connecticut 103, 111, 112, 117, 118, 121, 122, 134, 184, 216, 331
Connell, Mary 210
Connick, Charles 162
Connolly, John 135-137, 144-147, 166, 167
Continental Congress 28, 29, 188, 196, 200, 204, 205
convent inspection 113
Convent Station 190, 191
conversions 36, 138
Conway, James 72
Conwell, Henry 197, 207-212
Cooke, Terence 159, 161
Cooper, Francis 132
Cooper, Samuel S. 367
Corby, William J. 512, 515
Corcoran, Thomas 332
Cornwallis, Charles 110, 205, 265
corporation sole 150, 523
Correa, Nicolás 49
Corrigan, Michael 161
Corry, John 111
Costaggini, Filippo 261
Costello, Michael A. 344
Cottrill, Matthew 89, 91, 92
Council of the Indies 49
Crèvecoeur, Hector St. John de 127
Crioulo 78
Croatians 301
Cromwell, Oliver 117
Crosby, Bing 525
Cross, Bernard 35
Cross of the Royal Order of Charles III 52
Cuba; *also* Cubans 48, 112, 130, 192, 278, 305, 311, 349, 387, 389, 391, 392, 394, 395, 397, 404, 408-411, 412, 415-417, 437, 500
Cumberland Gap 449
Curley, Michael J. 294, 333
Curvin, Boniface 228
Cushing, Richard 65
Cutts, Adele 332

Cuyahoga County 430
Cuyahoga River 429
Cyrillic alphabet 234, 248
czarist regime 241

D
D'Aberville, Pierre Le Moyne 416
D'Estaing, Henri 366
Dabán, Juan 50
Dabler, William 441
Dablon, Claude 486, 487
Dahlgren Chapel 327
Dalai Lama 159
Daly, John 105
Damariscotta 89, 91-93, 97
Damariscotta River 89, 93
Damen, Arnold 531
Danish West Indies 34, 35, 37-41
Dant, James 465
Darnall, Molly 309
Daughters of Charity 133, 134, 139, 147, 290, 300, 330, 421, 422, 423-425, 557, 559, 560
David, John B. 453
Davis, Jefferson 361, 406, 424, 452
Davis, Jefferson, Jr. 368
Davis, Varina Anne "Winnie" 368
DeBarth, Louis 207
Declaration of Independence 22, 188, 200, 205, 241, 309
decree of suppression 26
de Gaulle, Charles 332
de Grasse, François 351
Delaware River 187, 196, 197, 199
Democrat; *also* Democrats, Democratic Party 93, 169, 458
de Montes, Torio 50
Denmark 34, 35, 37, 40
Department of Veterans Affairs — *see* VA
De Pere 555
deportations 117
Der Wahrheitsfreund 443
de Salamanca, Diego 46, 47
De Shon, George 182
De Smet, Pierre 278, 279, 565
Detroit 18, 167, 430, 443, 452, 457,

576

475-477, 479-482, 488, 489, 493, 498, 499, 509, 511, 520, 542, 556, 557
Detroit River 475, 479, 481
Devenish, Thomas 36
de Veuster, Damien 12, 565
Dewey, George 313
de Zayas, Manuel 50
Dickens, Charles 323, 444
Digest of Laws 109
Digges, Dudley 261
Digges, Thomas 329
diocesan synods 156, 445
Discalced Carmelites 23
Dismas House 307
Dittoe, Anthony 434
Dittoe, Jacob 433-438
Dittoe, Joseph 434
doctrinas 388, 391
Domingo, Placido 159
Dominica 39
Dominican; *also* Dominicans, Dominican Sisters 23, 34-36, 48, 51, 104, 120, 121, 123, 129, 135, 136, 144, 145, 207, 415, 417, 434-438, 441, 442, 452, 454, 456, 457, 489, 560
Dongan, Thomas 126
Dooley, Thomas A. "Tom" 516
Dorchester 63, 64, 66
Dosh, Lucy 459
Douay Bible 443
Dougherty, Dennis 242, 243, 470
Doughoregan Manor 287, 310
Douglas, Stephen A. 332, 437, 523
Douglas, William 187
Downes, William 120
Doylestown 429
draft riots 113, 156, 173
Drake, Francis 48, 389, 392
Drexel, Emma Bouvier 218
Drexel, Francis A. 218
Drexel, Katharine 217, 218
Druillettes, Gabriel 118, 487
Du Bois, Jean Baptiste 489, 493
Dubois, John 30, 147-149, 167, 169, 190, 343

Dubourg, Louis William 30
Duchesne, Rose Philippine 12, 565
Duggan, James 530, 531
du Guast, Pierre 90
Duncan, E. B. 270, 373
Duncan Phillips Art Gallery 270
Dungannon 441
Dunkers 254
Dunne, Frederic 469, 471
du Rhu, Paul 416
Dutch 34, 37, 38, 48, 128, 157, 256, 339, 557
Dutch Reformed Church 125, 126, 152, 165
Dutch West India Company 125
Dyer, Mary 69
Dyniewicz, Ladislaus 543
dysentery 48, 371

E

Early, Jubal 346
Early, Thomas J. 180
earthquake 51, 80, 360, 361, 505
Eastern Shore (Maryland) 310
East Liverpool 443
East River 157, 165, 166, 168-170, 173
Easton 310
Eccleston, Samuel 299, 300, 304, 330, 334
Edward VII 332
Egan, Michael 197, 206, 207, 211, 255, 267
Elgin Botanical Gardens 145
Elizabeth (empress) 332
Elizabeth (queen) 19, 27
Elkridge 310
Ellis, Richard 35
Ellsworth 84
Elyria 429
Emancipation Proclamation 304, 325
Emerald Guard 423
Emery, James Andrew 290
Empie, Adam 180
Encarnação, João Ignácio Azevedo 77

Enders, Joseph 261
Endicott, John 69
England 29, 126, 155, 182, 190, 196, 210, 253, 259, 283, 288, 291, 309, 332, 392
England, John 57, 208, 357-362, 368, 395, 396
English 14, 16, 17, 19, 20, 23-28, 30, 31, 34, 35, 37, 45, 58, 59, 65, 69, 76-78, 81, 89-92, 99, 101, 117, 118, 125, 128, 136, 145, 192, 195, 223-225, 229, 240, 244, 250, 254, 255, 259, 260, 262, 266, 268, 273-275, 277, 278, 334, 350, 353, 356, 357, 358, 366, 385-387, 390, 391, 393, 403, 412, 413, 417, 429, 436, 443, 449, 450, 452, 459, 469, 472, 477, 488, 489, 492, 493, 499, 505, 506, 523, 529, 551, 557, 559, 561, 565
English Jesuits 24, 26, 126, 274, 275, 486
English Test Oath 126
Entre Nous 191
Episcopalian; *also* Episcopalians 38, 70, 154, 313, 405
Erie Canal 71, 144
Erin Fraternal Association 167
Ernsten, Paul 228
Espeleta, José 417
Esperanza, Salvador de la 417
ethnic friction 30, 136, 562
ethnic parishes 30, 331
Eucharistic Congress 219, 533
Eudist Fathers 421, 505
Evacuation Day 66
Evangelicals 53
Ewing, Ellen 380
excommunicate; *also* excommunicated, excommunication 37, 151, 208, 209, 210, 394, 469, 547

F

faculties 15, 30, 128, 129, 137, 207, 208, 210, 317, 354, 358, 389, 424
Fairbanks, Charles W. 546

Fairfax County, Virginia 338
Fall River 77-79, 81
Farley, James A. 159
Farley, John 157, 158
Farmer, Ferdinand (Ferdinand Steinmeyer) 127, 188, 189, 197, 204
Farnan, John 167-169
Farragut, David 314, 425
Fathers of the Sacred Heart 135
Federalist Papers 28
Feehan, Patrick 545, 547, 549
Fenwick, Benedict 71, 104, 111, 135, 323, 356, 357, 442, 443
Fenwick, Edward D. 434-436, 438, 441, 452, 489, 490
Fernandes, Manuel Francisco 77
Fernandina 399
Fesch, Joseph 295, 442
festa; also festas 79, 80, 225
Ffrench, Charles D. 104, 136, 137
Fighting 69th 173
Filicchi, Antonio 133
Filipinos 524
Finck, Joseph 433, 434
Finn, William J. 525
Finnegan, Patrick 105, 118
fire 37, 42, 63, 64, 73, 78, 84, 119, 127, 146, 156, 159, 169, 175, 207, 222, 243, 250, 256, 275, 277, 280, 339, 347, 354, 360, 375, 376, 381, 383, 399, 405, 410, 419, 421, 427, 437, 438, 470, 476, 487, 503, 513, 523, 524, 530-532, 534, 544, 558, 561-563
First Earl of Bellamont 126
First Plenary Council 30, 223, 228, 331, 430, 480
First Vatican Council 99
Fitton, James 112, 118, 119
Fitzgerald, John 338
Fitzpatrick, John 57, 58, 64
Fitzsimmons, Thomas 213
Flaget, Benedict J. 30, 434, 435, 451, 453-458, 460, 464, 465, 500, 502, 503, 504, 506
Flagg, Ernest 313

Flagler, Henry M. 399, 400, 411
Florida 10, 16, 17, 22, 28, 48, 349, 350, 365, 368-370, 375, 385-400, 403-408, 410-412, 415-419, 421, 422, 426
Florida Keys 368, 405
Floyd, Olivia 275
Flynn, James 35
Foley, Thomas 524, 531, 544, 545, 549
Fond du Lac 492
Fordham University 160
Fort Adams 111, 112
Fort Dearborn 520, 521
Fort Duquesne 23
Fort Hamilton 167
Fort Jefferson 406, 408
Fort Kent 98
Fort Lafayette 372, 406, 407
Fort Pontchartrain 475, 488
Fort Pulaski 370, 371
Fort San Felipe 349
Fort Wayne 497, 505, 509
Fox Indians 555
Fox, James 471
France 17, 18, 24-29, 38, 56, 57, 90, 110, 118, 130, 145, 283, 289, 290, 295, 304, 322, 332, 353, 357, 366, 367, 368, 369, 372, 373, 399, 417, 420, 421, 423, 453, 457, 463-468, 470, 475, 476, 487, 488, 500, 503, 504, 505, 507, 509-513, 520, 521
Francis, John 417
Francis I 457
Franciscan Recollect; *also* Franciscan Recollects 17, 205, 254, 488
Franklin, Benjamin 27, 29, 283
Franklin and Marshall 254
Franklin Institute 218
Franz Joseph (emperor) 332
Frederici, Gaetano 191
Frederick the Great 266
Fredericton 99
Frederik III 34
Frederiksted 38, 41
freedmen 373

Freitas, Antonio 77
Fremont, John C. 173
French 14, 16-18, 22-27, 29, 30, 33, 34, 36-40, 48, 55, 56, 57, 69, 73, 81, 84-86, 90-92, 97-101, 106, 110, 118, 126-128, 134-137, 145, 147, 155, 179, 180, 204, 205, 213, 255, 265, 266, 268, 283, 289, 290, 305, 322, 332, 350, 351-353, 355, 357, 366, 367, 374, 385, 386, 387, 394, 398, 399, 416-418, 420-423, 425, 427, 453, 457, 464, 467-469, 475-477, 485, 487-490, 492, 493, 495, 497-501, 504-507, 509, 510, 512, 515, 519, 520, 529, 556, 565
French and Indian War 18, 20, 22, 165
French Canadians 78, 98, 101, 105, 499
French Gothic 63, 174, 375
French Renaissance 269
French Revolution 30, 56, 255, 266, 322, 453, 464, 476, 500, 501
French West Indian Company 34
Frenchville 98
Friend, Anthony B. 410
Friends of Ireland 167
Frontenac, Comte de 18, 475, 487

G

Gallagher, Simon Felix 352-355, 357, 358
Gallicanism 17
Gallitzin, Amalia 266
Gallitzin, Demetrius A. 265-268, 271
Gallitzin, Dimitri 266
Galveston 426, 541
Gamelin, Antoine 500
Gardiner, Harriet 503
Gardoqui, Diego de 127
Garibaldi, Giussepe 172
Gartland, Francis X. 369, 373, 405
Gary, Elbert 269
Gavazzi, Alessandro 172
gay rights; *also* gays 58, 158
Geiger, Adam 188
Geiger, Matthew 188

George, Henry 293
George III 321
George Rogers Clark Memorial 506, 507
Georgetown 85, 104, 105, 111, 136, 145, 184, 197, 255, 279, 321-327, 329, 339, 340, 353, 355, 356, 406, 420, 453
Georgetown Academy 290, 321, 322
Georgetown College 104, 105, 255, 323, 326, 339, 353, 406, 453
Georgetown University 85, 184, 322, 327, 356
Georgia 18, 20-22, 85, 350, 352, 353, 357, 365-371, 373, 374-376, 379, 382, 388, 391, 395, 397, 398, 406, 407, 471
Georgian Bay 485
Gerard, Alexander 205
German Catholics 147, 171, 188, 228, 254, 255, 269, 443, 504, 505, 521, 541, 556
Gettysburg 213, 259, 261, 292, 346, 459, 515
Ghione, Felix 407
Gibault, Pierre 498-500, 507
Gibbons, James 292, 300, 331, 357, 561
Gibbons, Thomas 292
Gibbs, George C. 400
Giffard, Bonaventure 21
Giorgetti, S. P. 39
Girard, Stephen 213, 233
Girard, Thomas 89
Glendale 429
Godefroy, Maximilian 455
Going My Way 525
Gooch, William 337
Good Shepherd Sisters 100
Gordon, Francis 550
Gordon, John 392
Gordon, Patrick 195
Goshenhoppen 188, 227-229
Gosselin, Antoine 98
Gothic 50, 58, 63, 65, 112, 145, 155, 167, 174, 183, 291, 294, 339, 375, 472, 476, 530

Grace Institute 158
Grace Lines 158
Grace, William R. 158
Grand Rapids 491
Grand River 491
Granger, Alexis 511, 512
Grant, Ulysses S. 182, 381, 559
Grassi, John 104, 135, 145
Great Depression 161, 296
Greaton, Joseph 195, 196, 200, 227
Greek Orthodox 393
Greek Revival style 138, 444
Greeks 392, 393
Greenville Treaty 520
Gregori, Luigi 512
Gregory XV 14
Gregory XVI 360
Grey Nuns 72
Gronchi, Giovanni 159
Gross, William 375
Guale Indians 388
Guardian Angel mission 519, 520
Guillet, Urbain 464
Gulf Coast 55, 415, 427
Gulf of Mexico 265, 393, 403-406, 416

H

Haetscher, Francis 489
Hagerstown 260
Hailandière, Celestine de la 506, 510, 511
Haile Selassie 332
Haiti 46, 133, 360
Hall, Thomas 295
Hamilton, Alexander 189
Hamilton, Henry 499
Hamilton, James 254
Hamilton, William J. 371, 372
Hamlin 100, 101
Hamtramck, John 500
Hanning, John Green 468
Hanover 259, 261, 464
Hardee, William 373
Harding, Charles 512
Harding, Robert 196, 203, 204, 211, 212

Hardin's Creek 450, 467
Harold, William 207
Harper, Catherine 112
Harper, James 148
Harper, Robert 343
Harrison, Benjamin 562
Harrison, William Henry 501, 502
Hartford 76, 81, 118, 119, 122, 150
Harvey, Thomas 126
Hassett, Thomas 394
Havana 389, 392, 395, 397, 399, 404, 407, 409, 410
Hawthorne, Nathaniel 73
Hayden, Basil 450
Hayes, Patrick 158, 161, 317
Hayes, Richard 356
Haymarket Riot 199
Hazelton 237-239, 244, 249
Head Start 307
Healy, James A. 85, 100
Healy, Patrick 85
Hecker, Isaac 524
Heeney, Cornelius 146, 169, 170
Heiss, Michael 561
Heister, Joseph 211
Henderson, David 182
Hennepin, Louis 555
Henni, John Martin 556
Henry, Patrick 498
Henry the Navigator 76
Henry VIII 45
Herard, Mathieu 37, 38
Hesburgh, Theodore 516
Hickey, James A. 334
Highland Falls 180, 182
Hill, Ambrose P. 345
Hispanic; *also* Hispanics 57-59, 192, 219, 256, 334, 477, 551, 563
Hobart, Henry 132
Hochwächter 444
Hofbauer, Clement 490
Hogan, William 207, 209
Holy Cross Brothers 531, 560
Holy Cross College 100, 112, 184
Holy Cross Fathers; *also* Congregation of the Holy Cross

23, 99, 100, 510, 512, 514, 530, 547, 551
Holy Cross, Kentucky 450, 459
Holy Cross nuns (France); *also* Holy Cross Sisters 330, 426, 511
Holy Cross Seminary 515
Holy Land 449, 459, 460, 463
Holy See 14-16, 21, 26, 38, 40, 45, 46, 48, 49, 85, 99, 135, 147, 153, 197, 206, 207, 211, 215, 249, 279, 290, 303, 305, 306, 340, 352, 355, 356, 360, 417, 418, 420, 422, 424, 452, 454, 456, 465, 467, 522, 547, 549, 558, 562
Holy Trinity (Augusta) 367
Holy Trinity (Chicago) 544-547, 551
Holy Trinity (Cincinnati) 443
Holy Trinity (Hartford) 118
Holy Trinity (Philadelphia) 205, 206
Holy Trinity (Somerset) 436, 438
homeless 43, 58, 84, 123, 199, 383
Homestead Steel Works 269
Hood, John Bell 381
Hooe, Robert T. 338
Hoover, Herbert 270
House of Representatives 181, 268, 359, 476
Howard, John Eager 289
Howard, Thomas 453
Howe, William 66, 204
Hudson Highlands 179
Hudson River 134, 147, 157, 180, 182
Hughes, John 138, 146-157, 161, 162, 171, 197, 316, 361, 370
Huguenot; *also* Huguenots 56, 350, 357, 385, 386
Humanae Vitae 333
Hunincq, Sylvanus 407
Hunter, George 196
Huntington, Jedediah V. 314
Huntsville 422
Hurley, Joseph T. 400
Huron Indians 485, 486, 555
hurricane; *also* hurricanes 37, 46, 49, 360, 361, 369, 411, 416, 503
Hurricane Hugo 42, 53, 361, 362

Hutchison, Anne 109

I

Idley, Joseph 127
Illinois; *also* Illinois River 17, 105, 346, 437, 452, 464, 476, 487, 498, 499, 504-506, 510, 519, 521-523, 529, 530, 536, 541, 545, 548
Illinois-Michigan Canal 530
Immaculate Heart of Mary Sisters 481
Immergrun 269-271
immigration 57, 80, 81, 85, 114, 132, 144, 190, 192, 222, 234, 241, 253, 254, 373, 411, 412, 422, 443, 505, 524, 542, 544
Incarnate Word Sisters 430
Indiana 322, 330, 339, 445, 450, 452, 497, 498, 501, 502-506, 509-511, 514, 521, 549
Indianapolis 506
interdenominational 183, 313, 315
interdict 197, 209, 211, 212, 240, 354-356, 397
International Eucharistic Congress 533
Iowa 182, 509, 531, 533, 561
Ireland, John 561
Ireland 23, 29, 30, 36, 72, 112, 117-119, 136, 144, 149, 170, 174, 190, 211, 270, 294, 344, 345, 346, 351, 356-358, 367, 380, 423, 522
Irish 17, 19, 20, 29, 30, 34, 35, 45, 56-58, 63-66, 69, 71, 72, 73, 76, 81, 84-86, 89, 92, 98, 100, 110-114, 117, 118, 120, 128, 129, 132, 135-137, 140, 144, 146-149, 154, 156-158, 165-169, 172, 173, 189, 190, 192, 198, 199, 204, 207, 217, 223, 224, 235, 236, 250, 255, 256, 260, 287, 294, 299, 300, 301, 344, 350-352, 355-357, 359, 360, 366, 367-369, 379, 381, 393, 405, 417, 422, 423, 426, 429, 430, 436, 443, 458, 480, 489, 495, 501, 529, 534, 543, 544, 547, 549, 550, 556, 557, 561

Irish Brigade (Illinois) 346, 523
Irish Brigade (New York) 156, 515
Irish Franciscan Brothers 268
Irish-American 147
Iroquois Indians 126, 350, 487, 555
Isoleri, Antonio 222-224
Italian; *also* Italians 57, 58, 65, 73, 86, 101, 110, 135, 153, 157, 158, 191, 198, 221, 222, 223-225, 244, 351, 375, 392, 404, 407, 411, 419, 447, 489, 495, 534
Italian Renaissance 480

J

Jackson, Stonewall 345, 346
Jacksonville 385, 399
Jamaica 128, 168, 330
James II 21, 126, 187, 253
James, John 24, 229
James River 90, 375
Jansenism; *also* Jansenist 25, 356, 451
Janski, Bogdan 542
Jaricot, Pauline 24
Jay, John 28, 131
J. Edgar Thompson Steel Works 269
Jefferson, Thomas 180, 343
Jefferson Medical School 213
Jefferson's Rock 343, 344, 346, 347
Jesuit Center for Spirituality 326
Jesuits; *also* Society of Jesus 16-27, 29, 30, 35, 40, 41, 48, 55, 85, 99, 104, 113, 126, 135-137, 145, 184, 197, 212, 228, 229, 255, 256, 260, 261, 273-275, 277-281, 305, 316, 322, 323, 338, 339, 349, 350, 355, 380, 387, 407, 408, 410, 411, 416, 421, 423-426, 434, 444, 456, 465, 480, 481, 485, 486-488, 490, 491, 493, 498, 509, 531, 555
Jewish synagogue 73, 183
Jews 34, 37, 362, 548
Jogues, Isaac 12, 16, 126, 485, 486, 506
John Carroll Society 332
John Paul II 59, 159, 176, 219, 250, 332, 362, 526, 533, 551

John XXII 506
John XXIII 10, 66, 261
Johnson, Andrew 293, 361, 407
Johnson, Lyndon B. 159
Johnson, Peter Leo 559
Johnston, Joseph E. 370
Jolliet, Louis 487, 519
Jones, Isaac 228
Jones, John Paul 314
Jones Point 338
Jones, William 48
Josephite; *also* Josephites 23, 306, 307, 325
Joubert, Nicholas 305
Julius II 16, 46
Juneau, Solomon 556
Juszkiewicz, Joseph 544

K

Kain, John J. 346
Kajsiewicz, Jerome 544
Kaminskas, Albin J. 240
Karalius, Joseph A. 242, 243
Karnes County 541
Kaskaskia 18, 105, 452, 476, 498, 499, 565
Katzer, Frederick F. X. 561, 562
Kavanagh, Edward 93
Kavanagh, James 89, 92, 93
Keating, Thomas 351
Keely, Patrick C. 58, 112, 174, 175, 512, 532
Keenan, Bernard 255
Kelly, Eugene (Mrs.) 157
Kelly, William 466
Kendall, Henry 38
Kennebec River 90, 91
Kennedy, Hyacinth 35, 36
Kennedy, John F. 59, 65, 114, 325, 332
Kennedy, Robert 159
Kenrick, Francis P. 197-199, 212, 215, 216, 219, 292, 369, 371, 397, 398, 457
Kentucky 56, 291, 434, 435, 437, 441, 442, 445, 449, 450, 451-460, 463-471, 473, 498, 499, 502-504, 506, 520
Keweenaw Bay 555
Key, Francis Scott 291
Key West 403-408, 410-412
Kickapoo Indians 555
Kilpatrick, Judson 261
King James Version 152, 458, 472
Kingdom of the Two Sicilies 25
Kinsella, Jeremiah 529, 530
Kiolbassa, Peter 542, 543
Kirby, John 368, 371
Kittanning Trail 265
Knights of Columbus (K. of C.) 121, 122, 284, 317, 415, 470
Knights of Labor 249, 293
Knights of Lithuania 244
Knights of Malta 159
Know-Nothing; *also* Know-Nothings, Know-Nothing Party 113, 114, 151, 422, 458
Kobrzynski, Simon 546, 547
K. of C. — *see* Knights of Columbus
Kohl, Helmut 159
Kohlmann, Anthony 135, 136, 144, 145, 148
Kolbe, Maximilian 284
Korea 317
Kosciuszko, Thaddeus 28, 179
Kozlowski, Anthony 547
Kroes, Peter 339
Kundig, Martin 556, 557, 560
Kweder, Joseph J. 244

L

Lady Elgin 560
LaFarge, Grant 331
Lafayette, Marquis de 28
Laffont, Jean 499
Lake Huron 475, 485, 486, 494
Lake Michigan 485, 487, 519-522, 530, 533, 556, 558, 559
Lalumière, Simon Petit 501
Lamy, John 565
Lancaster 253-256, 259, 380, 433, 435, 441, 450
Langdill, Arthur 189
Lange, Elizabeth 305
Langton, John A. 183
L'Arbre Croche 490
La Grande Trappe 464
Lanza, Mario — *see* Cocozza, Alfredo
Larissey, Philip 63, 76, 189
La Rocque, Mariano de 394, 409
La Salle, Sieur de 18, 555
Latrobe, Benjamin H. 290, 291, 294, 296
Laudonnière, René de Goulaine de 385
Laval, François 18, 487
Lavelle, Michael 158
La Vente, Henri Roulleaux de 416
Law of Liberty of Conscience 196
Laws of the Indies 52
League of Catholic Women 481
Leavenworth 535
Le Brun, Napoleon 216
Lee, Robert E. 184, 344-346, 426
Lee, Thomas Sim 331
Lefevere, Peter 30, 479, 480
legal title 160, 211, 212, 255, 327, 362, 367, 395, 404
Legion of Mary 59
Lehigh River 254
Le Mercier, Oliver 352, 353, 366, 367
Lemoine, John 366
Leopoldine Society 24, 490, 491
Leo XII 280, 418, 442, 457
Leo XIII 180, 218, 562
Le Propagateur Catholique 398
Letourno, Francis 480
Lewis, John 26, 212
Lewis, John L. 537
liberalism 542
Liberty Bell 200, 507
Lincoln, Abraham 156, 173, 292, 325, 330, 373, 408, 437, 459, 467, 559
Lincoln Administration 155, 370
Lincoln, Thomas 450
liquor 73, 152, 354, 487, 491, 501, 534

Lithuanian Alliance of America 237
Lithuanian Independence Day 241
Lithuanian Miners Union 239
Lithuanian parish 233, 235, 236, 241, 307
Lithuanian Roman Catholic Alliance 237
Lithuanians 65, 191, 234-239, 241, 301
Lithuanian Voice 237
Locust Grove 366, 367, 371
Logan Circle 215, 219
Long Island 134, 165-168, 171, 172, 176
Loras, Mathias 30
Lord Ashburton 98
Lord Baltimore — *see* Calvert, George
Lorentz, Maurice 188
Loretto, Kentucky 450, 459, 464, 465, 467, 470
Los Kayos Indians 403
Loughlin, John 171-175
Louis Philippe (the Citizen King) 457
Louis XV 22
Louisiana; *also* Louisiana Territory 16-18, 24, 38, 180, 303, 304, 325, 394, 398, 417, 426, 497
Louisville 306, 450, 456, 459, 464-466, 469-471, 504, 542
Louisville *Journal* 458
Loyola Retreat House 275
Ludwig (king) 563
Lulworth Castle 278, 288, 291
Lutheran; *also* Lutherans 34, 38, 41, 228, 254, 560, 561
Luther, Martin 45, 204
Lynch, Patrick N. 360, 361

M

Mackinac Island 485, 488, 489, 493, 495
Macon 85, 371, 374, 379
Madames of the Sacred Heart 481, 533
Madawaska River 97

Madeira 75, 77
Madeline Island 491
Madison, Dolly 330, 332
Madison, James 330
Mahanoy City 233, 235, 236, 240, 249
Maine 18, 56, 83-86, 89-93, 97-101, 105, 288, 409
Mallet, Pierre 500
Mallory, Stephen R. 404-407, 409
Malou, Peter Anthony 136, 137
Manchester 84
Mangin, Joseph 144
Manhattan 122, 125, 126, 133-135, 138-141, 143, 148, 154, 155, 157, 160, 165-167, 169-175, 438
Manogue, Patrick 565
Manso, Alonso 46, 47
manual labor 270, 310, 454, 514
Marèchal, Ambrose 30, 207, 279, 280, 290, 292, 353, 356-358, 418
Mariani, Gaetano 222, 223
Marietta 379
Maris, Roger 159
Marist Fathers 100
Maronite; *also* Maronites 140, 141, 247, 248
Marquette, Jacques 486, 487, 495, 519, 555, 565
Marquis de Grasse 351
married priesthood 249
Marrón, Francisco 389
Marshall, Adam 316
Martha's Vineyard 77
Martínez, Luis Aponte 45
Martínez, Pedro 387
martyrology 16
Mary Thomasina (nun) 400
Maryland 12, 13, 20-22, 24, 25, 29, 55, 90, 104, 105, 133, 145, 147, 168, 184, 187, 196, 212, 229, 259, 260, 265-267, 321-326, 329, 330, 333, 337, 338, 343-346, 351, 353, 357, 366, 367, 369, 408, 426, 433, 449, 450, 454, 459, 465, 486, 504, 557, 559, 565
Masillon 443

Mason and Dixon 259
Massachusetts 55-57, 63, 69, 75-77, 79, 81, 89-91, 93, 100, 111, 112, 155, 330, 438
Massachusetts Bay 19, 109
Massachusetts Bay colony 90
Mass houses 195, 260, 274
Masson, Peter 240
Matanzas River 387, 391
Mather, Cotton 63
Mathewson, Christy 536
Mathew, Theobald 72, 73
Matignon, Francis A. 56, 63, 70, 91, 110
Matthews, William 330
May, John L. 427
Mayne, Edward F. 396, 397
Maysville 449
Mazzone, Vito 224, 225
Mazzuchelli, Samuel 489
McCaffrey, James P. 426
McCalmont, Samuel 268
McCarthy, Edward 412
McCarthy, Joseph 332
McCarthy, Timothy 396
McCloskey, John 139, 156, 157
McCloskey, Patrick 166
McColgan, Edward 300
McDermot, James 119
McDonald, J. E. 407
McDonnell, Charles E. 174
McElroy, John 316
McEvoy, Christopher 36
McGean, James J. 139, 140
McGeough, Thomas J. 262
McGivney, Michael J. 121, 122
McGuire, John 399
McGuire, Michael 265-267, 271
McKenna, Joseph 181, 333
McKinley Administration 181
McKinley, William 182
McLaughlin, Thomas H. 191
McLoughlin, Hugh 176
McMahon, Lawrence 76, 120
McMullen, John 530-532
McNabb, John 287, 288
McNulty, William 190, 191

McQuade, Paul 70
McQuaid, John 145
Meade, George 213
Meagher, Elizabeth 119
Meals on Wheels 326
Meany, George 332
Medeiros, Humberto 78
mediator 208, 361
Medici, Paoli 160
Mehaney, Jeremiah 167
Melville, Herman 75
Ménard, René 486, 491
Mendoza, López de 386
Menéndez de Avilés, Pedro 349, 385, 387
Menet, John B. 493
Mennonite; *also* Mennonites 227, 254
Menominee Indians 555
Menomineeville 556
Mercedarian 417
Mermet, Jean 520
Mermet, Pierre 497
Merrick, Mary Virginia 333
Merrill 555
Merton, Thomas 471-473
Messenger of the Sacred Heart 198
Mestrovic, Ivan 512, 513
Methodist; *also* Methodists 20, 70, 77, 86, 152, 208, 221, 307, 351, 373, 381, 422, 453
Metropolitan Opera Orchestra 159
Meurin, Sébastien 497, 498, 501
Mexican War 191, 559
Mexico; *also* Mexicans 16, 17, 24, 26, 49, 121, 130, 265, 316, 387, 392, 393, 403, 404-406, 416, 436, 524, 530, 551, 558
Meyer, Albert 535
Miami 403, 404, 407, 410-412, 497, 519
Michigan 17, 442, 445, 475-477, 479-481, 485-495, 510, 511, 519-523, 530, 533, 555, 556, 558, 559
Miège, John 30
Mielcuszny, Adalbert 546

Miles, Richard P. 422, 457
military ordinariate; *also* military ordinary 158, 315, 317
military vicariate 317
Mill Hill Fathers 306
Milledgeville 379, 382
Miller, Peter L. 305
Milukas, Anthony 240
Milwaukee 530, 548, 551, 555-564
Milwaukee River 555, 556
Milwaukee *Sentinel* 558
Minnesota 442, 479, 489
Minorcans 392, 393, 426
Mirales, Juan 196
Mirault, Pierre Michel 366
missionaries 15-18, 23-25, 34, 35, 40, 65, 90, 91, 103, 126, 150, 187, 188, 196, 229, 259, 262, 266, 275, 288, 304, 306, 310, 329, 365, 404, 416, 429-431, 435, 441, 486, 487, 494, 497, 498, 502, 504, 509, 520, 555
Missionary Sisters of St. Francis 222
Missionary Society of St. Joseph 306
mission stops 24, 170, 188, 228, 388, 434, 451, 452, 555
Mississippi; *also* Mississippi River, Mississippi Valley 9, 10, 17, 18, 22, 26, 27, 29, 38, 260, 265, 288, 358, 365, 393, 415, 417, 421, 424, 427, 465, 476, 487, 497, 498, 519-521, 555, 556, 565
Missouri 278, 279, 444, 480, 499, 503
Missouri Compromise 93
Mobile 18, 27, 314, 372, 396, 397, 404, 415-427
Mobile *Register* 426
Moczygemba, Leopold 541, 542
Mohawk Indians 486
Molloy, Thomas E. 174
Molly Maguires 249
Molyneaux, Robert 29, 205, 212
Monahan, Michael 39
Monocacy River 260
Monroe Administration 280, 359

Montgomery 284, 367, 421, 425, 450, 504
Moore, James 350, 391
Moore, John 399, 410
Moran, George "Bugs" 535
Moravian; *also* Moravians 34, 36, 38, 254
Moreno, Angela 406
Morgan, François 497
Morgan's Raiders 459
Morris and Essex Canal 189
Morris, Andrew 132
Morris, Lewis 187
Morrissey, Patrick 119
Morse, Samuel F. B. 148
Morte, Peter 144
Mosley, Joseph 274
Most Holy Trinity (Brooklyn) 171
Most Holy Trinity (Detroit) 480
Most Holy Trinity (West Point) 179, 182-185
Mount Desert Island 90
Mount St. Mary's 12, 168
Mount St. Mary's College 147, 504
Mudd, Samuel A. 408
Mugavero, Francis J. 176
Mulledy, Thomas 280
Mulligan, James A. 346, 523
Mulligan's Irish brigade 346
Mundelein, George 174, 531, 533-536, 550
Murillo, Bartolomé Esteban 447, 457
Murphy, Christopher 375
Murray, John 167
Murray, Paddy 534
Murray, Patrick 495

N

Narragansett Bay 110, 111
Nashville 422, 450, 457, 469, 471
Natchez 27, 358, 418
National Archives 399
National Catholic War Council 317
national churches 31, 78, 223
national parishes 140, 191, 223, 224, 550

Native American Democratic Association 148
Native American Party 148
nativism; *also* nativist 57, 113, 114, 148, 151, 169, 172, 198, 199, 443
Naval Academy 113, 184, 310, 311, 313-315, 317, 318
Naval Academy Chapel 313, 315
Nazareth Academy 454, 456, 459
Neale, Francis 212, 322, 326, 329, 339
Neale, Leonard 104, 197, 279, 290, 322, 323, 353-356, 358
Nebraska 561
Nerinckx, Charles 450-454
Neumann, John N. 12, 216, 217, 221, 256, 310
Neves, Antonio G. 78
Nevis, Katherine 210, 211
New Albany 505
Newark 81, 150, 189, 190
New Bedford 75-79, 81
New Brunswick 97-101
Newcastle 89, 91-93
New Charter of Patroonship 125
Newell, Rebecca 113
New England 21, 27, 55-57, 63, 71, 75, 79, 81, 85, 89-92, 98, 105, 109, 112, 113, 117, 127, 179, 278, 357, 367, 524
Newfoundland 89, 90
New France 17, 18, 475
New Hampshire 71, 83, 103, 105
New Haven 117-123
New Orleans 16, 18, 25, 26, 38, 205, 218, 292, 361, 374, 394, 398, 404, 410, 416-419, 424, 455, 465
Newport 76, 109-114, 155, 310
New Riegel 429
New Spain 16, 17, 49, 51
New York 12, 16, 17, 19, 22, 25, 27, 28, 38, 57, 81, 84, 104, 113, 118, 125-141, 143-162, 165-172, 174-176, 179-181, 183, 184, 187-190, 196, 197, 205, 207, 210, 234, 269, 271, 291, 303, 306, 314, 316, 317, 331, 333, 350, 351, 353, 355, 358, 361, 370, 372, 375, 397, 399, 406, 430, 452, 456, 469, 470, 486, 513, 522, 523, 529, 536, 550, 564, 565
New York Literary Institution 135, 145
New York Protestant Association 148, 168, 169
New York Times 120, 380
Niles 548
Nixon, Richard M. 159
Nombre de Dios 386-388, 391, 393, 395, 399
Norridgewock 91
Northern Ireland 171, 207, 255
Northern Irish Orangemen 199
North River 141
Northway, Stephen 182
Northwest Territory 27, 433, 442, 476, 495, 499, 500, 502
Norumbega River 89
Norwich 112
Notre Dame 322, 330, 509-516, 530, 544, 547, 560
Notre Dame Sisters 84, 430
Nova Scotia 55, 69, 90, 97, 165, 287, 366
Novikof, Nicolai 159
novitiate 229, 278-280, 310, 322, 436-438, 472
Nugent, Andrew 129, 130

O

Oath of Allegiance 19, 22, 27, 361, 424, 464, 499
Oblates of Divine Providence 305
O'Banion, Dion 533-535
O'Boyle, Patrick A. 333
Obrecht, Edmond 469-471
O'Brien, Edward 120
O'Brien, Matthew 133
O'Brien, William 129, 130, 137, 166
O'Callaghan, Denis 65
O'Callahan, Joseph 317
O'Connell, William 59, 65, 85
O'Connor, John W. 535
O'Connor, Michael J. 268, 270, 305, 306
O'Daly, Thomas 50
Odell, Benjamin 181
Odin, John 361, 424, 541
O'Flaherty, Thomas 71, 72
Oglethorpe, James 22, 365, 391, 392
Ohio River 433, 444, 445, 449, 458
Ohio Valley 17, 27, 441
O'Keeffe, Cornelius G. 180, 181
O'Kelly, Patrick 556
O'Kennelly, J. F. 38
Old Catholic Church 547
Old Slavonic 248, 250
Old South Building 322
Old St. Patrick's 134, 135, 138, 143-153, 155-157, 166, 168, 171
Old Testament 295, 513
Old Town 17, 50, 90, 91, 340, 411
Olivier, Donatien 501
Olmstead, Frederick Law 154
Olyphant 249
O'Malley, Eugene 525
O'Meally, Thomas 211
O'Neill, Jeremiah F. 368, 374, 379
O'Neill, Thomas J. 294, 295
One Mile Tavern 289
Orangemen; *also* Orangemen's Day 147, 199
Order of St. Basil 249
O'Regan, Anthony 530
O'Reilly, Bernard 113
O'Reilly, Michael 394
O'Reilly, Thomas 380-382
Orinoco River 47
Orphans Asylum Society 151, 169
Orr, "Angel Gabriel" 173
Orthodox 25, 247, 250, 393, 543
Ottawa Indians 485, 491, 492
Our Daily Bread 296
Our Lady of Melleray 464
Our Lady of Mount Carmel 244
Our Lady of Siluva 244
Owings, Robert 259

P

Pacelli, Eugenio 159

Pacificator 370
Paldi, Angelo 480
Papal States 361
papists 35, 92, 109, 187, 350, 366, 458
parish missions 310, 398
parish records 39, 53, 98, 222-224, 240, 244, 262, 275, 280, 325, 389, 407, 408, 417, 421, 476, 480, 498, 520
parochial school; *also* parochial schools 42, 58, 65, 73, 81, 84-86, 105, 106, 112, 114, 131, 133, 139, 151-153, 157, 169, 170, 191, 198, 218, 224, 228, 230, 240, 243, 244, 256, 261, 271, 275, 284, 294, 296, 305, 307, 311, 323, 324, 333, 339, 340, 346, 362, 382, 400, 430, 438, 481, 495, 514, 523, 533, 537, 545, 551, 560, 561, 563
Parot, Joseph J. 546
Passaic River 189
Passamaquoddy Indians 90
Patapsco River 292
Paterson 134, 187, 189-192
patronato real 16, 17, 48
Patuxent River 277
Pauline Privilege 492
Paulist; *also* Paulists, Paulist Fathers 23, 182, 524, 525
Paul VI 159, 506
Pautienius, Simon 241
Pavarotti, Luciano 159
Pawtucket 111
Payet, Louis 489
Peckham, George 89
Pellentz, James 260
Pellicer, Andrew 426
Pellicer, Anthony D. 426
Pemaquid Point 89, 93
penal laws 19-23, 26, 27, 195, 253, 260, 273, 274, 277, 278, 287, 310, 337, 356
Penn, William 109, 187, 196, 227, 253, 254
Pennsylvania Packet 27
Penobscot Indians 90

Penobscot River 90, 91
Pensacola; *also* Pensacola Bay 395, 406, 407, 415-420, 424, 425
Pentecostals 53
Peoria 532, 561
Perdido River 395
Perkiomen Creek 227
Pernambuco 37
Perry, Matthew C. 404
Perryville 459
Peruvians 192
Petit, Benjamin 510
pew rents 138
Peyton, Patrick 12
Philadelphia 28, 31, 57, 127, 131, 147-149, 153, 172, 188, 189, 195-200, 203-208, 210-213, 215-219, 221, 222, 223-225, 227-229, 235, 236, 240, 242, 243, 248, 254-256, 260, 267, 291, 306, 310, 351, 355, 452, 457, 470, 513, 534, 565
Philadelphia Land Company 233
Philip II 47, 385
Philip III 49
Phillips, Marjorie 270
Pierrepont Distillery 166
Pierson, Philip 487
Pierz, Francis 489, 490, 492
Pilgrim Fathers 55
Pious Fund 24
Piret, Francisco 519
Piscataway Indians 273, 275, 486
Pittsburgh 267-269, 305, 449, 450, 523
Pius V 14, 387
Pius VI 29, 288
Pius VII 27, 132, 135, 209, 290, 355, 451, 452
Pius IX 39, 153, 155, 317, 361, 426, 465, 492, 512
Pius X 248, 280, 549
Pius XI 295, 536
Pius XII 159
plenary councils in Baltimore 30
Plessis, Joseph 137, 145
Plunkett, Robert 323, 326

Plymouth 90, 173, 233, 236, 238, 524
Polish National Alliance (PNA) 543, 545, 547, 550
Polish National Catholic Church 547
Polish Roman Catholic Union (PRCU) 543 545, 547, 550
political issue 445
Polk, James 316
polygamy 365
Ponce de León, Juan 46-48
Poor Clares 322, 443
popish recusant 19
Port Authority Trans-Hudson Corporation 140
Port of Spain 38
Port Tobacco Creek 25
Port Tobacco River 273
Porter, David D. (commodore) 404
Porter, David (governor) 199
Portier, Michael 30, 396, 397, 405, 418-423
Portland 83-86, 99, 100
Portugal; *also* Portuguese 14, 16, 25, 26, 37, 57, 75-81, 93, 128
potato famine 71, 144
Potawatomi Indians 509, 510, 520, 521, 555, 556
Potomac River 275, 291, 321, 323, 329, 337, 343-347, 486
Pottinger, George 466
Pottinger's Creek 450
Potts, Robert J. 244
poverty 38, 47, 49, 58, 132, 154, 223, 322, 340, 389, 390, 397, 398, 399, 425, 499, 520, 565
Power, John 118, 137, 138, 147
Prairie du Rocher 452
prefect apostolic 29, 55, 127, 129, 130, 189, 205, 278, 303, 321, 351, 499
Presbyterians 70, 126, 127
Priesterverein 561, 562
Prince Gallitzin Chapel House 271
prisoners 165, 307, 310, 311, 333, 345, 346, 370-373, 387, 408, 536, 565

pro-life activities 122
prohibition 20, 41, 73
Prohibition Era 533, 535
Propagation (or Propagation of the Faith) 14-17, 21, 29, 30, 36, 127, 128, 130, 134, 137, 211, 278, 304, 352, 354, 355, 358, 435, 451, 531
Prost, Joseph 40, 41
Protestant Bibles 172, 198
Protestant Protective Association 268
Protestants 20, 36, 41, 56, 57, 71, 84, 93, 119, 136, 148, 152, 200, 362, 366, 372, 395, 398, 409, 420, 422, 454, 455, 456, 468
Proust, Eutropius 465
Providence *Journal* 113
Providence Plantation 109
provincial council; *also* provincial councils 122, 156, 167, 195, 196, 292, 435, 445
Prussian 266, 549
public school; *also* public schools 112, 131, 151, 152, 169, 172, 191, 198, 229, 230, 270, 271, 311, 333, 368, 374, 399, 400, 458, 506, 531, 557
Puente, Juan Elixio de la 392
Puerto Rico; *also* Puerto Ricans 34, 37, 45-53, 192, 551
Pulaski, Casimir 28, 366
Purcell, John B. 398, 429, 443-446, 459, 559
Purcell, William 166
Puritan 57, 63

Q

Quaker; *also* Quakers 20, 70, 92, 126, 196, 200, 205, 338, 350
Quarter, Walter 522
Quarter, William 522-524, 529, 530
Quebec 17, 18, 23, 90, 97-99, 101, 105, 137, 145, 278, 283, 385, 415, 416, 486, 487, 498, 499
Quebec Act 27, 28, 204
Queen Anne's War 391
Queenstown 423

Quezon, Manuel 332
Quigley, James 533, 549
Quinlan, John 423
Quinn, Luke 344
Quinn, William 139

R

Raffeiner, John S. 171
railroad workers 299, 368, 379, 524
Rancé, Armand-Jean de 464
Rappe, Louis Amadeus 429
Rasle, Sebastian 91
Ray, Anthony 316
Raymbaut, Charles 485, 486
Reagan, Ronald W. 159
Recollects 17, 23, 488
Reconstruction 306, 339, 361, 380, 382, 398, 425
Red Mass 332
Redemptorist; *also* Redemptorists 23, 36, 39-42, 217, 256, 300, 309-311, 314, 375, 382, 398, 489, 490, 524
Reformation 182, 274, 393
refugees 29, 55, 110, 223, 273, 287, 305, 351, 352, 357, 366, 411, 412, 500
Reign of Terror 322
religious toleration 27, 34, 253, 254
Renwick, James, Jr. 154, 399
Résé, Frederic 24, 443, 489
Resurrectionist; *also* Resurrectionists, Resurrectionist Fathers 23, 456, 542, 544-549, 551
retreat 85, 269, 275, 290, 355, 456, 468, 473, 481, 499, 565
Revere, Paul 92, 94
Revolutionary War 27, 103, 179, 188, 196, 265, 289, 331, 337, 338, 366, 507
Reynolds, Charles B. 393
Reynolds, Frank 332
Rhode, Paul 549, 550
Ribault, Jean 386, 387
Richard, Gabriel 476, 489, 490
Richelieu, Jean du Plessis 17

Rico, John 210
Riney, Zachariah 467
riot; *also* riots 113, 148, 153, 156, 173, 198, 199, 215, 368, 458, 546, 547
Rivas, Biento 49
Rivet, John Francis 500-502
Rochambeau, Count de 28, 110
Roche, Kevin 122
Rock Creek Manor 283
Rockefeller Center 145, 157
Rockefeller, John D. 399
Rockland County, Georgia 471
Rockne, Knute 515
Rocky River 429, 431
Rodríguez, Blas 388
Rogel, Juan 349
Rogers, John 455
Rohan, William de 450
Romagne, James 92
Roman Catholic Society 166
Roman Catholic Volunteers 204
Roman Curia 65, 356
Romanian 248, 250
Romish priests 274, 338, 350
Roosevelt, Theodore 314
Rosati, Joseph 279, 418, 419, 520, 521
Rosecrans, Sylvester 459
Rosecrans, William 112
Rosensteel, Charles 284
Rousselet, Louis de 56
Royal Irish College 393, 417
Rubens, Peter Paul 447
Rule of St. Benedict 463, 470, 473
Russian; *also* Russians 41, 135, 234, 239, 241, 250, 266, 267
Russian Academy of Fine Arts 239
Russian persecution 234
Ruthenian 140, 248
Ruth, George Herman "Babe" 300
Ryan, Abram J. 426
Ryan, Dennis 92
Ryan, Joseph T. 315
Ryan, Matthew 351
Ryan, Patrick J. 235

S

sacramental records 188, 240, 316, 405, 447, 489
Sacred Heart Church (Bowie) 29, 280
Sacred Heart Church (Conewago) 266
Sacred Heart Church (Highland Falls) 182
Salas, Juan Pablo 404
Salem 69-73, 188
Salesian Sisters 191
Salt River 33
Salvador, Manuel G. 79
Sambrana, Diego de 389
Saint-Palais, Jacques 505
Sampson, William 314
San Antonio River 541
San Buenaventura, Francisco de 391
San José 48, 53
San Juan 45-49, 52, 53, 256, 390
Sandusky 429
Sanford, Paley 109
Santa Elena Island 349
Santa Rosa Island 415, 416, 424, 425
Santiago 278, 387, 415, 417
Santo Domingo 45, 46, 110, 305, 352, 357, 366, 389
Saracen 291
Satolli, Francesco 547
Sault Ste. Marie 485-487, 489, 490, 492-494
Savannah 352, 353, 357, 365-376, 382, 397-399, 404, 405, 408
Savannah Plan 374
Savannah River 365, 366
Schaeffer, Bernard 521
schism 30, 37, 197, 205, 209, 211, 353, 355, 547
Schneider, Theodore 188
Schneider, Thomas 227, 228
Schoolcraft, Henry Rowe 489
School Sisters of Notre Dame 311, 544
Schuylkill County 233, 235, 243, 244
Schuylkill River 218, 254

Schulte, Victor 558
Schwab, Cecelia 270
Schwab, Charles M. 265, 268-271
Schwab, Pauline 270
Schwenkfelders 254
Scoodic River 90
Scott, Winfield 98
Scranton 233, 547
Second Plenary Council 306, 494
Second Vatican Council — see Vatican Council II
secularism 542
Seeds of Contemplation 472
Sembratovych, Sylvester 247
Semmes, Raphael 375
senior citizens 176, 295, 427, 495
Serra, Junípero 12, 28, 565
Seton, Elizabeth Bayley 12, 130, 132-134, 166, 290, 305, 367, 454, 506
Seton, William Magee 132
Seven Years War 18
Severn River 313
Sewall, Charles 288
Seward, William 41, 152, 155
Shanahan, John 189
Shanahan, Thomas F. 379
Sharp, John K. 171, 175
Shea, John Gilmary 12, 55, 350
Shea, Nicholas 83
Shea, Thomas 279
Sheen, Fulton J. 161
Sheets, Millard 515
Sheil, Bernard J. 535-537
Shenandoah River 343, 345
Sheptytsky, Andrew 248
Sheridan, Philip 333
Sherman, John 380
Sherman, Thomas Ewing 380
Sherman, William Tecumseh 361, 370, 373, 380, 381, 512, 559
Shiloh 424, 472
Sibourd, Louis 166
Sicilians 301
Sidney 443
Silveri, Donato 225
Silvia, John A. 79

Simonton, John 404
Sioux Indians 486, 487, 555
Sisters of Charity 105, 157, 158, 167-170, 190, 191, 256, 459, 460, 481, 503, 531
Sisters of Charity of Nazareth 454
Sisters of Jesus and Mary 105
Sisters of Loretto at the Foot of the Cross 454
Sisters of Mercy 79, 86, 105, 112, 113, 119, 149, 270, 271, 300, 324, 360, 368, 369, 376, 382, 398, 399, 426, 523, 531
Sisters of Notre Dame 72, 311, 544
Sisters of Our Lady of Mercy 360
Sisters of Providence 307, 505
Sisters of St. Casimir 243
Sisters of St. Joseph 170, 198, 261, 373, 399, 493, 531, 532
Sisters of the Blessed Sacrament 217, 218
Sisters of the Blessed Virgin Mary 533
Sisters of the Holy Names of Jesus and Mary 408
slavery; *also* slaves 22, 28, 34-38, 47, 64, 117, 118, 133, 173, 268, 280, 304, 306, 325, 344, 345, 357, 359, 360, 365, 366, 369, 371, 373, 390, 391, 394, 397, 398, 408, 422, 500, 505, 559
Sliupas, John 237
Slocum, Henry W. 381
Slipyj, Josyf 250
smallpox 41, 403, 409, 557
Smith, Alfred E. 159, 270
Smith, Kate 332
Smith, Richard 38
Smithsonian Institution 155
socialism 542
Society for the Propagation of the Faith 24, 304, 374, 420, 422, 442
Society of Jesus — see Jesuits
Soleau, Vincent 41
Somerset 433-438, 441
Soriano, Manuel 50
Sorin, Edward 322, 510-514

soup kitchen 43, 106, 296, 326, 383, 551
South Bend 322, 509, 514
South Boston 57, 63-66
South End (Boston) 57-59
South End (Chicago) 537
Spain 16-18, 25, 26, 28, 37, 38, 45, 46, 49-52, 197, 278, 332, 351, 387, 390, 392, 393, 395-397, 404, 405, 415, 417, 447
Spalding, John Lancaster 561
Spalding, Martin J. 459, 466
Spanish 14, 16-18, 22, 24-26, 33, 34, 37, 39, 42, 45-50, 52, 53, 59, 73, 85, 127-129, 192, 196, 210, 219, 256, 268, 334, 349-351, 365, 385, 386, 387-395, 397, 399, 403-407, 412, 415, 416, 417, 427, 477, 498, 499, 506, 551
Spanish-American War 17, 45, 48, 85, 311, 314, 409, 410
Spanish Main 47
Spanish missions 16, 17, 25, 28
Spanish Renaissance 558
Spellman, Francis 160
spiritualities 206
Springer, Reuben 445
Springfield 434, 452
Spring Hill 372, 421, 423, 424, 426
St. Aloysius Academy 270
St. Augustine, Florida 349, 369, 370, 375, 404, 405, 408, 410, 416, 418-420, 426
St. Augustine (Isle Brevelle) 304
St. Augustine (Louisville) 306
St. Augustine (Philadelphia) 188, 199, 205, 206, 209, 221
St. Augustine (Washington, D.C.) 331
St. Basil's Church 98
St. Catherine's Island 365
St. Catharine's Junior College 454
St. Clement's Island 273
St. Croix, Maine 90
St. Croix, Virgin Islands 12, 33-43
St. Cyr, John Irenaeus 504, 520
St. Francis Borgia 14, 277

St. Francis College 268, 269, 271
St. Francis Seminary 556, 559
St. Gabriel's College 505
St. Ignace, Michigan 485, 487-489, 493, 495, 519
St. Ignatius Loyola 200
St. Ignatius Loyola (St. Ignace) 485, 495
St. Inigoes 105, 275, 291
St. Isaac Jogues 16, 506
St. James (Salem) 72, 78
St. Jerome River 497
St. John Baptist (Vincennes) 505
St. John Nepomucene (Lancaster) 254
St. John's Chapel 174, 175
St. John's High School 330
St. John's (New Haven) 119
St. John's River, Florida 385-387
St. John's River, Maine 98-101
St. John's (Utica) 134, 167
St. John's (Warrington) 425
St. John the Evangelist Church 148, 212, 215
St. John, Virgin Islands 35, 41
St. Joseph River 322, 509
St. Joseph's College (Alabama) 421
St. Joseph's College (Kentucky) 455, 456, 459, 465
St. Joseph's College (Ohio); also St. Joseph's Seminary 437
St. Joseph's Priory 436
St. Joseph's University 198
St. Lawrence River 17
St. Leonard Parent (New Brunswick) 101
St. Louis (Buffalo) 151
St. Louis, Missouri 279, 346, 380, 418, 419, 464, 480, 520, 521, 561
St. Louis (New Orleans) 205
St. Luce 98
St. Mary of the Springs 437
St. Mary's Academy (St. Augustine) 398
St. Mary's Academy (St. Mary's of the Lake) 511, 512
St. Mary's (Albany) 134

St. Mary's (Alexandria) 322, 329
St. Mary's (Annapolis) 314
St. Mary's Asylum 168, 170
St. Mary's (Baltimore) 369, 455
St. Mary's (Christiansted) 42
St. Mary's College 100, 147, 456, 504, 512
St. Mary's County, Maryland 273, 275, 449
St. Mary's Female Orphan Asylum 531
St. Mary's Hospital 425
St. Mary's Industrial School 300
St. Mary's Lake 515
St. Mary's (Milwaukee) 557, 561
St. Mary's (Mobile) 426
St. Mary's (New York) 138
St. Mary's (New Bedford) 76
St. Mary's (Philadelphia) 196, 197, 199
St. Mary's River 485, 486, 488, 489
St. Mary's (Rockville) 284
St. Mary's (Salem) 71-73,
St. Mary's Seminary 12, 266, 290, 292, 305, 306, 353, 367
St. Michael's Church (Pensacola) 407, 417
St. Michael's Church (Philadelphia) 199
St. Meinrad 505
St. Monica's (Boston) 63
St. Monica's (Chicago) 524
St. Monica's (Cincinnati) 446
St. Omer's 26, 309
St. Pallais, Maurice de 522
St. Patrick's Catholic Orphan Asylum 134
St. Patrick's Day 66, 156, 158, 204, 338, 369, 429, 431, 480, 557
St. Patrick's Seminary at Maynooth 23
St. Peter 209, 390, 393, 562
St. Peter and St. Paul 37
St. Peter Claver (Charleston) 306
St. Peter Claver (Washington, D.C.) 325
St. Peter's Anglican Church 392

St. Peter's (Baltimore) 288, 289, 293
St. Peter's (Charleston) 306
St. Peter's Island 365
St. Peter's (Milwaukee) 556, 557
St. Peter's (Montgomery) 504
St. Peter's (Rome) 121, 122, 296, 513
St. Peter's (Washington, D.C.) 329
St. Philip Neri Church 199
St. Raphael's Society 562
St. Remi's 101
St. Rose of Lima 434, 452
St. Thomas Aquinas 48, 51
St. Thomas College 435, 452
St. Thomas Manor 21, 212, 229, 274, 275
St. Thomas More Newman Club 123
St. Thomas Seminary 454, 455
St. Ursula 33, 48
St. Valentine's Day Massacre 535
St. Viator's College 536
St. Vincent de Paul Society 106, 149, 171, 173, 330
Stamp Act 27
stations of the cross 92, 161, 261, 375, 400, 512, 538
Stecher, Franz 261
Stevens, Thaddeus 255
Stanton, Edwin M. 373
Steinmeyer, Ferdinand — see Farmer, Ferdinand
Stokowski, Leopold 159
Stoughton, Thomas 130
Strain, James 71
strike; *also* strikes 33, 162, 239, 269, 326, 408, 411
Stritch, Samuel 535
Strupinskas, Andrew 234
Stuart, Jeb 261
Stuyvesant, Peter 125
Sulpician; *also* Sulpicians 23, 30, 136, 147, 279, 289, 290, 305, 353, 355, 369, 453-455, 476, 500
Sulzer, William 181
superstition 42, 359
suppressing the Jesuits 25
Susquehanna River 254

Susquehanna River valley 23
Syrian; *also* Syrians 58, 140, 191
Sztuczko, Casimir 547

T

Talbot, George 39
Tallahassee 388, 391
Tamillo, Jacob 547
Tampa 387, 407, 408, 410
Taney, Roger B. 292
Taunton 77, 81, 111
Tea Act 27
Tekakwitha, Kateri 12
temperance 72, 73, 218, 239, 557
temporalities 146, 160, 206, 503
Terre Haute 505, 511
territorial parishes 23, 31, 81, 191, 197, 223, 224, 307, 561
Test Oath 19, 22, 126, 254, 350
Texas 16, 17, 468, 541, 542, 545
Thayer, John 69, 70, 180
Thayer, Sylvanus 179, 180
The Bells of St. Mary's 525
The Man Who Got Even With God 468
The Official Catholic Directory 46
The Seven Storey Mountain 472
The Sign of Jonas 472
The Waters of Siloe 472, 473
Third Order Regular of St. Francis (TORs) 270
Third Plenary Council 306
Threlkeld, John 321
Tiffany and Company 161
Tiffany windows 314
Tilghman, William 209
Timon, John 151
Timucuan Indians 388, 390
Toa River 46
Tocqueville, Alexis de 138
Torrecilla 48, 52
Toucey, Isaac 314
tourism; *also* tourists 42, 53, 99, 105, 106, 123, 213, 261, 271, 296, 347, 376, 411, 427, 459, 494, 563
Toussaint, Pierre 132-134, 161

Trammell, Park 400
Trappist; *also* Trappists 145, 170, 463-472
Treaty of Ghent 330
Treaty of Paris 416
Trenton 188, 206
Trinidad 38, 39, 47
Trinitarian Fathers 347
Trinity Church (Chicago) 544, 546
Trinity Church (Philadelphia) 205
Trinity Church (Somerset) 436
Trinity Church (Washington, D.C.) 322, 324
Trinity Episcopal Church 127, 128, 130, 143, 144
trustee; *also* trustees, trustee system 39, 113, 128-132, 135-139, 143-151, 153, 155, 157, 158, 160, 166, 169, 190, 205-213, 236, 240-245, 255, 289, 291, 339, 351, 353, 355-358, 367, 374, 395, 397, 418, 419, 476, 480, 489, 502, 503, 520, 523, 544
Truth Teller 147
Tuite, Nicholas 34-36
Tuite, William 452
Turkalj, Joseph 515
Turnbull, Andrew 392
Turner, Peter 166, 168
Tuscaloosa 421
Tyler, John 332
typhoid 270, 300, 464, 487

U

Ukrainian 247-251
Uncles, Charles R. 306
Union Army 76, 99, 112, 156, 213, 229, 256, 316, 324, 325, 371, 373, 380, 381, 425, 459, 505, 512, 559
United Mine Workers of America 239
United States Catholic Miscellany 358
United States Steel Corporation 269
Universal Non-Sectarian Catechism 152
Universalist 76, 305

University of Detroit 482
University of Notre Dame 509, 510
Upper Matecumbe Key 403
Upper Peninsula 486-489, 491, 492, 494
Urban College 15
urban renewal 11, 59, 325
Ursuline; *also* Ursuline Convent 105, 173, 198, 360, 493
Ury, John 22
U.S. Air Force 183, 184, 494-495
Usannaz, Anselm 372
U.S. Army 184
U.S. Capitol Building 290
U.S. Coast Guard 184, 404, 412
U.S. Department of Housing and Urban Development 427
U.S. Joint Chiefs of Staff 332
U.S. Merchant Marine 184
U.S. Navy 213, 269, 311, 314, 404, 409
U.S. Virgin Islands 12, 33, 37, 38
Utica 104, 134, 167

V

VA (Department of Veterans Affairs) 315, 317
Vallee, Stanislas 100
Vallejo, José María 130
Valley Forge 204
Van Buren 97-101
Van de Velde, James 530
Van de Vyver, Augustine 346
Varela, José 397
Vatican Council I — *see* First Vatican Council
Vatican Council II 66, 192, 376, 472, 512, 513, 515
Vaughan, Herbert 306
Venezuela 47
Verot, Augustine 30, 369-375, 397-399, 407-409
Verrazano, Giovanni da 110
Vesque, Michel 39, 40
veterans' hospitals 315
vetoism 356
Viatorian Fathers 533, 536

vicariate 21, 99, 317, 369, 396-398, 417-420, 492-494
Vienna Boys' Choir 159
Vietnam 317
Vigo, Francis 498, 500, 502
Vincennes 18, 452, 453, 457, 497-507, 510, 511, 521
Vincennes *Gazette* 505
Vincentian; *also* Vincentians 23, 215, 216, 426
Virginia 20, 90, 110, 188, 229, 260, 293, 304, 326, 330, 357, 367, 369, 406, 450, 498, 499, 523
Vishinski, Andrei 159
visita 349
Visitation Convent 104, 322, 323, 356, 424
Voltaire [François-Marie Arouet] 152, 266
Von Scholten, Peter 38

W

Wabash; *also* Wabash River 265, 497-499, 504
Wagner, Robert F. 159
Wallabout Causeway 170
Wallace, James 356
Walsh, John A. 167-170
Walter, Henry 444
Wappeler, Joseph 254, 259, 260
War of 1812 144, 267, 290, 330, 436, 502
War of Spanish Succession 391
wardens 20, 39-41, 396, 397
Washington, George 110, 125, 179, 196, 204, 271, 325, 338, 343
Waters, Richard 169
Watson, Mary 352
Watters, Morgan 429
Wayne, Anthony 453
Weakland, Rembert G. 563, 564
Webster, Daniel 98, 99
Weiss, Hymie 534, 535
West Indian and Guinea Trading Company 34
West Indies 34, 35, 37-41, 49, 117, 367

West Park 429, 430
West Point 179-184
West River 310
Whealon, John 122
Whelan, Charles 128, 129, 450
Whelan, Peter 371, 372
Whig; *also* Whig Party 169, 305, 458
White, Andrew 273
White, Charles I. 330
White Marsh 277-280, 288
Whitfield, James 304
Wilderness Trail 449
Wilkinson, David 111
William of Orange 117, 253
Williams, John J. 58
Williams, Roger 109
Willing's Alley 195, 200, 208, 210, 221
Wilson, Frederick 314
Wilson, Samuel 452
Wilson, Woodrow 550
Wineman, Ferdinand 481
Wirz, Henry 371, 372
Wisconsin 235, 327, 442, 476, 486, 489, 550
Wisconsin River 486, 555
Witches Hill 69
Wolanski, John 248, 249
Wolfe, James 17
Wood, James F. 216
Woodley, Robert D. 111, 113, 118
World Trade Center 125, 140, 141
World War I 41, 158, 218, 234, 269, 317, 411, 549
World War II 100, 158, 183, 191, 199, 212, 250, 317, 325, 339, 430, 473, 512, 525, 537, 551
Wright Aeronautical Company 191

X

Xaverian Brothers 300
Xavier University (Cincinnati) 444, 481
Xavier University (New Orleans) 218

Y

Yankee clippers 64, 71
yellow fever 130, 206, 351, 369, 407, 409, 419, 421, 425
Yemassee Indians 416
Yorktown 28, 110, 265, 289, 351

Young Men's Bible Society 443
Young Men's Library Association 168
Young, Nicholas 435
Young, Notley 329

Z

Zanesville 433, 435, 441
Zemaitis, John A. 238, 239
Zeytz, Augustine 235
Zimmerman, Charles Adams 311